Professional
SQL Server™ 2005
Reporting Services

Paul Turley
Todd Bryant
James Counihan
Dave DuVarney

WILEY

Wiley Publishing, Inc.

Professional SQL Server™ 2005 Reporting Services

Published by
Wiley Publishing, Inc.
10475 Crosspoint Boulevard
Indianapolis, IN 46256
www.wiley.com

Copyright © 2006 by Wiley Publishing, Inc., Indianapolis, Indiana

Published simultaneously in Canada

ISBN-13: 978-0-7645-8497-8
ISBN-10: 0-7645-8497-9

Manufactured in the United States of America

10 9 8 7 6 5 4 3 2

1B/RV/QS/QW/IN

Library of Congress Cataloging-in-Publication Data:

Professional SQL Server 2005 reporting services / Paul Turley ... [et al.].
    p. cm.
  "Wiley Technology Publishing."
  Includes index.
  ISBN-13: 978-0-7645-8497-8 (paper/website)
  ISBN-10: 0-7645-8497-9 (paper/website)
  1. SQL server. 2. Client/server computing. I. Turley, Paul, 1962-
QA76.9.C55P79 2006
005.75'85—dc22
                        2005036108

For general information on our other products and services please contact our Customer Care Department within the United States at (800) 762-2974, outside the United States at (317) 572-3993 or fax (317) 572-4002.

Credits

About the Authors

Paul Turley

Paul Turley is a senior consultant for Hitachi Consulting. He architects database, reporting and business intelligence solutions for many prominent consulting clients. In addition to Reporting Services, he has created reporting solutions using Crystal Reports, Active Reports, and Access. Since 1988, he has managed IT projects, designed and programmed applications using Visual Basic 3, 4, 5, 6, ASP.NET, ADO.NET, and SQL Server. He obtained his MCSD certification in 1996 and other certifications include MCDBA, IT Project+, and Microsoft Solutions Framework (MSF) Practitioner.

He designed and maintains www.Scout-Master.com, a web-based service that enables Boy Scout units to manage their membership and advancement records online using ASP.NET, SQL Server, and Reporting Services.

Paul authored *Beginning Transact SQL for SQL Server 2000* and *2005*. He has been a contributing author on books and articles including *Professional Access 2000 Programming*, *Beginning Access 2002 VBA*, and *SQL Server Data Warehousing with Analysis Services*, all from WROX Press.

> *My deepest appreciation goes to my wife, Sherri, and our children: Josh, Rachael, Sara, and Krista for their support and understanding. Writing two books over the past year and a half has been a challenge for all of us. Rachael: You did a great job managing my screen shots. Sara, you are a champion and a fighter, and I appreciate your strength and example to everyone around you. Thanks to my folks and extended family who make me proud to be who and where I am.*
>
> *My appreciation to everyone at Hitachi Consulting for their support and contributions. Hitachi is a stellar organization with top-notch people who know how to get business done. Your support over the past year is appreciated.*

Paul contributed Chapters 1, 2, 4, 5, 6, 7 and Appendixes C and D to this book.

Paul may be contacted at pault@scout-master.com.

Todd Bryant

Todd Bryant has been creating custom data-focused applications and reporting solutions since the early eighties. He began using Microsoft technologies in 1998, and the love affair began. Todd has been contract programming, teaching, and developing custom courseware ever since. He is currently working half-time as a software architect for SoftWyre, a Little Rock, Arkansas, based software development company as well as training half-time at Netdesk Corporation in Seattle, where he concentrates on enterprise solutions, Com+ services, and object-oriented programming using both VB.NET and C#. His certifications include the MCSD, MCSE, MCDBA, and MCT certifications from Microsoft; the CNA certification from Novell; and both CompTIA's A+ and CTT+.

> *I would like to thank my family and friends for putting up with me during many months of late night work. I want to thankTodd Meister, our technical Editor. He was a joy to work with and made the process much more enjoyable.*

Todd contributed Chapter 13 and Appendix B to this book.

James Counihan

James Counihan started teaching himself binary in the early 1970s. He is now a Seattle-area consultant specializing in development on the .NET platform.

I wouldn't be where I am today if it weren't for the love and support of the people who care about me. Especially to my parents and sister, thank you!

James contributed Chapters 10, 11, 12, and Appendix A to this book.

Dave DuVarney

Dave DuVarney is a principal for Statera's Seattle office. He has broad technical knowledge stemming from his experiences as a software developer, a certified public accountant, and a technology trainer. Dave has been involved in multiple software development projects ranging from contract management systems to human rights auditing. He is proficient in numerous development languages as well as Microsoft business intelligence technologies. Most recently he has been consulting and delivering on SQL Server 2005 Analysis Services, Reporting Services, and Integration Services. Dave is the coauthor of Professional SQL Server Reporting Services.

I want to thank my wife Stephanie for putting up with another summer of weekends behind the computer. I'd also like to thank the other authors for giving so much of their time to make this second book a reality.

Dave contributed Chapters 2, 3, 8, and 9 to this book.

Acknowledgments

Our sincere thanks go to the members of the Reporting Services product team at Microsoft, who have been very supportive and accessible. A large portion of this book's content is a direct result of the numerous meetings and phone calls and hundreds of e-mails exchanged with our friends in the Reporting Services group at Microsoft. We've had the privilege of working with many folks at Microsoft on these two books over the past three years and greatly appreciate their many contributions. In particular, we'd like to thank Jason Carlson, Brian Welcker, Chris Hays, Carolyn Chau, Tudor Trufinescu, Lukasz Pawlowski, Fang Wang, and Rajeev Karunakaran.

A big *thank you* goes to Andrew Bryan at Dundas Software for his help with the charting features. The integration in the product is awesome, and your assistance and support have been invaluable.

Our editors at Wiley, Katie Mohr and Tom Dinse, have been terrific to work with, and Todd Meister did an awesome job on the technical review.

The Business Intelligence team at Hitachi Consulting has been a tremendous source of support and learning. Thanks for giving us the space to push the envelope. Special thanks to Hilary Feier, Mike Luckevich, Carr Krueger, Reed Jacobson, Tory Tolton, Ted Corbett, Martin Powdrill, Patrick Husting, Steve Muise, Stacia Misner, Jeanne Barnham, Scott Cameron, and too many others to mention by name.

Our consulting clients deserve a lot of the credit for affording us the opportunity to put this product in front of real businesses and corporate decision makers. The rules prevent us from acknowledging all of those we'd like to here. For the many with whom we've had the pleasure of sharing your work spaces, attending your meetings, and bringing your servers to a grinding halt while developing reporting solutions, you deserve our gratitude in a large measure.

Contents

Contents

Contents

Contents

Contents

Contents

Contents

Foreword I

Many people have asked me, "How can you be so passionate about reporting when it is so mundane?" To me, the most exciting thing about reporting is that it is so very common. Like basic transportation, everybody uses it in some way or another. A report is a piece of art meant to covey a message, but unlike traditional art, that message changes based on the data driving it. The potential to help, and be used by, millions of people and companies is one of the reasons I started writing software and eventually joined Microsoft. No other company can reach out to so many people by making great products accessible.

Reporting is a very broad topic covering areas ranging from packing lists and telephone bills to ad hoc analysis and Excel spreadsheets. When designing Microsoft SQL Server Reporting Services, I started with a simple definition for it: an information delivery platform. While this definition is also very broad, it did allow us to focus on our design, while leaving us significant room to expand in later versions. This book will help you understand the power of Reporting Services and to fully utilize its capabilities.

Information is not just data; it is data that has been transformed into something meaningful. This transformation is important. Any tool can read and display data; what people really need for doing their jobs is well-thought-out, correct, and pertinent information. There are many tools that let anyone with access to data build "views" or "reports." However, often these users are unfamiliar with all of the nuances of the data storage and can produce inaccurate results or inadvertently affect the performance of the data engine. Reporting Services acts as the official source so that there is only one version of the truth that everyone uses.

In the future, Microsoft plans to take this even further by integrating with Information Rights Management so that not only does the information come from a single source, but it is also certified, can expire, and is access-controlled even after it is delivered to the end user. The data does not always exist in one database or even come from a database. For those of us who have spent careers working with corporate data, this is a painful truth. Very few reports (or sets of reports that give you sufficient insight) come from a single source. Building some type of data mart or data warehouse is the best solution, but it is not always possible due to timing, policy, or budgetary constraints. Reports must be able to retrieve data from any source and combine them in a single report.

What good is information if you do not have it when you need it? Delivering information is more than just processing it and making it available; it is providing information when you need it, in any format, and on any device you have. The common case today is the ubiquitous online access via HTML in a browser. This is perfect when you have a computer and connectivity to the server. However, as we all know, nothing is perfect. We need the reports when we are on a plane, in a car, with the customer, at the game, on the production floor, and so on. This may include your pager, telephone, fax machine, laptop, paper, and other devices. We also need different capabilities: interactivity, pixel perfect printing, integration into applications like MS Excel for "what-if" scenarios and additional analysis, universal access via PDF, and so on. A single format and a single delivery channel is not enough, but how do you know which ones you will need? Reporting Services insulates you from these choices. All reports may be distributed in any channel or rendered in any format. Report design is independent of how it will be consumed. It is the responsibility of the system to provide the report as accurately as possible, given the constraints of the specific format or channel requested.

Foreword

Building a platform is very different from building a solution. In fact, the goals are in many cases completely opposed. A platform is successful if the developers and administrators have complete access to all aspects of the product. They need to be able to optimize, extend, restrict, embed, and replace parts of the product to meet their needs. This means that all of the APIs are available and documented, all formats are open and described, and every component is configurable or replaceable. While there are always restrictions due to the many tradeoffs in software design, this was the goal when building Reporting Services. Very much like Windows, SQL Server, or Visual Studio, Reporting Services is designed to enable developers to build on a solid foundation and mold it to meet the business needs in significantly less time and with more functionality, but without losing the flexibility and power of building it themselves.

Looking into the future, there's an endless list of features and scenarios that Microsoft will add to make the platform more powerful with little or no additional in-house development required. I have mentioned some, and there are many that haven't even been considered yet.

We look forward to hearing from all of our customers about what is important to them, and how we can make designing, building, and operating their information delivery systems easier, faster, and (I hope) more fun.

Jason Carlson
SQL Server Reporting Services Product, Unit Manager, Microsoft

Jason Carlson is the Product Unit Manager for SQL Server Reporting Services. He joined Microsoft in 1996 as a program manager for Visual Source Safe and Repository. In 1997, the Repository team joined SQL Server and Jason became the development manager for SQL Server Meta Data Services. In 2001, he built a team and started work on v1 of Reporting Services. Before joining Microsoft, Jason owned and operated an independent software development company. This company provided consulting and vertical software solutions for healthcare and telecommunications.

Foreword II

Agility. In business today, key decisions must be made daily or weekly rather than monthly or quarterly. Leading companies realize that to increase the speed of competitive response—their corporate agility—they need to delegate as much decision-making authority as possible to employees on the front lines. Real-time bidding systems, reverse auctions, accurate costing on spot production, build-to-order manufacturing, a worldwide labor force, and globalization are just a handful of the trends in today's business climate that demand better decisions faster.

To be successful in this new model, employees need the best quality information they can possibly get. Information must be accurate, timely, and reliable, and it must be the information they need. Whether your employees are trying to maximize revenues by intelligently attacking new markets or minimizing expenses through astute purchasing, they absolutely must have the right information at their fingertips.

Microsoft's release of SQL Server Reporting Services marks an important milestone in the world of business intelligence: information truly accessible to the masses. By building reporting functionality directly into Microsoft's Enterprise Data Platform, SQL Server, software developers and information architects can now count on the availability of a high-quality, scalable, and robust architecture on which to build their reporting systems.

For the past 20 years, business intelligence (BI) has been working its way deeper and deeper into the enterprise. Previously the domain of a handful of highly skilled analysts high in the corporate ivory tower, BI is now in the hands of line managers, department heads, and knowledge workers at the very edge of today's organizations.

In the past, dependable reporting systems could be horrendously expensive, with organizations forced to deploy robust reporting services only where the greatest gains could be realized. Microsoft's long-standing objective of reducing information technology cost to spur adoption is again evident in the SQL Server Reporting Services licensing model. This technology is licensed to anyone currently licensed for SQL Server and so essentially represents no additional cost. This is a fantastic development for software developers and users alike; it will dramatically increase the adoption and distribution of detailed, accurate, and timely reporting and will push quality BI even further down into the enterprise.

In this excellent book, the authors walk us through SQL Server Reporting Services from the basics of practical reporting through deployment and management of reporting solutions written for BI Solution architects, designers, and developers; it is certainly a most valuable resource.

David Cunningham
President & CEO, Dundas Software

Dundas Software has provided charting and graphing technology under license to Microsoft for inclusion in SQL Server and 2000 and 2005 Reporting Services. Dundas also offers aadditional data visualization charting and gauge extensions for Reporting Services as add-on products.

Introduction

Over the past three years, we've been using SQL Server Reporting Services to build reporting, business intelligence, and decision-support solutions for large and small companies. As consultants and instructors, we spend our time in front of many people who need serious solutions to meet business problems.

In 2003 and 2004, we wrote the first edition of *Professional SQL Server Reporting Services*. At that time, I knew that Reporting Services was going to be a big deal and I also knew that writing a book about something as substantial as this product, wasn't going to be a walk in the park—so I wanted to work with a capable, well-rounded team. Fortunately, I have had the pleasure of working with some very smart, hard-working individuals who love technology and solving problems. Reporting Services was a new product two years ago so we did a lot of research and learned some lessons along the way. Since then, we've learned even more by putting reporting solutions in front of many business users and consulting customers.

This book was written to cover the features of SQL Server 2005 Reporting Services. Although it doesn't address the differences, most of the material may be applied to SQL Server 2000 Reporting Services.

What We've Learned

I'm not saying that we know absolutely everything there is about this product—we're learning more about it on every project, but we've certainly made it our mission to be as versed as possible. Please bear with me as I toot my horn about those with whom I've had the pleasure to work alongside. For the first edition of this book, we worked primarily with the beta product. We have had many conversations with members of the Reporting Services product team at Microsoft as we put the product through its paces to learn what Reporting Services could and couldn't do. We did our homework, and we wrote about its wonderful capabilities. But as with most Microsoft products, we found that there are about 18 different ways to perform each task. Since then, we have deployed Reporting Services in dozens of corporate environments. We've helped business users understand their reporting needs and then designed reporting solutions for many types of organizations. We've integrated reports into web sites and portals, intranet sites, and desktop applications. We've trained hundreds of users, developers, and administrators and have presented at conferences. We've designed reports for savings and investment banks, support centers, software companies, sales and customer management system vendors, sportswear companies, and theme park and entertainment companies. We've learned a lot about how not to design reports and how to build reporting solutions more efficiently. This book is based on this foundation of experience.

Who Is This Book For?

There are a number of other books written about Reporting Services. Some are for beginners and others for serious developers and advanced report designers. Leonard Nimoy's character Mr. Spock once said that "the needs of the many outweigh the needs of the few." While this generally may be a true statement, we've made it a point to address the needs of the many without sacrificing the needs of the few. We wanted to write a book that would meet the needs of the broad audience of report designers, developers, administrators, and business professionals, without sacrificing any content. To meet this objective, we've divided this book into five sections: "mini-books," if you will. Depending upon your needs, you may spend more of your time focusing on the material in one of these sections and using the others for reference. This book is written for the novice report designer and the expert interested in learning to use advanced functionality. For the application developer, we will cover programming in reports and custom applications that integrate reports. You will also learn about report server administration and security issues.

A common practice among development groups at Microsoft is to profile their target users and to even give these personas names and profiles. As we've come to know more about the types of folks who use Reporting Services in various ways, we thought it might be interesting to do something similar. The following are descriptions of three fictitious people who are characteristic of the more common Reporting Services users we have worked with. See if you can identify with any of these descriptions:

Report Designer

Mary works in the financial group for a company that provides consumer services. She is a computer-savvy worker who possesses a wide range of office skills. She has worked in this group for several years and could easily do her boss's job. She understands her company's business processes, financial reporting practices, invoicing, and billing systems. She's not a computer genius but she knows her way around word processing, spreadsheets, e-mail, and simple database reporting. Mary started using Microsoft Access a few years ago and used the wizards to create some simple reports from data exported from the HR and customer billing systems. After a while, she learned how to write queries and build Access reports without the wizards, with custom formatting, groups, and summaries. Two years ago, she learned to use Crystal Reports to report on the data in the company's data warehouse. She has designed several reports with charts and pivots to analyze sales trends and profitability.

Mary's focus is out-of-the-box reporting, getting reports designed and deployed as easily as possible, using the tools readily available within the product. She may design standard server-based reports that users will access from a central report server via the corporate intranet. She may also want to create her own ad hoc, client-side reports from data models created by an administrator or more advance designer.

The following sections of the book will be of most interest to Mary:

> Part I: Getting Started
>
> Part II: Report Design
>
> Part III: Enabling End User Reporting with Report Builder

Application Developer

Joe has been writing database applications for several years, starting with small projects in Access and Visual Basic 5.0. In 2001, he began using Microsoft .NET programming tools and landed a programming position in the company's Information Technology group. Joe has designed many of the company's web sites and portals using the Visual Basic .NET and C# programming languages. Most of the reports Joe has created were written from scratch as custom web pages. He has worked a little with a few specialized reporting applications. He wants to add reporting capabilities to some of the company's custom business applications.

As far as Joe is concerned, writing simple reports is for others to do. His focus will likely be to add filtering, custom formatting, and conditional logic using program code and query script. He will also design his reports so that they fit right into applications as an integrated part of a solution. He may also want to create customized management utilities to automate report server maintenance routines.

Joe understands that Reporting Services offers many flexible options for integrating reports into different application interfaces. He may want to build reports into a custom Windows desktop application, web application, SharePoint Portal or mobile device application.

Joe will be most interested in these sections:

> Part II: Report Design
>
> Part V: Reporting Services Integration and the Reporting Services Web Services

Systems Engineer

Bob is our Network Engineer and Database Administrator. He is more concerned with the security and stability of the corporate servers than with the aesthetics and features of each report. He will want to make sure our report managers, designers, developers, and users, are organized into roles and that the report server is appropriately secured. Bob will install and configure options on the report server. He will schedule maintenance tasks, optimize the database and queries, and provide ongoing maintenance and disaster recovery.

Bob will find these sections most useful:

> Part III: Enabling End User Reporting with Report Builder
>
> Part IV: Report Server Administration

Business Leader

As a business owner, corporate executive or project manager; you may be the consumer of a reporting solution or the director of the development effort. Perhaps you have enlisted the services of a business intelligence consulting firm to architect a decision-support system to help you run your business. You need to be informed about your options and understand the capabilities of the products and technologies used to create your solution. This book will help you to understand these features and the choices necessary to put them into practice. The implementers of this solution will look to you for business requirements and feature choices. Chapters 1, 2, and 3 are a good place to start. The first section of Chapter 7 discusses how to define and manage reporting business requirements and specifications. This will serve as a communication forum between you and your report designers.

What Does This Book Cover?

This book is divided into five sections. These include "Introduction," "Authoring Reports," "Managing Reports," "Report Delivery," and "Advanced Topics," containing the following chapters.

Part I: Getting Started

Chapters 1, 2, and 3 provide an introduction to the capabilities and features of Reporting Services. You'll learn about its extensible architecture, which makes it a very powerful and flexible addition to nearly all existing business systems. This section will build a foundation of understanding upon which you will learn to design, deploy, manage, and, perhaps, customize business intelligence and reporting solutions.

Chapter 1, "What Can You Do with Reporting Services?," provides a high-level overview of the capabilities and opportunities to incorporate Reporting Services into your business environment. You'll learn about general application and reporting technology. You'll earn how to deliver important information on demand using subscriptions. You'll explore various solution types ranging from out-of-the-box reports to simple and advanced application integration.

Reports can be server-based or client-side reports embedded into an application. Report Builder reports also allow nontechnical users to create their own ad hoc reports without installing or learning to use special software.

Chapter 2, "Introduction to Microsoft SQL Reporting Services 2005," briefly discusses the history of Reporting Services and the architecture upon which it is built. You'll see that this is not just another reporting application but a new approach for accessing data and delivering results in a variety of formats, using different delivery methods. Each report definition is stored as an RDL file; a simple and portable standard XML file, making it easy to deploy a report to any server. Reporting Services can be completely secured. Reports may be managed and viewed using the Report Manager web interface or may be built into custom applications, using the provided `ReportViewer` controls or through custom rendering. Delivery options include scheduled subscriptions. Content may be cached to improve performance and conserve server resources.

Chapter 3, "Reporting Services Architecture," details the mechanics of the Reporting Services architecture. Reporting Services is implemented as an ASP.NET Web service, which provides a wealth of capabilities for enterprise-wide reporting. You will explore the different functional areas of Reporting Services and how they relate to user and business needs. You'll learn about the platform's features and the reporting lifecycle—from report design to delivery.

Part II: Report Design

Designing reports can be as simple as running a wizard or may be a highly complex development process to define advanced features. In Chapters 4, 5, 6, and 7, you'll learn about how reports actually process and render data and then how to use parameters and expressions to define creative report solutions.

Chapter 4, "Basic Report Design," starts with the fundamentals and teaches you to create basic reports using simple design tools. You'll learn the essentials about what you need to get started building basic reports using the Report Wizard and common report designer features. You'll be introduced to the fundamental building blocks of report design: report items and report layout properties.

After you explore the basics, you'll learn about grouping data, lists and data regions, using tables and the matrix reports, defining drill-through reports, and using charts. You'll also learn to write expressions and custom code to extend formatting and apply business logic, and to design reports for mobile devices.

Chapter 5, "Designing Data Access," reveals that reports are based on a data source and Reporting Services may be used to present data from many different data sources. You'll learn to define stand-alone and shared data sources, queries and data sets, and use parameters to filter data at the database and to filter data at the Report Server. You'll learn to use new parameter features introduced in the latest version of the product.

This chapter is a primer on Transact-SQL queries and stored procedures. You'll also learn to build reports using Analysis Services and the MDX Query Builder. Query examples are provided for Oracle PL/SQL, Sybase, and Access SQL dialects.

Chapter 6, "Advanced Report Design," helps you take design elements to the next level and learn to creatively use data groups and combinations of report items. Calculations and conditional formatting may be added by using simple programming code. Whether you are an application developer or a report designer, this chapter contains important information to help you design reports to meet your user's requirements and to raise the bar with compelling report features.

Chapter 7, "Report Solution Patterns and Recipes," takes you into the real world of business problems and reporting solutions. You'll start by learning how to document business requirements and to manage successful report projects.

This chapter presents report design from a different view: not the nuts and bolts but the overall pattern of design. We have assembled an extensive list of models and instructions to show you how to build several detailed report solutions to address a variety of specific business problems. This chapter serves as a practical guide to designing reports and building reporting solutions in the real world. It contains several examples of advanced report designs as recipes to solve specific business problems. You will apply the techniques you've learned in the previous three chapters to implement specific functionality.

Part III: Enabling End User Reporting with Report Builder

Report Builder technology puts simple report design into the hands of everyday users without requiring complex design tools. These two chapters introduce the Report Builder platform and the tools used to define data sources and semantic metadata models. Using the elements you deploy, your users can create simple reports without installing software or learning the intricacies of report design.

Chapter 8, "Reporting Services Report Models," shows you that a Report Model is the key component behind performing ad hoc end user queries. A model provides the means to navigate through either a SQL Server database or an Analysis Services database. This chapter will teach you to build a Reporting Services Report Model using sample data.

Chapter 9, "Report Builder," covers Report Builder, a platform for defining ad hoc reports using prepared data structures. You'll learn to use the Report Builder application with a familiar Microsoft Office interface for building reports. Using predefined report layouts, users can fulfill various reporting needs with ease. You'll learn to easily format, to sort and filter data, and to perform calculations. Finally, you'll learn how to manage and administer Report Builder models and reports.

Part IV: Administering Reporting Services

Report server administration has an important job: to keep data secure and available to the right users. Server-side reports can be configured and secured to optimize performance and to provide the right information to the appropriate user communities. Chapters 10 and 11 teach you to use all of the tools necessary to configure and manage your report server.

Chapter 10, "Report Management," teaches you how to use management tools and Reporting Services features to publish reports and manage execution and delivery. You'll learn to create automated scripts and custom solutions to manage all of the Report Server content. You'll revisit the stages of report execution from an administrator's point of view and learn how to optimize them. You'll also learn how to automate report delivery and server management.

Chapter 11, "Report Server Administration," is a comprehensive administrator's guide. You'll explore the related considerations for reporting requirements and deployment scenarios for Reporting Services. You'll learn about the configuration tools and utilities, backup and restore procedures, and monitoring a Reporting Services instance for issues and optimal performance.

Part V: Reporting Services Integration and the Reporting Services Web Services

Practically all of the built-in functionality in Reporting Services can be automated and preformed through custom program code. This includes report rendering and the core services of the reporting environment: data access, rendering formats, security, and delivery. Chapter 12 covers how reports may be integrated into applications, and Chapter 13 will teach you how to write custom extensions to the standard features of Reporting Services.

Chapter 12, "Integrating Reporting Services into Custom Applications," shows you that Reporting Services is a flexible reporting tool that can be easily incorporated in different applications. In this chapter, you'll learn to use URLs to access reports from document and web page links, use the Reporting Services Web service to programmatically render reports and use the ReportViewer controls to embed reports into custom Windows forms and ASP.NET web form applications. You'll learn to display reports in web portals using SharePoint Web Parts and other techniques. You can use programmatic rendering, URL or the ReportViewer controls to create custom report viewers and parameter interfaces. Examples are provided in C# and VB.NET.

Chapter 13, "Extending Reporting Services," shows you that Reporting Services is a robust and scalable product for enterprise report processing. In this advanced programming tutorial, you will learn to use this modular and extensible architecture. Programming classes, interfaces, and APIs give programmers the ability to customize, extend, and expand the product to support their enterprise business intelligence (BI) reporting needs. This chapter introduces you to most of the areas within Reporting Services that allow customization and some of the reasons that you may wish to extend the product. Developers can extend practically every feature by implementing their own security architecture and add custom data access, rendering formats, and report delivery mechanisms.

Chapter 13 is written for serious application developers using object-oriented programming techniques, with examples in C# and VB.NET.

Appendixes

The appendices at the end of this book include information for migrating Access Reports, a comprehensive Reporting Services object programming reference, Transact-SQL syntax, commands, and functions.

What You Need to Use This Book

To use SQL Server Reporting Services and to run the samples presented in this book, you will need:

- ❑ SQL Server 2005, any edition. An evaluation version of SQL Server and Reporting Services may be downloaded from Microsoft at www.microsoft.com/sql.
- ❑ Windows 2000, Windows Server 2003, or Windows XP Professional.
- ❑ Internet Information Services is required to install the Report Server.
- ❑ Pentium II class PC with a 500-MHz processor or better and at least 256 MB of RAM.

The complete source code for the samples is available for download from our web site at www.wrox.com. For programming examples, there are versions available in both Visual Basic .Net and C#.

Source Code

As you work through the examples in this book, you may choose either to type all the code manually or use the source code files that accompany the book. All the source code used in this book is available for download at www.wrox.com. Once at the site, simply locate the book's title (either by using the Search box or by using one of the title lists) and click the Download Code link on the book's detail page to obtain all the source code for the book.

After you download the code, just decompress it with your favorite compression tool. Alternatively, you can go to the main Wrox code download page at www.wrox.com/dynamic/books/download.aspx to see the code available for this book and all other Wrox books.

Errata

We make every effort to ensure that there are no errors in the text or in the code. However, no one is perfect, and mistakes do occur. If you find an error in one of our books, like a spelling mistake or faulty piece of code, we would be very grateful for your feedback. By sending in errata you may save another reader hours of frustration; at the same time, you will be helping us provide even higher-quality information.

To find the errata page for this book, go to www.wrox.com and locate the title using the Search box or one of the title lists. Then, on the book details page, click the Book Errata link. On this page, you can view all errata that has been submitted for this book and posted by Wrox editors. A complete book list including links to each book's errata is also available at www.wrox.com/misc-pages/booklist.shtml.

If you don't spot "your" error on the Book Errata page, go to www.wrox.com/contact/techsupport .shtml and complete the form there to send us the error you have found. We'll check the information and, if appropriate, post a message to the book's errata page and fix the problem in subsequent editions of the book.

p2p.wrox.com

For author and peer discussion, join the P2P forums at p2p.wrox.com. The forums are a web-based system for you to post messages relating to Wrox books and related technologies and interact with other readers and technology users. The forums offer a subscription feature to e-mail you topics of interest of your choosing when new posts are made to the forums. Wrox authors, editors, other industry experts, and your fellow readers are present on these forums.

At http://p2p.wrox.com you will find a number of different forums that will help you not only as you read this book but also as you develop your own applications. To join the forums, just follow these steps:

1. Go to p2p.wrox.com, and click the Register link.

2. Read the terms of use, and click Agree.

3. Complete the required information to join as well as any optional information you wish to provide, and click Submit.

4. You will receive an e-mail with information describing how to verify your account and complete the joining process.

You can read messages in the forums without joining P2P but in order to post your own messages, you must join.

Once you join, you can post new messages and respond to messages other users post. You can read messages at any time on the web. If you would like to have new messages from a particular forum e-mailed to you, click the Subscribe to this Forum icon by the forum name in the forum listing.

For more information about how to use the Wrox P2P, be sure to read the P2P FAQs for answers to questions about how the forum software works as well as many common questions specific to P2P and Wrox books. To read the FAQs, click the FAQ link on any P2P page.

Part I
Getting Started

1

What Can You Do with Reporting Services?

In 2003 and 2004, we wrote the first edition of *Professional SQL Server Reporting Services*. At that time, I knew that Reporting Services was going to be a big deal, and I also knew that writing a book on something as substantial as this product wasn't going to be a walk in the park—so I wanted to work with a capable, well-rounded team. Fortunately, I have had the pleasure of working with some very smart, hard-working individuals who love technology and solving problems. Reporting Services was a new product two years ago, so we did a lot of research and learned some lessons along the way. Since then, we've learned even more by putting reporting solutions in front of many business users and consulting customers.

What We've Learned

I'm not saying that we know absolutely everything there is about this product—we're learning more about it on every project, but we've certainly made it our mission to be as well versed as possible. Please bear with me as I toot my horn about those whom I've had the pleasure to work alongside. For the first edition of this book, we worked primarily with the beta product. We have had many conversations with members of the Reporting Services product team at Microsoft as we put the product through its paces to learn what Reporting Services could and couldn't do. We did our homework, and we wrote about its wonderful capabilities. But as with most Microsoft products, we found that there are about 18 different ways to perform each task. Since then, we have deployed Reporting Services in dozens of corporate environments. We've talked to business users to understand their reporting needs and then designed reporting solutions for many types of organizations. We've integrated reports into web sites and portals, intranet sites, and desktop applications. We've trained hundreds of users, developers, and administrators and have presented at conferences. We've designed reports for savings and investment banks, support centers, software companies, sales and customer management system vendors, sportswear companies, and theme park and entertainment companies. We've learned a lot about how not to design reports and how to build reporting solutions more efficiently. This book is based on this foundation of experience.

Who Uses Reporting Services?

Probably one of the most significant lessons of the past two years spent teaching training courses on Reporting Services is how diverse the demographics of the audiences are. I'm not talking about age and gender but the roles and backgrounds of those who design and implement reporting solutions. As an application developer, I was accustomed to teaching programmers and other technology professionals whose life quest is to make the world a better place by writing software. However, I quickly learned that there wasn't a stereotypical report designer. Some are very business-focused and aren't necessarily in love with technology and program code. Many are simply charged with managing or facilitating a line of business. They need tools to get information quickly and don't want to reinvent the wheel or work with cumbersome tools. The figures in the following table aren't substantiated by any kind of survey or study but are merely my objective observation of those who attend Reporting Services training classes.

Approximate Percentage	Role
15%	Business Managers
15%	System Administrators
30%	Software Developers
40%	Business Information Workers

Wait a minute! This is a book about creating reports to display information in meaningful and interesting ways. I can't just display this information in a boring list, so I've created a simple report and put it into a chart (an exploded, semitransparent doughnut chart to be specific) shown in Figure 1-1.

Of those who are working seriously with Reporting Services, have attended classes, or have engaged consulting services, about one-sixth are nontechnical business managers. Members of this role are mainly interested in the bigger picture: how reports can address their analytical needs and help them make informed decisions. These folks have little interest in the implementation details or the technology used to make it work. They direct people who can do the detail work.

System administrators consist of server system builders, hardware professionals, and database administrators. In smaller organizations, this role is often shared with the software developer. Administrators are typically concerned with the setup and ongoing maintenance of servers and the infrastructure to keep reporting solutions available and working. They typically spend their time and energy managing security and optimizing the system for efficiency.

The software developer represents slightly less than one-third of the audience. To achieve advanced reporting features, software developers will write complex queries and custom programming code to process business rules and give reports conditional formatting and behavior. Developers typically feel right at home with the report design environment because it's very similar to familiar programming tools.

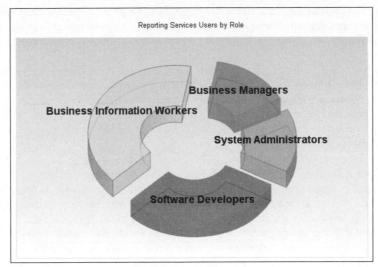

Figure 1-1

The largest group of reporting professionals is not the software developers or other technical experts. They have strong computer user skills, but they don't spend their time writing code and using tools like Visual Studio, Enterprise Manager, or SQL Server Management Studio. They are regular business users who need to design reports to run their businesses. As a software developer, coming to this realization was a wake-up call. As I taught Reporting Services 2000 classes for Microsoft, I often spent a large portion of the classroom time just teaching students to use the Visual Studio user interface. It was new to them and unlike any other application they were accustomed to. Report designers who have been using other tools such as Crystal Reports, for example, will typically be a little intimidated by the Reporting Services design tools because they may be unfamiliar and may seem to be more "raw" and developer-centric than what they're used to using. In order to take advantage of advanced report capabilities, these individuals must either acquire some simple programming skills or work with software developers to add custom code and expressions to their reports.

Application and Reporting Technology

The definition of reporting is changing. Like so many components of the computer/information industry, the lines between one thing and another have become very fuzzy. This applies to so many concepts in our industry. For example, many traditional desktop applications now run in a web browser. Are these client or server applications? These days it's hard to draw a line and categorize a business solution. Not long ago, if an application opened in a web browser it was considered to be a server-side application—all of the processing occurred on a web server. Likewise, if an application ran from an icon on your computer, it was a client-side application, where all of the files and processing occurred on your own computer. Have you attended an Internet hosted meeting or seminar? If so, you probably navigated to a site in your web browser, entered a meeting number, and, magically, you were looking at PowerPoint slides and a demonstration running on the presenter's desktop computer. Although you may have started from a web page and the conferencing application may have been started from your web browser, it was actually running in a client-side application, which you allowed to be installed on your computer, using advanced content-streaming technologies, allowing you to interact with the server-hosted conference.

What does this have to do with reporting? Quite a lot, actually. With Reporting Services, you will have the ability to integrate reports into applications in such a way that users may not be able to tell the difference between the two. With a little bit of programming code, reporting features can be extended to look and act a whole lot like applications. Where do applications stop and reports begin? When do reports start replacing application functionality? As I said, the lines are becoming blurred. Your task is to decide which tool best meets a need.

The exciting news is that you now have a tool that can do some incredible things. As my favorite super-hero's uncle said, "With great power comes great responsibility." If you are a simple report designer with simple needs, the good news for you is that using Reporting Services to design simple reports is . . . well, simple. If you are a software developer and you intend to use this powerful framework to explore the vast reaches of this impressive technology, I welcome you to the wonderful world of creative reporting. In this chapter, I will introduce the common reporting scenarios, beginning with the most basic and then moving to the more advanced. In subsequent chapters, you will explore these capabilities in depth and learn to use them in your own reporting solutions.

Information, Now!

Imagine that you are sitting in a presentation meeting at the corporate office of a key customer. You are a senior sales representative for a company that sells high-volume data backup systems, and the solution they decide on will be implemented in several regional data centers around the world. Your team has been preparing for this meeting for months. Your success depends on your ability to demonstrate your competence to the customer and a clear understanding of their needs. Your team has done their home-work, and you know the customer has a history of scanning printed medical records and storing them as image files. Based on this information, you are certain that a particular product will adequately provide the file backup facilities for their moderate volume of image files. You have made it a point to familiarize yourself with the capabilities of the system that appears to be the best fit.

During your customer's opening presentation, they tell you that they have recently made a huge investment into full-motion video-imaging equipment. Now they need a backup system that can handle large file capacities. They are prepared to make an investment that is substantially larger than what you had anticipated for a capable backup solution. Your company began to offer a large-scale solution just a couple of weeks ago, but you aren't very familiar with its capabilities. You've spent so much time preparing to sell the smaller system that you haven't had time to learn more about this new product. Your associate is doing introductions, and it will be your turn in about 15 minutes.

Discretely, you open your Pocket PC Phone and access the World Wide Web. You log in to your company's secure report server, select the product catalog report, choose the product category, and then *drill down* to the new product. The report has a *drill-through* option that lets you quickly view a detailed specification report for the new, high-volume backup system. After noting the pertinent specifications, you save this report to a PDF file and then choose the customer sales inquiry history report. Looking up this customer, you learn that someone named Julie made an inquiry about two months ago regarding video media backups from this very company.

Looking around the room, you find a name card with her name on it. You explore the details of this call, and you find that Julie had asked if you offer a solution comparable to a very expensive product from a competitor. Checking the competition's web site, you discover that the competing product Julie had mentioned uses older technology, has a smaller capacity than the new system, and costs considerably more. You save a report with all of the pertinent specifications to your memory card, hand the card to the administrative assistant sitting next to you, and ask that he make printed copies of the PDF file it contains.

Your colleague finishes her presentation and then introduces you. Taking another quick glance at the new product specs, you begin your introduction (see Figure 1-2).

Figure 1-2

You explain that one of your team's greatest strengths is your real experience and understanding of how business can change from day to day. In order to be responsive and competitive, it's necessary to adapt to these changes. You show the brochure for the midscale product and explain that this product would be an excellent solution for a company that just scans documents. But for digital video, a more capable solution is required. You share the product specification and qualify the product to meet your customer's needs. During your presentation, the administrative assistant returns with the printed specification report. Not missing a beat, you distribute copies to everyone and conclude your presentation. You make brief eye contact with your colleague, who raises an eyebrow just before your customer's chief decision maker, Julie, aggressively shakes your hand and thanks you profusely for your time and extra effort.

Solution Types

Reporting solutions come in a variety of sizes and shapes. These range from the standard Report Manager web interface to a completely customized application with integrated reporting features. The types of software solutions that might incorporate reporting include:

- ❑ Out-of-the-box, server-based reporting features, using reports created by report designers and deployed to a central web server.

- ❑ Client-side ad hoc reports created by users, on demand with the Report Builder tool using pre-defined data models.

- ❑ Reports integrated into web applications using URL links to open in a web browser window.

- ❑ Reports integrated into SharePoint Portal server applications using SharePoint Web Parts.

- ❑ Custom-built application features that render reports using programming code. Reports may be displayed within a desktop or web application interface or saved to a file.

Out-of-the-Box Reports

What does Reporting Services provide if you just want to use its simplest features right out of the box? Quite a lot, actually. Reporting Services uses the Microsoft Development Environment to design and deploy reports to a central web server. Prior to the release of SQL Server 2005, the development environment was exclusively part of Microsoft Visual Studio, a tool for serious application developers to create custom software. It still is, but now the development environment has been tailored to manage SQL Server databases, write queries, and design reports. Using this powerful tool is likely the most significant challenge for the new report designer.

Once you learn the basics of the development environment, designing reports and managing projects is actually quite easy. The report designer includes a simple Report Wizard that can lead you through designing common reports. Tabular, grouped, cross-tab, and chart reports are relatively easy to build just by following the wizard prompts and perhaps setting a few properties.

After a new report has been designed and tested, it can be deployed to a central report server where it will be available to all users through a simple web browser application called the Report Manager.

Beyond wizard-built reports, many aspects of more complex reports may be managed by creating simple programming expressions. An expression builder guides the designer through the simple use of functions and logical expressions that may be used to modify colors, visibility, and formatting aspects and to perform calculations. Because the expressions in Reporting Services are based on Visual Basic .NET, the power of conditional expressions is virtually limitless.

Server-Based Reports

It's important to understand the difference between SQL Server Reporting Services and a desktop reporting tool like Microsoft Access. Reporting Services isn't an application that you would typically install on any desktop computer. It requires Microsoft SQL Server, a serious business-class relational database management tool. For this and other reasons, Reporting Services is designed to run on a file server instead of a desktop computer. It also requires Microsoft Internet Information Services, a component of Microsoft Windows Server products.

Reporting Services is designed for business use. Therefore, it is a powerful tool that can literally scale to be used by thousands of users and can report on very large sets of data stored in a variety of database platforms. But just because Reporting Services is a business-sized product, this doesn't mean that reports have to be complicated or difficult to design.

Report users need to be connected to a network, or perhaps the Internet, with connectivity to the report server. When a report is selected for viewing from a folder in the Report Manager, it is displayed as a web page in the user's web browser. Optionally, the same report can be displayed in a number of different formats including Adobe PDF or Excel, or as a TIFF image. Reports may be saved to files in these and other formats for offline viewing. Reports may also be scheduled for automatic delivery by the report server by e-mail or may be saved to files. These features are standard and require only simple configuration settings and minor user interaction.

User-Designed Reports

Reporting Services in SQL Server 2005 introduces an alternative to predesigned, server-side reports. Standard reports are designed for users by a report designer or developer ahead of time and deployed to the server for users to select and display, print, or save to a file. This may be useful for standard reporting needs shared by most report users. However, savvy users cannot modify the design or these standard reports without access to the design and development tools. The Report Builder allows users to build their own reports on the fly, using prepared queries and data models. Using this option, the report designer or system administrator can prepare a variety of common data models to simplify and expose the underlying data sources in a concise form. This allows users to construct ad hoc reports using simple drag-and-drop techniques. These reports may be saved for others to use or to be built upon in later sessions.

The actual design work is performed using a client-side builder tool delivered on demand in the user's web browser. The user experience is quite simple. As far as the user is concerned, a new report is created using a simple web page selection and the Report Builder opens in a browser window without specifically installing a software package ahead of time. These reports are stored on the server in the same folder space as other reports. The Report Manager web interface is used to access and maintain standard Reporting Services reports as well as Report Builder reports and their associated data models.

The advantages of Report Builder reports are that they give users the ability to design and customize their own reports without involving a report designer or developer. Report styles and features include standard report layouts like columnar, hierarchal, pivot/matrix, and charts.

Report Builder reports cannot contain custom expressions or custom code. Data-formatting options are limited and the data models must be prepared ahead of time. Models may be created to mirror the details of source data tables or may be simplified. This allows the data model designer to hide sensitive data and to simplify complex data sources with alias columns aggregations and calculated data members.

Designing Reports

The report designer is integrated into the Microsoft Development Environment, which also is the platform used for the SQL Server 2005 design and administration tools. In Reporting Services for SQL Server 2000, report design was performed exclusively using Visual Studio. Now reports may be designed and created using either Visual Studio 2005 or the Business Intelligent Studio, both of which are implementations of the development environment.

Building standard, server-side reports in the designer can be as simple as 1, 2, 3: First, you create a data connection to the data source and dataset (query) for the report. The second step is to design the report layout using simple drag-and-drop tools. Formatting attributes are set by changing properties in the properties sheet or dialogs. The report may be previewed and debugged within the designer. The third and final step is to deploy the report to the report server. This may be done using a right-click menu action. The report designer, shown in Figure 1-3, supports this three-step paradigm with corresponding designer windows (located on the tabs) and features.

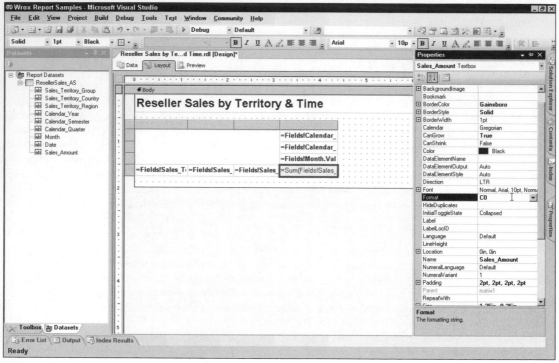

Figure 1-3

Report design is covered in Part II. You'll learn about the basics in Chapter 4 and about advanced techniques in Chapter 5. Chapter 6 will take you beyond the features and discuss several common business scenarios. In that chapter, you will learn techniques for designing the best reporting solutions to meet some common and unique challenges.

Client-side reports are a little different from Reporting Services' standard server-side reports. Because this feature is intended to give users the power to create and modify their own reports, it does not require Visual Studio or Business Intelligence Studio to be installed on their computers. First, a data model is prepared to support the reports users may build. These data models are stored on the report server with shared data sources and reports. The data model serves two important purposes: It provides a simplified view to hide the complexity of relational or hierarchal data. Second, it allows the data model designer to control access to sensitive or irrelevant data stored in the database. When a user wants to build a report from the Report Manager, the Report Builder design components are downloaded and activated in the user's web browser. This design environment shares common features and characteristics with the report designer but is simpler to use and specifically designed for creating these client-side reports (see Figure 1-4). Report Builder reports are automatically laid-out and formatted for ease of use. Finished reports may be stored on the server for reuse.

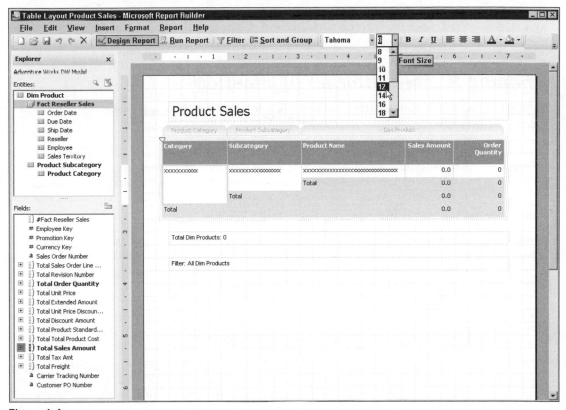

Figure 1-4

Part III, including Chapters 8 and 9, thoroughly covers client-side reporting concepts, data model preparation, and the Report Builder design environment.

Simple Application Integration

There are a few options available for integrating reports into business solutions. Using reports from an external application isn't hard to do, but choosing the right technique depends upon the type of application and the desired behavior of the report interface. Even with all of these options, you may still have a few different implementation choices. There are two recommended methods for rendering reports in a custom implementation which include:

❑   A standard web request using a Uniform Resource Locator (URL).

❑   A report embedded into a Windows or web application using an IFrame, Browser control, or ReportViewer control.

❑   A programmatic web request using the Simple Object Application Protocol (SOAP).

The first option is much easier but may be used in a variety of different ways. In its simplest form, a hyperlink is used to open the report in the web browser. The user uses a standard toolbar to provide parameters for filtering and other report options.

Launching Reports from an Application

Hyperlinks and application shortcuts can easily be added to documents and custom applications. Using this simple technique, report links can be added to Windows forms, documents, and web pages.

Much of the standard report viewing environment may be controlled using parameters passed to the report server in the URL. By incorporating these commands into a hyperlink, reports may be displayed with or without toolbar options and features. You can change the zoom factor and modify the rendering format. For example, clicking a link for one report may open it as a web page in HTML, and another link for a different report may open it in Excel or the Adobe Reader.

Reports may be designed to prompt users for parameter values used to filter data and to modify the report format and output. These parameters may also be incorporated into a URL string. This way one hyperlink will display a report with one set of data, and another hyperlink will display the same report with different data. Parameters can even be used to change display attributes such as font sizes and colors, and to hide and show content.

User Interaction and Dynamic Reporting

There are many opportunities to use report features to provide a rich user experience. In the past, many reports were nothing more than a list of values with totals. Now reports can be a starting point that can guide users to the information they need to make decisions. Report elements, such as text labels, column headers, and chart points can be used to navigate to different report sections and to new reports. Since navigation links may be data-driven and dynamically created based on program logic, report links (see Figure 1-5) may also be used to navigate into business applications. Imagine using your reports to launch programs and to navigate to document libraries and online content!

Dynamic reporting means that the content and layout of a report can change as the user selects parameter values or clicks on different items. Summary headers, shown in Figure 1-6, may be used to expand and collapse detail sections, giving users the ability to drill down to more specific information.

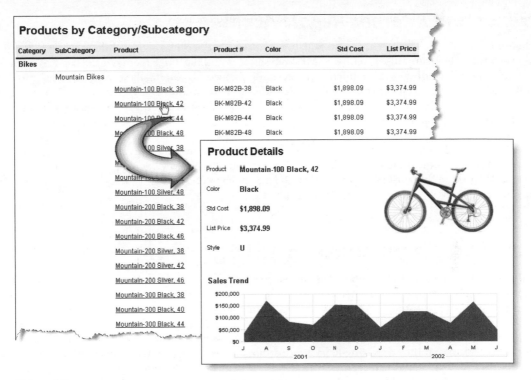

Products by Category/Subcategory

Category	SubCategory	Product	Product #	Color	Std Cost	List Price
Bikes						
	Mountain Bikes					
		Mountain-100 Black, 38	BK-M82B-38	Black	$1,898.09	$3,374.99
		Mountain-100 Black, 42	BK-M82B-42	Black	$1,898.09	$3,374.99
		Mountain-100 Black, 44	BK-M82B-44	Black	$1,898.09	$3,374.99
		Mountain-100 Black, 48	BK-M82B-48	Black	$1,898.09	$3,374.99
		Mountain-100 Silver, 38				
		Mountain-100 Silver, 48				
		Mountain-200 Black, 38				
		Mountain-200 Black, 42				
		Mountain-200 Black, 46				
		Mountain-200 Silver, 38				
		Mountain-200 Silver, 42				
		Mountain-200 Silver, 46				
		Mountain-300 Black, 38				
		Mountain-300 Black, 40				
		Mountain-300 Black, 44				

Product Details

Product **Mountain-100 Black, 42**

Color **Black**

Std Cost **$1,898.09**

List Price **$3,374.99**

Style **U**

Sales Trend

Figure 1-5

Products by Category/Subcategory

Category	SubCategory	Product	Product #	Color	Std Cost	List Price
⊞ **Accessories**						
⊞ **Bikes**						
⊟ **Clothing**						
	⊞ Bib-Shorts					
	⊞ Caps					
	⊟ Gloves					
		Full-Finger Gloves, L	GL-F110-L	Black	$15.67	$37.99
		Full-Finger Gloves, M	GL-F110-M	Black	$15.67	$37.99
		Full-Finger Gloves, S	GL-F110-S	Black	$15.67	$37.99
		Half-Finger Gloves, L	GL-H102-L	Black	$9.16	$24.49
		Half-Finger Gloves, M	GL-H102-M	Black	$9.16	$24.49
		Half-Finger Gloves, S	GL-H102-S	Black	$9.16	$24.49
	⊞ Jerseys					
	⊞ Shorts					
	⊞ Socks					
	⊞ Tights					
	⊞ Vests					
⊞ **Components**						

Figure 1-6

Intranet and Internet Report Access

One of the marvelous things about the SQL Server Reporting Services architecture is that it is based on modern Internet technologies, namely XML Web services and the .NET Framework. The Report Server, running under Windows Server Internet Information Services, is essentially a complete web portal. At its core the Reporting Services exposes all of its features and capabilities as a Web service. This means that there are virtually no practical limits to how the features of reports and the report server may be expanded to meet specific needs.

At the simplest level, this simply means that reports may be accessed by privileged users who are connected through a corporate Internet (network) or through the World Wide Web. Reports may be made available through the out-of-the-box Report Manager web page interface or may be built into custom applications, as you will see in subsequent chapters.

Seamless Application Integration

How and why you would build reporting into a custom business application is a big question. Although there are some common (and rather simple) techniques, there isn't just one way to incorporate reports into a business environment. Whether you want your users to simply link to a report in a standard browser-based report viewer or to have report content seamlessly melded into a custom application user interface, there are a handful of methods to get there. Whatever the chosen technique, users need not even realize that they are using Reporting Services to view their content. In fact, they may not even realize that they are viewing a report. From the users' perspective, their experience is simply a convenient and smooth flow of information as they navigate from one simple interface to another, without ever leaving your business solution.

Part V will help you explore opportunities for integrating Reporting Services reports into applications and business solutions. Chapter 12 will show you different techniques for including reporting features into Windows and web applications. You will learn how to program the Reporting Services Web service to gain control over the report rendering process and to manage reports through custom applications.

Web Application Integration

It's impossible to know for sure but by some estimates, as many as 60 to 80 percent of all desktop business applications have been replaced by browser-based applications, most in the past five years. The power of the web and Internet technologies has drastically changed the way we use our computers. For this reason, web applications have come a long way in just the past few years. Once stodgy, static web pages, many "web sites" have been replaced with interactive information portals and dynamic application interfaces that provide feedback and tactile response to user interaction.

The page paradigm has turned once standard gray window dialogs into artistic-yet-efficient, fashionably color-coordinated, data input and management screens. One of the reasons that Reporting Services integrates so easily with modern web applications is that it natively supports HyperText Markup Language (HTML), the standard markup language used to create web pages. Techniques may be used to incorporate reports into a web application in a variety of ways:

- ❑ Hyperlinks to navigate the web browser window to a report.

- ❑ Hyperlinks to open reports in a separate web browser window, with control over report display and browser features.

- ❑ Embedding reports into a page using a frame, IFrame, or ReportViewer web control.

- ❑ Programmatically feeding report content to an Active Server Page (ASP or ASPX) using server-side custom code.

- ❑ Programmatically writing reports to files available for downloading from a web site.

- ❑ Using a web part to embed reports into a SharePoint Web Portal.

The fact is that there are a lot of creative ways to integrate reports into a web application. These techniques range from very simple, requiring little more than a little HTML script, to very complex, custom methods. And if it's not enough to be able to embed reports into custom web pages, it's also possible to use custom program code to embed additional content into reports. Imagine the possibilities . . . actually, you don't have to imagine anything. Just keep reading!

Portal Integration

As web technologies and products have matured, a new breed of web applications has evolved. Most web sites consist of several HTML page files, which contain mainly text content. Portal frameworks, like Microsoft SharePoint Portal Server, Plumtree, E-Portal, K-Station, and DotNetNuke have replaced many large, complex web sites. A portal server takes much of the programming out of web site construction by providing a framework and the building blocks to assemble an intricate web site from modules. Most of the content is managed in a database rather than in physical pages.

A Reporting Services report can integrate with portal sites in some of the same ways that it integrates standard web pages: by using IFrames and hyperlinks. SharePoint integration is particularly easy for nondevelopers because it involves the use of simple menu options rather than writing script or program code. Adding the report viewer web part to a portal site page is as easy as dragging and dropping it into a page zone and then setting some simple properties. Microsoft offers a simple portal framework with limited features with Windows Server, called Windows SharePoint Services (WSS.) The full-featured, corporate-scale edition, SharePoint Portal Server, is a separate product that adds features and advanced scalability to the WSS foundation.

Windows Application Integration

Reports may be viewed in custom Windows desktop applications using one of two techniques. The ReportViewer control or embedded web browser may be used to view server-based reports in a form. These reports are still managed on the Report Server and maintain all of the security settings and configuration options defined by an administrator. Queries and data access are still performed on the server. The other option is to embed these reports directly into the client-side application. The Windows forms ReportViewer controls can act as a lightweight report-rendering engine. This means that reports built into a custom application can run independently from the report server. Figure 1-7 show a report rendered on a Windows form using the ReportViewer control.

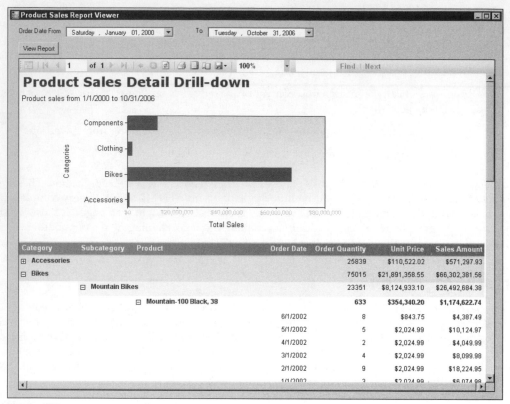

Figure 1-7

Managing and Customizing the Report Server

Reports may be delivered in a variety of ways (not just when a user navigates to a report in real time). Reports may be automatically rendered to server cache, so they open very quickly and don't burden data sources. They may be delivered via e-mail and to file shares on a regular schedule. Using data-driven subscriptions, reports may be "broadcast" to a large audience during off-hours. Each user may receive a copy of the report rendered in a different format or with data filtered differently. You will learn to plan for, manage, and configure these features.

Chapter 11 (in Part IV) will guide you through report server administration. You will learn how to optimize, back up, and recover the ReportServer database, Web service, and Windows service. You will learn to use the management utilities, configuration files, and logs to customize the server environment and to prevent and diagnose problems.

Chapter 13 covers programmatic extensions to the Report Server. You will learn to write custom data source, rendering, delivery, and security extensions. That chapter will show you how to build new features on top of the Reporting Services architecture. As a report designer or business manager, you will learn of these powerful capabilities, enabling you to address specialized requirements and to direct application developers to develop custom extensions. As a system administrator, you will learn to enable custom extensions and define appropriate security allowances to enable custom extensions to run on your report server. As a custom extension developer, you will learn how to use the Reporting Services object model to extend the features of reports and your server, to solve business problems and enable advanced capabilities.

Summary

Different people will use Reporting Services in different ways. Our goal is to address the needs of the broad community of power users, report designers, solution architects, system administrators, and business managers. For some, the material contained in sections of this book will help them build and deploy reporting solutions to meet their needs. For others, it may open their eyes to powerful capabilities beyond their skillset and to work alongside other professionals as educated members of a project team.

As a nonprogrammer report designer using Reporting Services, you are likely to learn to write some custom expressions and program functions to meet specific reporting needs. Perhaps this is as far as you will need to take Reporting Services. For the vast majority, this is enough to design, build, and deploy reports with capabilities far greater than any other reporting tools you may have used in the past. If you are a serious programmer, then your needs are probably a little different from those of the casual report designer. For the custom business solution developer, there are very few boundaries set by limitations of this product. With some creativity and the techniques you will learn in the chapters ahead, you will take reporting further than you have before and provide your users with real business intelligence rather than just the ability to print out data.

Reporting Services takes data accessibility to the next level. Microsoft is making good on its promise of making information available "any time, any place, and on any device." Reports may be designed using specific rendering formats and page sizes to support mobile devices, the browser window, Office documents, and — oh yes — the printed page.

Introduction to Microsoft SQL Server Reporting Services 2005

SQL Server Reporting Services (SSRS) 2005 expands on Microsoft's first release of its reporting platform. In 2003, Microsoft released Reporting Services as an addition to the suite of SQL Server 2000 products. Reporting Services was originally intended to be a part of the overall SQL 2005 release. However, the Reporting Services team found an opportunity to launch the product early. To their credit, the release was extremely successful. Reporting Services has been one of the most adopted version 1 products from Microsoft. That being said, it was still a version 1 product and had some room for polishing and fine-tuning. Features are selected from a long "wish list" in order of priority. It's a long list containing essentials and nonessentials, and some items that may never make it into the final product. Additional items from this list are added with each version and service release.

In this chapter, you learn:

- ❑ A new approach for accessing data and report delivery is part of the extensible architecture of the Reporting Services platform.

- ❑ How each report is stored in a simple and portable report definition Extensible Markup Language (XML) document file using a standard called RDL.

- ❑ That Reporting Services can be completely secured and highly customized. Reports may be managed and viewed using the Report Manager web interface or may be built into custom applications using provided report viewer controls or custom rendering.

- ❑ A range of delivery options, including scheduled subscriptions, allowing users to receive reports as files or e-mail items. Report content may be cached in a variety of ways to improve performance and conserve server resources.

In the 2000 release, Microsoft spent a significant amount of time making sure that the underlying platform was extensible, scalable, and generally well architected. I believe this was the right decision when looking at the long-term use of this product. Focusing heavily on the platform did require that some end user features be held until further releases. What we are seeing in the SSRS 2005 is a major addition of some of the most commonly requested features. Some of these include multi-select parameters, sortable headers, and a number of user enhancements. The major improvement comes with the new Report Builder application. Report Builder allows users to easily create their own reports with a friendly Microsoft Office–like interface.

If you are impressed by the capabilities of the .NET Framework, Web services, SQL Server, and ASP.NET, you should know that by using these technologies Reporting Services takes data accessibility to the next level. Microsoft is making good on its promise of making information available "any time, any place, and on any device." Reports may be designed using specific rendering formats and page sizes to support mobile devices. There are many other reporting tools with impressive capabilities, but none of them is quite like this one.

This chapter will introduce several topics that will be covered in greater detail later in the book. This will be a high-level view of the need for and purpose, capabilities, and mechanics of SQL Server Reporting Services.

Traditional Application Reporting

In many business applications, reporting is an afterthought. When designing systems, there is a great deal of time spent on workflow, data elements, and the user interface. Systems take significant amounts of time to design, build, test, and deploy. In the end, many organizations end up with a tool well suited for collecting information and improving productivity. However, reporting is usually lacking. It seems that people usually see reporting as a simple add-on that can be completed with relative ease.

The reality is that good reporting takes the same type of solid planning and design done in the original application. You need to clearly define what it is the user is looking for, how he or she is going to use it, and how often it needs to be available. Without proper planning, queries became complicated and difficult to support. Reports run slowly and are prone to errors.

To avoid these difficulties, you need a plan. In a perfect world, you would architect the database and application around your reporting needs and would completely understand your users' requirements before designing the system. In the real world, you may understand some of the users' needs ahead of time, but chances are that new reports will be requested long after the other features are in place.

According to Frederick P. Brooks's *The Mythical Man-Month*, it's usually a good idea to learn from and throw away your first few attempts at almost any design. I typically try to develop reports in stages, realizing that the first attempt will be a prototype. My experience has been that when you gather the initial requirements, users will ask for a handful of different reports based on some specific criteria. After the solution is deployed and people begin to use it, others will almost inevitably realize that they, too, would like reports to help make their jobs as easy as their associates'. As users realize what kinds of information they can get, they will find new and exciting ways to sort, filter, group, pivot, and slice and dice their data — in ways they never thought possible. That is, until you show them the possibilities.

Today's Reporting Requirements

Static, printed reports may be an acceptable format for a list of products and prices or for a company but not for the majority of the information people use to make important decisions today. Business decision makers need pertinent information, and they need to view it in a manner that applies to that person's role or responsibility. Since most users deal with information in a slightly different manner, you can create hundreds of reports, each designed for a specific need. Alternatively, you can create flexible reports that serve a broader range of user needs. For example, a sales summary report could be grouped or filtered by the salesperson's region, or by customer type, and include information for the week, month, quarter, or year or for a specific product category. To produce individual reports for each of these needs would be time-consuming and cost-prohibitive. Besides, computer users are savvier than they were a few years ago and need to have tools that help them make informed decisions, not just look at the numbers.

I recall working at Hewlett-Packard several years ago in a manufacturing site IS group. Every Thursday a report card would come around. There were several regularly scheduled reports that the mainframe system produced on a weekly and monthly basis. Users, typically department managers, would subscribe to these reports that were then printed in another building and delivered by hand to each subscriber. Many of these reports were little more than a huge list of numbers and text printed on continuous, fan-fed paper — some as large as 500 pages. I watched inquisitively as managers would meticulously scan through the pages, highlighting and circling figures of interest. Some would bind them into large books and give them to their administrative assistants to go through with a 10-key calculator and add up all of the figures they had highlighted.

At the end of the month dumpsters full of these reports were hauled off to landfills and recycling centers as their usefulness quickly came to an end. I spent nearly two years developing a reporting application for this group using Microsoft Access. We originally planned for 8 to 10 reports in this application. But as time went on, and users began to rely on the reports to perform their jobs, they would ask for the same reports with different sorting, grouping, and selection criteria. In the end, we deployed some 25 to 30 reports, most of which were variations on the few original reports.

Business Intelligence Defined

The previous section discussed the importance of adding reporting to your applications. Reporting can answer a number of business questions, but it only represents a portion of what we call business intelligence (BI).

BI seems to be a very popular industry term right now. Like many popular industry terms, there is generally a lot of confusion about its actual meaning. So, we need to add a little clarity about what BI actually means. To us, BI is the ability to gather information, make a decision on the information, implement a change in your business, and then measure the effects of the change. Figure 2-1 shows the circular nature of BI.

Business executives understand that it's important to have good data. They reason that good data should lead to good decisions, and good decisions mean good business. This makes sense, right? A very common scenario today is that businesses trying to get that edge will invest in expensive Enterprise Resource Planning (ERP) systems that effectively gather and store mountains of customer, product, and sales information. Mission accomplished? Wrong! These days, the time between data entry and consumption is very short, almost instant. More effective data-gathering mechanisms result in data silos and data warehouses populated to the gills with all kinds of facts.

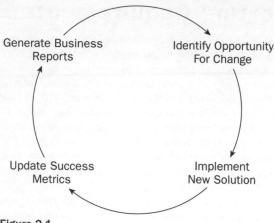

Figure 2-1

The new generation of business workers is informed and empowered to make decisions. They need tools to get useful information and respond to changes. Having data available is useless unless it has business value and can be used to effectively make informed decisions.

A fundamental fact in business is that the people who gather and collect data are often not the people who use that data or need access to the information that the data represents. Business executives, managers, and analysts make strategic decisions every day that may affect many people, the direction of their organizations, and ultimately, the way people and organizations will go about conducting business in the industry. These decisions are largely driven by the relative height of a bar displayed in a chart or a few numbers printed on a piece of paper. Having capable reporting tools doesn't necessarily solve this problem. Most businesses don't know how to effectively use the products they own. A reporting tool is of little value if it's complicated and difficult to use.

This presents some fundamental challenges, such as collecting comprehensive, accurate, and meaningful information; storing it in a form so it continues to represent the facts; and presenting the information in a concise and unbiased form. On the surface, it seems like a simple task.

Automation to the Rescue — a Scenario

I'll share an example of this kind of challenge. Several years ago, I spent a few months developing a reporting system for the operations group at a paper mill in the Pacific Northwest. The old mill is located in a small, remote town, and many of the people operating the mill have been working there all of their lives. As is common in the pulp and paper industry, the mill has changed ownership a few times and is currently operated by a very large paper and office supply company.

As time went by and technology changed, several different computer systems were incorporated into the operation of this mill; an IBM 360 and an AS/400 system were used to manage customer orders and production history records. The original inventory management system is still in place. It's a very old, special-purpose computer that stores most of its data in a single, flat text file. All of its components are redundant, and it hardly ever needs significant maintenance. Shortly before I arrived, a Windows server box was installed with a SQL Server database and an application that would replicate production and inventory data from the existing database systems. Management within the parent company believed that they didn't have a handle on the rates of material consumption and product quality. They wanted a reporting system that would give them the figures they needed to make adjustments to their ordering and pulp production processes.

Over time, orders would be placed for certain grades of pulp. The system would calculate quantities of ingredients needed to produce a batch — typically to fill an order for a customer. The order would be sent to the production floor, where workers had newly installed controls used to ensure the accurate delivery of pulp ingredients. Different batches of product continued to be produced with varying degrees of quality, and management's ability to track the consumption of these materials didn't significantly improve. Management continued to invest in reporting solutions. They bought and developed software to look for trends and perform statistical analysis but to no avail.

After several months and hundreds of thousands of dollars invested, the product quality didn't really improve much. Finally, one of the IT managers put on a hard hat and walked down to the production floor to observe the process. What he learned was a simple lesson: When the orders arrived on their computer workstations, workers were printing the orders and then putting them aside. They had overridden the automated controls and were using the same manual techniques to make paper that earlier generations had been using for decades. It was a matter of tradition and pride, and they weren't about to let some computer do their job for them.

The initial reporting solution was elegant and technically capable. The calculations were accurate and the report presentation was appropriate. However, the solution didn't fully support the process. This cultural hurdle was eventually overcome (workers were instructed to use the automated systems if they wanted to keep their jobs), and the product and process improved. A report is only as good as the data it presents, and the data is only as good as the information used for collection. The information is only as good as the process that it represents.

Challenges of Existing Reporting Solutions

For over 10 years, Microsoft offered only one product with substantial reporting capabilities. Designed to run as a single-user or a small workgroup desktop application, Microsoft Access is a capable database and reporting solution. In Access 2000, Access Data Projects were added. This extension of the product works well against a SQL Server back end in a LAN environment. In Visual Studio 6, an integrated reporting tool was offered for Visual Basic 6, but its capabilities were meager at best. Developers at that time thought this was a glimpse of things to come in subsequent versions of Visual Studio.

Due to the lack of a unified, consistent approach for reporting, many developers have had to revert to creating their own custom solutions. One case in point is the reports starter kit project available on the ASP.NET development support site (www.asp.net). The developers did a bang-up job creating a web-based reporting solution using ASP.NET datagrids and datalist controls. They even made their own pie charts using line-drawing objects. This effectively proves that .NET is a powerful arsenal of programming tools. However, it also makes the point that we have lacked a strong reporting platform to round out Microsoft's front-line development and database suite.

When Visual Studio .NET was released in 2002, I was a little disappointed because the only integrated reporting component was a limited-use version of *Crystal Reports*. Now, before I get myself into too much trouble with folks who may be loyal to this product, I'll say that Crystal Reports is a capable reporting tool. However, it's neither a part of Microsoft's strategic direction nor does it behave like, or integrate tightly with, other Microsoft products. The version of Crystal Reports that is installed with Visual Studio is limited to five concurrent users (and the term *concurrent* is subject to some serious interpretation). Now that Crystal Reports has changed hands once again (acquired by Business Objects), it will be interesting to see how this affects the direction of this well-known product.

Notably, the most remarkable change in the industry over the past few years has been the opportunity and need to exchange information over the Internet. Previous technologies simply don't provide the means to access application components across the Internet. Component architectures such as COM, DCOM, and CORBA were designed to communicate across secure local area network (LAN) and wide area network (WAN) systems, which required a substantial infrastructure investment. Connecting business trading partners and even regional sites was often cost prohibitive and logistically infeasible. Few options existed for reporting over the web. At best, a list or table filled with data could be viewed in custom-built, server-side web page solutions using Active Server Pages (ASP) or Common Gateway Interface (CGI). Each page had to be carefully designed and scripted at the cost of dozens, or sometimes hundreds, of programming hours.

With the recent maturity of the web, a new generation of mobile devices is evolving that can connect users to company resources, e-mail, documents, and databases. These laptop, hand-held, palm-top, and wrist-worn devices open new doors of opportunity and present new challenges for data presentation.

To gain access to useful and readable information, data must be accessible over available communication channels (such as corporate networks and the Internet), easy to access, secure, and available in a variety or formats so that it may be viewed using available document readers or browsers — all compatible with different devices. Did I mention the need to support different *operating systems (OSs)*, applications, and perhaps, without the installation of any custom software on the client device? This is the challenge.

How Does SQL Server Reporting Services Meet This Challenge?

SQL Server Reporting Services is a server-side reporting platform that meets all of these requirements and more. It can obtain its data from a variety of data sources that you can access using modern programming tools. That data may be grouped, sorted, aggregated, and presented in dynamic and meaningful ways. The structure of the data and the presentation elements may be transmitted across practically any communication medium, using an industry-standard format, to just about any type of client or server computer or device. The resulting content may then be displayed in many standard formats using browsers and document readers. Further, the data itself may be consumed by standard and custom applications to be further parsed, imported, manipulated, and consumed. It's a truly remarkable innovation with incredible possibilities.

Since Reporting Services is based on .NET, it offers the advantage of integrating tightly with the Windows platform and benefits from the performance, scalability, and security inherent to the .NET Framework. When used in concert with BackOffice products like SharePoint Portal, it can provide a comprehensive enterprise solution with little programming effort. Reporting Services can be used with ASP.NET and other .NET programming tools to produce highly customized, special-purpose solutions.

Chapter 3 discusses the specific Reporting Services architecture that is used to perform all of this magic. In brief, functionality is exposed through an XML Web service that may be accessed across a LAN or across the web. Reports may be rendered in program code or they may be accessed through a simple web address—like any other web page. Reports may be rendered in several formats. These include different flavors of HyperText Markup Language (HTML) to provide compatibility with different browsers and devices, the Adobe Acrobat *Portable Document Format (PDF)* for uniform presentation and printing, as a graphic file, and in Microsoft Excel so users can slice, dice, pivot, and reanalyze the data. Content may also be rendered in XML and CSV (Comma-Separated Values) formats to import and exchange data with a variety of applications.

Business Intelligence Solutions

Traditionally, BI solutions have been very costly and only accessible to large businesses that could afford them. *Customer Relationship Management (CRM)* systems, *Online Analytical Processing (OLAP)* systems (or data warehouses), and analysis solutions have been available for many years from specialized vendors. However, they require costly deployment, training, and maintenance. By contrast (this is the part I like the best), Reporting Services is available at no additional cost if you install it on a computer with a licensed instance of SQL Server. In a single-server installation, you don't need an additional license and you can use it royalty-free—so long as your database and server products are appropriately licensed.

Comparatively speaking, collecting data is the easy part. Most companies have been doing this for decades, but how they utilize all of this data is often another story. There is no doubt that effectively collecting data may not be so easy, but it's something businesses have been doing for quite some time. Most companies have untold mega-, giga-, or even terabytes of "important" archived data residing in documents, spreadsheets, and various databases on backup tapes, disks, and folders throughout their enterprise—with no hope of fully utilizing and gaining significant value from it all.

According to Tommy Joseph of Disney Interactive Group, "BI is about more than just tracking product sales. It's about measuring performance, discovering patterns and trends, and measurable forecasting through statistical analysis."

An effective BI solution provides visibility to important facts at all levels of an organization and gives people access to uniform data from different sources using familiar and easy-to-use applications. It ties together applications, documents, and data sources in a manner that lets people collaborate and communicate effectively.

BI systems are no longer a luxury but a necessity in many business environments. Today, having access to timely information can make the difference between having a competitive edge and being left in the dust behind competitors.

Who Uses Reports and Why?

In almost any organization, there is a universal condition that people in different roles and at different levels have different perspectives on information. This is typically most apparent in large corporations, where executive leaders who make financial and market-direction decisions have less exposure to the daily processes of the company than the line-level workers. Ask any executive, and he or she will tell you that the line-level worker doesn't have a broad perspective regarding the challenges and direction of the organization at a high level. Conversely, ask most of the line-level workers in the organization, and they will tell you that the upper management and executives don't share their perspective of "real problems" and the daily pulse of the company. To a point, this is the natural condition of a healthy organization.

Bill Gates has spoken extensively about the *information worker* of the twentieth century. At all levels within an organization, people who have convenient access to accurate and appropriate information are empowered to make informed decisions that benefit the organization and the individual. This is rapidly becoming the case throughout many industries today and continues to change the way people work and are managed. Although this paradigm shift may be occurring for many people, organizations often struggle to provide the resources necessary to support workers who are eager to use information to make a difference in their environments.

Executive Leadership

Leaders simply must make informed decisions. They must fully understand their business environment and the competitive climate in which they operate. Access to market conditions, customer needs, and financial information can often make the difference between decisions that produce success or jeopardize the organization.

Decision support systems provide interfaces for executive leadership through dashboards called *Executive Information Services (EIS)*. Reporting Services installs with a simple web interface and enhances integration with executive consoles through SharePoint Portal services and third-party solution integration.

Managers

Inefficient business processes can no longer remain the status quo. Customers demand results and simply will not tolerate services or products that don't meet their expectations. Customers have choices and will quickly switch to a competitor if their needs are not met. Managers need the information necessary to drive customer satisfaction and make corrections, directing business processes and the effective use of people and other important resources.

Information Workers

In businesses today, workers are educated and given more freedom to solve problems and effect change. This category could be applied to workers at various levels within an organization, including the managers and higher-level workers. Often, the customer service representative or service provider will be the only human interface a customer has with an organization. That person must be empowered to collect and retrieve information quickly and accurately. They must also be empowered to make corrections to—and to work with, not against—unyielding business processes. In the past, workers simply had to accept the way information was presented to them, as well as the inefficiencies of most automated systems. With greater demands on businesses, workers simply must have the means to acquire accurate and concise information that meets their needs—in order to work efficiently.

Customers

Many businesses can't afford to put people in front of their customers on a routine basis. Customers who can get the information, services, and assistance they need may not demand that someone help them when it's not warranted. By making regular services available through customer-friendly automation and information portals, you can afford to offer assistance to customers who really need special attention. Customers often need to look up account and transaction histories, order status, and shipping information. Making these services available through a web browser, e-mail, or a mobile device can provide a greater degree of customer satisfaction.

Vendors and Partners

Like customers, business vendors may need to interface with an organization to place orders, schedule service calls, and obtain status information. Making this information available in the most appropriate form will improve efficiency and ultimately business-vendor partnerships. Business vendors are often more accepting of special procedures and automated systems. Vendors can be trained to use more sophisticated systems to obtain product information, service orders, invoices, and other business-related information. Systems may be designed to interface and automate the download or exchange of information that enable a partnering business to work cooperatively.

Reporting Solution Alternatives

The following section discusses some common reporting solution alternatives. The alternatives usually represent an evolution in a company's reporting sophistication. Generally, organizations start with some main reports from an OLTP (Online Transaction Processing) system. Once they meet the limitations of the OLTP system, they evolve their reporting into data warehouses. Eventually, even more complex reports and interactivity are required. This usually leads to the implementation of an OLAP system. We will take a look at each of these alternatives and their relative advantages.

Reporting with Relational Data (OLTP)

Transactional databases are designed to capture and manage real data as it is generated, for example, as products are purchased and as services are rendered. Relational databases are designed according to the rules of normal form and typically have many tables, each containing fragments of data rather than comprehensive information or business facts. This helps preserve the integrity and accuracy of data at the detail level, but it presents challenges for deriving useful information from a large volume of transactional data. In order to obtain information with meaningful context, tables must be joined and values must be aggregated.

For simple report requests, this usually is not an issue. Take the example of an invoice. An invoice is a simple report. It displays custom information along with detail for a small number of transactions. For this type of report, querying an OLTP system is not very costly and the query should be relatively straightforward. However, users will eventually move past these simple reports as they start to look for information for an entire year or product line. Developing these types of reports will eventually consume considerable resources on an OLTP system as well as require increasingly difficult queries. Although relational database systems may support complex queries, reporting against these queries routinely could prove to be slow and inefficient.

Relational Data Warehouses

I have seen many organizations evolve away from reporting on their OLTP data. Usually their first step is to create a carbon copy of the OLTP system on another server. This alleviates the resource constraints on the original system, but it does not solve the issues around increasingly difficult queries. OLTP systems simply are not organized in a logical reporting structure.

To deal with increasing reporting needs, an entire industry has evolved to simply handle reporting. From this industry, individuals such as Ralph Kimball have refined standard patterns and methodologies for developing data warehouses. A common misconception is that a data warehouse is simply a denormalized transactional system. In reality, a data warehouse is another form of relational database that is organized into a reporting-friendly schema. Data is centered around what is known as a "fact" table. A fact table relates to business processes such as orders or enrollments. Radiating out from the fact table are dimensional tables. Dimensional tables contain attributes that further define the facts. These attributes could contain product names, geographic sales locations, or time and date information.

Relational data warehouses can significantly improve query performance on large data sets. However, they too have related drawbacks. These drawbacks generally relate to the fact that data is still stored in a relational format. Relational databases require joins to combine information. They also require aggregate functions to calculate summary-level detail. Both joins and aggregate functions can slow queries on very large sets of data. Relational databases also do not understand inherit associations in the data. Take the example of a product table. Each product table has a related subcategory and each subcategory has a related category. If you need to create a report that is product sales with its percentage makeup of each related subcategory, you have to understand the relationship and write it in your query. The same holds true for time relationships. If you need to create a report that contains year-to-date information, you need to understand what the current date is as well as all the related periods in the same year. These things are possible in SQL queries but take additional effort and require more maintenance. That moves us into our next type of reporting alternative: OLAP.

Reporting with Multidimensional Data (OLAP)

Multidimensional databases take a much different approach to data retrieval and storage than relational databases. Multidimensional databases are organized into objects called cubes. Cubes act as a semantic layer above your underlying database. These databases can contain numerous different relationships and very large sets of aggregate data.

As a multidimensional database, information can be aggregated across many dimensions. This data is preprocessed into the multidimensional structure. Because it is preprocessed, query times are significantly reduced for large additive data sets. Multidimensional databases also have the advantage of understanding relationships between and across dimensions. This opens the door to creating calculations and reports that would be extremely difficult in a relational database.

Imagine that a user asks you to create a report that displays the top five customers with their top three products by this year's sales amount and compared to last year's sales amount. Writing a SQL query to return the top five customers is fairly straightforward. However, returning each one's top three products would require additional subqueries because the relational database does not understand the association between products and customers. The final part of the request can prove even more burdensome. Returning a single year's data is easy, but nesting that data next to last year's data can prove almost impossible. The SQL query for the above scenario would most likely contain a number of nested queries as well as some creative use of temporary tables. Besides being a terribly complex query, it probably would not perform that well. On the other hand, Multidimensional Expressions (MDX), the language used to query multidimensional databases, can handle this in a few simple calls—not because MDX is a more advanced language, but simply because the underlying database understands the associations in the data and has stored this information for quick retrieval.

Microsoft has made major enhancements to its multidimensional database product called Analysis Services. Reporting Services 2005 adds improvements for working with Analysis Services databases. There is a new query designer that assists you in writing the underlying MDX. There is also support for creating Reporting Models that allow ad hoc access to OLAP data. Creating Reporting Models for Analysis Services 2005 is covered in more detail in Chapter 8.

The Reporting Lifecycle

Chapter 3 discusses the reporting lifecycle in greater detail with the architecture that supports this process. Creating a functional reporting solution requires an understanding of user and business requirements. Existing data sources must be considered and new data stores must be designed to meet reporting needs. From this perspective, the process of creating useful reports consists of three activities:

❑   **Authoring:** With the available tools, reports are authored using the *Report Designer* in Visual Studio .NET. This interface is used to create data sources, queries and data sets, and the report definition.

❑   **Management:** Report management is performed using the *Report Manager*, a web browser interface used to manage and deploy report definition files, shared data sources, and configuration settings; it can also be used to view and export report data.

❑   **Delivery:** Reports may be delivered to a user *on demand* through the Report Manager or a custom application; it can also be scheduled for delivery through *subscriptions*. Reports can be delivered in the form of a web page, document, file, or even via e-mail.

Report Delivery Application Types

In the past, reporting solutions were typically delivered through a desktop application of some kind. Data was queried in real time, and of course the application had to be connected to the data source. Users also had limited opportunity to save reports for later viewing and usually printed them on paper.

Now we have many opportunities to view and interact with reports in environments where it may not be possible (or feasible) to connect to data stores. Reports may also be presented in different forms that offer multiple capabilities and compatibility with various devices and software.

Web Browser

Web browser–based solutions have become popular for a number of reasons. User accessibility takes on a whole new definition when special software isn't required on the client computer. Of course, a web browser makes information available for viewing over the World Wide Web, but browser-based solutions are also a compelling means to deliver information in a controlled business enterprise environment. Whether users access resources within their corporate intranet environment or over the web, the browser paradigm has significantly changed the approach to application delivery.

Some of the traditional challenges with browser solutions are the lack of consistent support for client-side script and components. These issues have largely been resolved with server-side rendering mechanisms that output product-independent HTML content. For viewing offline content, HTML documents require links to external files, such as images, sounds, and video. These issues have also been resolved by using a Multipurpose Internet Mail Extensions (MIME)–encoded format called *MHTML* or *Web Archive* to encapsulate binary content within the page definition. Although not supported in all browsers, this format is a viable means to deliver extensible report content for live and offline viewing. HTML 4.0 works on different types of computers across the Internet and within a LAN on newer web browsers, and HTML 3.2 works with older browsers and on portable or hand-held devices.

Office Applications

Microsoft Office brings together a tremendous assortment of capabilities to assist report users at all levels. Microsoft Excel has been the mainstay tool for data collection and analysis. By rendering a report into Excel, the data may easily be reformatted, modified, or analyzed using formulas and calculations. This capability has been around for several years, but it required writing custom code to use the Excel object model from Access or Visual Basic to produce report data in Excel—this process was tedious at best. Now, pushing complex report data into a useful and well-formatted Excel document is simple.

Microsoft Access continues to be the office worker's database of choice. Data tracking and management solutions can be created with minimal cost and effort. Report Services may be used to exchange and import data into an Access database using XML or CSV formats. Access and Excel both provide the Office Web Components that may be used to view pivot tables and charts. These components duplicate the functionality of the Matrix and Report Services *chart* items but might give users a more convenient option for analyzing data.

Programmability

The possibilities for incorporating report features in your own applications are impressive. All of the features of the Report Manager can be duplicated in many cases and can be extended through program code. Reports may be viewed in place within an application by using an external web browser window, integrated browser control, or a custom report viewer component. Report content may be rendered to a file for persistent storage to directly into a viewer or browser.

Subscriptions

Subscriptions allow users to receive or gain access to reports on a regular schedule. Reports are delivered by e-mail or saved to files where they may be viewed offline at the users' convenience. Report subscriptions may be set up for an individual user or large groups of users using data-driven subscriptions. To put this into perspective, effectively, reports may be delivered to any individual or size group of users in practically any readable format at any place and any time.

Report Formats

In addition to the three HTML rendering formats, you can use document types to control formatting elements, printing layout, and adding other capabilities. The PDF document format remains the most popular means for ensuring that documents are formatted exactly as they were intended. Rendering a report to a Microsoft Excel workbook gives users the ability to continue to massage data and perform calculations.

Importing Data/Exchanging Data

Not all "reports" may be intended to be read or printed. Reporting Services provides two report rendering formats that can be used for export/import and data exchange. Using either the *Comma-Separated Values (CSV)* or XML formats, Reporting Services provides a very convenient mechanism for intersystem data exchange or pushing data out to a trading partner. Imagine that your system automatically sends invoices and shipping manifests to your order-fulfillment vendor at the end of the day via XML file attachments to e-mail.

Ad Hoc Reporting

Another important component of a reporting platform is the ability for users to easily create their own reports. The major new feature of Reporting Services 2005 is the introduction of Report Builder. Report Builder is comprised of two major components: Report Models and the Report Builder client. Report Models allow you to create a semantic layer on top of SQL Server or Analysis Services data. The semantic layer provides an easy-to-understand model for the user to navigate. Users will not have to understand how to query the underlying database to create reports. The Report Builder gives users an easy-to-use interface for building reports. The Report Builder client leverages information from the Report Model to easily build structured reports. Chapters 8 and 9 will discuss how to create Report Models and how to access this data using Report Builder.

System Requirements

The hardware system requirements for Reporting Services are very similar to those for SQL Server. The default installation will place the Report Manager, Reporting Services, and the Report Server database on the same physical server, but this configuration is not a requirement. These components may be installed on three separate servers.

The Report Server and the Report Manager servers must be running *Internet Information Services (IIS)* 5.0 or higher with ASP.NET, and the .NET Framework 1.1 or higher. The Report Server Database requires any edition of SQL Server 2005.

Editions of Reporting Services correspond to editions of SQL Server 2005 and include Enterprise, Standard, Workgroup, Developer, and Express editions. Like SQL Server 2005, Standard Edition is a good solution for a single-server environment with a moderate number of users.

The following table shows the features for each edition of SQL Server Reporting Services 2005 (from `www.microsoft.com/sql/2005/productinfo/rsfeatures.mspx`).

Report Server

Feature	Express	Workgroup	Standard	Enterprise	Comments
Data Source(s)	Express 1, 2	Workgroup 1, 2	X	X	SE and EE support all data sources (OLAP and Relational)

Table continued on following page

Feature	Express	Workgroup	Standard	Enterprise	Comments
Rendering	Excel, PDF, Image (RGDI, Print), DHTML	Excel, PDF, Image (RGDI, Print), DHTML	X	X	Standard Edition and Enterprise Edition support all output formats
Management	Report Manager	X	X	X	Workgroup, Standard, and Enterprise editions support SQL Server Management Studio and Report Manager
Caching			X	X	
History			X	X	
Delivery			X	X	
Scheduling			X	X	
Extensibility			X	X	Can add/remove renderers, data sources, and delivery
Custom Authentication		X	X	X	
SharePoint Integration			X	X	
Scale-Out Report Servers				X	
Subscription			X	X	
Data Driven Subscription				X	
Role Based Security	Fixed Roles	Fixed Roles	X	X	Standard Edition and Enterprise Edition can add roles
Report Builder		X	X	X	
Report Builder Data Sources		Workgroup 1, 2	X	X	
Model Level Security			X	X	
Infinite Clickthrough				X	

Reporting Services Components

The following section will take a broad look at the different Reporting Services components. We will discuss some of the main server components, then move on to client tools, and finally look at options for help and building samples.

Server Components

Server components include the Report Server and the Report Manager. Components consist of a Windows service that runs continually on the server computer, a .NET Web service hosted in IIS, and two SQL Server databases. The Report Server databases can be installed on only one instance of SQL Server per physical database server computer. The databases need not reside on the local Report Server computer, but the server must be a member of the Windows domain or a server trusted by the domain.

Report Manager is an ASP.NET application that exposes reports, configuration, and administrative features through a web-browser interface.

The Report Manager requires IIS 5.0 or greater to be running on the Report Server computer. The .NET Framework version 1.1 also must be installed on the server. This is an included feature of Windows Server 2003. On a Windows XP Professional system, Service Pack 1 (SP1) is required. Windows 2000 Professional, Server, and Advanced Server require SP4. Windows XP Home Edition is not supported.

Client Components

Client components include the SQL Server Management Studio and the Business Intelligence Development Studio. SQL Server Management Studio is the common administration interface for all SQL Server products. Business Intelligence Development Studio uses the Visual Studio shell to allow creation of reports and report models. The client components can reside on a different server than the Report Server.

Getting Help with Books Online

The documentation for Reporting Services is contained within SQL Server Books Online. All Reporting Services–related documentation is contained in only one source. If you plan to install the server and client tools on different computers, you should consider including the Books Online with both installations.

Adventure Works Sample Databases

There are three sample databases that you can use to work with SQL Server Reporting Services. They include:

❑ **AdventureWorks:** SQL Server OLTP database for fictitious Adventure Works company.

❑ **AdventureWorksDW (relational):** SQL Server data warehouse based on the AdventureWorks OLTP database.

❑ **AdventureWorksDW (OLAP):** Analysis Services OLAP database based on the AdventureWorkDW data warehouse.

You can use all three of these databases to create sample reports. Throughout this book, we will primarily use the AdventureWorksDW database. It will be helpful to install the sample from the SQL Server 2005 installation media.

Administrative Tools

Command-line utilities provide scripting and command-level access to server management, deployment, and configuration features. These capabilities are thoroughly discussed in Chapter 11.

Command-Line and Unattended Installation

The setup may be run using command-line switch to automate the installation process. This capability is provided by the standard Windows Installer 2.0. Although there is no command-line interface, the setup process may be scripted and settings can be specified.

Log Files

Reporting Services records event information in the standard Windows Application Log and in specific log files. Report execution logging is enabled by default and may be configured in the Report Manager. Specific settings for the Report Server are stored in the RSReportServer.config file. More granular tracing information may be captured in log files for a variety of application and server events and system errors. These logs may be helpful in analyzing usage and debugging specific problems. The log files are auto-generated using time-stamped names. Further configuration and logging information can be found in Chapter 11.

Designing Reports

Starting in Chapter 4, we will deal with the essentials of report design and will take more specific design elements to the next level. Reports fall into a few design categories, which will be covered next.

Form Reports

A report can display a single record on a page with data from a table, calculations, and just static text. Form reports can be used to print or display a letter, invoice, contract, or informational sheet.

Tabular Reports

This is a fundamental style for reports that have repeated rows of data called data regions. Tabular data is repeated in free-form bands or table rows with rows and columns. Either the list or table items may be used to produce a tabular report in various layouts. Column headers can be displayed for each column in a table, and subtotals and summary information may be displayed in table or group section footers.

Groupings and Drill-Down

Records in a report may be sorted and grouped. Each group can be collapsed and expanded to drill down into more detail. This capability gives users the ability to explore large sets of data without the need to scroll though long, multipage reports. The report may also be printed in its expanded form.

Drill-Through Reports

A drill-through report can be any standard form, tabular, or pivot table report that contains links to a separate report. Any textbox item may used as a link to provide drill-through capability. Key values are hidden with the link and passed as a parameter to the target report for filtering.

Multicolumn Reports

A report may contain multiple columns. List or tabular rows are repeated vertically within a column and then *snake* from one column to the next, filling the page. This type of format is ideal for optimizing page space for labels and contact information.

Matrix

A matrix is like a cross-tab or a pivot table in which the rows and columns roll up summary values and may be expanded or collapsed to expose more or less detail. It is a simple and easy-to-use control, much like the datagrid control in ASP.NET.

Charts

Charts are used to display a graphical representation of data, typically aggregated along at least two axes. Common types of charts are bar and column, pie and donut, line, area, and scatter charts. More specific types of charts like stock and bubble charts are more specialized.

Data Sources

Reports can obtain data from standard data providers supported by the .NET Framework. In addition to SQL Server, this list includes Oracle, Access, Excel, Informix, DB2, and any other databases and data sources accessible via an OLE DB provider or Open Database Connectivity (ODBC) driver. Nonrelational sources such as Active Directory Services, Exchange Server, and OLAP sources such as Analysis Services can be queried. Developers can create custom data provider extensions — when an OLE DB provider or ODBC driver does not exist — to make practically any type of data accessible to a report.

Queries

Each report contains a query expression within its definition. A standard Transact-SQL query builder tool is incorporated into the report designer, capable of producing complex query expressions to be stored in the report. Although this is the de facto behavior of the designer, keeping queries in the report may not always be the best practice. Using a view or stored procedure from a SQL Server database can be a far more efficient method to query enterprise data. Parameters passed to a stored procedure cause the precompiled query to be processed on the database server before data is transferred across network connections.

OLAP Reporting

Decision-support databases come in many sizes and shapes. In its simplest form, a reporting data source can be a relational database with a few tables that can be queried more easily with some joins to other tables. Unlike transactional databases (often called Online Transaction Processing, or OLTP, systems), OLAP databases are designed for efficient read-only access and reporting.

Large-scale OLAP databases require special storage and retrieval engines. Data may be managed in a cube structure, which enables values to be summarized and aggregated into slices and pivots. Microsoft provides SQL Server Analysis Services as its OLAP database product. Integration with Analysis Services has been significantly improved in Reporting Services 2005. When querying an Analysis Services 2005 database, you can use the Analysis Services provider to invoke the new MDX query editor. The MDX query editor allows you to visually create queries, add parameters, and display Key Performance Indicators (KPIs).

You can also use the OLE DB provider for OLAP to query both Analysis Services 2000 and 2005. Using the OLE DB provider requires coding of MDX in Reporting Services generic query designer. It is a bit more complicated than the MDX query designer, but it does allow much more control over the query sent to the Analysis Services database.

Using Business Intelligence Development Studio

The Business Intelligence Development Studio (BIDS) leverages Visual Studio 2005. When you launch BIDS, you might notice that the application title bar actually displays Visual Studio 2005. BIDS is freely available with the installation of SQL Server 2005. It contains project templates for creating Reporting Services Reports and Reporting Services Report Models as well as other BI-related projects. Unlike the full Visual Studio 2005 product, it does not include templates for creating Windows- or Web-based applications using languages such as C# and VB.NET. It replaces several different development tools in previous versions. BIDS is the main developer tool available to design and build reports for SQL Server Reporting Services. Because of the extensibility of Reporting Services and the RDL XML grammar, other design tools are available from third parties.

Report Wizard

The Report Wizard is a simple way to get started creating reports. It leads a designer though all of the steps necessary to build a simple report interface. New designers will find it an easy, uncomplicated tool for creating or choosing a data source, creating a query, selecting fields for the header and grouping and displaying values, and choosing report styles and format options. After completing the wizard, the report design may be extended and tuned to provide more functionality.

> **Experienced designers will likely not find the wizard helpful as they become more familiar with the design process and may prefer to have more control of these options.**

The .NET Framework

The Microsoft .NET Framework is a completely new direction for Microsoft and replaces the *application programming interfaces (APIs)* and object technology of the past. It's far more than a marketing strategy or a product. It gives application developers the objects and building blocks to create powerful applications of all kinds. Design and debugging features are also available in it to help developers through the tedious application development process. Utilities and compilers enable applications to be configured, compiled, and deployed. A runtime environment manages execution, resource allocation, security, and interoperability with other services, servers, and operating systems.

The main thing to understand about .NET is that it is a core component of Windows, and it supports applications at many levels. The runtime and the development support tools are free. Visual Studio 2005 is a development tool that gives developers convenient access to these design and development capabilities.

Reporting Services is built on the .NET platform. The Report Server runs as a Windows service and is a .NET-managed assembly. Rendering and management features are exposed as an ASP.NET Web service. The Report Manager is an ASP.NET web forms application. Finally, the report metadata, subscriptions, and configuration information is managed in a SQL Server 2005 database accessed through the SQL Server ADO.NET data provider. As you can see, Reporting Services is purely a .NET solution.

Extending Reporting Services

On the advanced end of the opportunity scale, reports can be extended and enhanced in a variety of ways. At the core of the Reporting Services architecture is a set of extendable programming interfaces that enable the use of custom components written with .NET programming tools. Custom extensions are discussed in Chapter 13.

Data Processing Extensions

The .NET Framework includes native support for connecting to standard data sources using the SQL Server, OLE DB, ODBC, and Oracle .NET data providers. However, to report on nontraditional types of data, developers can create custom data processing extensions to expose practically any type of data as a data provider. For instance, a cache of in-memory data could be used as a data source rather than data written to disk. Another example would be data stored in files using a proprietary format.

Delivery Extensions

Reporting Services supports subscription delivery via e-mail or file output with no additional programming work. Additional delivery options can be added by creating a custom delivery extension. Using a custom solution, reports could be sent to a message queue, File Transfer Protocol (FTP) site, or practically any other destination.

Security Extensions

Out of the box, Reporting Services uses Windows integrated security through IIS. This allows you to secure Report Server objects using standard Windows users and groups. There are times when this configuration isn't the best or even a possible solution. One client we've worked with had their own Internet-based solution. The solution used custom authentication and authorization code that was not compatible with

Windows. The client needed a way to ensure secure access to reports. We created a custom security extension that used their existing code to allow user access. By extending the security infrastructure, we were able to leverage all of Reporting Services' features.

Rendering Extensions

The final extension type is the rendering extension. Say that you had a requirement to deliver reports in a Rich Text Formatting (RTF) format. You could use the standard rendering interfaces to create the next extension. Once the extension was created, it would be available for every report, even those reports that have been archived as snapshots. Creating rendering extensions is not a trivial task. You must account for all of the different report elements and how they will be displayed. However, it does open the door for third-party companies to extend the Reporting Services infrastructure.

Scripting

Most report management and delivery features may be automated through a simple scripting interface. A single utility executable, rs.exe, is used to obtain access to the vast capabilities of the Report Services Web service. You can create scripts to manage batch processing of reports or programmatically manipulate any exposed functionality of reporting service. Capabilities are similar to that of the Web service proxy used in .NET programming code, but a scripting solution is a simpler approach that doesn't require complex programming or a compiled project. Scripting is an ideal approach for system administrators to create simple maintenance, deployment, and ad hoc delivery solutions.

Subscriptions

Subscriptions enable users to request reports to be delivered to them automatically. Based on a schedule (single-instance or recurring) reports may be delivered using any available deliver extension (e-mail, file, or custom) in any available rendering format. Subscriptions can be either standard, where a user requests the scheduled delivery of a specific report, or data-driven, where a group of users can request the scheduled delivery of one or more reports. This is an extremely powerful tool that can be used to provide report content in an efficient manner to users in practically any location or work schedule. Chapter 10 will lead you through this compelling feature.

Securing Reports

Reporting Services uses a role-based security model that is installed and configured by default. This model is highly extensible and may be changed after installation to use a custom authentication component.

In order for sensitive data to be protected from intrusion, it should be encrypted both at the Report Server and in the web browser or client application. The preferred method to do this is to use Reporting Services' built-in support for certification-based encryption over the *Secure Sockets Layer (SSL)*. Implementing SSL will automatically redirect web requests to an address at the same location using the https:// prefix. This enables bidirectional encrypted streaming of all data over port 443 (by default) rather than the standard HTTP port 80. Reporting Services supports levels of automatic encryption, which are detailed in the section that follows. There is currently no maintenance interface for this setting through the Report Manager or any other provided utility.

You will need to obtain a digital certificate from a certificate authority such as Verisign, AuthentiCode, or Thawte. These companies will sell or lease the certificate for a specified period of time for a few hundred dollars per year. The authority will do a background check on your business to verify you are legitimate. Configuring the certificate is actually quite easy. This is performed using the IIS management console and setting the properties for the ReportServer web folder.

To enable encryption in Report Services, edit the RSReportServer.Config file using Visual Studio or a text editor and set the SecureConnectionLevel element to a value from 0 to 3.

The Report Manager

The Report Manager (shown in Figure 2-2) is a web-based interface that provides both user-level access to reports and administrative features to configure security, subscriptions, report caching, and data access.

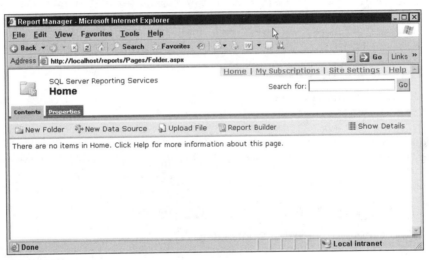

Figure 2-2

This web application is used to perform report and server administration as well as report delivery. Users may use it to simply navigate to reports, provide parameter values, and view them. The Report Manager will be discussed in detail in Chapter 10.

Designing Reports

In this release of Reporting Services, reports are designed and created in the Business Intelligence Development Studio using a special type of project especially for report design. Simple reports can be built with little effort using the report wizard. The wizard leads the user through all of the steps necessary to produce a variety of useful but simple report designs. Chapter 4 will lead you through a series of exercises to get you started with simple report design and lay the foundation of the report design elements. Chapter 5 covers the spectrum of report design items, data ranges, and formatting tools. By using groupings, you can design multilevel, hierarchical reports. Drill-down reports let users interactively expand groupings and discover more detail without having to navigate through many pages of content. Drill-though reports let users navigate from one report to another, passing filtering parameters to obtain detailed information about items in the report. Navigational links may also be used to drill through to external resources like web pages, documents, and e-mail links. Chapters 6 and 7 look at data access as well as some best practices and tips.

Charts are useful for aggregating values and presenting a series of data for comparison. A number of standard charts are available including bar, column, line, area, pie, and doughnut charts. Specialized charts types such as scatter, bubble, and stock charts are used with multidimensional data and values in distinct ranges.

Report formatting and content may be enhanced by using program code in a few ways. Custom functions may be written in a block of code that is embedded into the report. These functions may then be called in various property expressions providing conditional formatting and business rules. More complex code routines may be built into a class library and exposed to reports as custom assemblies. An assembly is deployed to the Report Server and may be shared by many reports. Finally, custom extensions may be written to replace or extend inherent data source and rendering capabilities, providing custom capabilities beyond those built into the product.

URL Access to Reports

The Report Manager environment is the default entry point and a convenient, comprehensive interface to view reports. However, one easy method to view a report is to simply navigate to the report's web address provided by the Report Server. URL query string parameters are used to specify a variety of options, including rendering formats, filtering parameter values, and display options. This is a simple method for managing and using reports right out of the box — without additional programming or configuration.

Rendering Reports in Program Code

Possibly the most unique characteristic of Reporting Services is the way it renders report content. Unlike traditional report solutions that use a proprietary, custom viewer to render the report content, at its core, Reporting Services is built on a programmatic interface (an XML Web service) that outputs the entire contents of reports in several different file or rendering formats. This capability gives programmers an incredible range of options for creating custom solutions:

❑ On a simple web page, users could click a link to display a custom report in their web browser using simple URL rendering.

❑ In a custom ASP.NET web application, users provide filtering criteria on a web page, click a button, and view the resulting report in a secondary browser window without navigating off the application's web site.

❑ In a desktop application, users provide filtering criteria and view the report within the desktop application form.

❑ Custom reports are saved to an Adobe Acrobat (PDF) file that may be viewed offline on a laptop, Pocket PC, or other mobile device.

An in-depth discussion of programmatic rendering may be found in Chapter 12. Even for the novice programmer, creating these kinds of solutions is relatively simple and may be accomplished with just a few lines of program code.

Report Definition Language

Rather than defining a proprietary specification for individual report definitions, our friends at Microsoft took a very different approach. They chose to publish an extensible and well-documented standard. The entire set of instructions that define a report are stored in a single XML document using an RDL XML grammar. If necessary, property values for elements of a report's design could be modified with a text editor. If someone wanted to build a report design tool, he or she would simply need to output the appropriate XML tags to an RDL file. This also makes it easy and convenient to send the report definition to someone or to deploy a report to another server.

Deploying Reports

Reports are defined in an RDL file, but the report's definition is stored in the Report Server database once it has been deployed to the server. Report deployment may be performed in at least three different ways. In Visual Studio 2005, the project defines a corresponding web folder on the target Report Server. Building a report project will deploy reports to a designated target Report Server. The Report Manager web interface may be used to deploy individual reports manually by simply browsing for and selecting the RDL file. The Reporting Services Web service may be used to deploy reports programmatically using methods of this multipurpose object. Chapter 10 will explore each of these options and detail deployment techniques and related considerations.

Designing and Architecting Report Solutions

Reporting Services does offer an out-of-the-box solution. Reports can be designed in Visual Studio 2005, deployed to a server, and viewed using the Report Manager web interface quite easily. However, for custom applications or to meet specific business needs, this may not be the ideal solution. Reporting Services is an extensible service with several options for designing, managing, deploying, rendering, and delivering reports to users.

Chapter 12 discusses these options and consider how understanding your business requirements should lead to the most ideal solution. You will look at different business cases and how a reporting solution fits into the overall picture to meet business and users' needs now and in the future.

Third-Party Product Integration

Probably one of the most compelling aspects of the Reporting Services extensible architecture is its ability to integrate seamlessly with business solutions. This means that it can not only become part of a custom-built business solution but also folds very neatly into commercial product offerings. The SQL Server database product has become a core component of third-party CRM, financial, ERP, and business analytics solutions. Now Reporting Services is working its way into many shrink-wrapped products as well. Reporting Services can be incorporated into a custom application without the user ever knowing that they are using a different product. It integrates with many development environments so much more easily than other reporting products. I'd like to briefly showcase two of the industry's leading business intelligence and reporting solutions that have integrated Reporting Solutions into their product suites.

Panorama Enterprise Reporter

Panorama Software has incorporated SQL Server Reporting Services into their Enterprise Reporter solution to not only utilize the report delivery features but also allow for browser-based report design. Full-featured server-side reports may be designed using familiar drag-and-drop techniques without installing development software on the client. They have also implemented a template paradigm for queries, filters, parameters, and report styles to encourage design reuse. This puts report creation capabilities into the hands of anyone in the organization without complicated software.

Their reporting solution tightly integrates with Panorama NovaView(tm), Panorama's enterprise analytics tool which provides comprehensive and robust analytic functions that enable users to identify and understand the catalysts driving business results. Panorama Enterprise Reporter and Panorama NovaView include navigation paths which allow reports and application components to integrate without the perception of multiple products or technologies.

For details on Panorama Software, visit www.panorama.com.

ProClarity for Reporting Services

ProClarity for Reporting Services integrates the structured world of production reporting with ad hoc analytics, providing what they call "insight beyond the report." ProClarity integrates with Reporting Services with a sophisticated Report Wizard that provides a rich, graphical add-in for Report Designer that automates the process of creating and editing OLAP datasets and provides "one-click" analysis of OLAP reports.

The ProClarity Professional OLAP reporting tool contains an "Export to RDL" feature to generate reports directly from their application. Formatted "Drill-to-detail" — leveraging SQL Server Analysis Services cell-level actions — provides highly formatted details behind OLAP aggregations. The ProClarity Dashboard Server incorporates Reporting Services reports and ProClarity Analytics in comprehensive BI Performance Dashboards. Reports and analytics may be deployed with common filters and selection controls so that all dashboard content is delivered in-context to the business user.

Visit www.proclarity.com for more information about ProClarity.

Summary

At this point, you should understand that Reporting Services isn't just another reporting application. The key points in this chapter are:

❑   Reporting Services uses a new approach for report delivery. Each report has a data source that may be shared with other reports. A data source can obtain data from practically any database product or data provider.

❑   Report definitions are stored in an XML document format called RDL. Out-of-the-box reports may be designed in the Business Intelligence Development Studio, but third-party and custom solutions may be used to create and design reports as well.

❑ Reporting Services can be completely secured and highly customized. The Report Manager is provided to simplify server, user, and report management. Solutions may be simple and easy to implement, or they may be completely customized and integrated into your custom-built software.

❑ Reports may be delivered using snapshots and subscriptions that are either pulled by the user in real time, or pushed by the server on a schedule. Using these capabilities, valuable system resources are conserved since reports are rendered less often and can be cached in the Report Server database.

The next chapter will help you understand the architecture that makes Reporting Services work. You learn about the nuts and bolts that give this impressive product the ability to provide scalable and extensible reporting solutions. Throughout the book, you build on this foundation as you learn to design, manage, and deploy your own reporting solutions.

3

Reporting Services Architecture

This chapter looks at how SQL Server Reporting Services (SSRS) operates. You will explore the different functional areas of Reporting Services and how they map to general report platform requirements. The first part of the chapter discusses general reporting platform concepts including platform features, report design, and report delivery. Once you have a general understanding of reporting platforms, you'll see how platform features are implemented in Reporting Services.

In any reporting platform, there are four main components: report design, report delivery, administration, and programmability. In this chapter, I discuss the overall Reporting Services architecture and how it implements each of these four functional components. This chapter focuses primarily on how Reporting Services implements its features. Later chapters discuss why those features are important and how they should be used.

This chapter covers:

❑   Reporting lifecycle

❑   SSRS platform overview

❑   SSRS XML Web service

❑   SSRS Report Server

❑   Report delivery

❑   Report design

Reporting Lifecycle

To understand the needs of a reporting platform, you need to first understand the reporting lifecycle. Reporting platforms can be evaluated by their support for the following areas: authoring, management, and delivery. You look at each of these phases later to see how Reporting Services implements them. Figure 3-1 shows the basic reporting lifecycle.

Figure 3-1

Authoring

Authoring is the process of creating and publishing reports. There are two primary methods of report development: end user developed reports and report analyst developed reports. There are some distinct differences between these two methods. End user developed reports generally require a much simpler interface. This interface needs to make report layout and formatting quite simple as well as give end users a way to understand the underlying data. Report analyst developed reports generally consist of a more robust report authoring environment and usually require a better understanding of how to query the underlying data source. Both methods of report development are usually necessary to support an enterprise reporting solution. Below are the common features to expect from a report authoring environment:

- ❑ Connects to multiple data sources.
- ❑ Query editors for previewing and returning source data.
- ❑ Report layout designers.
- ❑ Report parameters editors.
- ❑ Expression editor for creating formulas and building dynamic formats.
- ❑ Ability to set report properties such as height and width.

These capabilities are key to the initial report development. They must be flexible enough to handle complex report requirements as well as easy enough for end users to use effectively. Later, this chapter discusses report authoring in Visual Studio 2005 and the Report Builder.

Management

After developing a report, it must be deployed to some location where users can access it. After publishing, the reporting lifecycle moves into the management phase. This phase includes setting properties that allow end user access and take into consideration different environments. Some of those properties include:

- ❑ Data source connection information.
- ❑ Default parameter values.

❑ Report security settings.

❑ Report caching options.

❑ Report execution schedules.

❑ Report delivery schedules (subscriptions).

The management phase is generally performed by system administrators. Most of the user access to reports is defined in this phase.

Delivery

The delivery phase consists of end users accessing reports. There are two common delivery concepts for accessing reports: push delivery and pull delivery. Push delivery consists of reports being sent to the end user. This might include e-mails, files moved to a file share, or reports sent directly to a printer. The basic ideas is that a report is executed on a given schedule and when completed, it is sent to the user. Push delivery on the other hand consists of the end user accessing some sort of application containing reports. This could be a web portal such as SharePoint or simple links in a custom-built application. Below are some common features of the delivery phase:

❑ End user interface for report browsing.

❑ Scheduled report distribution.

❑ Parameter selection.

❑ Multiple output formats.

A good reporting platform will support both push and pull delivery and the ability to embed delivery functions into custom applications.

Now let's take a deeper look at the physical architecture of Reporting Services 2005.

Reporting Services 2005

This section covers the core components of Reporting Services 2005. This discussion will provide you with a better understanding of the pieces that must come together to create an overall reporting solution.

Platform Overview

As you saw in the previous section, the reporting platform can be broken into three main phases: authoring, management, and delivery. Now you'll take a look specifically at Reporting Services 2005 and see how the platform encompasses these three phases.

The first thing we need to identify is that Reporting Services really is a platform. Microsoft has created a tool that provides the infrastructure for building robust reporting solutions. This platform consists of a few major components: Reporting Services XML Web service, Report Server, and Reporting Services Catalog. In this section, you will be primarily concerned with functionality that enables the managements and delivery phases of the reporting lifecycle. The next section discusses the features that support authoring.

Figure 3-2 shows an overview of the Reporting Services platform. It illustrates the three main components. Understanding the three main components will better assist you in designing and implementing Reporting Services solutions.

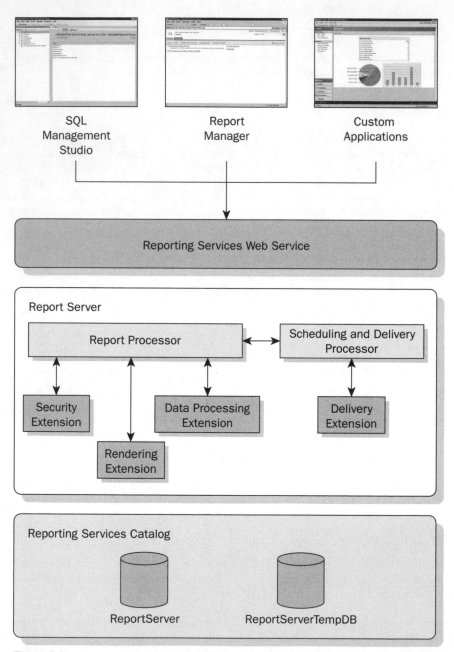

Figure 3-2

Now that you have seen the overall picture of the Reporting Services platform, let's dive into each of the three main components.

Reporting Services XML Web Service

Microsoft chose to use a Web services interfaces to expose the functionality in Reporting Services. This is important for a couple of reasons. First, it opens the platform to other programming languages. Because Web services are built on open standards and use XML to transfer information, Reporting Services can be implemented in almost any platform that supports HyperText Transfer Protocol (HTTP) and XML. Second, Web services allow for communication across networks. Using HTTP, messages can be sent across firewalls and help developers easily implement distributed systems.

So, what does the Reporting Services XML Web service do? As you navigate through the report manager or SQL Management Studio, you can perform a number of publishing, rendering, and management functions. All of these functions work against the Reporting Services Web services. Microsoft does not use any APIs not exposed to the developer. So, you can do anything in code that Microsoft does in Report Manager or SQL Management Studio.

Here are a few quick examples of where the authors have leveraged the Reporting Services Web services:

❑ **Report Deployment:** We have used RSS scripts (discussed in Chapter 10) to build automated setup routines. These routines use the Reporting Services Web services to enumerate a folder and deploy all report files contained within that folder.

❑ **Report Management:** We have also used the Reporting Services XML Web service to set up subscriptions through a custom interface. Often applications require leveraging features of the Reporting Services platform such as subscriptions without using the Report Manager interface. Through the Web services, we have embedded a subset of the subscription functionality into applications.

❑ **Report Rendering:** The most common use of the Reporting Services XML Web service is adding report rendering functionality into custom applications. There are three main items that most report viewers require: report list, parameters selection, and report rendering. All three functions can be performed through Web services to easily build your own look and feel around the Reporting Services platform. Chapter 12 will go into greater detail on rendering reports within your own application.

Reporting Services takes advantage of standard Microsoft technologies to implement its Web services interface. The Web service is hosted within Internet Information Services (IIS) and uses the .NET Framework. Both components provide the backbone infrastructure. IIS performs web request handling and routing along with some security features. The .NET Framework provides classes for consuming and publishing the web services interface.

A full breakdown of the Reporting Services XML Web service is located in Appendix B.

Report Server

The Report Server is the main engine behind reporting services. Its primary function is to process and deliver report information. You could think of it as the true core of Reporting Services. This core is made up of five main components: report processor, data source extensions, security extensions, rendering extensions, and delivery extensions. Each of the four extensions implements interfaces that allow users to extend the engine to fit their needs. Through this section, you explore each of the components and develop a basic understanding of their functionality.

Report Processing

Report processing is the main driver in the Report Server. This process is responsible for handling user requests for reports and report models and returning the appropriate data. Along with this task it also performs caching of reports to improve performance.

> *The main job of the Report Processor is to combine the report definition and report data to return a formatted output to the user.*

Figure 3-3 is an illustration of a basic report request and how the Report Processor handles it.

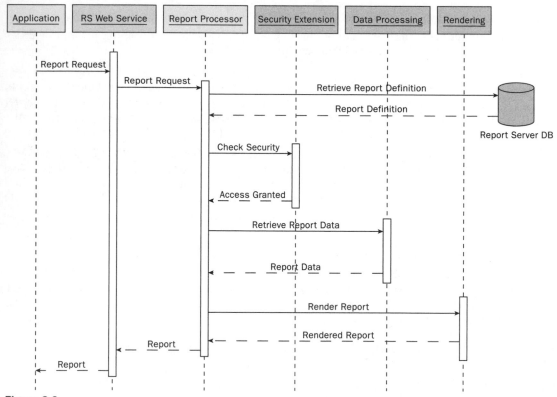

Figure 3-3

Let's take a look at some of the major tasks handled by the Report Processor.

Report Request Handling

When a report request is received, the report processor takes the following steps:

1. It determines which report is being asked for and retrieves the report definition from the Report Server database.

2. The user's credentials are validated against the report being requested.

3. The report processor asks for the report data. This call is made into the data processing extension.

4. Once the data is retrieved, the report processor combines the data and definition into an intermediate report format. This intermediate report is output format neutral so that it can be rendered using any of the available rendering extensions.

5. Once the intermediate report is created, it is cached for later use based on the execution setting of the specific report.

6. Finally, the intermediate report is sent to the rendering extension and the formatted output is returned.

Next, you take a look at some of the items involved in this process.

Report Definition

The report definition is an output-format neutral representation of the report. Reporting Services was designed to support numerous output formats, so the report definition is not aware of how the report will actually be rendered. The report definition defines the data source and layout of the report as well as parameters and default settings. Some of the layout items include tables contained within the report, their position in the report, and the number of columns. Data source information includes the connection string information for the database, the query to process, and any timeout and credential information.

Microsoft has published their report definitions as part of the Report Definition Language (RDL). RDL is an open specification that developers can use to either create their own report authoring tools, design their own output formats (rendering extensions), or manipulate the definition programmatically. Several companies have already take advantage of this open specification. Cizer Inc, has used RDL to create their own web-based report authoring tool. Hitachi Consulting has used RDL to automatically convert legacy reports into Reporting Services as well as manipulate report text for localization.

> *For the full RDL specification, check out:*
> `www.microsoft.com/sql/reporting/techinfo/rdlspec.mspx`.

Once the report definition and data are combined, they form what is called the intermediate format.

Intermediate Format

The *intermediate format* is an internal format of the report used by Reporting Services. This format is used for both rendering and caching. It is a combination of both data and structure, which means that if there is a table defined in a report and linked to a specific data set, the intermediate format will contain all the rows and columns that identify that table. However, it does not contain specific rendering information such as a <td> tag for an HTML output. The size of the intermediate format will depend on how much data is returned.

Caching

The report processor also handles the caching of reports. One of the key resources in a reporting solution is the reporting data source. To reduce the load on the data source, caching is implemented to store query results for future use.

Caching is beneficial in a number of scenarios. In many reporting solutions, the reporting database is processed on a given schedule. This is especially true when dealing with data warehouses. Say that a reporting database is only processed once per day. In this case, it is a waste of resources to continuously query a database when the information will not change. In this scenario, caching report data can be very beneficial.

Another common scenario is simply a single user moving through the same report data. If a user views a report in a web browser and then decides to export those results to Excel, rerunning the query would be wasteful. The data has already been retrieved, it simply needs to be presented in a different format.

There are three main types of caching in Reporting Services: session cache, cached instance, and snapshots. The next three sections explore the different caching options.

Session Cache

Since Reporting Services works over HTTP, it must maintain some information about each user request. This information is referred to as a *session*. If the same user asks for the same report within a short period, it does not make sense to query the information again. So, when a user makes an initial request, the report definition and data are stored in the session cached. The session cache is persisted in the ReportServerTempDB — more on this later — for each user. The duration of the session information is determined by settings on the Report Server. The default length is 10 minutes. Any report that does not have specific execution options set, cached instance or snapshot, will take advantage of session caching.

Cached Instances

Cached instances also store the report definition and data, but they have one specific identifier. They will expire at a given time. This time frame could be a matter of minutes, hours or days. It can also be a specific time period, say every night at midnight.

With a cached instance, the specific start time is not defined. Reports with this execution setting are cached when the first user asks for the report. That user will have to wait while the query is executed and the intermediate format is built. Subsequent requests for the report will take advantage of the cached intermediate format.

Once the report reaches its expiration time, it will be removed from the cache. The next request to the report will rerun the query, recreate the intermediate format, and repopulate the cache.

This caching strategy is perfect if you have slowly changing data or if frequent data changes are not critical to business decision making.

Snapshots

The final type of caching strategy is referred to as *snapshots*. Like the name implies, it is a copy of the data at a given point in time. Unlike cached instances, snapshots have a defined start time and no definite end time. Let's say you have a group of users that needs summary reports every Monday at 7:00 am for a weekly status meeting. You are in the data warehousing group and have jobs that process data late Sunday night in preparation for the meeting. Once the data is processed, it does not change. This data is also very large and takes a significant time to query. In this case, it makes sense to store the reports after the information is available. This way, people can come in on Monday, run their reports and get quick response times.

Working from the example above, a week goes by and you are again ready to run your reports. In this case, you would probably not want to get rid of last week's reports. Instead, you would want to archive them for historical purposes. With snapshot caching, you can specify which reports to store in history and how many to store. In this setup, as soon as a snapshot is created, an identical copy is stored in history. Then when your data updates and a new snapshot is created, a historical view will be available for the users.

Now that you have seen the main report processing engine, you next take a look at each of the components it leverages.

Data Processing Extensions

All data is returned to the report processor through data processing extensions. Data processing extensions can be created for just about any type of data. There are also a number of data processing extensions supported by Reporting Services.

Some of the common tasks performed by a data processing extension include:

- ❑ Connecting to the data source.
- ❑ Passing and retrieving parameter collections.
- ❑ Executing commands against a data source.
- ❑ Returning data readers from a data source.
- ❑ Providing methods to read information from the data source.
- ❑ Implementing transactions on a given data source.

Figure 3-4 shows a basic breakdown of data processing extensions.

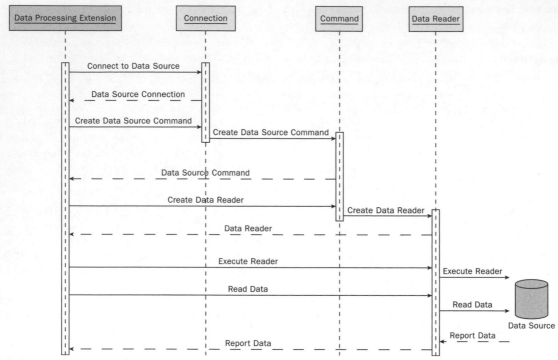

Figure 3-4

Let's take a look at some of the support providers in SQL Reporting Services 2005.

Supported Providers

Reporting Services supports the .NET managed providers as well as custom extensions for returning data. The .NET managed providers include SQL Server, OLE DB, and Oracle. Managed providers take full advantage of the .NET Framework. Using these providers, users should be able to connect to just about any data source. Let's take a look at some of the common Reporting Services data extensions.

SQL Server Provider

Using the SQL Server provider, users can retrieve data from SQL Server tables, stored procedures, views, and user-defined functions. The SQL Server managed provider is optimized to connect to SQL Server. Extra layers such as OLE DB and ODBC have been removed to improve performance.

When using the SQL Server provider, users can also take advantage of the SQL Query Designer. This designer allows users to visually build SQL queries taking away some of the complexities of the language. The SQL Server provider will work with both SQL Server 2000 and 2005.

Oracle Provider

Although Reporting Services uses SQL Server to store its metadata, you can use Oracle as a source for your reports. Like the SQL Server managed provider, the Oracle provider is optimized for Oracle and removes extra layers such as OLE DB and ODBC.

Analysis Services 2005 Provider

A welcome addition to Reporting Services 2005 is the Analysis Services 2005 provider. This provider allows users to connect to the Analysis Services Unified Dimensional Model (UDM) and retrieve multi-dimensional data. The UDM gives users a semantic model that understands data relationships and aggregation. Access to the UDM is implemented using Multidimensional Expressions (MDX).

From a reporting perspective, MDX is an extremely powerful query language. MDX understands and can work with data relationships. It can also perform coordinate-based calculations to build Excel-like formulas.

Along with the power of MDX comes a bit of complexity. Most people have the perception that MDX is a challenging language. It is my opinion that MDX is no more challenging than SQL; it just takes some practice. Once you have a fundamental understanding of the language, common report tasks can become trivial. In the meantime, you can use the MDX Query Builder provided by the Analysis Services data extension. This query builder allows users to drag and drop measures and dimensions to form a result set. It also allows users to specify parameterized dimensions that will then appear in the reports.

OLE DB Provider

The OLE DB provider gives report writers a great deal of flexibility. Using this provider, you can query a number of different data sources. The following is a list of just a few:

❑ Microsoft Analysis Services 2000

❑ Microsoft Access

❑ Microsoft Excel

❑ Microsoft Directory Services

❑ OLEDB for ODBC

Data source extensions are the first key to the Reporting Services platform. They allow report writes to access a large array of data sources, and if there is no provider present, a new data source extension can be developed. In the next section, you will look at rendering extensions.

Rendering Extensions

Reporting Services supports a number of different rendering extensions. When creating a report in Reporting Services, you are creating it in a neutral output format. In the report, you define the query, the fields, and how they should be laid out on the page. It is the job of the rendering extension to take this information and combine it with report data to create a formatted output. In this section, you look at some of the supported extensions.

Excel

The Excel rendering extension takes report data and outputs it to a spreadsheet. This is an extremely common format for many users. Excel is especially useful for those users wanting to perform further analysis on the information.

Excel rendering in some reporting platforms can tend to cause formatting problems. This is due to the report design methods used in other tools. Microsoft Access is an example of a banded report designer. In this type of designer, users have detailed header and footer bands to deal with data set information.

This allows for a great deal of flexibility but doesn't translate well into rows and columns. If a heading and its associated data item are misaligned by a couple of pixels, it is difficult for the rendering extension to determine that those two items should be aligned in a single column. Some banded tools will take these separated items and create two different columns. This type of output generally results in a spreadsheet that requires a large amount of manipulation to format correctly.

Reporting Services does not use a simple banded report design. Instead, it uses objects that are laid out within a page. Two of the main objects used to display repeating data are the table and matrix controls. Both controls understand rows and columns. So, when you use these types of display items, exports to Excel more closely resemble the original report.

PDF

Microsoft also provides a rendering extension for the PDF format. This format is one of the most popular formats for sharing documents. It is clean and easy to read with exceptional printing capabilities. You would most likely choose this format for reports that are widely distributed but not analyzed by the end user. Reports that are in PDF format cannot be altered. Examples of where PDF would be appropriate are invoices, inventory pick tickets, weekly sales summaries, and public financial documents.

PDF also supports document maps. Document maps are a feature in Reporting Services that allow you to define bookmarks within a report. Once the report is rendered, users can click on links to easily navigate to different areas of a report. This functionality can be leveraged to create a table of contents for larger reports.

End users can download Adobe Acrobat Reader for free and do not need a license to distribute PDF documents generated by Reporting Services.

HTML

The most common output format for reporting in Reporting Services is HTML. Reports can be rendered in HTML 4.0 or HTML 3.2. The .NET Framework identifies the browser support of the user and renders the report in the appropriate format.

HTML rendering is good for interactive reports. By navigating to a web site, a user can easily manipulate report parameters to find specific information. HTML rendering also supports dynamic visibility, which gives users the ability to drill down to more detailed information. Document maps can also be used to help navigate large reports.

The downside to HTML rendering is its lack of ability to print. Web pages have never been good for printing and that does not change with Reporting Services. Users can export reports to formats such as PDF or TIFF for printing but generally do not like to take that extra export step to create a printed report. To solve this problem, Reporting Services now supports client-side printing. Client-side printing is implemented by running an ActiveX control in the user's browser that builds a print-ready format. This method of printing from the web is not new. The Crystal Reports web control uses a similar process.

Web Archive (MHTML)

Web Archive or MHTML is commonly found in e-mail messages. MHTML stands for MIME Encapsulation of Aggregate HTML Documents. That is an extremely long name that basically means images, style sheets, and other referenced-type information in an HTML document is embedded into the MHTML document. This allows a single document to be sent to a user without having dependencies on external resources.

MHTML documents are useful when creating reporting subscriptions delivered by e-mail. MHTML will allow you to send a formatted report directly to a report user without an associated attachment. Not all e-mail products support MHTML, so check with your user community before choosing this output format.

CSV

The Comma-Separated Values (CSV) format takes the report definition and data and transforms it into a flat file. This output is appropriate for exchanging data. You might have customers with legacy systems that are very good at parsing and consuming flat files. In this case, you might electronically send reports in CSV format to these users. However, Reporting Services is not meant to be a data exchange tool. For true system integration, look to products like Microsoft BizTalk Server and Microsoft Integration Services.

TIFF

Tagged Image File Format (TIFF) is a widely used format for storing document images. Many facsimile programs use this standard for transferring data. Many organizations also store archived documents in this format. Reports rendered in TIFF would be excellent candidates for document management systems such as Windows SharePoint Services. Historical snapshots of reports could be transferred to document management systems and then removed from the Report Server. This would allow users to take advantage of common document management features such as indexing and searching.

XML

Extensible Markup Language (XML) is another format commonly used for extracting report information into a data exchange format, similar to CSV. CSV and XML can serve a similar purpose; however, XML is a much more powerful format. XML is a structured markup language that lets you define data schemas. Reporting Services uses this markup in a number of areas. When reports are rendered as XML, they include both the report definition and data. XML files are ideal for exchanging information. You could send XML rendered reports to customers or other applications for additional processing.

Delivery Extensions

Delivery extensions can be used to render reports on a given schedule and to a given output. Delivery extensions take advantage of existing rendering and data source extensions. Report Services supports delivery of reports to e-mail and file shares. Developers can create their own delivery extensions. Some delivery extension examples the authors have dealt with include:

- ❏   Delivery directly to a printer for high volume billing reports.
- ❏   Delivery of reports to a SharePoint portal site.

Delivery extensions use a series of classes to handle notifications and process report stream outputs. These classes are called from the Scheduling and Delivery Processor. The next section explores the Scheduling and Delivery Processor.

Scheduling and Delivery Processor

The Scheduling and Delivery Processor has two major functions: working with report execution schedules and delivering reports through delivery extensions. These functions hinge on the use of Microsoft's SQL Server Agent and the Reporting Services Windows service. When scheduling a report, a new SQL Server Agent job is created. That job contains a call to a single stored procedure on the Report Server database. When the agent runs the scheduled job, the stored procedure places a single record in the Event table of the Report Server database. The Reporting Services Windows service queries this table on a regular basis. As soon as the record is present, the Reporting Services Windows service starts the Scheduling and Delivery Processor. Figures 3-5 and 3-6 illustrate creating a subscription and processing subscription events with the Scheduling and Delivery Processor.

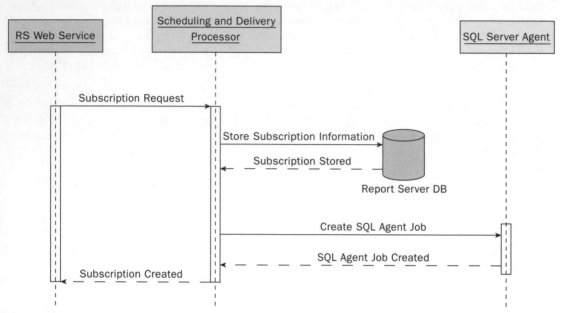

Figure 3-5

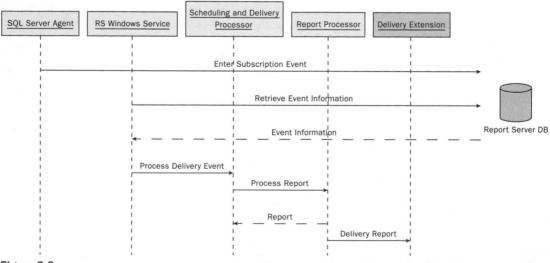

Figure 3-6

Now that you have seen the Scheduling and Delivery Processor, you'll next explore some of the features that make it work.

Scheduling

Reporting Services 2005 has the ability to create sophisticated execution schedules for reports. When creating a delivery schedule, Reporting Services stores the schedule information in the Report Server database. It also creates an SQL Server Agent job referencing the schedule. Both users and administrators can define schedules for report execution and delivery.

Subscriptions

Subscriptions deal with the mode in which reports are delivered to the end user on a given schedule. Users can have reports delivered via e-mail, a file share, or a customized delivery extension. There are three different types of subscriptions available in Reporting Services: standard subscriptions, data-driven subscriptions, and event-based subscriptions. In this section, you look at the three different types of subscriptions.

Standard Subscriptions

Individual user subscriptions can be created through SQL Management Studio, Report Manager, or a custom application via the Reporting Services Web service. When setting up a standard subscription, information such as parameter values and rendering format can be set along with a schedule for report delivery.

With standard subscriptions, users can define their own schedule for receiving a report. This is important for small-scale reports and gives users a great deal of freedom in how they receive certain information.

Data-Driven Subscriptions

Data-driven subscriptions allow for scaling out a report subscription. Subscriptions can be created for a large number of users and include different rendering parameters, report parameters, and delivery options for each individual. This allows you to create a very customized report experience for users with a minimal amount of work.

Think of a large retail organization where each store in the organization has a store manager. Each week the store manager receives the sales numbers from the previous week. The report is identical for each manager except for the reference to the actual store. So, using data-driven subscriptions, you could dynamically set the store report parameter for each report and then e-mail individual reports to each manager. In the end, you have created only one report but quickly tailored it for a number of different users.

Setting up data-driven subscriptions is very straightforward. Similar to a standard subscription, you have two main sets of data to configure for the subscriptions: report information including parameters and delivery information such as an e-mail address. Data-driven subscriptions use a relational table to store the report and delivery information. Because it is stored in a relational table, you can customize it for each record that is created.

In both standard and data-driven subscriptions, the delivery of these reports is event-driven. In the next section, you look at the two types of delivery events.

Schedule-Based Events

One of the common methods of determining when reports are to be delivered is doing so through some sort of schedule. The report could be delivered every month, week, or day, or at any such predetermined interval of time. Reporting Services gives users a number of different options when setting schedules. These schedules can be either specific to a given subscription or shared through Reporting Services.

Let's imagine that your organization has a set of reports that have their underlying data updated every Sunday evening. Executives can use this information for a Monday morning meeting. You could define a shared schedule that contains information such as "Weekly, Monday, 6 am." This shared schedule could then be used for any number of reports. If later you decide that sending the report at 6 am does not meet new requirements, you could simply edit the shared schedule and thereby change the schedule for each report using it.

Snapshot Update Events

Delivery of reports can also be triggered by the update of snapshot reports. Many reports in an organization have set intervals after which they are updated. For example, data for a monthly sales report is always updated on the last day of the month. Once this has happened, the data is frozen and does not change for an entire month. If you want to create a report from this information, does it make sense to query the database each time the report runs? No, the information at this point is static. So, you create a snapshot of the data at the end of each month and store the entire report. At this point, when users display the report you no longer have the overhead of a database call.

If you were going to update your reports according to a given schedule, it would only make sense to deliver them to the appropriate users when they are ready. Reporting Services allows users to set their subscriptions based on updates to snapshots. With this method, you do not have to worry about setting a defined time when you think the report will be done processing; instead, it will send off the delivery when report processing is finished.

Supported Delivery Extensions

Delivery extensions are tied heavily to the Scheduling and Delivery Processor. They are used when sending subscriptions to users. Microsoft has provided two delivery extensions and given users the ability to develop their own. Reporting Services comes with two delivery extensions: e-mail and file share. In this section, you look at the two base extensions.

E-mail

The e-mail delivery extension allows users to receive reports directly in their inbox. You can specify the rendering format that you would like the report to be delivered in and whether or not to include a web link to the report. Depending on the rendering extension used in the report, users either will see the report directly in their mailbox or receive it as an attachment. As mentioned earlier, you could use the Web Archive (MHTML format) to embed reports and their images in an e-mail message.

> *To send e-mail deliveries, Reporting Services must be able to communicate with a valid Simple Mail Transfer Protocol (SMTP) server. This setting is initially set when installing and configuring Reporting Services.*

File Share

Reports can also be delivered directly to a file share. For this, Reporting Services must have write permissions to the share. You can specify credentials to use when sending reports to a file share.

Custom Delivery Extensions

Along with the supported extensions, Reporting Services allows for the creation of custom delivery extensions. Some of the common delivery extensions we have come across include printer delivery extensions. One client had to print a large number of reports every month, approximately 200,000. We created an extension that interfaced directly with the printer delivery and was able to effectively process all reports each month.

Security

The final component you will look at is the Reporting Services security extensions. Reporting Services relies on security extensions to handle both authentication and authorization. The default security extension in Reporting Services supports Windows authentication. In a number of scenarios, this is an acceptable method. However, there are those solutions that cannot rely on users' having a trusted Windows account.

In one client scenario, we were working with a solution provider that sold a hosted web application. The client was interested in providing reporting through Reporting Services over the Internet. The client's solution implemented its own authentication and authorization logic. To implement Reporting Services, we needed to hook into this authentication and authorization logic. Our final solution included a custom security extension that called the client's application logic to authenticate a user. Once we had the user's authentication information, we could easily implement different types of security within our solution.

Often, developers are hesitant to create their own security extension. We have seen that many people try to implement their own type of security logic on top of reporting services instead of working with the security extensions. It has been our experience that working around the security model instead of within it usually represents more work and less functionality. By implementing a Reporting Services security extension, you take advantage of the platform architecture and can implement all of the Reporting Services features that hook into it.

Reporting Services Windows Service

Another major component of Reporting Services is the Reporting Services Windows service. One of the major functions of this service is the execution of scheduled tasks. Entries are written to the Event table in the ReportServer database using SQL Server Agent. By default, the Reporting Services Windows service queries this table every 10 seconds. Once it finds an entry, it performs any processing required by the event.

Reporting Services Catalog

Reporting Services relies on SQL Server for storing its metadata. This allows for greater scalability in large reporting applications. This also allows you to take advantage of features inherent to SQL Server such as backup and transaction logging.

Reporting Services uses two SQL Server databases to store data: ReportServer and ReportServerTempDB. In the next section, you look at each database and learn how they are used.

ReportServer Database

The ReportServer database is the main store for data in Reporting Services. It contains all report definitions, report models, data sources, schedules, security information, and snapshots. There are a series of tables for each functional area. The database schema is open and generally easy to follow.

Updating or querying these database tables is not recommended, but an understanding of how they are arranged should give you a better understanding of how Reporting Services works.

The following table lists some of the tables in the ReportServer database and their related functions.

Table Name	Function
Resources	
Catalog	Contains report definitions, folder locations, and data source information.
DataSource	Contains individual data source information. Data source information is maintained separate from report definitions to ensure it is not overwritten when reports are republished.
Security	
Users	User name and security ID (SID) information for authorized users.
Policies	Listing of references to different security policies.
PolicyUserRole	Association of users/groups, roles, and policies.
Roles	List of defined roles and the tasks that the role can perform.
Snapshots and Snapshot History	
SnapshotData	Information used to run an individual snapshot, including query parameters and snapshot description.
ChunkData	Stores the report snapshots. Snapshots contain both report definition and data. There are also certain records containing rendered snapshot output for quicker rendering.
History	Stores a reference between stored snapshots and the date they were captured.
Scheduling and Report History	
Schedule	Contains information for different report execution and subscription delivery schedules.
ReportSchedule	Association between a given report, its execution schedule, and the action to take.
Subscriptions	Listing of individual subscriptions, including owner, parameters, and delivery extension.
Notification	Subscription notification information such as date processed, last runtime, and delivery extension.

Table Name	Function
Event	Temporary storage location for event notification. Populated by SQL Server Agent and then executed by the Reporting Services Windows service.
ActiveSubscriptions	Subscription success/failure information.
RunningJobs	Currently executing scheduled processes.
Administrative	
Configuration	Reporting Services configuration settings. These should only be administered using the Reporting Services configuration utilities.
Keys	Listing of public and private keys for data encryption.
ExecutionLog	List of reports that have been executed, when they started execution, when they finished execution, the user making the request, and the parameters used.
Report Models	
ModelDrill	Contains information used when implementing Report Builder infinite drill-down feature. Lists reports and their associated report model.
ModelItemPolicy	Association among a given report item, model, and policy.
ModelPerspective	Association between a given report model and its perspectives.

> When working with Reporting Services, it is important to pay close attention to the ReportServer database. It contains all critical information related to Reporting Services and should be backed up on a regular schedule.

ReportServerTempDB

As the name implies, the ReportServerTempDB database stores temporary Reporting Services information. User session information is stored in the ReportServerTempDB. Because Reporting Services communicates using HTTP, no state is maintained between the client application and server. Session state about the reports that the user is running must be stored between each server call. The ReportServerTempDB stores this information in a SessionData table.

ReportServerTempDB also stores report cache information. When a report is set as a cached instance, there is no definite time when that report is executed. It depends on which process requests the report first. Once the report is executed, the intermediate format and data are stored in the ReportServer TempDB database. If this database were to fail, the cached information would be lost. But, since it is executed when a user views the report, there is no real loss of information. Snapshots, on the other hand, are not stored here. Their execution time is usually at a set moment to ensure that the data on the report is correct. Therefore, this information is stored in the more permanent ReportServer database.

Reporting Services will not be able to function without the ReportServerTempDB database.

The following table lists some of the tables in the ReportServer database and their related functions.

Table Name	Function
ChunkData	Stores report definition and data for session cached reports and cached instances.
ExecutionCache	Stores execution information including timeout for cached instances.
PersistedStream	Stores session level rendered output for an individual user.
SessionData	Persists individual user session level information, including report paths and timeouts for given session information.
SessionLock	Temporary storage to handle locking of session data.
SnapshotData	Stores temporary snapshots.

It is not necessary to back up the data in the ReportServerTempDB.

Execution Information

As mentioned earlier, it is not recommended that you view or modify the underlying SQL Server tables. It is also very difficult to analyze execution information in the ReportServer database.

However, there is a good deal of information about report execution stored in the ReportServer database. To make access to this information easier, there is a sample Integration Services package that will extract report execution data and expose it for reporting.

Along with the Integration Services packages, there are sample reports that demonstrate how to expose execution information. To access these samples, you must install the Server Management Samples included in the setup CD.

Report Design

Good report design is core to any reporting platform. If reports are not easy to create and edit, adoption of the product will suffer. When Reporting Services 2005 was released, Microsoft took an interesting approach to report design. Essentially, it decided to create a standard that could be extended by third parties and Microsoft. This standard, know as Report Definition Language (RDL), has opened the door to a number of outside tool vendors, allowing them to create their own report design utilities. This section looks at the different report design options and how they can be leveraged.

Visual Studio 2005 Report Designer

Visual Studio 2005 has become the standard development environment for a number of Microsoft products including Office, Integration Services, and Analysis Services. Reporting Services 2000 leveraged Visual Studio as its development interface. In SQL Server 2005, Microsoft has created a new tool called the Business Intelligence Development Studio.

The Business Intelligence Development Studio is based on the Visual Studio 2005 shell. When installing any of the Business Intelligence products (Analysis Services, Integration Services, and Reporting Services) the Visual Studio 2005 shell is also installed. Along with the shell, project templates are installed for each of the Business Intelligence products. Reporting Services includes wizards for creating reporting projects and individual reports. It also contains templates for creating new shared data sources and blank reports. Chapter 4 discusses report design in greater detail.

Once Visual Studio 2005 is installed, users can create a new report project. Within the report project, users can define the data sources and queries used to drive reports, layout, and parameter inputs. Visual Studio is a robust development tool and is primarily targeted toward developers and analysts who are comfortable in a richer environment. However, there is a large need for users to create their own basic reports. The next section covers how Report Builder has opened up report creation to a larger audience.

Report Builder and Report Models

Report Builder is arguably the biggest enhancement to Reporting Services 2005. It is a major component in creating a true reporting solution. Report Builder is intended to give end users the ability to create their own reports. One of the keys to this functionality is giving users an understandable data model that they can easily leverage.

In 2004 Microsoft purchased the company ActiveViews. ActiveViews had technology that allowed developers to create a user-friendly data model on top of an existing database. This model enabled end users to create reports without knowing the underlying database query syntax or schema. The Reporting Services team has taken this technology and incorporated it into Reporting Services 2005. Now, developers can build new Report Model projects and end users can work with them from the Report Manager. Chapters 8 and 9 will detail Report Models and the Report Builder.

Third-Party Designers

Because RDL is an open standard, there are a number of third parties that have also created tools for developing reports. The three most recognizable names are Proclarity, Panorama, and Cizer. Proclarity and Panorama are both developers of OLAP front-end tools. With the introduction of Reporting Services, they have used their own engines to help developers query multidimensional data and build Reporting Services reports on top of it. Cizer took advantage of RDL and created a suite of products around Reporting Services. Cizer's products include browser-based report design interfaces and a Microsoft MapPoint integration component that allows users to include map data within their views.

Now that you have seen the different engine components as well as report design tools, you are going to look at how reports are exposed to end users.

Report User Interface

As was described earlier, Reporting Services is a platform for building reporting solutions. Outside of a flexible report processing engine and variety of development tools, a platform must provide mechanisms for displaying reports to end users. In Reporting Services 2005, there are a number of ways to expose your reports to others. In this section, you look at how you can expose reports through the Report Manager, SharePoint Web Parts, Visual Studio controls, and custom user interfaces.

Report Manager

Report Manager is the default mechanism for exposing reports to the end user. When you install Reporting Services 2005, two virtual directories are created. One of these is the Report Manager directory. Report Manager is a web-based application that communicates with the Reporting Services Web service. It can display a list of folders and reports to end users for browsing. It also provides mechanisms for users to create and modify their own subscriptions.

This interface is easy to deploy since it is included with the product. However, it does not offer a great deal of flexibility in the user interface. There are techniques that you can use to customize the styles used by the interface, but you cannot rearrange or modify how different parts of the application are organized or look. The next few sections talk about other methods for exposing reports. Each one requires an increased level of custom development to implement.

SharePoint Web Parts

One of the easiest ways to incorporate Reporting Services into another application is through the use of SharePoint Web Parts. The SharePoint Web Parts include a Report Explorer and Report Viewer. These controls can be used to embed Reporting Services reports into an existing site. Implementation of these web parts takes a general understanding of both Reporting Services and SharePoint.

If you are not using SharePoint as part of your user interface, you can consider a few Visual Studio Controls to accomplish this integration.

Visual Studio Controls

Reporting Services 2005 includes two Report Viewer controls for embedding reports into custom applications. These controls include an ASP.NET control as well as a Windows control. Both controls can communicate with the Reporting Services XML Web service to render reports. The Windows control is a major improvement in Reporting Services 2005. It includes a local processing mode that allows developers to supply report definitions and data sets within their own applications. This functionality enables the creation of offline applications that still take advantage of the Reporting Services Report Processing.

For the greatest flexibility, users can create their own user interfaces through the Reporting Services XML Web service.

Custom User Interface

The Reporting Services XML Web service contains a new Execution endpoint that allows developers to more easily create their own user interfaces. This endpoint exposes methods for rendering reports into various formats. Once the report is rendered, developers can take the output and send it to their own web processing code or some other custom interface.

This method provides the most flexibility in creating a user interface but also requires the greatest degree of skill. Many implementations of Reporting Services will incorporate some combination of the User Interface choices identified above. In Chapter 12, you take a close look at implementing each of the User Interface options, and we discuss what you need to consider when designing your own solutions.

Summary

This chapter covered the basics of Reporting Services. It started with a look at the different reporting phases: authoring, management, and delivery. The authoring phase dealt with developing the reports. In the management phase, you set individual properties of the reports such as data sources and security rules. In the delivery phase, you looked at the different methods to giving access to end users.

After the discussion of these phases, you saw the features of Reporting Services that support them. Visual Studio 2005, Report Builder, and third-party tools can be used to create report definitions. Once reports are created, they can be published to the Report Server. Using Report Manager or SQL Management Studio, you can update and maintain report information. If users need to view reports, they can use the Report Manager, SharePoint Web Parts, Visual Studio controls, or custom code.

Finally, you looked at the specific components of Reporting Services. You started by looking at the Reporting Services XML Web service and seeing how the Reporting Services interface is exposed. Next, you looked at the Report Server and learned about report processing and scheduled delivery. The last component dealt with the storage of metadata in the ReportServer and ReportServerTempDB databases.

After reading this chapter, you should understand the following:

- ❑ Authoring, management, and delivery in the reporting lifecycle.
- ❑ The major components of Reporting Services.
- ❑ Tools available to create Reporting Services reports.
- ❑ Methods for delivering reports to end users.

In the next chapter, you see techniques and concepts that can be used to build your first reports.

Part II
Report Design

Chapter 4: Basic Report Design

Chapter 5: Designing Data Access

Chapter 6: Advanced Report Design

Chapter 7: Report Solution Patterns and Recipes

Basic Report Design

One of my pet peeves is someone giving me too much information in response to a simple question. At times the easiest way to get from point A (in this case, not knowing how to create a report) to point B (having a working report) is a simple matter of learning *what* to do, not necessarily *how* to do it all. Don't get me wrong; *how* is an important question that deserves a thorough explanation — at the right time. Unlike many college courses that are filled to the brim with information about the history and concepts related to a topic with no direction regarding what a person should actually do with this information, my goal is to give you some practical guidance right upfront. I'll deal with the details later on.

The next three chapters will teach you all about report design. I will start with a high-level view of the mechanics of report design (*what* to do). After you understand the fundamentals of common report construction, you'll learn more about how reports actually process and render data. With this knowledge under your belt, you will be better prepared to exercise your creativity and will know how to put all the pieces together to create effective reports.

- ❑ Chapter 4 teaches you the essentials: *What* you need to do to get started building basic reports using the report wizard and common report designer features. The second half of that chapter introduces the fundamental building blocks of report design: report items and report layout properties.

- ❑ In Chapter 5 you learn about the design elements that may be used to create more advanced reports. I'll show you *how* to use different tools and techniques to implement different features. Many of the topics in the chapter you are now reading will be revisited in Chapter 5 in a more advanced context.

- ❑ Chapter 6 is once again about *what* to do. We have assembled step-by-step instructions to show you how to build specific report solutions to address a variety of business problems.

Report Design 101

You're going to learn how to design reports using the Report Wizard — the simplest of all methods. If you are new to report design and Visual Studio, I think you will find the Report Wizard to be a convenient way to design simple reports. If you are an experienced report designer or application developer, or if you need to learn to design complex, custom reports, you're likely to use the Report Wizard a few times and then leave it behind.

Let's take a look at the big picture of designing reports in SQL Server Reporting Services. We will examine most of the important features of Reporting Services just to get an idea of what you can do with the product. We'll also point you to later chapters to get more information and to learn about the details. We will be using Visual Studio 2005 to design and create reports. Although there have been some enhancements, the report designer in Visual Studio .NET 2003 and Visual Studio 2005 are very similar. In case you have used the earlier version, I'll point out some of the differences. To duplicate all of the report examples in the book, you may use any edition of Visual Studio 2005.

Before you read on, you need to get your bearings and get a sense of this chapter's direction. In any technical book, it's necessary to get every reader at a basic level of understanding before moving on to advanced material. Different readers may have varying levels of expertise or experience with Visual Studio, so let's start with the basics. Don't worry — whether you've never seen Visual Studio before or you are a tenured Visual Studio developer, we're going to cover the right material at the right depth at the right time. If you have used Visual Studio for application development, please be patient as you read through the next section. If you have never written a line of code in your life or if you are new to Visual Studio, you're in luck.

This chapter covers the following topics:

- ❑ Using the Report Wizard.
- ❑ Importing reports.
- ❑ Planning for extensibility.
- ❑ Report items and data regions.
- ❑ Formatting considerations.
- ❑ Pagination and printing considerations.

We're covering all the essentials in the chapters in Part II of this book. This chapter contains a series of walk-through exercises that are intended to lead you step by step through some basic report design.

Using the Report Wizard

To get acquainted with the basic mechanics of reports, let's start with a quick tour of the Report Wizard used to create a simple, tabular report. The Report Wizard will take you through all of the steps necessary to design a basic report. From that point, you can make adjustments and add more features to your report.

To get started, open SQL Server Business Intelligence Studio, as shown in Figure 4-1.

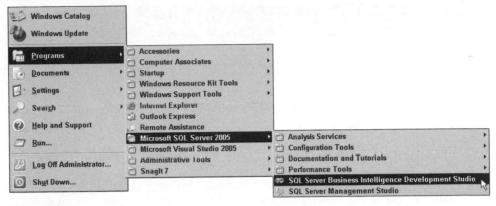

Figure 4-1

Later in this chapter, you'll learn more about the features of the design environment. Click the leftmost button on the toolbar to create a new project (see Figure 4-2).

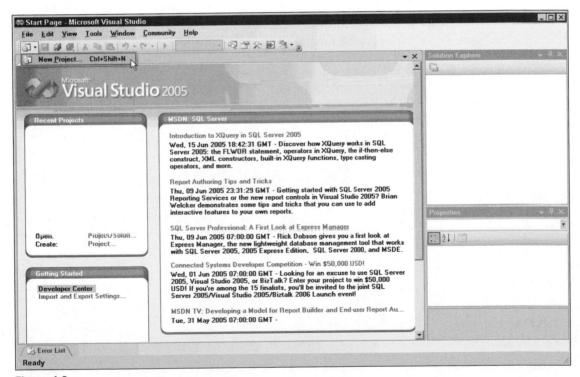

Figure 4-2

The Reporting Services installation adds a project type category to the Microsoft Development Environment called Business Intelligence Projects. Choose this group, select the Report Server Project template, and enter a name for the project. This creates a new report project, as shown in Figure 4-3.

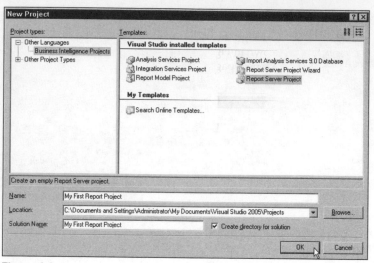

Figure 4-3

Incidentally, the Report Server Project Wizard and the Report Server Project items have similar behaviors. The Report Server Project Wizard option simply saves a step and takes you straight to the Report Wizard.

Figure 4-4 shows the Solution Explorer window, which is displayed in the upper-right pane of the design surface. This is a tree view showing components of the new report project. As you see, the project name is displayed above folder icons used to group Shared Data Sources and Reports. Right-click the Reports icon, and choose Add New report from the menu. This action opens the Report Wizard.

Figure 4-4

The Report Wizard

The Report Wizard will lead you through the basic steps for creating a new report. The first page of the wizard dialog is a splash screen, shown in Figure 4-5, containing instructions and introductory information. Click the Next button to move to the next page.

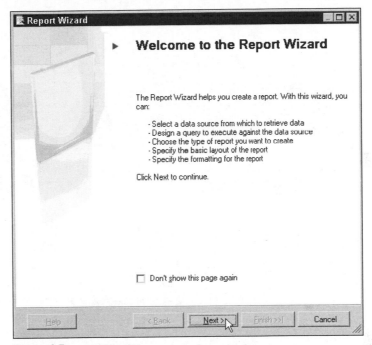

Figure 4-5

Establishing a Data Source

Since you have no data sources created yet, let's add one. It usually makes sense to use a name that indicates the name and location of the database. In this example, you will use the AdventureWorks sample database that installs with Reporting Services. Make sure the New data source radio button is selected and type the database name into the Name text box as you see in Figure 4-6.

Leave the Type set to Microsoft SQL Server, and then click the Edit button. This opens the Data Link Properties dialog to set up a connection string shown in Figure 4-7. If you have used other Microsoft products that use SQL Server, this interface should be familiar to you.

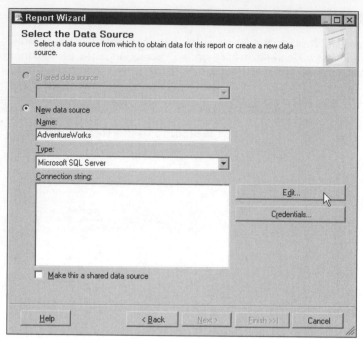

Figure 4-6

Figure 4-7

There are three steps to complete this dialog:

1. Select the database server from the drop-down list. Since you're using the database server installed on the local computer, enter LocalHost. If this were a production application, you could select the name of any server on your network from the list and then type the server name or enter an IP address to connect to a server over the Internet.

2. To use integrated Windows security, select the first radio button reading Use Windows Authentication. You would use the second option if you were using the SQL Server security model. If that were the case, your database administrator would provide this information.

3. Finally, select the AdventureWorks database from the drop-down list. You may use the Test Connection button to validate the settings. When you click the OK button, a connection string is generated and returned to the Report Wizard dialog, as shown in Figure 4-8.

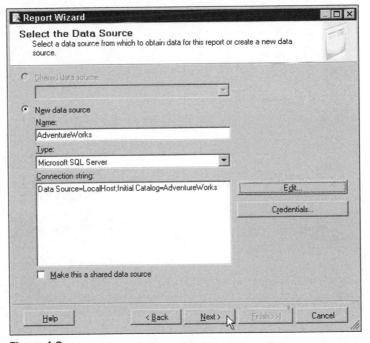

Figure 4-8

Selecting the check box labeled Make this a shared data source will cause this data source to be available to other reports. This simple but important feature is quite powerful and will save you a tremendous amount of time and effort. By creating a central data source for all reports on the server, connection and database information may be changed in only one place to affect all your reports. This is preferable to the traditional approach, where each report must be updated separately. That can be very inconvenient when the system administrator moves your database to another server or when you migrate your reporting solution from the development environment to your production server.

So far, the Report Wizard has created a report project and has led you through creating a shared data source. There isn't much to see yet. You need to continue to work through the pages of the wizard before you see any results. In an established report project, you would create a new report using the shared data source you created earlier.

Building a Query

The next wizard page prompts you for a query string, as shown in Figure 4-9. If you are using a SQL Server database as the data source, this is a Transact-SQL SELECT statement used to retrieve the data for the report. For simple queries, you can simply type a Transact-SQL expression into this box. For most queries, you'll probably want to use the Query Builder option.

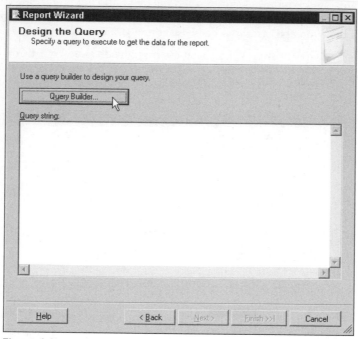

Figure 4-9

More complex reports may be based on more than one query. In fact, data can even be obtained from multiple data sources in a single report. Click the Query Builder button to open the Transact-SQL Query Builder dialog. The Query Builder has two different modes. Figure 4-10 shows the Generic Query Designer. This window is little more than a simple text editor with no error checking, validation, or code-generation features. Use it to write queries for data sources other than SQL Server or complex queries the Graphical Query Designer isn't equipped to handle.

Click the leftmost toolbar button to switch to the Graphical Query Designer. The tooltip label on this button is the opposite of what I would normally expect. It displays the current state of the query designer rather than the state after clicking the button.

This dialog box is common to several Microsoft products. In Reporting Services for SQL Server 2000, there were no toolbar controls available in this dialog screen and all functionality was available from a pop-up menu. The toolbar, shown in Figure 4-11, has been added in Reporting Services for SQL Server 2005.

If you've never created a query before, the following steps will take you through the process, and, with a little practice, you'll see that it's pretty easy.

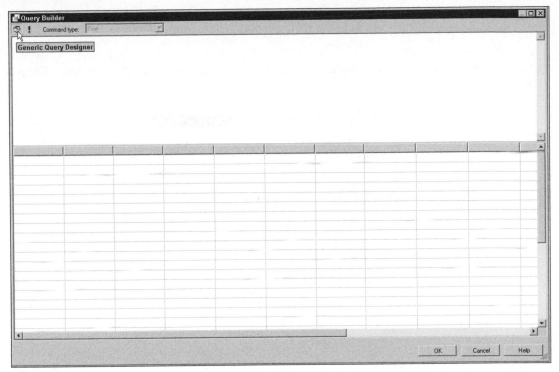

Figure 4-10

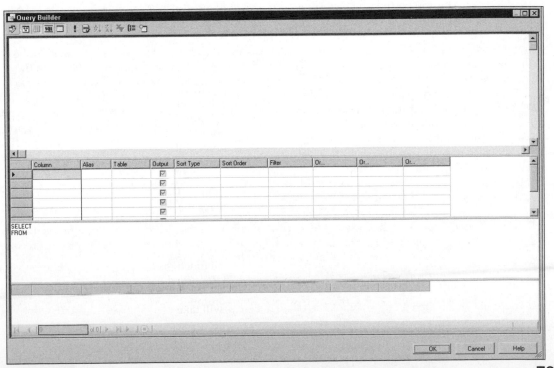

Figure 4-11

You'll take a closer look at the features of the query designer in Chapter 5. For more information about writing Transact-SQL queries, refer to *Beginning Transact-SQL* by Paul Turley, also from Wrox (ISBN 076457955X).

Click the Add Table toolbar button on the right side of the toolbar to display the Add Table dialog, as shown in Figure 4-12:

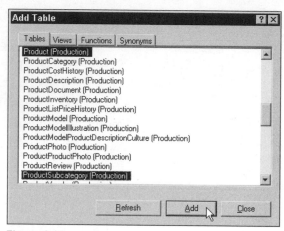

Figure 4-12

Select the Product table from the list and then click the Add button. Repeat this action for the ProductSubCategory table. This adds these tables to the top pane of the Query Builder as in Figure 4-13. Click the Close button on the Add Table dialog. You need to include four columns in the report so let's add them to the query.

In the ProductSubCategory table window, check the Name column. You should see it added to the column list and to the SQL statement, which is in the third pane of the Query Builder window. In the Product table window, check the Name, ProductNumber, and ListPrice columns. Note that they are added to the columns pane grid in the order they are checked. When two or more columns are added with the same name (as is the case for the two Name columns,) an alias is created with a default name. You will define explicitly named aliases for both of these columns: type SubCategory in the first row and ProductName in the second row for the ProductSubCategory and Product Name columns, respectively. You will also need to sort the results by these columns. This may be done by setting the Sort Type for the columns to Ascending. Note that the Sort Order values are set in the order you selected the Sort Type. You can also set up sorting within the report definition; however, having the data presorted from the database, as you have done here, is far more efficient.

To test the query results, right-click in the top pane again, and select Run from the pop-up menu. The query results are displayed in the lower pane in this window. You should see that the product records are ordered by the SubCategory and then the ProductName columns.

When you click the OK button in the Query Builder window, the query string is returned to the Report Wizard dialog, as in Figure 4-14. Click the Next button to continue.

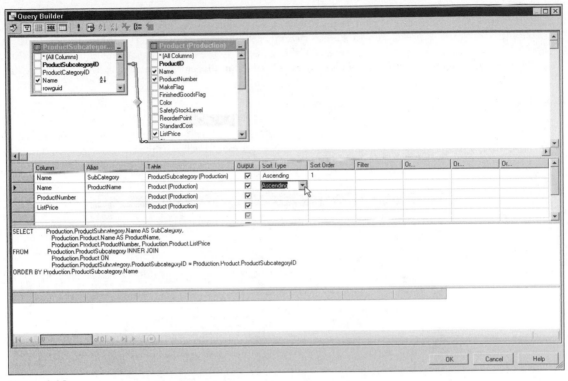

Figure 4-13

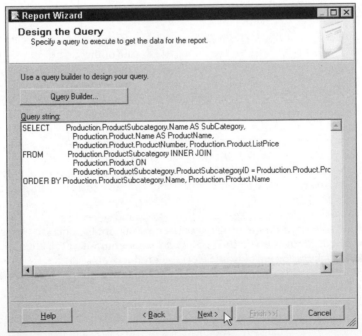

Figure 4-14

The Query Builder does one very simple thing: It creates the Transact-SQL expression that you see in the Query string box in this page of the Report Wizard. If you know your way around Transact-SQL, you can simply type the expression into this box or into the SQL pane of the Query Builder Window. You can also go back and make changes if necessary either directly to the query string or using the Query Builder dialog. In a later example, a stored procedure will be used in place of the query string.

Defining the Report Structure

The following pages will guide you through specifying report design elements such as the style, layout, data sorting, and grouping. In an effort to keep things simple, specify a Tabular style with all data fields in a single detail section, as in Figure 4-15.

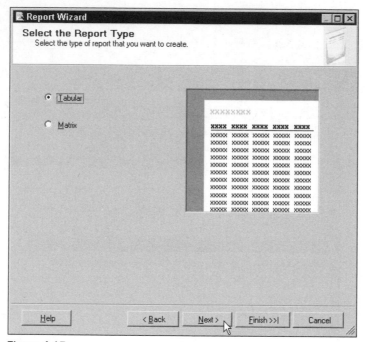

Figure 4-15

This report will simply be a list of records and is known as a Tabular report. Click the Next button to go to the next page (shown in Figure 4-16), which is used to design a table control that will display rows and columns of data. In this simple report, you will not be using any groupings so all four fields will be added to the Details section.

On the Choose the Table Layout page (not shown,) simply accept the default setting and click the Next button. This report will be grouped on the SubCategory column. Select this field from the Available fields list, and then click the Group button. Select the ProductName, ProductNumber, and ListPrice fields from the Available fields list and click the Details button in that, and then click the Next button, as shown in Figure 4-17.

The Report Wizard will create controls with coordinated fonts and colors using one of five different themes. These properties may be modified in the designer later. Retain the default Corporate setting, and click Next.

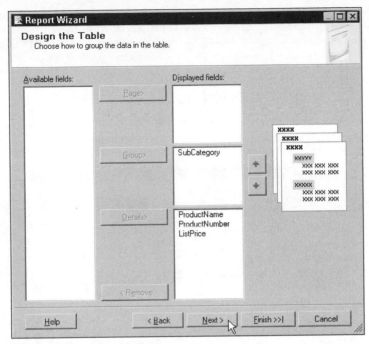

Figure 4-16

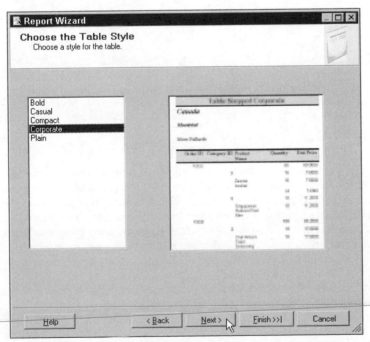

Figure 4-17

As you create other reports, you will have the opportunity to define your own look and feel by using fonts, colors, borders, and graphics. The Report Wizard sets many of these properties for you using the style templates you see on this page. If you like, all of these properties can be changed in the Report Designer.

Specifying the Deployment Location

The first time the Report Wizard is used in a report, the dialog box shown in Figure 4-18 is displayed, prompting for the Report server path and Deployment folder name.

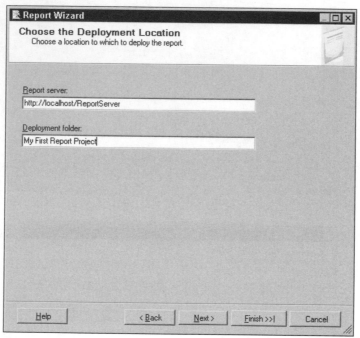

Figure 4-18

The default URL is used for the Report server. Unless you intend to use a different server, leave this value as it is. Enter a folder name for the Deployment folder. This folder will be created and displayed in the Report Manager and will contain all of the reports defined within this project. It's important to note that these folders do not correspond with folders in the file system. The hierarchy of folders is actually stored in the Report Server catalog database and can be based upon functional or operational classification. This method simplifies making related reports available to various user roles. Folders may be useful for grouping reports categorically and searching and securing reports as a group.

When Reporting Services is installed, a web folder is created on the server and is managed by Internet Information Services (IIS), which exposes this path as a URL or web folder. The URL you see in Figure 4-19 is the default location, if you are developing reports on the Report Server. If you are developing on another computer, you should enter a URL that points to that Report Server's installation path, most likely http://yourservername/ReportServer. If you're not sure, talk to your server administrator. The Deployment folder isn't really a physical folder. It's a virtual path that is managed and exposed by Reporting Services through the web server. You'll see this folder when you use the Report Manager later on.

Finally, enter a Report name, call this report Products by Subcategory as in Figure 4-19, and click the Finish button. The report name is used to name the report definition file in the report project and will be the title of the report displayed for users in the Report Manager.

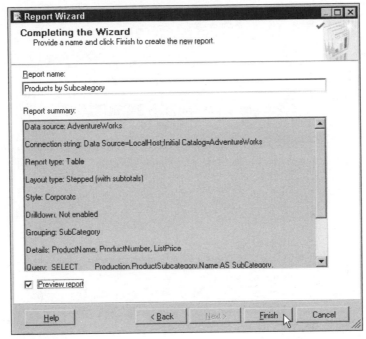

Figure 4-19

The Report Designer

Completing the Report Wizard causes the report to be built and the Report Designer to be displayed in either Layout or Preview mode. The Report Designer has three tabs along the top:

❑   **Data:** This displays the query designer used in the Report Wizard.

❑   **Layout:** This is used to create or alter the report design.

❑   **Preview:** This is used to view the report with data.

Visual Studio 2005 contains several useful designer windows that are automatically hidden by default. These windows are accessible when you hover the mouse pointer over icons positioned along the left and right edge of the designer window. As you can see, some of these icons are labeled and some are not. (You take a closer look at the Toolbox, the Fields, the Solution Explorer, and the Properties designer windows after this tour.)

The next thing you should see is the actual report in Layout view. The Report Designer is now a component of the Microsoft Integrated Development Environment (that is, Business Intelligence Studio or Visual Studio) and uses many of the windows and tools that are built into the Visual Studio product.

You'll be taking a look at a number of these tools as you continue. The Report Wizard can also decipher intelligent column labels from the column names. Note that each column header has a space between the words that were delineated using capital letters, as in Figure 4-20.

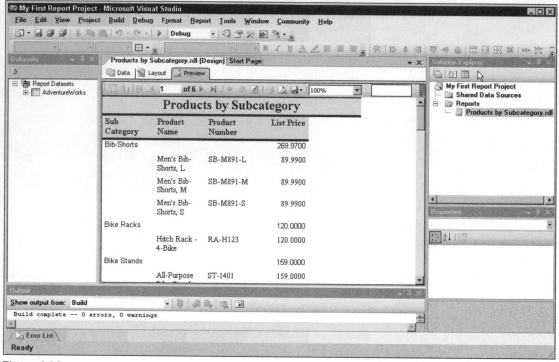

Figure 4-20

Scale Units

Let's take a short break from the wizard and discuss some important information you need to understand before you move on. Notice that these examples were created on a computer configured with US/English regional settings. As a result, all of the scaling units are set to inches. If your computer is configured for another culture or regional setting, your environment may use metric units.

It's also important to understand how a report fits onto a page. The report content fits onto a design element called the *Body*. The report defines the page for printing and displaying purposes with associated margins. The relationship between these two design elements will be discussed shortly.

American SAE, pixels, and metric scale units may be used for the report, body, margins, and control size measurements. The designer will automatically use either inches (in) or centimeters (cm) depending on the current locale setting in Windows. This example uses inches with the default US letter 8.5in x 11in page size. If you are using metric units or a different page size, please make the appropriate adjustments. For example, if you are designing reports for A4 paper, the report width and height should be set to 21.0cm and 29.7cm, respectively.

Note that the Report Designer is currently only 5 inches wide and that the grid containing the fields partially fills this space. You need to make some adjustments to use the available space.

You should be able to use all of the available space to fill your target page size. Apply the following formula to calculate the report page width:

```
Report Width = Body Width + Left Margin + Right Margin
```

You can set the report size by either resizing the report body in the designer with the mouse or by setting the Height and Width values in the Properties window. Although it usually makes sense to match the report size to the paper size for printed reports, the report width may be set as wide as 160 inches.

Click on the report background and view the Properties window (either right-click and choose Properties or just click the Properties tab on the right side of the designer). Verify that Body is displayed in the drop-down list at the top of the Properties window. Now, click the small plus sign next to Size to expand this item and set the properties, as shown in Figure 4-21.

Figure 4-21

To set the report margins, select Report from the drop-down list and expand the Margins item. Change the Left, Right, Top, and Bottom margins, as shown in Figure 4-22.

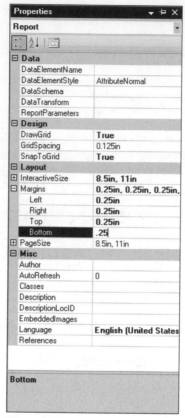

Figure 4-22

Here's a quick review: The report body contains the actual report content. This area must fit within the area defined for a page of the report. Using the Properties window, set the report dimensions to 8.5 inches wide by 11.0 inches tall with the left and right margins set to 0.25 inches each. This leaves 8.0 inches of available width for the report body. To use all of this horizontal space for report data, set the body to be 8.0 inches wide.

With the report and margins set correctly, you can reformat the report (see Figure 4-23). For the list of repeated data, the wizard added a table with columns bound to the four fields you exposed in the query. Sizing these columns for optimum space is a simple matter of trial and error. The first order of business is to select the table and resize it to fill the report body.

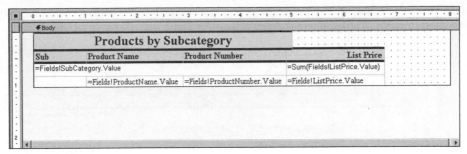

Figure 4-23

To select the entire table (rather than a specific cell) click anywhere in the table and then click on the gray box at the top-left intersection between the column and row headers. This is shown in Figure 4-24.

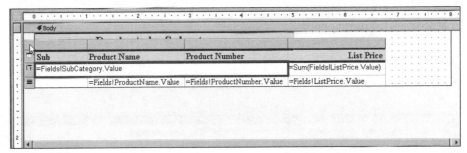

Figure 4-24

This will display a selection box around the table with resizing handles as shown in Figure 4-25. Grab the table on the right side and drag it to fill the report body.

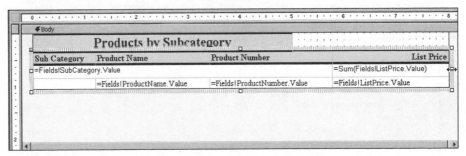

Figure 4-25

The text box immediately above the grid may also be resized. Grab the right handle as shown in Figure 4-26 and drag to resize the text box to the same width as the grid.

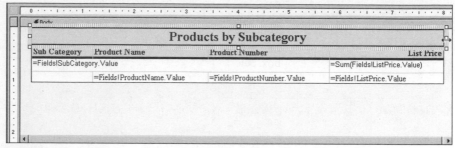

Figure 4-26

Using the column headers at the top of the grid, resize each column. You can switch between Layout and Preview to see how the data looks in the report. With a little adjustment to column sizes and text alignment, the table may easily be formatted so text in each cell doesn't wrap and the report appears balanced. Let's fix the report heading. You can edit the heading text right in the text box.

Select the Preview tab to view the completed report, as shown in Figure 4-27.

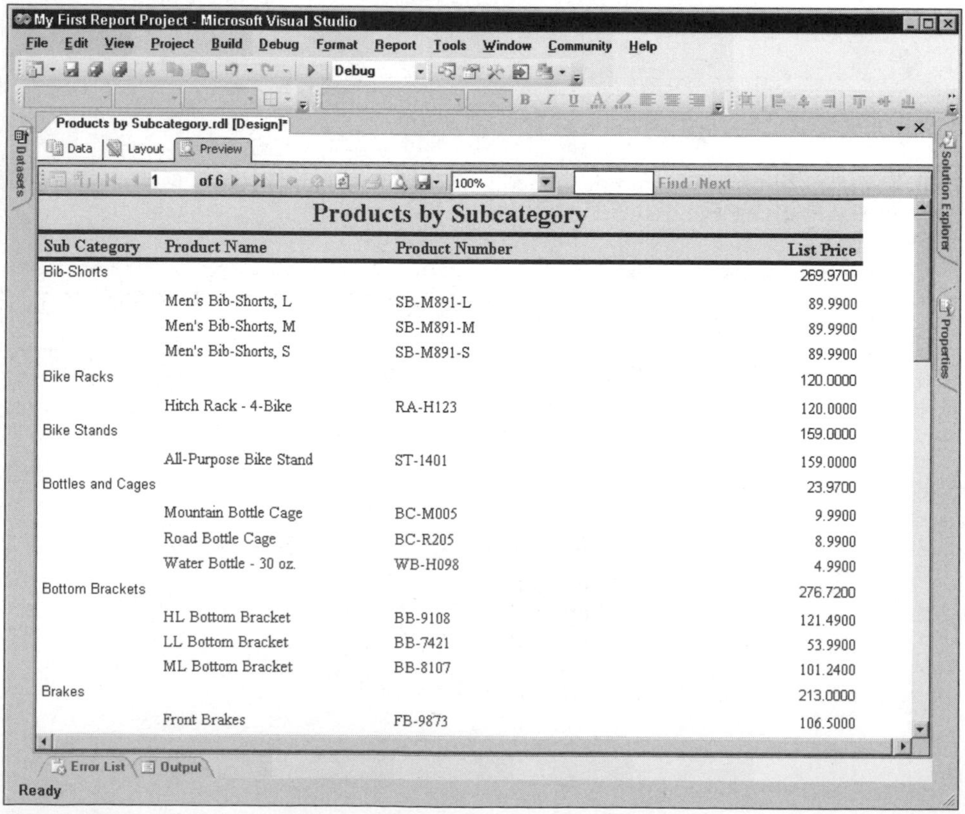

Figure 4-27

Currency Format

Just one more little tweak and this report will be done. The wizard doesn't take care of any specific data formatting. This means that numbers and dates may need some adjustments to look presentable. I'll discuss this in detail toward the end of this chapter. For now, here are some simple instructions to display the list price value as currency. For each of the two text boxes in the ListPrice column, click on the text box and then hover the mouse pointer over the Properties tab on the right side of the designer. This displays the properties sheet for the selected text box. Select the Format property, and then type **C2** (see Figure 4-28). This is the standard regular expression to format a currency value with two decimal positions.

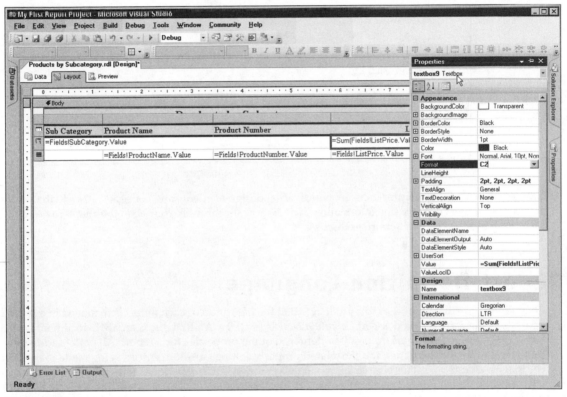

Figure 4-28

That's it! You've created your first report using the Report Wizard. You can go back and make changes to the report design by opening it from the Visual Studio Solution Explorer. In the future, you may find it more effective to create reports without the wizard, where you have more control and don't have the tool making so many decisions for you. To get more practice, you may want to design additional reports using different data sources, queries, or other options. At the very least, you'll end up with a few attempts that didn't go so well and some reports that worked. On one of my kids' favorite Saturday TV programs, the teacher character would always say, "Get dirty, make messes, and don't be afraid to try things." That concept applies here. Figure 4-29 shows the report in Preview.

Products by Subcategory			
Sub Category	**Product Name**	**Product Number**	**List Price**
Bib-Shorts			$269.97
	Men's Bib-Shorts, L	SB-M891-L	$89.99
	Men's Bib-Shorts, M	SB-M891-M	$89.99
	Men's Bib-Shorts, S	SB-M891-S	$89.99
Bike Racks			$120.00
	Hitch Rack - 4-Bike	RA-H123	$120.00
Bike Stands			$159.00
	All-Purpose Bike Stand	ST-1401	$159.00
Bottles and Cages			$23.97
	Mountain Bottle Cage	BC-M005	$9.99
	Road Bottle Cage	BC-R205	$8.99
	Water Bottle - 30 oz.	WB-H098	$4.99
Bottom Brackets			$276.72
	HL Bottom Bracket	BB-9108	$121.49
	LL Bottom Bracket	BB-7421	$53.99
	ML Bottom Bracket	BB-8107	$101.24
Brakes			$213.00
	Front Brakes	FB-9873	$106.50
	Rear Brakes	RB-9231	$106.50

Figure 4-29

The remainder of this chapter focuses on individual design elements and concepts rather than the overall process. You will apply this information in another walk-through exercise in the chapter where designing more advanced reports is discussed.

Report Definition Language

One very compelling aspect of this product is that the definition of each report is managed in a standard, text-based file format called *Report Definition Language* (RDL). An RDL file is an XML document with a standard definition for markup tags that define all of the properties for a report. All objects added to a report in the Report Designer and the related property settings result in entries being made to the RDL content for that report. This simple approach makes it easy for independent software vendors and custom solution developers to generate a report definition from a variety of sources and tools. It also makes it easy for report designers and developers to open the report definition in a text editor to make changes outside of the report designer. Contrast this with the proprietary binary formats used in other popular reporting products.

As an example, the following is a small snippet of an RDL file content describing a Textbox report item:

```
<Textbox Name="textbox1">
  <Style>
    <PaddingLeft>2pt</PaddingLeft>
    <PaddingBottom>2pt</PaddingBottom>
    <PaddingTop>2pt</PaddingTop>
    <PaddingRight>2pt</PaddingRight>
  </Style>
```

```
        <Top>0.25in</Top>
        <rd:DefaultName>textbox1</rd:DefaultName>
        <Height>0.25in</Height>
        <Width>1in</Width>
        <CanGrow>true</CanGrow>
        <Value />
        <Left>0.375in</Left>
    </Textbox>
```

Report Migration and Integration

We are beginning to see applications and products that have the ability to create report definitions for Reporting Services. The Extensible Report Definition Language allows reports to be created, converted, or modified by custom tools. For example, we've worked with products from Panorama and Cizer that provide custom report designer front ends within their own web browser–based business intelligence reporting applications. These products put report design capabilities in front of corporate business users without installing complex desktop report-authoring software.

Because RDL is simply an XML grammar, building reports can be performed programmatically with relative ease. Because of the complexities of parsing and deciphering proprietary report formats, converting existing reports from other products is more complicated. To date, there are no universal report conversion utilities on the market. The capability to perform report conversion is a common request from businesses that have already invested in older, expensive reporting products and want to migrate to Reporting Services. Hitachi Consulting offers report migration as service rather than a product for this reason. If this is an option that you or your company is considering, report migration may be more cost-effective than starting from scratch.

A point to consider is that the fundamental approach for designing reports most effectively may be quite different using different products. A "converted" report (one you designed in another tool) may not run efficiently and may deny you the flexibility to use Reporting Services to its full capability.

Importing Access Reports

Using the Report Designer, you have the ability to import reports from Microsoft Access. Access has an excellent report writer and has long been the only real substantial reporting tool in the Microsoft armada of products. Since the early 1990s, Access was the product of choice for creating reporting solutions and still is for many desktop solutions. Its greatest limitation, however, is that Access must be installed on the user's desktop and can effectively be used only in a single-user or small-network environment.

If you are already familiar with creating reports in Access, this may be a good starting point to learn report design in Reporting Services. Most basic Access reports can be imported very nicely. There are some functions and expressions used in Access that are not supported, and Access reports that run program code behind them will likely not work without some adjustments. These details are explained in Appendix A, but the short version is that most basic report functionality will work. Grouping and sorting features are preserved, as are most expressions and formatting. The use of domain functions and any custom code is not supported.

Plan for Extensibility

If your goal is to create a reporting solution that will work for users with different needs, there are a number of things to be considered. The users may need to:

❑ Access reports from a web-enabled hand-held device or cell phone.

❑ Download reports for offline viewing.

❑ View reports in different web browsers.

Reporting Services can meet all of these needs if you understand the requirements and plan ahead. Let's briefly discuss some of these design considerations.

Browser Compatibility

A solution should be designed to meet the needs of the least-capable user or platform. The optimal design for the web has always been a moving target. If, when designing reports, you view them only in the latest version of Internet Explorer, you may not be aware of incompatibilities or design issues for other browsers. Creating solutions independent of the client platform for a diverse audience will always be challenging, with a certain degree of unpredictability.

Reports with interactive design elements such as *drill-down* and *auto-hide* sections, for example, generate client-side JavaScript. This script runs in the user's browser to produce effects and interactive functionality. Theoretically, pages containing many JavaScript functions should run in newer versions of Internet Explorer, Netscape Navigator, and other browsers. In a report, scripted features include documentation maps, bookmarks, and show/hide features (used for drill-down reports). On the standard report toolbar, scripted features provide the ability to zoom, search, refresh, export, and request help.

Another variable to consider when using HTML is the font typeface and size. If you make a point to use common fonts, this is not typically an issue. However, the user's configuration isn't always predictable. Font files on the user's computer can be uninstalled or deleted and default font sizes can be changed in the browser. A popular solution for unpredictable HTML results is to use a proprietary document format typically read in a downloadable viewer. Rendering reports to an *Adobe Portable Document Format* (PDF) document will ensure that reports are displayed and printed consistently.

Offline Viewing

Reporting Services can render reports in three different forms of HTML, including MHTML (or Web Archive). As mentioned in earlier chapters, MHTML is a fairly recent standard that encapsulates content that would normally be linked to separate files, typically graphics, into a single document. Using this format simplifies web content rendering for portability, but it isn't supported in all browsers (including Pocket Internet Explorer). Even when using standard HTML format, most report files will be self-contained with the exception of any graphics. If all of the content is contained in one file, it will be easier to download and view offline. If your users are consistently using Internet Explorer or a browser you have tested thoroughly, consider rendering reports in MHTML to preserve embedded graphics content. If you don't have that kind of control over the user's environment, PDF document rendering may be the best choice.

Another possibility is to allow the user to download report content into a storage file and then render the content using your own client-side solution. Reports rendered as *Comma-Separated Values* (CSV) can be opened in Microsoft Excel, where the user can format or further manipulate the data. Data saved to an XML file may be imported or read using Excel, Word, or a custom application. The Excel rendering format currently supports Microsoft Excel versions 2002 and 2003 only.

Mobile Device Support

Portable electronic devices are available in different sizes and shapes. This medium could prove to be a very convenient reporting solution for users who need to get information on the go. Web-enabled cellular phones generally fit into three categories:

- ❑ The Pocket PC and Palm OS devices with integrated cellular phones have the advantage of a relatively larger display (240 by 320 pixels) and a more traditional-style web browser.

- ❑ The new generation of *Smart Phones* runs a slightly scaled-down version of the Windows CE operating system with a smaller display (176 by 220 pixels) and fewer features but in a more convenient size.

- ❑ The standard web-enabled cell phone. It's hard to find a new cell phone that doesn't offer the capability to surf the web. Most of these phones have very small displays, and many will only display text.

The simple fact is that you can develop reporting solutions using Reporting Services for all of these devices, making it possible and convenient for users to access information wherever they are.

Of course, screen size is one of the most significant limitations, so reports may simply be scaled down to a smaller page size to fit a smaller screen size. The Pocket PC and Smart Phone browsers will run client-side JavaScript to support drill-down and other such effects. To support less capable devices, you can design simple text reports rendered in HTML.

Report Items and Data Regions

Reports consist of items and regions that define the placement and format of data from a data source. What's interesting is that the Reporting Services architectural specification calls these things "controls." Application developers familiar with text boxes and tables are also likely to refer to them by the same name. However, the official term is *Report Item* — and that's what we call them in this book.

In the Report Designer, you can place items or draw them onto the report body. If you have worked with Visual Basic or Access forms, you are familiar with the practice of placing controls on forms. This is pretty much the same environment. When you add a new report to a report project in Visual Studio 2005, the designer is displayed in the Layout view. Much of the Visual Studio functionality is exposed using various utility windows. On the left side of the designer, you will find the Toolbox, which contains all of the available report items, as shown in Figure 4-30. The Toolbox may be set to auto-hide by using the pushpin icon in its toolbar.

Figure 4-30

Textbox Report Item

The Textbox item can be used to display data from a data source, calculations or expressions, or static data, much like a label control in a Windows forms project. When you drag fields from the Fields list onto the Report Designer, *bound* Textbox items are created. Common expressions can refer to a field in the report.

The example shown in Figure 4-31 shows a Textbox used as a label and another Textbox bound to the LastName field of the report data source.

Figure 4-31

Right-click the Textbox and select Properties from the pop-up menu to display the Textbox Properties dialog, as shown in Figure 4-32.

Properties may also be viewed and set by using the standard properties sheet located to the right of the designer. This window may be pinned out or will auto-hide by default. As shown in Figure 4-33, this window contains quite a bit more detail than the custom properties window. However, the property information is not as conveniently organized. Right-click to get to the most-common properties, and use the properties sheet when you need to set other properties.

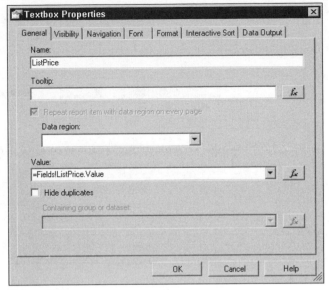

Figure 4-32

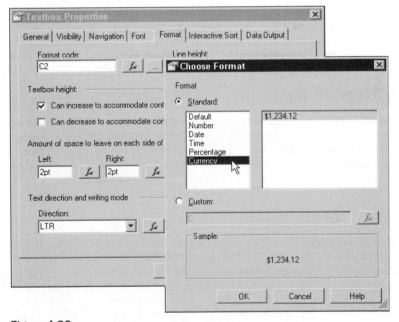

Figure 4-33

Line Report Item

Lines may be drawn in any direction and may be set to a variety of styles and colors, as displayed in Figure 4-34. The properties for a line are simple and mostly set using the Properties window or designer toolbar.

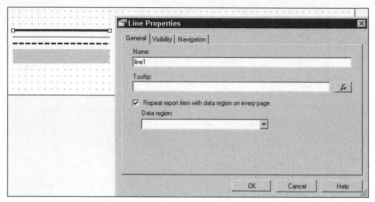

Figure 4-34

Some clever techniques are used to render lines in HTML. Reporting Services will typically try to render content using the most effective way possible. For example, when outputting standard HTML, lines may be rendered as table borders, as a `DIV` tag filled using a JavaScript function, or even using *Virtual Reality Modeling Language* (VRML) commands. Like all reports, it's the job of each format rendering extension on the report server to use the appropriate technique to build each report element output.

Rectangle Report Item

A rectangle item can have many different uses. A rectangle is simply used to visually separate a region of the report. It may be used to visually contain other items. If items such as text boxes, grids, and so on are placed into a rectangle, all these items can be moved together by simply moving the rectangle. A rectangle may also be used as a data container for data items and can be related to and repeated with a parent container (see Figure 4-35).

Image Report Item

Images can be embedded into the report, linked to an external file, or obtained from a data source. Images can be of the BMP, GIF, JPG, JPE, PNG, or X-PNG type. Adding an image in the designer is pretty straightforward. A critical factor is that images are sized and cropped prior to being added to a report. You can resize the image in the Report Designer, but this will not result in a smaller file size. Use a graphics editing tool like the Office Picture Library, Adobe PhotoShop, or Macromedia Fireworks to resize or crop the image and then save it to a new file. You can scale and fit an image to fit the image item container, but it's advisable to use image files that are already the correct size. This conserves disk space, improves performance, and prevents image distortion.

Drag and drop an image item from the Toolbox onto the report. This will launch the Image Wizard dialog (see Figure 4-36). Select the method you want to use; the image can be from a table in the database or a file and may be linked or embedded into the report. Getting external image files to render correctly can be a bit tricky at times due to file access permissions on the server. If in doubt, it may be easiest to either store the image in the database or embed it into the report definition.

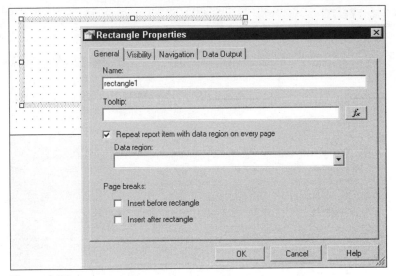

Figure 4-35

Figure 4-36

Embedded images are encoded as text and stored in the report definition file. Although this increases the size of the RDL, it can simplify the deployment and configuration. Selecting the Project option will result in a linked image using a file found in the project folder. Selecting the Database option will allow you to extract an image stored in an `Image` or `Binary` type column within a database, exposed through your data set. The Web option allows you to use a URL to reference an existing file either on the report server or elsewhere.

Keep the default selection Embedded and click Next to show the image selection page shown in Figure 4-37. Click New Image and find your image file.

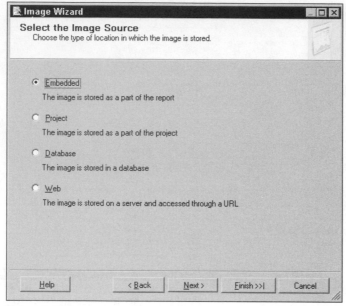

Figure 4-37

When you click Next, a summary is displayed with information about the image (see Figure 4-38).

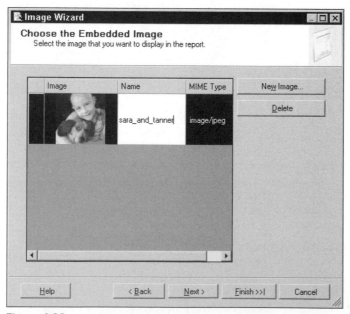

Figure 4-38

If your picture data is stored in the database and the Database option is selected, the database field page is displayed in the wizard. This gives you the option to derive an image file type from the image, as in Figure 4-39.

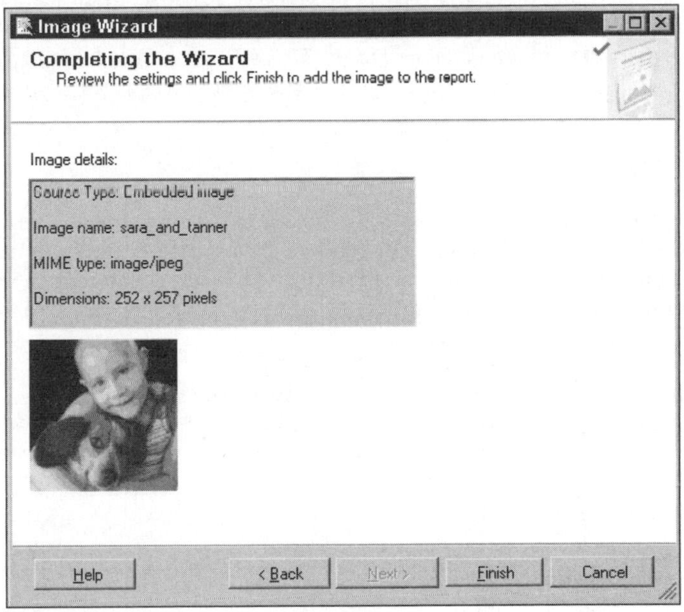

Figure 4-39

Generally, the JPEG format is most conservative and PNG graphics are higher quality and more flexible. The GIF and JPEG formats are most widely used on the Internet and are supported by all web browsers. The GIF and PNG formats support transparency, but I have not had good results with transparent images in Reporting Services. As a rule, if you need an image to appear nonrectangular (such as an icon and indicator graphic), set backgrounds to white over a white report area, as shown in Figure 4-40.

Figure 4-40

Images, Background Color, and Transparency

The image item doesn't have a `BackgroundColor` property. If an image is placed on the report body or a container item with a background color, transparency effects will work as you would expect. If you place an image in the cell of a table, the image replaces the text box that would normally occupy the cell, which prevents that cell from having a background color. To work around this, place a rectangle in the table cell and then place the image in the rectangle. This will give you the ability to set a background color and then allows a transparent graphic to share the same space as the colored cell area.

Subreport Item

A *subreport* is a container for another report embedded into a parent report. The subreport can contain practically any other report with its own, independent data source. It can optionally have its data linked to a key or value in the main report, often referred to as a master/detail report. Subreports are an important element in complex report designs. Figure 4-41 shows a simple report containing a master record and related detail records in the subreport.

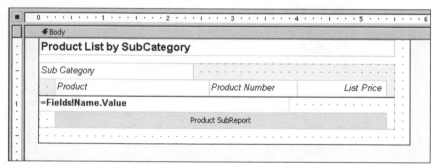

Figure 4-41

The design details of the subreport are not visible in the designer. This report is designed separately and then inserted into the main report as a subreport item.

Be cautious about using subreports with large results. This report item is appropriate for embedding unrelated content within a report that is bound to a different data source or for detail rows related to few master records. Although this may be a useful technique for consolidating reusable report content, it can be very inefficient when compared with some other techniques. For example, if you create a complex query to return all related data in a single result set; a single table item may be used in place of the subreport and may prove to be more efficient.

Chart Report Item

The chart functionality in Reporting Services is really a simplified version of charting components that Microsoft has licensed from Dundas Software. It's a very capable and easy-to-use charting solution with a variety of available chart types.

Probably the most common and most recognizable chart type is the column chart. The example in Figure 4-42 shows sales data for a given year, grouped by quarter and the sales territory. The total sales amount is plotted on the Y-axis (columns) of the chart.

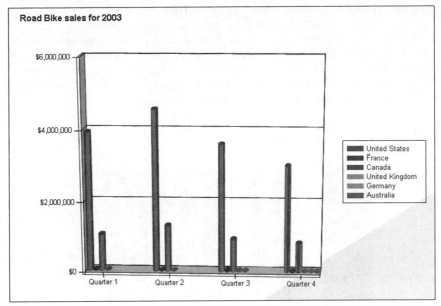

Figure 4-42

Bar charts and column charts are pretty much the same. You can tilt your head to the side to get the same view as the other. Figure 4-43 shows the same data in a bar chart with values plotted on the X-axis (rows).

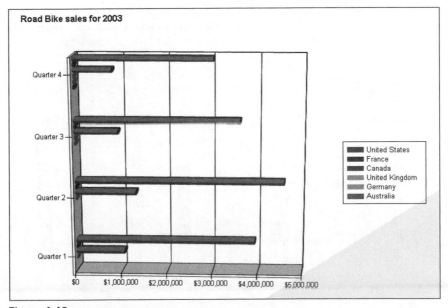

Figure 4-43

In addition to the standard, single-bar view, the stacked view provides a consolidated look at a series of values by using fewer bars or columns. Each bar is like a mini-pie chart where each value in the bar's range is in proportion to the others. Figure 4-44 shows a standard stacked column chart. A series of related values is stacked in the column to show the aggregate sum of values and their proportional values. A variation, the 100% stacked bar or chart, displays each bar with the same height or length as others, regardless of the total values. This type of chart is useful for comparing values within the bars' range but not for comparing the aggregates represented by each bar.

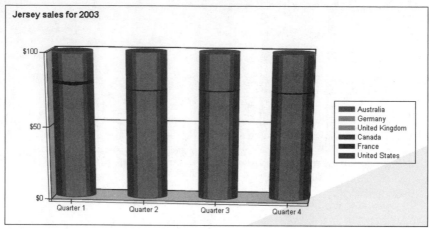

Figure 4-44

One of the most powerful features of the chart item is the ability to group data within each axis. Figure 4-45 shows a simple column chart with two field groups defined on the X-axis, representing related categories. Columns are grouped by quarter and then by the sales territory country.

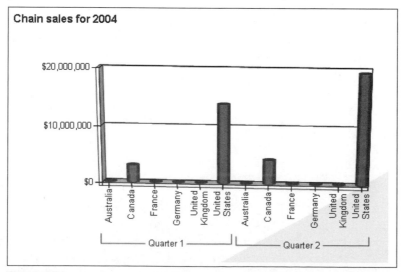

Figure 4-45

Pie charts put proportional values into perspective. This type of chart comes in two pastry types: pie and doughnut. Values are presented visually as a percentage of the total for all values in a series. Pie and doughnut chart views may be either *Simple* or *Exploded*. The exploded presentation may help to visually separate values, especially the smaller slices. These types of charts can be useful for placing values into comparative perspective (see Figure 4-46).

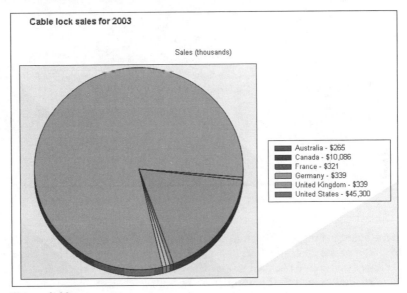

Figure 4-46

The example in Figure 4-47 shows a bubble chart. The size of the bubble represents values on a third dimension, in addition to X- and Y-coordinates. Imagine that the bubbles are the same size and that those "closer" to you appear larger.

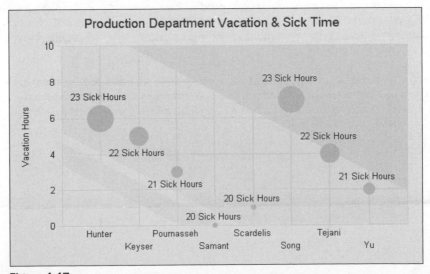

Figure 4-47

A stock or candlestick chart plots three or four values in a range. The stock chart shown in Figure 4-48 plots prices, including the lowest purchase, last purchase, and the sales price. This may be useful for displaying relative profit margins and cost variance.

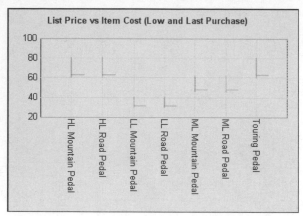

Figure 4-48

In addition to the standard report items that ship with the product, application developers and third-party companies can create custom report items (CRI) that may be installed and used in the designer. In Chapter 7, I'll show you how to use the Dundas Chart for Reporting Services custom report items. These are advanced charts that exceed the capabilities of the built-in charts you just looked at. You are likely to see more CRI suites for Reporting Services that will add even more capabilities to your reports.

Drill-Down and Drill-Through Reports

Although related, these are two different features. A drill-down report, shown in Figure 4-49, contains related groups or sections of information. Each section can be expanded or collapsed to show or hide pertinent information. In the following report, product categories only are displayed when the report opens. Using the expand icon next to a category, the category group (in this case, Clothing) is expanded to reveal a group of related subcategories. Expanding a subcategory (such as Bib-Short) reveals individual products within the subcategory.

A drill-through report may or may not include some drill-down functionality. Items shown in the report may represent sections or more detailed information that may be viewed in a separate report. These key items are displayed as hyperlinks and when a user clicks a link, a separate detailed report is displayed for the item selected, as shown in Figure 4-50.

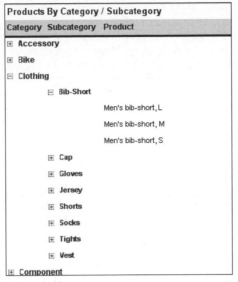

Figure 4-49

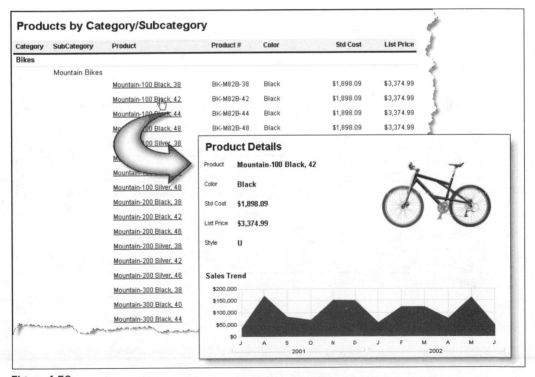

Figure 4-50

Tabular Reports

One of the most fundamental reports is a simple list of record values arranged in rows and columns. Typical tabular reports display column headers above repeated row values. Rows may also be grouped categorically and may be followed by totals, subtotals, or other aggregate values pertaining to a grouping or the entire report.

The two common techniques used to obtain this design are by using either the grid control or the list control. The grid control makes it easy to format rows and columns with column headers and supports groupings, headers, footers, and multiple-row sections.

Grouping Data

Tabular or matrix data may be sorted and grouped on one or multiple levels. The table, list, and matrix controls support this functionality. Groupings may be based on field values or expressions that may include conditional qualifiers, functions, and combined values from multiple fields.

When values are grouped, they may need to be aggregated. This means that a row in the report layout represents a *rollup* of multiple rows from the data source (such as the sum or average of a range of values). After introducing the data region items used to perform grouped operations, let's take a closer look at the aggregate functions that are used as rollup values within the group.

Table Report Data Region

The example in Figure 4-51, using a table, contains three groupings for product records on the Category, Sub Category, and Product fields.

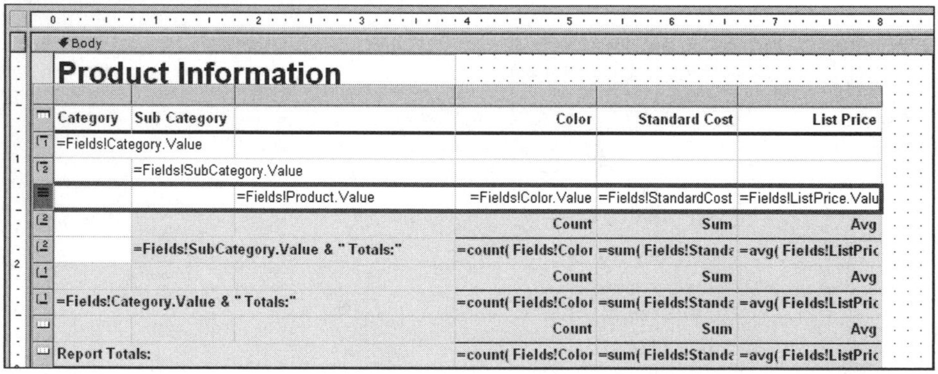

Figure 4-51

List Report Data Region

Using embedded list items allows greater flexibility over the formatting and placement of individual report items. The list control may also be used as the basis for a more complex report with embedded subreports, lists, matrices, or grids. Figure 4-52 shows a preview of a report with groupings created using nested list items. The list item is useful for creating groups of repeated data that aren't constrained to a tabular format.

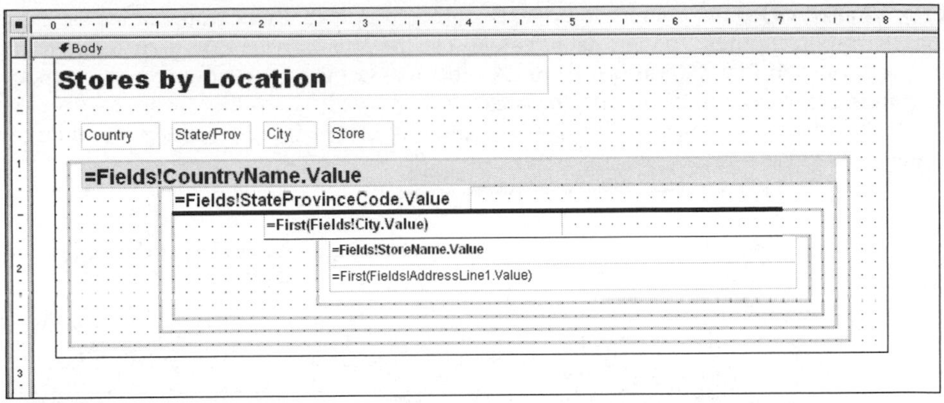

Figure 4-52

In the design for this report, there are four list controls placed inside one another. Data groups have been created for each of the lists to organize them into a hierarchy. For the sake of clarity in this demonstration, each list control is drawn well inside its parent list, and the borders are made easier to see, as in Figure 4-53. It is common for the list borders to share the same line space if you don't need to create additional white space around data elements typically on the right side and bottom borders.

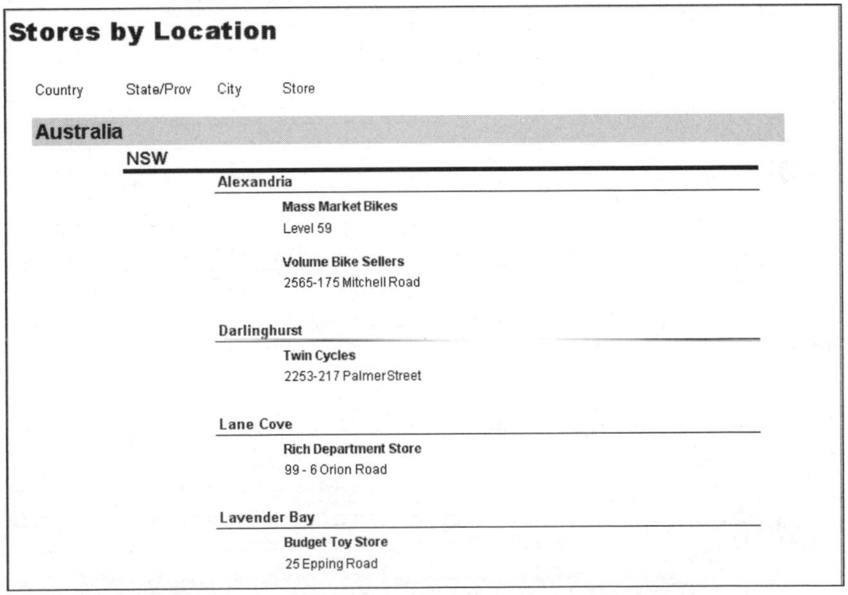

Figure 4-53

Matrix Report Data Region

The matrix item produces a pivot table with automated drill-down functionality on both axes. This matrix report contains the same groupings for row data as the previous report and also contains column groupings for Product Category and Sub Category fields. The aggregate value in the center cells is the sum of product sales for the intersection of each of the groupings. By default, values are aggregated and rolled up within groupings. To view detail values, use the plus sign (+) icon to drill down in one axis (rows or columns) and then do the same for the other axis. Figure 4-54 shows a matrix report that has been expanded to show details on both the axes.

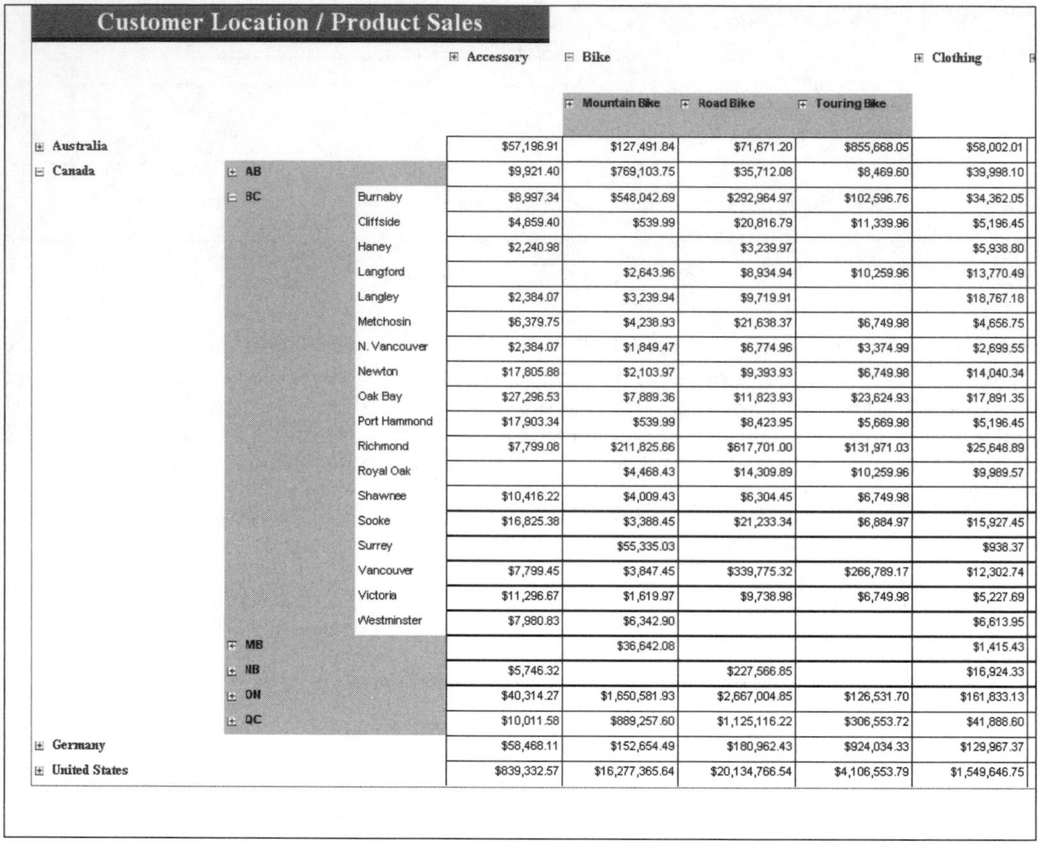

Customer Location / Product Sales

			⊞ Accessory	⊟ Bike			⊟ Clothing
				⊞ Mountain Bike	⊞ Road Bike	⊞ Touring Bike	
⊞ Australia			$57,196.91	$127,491.84	$71,671.20	$855,668.05	$58,002.01
⊟ Canada	⊞ AB		$9,921.40	$769,103.75	$35,712.08	$8,469.60	$39,998.10
	⊟ BC	Burnaby	$8,997.34	$548,042.69	$292,964.97	$102,596.76	$34,362.05
		Cliffside	$4,859.40	$539.99	$20,816.79	$11,339.96	$5,196.45
		Haney	$2,240.98		$3,239.97		$5,938.80
		Langford		$2,643.96	$8,934.94	$10,259.96	$13,770.49
		Langley	$2,384.07	$3,239.94	$9,719.91		$18,767.18
		Metchosin	$6,379.75	$4,238.93	$21,638.37	$6,749.98	$4,656.75
		N. Vancouver	$2,384.07	$1,849.47	$6,774.96	$3,374.99	$2,699.55
		Newton	$17,805.88	$2,103.97	$9,393.93	$6,749.98	$14,040.34
		Oak Bay	$27,296.53	$7,889.36	$11,823.93	$23,624.93	$17,891.35
		Port Hammond	$17,903.34	$539.99	$8,423.95	$5,669.98	$5,196.45
		Richmond	$7,799.08	$211,825.66	$617,701.00	$131,971.03	$25,648.89
		Royal Oak		$4,468.43	$14,309.89	$10,259.96	$9,989.57
		Shawnee	$10,416.22	$4,009.43	$6,304.45	$6,749.98	
		Sooke	$16,825.38	$3,388.45	$21,233.34	$6,884.97	$15,927.45
		Surrey		$55,335.03			$938.37
		Vancouver	$7,799.45	$3,847.45	$339,775.32	$266,789.17	$12,302.74
		Victoria	$11,296.67	$1,619.97	$9,738.98	$6,749.98	$5,227.69
		Westminster	$7,980.83	$6,342.90			$6,813.95
	⊞ MB			$36,642.08			$1,415.43
	⊞ NB		$5,746.32		$227,566.85		$16,924.33
	⊞ ON		$40,314.27	$1,650,581.93	$2,667,004.85	$126,531.70	$161,833.13
	⊞ QC		$10,011.58	$889,257.60	$1,125,116.22	$306,553.72	$41,888.60
⊞ Germany			$58,468.11	$152,654.49	$180,962.43	$924,034.33	$129,967.37
⊞ United States			$839,332.57	$16,277,365.64	$20,134,766.54	$4,106,553.79	$1,549,646.75

Figure 4-54

The matrix control takes care of the grouping functionality in this report. As you can see in Figure 4-55, the design is fairly simple.

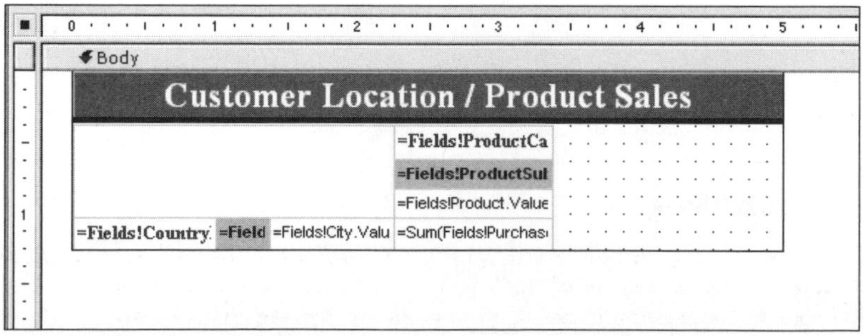

Figure 4-55

Subtotals

Although Reporting Services generically refers to these types of expressions as subtotals, they may be used to perform any aggregation of grouped data. Subtotals may be added to a table's footer row, to the list control, or in the detail or grouping cells of a matrix. The following table is a list of aggregate functions supported by Reporting Services.

Avg	Average for all values in a range.
Count	Count of all non-null values in a range.
CountDistinct	Count of unique values in a range.
CountRows	Count of all rows in a range, regardless of null values or uniqueness.
First	First value in a range based on current sort order.
Last	Last value in a range based on current sort order.
Max	Highest value in a range.
Min	Lowest value in range.
StDev	Standard deviation of non-null values.
StDevP	Population standard deviation of non-null values.
Sum	Sum of all values in a range.
Var	Variation of non-null values.
VarP	Population variance of non-null values.

Using the table item in Figure 4-56, let's take a closer look at the summary rows and their aggregated values. In this example, a table that has groupings on the Category and SubCategory fields is created. Note that the grouping numbers in the row markers next to each row indicate the grouping level. The detail row is selected and sandwiched between grouping levels 1 and 2. In the grouping footers and the report footer, the aggregate functions Count, Sum, and Avg are used for the Color, StandardCost, and ListPrice columns. In this report, an additional row is added for each of the grouping footers for the columns (see Figure 4-56).

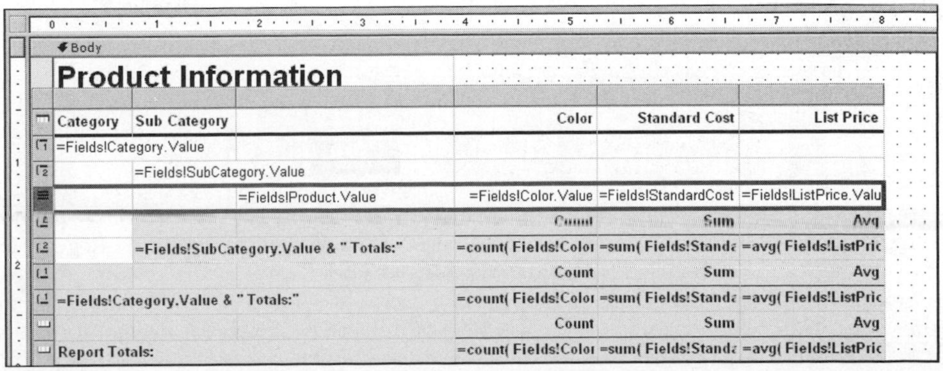

Figure 4-56

Aggregate expressions may be entered in different ways. The expression may be typed directly into the text box or into the value property using the property sheet window or customer property page window. Next to each applicable property, a button can be used to open the Expression Builder dialog box, which can be used to assemble the expression. This is discussed in detail in Chapter 6.

Here is a condensed view of the same report shown in the print preview. Since you are using the `Count` function on the `Color` field value, rows that don't have a value in this column (the value is `Null`) have a count of 0. First you see four sections with subtotals for the Sub Category field, and then, further down the page, you see rollups for the Category and then for the entire report, as shown in Figure 4-57.

Formatting

Many data values need to be formatted appropriately because the default formats are usually not acceptable. The following table shows common SQL Server data types and their unformatted defaults.

Data Type	Default Display	Example
Float	Large number of decimal positions with no rounding r truncation. Large numbers with no thousand separators or scientific notation.	123456789.123456 1.23456789012346E+19
Decimal	Large numbers with no thousand separators. The number of decimal positions is defined by column's scale attribute.	123456789.1234
Int, SmallInt, BigInt	Large numbers with no thousand separators.	123456789
Money	Up to four decimal positions. Large numbers with no thousand separators.	123456789.1234
Date	Always displays date and time. Seconds included.	11/1/2003 3:34:26 PM
Bit	Displays the words True or False.	True False

If these values are not what you want to see in your reports, you will need to use the `Format` property of each control to change them. The formatting capabilities of Reporting Services controls are based on the formatting mechanics in the .NET Framework and use a form of *regular expressions*. Regular expressions are very powerful and can be used to format values in just about any way imaginable. Expression strings can range from simple to extremely complex. If you need to learn more about the advanced use of regular expressions, search the Visual Studio online help or the MSDN library for *Regular Expression Language Elements*. For most of your needs, however, we'll show you how to use the basics.

Product Information

Category	Sub Category	Color	Standard Cost	List Price
Accessory				
	Bike Racks			
	Hitch rack - 4 bike		$66.00	$120.00

		Count	Sum	Avg
Bike Racks Totals:		0	$66.00	$120.00

	Bike Stand			
	All-purpose bike stand		$87.45	$159.00

		Count	Sum	Avg
Bike Stand Totals:		0	$87.45	$159.00

	Bottles & Cages			
	Mountain bottle cage		$5.49	$9.99
	Road bottle cage		$4.94	$8.99
	water bottle 30 oz		$2.74	$4.99

		Count	Sum	Avg
Bottles & Cages Totals:		0	$13.18	$7.99

	Tires & Tubes			
	HL Mountain Tire		$19.25	$35.00
	HL Road Tire		$17.93	$32.60
	LL Mountain Tire		$13.74	$24.99
	LL Road Tire		$11.82	$21.49
	ML Mountain Tire		$16.49	$29.99
	ML Road Tire		$13.74	$24.99
	Mountain Tire Tube		$2.74	$4.99
	Patch kit with 8 patches		$1.26	$2.29
	Road Tire Tube		$2.19	$3.99
	Touring Tire		$15.94	$28.99
	Touring Tire Tube		$2.74	$4.99

		Count	Sum	Avg
Tires & Tubes Totals:		0	$117.87	$19.48

		Count	Sum	Avg
Accessory Totals:		5	$547.87	$34.35

		Color	Standard Cost	List Price
	LL Mtn Rear Wheel	Black	$64.93	$87.75
	LL Road Front Wheel	Black	$63.32	$85.57
	LL Road Rear Wheel	Black	$83.30	$112.57
	ML Mtn Front Wheel	Black	$154.68	$209.03
	ML Mtn Rear Wheel	Black	$174.66	$236.03
	ML Road Front Wheel	Black	$183.80	$248.39
	ML Road Rear Wheel	Black	$203.78	$275.39
	Touring Front Wheel	Black	$161.33	$218.01
	Touring Rear Wheel	Black	$181.31	$245.01

		Count	Sum	Avg
Wheel Totals:		14	$2,288.83	$220.93

		Count	Sum	Avg
Component Totals:		292	$127,300.45	$540.62
		Count	Sum	Avg

Figure 4-57

Standard Formatting

Standard, one-character strings may be used to specify formatting options for numbers and dates. One advantage of using standard format strings is that culture-specific formats are automatically applied. Depending on the application of the report, this could also be undesirable. For example, if a user whose local computer was configured for a European regional locale were to view an invoice, he or she might think they were buying a bike for a thousand Euros instead of a thousand U.S. dollars. In such as case, it might be best to explicitly format the currency as U.S. dollars and then use a general format for dates, so they appear to the European user in their native format. The best way to do this is to use standard formatting strings for both the currency and date text boxes and then set the Locale property for the currency to the EN-US locale. Leaving this property blank for the date will cause it to be resolved when the report is rendered based on the client settings.

There is plenty of information on this subject in Reporting Services Books Online. Unfortunately, there is also a lot of extra information that just doesn't apply to most reporting needs. The objective is to keep this simple and show you only what you really need to know for the majority of reports. The following table lists the common format strings that apply to numeric data types.

Format	Description	Example
C	Currency	$123,456,789.12
D	Decimal *followed by optional precision specifier*	123456789 000123456789 using D12
E	Scientific notation *followed by optional precision specifier*	1.234568e+008 1.234567891234+008 using E12
F	Fixed-point *followed by optional precision specifier*	123456789.12 123456789.123400000000 using F12
P	Percent *followed by optional precision specifier*	12.35%

The next table lists the common format strings that apply to date and time data types.

Format	Description	Example
d	Short date	11/1/03
D	Long date	Saturday, November 01, 2003
t	Short time	3:34 PM
T	Long time	3:23:26 PM
f	Full date and time	Saturday, November 01, 2003 3:34 PM
F	Full date and time	Saturday, November 01, 2003 3:34:26 PM
g	General date and time	11/1/03 3:34 PM

Format	Description	Example
G	General date and time	11/1/03 3:34:26 PM
M or m	Month	November 01
Y or y	Year month	November, 2003

Explicit Formatting

In addition to the standard formatting techniques, you may also use an explicit format string to get more control and deal with specific format needs. Keep in mind that the formatted output will be the same for dates and currency even if the locale setting is changed for the server.

Again, the Reporting Services Books Online contains detailed information about specific formats for string elements, so we won't rehash that information here. What we will do, however, is show a few common examples of explicit formatting. You can find the details about this topic under the topics "Custom Numeric Format Strings" and "Custom DateTime Format Strings" in Books Online. The following table is a summary of some common format expression elements.

Format Element	Type	Description	Example
Yyyy	DateTime	Four-character year	2004
Yy	DateTime	Two-character year	03
MMMM	DateTime	Month, full name	August
MMM	DateTime	Month, three characters	Aug
MM	DateTime	Month, two numerals	09 or 11
M	DateTime	Month, one or two numerals	9 or 11
Dddd	DateTime	Weekday, full name	Saturday
Ddd	DateTime	Weekday, three characters	Sat
Dd	DateTime	Day, two numerals	04 or 15
D	DateTime	Day, one or two numerals	4 or 15
Hh	DateTime	Hour in 12-hour time, two numerals	08 or 10
H	DateTime	Hour in 12-hour time, one or two numerals	8 or 10
HH	DateTime	Hour in 24-hour time, one or two numerals	08 or 23
H	DateTime	Hour in 24-hour time, one or two numerals	8 or 23

Format Element	Type	Description	Example
Mm	DateTime	Minutes, two numerals	35
Ss	DateTime	Seconds, two numerals	45
Tt	DateTime	12-hour time using AM or PM	AM or PM
T	DateTime	12-hour time using A or P	A or P
0	Number	Required numeral placeholder	09
#	Number	Optional numeral placeholder	
%	Number	Percentage	.95 = 95%
. , : - /	Any	Literals	123.45 1,234 12:34 PM

Let's use a common scenario as an example. Say that your company has offices around the world and follows a corporate standard to use European-style dates, regardless of where users are located. Instead of letting the system decide how to format dates, you want them to be explicitly formatted using your corporate standard.

If you set the Format property of the date type controls to the string MMMM d, yyyy, the resulting date will be displayed in this format: November 1, 2003.

Conditional Formatting

Under certain conditions, you may need to alter the format of a value based on an expression related to other fields or conditions in the report. The use of different functions and expressions will be discussed in Chapter 6. For now, let's take a look at a couple of examples to explore the concept and some techniques. The following is simply an example to demonstrate how regional formatting can vary and is not a common business solution.

Let's say that your company has locations in England, Germany, and the United States, and, for whatever reason (remember, we're making this up), you want different rows to display information formatted for the corresponding locales. Each row in the underlying table includes a column named MyLocale that holds your own two-character code for the locale. The industry has a five-character standard known as the RFC1766. Your codes are loosely translatable to this standard. Based on the anticipated values in this column (UK, DE, or US), you will display currency and date information in the corresponding format. The objective will be to format the date and currency values as shown in the following tables.

Value	Locale	Formatted Value
November 1, 2003	US	11/1/03
"	UK	1/11/03
"	DE	1.11.03
12345.1234	US	$1,234.12
"	UK	£1,234.12
"	DE	1.234,12€

A control's property may be set to an expression that will actually parse and set the property value for the row as it is rendered. There are a few techniques to do this; one is to use the Immediate If or IIf function. This works if you have one condition to test and two possible outcomes. A more powerful technique is the Switch function. It works like the Switch statement in C# and like the Select Case statement in VB rolled into one. This technique will be used to set the Format property of the date. For the text box that will display this value, use the following expression:

```
=Switch(Fields!MyLocale.Value="DE", "d.MM.yy", Fields!MyLocale.Value="UK",
"d/MM/yy", Fields!MyLocale.Value="US", "M/d/yy")
```

The currency value could be set the same way, except that the German form would be difficult to contend with, since periods are used to designate the thousand separator and a comma is used for decimals. In the German language, these characters have the opposite meaning. Fortunately, each control has a Language property that is equipped to handle this and many other language- and culture-specific idiosyncrasies. By dynamically manipulating this property in the same manner, you can reach your objective. Using the Switch function, you can translate your two-character codes to the industry standard that uses five-character codes. The following expression can be used to change the Language property of the currency text box:

```
=Switch(Fields!MyLocale.Value="DE", "de-DE", Fields!MyLocale.Value="UK", "en-GB",
Fields!MyLocale.Value="US", "en-US")
```

Again, this is an example of one possible business problem and one possible solution. If this were a real situation, it might make more sense to store the actual culture information string in the table and simply set the Language property of the control to that value pulled directly from the table. By the way, all of the supported culture information strings can be found in the MSDN library under the search key CultureInfo. The sample report in Figure 4-58 shows the final result using the formatting examples just discussed.

Conditional Formatting Example

Locale	Date	Money
UK	11/1/2003	£123,456,789.12
DE	01.11.2003	123.000.000.000,01 €
US	11/1/2003	$98,765.43
DE	01.11.2003	1.234.567,12 €
US	11/1/2003	$1,234,567.12
UK	11/1/2003	£1,234,567.12

Figure 4-58

Multiple Columns

A report can display list values in multiple columns. Values in a column *snake* from top to bottom and then left to right. It's important to note that Reporting Services can only do so much in HTML and that some multicolumn reports can't be rendered in some (or possibly any) versions of HTML, so your only option may be to render these reports in PDF format.

Columns are defined for the body of a report. When the Columns property for the body is set to a value greater than 1, the report page width should be set according to the following equation:

```
Report Page Width >= (Body Width x number of columns) + (ColumnSpacing x (number of
    columns - 1))
```

For example, a report, that has a body width of 2.5 inches with three columns and the column spacing set to 0.25 inches will yield a report width of 8 inches. If the report's left and right margins were set to 0.25 inches each, this should fit neatly into an 8.5-inch page width.

The layout window shown in Figure 4-59 shows a report designed with these dimensions and property settings.

Figure 4-59

This report is very simple and contains no headers or footers. You can add them to this report, but the options are limited. You are limited to the width of the report body and the header will only show above the first column. In order to use a report header wider than 2.5 inches in this example, you have to create another report and use the multicolumn report as an embedded subreport. You learn more about creating subreports in Chapter 6. Keep in mind that some rendering formats (such as HTML) have difficulty with multicolumn reports. Use this feature carefully and make sure that you test your report design using all the rendering formats you plan to support. I have made a point to redesign multicolumn reports to avoid this limitation whenever possible.

Pagination Control

Unlike traditional reporting tools such as Microsoft Access, Reporting Services doesn't have one specific report viewer. Since reports may be rendered in different formats and viewed in different browsers or document viewers, page handling may be different for various rendering formats. For PDF and TIFF formats, reports will naturally be paginated as the content exceeds the usable page height. In cases where you need content to paginate uniformly, you can force page breaks using a number of different data containers or data ranges. For each of the following report items, right-click on the item and select Properties from the pop-up menu to view the related properties dialog.

Page Breaks for a Rectangle

You can set a page break to occur before or after a rectangle. Using the properties dialog or properties sheet for a rectangle, set one or both of the page break properties, as seen in Figure 4-60. If all you want to do is set a page break at a specific location in a static report, you can use a rectangle with no border to do this.

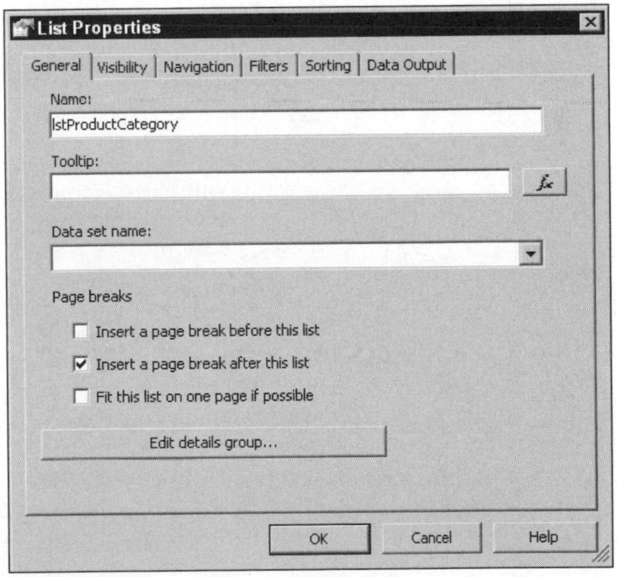

Figure 4-60

These options are similar for each report item and may be set using either the properties dialog or the designer's properties sheet.

Page Breaks for a List

Since the list item is designed to repeat a group of bound report items, it is a natural place to force a page break. Set these properties using the List Properties dialog. In addition to breaking before or after the entire range of listed items, you can cause a list to fit onto one page if the rendered content permits this to happen. If this property is checked, the rendering engine will test the length of the listed data and move the entire list to the next page so that it fits.

Page Breaks for a Table

The table can have page breaks defined in much the same way that they are for a list item. A page break may be set to occur immediately before or after the table. You can also try to fit all of the table data on one page, in which case a page break will occur before the table. Breaks may be specified within the table at data groupings. Grouping and sorting will be covered in greater detail in the next chapter. Once a grouping has been defined for a table, the grouping and sorting properties dialog is accessible by selecting the grouping row in the table. Either right-click on the row selector and select Edit Group from the pop-up menu or choose Grouping/Sorting from the standard Properties window.

Page Breaks for a Group

In the Grouping and Sorting Properties dialog, shown here in Figure 4-61, page breaks may also be forced before or after the grouping.

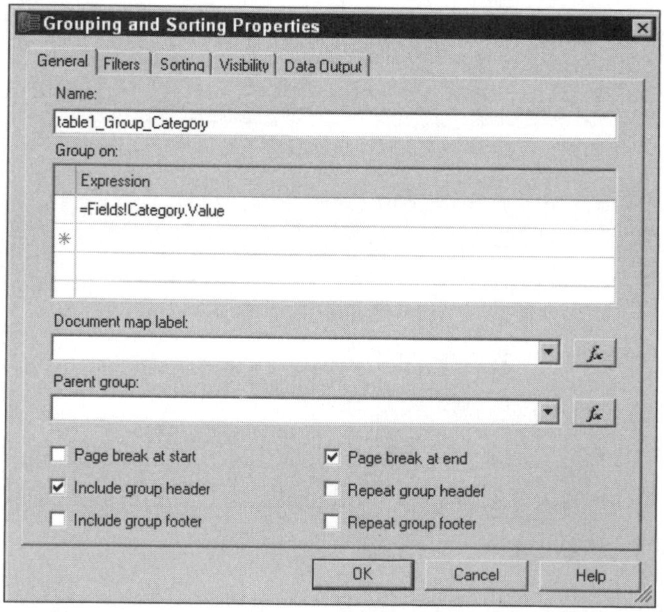

Figure 4-61

Page Breaks for a Matrix

The matrix page break options are the same as for the table report item. As the matrix rows are expanded, data will automatically span pages. If the content fits on one page and the Fit this matrix on one page if possible option is checked, a page break will be placed before the content. You can also force a page break immediately before or after the matrix content.

Page Breaks for a Chart

Page break properties for charts are available only in the standard Visual Studio properties window and not in the custom properties dialog for the chart. You may set a page break immediately before or after a chart by setting the Page Break At Start and Page Break At End properties, respectively.

Printing Considerations

An important issue to keep in mind is that unlike many other reporting tools, Reporting Services may be displayed using a variety of report viewers or browsers. In the first generation of Reporting Services, this posed a significant limitation for users printing reports. Today, there are two different options for report printing: It can be managed by the application used to view the report, or users may print reports from the Report Manager Web interface using the client-side print management control. Each rendering format has its limitations and idiosyncrasies that can affect printed output. Rather than relying on the printing features of Internet Explorer, Microsoft Excel, or the Adobe Acrobat Reader to print from these different rendering formats; reports may be printed directly from the Report Manager using a simple print dialog with pagination, margin, and page selection options. This ActiveX control runs as a client-side component and will be installed on the user's computer the first time it is used.

In cases where international users might need to access and print your reports, you may need to specify a page size that will accommodate different paper sizes. For example, if you anticipate that a report will be read and printed in the United States and Great Britain, the report content should fit on both U.S. letter and A4 paper sizes (see Figure 4-62).

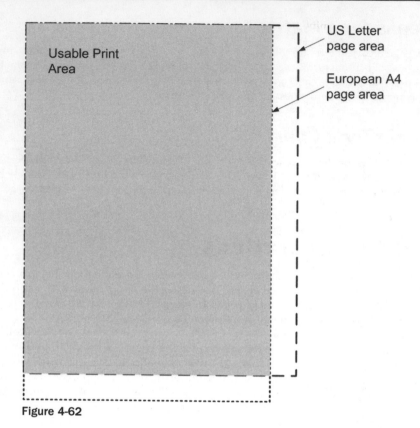

Usable Print Area

US Letter page area

European A4 page area

Figure 4-62

Summary

The purpose of this chapter was to introduce the Report Designer and get you started on designing a report. Several features and design considerations were mentioned but not discussed in depth. In brief, you learned:

- ❑ How to use Report Wizard to create a simple, tabular report.

- ❑ The fundamental building blocks, which include defining a data source and data set query, grouping, and basic table layout.

- ❑ Reports are deployed to the report server using the settings defined in a report project.

- ❑ The basic use and function of each report item and how they are defined in the Layout tab of the Report Designer.

This has given you an overview of a Report project in the SQL Server Business Intelligence Studio or Visual Studio 2005 and the basic features of the Report Designer. Furthermore, importing reports from Access will allow you to leverage existing report solutions. You can also use the features of Access you already understand as a learning tool. Designing reports for extensibility with different user environments, including different browsers, computers, and mobile devices, was also covered.

Different reporting formats can ensure formatting control and compatibility. Report items can be used to display static values as well as data from a data source. Simple items such as text boxes may be repeated and grouped in data ranges and list-type containers. More sophisticated report items such as the list, table, and matrix may be used to create tabular and pivot reports that perform functions like aggregate, subtotal, and group and provide drill-down and drill-through functionality.

Data formatting can be achieved using simple, standard format strings, explicit format expressions, and conditional logic that uses programming functions and expressions. Several report items can be used to paginate a report statically or based on the size and content of data regions.

By now, you should be comfortable using Visual Studio to create and extend a simple report project. The next two chapters will expand on what you learned. Chapter 5 will address queries and accessing data and then Chapter 6 will show you how to take report design to the next level.

5

Designing Data Access

In nearly all cases, reports are based on a data source of some kind. Therefore, the first order of business when designing a report is to create a connection and define the queries necessary to retrieve the report data. This chapter will discuss the essential first steps of report design—how to consume data. Although this is typically simple and straightforward, there are a number of options to be considered when designing data sources and queries. Although SQL Server Reporting Services is packaged with the SQL Server database product, it may be used with other database products as data sources. This chapter discusses the following topics:

- ❏ Creating stand-alone and shared data sources.
- ❏ Designing queries and data sets.
- ❏ Using parameters to filter data at the database.
- ❏ Using parameters to filter data at the Report Server.
- ❏ Using Analysis Services and the MDX Query Builder.
- ❏ Obtaining data from other data sources.

Every report will have at least one data source (with the rare exception of a special-purpose report that doesn't use any data). The simplest of reports will have a single data source to provide data for a single data set. The data source defines a connection as a string of text stored either in the report definition file or in a separate shared data source file that can be shared among several reports. This connection information may include security credentials. The data set defines a query expression or a reference to query objects stored in the database. The data set is also contained within the report definition. Figure 5-1 depicts how data flows to the report. The data source provides the ability to connect to the database, and the data set contains a query expression that populates the report with data.

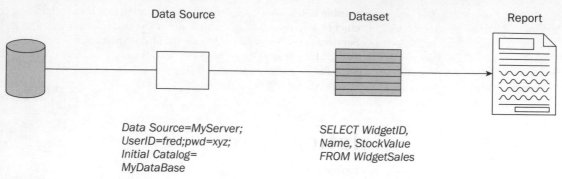

Figure 5-1

More complex reports may require multiple data sets to provide data for different data ranges or items in the report or to feed values to parameter value selection lists. Data sets can be based on query expressions from the same data source, as shown in Figure 5-2.

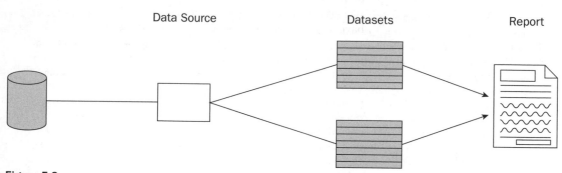

Figure 5-2

Multiple data sets can get their data from multiple data sources. This model would enable a report to have parameter selection values be obtained from a local database and report data to be obtained from a central data store. In some cases, data regions, subreports, and various report items might obtain data from multiple sources through associated data sets, as shown in Figure 5-3.

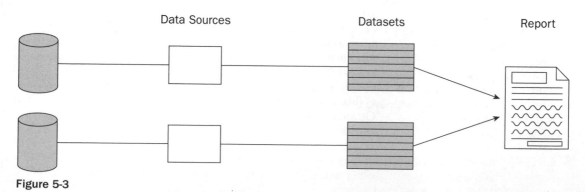

Figure 5-3

As you can see, almost anything is possible in terms of combining data sources and data sets. Data sources can be practically any database product or any data source you can query by means of standard connection libraries or drivers. Reporting Services consumes data using the .NET data providers, which include support for SQL Server, Oracle, and all OLE DB providers. These include almost any database product that supports ODBC access or a capable ISAM driver. Data sets in Reporting Services are always read-only, so there is no need to specify cursor types or locking options.

Reporting for Relational Data

In the previous chapter, you briefly looked at using the Query Builder. Now you'll take a closer look at how queries are created and how data is provided for a report. At this point, it's important to understand the basic building blocks for reports. The discussion will begin with some of these fundamentals. You will go through several short walk-through exercises, so you can see and experience how it works. I am assuming that you have used Visual Studio 2005 and you have created a report using the Report Wizard.

If you are a .NET programmer, as I am, you may have seen the term "data set" and thought, "I know what a data set is, and I use them all the time in .NET data access program code, so I should have a leg up on doing data access in Reporting Services." If you are not a .NET programmer, you're already a step ahead of those programmers who have to relearn the application of this term. By the way, if you are not a .NET application developer, you don't need to concern yourself with this at all.

Why does the term "data set" mean two completely different things? We ran out of new words in the English language a long time ago. Everyone knows that to be environmentally responsible we need to recycle, so this is what we're doing—recycling words and phrases. This one is a classic example. In Reporting Services, you have the concept of a query in the report definition that provides data values for the report output; our good friends at Microsoft decided to call this a *Dataset*. If you have worked at all with programmatic data access in the .NET Framework, you should know that a Dataset is also an object that stores a cache of data (perhaps from a query) as an XML structure in memory. Although these two items may both handle data and deal with queries, result sets, and binding values displayed in a report, they are two very different concepts. Now, since we have that straightened out, try this: If you were to create a custom data source extension in program code, you might use an ADO.NET Dataset that would serve as the Dataset for a report!

Query Basics

Reporting Services has the ability to obtain data from a variety of data sources. Nearly all relational database products are queried using a form of *Structured Query Language (SQL)*, which means that a query created for one database product (say, Microsoft Access) may be portable to a different data source (perhaps Oracle or SQL Server). Most database products implement a form of SQL conforming to the ANSI SQL standard. SQL Server, for example, conforms to the ANSI 92 SQL standard, and other products may conform to other revisions (like ANSI 89 SQL or ANSI 99 SQL). Beyond the most fundamental SQL statements, most dialects of SQL are not completely interchangeable and will require some understanding of their individual idiosyncrasies.

Other specialized database products may use a different query language. Microsoft SQL Server Analysis Services is a data storage and retrieval product that uses multidimensional cube structures to organize complex data for decision-support systems.

The main point here is that you can use whatever query language your database product understands. Reporting Services provides a query editor designed especially for Transact-SQL and a generic editor that will accommodate other query languages and SQL dialects.

Data Sources

A data source contains the connection information for a data set. Data sources either can be created only for a specific report data set or may be shared among different reports. Since most reports will get data from a common data source, it often makes sense to create a shared data source. There are a number of advantages in using shared data sources. Even if you don't have several reports that need to share a central data source, it takes no additional effort to create a shared data source. This may still be advantageous in this case as the data source is managed separately from each report and can be easily updated if necessary. Then, as you add new reports, the shared data source will already be established and deployed to the Report Server.

In a Visual Studio report project there are three different ways to create a data source:

❑ Creating a data source in the Report Wizard.

❑ Creating a data source from the Project Add Item template.

❑ Creating a data source when defining a data set.

Let's look at each of these in detail.

Creating a Data Source in the Report Wizard

For this exercise, you may create a new report project or open an existing report project. From the Solution Explorer, right-click the Reports folder and choose Add New Report to launch the Report Wizard. The first page in the wizard will give you the opportunity to select an existing shared data source or create a new data source, as shown in Figure 5-4.

Creating a Data Source from the Project Add Item Template

In the Solution Explorer, point to Reports. Right-click, and choose Add⇨Add New Item. The options in this dialog include Report Wizard, Report, and Data Source. Selecting the Data Source option creates a shared data source.

The following is an example of the standard Data Link Properties dialog used to define a data source. If your database server was named DWServer, this name would be selected or entered in the first box, under step 1 in this dialog, as shown in Figure 5-5.

If you are working with a local development database server installed on the same computer, you can enter . (a period) or **localhost**. Otherwise, enter the name of the database server. In step 2, you choose the security authentication method to be used by the database server to check security credentials. SQL Server may be configured to use Integrated Windows Security or both SQL Server Security and Integrated Windows Security. In a development environment, integrated security is a simple choice.

Finally, you select or type the database name.

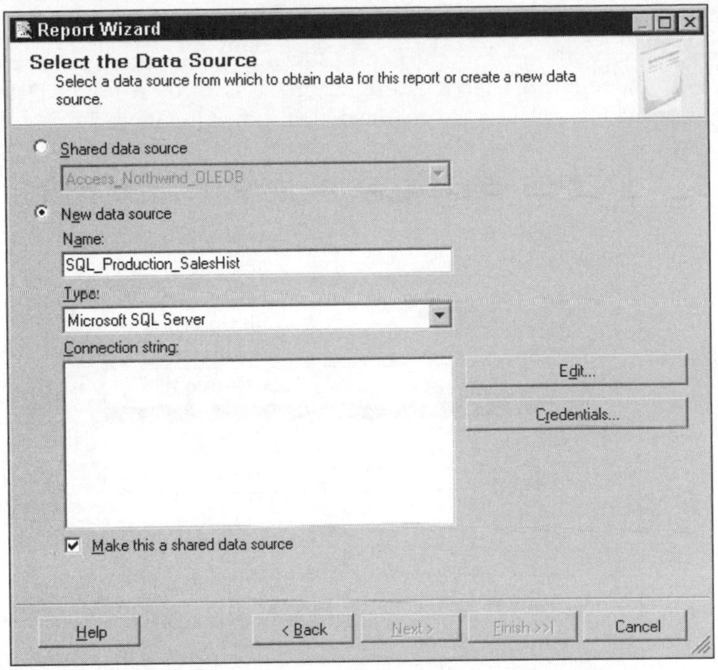

Figure 5-4

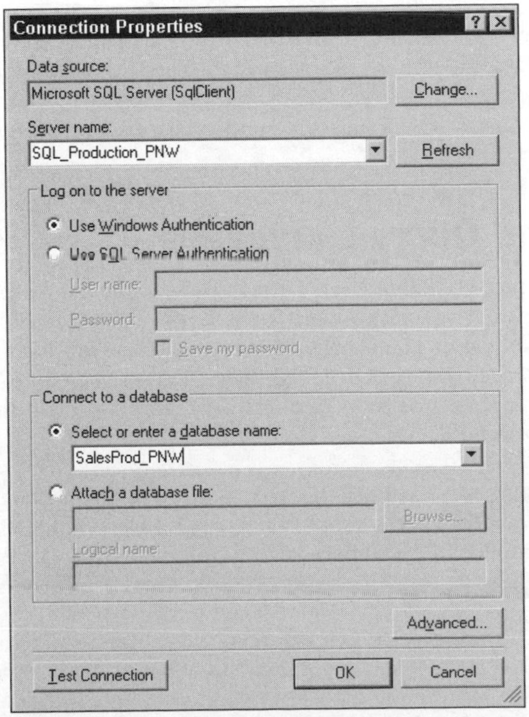

Figure 5-5

Creating a Data Source When Defining a Dataset

If you create a new report without using the Report Wizard, data sources are selected or created from the report designer. With the report open in the designer, make sure you're on the Data tab. From the Data set drop-down list, select New Data set to get the dialog shown in Figure 5-6.

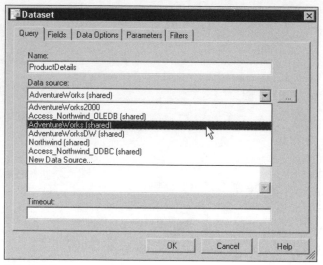

Figure 5-6

Select a New Data Source from the data source drop-down list, and this will open the Data Link Properties dialog with the same options as selecting the Data Source new item template.

Regardless of the method used, a data source is simply a connection string saved into the report definition or shared data source file.

Data Sources and Query Languages

The examples in this chapter will all use SQL Server 2005 sample databases. When creating a data source, if you choose any data provider other than SQL Server, queries must be written in the query language appropriate for that product. For most relational database products, this will be a dialect of SQL. For example, Oracle uses a version of SQL called PL/SQL, and Microsoft Access understands Access SQL. Some providers require unique types of query expressions or scripting code specifically designed for that data source environment.

When defining a data set's query expression, the designer will display one of the two similar query windows. If you are using the SQL Server data provider, the Transact-SQL Query Builder will be displayed. In the case of another data provider that uses another query language or dialect of SQL, a generic query window is displayed.

To query cube structures in Analysis Services, a specialized expression language called Multidimensional Expressions (MDX) is used. The current implementation of Reporting Services supports MDX with some limitations. Unlike the Cube Browser in Analysis Services and other specialized multidimensional data query tools, reports are based on data that is flattened to two-dimensional structures and represented as rows and columns like a SQL query.

In this sample MDX query expression for the AdventureWorks DW OLAP database (included in SQL Server 2005 Analysis Services):

```
" SELECT  { [Measures].[Sales Amount] } ON COLUMNS,
  { ([Reseller].[Reseller Type].[Reseller Name].ALLMEMBERS * [Ship
Date].[Calendar].[Month].ALLMEMBERS ) }
  ON ROWS FROM [Adventure Works] "
```

I will cover the use of Microsoft Analysis Services and other data sources later in this chapter in the section "Reporting for Analytical Data."

Filtering Techniques

When retrieving report data from a data source, it's important to consider the most efficient means for filtering report data based on the user's selection criteria. Many databases contain large amounts of data. Therefore, it is always important to retrieve just the right amount of data required for reporting. At times, a report will only be used to view data for a narrow range of values, and at other times the user may specify different criteria, causing the report to render a varied range of related values. In the case of a narrow range of possible values, it makes more sense to retrieve only the associated data. However, if users will specify different criteria during a session—causing the data source to be requeried multiple times—it could prove to be slow and an inefficient use of resources.

In Figure 5-7, parameters presented to the data source cause data to be filtered and return only the data for a single rendering of the report. The data set represents the database server's result set on the client side (the Report Server). As you see in the diagram, this is small volume of data since it has already been filtered at the database.

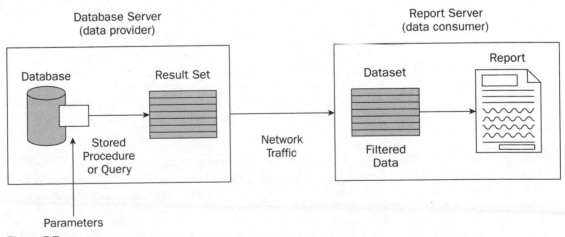

Figure 5-7

By passing selection criteria parameters at the database object level, network traffic can be greatly reduced and the report is rendered more efficiently. However, if the user will be providing different parameter values to render several views of the same report within a session, the database will be queried repeatedly, perhaps resulting in longer overall wait times and much of the same data will be moving across the network multiple times. In Figure 5-8, a larger volume of data is returned from the database server since it is unfiltered. Filtering then occurs by using report parameters on the Report Server.

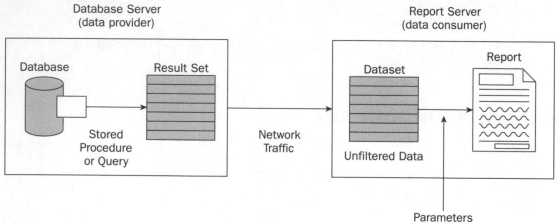

Figure 5-8

If all of the data necessary for each query to be executed in a user's session is obtained in one result set, it will result in a greater volume of network traffic for a single execution. However, it may reduce subsequent report rendering times.

Selection parameters may be applied to data at the report level rather than at the data source. Since all of the data is cached (held in memory), reports will be rendered much faster. This technique can reduce the overall network traffic and rendering time.

You certainly don't want to retrieve unnecessary data from the data source, so a combination of these two techniques may be the appropriate solution, depending upon specific reporting needs. For example, if you are a regional sales manager and you wish to get sales summaries for each of the territories within your region, you may begin your session by retrieving all of the regional sales data for a range of dates. For each territory report, this data is simply filtered down to the territory level.

Parameter Concepts

Although I don't believe this to be overly complicated, at first I found the whole parameter puzzle to be a little confusing until I had a chance to do some creative things with parameters in both queries and report expressions. To lessen your agony (and hopefully shorten your learning experience,) I'll explain how parameters are defined in simple queries and reports, and I'll also explain how you may need to use (and define) parameters in more complex reports.

There are two (and possibly three, depending on your query technique) different types of parameters with which you may contend in report design: data set parameters and report parameters. Data set parameters may be derived from database objects such as stored procedures and user-defined functions. Figure 5-9 shows you that there may be three different layers in the design process where you may encounter parameters.

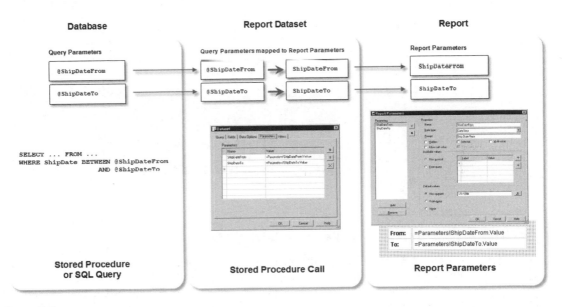

Figure 5-9

When using SQL Server as the data source, parameters are defined in the SQL syntax by prefixing the names with a single @ symbol. In a stored procedure, these parameters are defined first and then used in the procedure body much as you would use an ad hoc query. The report designer generates corresponding report parameters. The third section of Figure 5-9 shows the Report Parameters dialog open with the two derived parameters. If you use the Graphical Query Builder or Generic Query Designer to write a typical Transact-SQL statement, the report designer will resolve data set parameters and database object parameters and create corresponding report parameters automatically. Data set parameters are mapped to report parameters in the Data set Properties dialog, shown in Figure 5-10. This dialog is accessible from the ellipsis (...) button next to the data set drop-down list in the Data tab of the report designer.

For basic queries, the report designer will populate this dialog and match the parameters for you. However, if you have created a complex or unusual data set query, you may need to match the data set and report parameters manually. Parameter resolution is performed on a number of events, which include when the refresh button is pressed, when another data set is selected, or when moving off of the Data tab in the report designer.

> When working with unusual queries that may require manual intervention, I recommend that you keep a backup copy of the last working version of the report and copy the query text to Notepad just in case you need to revert to it.

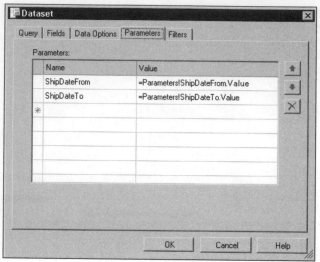

Figure 5-10

Filtering Data with Query Parameters

Parameters are often used to filter data at the data source. Whether the data is to be filtered within the report or not, filtering at least some of the data within the database is an essential technique for most report solutions. If you have created parameterized stored procedures in SQL Server, you are already familiar with this pattern. The technique applies to stored procedures and query expressions that use very similar syntax. Let's start with a simple ad hoc query expression and then we'll move on to creating a stored procedure.

Query parameters begin with the @ symbol and must conform to the naming convention standards for Transact-SQL identifiers. The name should not contain spaces or certain punctuation characters and can't begin with a numeral; for simplicity, just use letters. In stored procedures, parameters must be declared before they are used. In an ad hoc query, simply make up parameter names when you need them. In the WHERE part of a SQL statement, use a parameter to represent a variable valuable as follows:

```
SELECT * FROM Products WHERE ProductID = @ProductID
```

In this case, the parameter has the same name as the corresponding field name, but this isn't necessary. If you want to use the Query Builder to create a more complex query, parameters may be specified in the Criteria column of the builder grid. This is shown in Figure 5-11.

In this example, rows will be returned for records where the ListPrice column value is less than or equal to the value specified using the @ListPriceMax parameter.

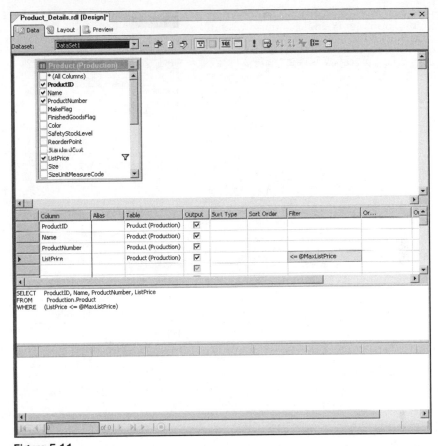

Figure 5-11

Report Parameters

In addition to report parameters derived from data set parameters, you may add report parameters of your own. These report parameters (that do not have corresponding query parameters) can be added to support additional report functionality, such as hiding and showing report sections, page numbers, and dynamic formatting.

The following example demonstrates some simple report parameters used to dynamically set values on the report. Later we'll apply this technique to some practical report features. This example is intended to demonstrate two very simple report parameters for academic purposes.

Create a new report without using the wizard. You can do this by selecting Add and then Add New Item from the Solution Explorer's right-click menu; select Report from the report item templates in the Add New Item dialog. Do not specify a data set for the new report, and then switch to the Layout view in the report designer.

Report parameters are added using the Report Parameters dialog. Select the Report item in the Properties window and click the ellipsis (...) button next to the ReportParameters property.

As you see in Figure 5-12, the ReportTitle parameter is a string value with the default set to Report Title. The TextColor parameter is similar and has a default value set to Blue.

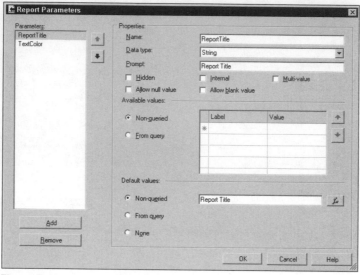

Figure 5-12

Drag two text box items from the Toolbox window onto the body of the report in the report designer. Normally it's a good idea to give items an appropriate name (especially if they are to be referenced in an expression), but this isn't necessary in this simple example.

Set two properties for these text boxes: the Value property for each text box and the Color property of the second text box, according to the following instructions. The designer displays the value property in the text boxes, but it's a good idea to change these property values in the standard properties window or the custom text box Properties dialog (right-click the text box and choose Properties).

The first text box will get its value from the ReportTitle parameter. Set its Value property to **=Parameters!ReportTitle.Value** and set the Value property of the second text box to **="This Text is " & Parameters!TextColor.Value**. Select the second text box and set its Color property to **=Parameters!TextColor.Value** (see Figure 5-13).

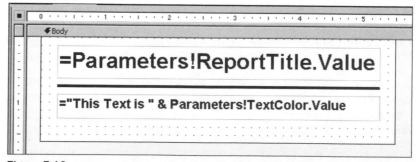

Figure 5-13

You can also change the FontSize *and* FontWeight *properties if you prefer to dress things up a bit more. I've also added a line to the report.*

Now, click the Preview tab and notice what happens. The ReportTitle and TextColor parameters are displayed in the header of the preview window with the default values, and these values are displayed in the report.

Try changing the ReportTitle and Color using the parameter fields in the header, and click the View Report button to refresh the report preview. The first text box should display the text entered into the ReportTitle parameter, and the second text box should not only display the specific color name but the text should also be displayed in that color, as in Figure 5-14.

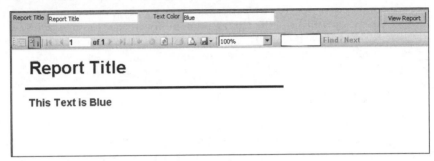

Figure 5-14

As you can see, this is an effective way to feed values to the report to be used in expressions. We will expand this technique to provide filtering and dynamic formatting.

Basing a Parameter on a Query

Whether report parameters are derived from query parameters or created within the report explicitly, they may be used for a variety of things in the report. Often, it will make sense to let your user select from a list of items to supply a parameter value. Parameter items may be populated from a static list or from a data-driven query.

Parameter values can be selected from a data source through a data set that is set up within the report designer like any data set you would use for the report itself. A report may contain any number of data sets, some to supply parameter values and others to supply data for items within the report.

Using the sample Northwind database for a simple example, your report may be driven by a data set that selects records from the Products table where the CategoryID matches a user-specified parameter value. The CategoryID parameter values would be based on another data set that selects the CategoryID and CategoryName columns from the Categories table. In Report Manager, the user simply selects a category name from a drop-down list, and then the report is viewed showing only products that match the selected category.

In the upcoming walk-through exercise, you will create different parameters that will not only drive the report but will filter the values for multiple related parameters.

Cascading Parameters

The behavior I just described is what we call *cascading parameters*. This is a feature in the Report Manager that allows one parameter value selection to cause another parameter list to be populated with related values. There will be times when you may want to filter a list of parameter values based on another parameter selection. In the earlier example for product categories and products, let's say that the selection from the Products table is to provide another parameter value that will be used to generate a report of sales records for the selected product. In this case, you may want to select the category first. This would give you a filtered list of products that would be used to select a specific product. The product selection would then be used to render the sales report.

I'll use another example from the AdventureWorks2000 database. I'll raise the bar just a little more and create three different parameters to drive a fairly simple walk-through example. The outcome of this exercise will be a report showing stores in a given location. You will be prompted to select a country. When the country is selected, related states or provinces will be listed. Making a selection from this list will make cities available. Selecting an item from this list will drive the report data—a list of stores in the selected city.

This walk-through requires that you either complete the steps in the preceding chapter or that you already know how to create a report project and a shared data source.

To begin with, add a new report to a Visual Studio report project. From the Solution Explorer, right-click on Reports and choose Add and then Add New Item. Select Report from the templates list and give it any name you like. I'm calling mine Cascading_Parameters. I know that it's not very imaginative, but it makes the point.

In the report designer, you should be looking at the Data tab at this point. Drop down the list labeled Dataset and select New Dataset. The dialog shown in Figure 5-15 will appear.

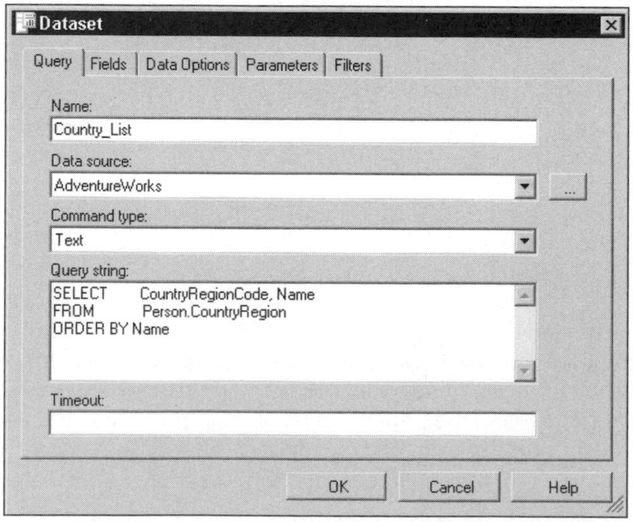

Figure 5-15

Enter the name **Country_List** for the new data set. Select or create a shared data source for the AdventureWorks database (the one you created in the previous chapter), and then click the OK button to move to the Query Builder window.

Rather than going through the whole Query Builder procedure, here is the SQL statement to type into the SQL pane. Place the cursor in the third pane down in this window (between the two grids) and type the following code:

```
SELECT      CountryRegionCode, Name
FROM        CountryRegion
ORDER BY    Name
```

Note that the carriage returns and most of the spacing are optional. The only critical spaces are between the words ORDER and BY. Everything else should have one or more spaces. This query doesn't use any parameters since it won't be filtered.

Drop down the Dataset list, choose New Dataset, and repeat the preceding steps to create a new data set called StateProvince_List. The SQL expression for this data set can also be typed into the Query Builder window:

```
SELECT      StateProvinceID, StateProvinceCode, CountryRegionCode
FROM        Person.StateProvince
WHERE       CountryRegionCode = @CountryRegionCode
ORDER BY    StateProvinceCode
```

If you used the Query Builder to create this expression, there may be some additional parentheses. These are unnecessary and, again, the spacing and returns are not particularly important.

This expression does include a parameter, @CountryRegionCode, which will get its value from a row selected from the previous data set. A corresponding parameter will be created for the report called CountryRegionCode.

Drop down the data set list and create a third data set called City_List. Like the last data set, this one also includes a parameter that will get its value from the selected state or province. Type the following SQL statement for this data set:

```
SELECT      StateProvinceID, City
FROM        Person.Address
GROUP BY    StateProvinceID, City
HAVING      StateProvinceID = @StateProvinceID
ORDER BY    City
```

There is no table exclusively for cities, so you can use the Address table and grouping on the City column to eliminate duplicates. This query will return a list of cities for the selected state or province by using the StateProvinceID parameter.

Finally, you will need to create the data set for the report itself. The SQL for this is going to be a little more complicated. Due to the normalized design of the AdventureWorks2000 database, it takes several tables to take you from a city to a store with the necessary report values. Let's use the Query Builder for this one.

If you prefer, you may skip the following Query Builder steps and type the SQL statement directly into the SQL pane.

Add one more data set and call it Stores_By_City. Use the toolbar to switch to the Graphic Query Designer and click the Add Table toolbar button (or right-click the top pane and choose Add Table) and add the tables illustrated in Figure 5-16 in the following order: Address, CustomerAddress, Customer, Store, StateProvince, and CountryRegion.

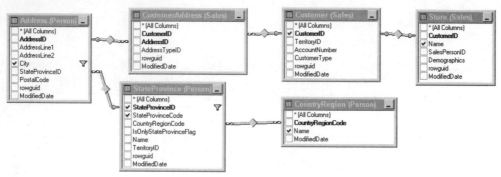

Figure 5-16

The joins will be added automatically by the Query Builder. An additional join will be added between the StateProvince and CountryRegion tables. To remove the join, click once on the line and then press the delete key.

In the second pane, select the table columns in the order you see here. You can either use the drop-down lists in the grid for the column and table or check them in the table diagram in the first pane. Since the Store and CountryRegion tables both contain columns called Name, you can use aliases to make these column names more descriptive. Enter the alias names as you see in the grid in Figure 5-17.

Column	Alias	Table	Output	Sort Type	Sort Order	Filter	Or...	Or...	Or...
CustomerID		Customer (Sa...	✓						
Name		Store (Sales)	✓						
Name	CountryName	CountryRegi...	✓						
StateProvinceCode		StateProvinc...	✓						
City		Address (Per...	✓			= @City			
StateProvinceID		StateProvinc...	✓			= @StateProvinceID			

Figure 5-17

Finally, enter the query parameters @StateProvinceID and @City as you see here. This data set should be complete. To check it, compare this SQL statement with the one in the Query Builder:

```
SELECT      Sales.Customer.CustomerID, Sales.Store.Name,
            Person.CountryRegion.Name AS CountryName,
            Person.StateProvince.StateProvinceCode, Person.Address.City,
            Person.StateProvince.StateProvinceID
FROM        Sales.Customer INNER JOIN Sales.CustomerAddress
        ON Sales.Customer.CustomerID = Sales.CustomerAddress.CustomerID
        INNER JOIN Sales.Store
```

```
              ON Sales.Customer.CustomerID = Sales.Store.CustomerID
              INNER JOIN Person.Address
              ON Sales.CustomerAddress.AddressID = Person.Address.AddressID
              INNER JOIN Person.StateProvince
              ON Person.Address.StateProvinceID = Person.StateProvince.StateProvinceID
              INNER JOIN Person.CountryRegion
              ON Person.StateProvince.CountryRegionCode
              = Person.CountryRegion.CountryRegionCode
   WHERE      (Person.Address.City = @City)
       AND    (Person.StateProvince.StateProvinceID = @StateProvinceID)
```

Let's now look into configuring parameters.

Switch to the Layout tab and select the Report item from the Properties window drop-down list. Click the ellipsis button next to the `ReportParameters` property. This opens the Report Parameters dialog, as seen in Figure 5-18.

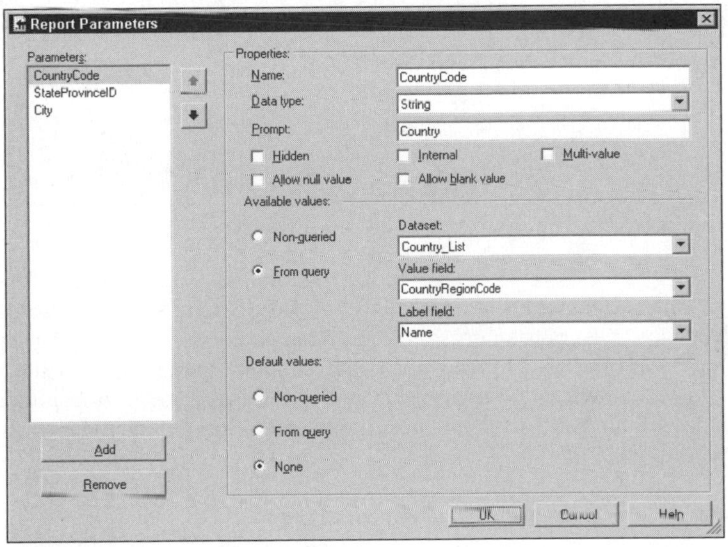

Figure 5-18

The `CountryCode` parameter will get its values from the Country_List data set. Like most typical lookup tables, the key value is not intended to be a user-readable value but is used to indicate the selected country for related tables through a foreign key relationship.

Select this parameter in the Parameters list box and then enter **Country** for the prompt. This is the caption the user will see next to the parameter drop-down list when they view the report. Ensure that all of the check boxes are unchecked to indicate that the user must select a value from the drop-down list.

The parameter drop-down list will display values in the Name column and return the corresponding value in the CountryRegionCode column. Set the `Label field` and `Value field` properties accordingly. Finally, indicate that there is no default value by selecting the last radio button, and click OK when you're done.

We will repeat this process for the other two parameters. Use the following Report Parameters screen diagram to set these properties.

The StateProvinceID parameter is configured as shown in Figure 5-19.

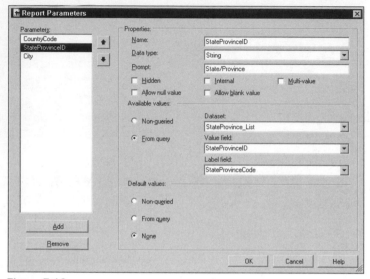

Figure 5-19

The properties for this parameter are set much like they were before. This time use the StateProvince_List data set as the drop-down list data source. You should remember that this data set contains a query parameter called CountryRegionCode. The reporting engine is smart enough to make the connection between the Value field of the previous parameter's data set and this data set's corresponding parameter. One parameter selection will filter the list for the next parameter as long as the parameters are listed in their order of dependency.

The final parameter, City, is configured, as shown in Figure 5-20.

Much like the previous parameter, the City parameter gets its value list from the City_List data set, which contains a query parameter related to the value field selection for the StateProvinceID parameter.

Designing the report is easy. I've made it a point to size the text box items so that you can read their value properties in this view of the report designer (see Figure 5-21).

The wide rectangle at the bottom of the report body is a list item. Drag this from the Toolbox to the report body first and set its DataSetName property to Stores_By_City. The Toolbox is located on the left side of the Designer window and has a little wrench-and-hammer icon.

The easiest way to create data-bound text boxes is to drag fields from the fields list (located on the left side near the Toolbox). With the fields list open, drop down the list at the top and select the Stores_By_City data set. Now, drag the CustomerID and Name fields onto the list item you created earlier.

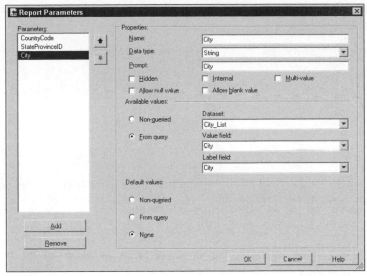

Figure 5-20

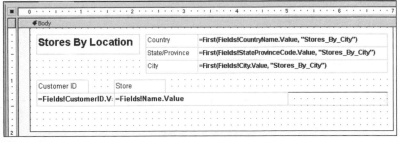

Figure 5-21

From the Toolbox, drag two text boxes above the list and change the Value properties to Customer ID and Store, as shown in Figure 5-22. The Stores By Location, Country, State/Province, and City text boxes are also unbound and serve only as static labels.

Drag and drop the CountryName, StateProvinceCode, and City fields to the right of the corresponding text boxes near the top of the report body.

Note the value of these three items contains some additional information. An aggregate function (like the First function used here) is necessary when an item isn't contained in a list, grid, or other container item that repeats rows of data. Since this report defines more than one data set, the data set name is required in the second argument of the First function.

With these settings in place, you should be able to preview the report and see the results. Switch to the Preview tab and select a country from the drop-down list.

As shown in Figure 5-22, select United States from the list and the State/Province parameter list is enabled.

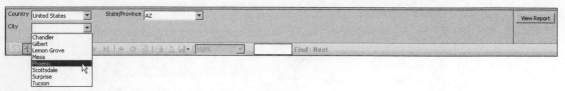

Figure 5-22

Drop this list down and you will see that it contains only states in the United States. Select AZ for Arizona and the City parameter list becomes available.

Drop down the City list, select Phoenix, and click the View Report button, as shown in Figure 5-23.

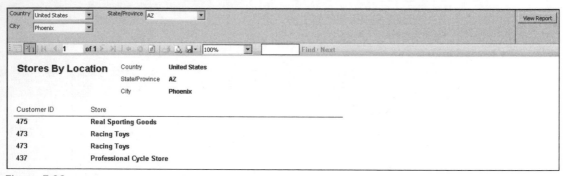

Figure 5-23

As you can see, the report manager offers a great deal of built-in functionality for using parameters with very little effort. Even in Microsoft Access, getting this kind of behavior would have required writing some code.

Multi-select Parameters

This new feature in SQL Server Reporting Services 2005 takes parameterized reports to the next level. Any parameter based on a select list, either static or data-driven, can be a multi-select parameter. Setting up multi-select parameters is quite easy. Working with them in queries can take just a little more effort, but in all, it's not hard to build a report using this feature. If you are using Analysis Services, the MDX query builder creates multi-select parameters and all of the supporting query script from start to finish. If you are using SQL, it does not. The following example takes you through the steps to create a SQL report with a multi-select parameter.

I'm going to work backwards to show you the mechanics of the process. This simple report will display a list of products for selected product subcategories. Before I create the SQL query for the main data set, I'd like to show you how the parameter is configured. Figure 5-24 shows the Report Parameters dialog for my ProductSubCategory parameter. To enable this feature, I simply check the Multi-value property box.

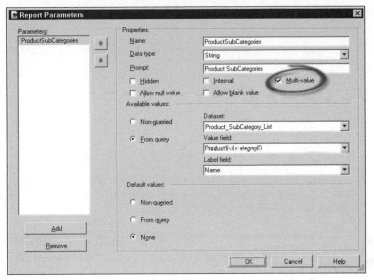

Figure 5-24

This does two things. First, it changes the value returned to the @ProductSubCategories query parameter. Now, I'll show you the query that provides the values for this parameter. This is the SQL query for a data set called Product_SubCategory_List:

```
SELECT        ProductSubcategoryID, Name
FROM          Production.ProductSubcategory
ORDER BY Name
```

As you see, the parameter value is provided by the ProductSubCategoryID column, an Int type identity key value. But when multiple values are selected and this parameter is passed back to the main data set, the parameter value is converted to a string containing a comma-delimited list of keys. This is just the right thing for use with the Transact-SQL IN() function. In a single-select query, the WHERE clause would look something like this:

```
WHERE ProductSubCategoryID = @ProductSubCategoryID
```

But, in a multi-select enabled query, the parameter is passed to the IN() function like this:

```
WHERE ProductSubCategoryID IN( @ProductSubCategories )
```

Here's the entire query:

```
SELECT        *
FROM          Production.Product
WHERE         ProductSubcategoryID IN ( @ProductSubCategories )
```

When the deployed report is run in the Report Manager, the parameter drop-down list is replaced with a drop-down check box list. You see this in Figure 5-25.

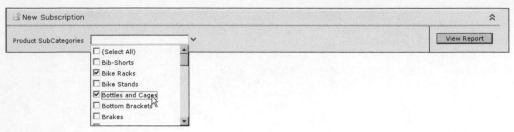

Figure 5-25

An interesting fact is that there is no such thing as a drop-down check box list in HTML. So, how is this possible? This feature is implemented using some very creative JavaScript programming. Finally, the rendered report is displayed in Figure 5-26.

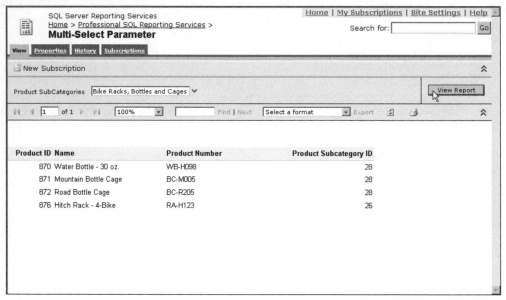

Figure 5-26

Notice that the collapsed parameter list shows a comma-delimited list of subcategory name values rather than the key values that were passed into the query. This is because the list displays the selected members using the `Label` property rather than the `Value` property of the parameter.

Here's an interesting challenge: I told you that the query parameter returned a comma-delimited list of selected values to use with the `IN()` SQL function. I would like to display a similar list, perhaps of the user-friendly Label values in the report header to document the selected items from the parameter list. However, when I reference the parameter in an expression (using either `Parameters!ProductSubCategories.Value` or `Parameters!ProductSubCategories.Label`), this returns an error. I can check the query parameter mapping in the data set, and it's set to `Parameters!ProductSubCategories.Value` as you would expect. How is this possible?

When you check the box in the Report Parameters dialog to enable the Multi-value feature, the parameter value (and `Label`) properties are managed as an array instead of single value. If you use the expression builder to reference the parameter, you'll see that it references only the first element in the multi-select list, using index zero:

```
=Parameters!ProductSubCategories.Label(0)
```

Why *zero* and not *one* for the first element? It's a programming thing. In Visual Basic, when arrays and collections are enumerated, the first index value is *zero*. This means that if there were four elements, the indexes would be 0 through 3.

Now, back to the query for the main data set. Behind the scenes, the array is parsed and selected values are converted to a comma-delimited list for use in the query. To use these values in a similar manner within the report requires some programming. The following Visual Basic function may be used to convert the parameter `Label` property array into a string value for use in the report header (see Figure 5-27):

```
' ***********************************************************************
'
'   Accepts parameter array of any data type
'   and returns a comma-delimited string of
'   parameter values.
'
'   Paul Turley, 11/17/06
'
' ***********************************************************************
Function ParameterList(ByVal Parameter As Object) As String
        Dim sParamItem As Object
        Dim sParamVal As String = ""

        For Each sParamItem In Parameter
            If sParamItem Is Nothing Then Exit For
            sParamVal &= sParamItem & ", "
        Next
        '-- Remove last comma & space:
        Return sParamVal.SubString(0, sParamVal.Length - 2)
    End Function
```

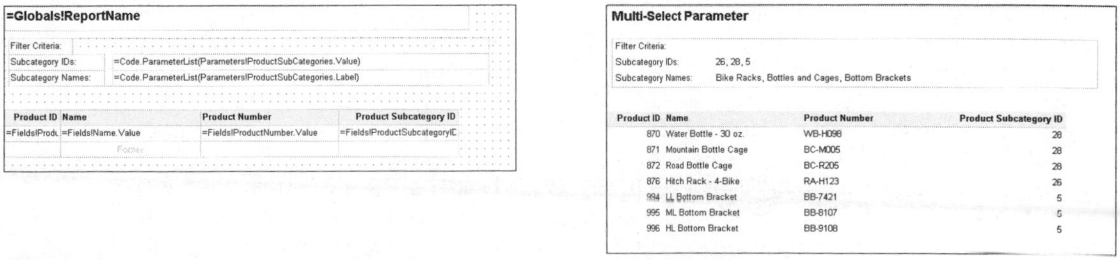

Figure 5-27

Using Stored Procedures

What the best way to go about querying a data source is will depend highly on your requirements. Refer back to the earlier discussion about filtering techniques where processing parameters (on the database server, the client, or both) affects performance, efficiency, and the flexibility of your reporting solution. Handling parameters on the database server will almost always be more efficient, while processing parameters on the client will give you the flexibility of handling a wider range of records and query options without needing to go back to the database every time you need to render the report.

Using a parameterized stored procedure is typically the most efficient means for filtering data since it returns only the data matching your criteria. Stored procedures are compiled to native processor instructions on the database server. When any kind of query is processed, SQL Server creates an execution plan, which defines the specific instructions that the server uses to retrieve data. In the case of a stored procedure, the execution plan is prepared the first time it is executed and then it is cached on the database server. In subsequent executions, results will be returned faster since some of the work has already been done. Stored procedures for SQL Server can be created in three different places: the SQL Enterprise Manager, the SQL Query Analyzer, or Visual Studio's integrated Query Builder.

In the next exercise, you create a stored procedure that will be used to create a columnar report. This is performed using the Server Explorer to obtain a connection to the database server and then manage objects on the server.

In Visual Studio open, you can see the Server Explorer (located on the left side of the designer by default). If it's not there, you can enable this window using the View menu. To manage the objects in a database, you must first define a connection to your database server. To do this, right-click the Data Connections item and choose Add Connection from the menu. The Add Connection dialog is very similar to the one you used to define a report data source. After saving the connection, expand it using the plus sign and then right-click on Stored Procedures. From the pop-up menu, select Add New Stored Procedure, as shown in Figure 5-28.

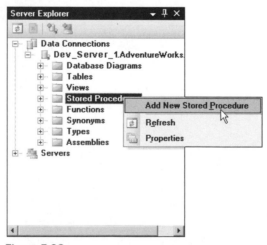

Figure 5-28

This action will open a new Designer window to create a new stored procedure. The text in Figure 5-29 demonstrates the basic structure of a simple stored procedure.

```
CREATE PROCEDURE dbo.StoredProcedure1
    /*
    (
    @parameter1 int = 5,
    @parameter2 datatype OUTPUT
    )
    */
AS
    /* SET NOCOUNT ON */
    RETURN
```

Figure 5-29

You will replace the procedure name and parameters and add a Transact-SQL statement to complete the procedure.

Note that the line numbers shown in the left side of the code window are an optional feature of the Visual Studio editor and are not part of the stored procedure text. If you don't see them, don't worry about it.

Highlight the procedure name (dbo.StoredProcedure1) and replace it with spGetStoresByLocation. Highlight all of the green-colored text in the block including the /* and */, delete it, and replace it with:

```
@StateProvinceCode Char(2),
@City              nVarChar(30)
```

The spacing and indentation isn't important. Highlight and delete the text /* SET NOCOUNT ON */ and then right-click in this location. From the pop-up menu, select Insert SQL. In the Query Builder, type the following into the third pane down (between the grids in the second and fourth panes):

```
SELECT    Sales.Store.Name AS StoreName, Person.StateProvince.StateProvinceCode,
          Person.StateProvince.Name AS StateProvinceName, Person.Address.City
FROM      Sales.Customer
          INNER JOIN Sales.Store
          ON Sales.Customer.CustomerID = Sales.Store.CustomerID
          INNER JOIN Sales.CustomerAddress
          ON Sales.Customer.CustomerID = Sales.CustomerAddress.CustomerID
          INNER JOIN Person.Address
          ON Sales.CustomerAddress.AddressID = Person.Address.AddressID
          INNER JOIN Person.StateProvince
          ON Person.Address.StateProvinceID = Person.StateProvince.StateProvinceID
WHERE     (Person.StateProvince.StateProvinceCode = @StateProvinceCode)
      AND (Person.Address.City = @City)
ORDER BY Person.Address.City, StoreName
```

Again, using spaces and indentation (as well as carriage returns) is not mandatory, but is a good practice for increasing the clarity of code and reducing errors. If you are familiar with the Query Builder, you can build this query in the table diagram and column grid panes rather than typing all of this into the SQL pane. Close this window and confirm that you want to save changes and update the stored procedure with this expression. The finished stored procedure should appear as shown in Figure 5-30.

Go ahead and close this window and save any changes if prompted. The stored procedure should show up in the Server Explorer tree under the stored procedures branch.

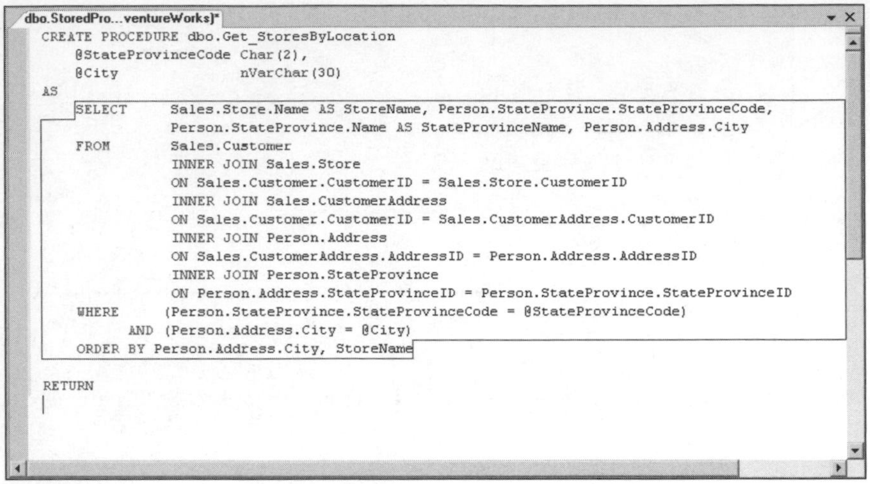

Figure 5-30

Next, create a new report and use this stored procedure as the data set. In the Solution Explorer, right-click on Reports and select Add⇨New Item. In the Add New Item dialog, select Report and enter the report name **Stores By Location**. Click Open to create the new report. On the Data tab of the report designer, drop down the Dataset list and select New Dataset. In this dialog, enter **StoresByLocation** for the data set name and then select or create a data source for the AdventureWorks database.

You created a shared data source for this database earlier. You can refer to that exercise to create it if the shared data source isn't available in this project.

Change the Command type from Text to StoredProcedure and then type the stored procedure name, **spGetStoresByLocation**, into the Query string box. Click OK when you're done. See Figure 5-31.

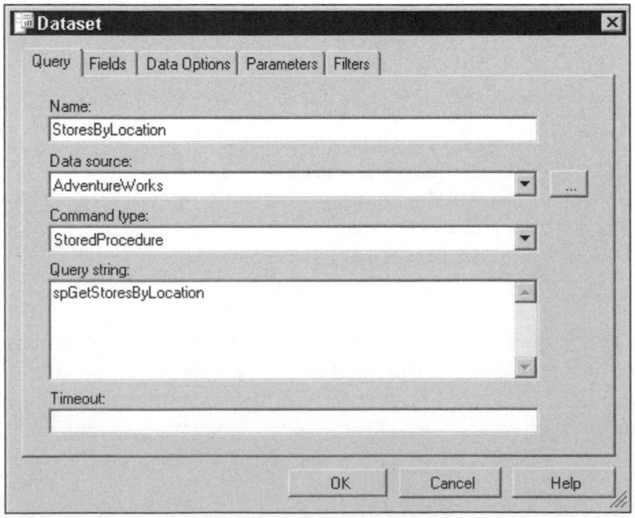

Figure 5-31

The designer's appearance will change to a grid with the stored procedure name in a drop-down list at the top right.

Click the Execute button (dark-red exclamation mark icon) to test the data set and run the stored procedure. You will be prompted for the two parameter values, @StateProvinceCode and @City. Enter two valid values, and click OK to view the results. Figure 5-32 shows an example.

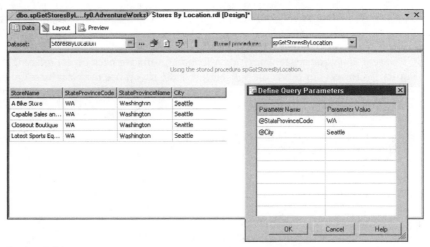

Figure 5-32

The data set is used exactly as before. The stored procedure parameters become report parameters.

Filtering Data with Report Parameters

So far you've only filtered data at the database level. In cases where users may be using the same report in one sitting to view data for different criteria, it may be more effective to retrieve a larger result set from the data source and then filter the report data on the report server.

As you've already seen, parameters defined in a query or stored procedure that serves as report data set are pulled into the report as report parameters. You can also define your own parameters and use expressions to filter data at the report level.

We're going to use both product categories and subcategories for report parameters. The category will be filtered in the data set (at the SQL Server), and the subcategory will be filtered in the report (on the report server).

Add a new report to a project. Use the AdventureWorks shared data source. Created a new data set named ProductsByCategory and apply the following SQL expression in this data set:

```
SELECT      Production.Product.ProductID,
            Production.Product.Name AS ProductName,
            Production.ProductSubCategory.Name AS SubCategoryName,
            Production.ProductCategory.Name AS CategoryName,
```

```
            Production.ProductSubCategory.ProductCategoryID,
            Production.Product.ProductSubCategoryID
FROM        Production.Product INNER JOIN Production.ProductSubCategory
            ON Production.Product.ProductSubCategoryID
            = Production.ProductSubCategory.ProductSubCategoryID
            INNER JOIN ProductCategory
            ON Production.ProductSubCategory.ProductCategoryID
            = Production.ProductCategory.ProductCategoryID
WHERE       Production.ProductSubCategory.ProductCategoryID = @CategoryID
ORDER BY    Production.Product.Name
```

Note that SQL Server 2005 queries now include a schema prefix for each object reference (*Production* in this query) similar to the owner prefix for SQL Server 2000. If you use the Graphical Query Designer and type or paste SQL without the schema prefixes, the query designer will try to add the schema prefix to every table reference.

You're going to create two more data sets to populate parameter drop-down lists and set up a cascading relationship between the two parameters.

Using the same data source, add another data set and name it CategoryList. Type this text into the third pane of the Query Builder:

```
SELECT      ProductCategoryID, Name
FROM        Production.ProductCategory
ORDER BY    Name
```

And add one more data set, named SubCategoryList, using this text:

```
SELECT      ProductSubCategoryID, Name, ProductCategoryID
FROM        Production.ProductSubCategory
WHERE       ProductCategoryID = @CategoryID
ORDER BY    Name
```

With the report designer Layout tab selected, select the Report item from the properties window drop-down list and find the ReportParameters property. Click the ellipsis button next to this property. This will open the Report Parameters dialog. Note that the CategoryID parameter has been added to the report parameters, as expected. Click the Add button to add a new parameter and name it SubCategoryID. Leave all of the other settings at default values to keep things simple. Click OK to close the Report Parameters dialog.

Now switch back to the Data tab, select the first of these three data sets from the Dataset drop-down list and click the ellipsis next to the data set name. On the Dataset dialog, switch to the Filters tab. There are three required elements for a filter expression — the Expression (what you want to filter), Operator (how you're going to compare a value), and Value (the source of the filter value). For the expression, drop down the list and select =Fields!SubCategoryName.Value.

Leave the equality operator set to = and then drop down the Value list and select Expression. This opens the expression builder. Use the controls to select the SubCategoryID parameter and use the Insert button to move it into the expression box on the right side of this dialog. The resulting expression should be =Parameters!SubCategoryName.Value.

Modify the first expression using the CInt() function, and place parentheses around the field expression. Some value comparisons don't resolve data types correctly. If such a comparison results in a data type conversion or casting error, it can be corrected by explicitly converting the expression to the correct data type, as you've done here with the field expression to explicitly convert it to an integer. To be on the safe side, you can use Visual Basic–type conversion functions with any expression or value. See Figure 5-33.

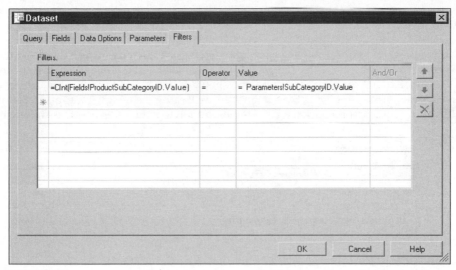

Figure 5-33

The Filters expression builder has an interesting feature. The And/Or column doesn't allow an explicit selection to be made. It will automatically set the logic to Or only when a redundant expression is used with a different value. If you want to use a more complex expression (for example, if you wanted to bring back all products for a category if no subcategory was selected), you can enhance the expression manually as a single expression. However, it would be very difficult to do this line by line using this tool. For more information about advanced filtering techniques, take a look at Chapter 6.

Finally, switch to the Layout tab, and open the Report Parameters dialog from the Report menu. Associate the SubcategoryID and CategoryID parameters with their corresponding data sets as we've done in previous exercises. Make sure that these parameters are listed in this order.

> You have the opportunity to filter data in several different places, so plan carefully when you intend to use report filtering. For example, if you created a report with a grouped table and a chart, you would be able to define filters for the data set, the table, the table group, and the chart. As a rule, I recommend defining report filters in the data set unless you have a compelling reason to do it elsewhere.

Now that you have the data sets and parameters set up, you can actually create a report. We'll keep it simple. In the Layout tab, drag a text box to the report body, click on it to set focus, and type the report title **Products by Category/Subcategory**. Add a table to the report just below the text box and stretch it to fill the width of the report.

Click once in the table and then select the table by clicking the top-left corner selector to select the table. Select the DatasetName property in the properties window for the table, and select the data set ProductsByCategory. From the fields list on the left of the designer, drag the ProductName, CategoryName, and SubCategoryName fields into the detail row's first, second, and third columns, respectively.

Dress up the grid by selecting the header row (click once on the grid and use the row selector on the left to select the header row) and using the report formatting toolbar to make the text bold. Use the property window to set the `Border Style|Bottom` property to `Solid` and the `Border Width|Bottom` to `2pt`.

Switch to the Preview tab. You should be prompted to select a category using a drop-down list. The category selection will populate the `CategoryID` query parameter and retrieve records from the database into memory. Select any category value, and you should be prompted to select a subcategory. This is the report parameter `SubCategoryID`. Selecting a value will cause the filter to be applied, and the resulting data will be fed to the report. Click the View Report button to render the report, as shown in Figure 5-34.

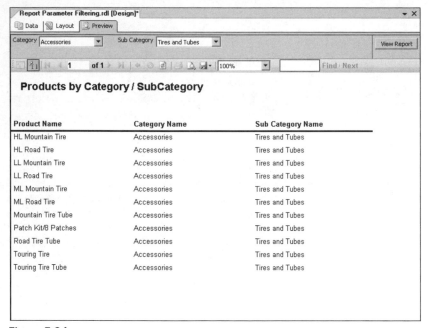

Figure 5-34

The category parameter filters data at the database, as shown in Figure 5-35.

The resulting data is cached in memory on the Report Server, where the subcategory filter further limits results.

You could easily extend the design of this report using more complex items, sorting, and grouping. The data set query could also be replaced with a stored procedure. With these building blocks, you now have the capability to create efficient reports that move the appropriate volume of data across network connections and allow users to use filtering criteria without needing to requery the entire data set.

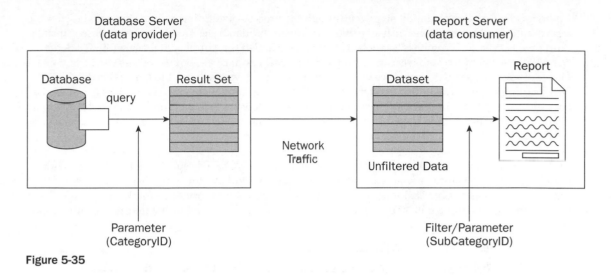

Figure 5-35

Reporting for Analytical Data

In recent years, advanced reporting and data analysis systems have spurred the popularity of an entirely different category of database systems. With businesses storing more data than ever before in complex transactional databases, it has become increasingly difficult to aggregate large volumes of data effectively for reporting. Decision-support databases store preaggregated data in multidimensional cubes rather than relational tables. The fact is that many data warehouse systems may utilize some combination of relational and multidimensional storage. Decision-support database engineering is quickly becoming a highly specialized field.

One of the most significant differentiators is the language used to query these special databases. One of the most popular query languages is MDX, or Multidimensional Expressions language. A cousin of SQL, it shares some common clauses and statements, but MDX is tuned to work with structures like tupples, cubes, measures, and slices, rather than relationships, tables and fields.

SQL Server Analysis Services

By design, Analysis Services data is hierarchal and multidimensional. Rather than storing individual transactions and aggregating values (or "crunching numbers") each time a query is executed, aggregated values are stored at predefined grouping levels. The multidimensional data views are called cubes, which contain dimensional members (dimensions) and fact members (measures and calculations). Dimensions typically define a hierarchy of grouped values. Analysis Services is optimized for reporting. In the course of the evolution of business data systems, relational database systems often reach a point of critical mass, where the data becomes so voluminous and complex that queries run too slow. A large number of users and systems sharing and modifying data can create contention for server resources, and this slows query performance. Data warehouses and data marts implemented using Analysis Services allow many concurrent connections with much faster query performance.

In the following example, I will step you through the process of defining a data source and data set for a report based on the Analysis Services AdventureWorksDW database. This sample database is installed with SQL Server 2005 Analysis Services. If you have installed the sample database with SQL Server to the default installation path, you will find the Setup package at `C:\Program Files\Microsoft SQL Server\90\Tools\Samples`. Once installed and connected, you will be able to use this database to build sample reports following the steps in this section. I assume that Analysis Services is installed and configured, and that you have sufficient permissions to browse cubes and retrieve data. If not, you may need to have a chat with your resident database administrator. Start by bringing their favorite beverage. I find this to be an effective means for getting things done.

In this example, I will give basic steps to design an entire MDX-based report, but I will not provide detailed instructions for every single step. By now, you should have the necessary survival skills to work with these tools and controls. I will offer the basic instructions to complete a simple matrix report so you can see the results of the data source and query. You will learn more about the matrix and other report items in subsequent chapters.

> **In order to complete the following exercise, you will need to have SQL Server 2005 Analysis Services installed and running. You will also need to have the AdventureWorksDW Analysis Services database generated and loaded on your server.**

If you don't have the AdventureWorksDW database available, make sure that you have installed SQL Server with all of the sample databases. This database is generated using Visual Studio. Find the `AdventureWorks.sln` file in the AdventureWorks Analysis Services Project folder under your SQL Server 2005 installation path. Open this solution in Visual Studio, and simply run the project. This connects to the relational AdventureWorksDW database, generates the Analysis Services database, processes and populates all of the cubes and associated objects, making this data available to Analysis Services.

Going beyond the very basics with Analysis Services would take us pretty far off topic and beyond the scope of this book. For more information about SQL Server Analysis Services and MDX query programming, please refer to the Wrox Press book *Professional SQL Server Analysis Services 2005 with MDX* by Sivakumar Harinath and Stephen R. Quinn.

Creating a Data Source

The first step, of course, is to create a data source to the SQL Server Analysis Server. I will be using my local computer. I add a new shared data source to my report project and the Shared Data Source appears as in Figure 5-36. By default, the connection type will be set to use the SQL Server relational database engine. This will actually be changed in the next dialog. Give the data source a name, and then click the Edit button. In case you have the connection string information, you can select the provider from the Type list, type the Connection string, and then skip ahead to Figure 5-37.

This opens the Connection Properties dialog that you see in Figure 5-37. Use the Change button on this dialog (shown in Figure 5-38) if it is not set to connect using the Analysis Services provider.

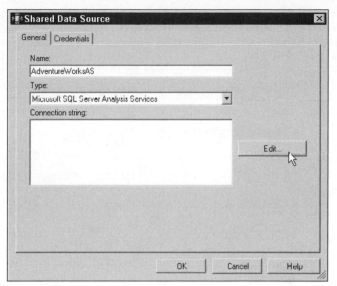

Figure 5-36

Figure 5-37

If you need to change the data provider, you will use the Change Data Source dialog, shown in Figure 5-38. Select the Data source for Microsoft SQL Server Analysis Services and verify the Data provider selection is the .NET Framework Data Provider for Microsoft Analysis Services. Click the OK button to return to the previous dialog.

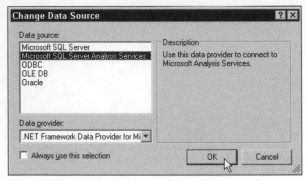

Figure 5-38

My Analysis Server is my local machine, so I have entered **localhost** for the Server name (see Figure 5-39). You will need to enter your server name here if the Analysis Server isn't local. Select the Analysis Services database using the lower drop-down list, and then click the OK button.

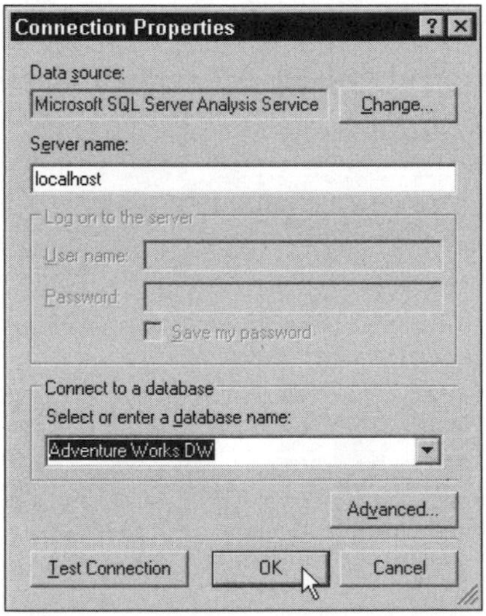

Figure 5-39

As you see in Figure 5-40, this generates a connection string. If you have this information, you can skip the previous steps and type this text directly into the Connection string text box. In either case, after the provider type and connection string have been entered, select the Credentials tab.

Shared Data Source
General
Credentials
Name:
AdventureWorksAS
Type:
Microsoft SQL Server Analysis Services
Connection string:
Data Source=localhost;Initial Catalog="Adventure Works DW"
Edit...
OK
Cancel
Help

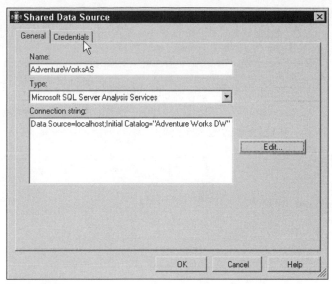

Figure 5-40

Just like the SQL Server relational database engine, there are a few different ways to authenticate when making a connection. On the Credentials tab, shown in Figure 5-41, select the first option, Use Windows Authentication. When completed, click the OK button.

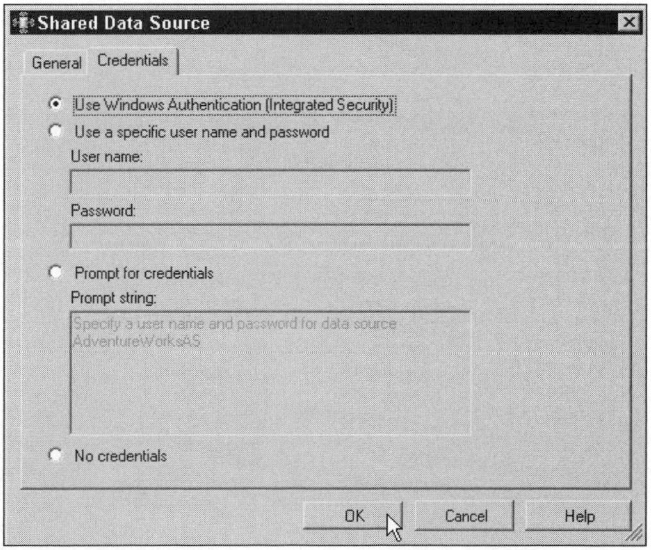

Shared Data Source
General
Credentials
Use Windows Authentication (Integrated Security)
Use a specific user name and password
User name:
Password:
Prompt for credentials
Prompt string:
Specify a user name and password for data source AdventureWorksAS
No credentials
OK
Cancel
Help

Figure 5-41

Chapter 5

Creating a Report

Now add a new report. I want to define this report manually, so I will right-click the project in the Solution Explorer and then choose to add a new item. This opens the Add New Item dialog shown in Figure 5-42. Choose the Report template and then give the report a descriptive name as I've done here. Click the Add button to create the RDL file, and add the new report to the project.

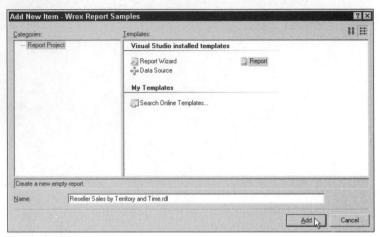

Figure 5-42

On the Data tab in the report designer, create a new data set and assign it the shared data source you just created. Assign the name **ResellerSales_AS**, and click the OK button to move on. Figure 5-43 shows the familiar Dataset dialog.

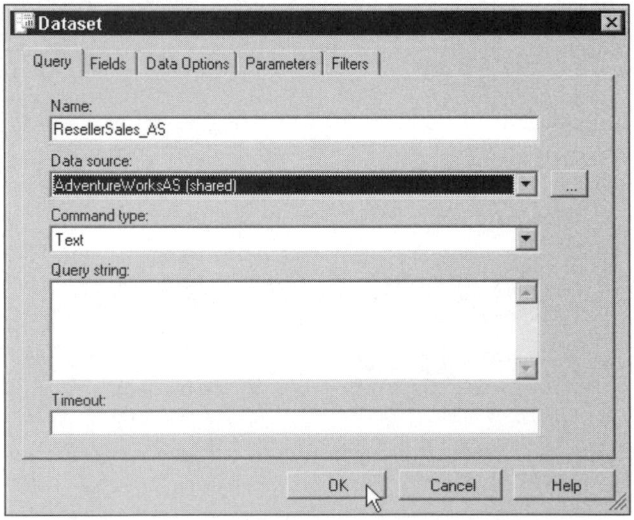

Figure 5-43

When you click the OK button without entering text into the Query String text box, this will open the query designer. Because the data source is configured to use the Analysis Services data provider, this will open the MDX graphical Query Builder shown in Figure 5-44.

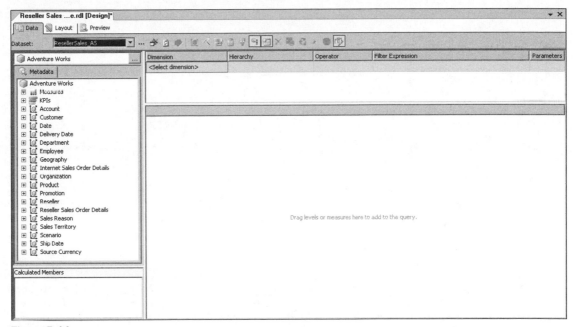

Figure 5-44

If the database has multiple cubes defined, a cube may be selected from the selection box in the top of the left pane. The cube structure is displayed in the Metadata window. For this cube, you can see tree view node icons representing measures, KPIs, and dimensions.

For each dimension, you may expand the node to view its hierarchy and you may drag all or part of the dimension levels onto the query design surface. Dragging a dimension level to the designer will include the selected level and all dependent levels. For example, if a Time dimension includes Year, Quarter, Month, and Day and you were to expand and then drag the Month level, this would include the Month and Day as columns. The columns for any level may then be removed if they are not required. You will include all levels for two dimensions in the following example.

Flattened Hierarchies

Reporting Services is designed to use two-dimensional queries and does not fully take advantage of some of the capabilities of MDX. For this reason, all MDX queries define only columns rather than rows. Using capable report items such as the matrix and charts, these two-dimensional results may be transformed back into multidimensional data presentations.

To define the first set of columns, drag the Sales Territory dimension onto the query design surface. You will see the mouse pointer change to indicate the drag-and-drop action and a red bar will appear on the left side of the designer (see Figure 5-45).

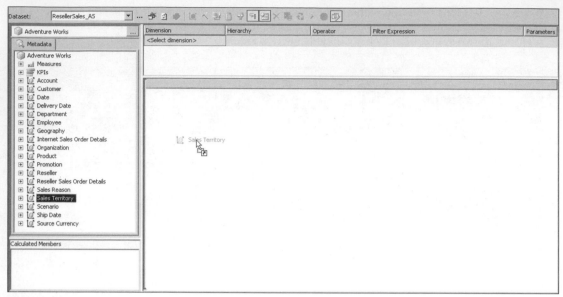

Figure 5-45

When the mouse is released and the dimension is dropped, three columns are added for the corresponding levels of this dimension, in order of their hierarchal rank. Repeat this process using the Delivery Date dimension. Be careful to drop this item to the right of the existing columns (see Figure 5-46).

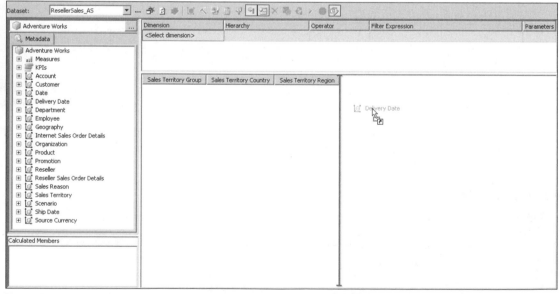

Figure 5-46

When this dimension is dropped, five new columns are added for the levels defined for specific time periods (see Figure 5-47).

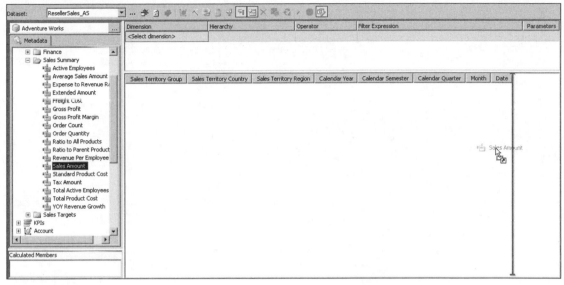

Figure 5-47

Expand the Measures node and then the Sales Summary folder. Several measures are defined for different calculations and values. Drag and drop the Sales Amount measure to the rightmost position in the column list. As soon as you do this, the query design will immediately return dimension and preaggregated measure values. This is the default behavior of the MDX query builder. For very large databases, it may take time to return results, especially if dimension members are added in an unusual order. To improve performance, you can toggle the Auto Execute mode using the toolbar option indicated in Figure 5-48.

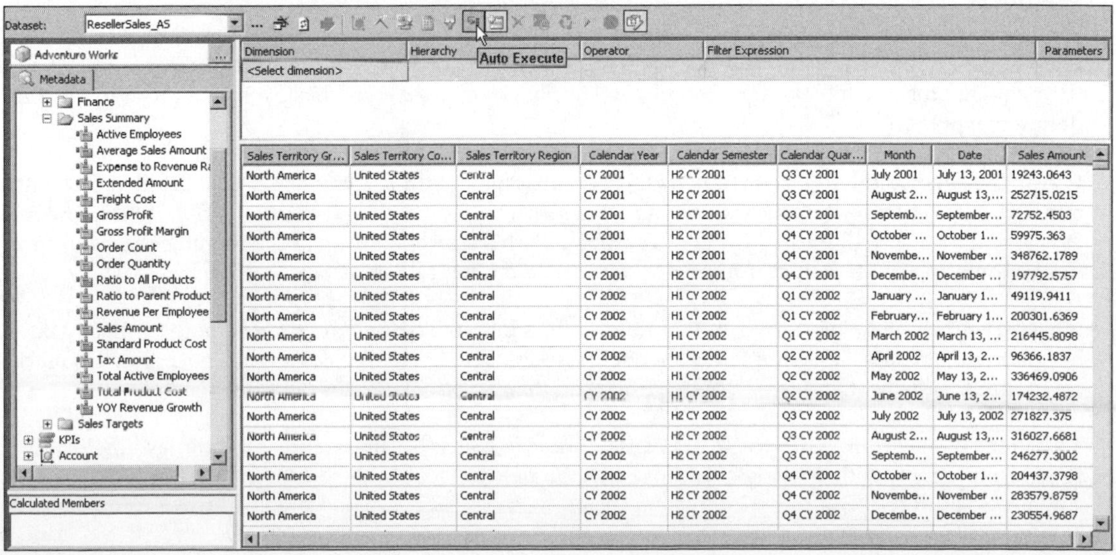

Figure 5-48

The underlying query is a Multidimensional Expression (MDX.) Figure 5-49 shows the query after switching to the MDX mode using the rightmost toolbar button. Unlike the Transact-SQL graphical query designer, the MDX Query Builder does not translate MDX into graphical form. If you enter a query manually or make any changes to an existing MDX expression, you cannot switch back to design graphical mode without losing your work.

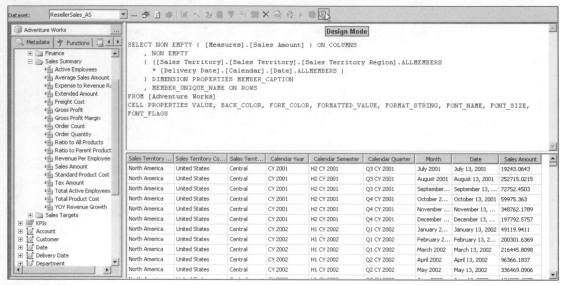

Figure 5-49

For the first phase of this example, the data set is complete. Before you continue, save the work you've done so far by clicking the Save All button on the toolbar.

Designing the Report

This section is about designing data access for Analysis Services, but to see the results of the MDX query I just built, I'd like to finish this report. You'll learn more about the features of the matrix report item in the next chapter. For this demonstration, I'm simply going to give you basic instructions without a lot of detailed explanation.

Figure 5-50 shows the report designer's Layout tab. The first thing I've done is added a text box with a title for the report. Add a matrix item and drag the first field, Sales_Territory_Group, to the row cell. When you drag a field into a Rows or Columns cell, this creates a group and generates the appropriate field expression in the Value property for the corresponding cell's text box.

Next, drag the Sales_Territory_Country field to the same cell. Before you drop it, note the heavy vertical bar that will indicate a position to the left or right of this cell. Move the mouse pointer so that this marker is on the right side, as it appears in Figure 5-51, and then release the mouse to drop the field.

This creates related field groups in a specified order to match the hierarchy of the dimension levels. Repeat this action with the Sales_Territory_Region field to create a third group. You can see the second row group added in Figure 5-52 while I'm dropping this field to created the third row group.

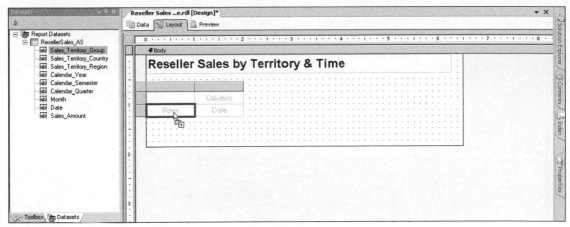

Figure 5-50

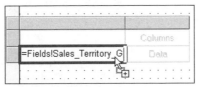

Figure 5-51

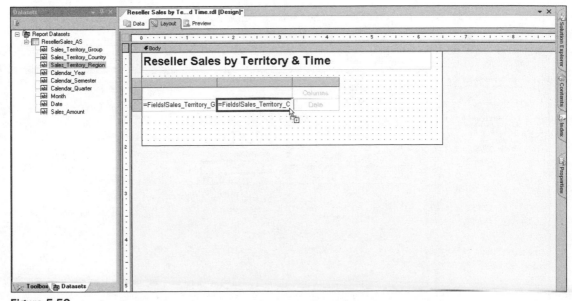

Figure 5-52

To create the column groups, drag the Calendar_Year field to the Columns cell. Add the Calendar_Quarter and Month columns in turn to the bottom of each parent cell, as shown in Figure 5-53. Note that there are fields (levels) in this hierarchy I have chosen not to use in the report.

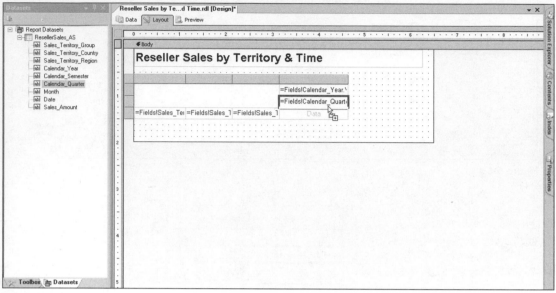

Figure 5-53

Finally, drag the Sales_Amount measure value from the fields list to the Data cell, as shown in Figure 5-54.

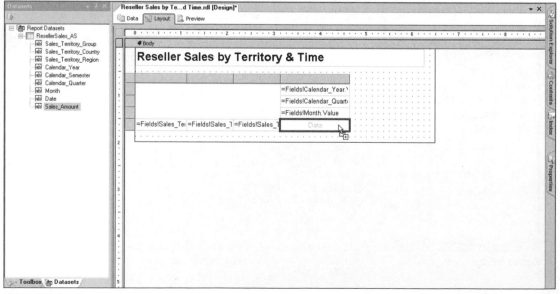

Figure 5-54

I'd like to implement drill-down functionality, so the matrix only displays aggregate values at the highest level until you expand these groups to see more detail. I will hide all subordinate row and column groups and set the visibility to be toggled using their parent group. I'll work through the groups from the inside out. Begin by right-clicking the cell for the Sales_Territory_Region field. From the menu, select Edit Group, as shown in Figure 5-55.

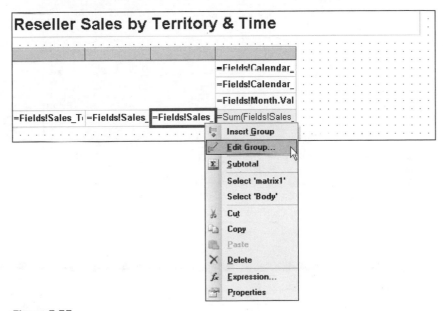

Figure 5-55

Switch to the Visibility tab on the Grouping and Sorting Properties dialog, as shown in Figure 5-56. When using the drag-and-drop technique to define groups, each cell's text box is given the same name as the field. Set the Initial visibility property to be Hidden, and then type the name of the parent level for the toggle item into the Report item box.

You'll recall that the row groups are defined as Sales_Territory_Group, Sales_Territory_Country, and Sales_Territory_Region, in order. Since I'm working with the Sales_Territory_Region group, the toggle item will be the Sales_Territory_Country field (actually, this is the text box for this group, but it has the same name).

Repeat these steps for the Sales_Territory_Country group, setting the toggle item to be Sales_Territory_Group. For the column groups, start at the bottom and work up. Right-click the Month column cell and set its toggle item to be Calendar_Quarter. For the Calendar_Quarter group, set the toggle item to be Calendar_Year. Make sure that the Initial visibility property for these groups is Hidden. Don't make any changes to the Sales_Territory_Group and Calendar_Year groups.

The Sales_Amount value cell should be set to display currency. This may be done using the Format property, as shown in Figure 5-57. Set this property to C0 to use a currency format with no decimal.

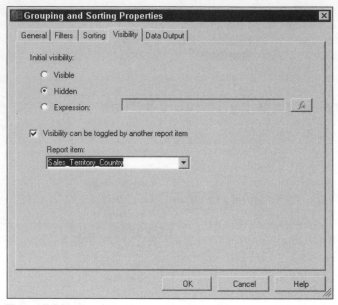

Figure 5-56

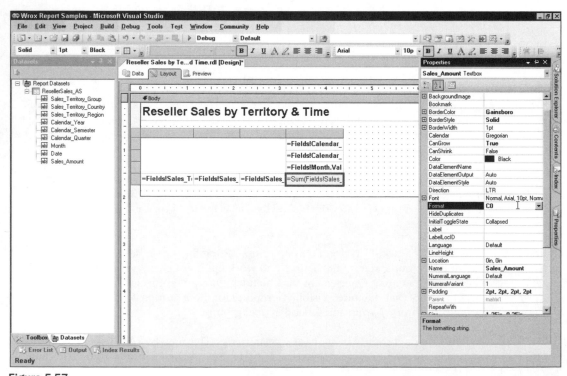

Figure 5-57

Select the rightmost column using the column header and use the Report Formatting toolbar to right-align the text. This screen is shown in Figure 5-58.

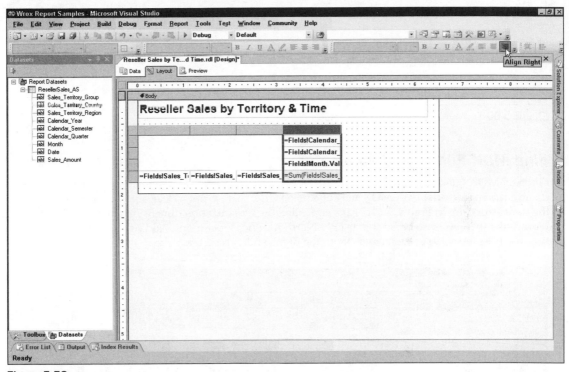

Figure 5-58

To make my report more readable, I'll set the Value cell with a WhiteSmoke BackColor and set the BorderColor and BorderStyle properties as shown in Figure 5-59.

Figure 5-59

The report is ready for preview. Figure 5-60 shows the Reseller Sales Territory & Time report with some rows and columns expanded. You should be able to expand and collapse groups to display detail at different levels.

Reseller Sales by Territory & Time

| | | | CY 2001 | | | | CY 2002 | CY 2003 | CY 2004 |
| | | | Q3 CY 2001 | | | Q4 CY 2001 | | | |
			July 2001	August 2001	September 2001				
North America	United States	Central	$19,243	$252,715	$72,752	$606,530	$2,625,640	$3,008,352	$1,
		Northeast	$21,598	$71,553	$124,320	$351,075	$2,443,902	$2,867,805	$1,0
		Northwest	$133,787	$333,187	$272,224	$1,311,804	$4,358,692	$5,644,545	$4,0
		Southeast	$139,164	$301,907	$138,203	$869,647	$2,816,686	$2,432,293	$1,
		Southwest	$141,336	$407,928	$497,208	$1,461,350	$7,589,292	$8,776,353	$5,

Figure 5-60

Adding MDX Filters and Parameters

Filtering MDX queries is quite different than it is with SQL queries and in many ways is easier. One of the unique characteristics of MDX and cube data is that there is not a clear separation of the data from the data structure. In Figure 5-61, I have expanded the Organization dimension to expose its members. I would like this report to be limited to only North America Operations. Adding this filter is simple: Drag the North America Operations member to the filters and parameters pane in the MDX Query Designer.

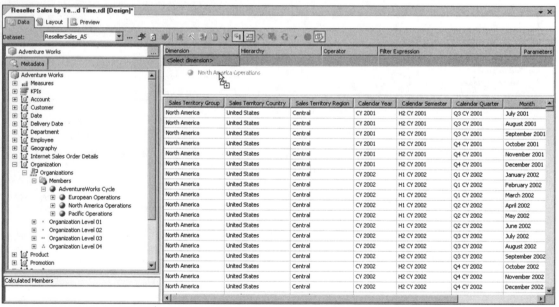

Figure 5-61

This creates an expression to filter the report data from the cube. The results are refreshed to reflect this change to the query. Filter selections are not exposed to users by default. I'd like to add another filter that may be controlled with user-selectable values, so in addition to a filter expression, I'd like to create two parameter lists to enable the user's selection of a range of years for the delivery date.

First, drag and drop the Delivery Date dimension onto the filters and parameters pane in the MDX Query Designer. The second drop-down list, shown in Figure 5-62, contains the members of the dimension hierarchy. Use this to select the Calendar Year.

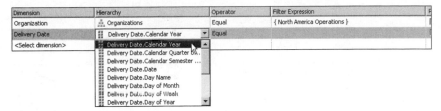

Figure 5-62

The Operator is set to Equal by default. Change this selection to Range (Inclusive) as I've done in Figure 5-63. This will change the Filter Expression options.

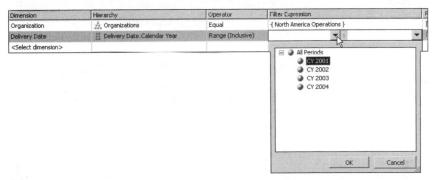

Figure 5-63

Now two drop-down lists are displayed in the Filter Expression column. Use the first drop-down lists to expand and select the first year on the list. Figure 5-64 shows that this is the year 2001. Use the second drop-down list to select the year 2004.

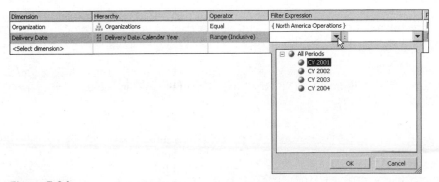

Figure 5-64

Since I want the user to be able to change this range and modify the filtered report data, parameters must be created in the report user interface. This is done by checking the boxes in the Parameters column (see Figure 5-65). Two check boxes are displayed so that either or both of the filter criteria may be either parameter-based or hard-wired in the query.

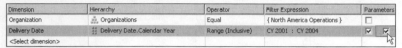

Dimension	Hierarchy	Operator	Filter Expression	Parameters
Organization	⚏ Organizations	Equal	{ North America Operations }	☐
Delivery Date	⚏ Delivery Date.Calendar Year	Range (Inclusive)	CY 2001 : CY 2004	☑ ☑
<Select dimension>				

Figure 5-65

On the Layout tab of the report designer, the Report Parameters dialog may be displayed from the Report menu. Figure 5-66 shows the two parameters automatically created from the MDX Query Designer filter selections.

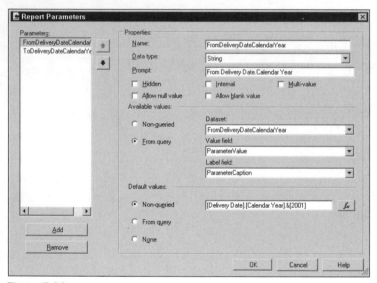

Figure 5-66

Using the Preview tab to view the report, you can see the two parameter value lists displayed in the parameters report toolbar. Figure 5-67 shows the first year of the range changed from 2001 to 2002.

After making this selection, click the View Report button to apply the filter and execute the report. The report is displayed in Figure 5-68. I've expanded some of the row and column groups to show more detail.

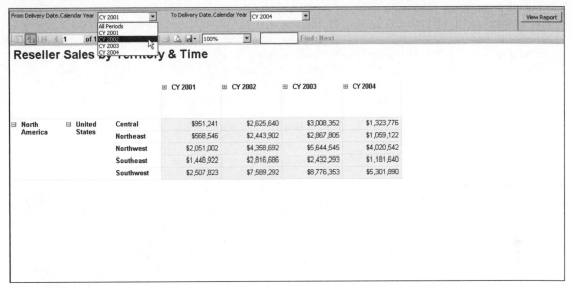

Figure 5-67

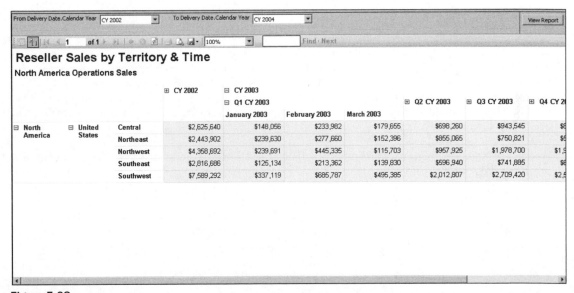

Figure 5-68

Using Other Data Sources

After using Reporting Services with SQL Server databases and then later with others, I realized that I had become a bit spoiled. It's true that you can use practically any standard database product as a data source for reports; you're not going to have the assistance of the graphical query builder and other auto-mated features of the report designer. Nevertheless, Reporting Services can work with the language syntax and features of most databases; you'll just need to do some of the easy stuff yourself. This section showcases a few different products we've used as data sources. One point to keep in mind is that the compatibilities and behaviors will be influenced by a number of factors.

The technique demonstrated a little later in the chapter with an Access query (see "Building a Query in a String Expression") is a universal pattern that applies to all database products. I strongly recommend that you take a look at this technique because it will be useful to you at some point, regardless of the data source you will use for reporting.

Microsoft Access

Microsoft Access is built on top of the JET Database Engine with data stored in a single MDB file. This is simple and convenient for small, portable databases. However, Microsoft continues to take steps to replace JET databases with SQL Server and the desktop implementations of SQL. These include the SQL Server 2000 Desktop Database Engine (MSDE) and SQL Server 2005 Express Edition. As a desktop application, Access may also be used as a front end to SQL databases. If you have the luxury of building a new database solution, it may be best to use one of these newer products in place of older Access data-bases. But if you have existing solutions based on older Access databases, it will likely be easier to con-tinue to work with them in their present form.

There are two standard data providers that may be used to connect to Access databases. The JET 4.0 .NET OLE DB provider is newer and should be a little more efficient than using the older Access ODBC driver. The fact is that the data provider is rarely going to be a performance bottleneck, so this is proba-bly a moot point. The OLE DB provider is typically easier to use and more efficient. One of the nice fea-tures of the new data provider is that it will accept Transact-SQL and translate it into Access-specific syntax. Although Access SQL and Transact-SQL are very close, there are some subtle differences. This feature enables the report designer to utilize the Transact-SQL graphical query builder when a data set uses a JET data source.

Figure 5-69 shows the Connection Properties dialog used when defining an Access database connection using the JET OLE DB provider:

Note that the default security credentials used with an unsecured Access database are the Admin user with a blank password. Even if you were to explicitly provide this information and check the Blank password box, the dialog doesn't show these values. This is so because the data provider knows to use default credentials when the database hasn't been secured.

The connection string and credentials are shown in Figures 5-70 and 5-71.

Select the Credentials tab to view or modify the user authentication information.

Access has some minor quirks that you should be aware of. Any file-based data source can present a challenge for Reporting Services because the service must have the necessary security access to open the database file. If the MDB file is on the report server, this shouldn't be a concern, but if the file is on another network share, it may be. If you get file-sharing errors, make sure that Reporting Services ser-vice runs using a network account that has privileges to open the Access database file and its containing folder.

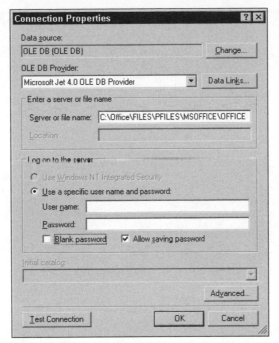

Figure 5-69

Figure 5-70

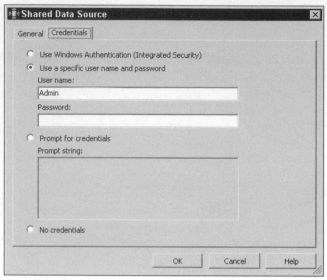

Figure 5-71

Parameterized Access queries have always presented a challenge in custom code, outside of simple Access forms applications. The JET database engine has difficulty resolving parameter values passed into queries and may report errors even if the values are passed using the correct data type and format. For example, the following Access query defines and then uses two parameters to filter order records in the Northwind sample database:

```
PARAMETERS [ShipDateFrom] DateTime, [ShipDateTo] DateTime;
SELECT Orders.ShippedDate, Orders.OrderID, [Order Subtotals].Subtotal,
Format([ShippedDate],"yyyy") AS [Year]
FROM Orders INNER JOIN [Order Subtotals]
    ON Orders.OrderID = [Order Subtotals].OrderID
WHERE (((Orders.ShippedDate) Is Not Null And (Orders.ShippedDate) Between
[ShipDateFrom] And [ShipDateTo]));
```

Even when the `ShipDateFrom` and `ShipDateTo` query parameters are correctly mapped to corresponding report parameters, the report runs with an error. If you are connecting via the JET OLE DB provider, it reports this error:

```
No value given for one or more required parameters.
```

If the Access ODBC driver is used, the native JET error is reported:

```
Too few parameters. Expected 2.
```

The easiest way I've found to work around the Access query parameterization issue is to build the query string using an expression rather than to rely on this feature. It's not hard to do. The first step is to define the parameters in your report. Figure 5-72 shows one of these two parameters in the Report Parameters dialog. On the report designer's Layout tab, use the Report menu to select Report Parameters... to open this dialog.

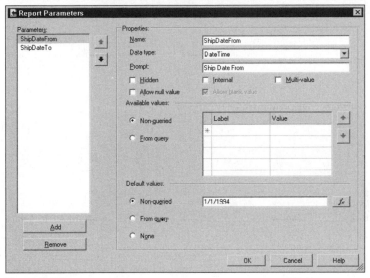

Figure 5-72

With the report parameters in place, they can be referenced in the data set query expression. There is no need to change the parameters or any other properties of the data set because this will be handled in the expression.

Building a Query in a String Expression

This technique can be used typically when other options, such as using the graphical query builder and defining query parameters, won't work in the designer. Any expression may be used to build a text string and can include Visual Basic functions and custom code. The resulting string is simply presented to the database engine through the connection's data provider. No other parsing or processing is performed. The query expression must be entered using the Generic Query Designer window for the data set, as shown in Figure 5-73.

Because this is a Visual Basic expression, double quotation marks are used to encapsulate literal text. Line breaks cannot be used without terminating and concatenating the string using the + or & character. Parameters values are concatenated into the query string with appropriate delimiters. The two parameter expressions refer to the parameters I defined in Figure 5-72.

Note that this is an Access SQL query rather than Transact-SQL. Pound-sign characters are used to delimit dates rather than single quotation marks.

Some variations of this technique can be useful to meet specific needs. Rather than building the entire query string in the dataset designer, you can call a custom Visual Basic function to do the work in programming code. Parameters could be passed to this function that returns the entire query.

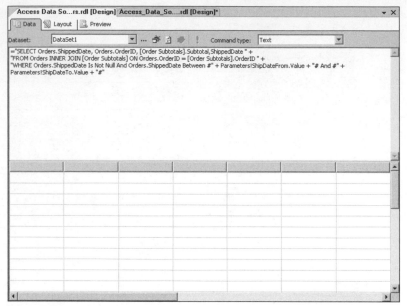

Figure 5-73

> An unfortunate side effect of using this expression query technique is that the dataset designer will not allow you to execute the query. If you need to make any changes to the query expression that will update the fields available to the report, you must convert the query back to a SQL expression (by removing the = and " characters), execute the query, and update the fields list using the Refresh button. Another option is to manually edit the fields list.

I recommend that you paste the expression into Notepad or SQL Server Management Studio, modify the expression in the dataset designer to update the fields list, and then paste the expression back into the designer. This will save effort and give you an "undo" option if things don't go well.

Microsoft Excel

As a quick-and-easy data source, Excel is a great tool. I am continually amazed by the proliferation of Excel spreadsheets as production enterprise databases used in large business. Even at Microsoft, this practice is commonplace. I think this is largely due to the fact that business data comes from business people, and business people use Excel. I'll leave the data management and consolidation discussion for another time. The fact remains that a lot of important data exists in Excel files, and you can create reports to view this data as you would with any database system.

Oracle P/L SQL

Connecting reports to an Oracle database is quite easy to do. Depending on the version of Oracle and the Oracle client software, you can use the ODBC, Simple OLE DB, or native Oracle Client data providers.

The native Oracle Client provider is preferred and is simple to use. When creating a data source, choose Microsoft OLEDB Provider for Oracle; enter the server name and the user name and password required to log in to the Oracle database server.

Oracle PL/SQL is an ANSI-compliant dialect that is very similar to Transact-SQL in most regards. Newer implementations use the ANSI join syntax rather than the '=', '*=', and '=*' syntax in the WHERE clause to denote joins. This style was popular until just a few years ago and its use is still habitual for many Oracle SQL query designers.

Oracle has a handful of data types that are equivalent to T-SQL types. Since reporting services uses .NET data types used in Visual Basic .NET expressions, it's advisable to explicitly convert field values when used in expressions. Use the Visual Basic conversion functions (that is, CStr(), CDbl(), CInt(), CDate(), CBool(), and so on) liberally.

The syntax for PL/SQL variables and parameters is quite different from Transact-SQL. Rather than prefixing them with a @, these items are prefixed with a colon (:). Variables used in PL/SQL script may be assigned a value when they are declared. T-SQL doesn't allow this. Here is a brief example of a parameterized PL/SQL expression:

```
SELECT
       SL.STORE_CODE
     , SL.LOCATION_NAME
     , SL.TELEPHONE_NUMBER AS LOCATION_PHONE
FROM STORE_LOCATION SL
  INNER JOIN REGION R ON R.LOCATION_ID = SL.LOCATION_ID
WHERE SL.STORE_CODE = :STORE_CD
```

Testing for equality with a numeric type works as you would expect. However, character type comparisons may be performed using the LIKE operator. String concatenation is performed using double pipe-symbol characters rather than the plus sign used in T-SQL.

```
SELECT
       SL.STORE_CODE
     , SL.LOCATION_NAME
     , SL.TELEPHONE_NUMBER AS LOCATION_PHONE
FROM STORE_LOCATION SL
  INNER JOIN REGION R ON R.LOCATION_ID = SL.LOCATION_ID
WHERE SL. LOCATION_NAME LIKE '%' || UPPER(:STORE_NM) || '%'
```

Sybase Adaptive Server

Adaptive Server's query language is most similar to SQL Server because these products share some history. Like SQL Server, Sybase databases can implement stored procedures for modularized, more efficient query processing. Overall, I've found Adaptive Server to be fairly easy to use with Reporting Services, but it may require a little extra effort to prepare SQL queries. Simple queries can be written using the Generic Query Designer. Stored procedures are executed using a string expression similar to the following example:

```
="spMonthEndSalesByCust '" + Parameters!MonthEndDateMonth.Value,
Parameters!monthEndDateYear.Value + "'"
```

There are some known minor data type incompatibilities with report parameters. In particular, you may find it easier to use String-type parameters for dates rather than the native Date type. If you use date or numeric parameters, you may need to convert them in the query expression. Since SQL queries and stored procedure calls are assembled as a string expression, parameters need not be converted to explicit types. Type conversion will be performed by the database engine.

The report server and development computer will need to have the Sybase ASE OLEDB Provider installed and configured correctly. This will enable you to create connections using the Microsoft Simple OLEDB Provider with the installed Sybase client components.

Best Practices

Use shared data sources to reuse the connection information. Data sources are not redeployed by default. Remove the report and data source file from the report server and redeploy the data source to update connection information and certain report metadata.

When using complex query expressions, keep a copy of the last working query script in a separate query tool window or in NotePad.

When using an expression for a data set (i.e., ="SELECT..."), if changes are made to the query expression, you may need to remove the string encapsulation characters from the text to run the query. Make a point to execute the query and click the Refresh toolbar button to update the report fields definition.

Filter in the data set or stored procedure to reduce network traffic and reduce report server processing overhead. Filter data in the report to reuse the same result set and improve response time for longer, interactive report sessions.

Plan ahead and filter data consistently in the data set, report item, or group.

In MDX queries, add and configure parameters before making any manual changes to MDX script. You cannot modify or view the query using the graphical MDX Query Designer after making manual changes.

Summary

This chapter covered the following:

- ❏ Each report typically has at least one data set, which defines a data query. Each data set will have a data source that may be stored in the report or the report project as a shared data source. Additional data sets may be used for different report items or to populate parameter lists.

- ❏ A data set may be designed using either the Generic Query Designer or the Graphical Query Designer. Most queries built on SQL Server databases are most easily designed using the Graphical Designer.

- ❏ Data may be filtered in the data set query, which is typically processed on the database server, or within the report. Report filters may be defined at the data set, at the report item, or within a group. These options cause more data to be sent to the report server but may help prevent multiple, long-running queries if users spend time interacting with a single report.

❑   Parameters may be used to drive advanced report features such as cascading parameter selection.

❑   SQL Server Analysis Services may be used to simplify complex report queries by storing preaggregated values in multidimensional cubes.

❑   The MDX Query Designer may be used to define data sets for Analysis Service queries and related parameters with little or no understanding of the MDX query language.

❑   Reports may use many different data sources that use different SQL dialects and query languages. Any data source may be used as long as it supports an ODBC driver, OLE DB provider, or .NET data provider that returns rows and columns or data.

Defining data sources and data sets to manage data source queries is the starting point for almost any data-driven report. It's essential to understand basic data storage and query architecture to achieve the best design. Data can be filtered within the database server or in the report. Making the correct choice and finding the best combination of these options will improve performance and provide flexibility with the least degree of overhead.

Defining shared data sources in your projects makes it much easier to maintain data connections for all of your reports as a group. Changing the database location or security credentials becomes a much simpler proposition. The data sets for your reports define queries for retrieving data and may be used as the source for the report and repeatable data regions or to provide data value for report parameters.

An ad hoc query expression is stored in the report within the report definition, and a stored procedure is stored in the database. Using stored procedures is an effective means for processing parameters and filtering data before sending it to the report, while using a report filter lets you reuse the data you've already retrieved. A combination of these parameterized filtering techniques may be an optimal solution for more complex reporting needs.

Advanced Report Design

In Chapter 4, you learned about the basic components of report design, but now you take each of these elements to the next level. The real power behind Reporting Services is its ability to creatively use data groups and combinations of report items. Calculations and conditional formatting may be added by using simple programming code. Whether you are an application developer or a report designer, this chapter contains important information to help you design reports to meet your user's requirements, and to raise the bar with compelling report features.

This chapter covers:

❑   Grouping data.

❑   Lists and data regions.

❑   Creating a tabular report using tables.

❑   Matrix report.

❑   Links and drill-through reports.

❑   Using charts in reports.

❑   Using custom code to extend formatting and apply business logic.

❑   Designing reports for mobile devices.

At this point, you should be comfortable using Visual Studio 2005 to create and add reports to a project, and you should be familiar with the basic mechanics of the designer. If you are new to this environment, please work through the exercises in Chapter 4 before you read on.

We will no longer be using the Report Wizard throughout the remainder of the book. You should be able to add a new report to a project, create or select a shared data source, create a data set, and add items to the Report Designer by now. This chapter will provide directions for using nearly all of the design elements mentioned here.

Although you will be exploring more advanced report design techniques, I've made it a point to keep the data sets very simple. In a few cases in subsequent chapters where I do use complex queries, you may download these examples from the book's companion site at P2P.com and paste the script into a new report. For most of the examples, you'll simply use a list of products with categories and subcategories. This will help to keep things simple while focusing on report design features rather than the intricacies of the data.

Chapter 4 covered using items and data regions in a report. In particular, you used the wizard to generate a tabular report with a *table data region*. In this chapter, you will start by repeating this exercise, only with a greater level of detail to create a report to your own specifications.

Anatomy of a Text Box

The text box is one of the most fundamental and most common report items. Generally, all text and data values are displayed using text boxes. The cells of a table and matrix contain individual text boxes. In addition to the text displayed, there are several useful properties used to manage the placement, style, and presentation of data. `Font` properties, `Color`, `BackGroundColor`, and `BackGroundImage` properties make it possible to dress up your report data with tremendous flexibility.

The `BorderStyle` properties of a text box are similar to those of other report items (such as a rectangle, list, table, and matrix.) Once you have mastered the text box properties, you should be able to use these other items in much the same way. When using a table, group separation lines are created by setting the border properties for text boxes in header and footer rows (typically by selecting the entire row and setting the text box properties as a group).

Three property groups are used for borders. In the Properties window, these groups are expanded using the plus sign (+) icon to reveal individual properties. The group summary text can actually be manipulated without expanding the properties, but it's usually easier to work with specific property values. The `BorderColor`, `BorderStyle`, and `BorderWidth` properties each contain a Default value that will apply to individual properties (that is, Left, Right, Top, and Bottom) that have not otherwise been set. This provides a means to set general properties and then override the exceptions. By default, a text box has a black `BorderColor` and a 1-point `BorderWidth` with the `BorderStyle` set to `None`. To add a border to all four sides, simply set the `Default BorderStyle` to `Solid`. Beyond this, individual properties may be used to add more creative border effects. Figure 6-1 shows two text boxes with a variety of border styles. The second text box corresponds to the property settings shown in the selection of the Properties window.

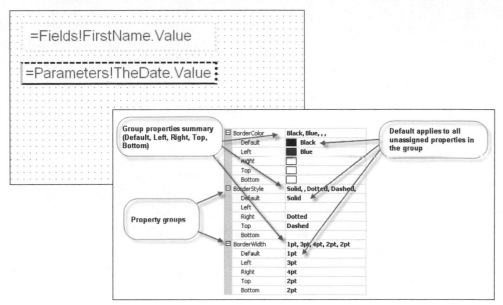

Figure 6-1

Here's a shortcut that may save you some work: You can set groups of properties by either expanding the properties group and setting the individual members or you may use the group summary line. For example, if you wanted to set the BorderWidth properties for multiple text boxes to be the same as the one shown in Figure 6-1, you could copy all of the values from the BorderWidth property group summary (*1pt, 3pt, 4pt, 2pt, 2pt*) and paste this text into the same line for the target text boxes. Report items that support the same properties may be selected as a group and set at one time, using the properties window for the common group selection.

> **You may simply type or paste all of the property values, separated by commas, on the properties group summary. This makes it easy to copy and paste a group of properties to multiple report items.**

Most report items support Padding properties, which are used to offset the placement of text and other related content within the item. Padding is specified in points. A unit of measure from the printing industry, a PostScript point equates to 1/72 of an inch or approximately 1/28 of a centimeter. In Figure 6-2, I've diagrammed a text box with padding margins. These are shown with the corresponding Padding section of the properties window.

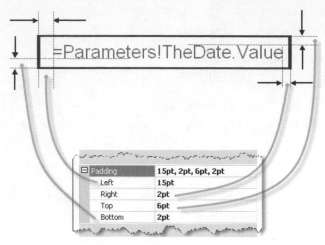

Figure 6-2

Grouping Data

This is one of the fundamental constructs of nearly all reports. Data groups provide a mechanism for organizing data into hierarchies and may be used to create section breaks and subtotals. Groups are used in different report items to implement specific features. Once you have defined a group in any report item, you should be able to do the same in any other item, although the design user interface may vary slightly for different types of items. There is no limit to the number of groups that may be added for any item.

Figure 6-3 shows the Grouping and Sorting Properties for a group defined in a table.

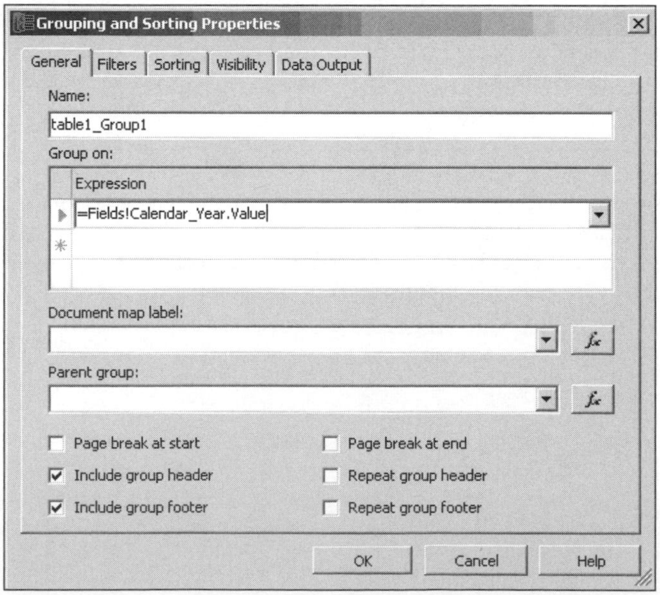

Figure 6-3

A group is defined in the Group on section of this dialog and is typically based on a field expression. This means that as rows are read from the data set, each time the field's value changes, a new group section or header is rendered. The group expression can include multiple fields, conditional expression, or Visual Basic function. It can be practically anything that returns a value. In the following sections, you will see how groups are applied within different report items.

Data Regions

A data region is a report item that repeats rows of data. For every row returned by the data set, a row, cell, or some other visual element will be created within the report body. The simplest and most common data regions are list items and tables, which extend the vertical space by adding a row in the report for every row of data. More sophisticated data regions, such as the matrix and chart items, add cells to extend the report either horizontally or vertically, or generate charting elements such as columns, bars, points, slices, and bubbles.

The report itself actually does little work to represent data. The report items placed in the body of the report are largely responsible for performing this task. When compared with most common reporting products, this is a different approach and adds a great deal of flexibility to the report design. Since report items may be placed practically anywhere in the body of the report, and many items can be used as containers for other items, this enables a great deal of creativity. Multiple report items can present independent sections of data side by side, on the same report. Essentially this creates multiple reports within a report. Report items placed within containing report items may present multiple nested reports or repeating sections of detail. Unique report designs are possible using this technique.

Using the List Item

The List item is the simplest of all data regions. One list visually represents one group, and the body of the list is simply repeated for each underlying data row. Using the properties for the list, it is associated with a data set. After placing a List item on the report, fields dragged from the Datasets window (previously called the Fields window in SSRS 2000) will bind the list to the data set and create data-bound text boxes. The example in Figure 6-4 shows formatted text boxes used for labels and values and a line used a row separator. The text box on the right contains an expression to calculate a product's profit margin by subtracting the StandardCost from the ListPrice field values.

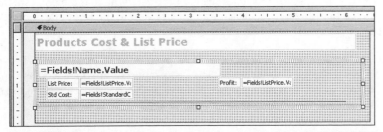

Figure 6-4

Like most report items, properties for the list may be set using the standard properties window or the custom properties dialog. Figure 6-5 shows the standard properties window. To select the list item, click on the border line to display the selection handles. The selected item appears in the topmost drop-down list in the properties window.

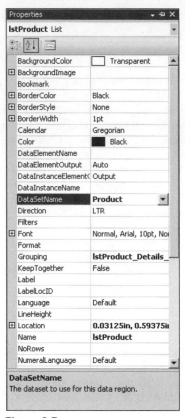

Figure 6-5

I've already defined a data set for this report called Product. Note that the DataSetName property was set when I dragged a field from this data set into the list item in the report designer. I'll set the Grouping in the next step.

Properties may also be set using the list item custom properties dialog. With the list selected, right-click and select Properties from the pop-up menu. The List properties are displayed as a modal dialog that must be closed before working with any other features of the report designer. Figure 6-6 shows this dialog with the same property settings as the previous property window.

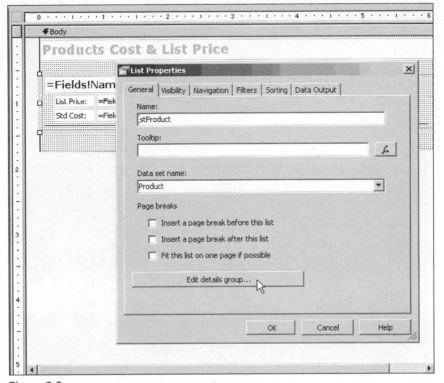

Figure 6-6

In order to define the details group for this list, either select the Grouping property in the properties window and then click the ellipsis button (...) or use the List Properties dialog and click the Edit Details Group... button. Either of these options will open the standard Grouping and Sorting Properties dialog that was shown earlier in Figure 6-3.

Figure 6-7 shows what the report looks like in Preview.

To demonstrate how the list can be used as a container for other data range items, I've added a chart item to the list that is selected in Figure 6-8. Since the list contains a detail group that returns only one record at a time and the chart is configured to recognize this parent group, the chart has visibility to this level of detail. In other words, each instance of the chart sees only one product record. You'll learn more about configuring the chart later in this chapter.

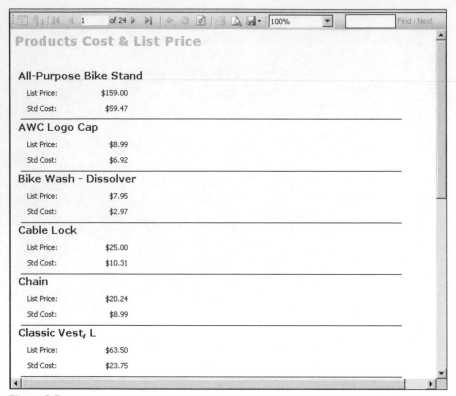

Figure 6-7

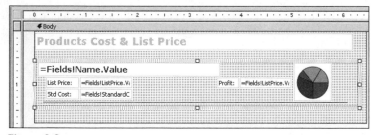

Figure 6-8

Figure 6-9 shows this report in preview. Each row of the report displays a pie chart with the calculated profit as a percentage of the ListPrice field value.

Figure 6-10 shows another example with a table placed within the list. The table must be bound to the same data set and must be grouped at the same level as the list.

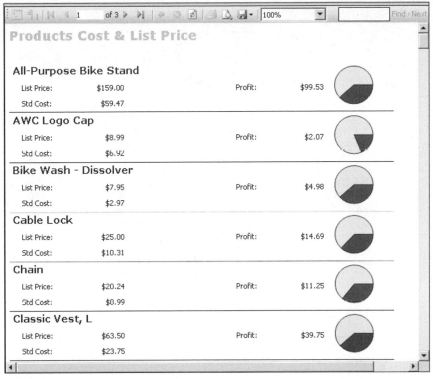

Figure 6-9

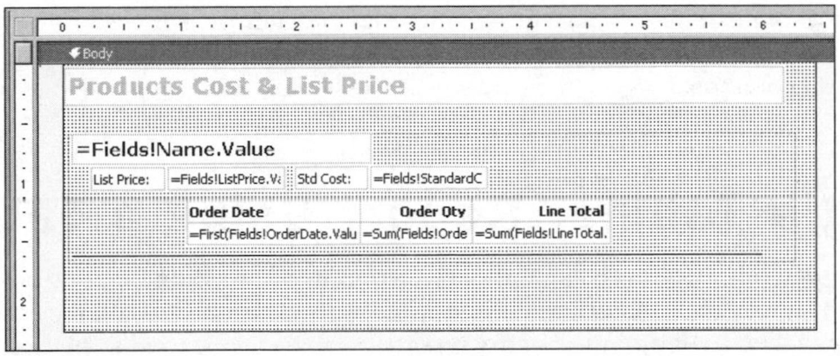

Figure 6-10

In Figure 6-11, you can see that the table displays only sales order rows for the product name displayed by the list.

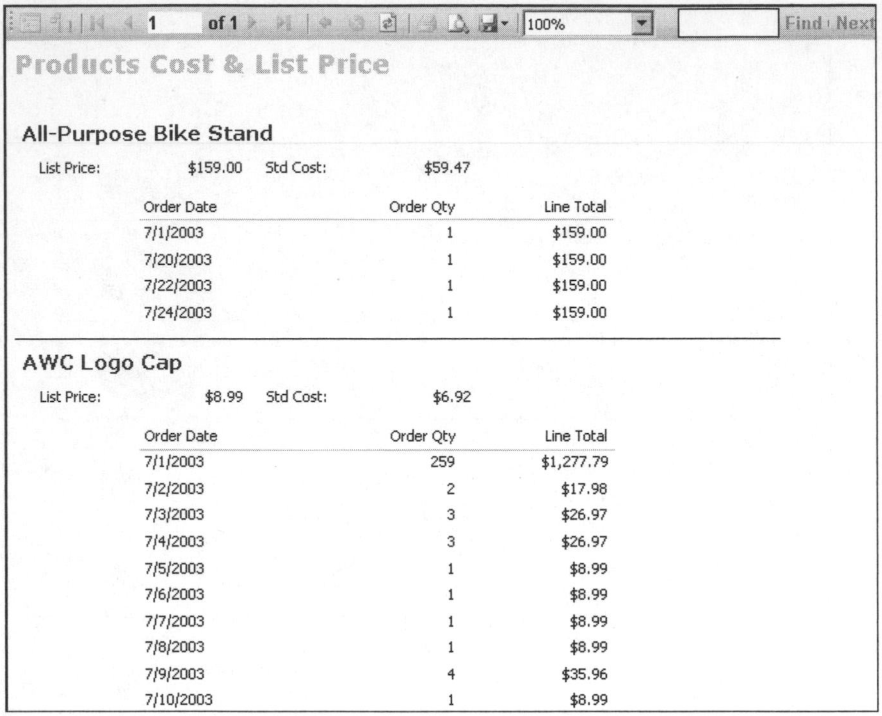

Products Cost & List Price

All-Purpose Bike Stand

List Price: $159.00 Std Cost: $59.47

Order Date	Order Qty	Line Total
7/1/2003	1	$159.00
7/20/2003	1	$159.00
7/22/2003	1	$159.00
7/24/2003	1	$159.00

AWC Logo Cap

List Price: $8.99 Std Cost: $6.92

Order Date	Order Qty	Line Total
7/1/2003	259	$1,277.79
7/2/2003	2	$17.98
7/3/2003	3	$26.97
7/4/2003	3	$26.97
7/5/2003	1	$8.99
7/6/2003	1	$8.99
7/7/2003	1	$8.99
7/8/2003	1	$8.99
7/9/2003	4	$35.96
7/10/2003	1	$8.99

Figure 6-11

The list item works well when repeating graphical items such as images and charts. Although the list offers a great deal of flexibility, it can require quite a lot of detail work if used for complex columnar reports and those with multiple levels of grouping. Consider using a table instead of a list when all data fits into rows and columns.

Creating a Tabular Report Using a Table

The Table data region is the most commonly used report item for columnar-style business reports. One of the most significant lessons I've learned while designing reports with the earlier versions of this product is to use tables to design most of my reports. A table may be used in place of a List item in many cases and offers more structure and built-in functionality. A table may be used to create reports with multiple levels of groupings and drill-down functionality. As you've already seen, groups give you the ability to organize repeated data within hierarchies and related groups. The table naturally supports this design paradigm.

I'd like to start with a simple example using a simple query, similar to the one used in Chapter 4. If you'd like to follow along, create a new report and add a new data set called Products_by_Subcategory_and_Category. Follow the instructions I gave when you stepped through the Report Wizard. Using this query, we will create a simple report that demonstrates the use of groupings within a table. After demonstrating groupings in a multilevel grouped table, drill-down and drill-through capabilities will be added.

Type the following SQL expression into the third pane of the Query Builder or use the techniques illustrated in Figure 6-10 to design the query using the Graphical Query Design tools:

```
SELECT
      Production.Product.ProductID
    , Production.ProductCategory.Name AS CategoryName
    , Production.ProductSubcategory.Name AS SubCategoryName
    , Production.Product.Name AS ProductName
FROM
      Production.Product
      INNER JOIN Production.ProductSubcategory
      ON Production.Product.ProductSubcategoryID =
      Production.ProductSubcategory.ProductSubcategoryID
      INNER JOIN Production.ProductCategory
      ON Production.ProductSubcategory.ProductCategoryID =
      Production.ProductCategory.ProductCategoryID
ORDER BY
      Production.ProductCategory.Name
    , Production.ProductSubcategory.Name
    , Production.Product.Name
```

Figure 6-12 shows this query in the Graphical Query Designer.

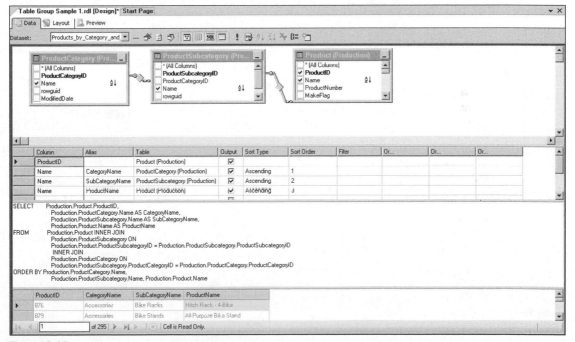

Figure 6-12

Switch to the Layout tab and drag a Table item from the Toolbox to the report designer. Click on the table, and then click the gray table selector handle on the top left to select the entire table.

Selecting a table is simple but may not be obvious: First, click anywhere in the table to view the row and column selector handles, and then click the table selector handle in the corner to select the table (see Figure 6-13).

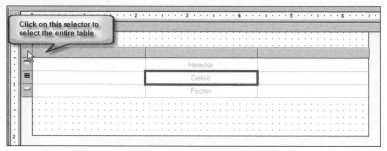

Figure 6-13

This should display a border with selection handles around the table as in Figure 6-14.

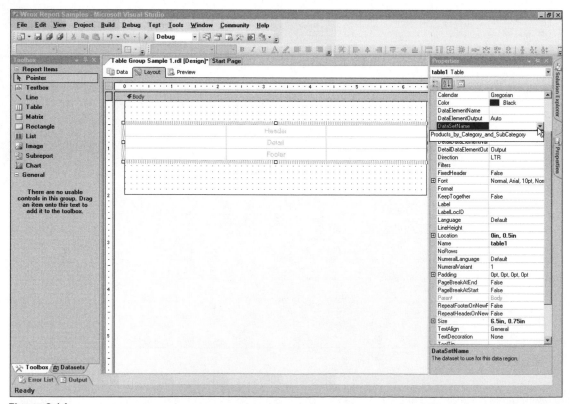

Figure 6-14

In the properties window, select the `DataSetName` property and, in the drop-down list, select the new data set name. If you drag and drop a field from the Dataset window to any cell of the table, this property will be set automatically. In case you need to change the data source for a table or if the name of the data set were to change, it's important to know how to change this value.

Groups are added directly to the table item using the right-click menu and a custom properties dialog window. Table groupings can have an associated header and footer row. Cells in these rows contain text boxes (by default) that can be used to display column values for the grouping level. Different columns can be used to indent grouped values, or you can use the padding property of a text box to achieve more precise control.

By default, a table contains a detail row and a header and footer row. You can add and remove rows for each of these areas and to any group using the right-click menu from the row handles. Figure 6-15 shows the Detail tooltip. Tooltips are visible as you hover over each row selector handle.

Figure 6-15

You will add two groups. One each for the `CategoryName` and `SubCategoryName` fields. Groups are added in top-down order (not from the inside out), so you will add the `CategoryName` group first. Right-click the detail row handle and select Insert Group from the pop-up menu, as shown in Figure 6-16.

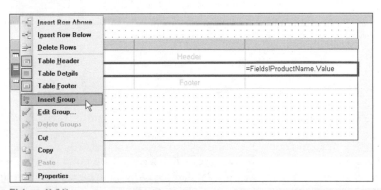

Figure 6-16

The Grouping and Sorting Properties dialog is displayed with a default name for the new grouping. For a complex report, you may want to devise a more intuitive naming convention than the one offered by the Designer. Note this dialog includes the following features:

❑ Name is used for identifying and referring to this group in expressions.

❑ Group on may contain one or more expressions, typically fields, to group on.

❑ Document map label is a field value, an expression, or text that will be used in the document map for the report.

❑ Parent group may be used to create a hierarchy of nested groupings. This property is not necessary for multiple groups in the same table.

❑ Page break options may be used to force a page break.

❑ Header and footer options enable group header and footer rows.

For simplicity, just add the group field name to the end as you see in Figure 6-17. In the Expression box, drop down the list from the first row of the grid and select =Fields!CategoryName.Value.

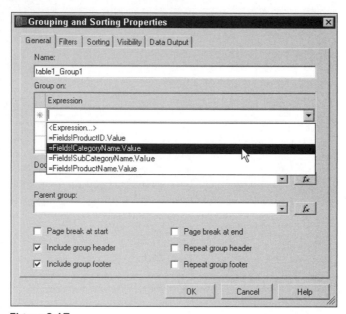

Figure 6-17

Switch to the Sorting tab and choose the same field to ensure that records are sorted correctly prior to grouping on this field value, as shown in Figure 6-18. It's typically a good idea to sort records in the data set query in the same order they will be presented in the report. However, since grouping and sorting can be dynamically changed using expressions, make sure that records are sorted in the same order that they are grouped. Doing otherwise will cause some strange results. If you plan to sort rows differently from the way they are returned by the data set, choose the appropriate field expression from the drop-down list in the first row of the Sort on grid. You may subsort on different field values by choosing subsequent field expressions in multiple rows in this grid.

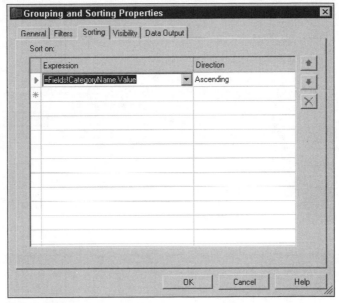

Figure 6-18

Click OK to close the Grouping and Sorting Properties dialog. Right-click on the detail row handle again and repeat the same process for the ProductSubCategory field.

Adding the fields to the table is a snap. Just drag and drop them from the Dataset window on the left. Place the CategoryName in the first cell in the group 1 row. Drag the SubCategoryName field to the second column on the group 2 row, and drag the ProductName field to the third column on the detail row, as shown in Figure 6-19.

Note that the table headers have text added and that the mixed-case field names are parsed appropriately. The report should be functional at this point, although it needs a little cosmetic work. Select the header row by clicking in the table and then on the header row selector handle. This selects all of the text boxes in this row. Using the properties window, set the BorderStyle_Bottom property to Solid and the BorderWidth_Bottom property to 2pt. Text fonts and styles can be set using the properties window or the layout toolbar. Using either method, set the FontWeight for the text in this row to Bold. The properties window is shown in Figure 6-20.

Finally, remove the unused footer rows. Select the group and table footer rows and then press the Delete key. What the report looks like in preview is shown in Figure 6-21.

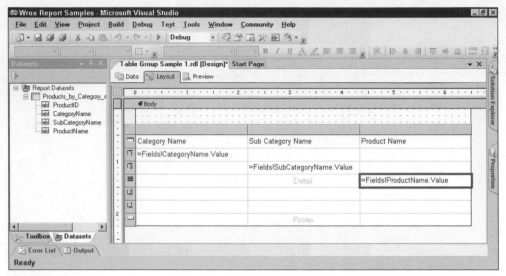

Figure 6-19

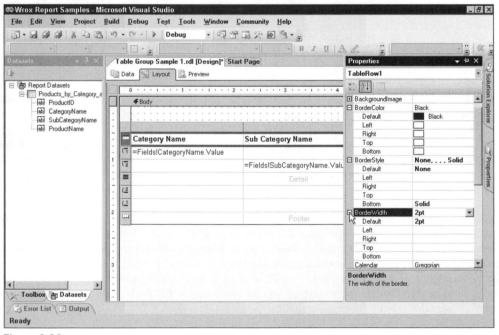

Figure 6-20

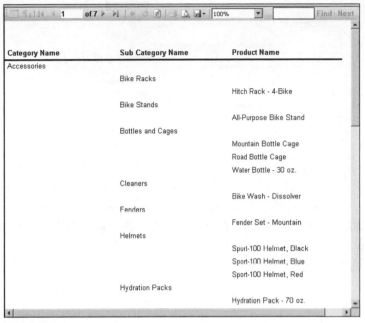

Figure 6-21

Column Placement and Indentation

One of the typical challenges associated with a table is that horizontal space is limited. There are two common techniques for dealing with these limitations. The first technique you'll use in this example is to merge columns together, which will give values more space, even with the column spacing reduced. This effectively extends the first cell in the range and hides other cell values. You may find it necessary to abbreviate column headings, so you can resize the columns and get the desired effect.

The column space used in our report by the CategoryName and SubCategoryName group fields would be unacceptable if I needed this space for other fields. I'm going to resize these columns to make room for some additional fields. I've added four more fields to my data set query: ProductNumber, Color, StandardCost, and ListPrice. To add additional columns to the table, I right-click on a column header and select an option to insert a new column from the pop-up menu, as shown in Figure 6-22.

I'll repeat this step to create the four columns and then drag and drop the fields from the Dataset window to the new cells in the detail row. In Figure 6-23, you can see that the CategoryName and SubCategoryName fields and the table header text for the new columns no longer fit.

To fix the column headers, I'll change the text using abbreviations. Since I have room for the CategoryName and SubCategoryName field values in adjacent cells, I can merge these cells. Simply drag across all of the cells, right-click, and select Merge Cells from the pop-up menu, shown in Figure 6-24.

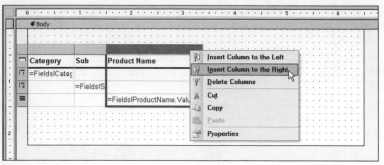

Figure 6-22

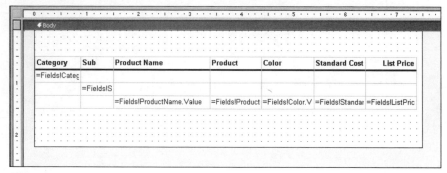

Figure 6-23

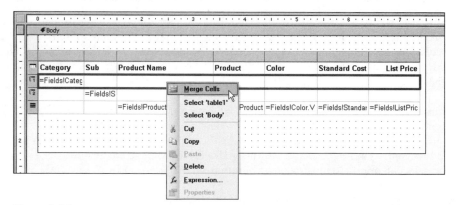

Figure 6-24

Once cells have been merged, column changes are not allowed. It's generally not a good idea to merge cells until you have completed the rest of the table design work that may involve adding or removing columns.

Two of these columns contain currency values that need to be formatted. I'll change the `Format` property to standard currency. The custom properties dialog for a text box contains a format selection list. You can also use this dialog or the properties window to type a format string. In this case, the format string for standard currency is a capital letter C. The formatting options for a text box are shown in Figure 6-25.

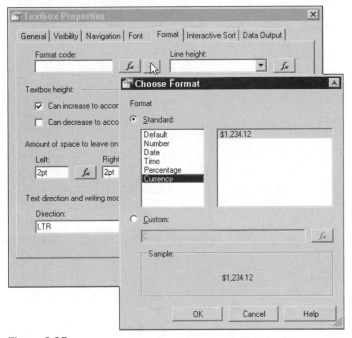

Figure 6-25

Figure 6-26 shows the report in preview after making these changes.

Indent with Padding

If you want values to be indented or staggered, you can work around the restrictions of column placement and widths by using the Padding properties of a text box. Padding may be applied to the left, right, top, or bottom of a text box and simply provides a margin of space between the border and contained text.

To demonstrate, I will save a copy of the report we have been using in the previous example. In the new report, I will remove the two leftmost columns and place the `CategoryName`, `SubCategoryName`, and `ProductName` fields in the same column. For the reason I mentioned above, I cannot remove these columns without first splitting the merged cells back apart. Figure 6-27 shows the new report in design and preview. As you can see, with all three group fields in the same column, it looks very confusing.

To correct this, I change the left padding property for each of the data-bound text boxes in the first column. The group 1 header padding is left at 2 points, the group 2 header is set to 12 points, and the detail row text box is set to 24 points. For reference, there are 72 points to an inch and about 28 points to a centimeter.

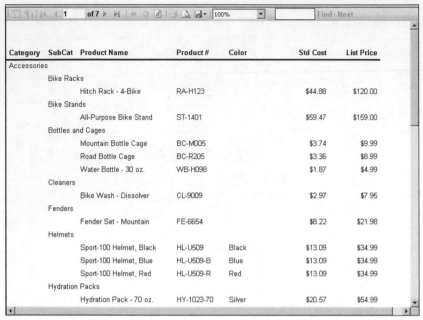

Figure 6-26

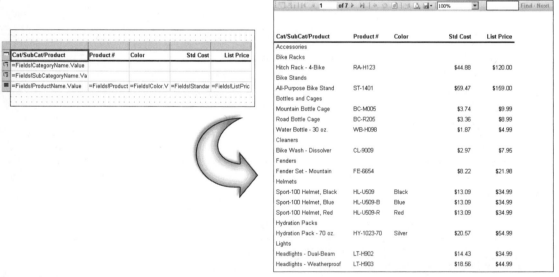

Figure 6-27

I've also added two additional rows to the table header, used the same padding for the corresponding heading text and changed the background color to dress things up a little. The result is shown in Figure 6-28.

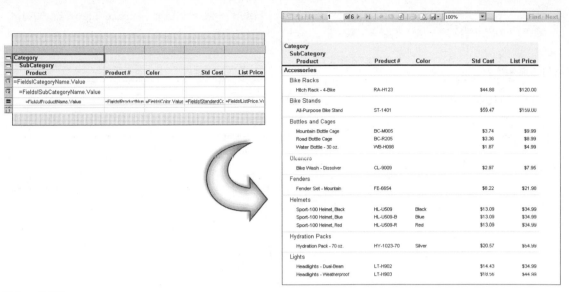

Figure 6-28

Headers and Footers

Page headers and footers can be configured so that they are displayed and printed on all pages or omitted from the first and/or last pages. Unlike many other reporting tools, there is no designated report header or footer. This is so because the report body will act as a header or footer, depending on where you place data region items. If you were to place a table an inch below the top of the report body, this would give you a report header 1 inch tall. And since there is no set limit to the number of data regions or other items you can add to a report (and you can force page breaks at any location), all of the space above, below, and in between these items is essentially header and footer space.

You have a lot of flexibility for displaying header and footer content. In additional to the standard report and page headers and footers, data range sections can be repeated on each page, creating additional page header and footer content. Figure 6-29 shows a table report with each of the header and footer areas labeled.

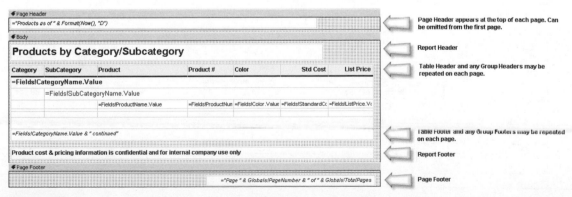

Figure 6-29

I've shortened the page height on this report to 5 inches in order to conserve space. Figures 6-30 and 6-31 show two rendered pages for this report.

Products as of Tuesday, July 26, 2005

Products by Category/Subcategory

Category	SubCategory	Product	Product #	Color	Std Cost	List Price
Accessories						
	Bike Racks					
		Hitch Rack - 4-Bike	RA-H123		$44.88	$120.00
	Bike Stands					
		All-Purpose Bike Stand	ST-1401		$59.47	$159.00
	Bottles and Cages					
		Mountain Bottle Cage	BC-M005		$3.74	$9.99
		Road Bottle Cage	BC-R205		$3.36	$8.99
		Water Bottle - 30 oz.	WB-H098		$1.87	$4.99
	Cleaners					
		Bike Wash - Dissolver	CL-9009		$2.97	$7.95

Page 1 of 23

Figure 6-30

Products as of Tuesday, July 26, 2005

Category	SubCategory	Product	Product #	Color	Std Cost	List Price
	Panniers					
		Touring-Panniers, Large	PA-T100	Grey	$51.56	$125.00
	Pumps					
		Minipump	PU-0452		$8.25	$19.99
		Mountain Pump	PU-M044		$10.31	$24.99
	Tires and Tubes					
		HL Mountain Tire	TI-M823		$13.09	$35.00
		HL Road Tire	TI-R982		$12.19	$32.60
		LL Mountain Tire	TI-M267		$9.35	$24.99
		LL Road Tire	TI-R092		$8.04	$21.49
		ML Mountain Tire	TI-M602		$11.22	$29.99
		ML Road Tire	TI-R628		$9.35	$24.99
		Mountain Tire Tube	TT-M928		$1.87	$4.99
		Patch Kit/8 Patches	PK-7098		$0.86	$2.29

Accessories continued

Page 3 of 23

Figure 6-31

Note the page header containing the date at the top of this page, the repeated table header, and the table footer showing the continuation of the CategoryName group, and then the page footer with the page number and page count.

There are some restrictions regarding the content you can include in page header and footer sections that can be easily worked around. Field references are not allowed in these areas because the page header and footer are added to the final report output after the data is processed. Pagination is a feature of each report format–rendering extension so the report engine has no knowledge of page placement at the time of the initial report content rendering. You do have access to several resources such as global variables, parameters, and report items. A simple technique for including data in the page header and footer is to place a text box in the report body with the desired field reference and then refer to this report item from the header or footer.

Add a page header and footer by selecting Page Header and Page Footer from the Report menu while the report is open in Layout view. Select Report Properties from the Report menu. This is where you can optionally leave a page header or footer off the first or last page of the report.

Now that the page header and footer are visible in the report designer, drag the report title text box into the header area. You'll also replace the header row of the table with text boxes in the page header. Add text boxes, and label them with the same text as the columns in the table header row. To separate the headings from column values, add a line, and place it immediately below the row of text boxes. Resize the page header area as needed.

In the report body, click on the table and then right-click the row selector to the left of the table header. Choose Delete Rows to get rid of the header row. Resize the report body as needed. Finally, in the report footer section, place a horizontal line and a text box item below it.

Aggregate Functions and Totals

Reporting Services supports several aggregate functions, similar to those supported by the Transact-SQL query language. Each aggregate function accepts one or two arguments. The first is the field reference or expression to aggregate. The second, optional argument is the name of a data set, report item, or group name to indicate the scope of the aggregation. If not provided, the current item scope is assumed. The following table lists the aggregate functions available in Reporting Services.

Function	Description
AVG()	The average of all non-null values.
COUNT()	The count of values.
COUNTDISTINCT()	The count of distinct values.
COUNTROWS()	The count of all rows.
FIRST()	Returns the first value for a range of values.
LAST()	Returns the last value for a range of values.
MAX()	Returns the greatest value for a range of values.

Table continued on following page

Function	Description
MIN()	Returns the least value for a range of values.
STDEV()	Returns the standard deviation.
STDEVP()	Returns the population standard deviation.
SUM()	Returns a sum of all values.
VAR()	Returns the variance of all values.
VARP()	Returns the population variance of all values.

In addition to the aggregate functions in the previous table, the functions listed in the following table behave in a similar way to aggregates but have special features for reports.

Function	Description
LEVEL()	Returns an integer value for the group level within a recursive hierarchy. The group name is required.
ROWNUMBER()	Returns the row number for a group or range.
RUNNINGVALUE()	Returns an accumulative aggregation up to this row.

Examples of aggregate function expressions and recursive levels are found in the following sections for table and matrix report items.

Using the Expression Builder

You've already used a few expressions in the basic report design work you've done so far. Any field reference is an expression. In the Grouping and Sorting Properties dialog, you used a field expression. In the report shown in the previous example, I used an expression to show the page number and total pages so that it reads "Page X of Y." Expressions are used to create a dynamic value based on a variety of global variables, fields, and programming functions. Expressions may be used to set most property values based on a variety of global variables, field values, and calculations. Let's take a quick look at common methods to build simple expressions.

To display the page number and page count, add a text box to the page header or footer. Right-click the text box and in the drop-down list select Expression. Use the Edit Expression window to create the expression. There are two different ways to enter an expression. The first method is to select and paste items from the object tree and member lists (shown in Figure 6-32). You can either double-click an item or click the Paste button to add items to the expression. The other method is simply to type text into the expression text area. As you type, you may use the IntelliSense Auto List Members feature to provide drop-down lists for known items and properties. When you type a known object (for example, Globals or Fields) followed by a period or exclamation mark, a list of members will appear at this location. You may continue to type or select a list item using the mouse or keyboard arrow keys. When the appropriate list item is highlighted, use the Tab key to select it from the list.

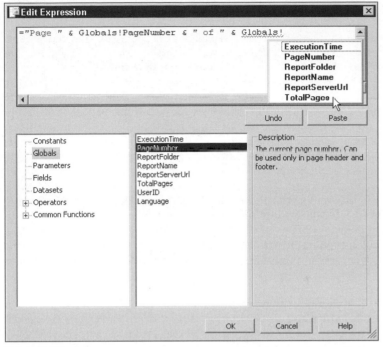

Figure 6-32

Begin by typing `="Page " &` in the Expression box, and then click the Globals item on the object tree view. All related members are listed in the adjacent list box. Double-click the PageNumber item in the list. Place the cursor at the end of the text and type the text `& " of " &`. and then select and insert the TotalPages field. The finished expression should read as follows:

```
="Page " & Globals!PageNumber & " of " & Globals!TotalPages
```

The Edit Expression window (also called the Expression Builder) should appear as shown in Figure 6-32.

The term *Globals* applies to a set of variables built in to Reporting Services that provide useful information such as page numbers. A list of available global variables, fields, and parameters may be found in the Expression Builder.

As I said, you'll see this dialog again. In fact, it's something that you will likely use quite a bit. In the properties window, many property values can be set by using the drop-down list to select the item labeled <Expression...>. In the custom properties dialog for each report item, the Expression Builder dialog is invoked using the buttons labeled f_x adjacent to each property value. In the previous chapter, you learned how parameter values are passed into a query to limit or alter the result set. Parameters may also be used within the report to modify display characteristics by dynamically changing item properties.

In the next chapter, you learn techniques for using expressions with parameters, global variables, and simple programming code to extend report functionality.

Drill-Down Reports

A *drill-down report* is an interactive report that allows the user to expand and collapse grouped sections to discover more detail as needed. In recent years, users have become accustomed to this type of tree view navigation in common software, so it has become an intuitive user interface metaphor. Interactive reports give users more options and reduce unnecessary screen space used by data that users need not view. They can drill down further as suits their need to view more specific details. Drill-down reports are designed to be interactive, but they usually work well on the page. Different report-rendering formats treat drill-down reports a little differently. In HTML and Excel, reports will behave as they do in the report designer. However, PDF and image-rendered reports don't support the dynamic drill-down functionality. When exported from the Report Manager, these reports will have sections expanded and collapsed as they were at the time they were exported.

The magic of drill-down reports is that rows and sections are simply hidden and displayed based on a toggle item. This means that a value item (like a text box) is used to toggle the hidden property of rows and other report items. A plus sign (+) is displayed to the left of the toggle item. Each time the user clicks the icon, the hidden property for the associated row items is toggled between the value True and False, and the icon toggles between a plus (+) and minus (–) sign. The rows must also be set up to collapse when they are hidden.

Using the Products and Categories report from the previous example, the detail row and SubCategory header row must be hidden and set up to toggle. As drill-down visibility is managed at the group level, you need to define a group for the detail row. Select the detail row using the row selector, right-click, and choose Edit Group to show the Grouping and Sorting Properties dialog. Select `=Fields!ProductName.Value` from the drop-down list in the first row of the Expression list box, as shown in Figure 6-33.

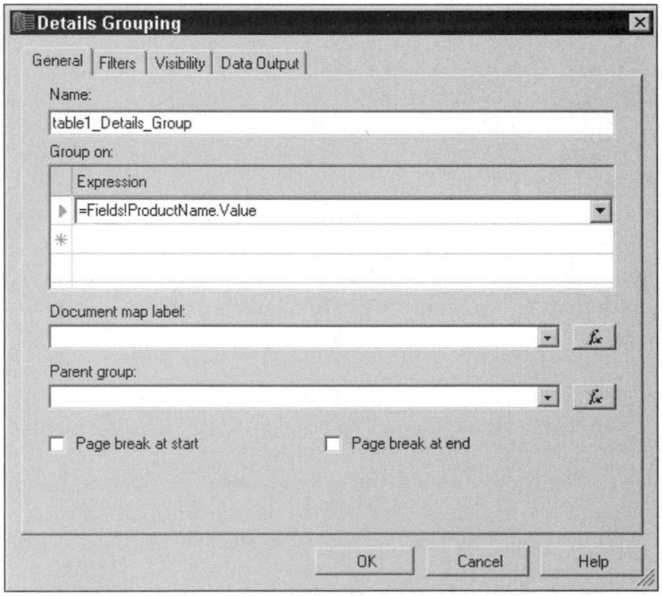

Figure 6-33

The toggle items (in this case, the CategoryName and SubCategoryName text boxes) should be named appropriately because they will be referenced in expressions. Since I defined these items using the drag-and-drop technique, the text boxes have the same names as the fields to which they are bound. If they had not been created this way, they may have arbitrary names (like TextBox17 and TextBox43). Make it a point to rename any report items that may be used in expressions.

I like to prefix report item names with the abbreviated form of the item (such as txt for text box, tbl for table, and img for image). This is a matter of preference and isn't necessary in simple reports.

On the Visibility tab, change the initial visibility to Hidden and then the check box labeled Visibility can be toggled by another report item. This enables the report item drop-down list. Select the SubCategoryName item in the Report item drop-down list. The SubCategoryName text box is in the second column of the SubCategory group row. It will be used to toggle the visibility of the row (see Figure 6-34). I have found this item selection to be a little unpredictable, and some items may not be listed as they should. In any case, if you don't see the report item you expect, just type it into the list text area.

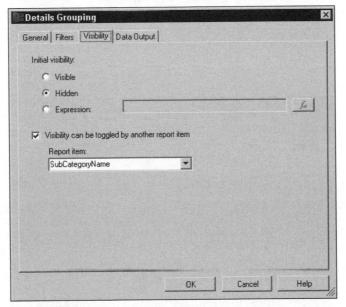

Figure 6-34

The same process should be repeated for the SubCategoryName row group. Select this row using the row selector, and repeat these steps. On the dialog, choose the Visibility tab and set the initial visibility to Hidden and use the CategoryName report item to toggle the visibility of this grouping. Click OK to save the settings. Figure 6-35 shows the preview for this report with all detail hidden in its initial state.

Figure 6-36 shows the same report with both groups drilled open. Note the standard "finger" mouse pointer used to toggle the group rows.

Use the (+) icons to drill down into a CategoryName or SubCategoryName rows. As you see, the report now becomes interactive, and users can customize the display of the report by viewing only the information that they need.

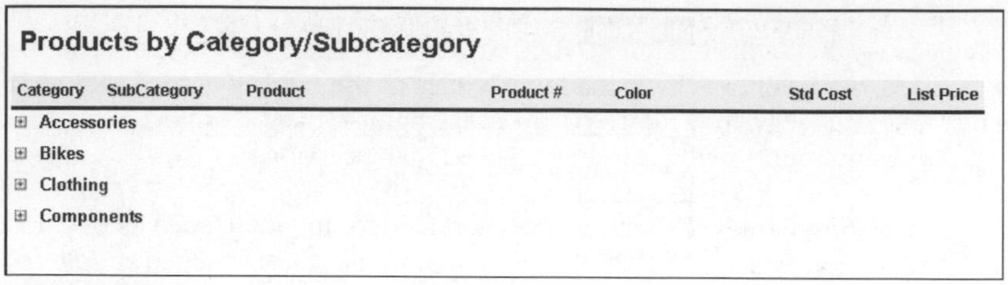

Products by Category/Subcategory

Category	SubCategory	Product	Product #	Color	Std Cost	List Price
⊞ Accessories						
⊞ Bikes						
⊞ Clothing						
⊞ Components						

Figure 6-35

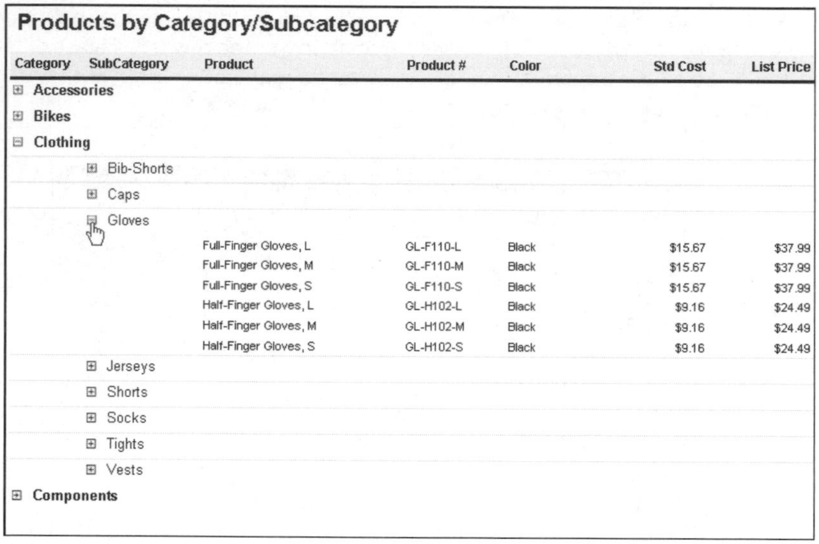

Products by Category/Subcategory

Category	SubCategory	Product	Product #	Color	Std Cost	List Price
⊞ Accessories						
⊞ Bikes						
⊟ Clothing						
	⊞ Bib-Shorts					
	⊞ Caps					
	⊟ Gloves					
		Full-Finger Gloves, L	GL-F110-L	Black	$15.67	$37.99
		Full-Finger Gloves, M	GL-F110-M	Black	$15.67	$37.99
		Full-Finger Gloves, S	GL-F110-S	Black	$15.67	$37.99
		Half-Finger Gloves, L	GL-H102-L	Black	$9.16	$24.49
		Half-Finger Gloves, M	GL-H102-M	Black	$9.16	$24.49
		Half-Finger Gloves, S	GL-H102-S	Black	$9.16	$24.49
	⊞ Jerseys					
	⊞ Shorts					
	⊞ Socks					
	⊞ Tights					
	⊞ Vests					
⊞ Components						

Figure 6-36

Creating a Document Map

This is a simple navigation feature that allows the user to find a group label or item value in the report by using a tree displayed along the left side of the report. It's sort of like a table of contents for report items, which can be used to quickly navigate to a specific area of a large report. You typically will want to include only group-level fields in the document map rather than including the detail rows.

> *The document map is limited to the HTML, Excel, and PDF rendering formats. In Excel and HTML formats, the document map may not survive when saving report files to an older document format, such as Pocket Excel on a Pocket PC device.*

This example will use a version of the drill-down report, only with the visibility properties set back to defaults. You will add the CategoryName and SubCategoryName groupings to the document map. In the Grouping and Sorting Properties dialog for the Category row (group 1), drop down the Document map label list, and choose the =Fields!CategoryName.Value item (see Figure 6-37).

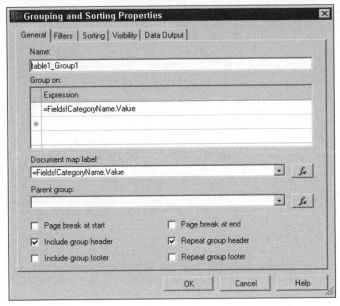

Figure 6-37

Click OK to close the dialog, and then do the same for the SubCategoryName row group.

Be careful and specify the document map label property only for items that you want to include in the document map. For example, if you specify this property for a grouping (as has been done here), don't do the same for a text box containing the same value. Otherwise, you will see the same value appear twice in the document map. A report with a document map is illustrated in Figure 6-38. The report name is the top-level item in the document map, followed by the product Category and Subcategory names.

Category	SubCategory	Product	Product #	Color	Std Cost	List Price
Accessories						
	Bike Racks					
		Hitch Rack - 4-Bike	RA-H123		$44.88	$120.00
	Bike Stands					
		All-Purpose Bike Stand	ST-1401		$59.47	$159.00
	Bottles and Cages					
		Mountain Bottle Cage	BC-M005		$3.74	$9.99
		Road Bottle Cage	BC-R205		$3.36	$8.99
		Water Bottle - 30 oz.	WB-H098		$1.87	$4.99
	Cleaners					
		Bike Wash - Dissolver	CL-9009		$2.97	$7.95
	Fenders					
		Fender Set - Mountain	FE-6654		$8.22	$21.98
	Helmets					
		Sport-100 Helmet, Black	HL-U509	Black	$13.09	$34.99
		Sport-100 Helmet, Blue	HL-U509-B	Blue	$13.09	$34.99
		Sport-100 Helmet, Red	HL-U509-R	Red	$13.09	$34.99
	Hydration Packs					
		Hydration Pack - 70 oz.	HY-1023-70	Silver	$20.57	$54.99

Document Map Sample 1
- Accessories
  - Bike Racks
  - Bike Stands
  - Bottles and Cages
  - Cleaners
  - Fenders
  - Helmets
  - Hydration Packs
  - Lights
  - Locks
  - Panniers
  - Pumps
  - Tires and Tubes
- Bikes
- Clothing
- Components

Products by Category/Subcategory

Figure 6-38

The document map may be shown or hidden using the leftmost icon in the report designer's Preview or the Report Manager Report View toolbar.

Links and Drill-Through Reports

Any text box or image item can be used for intrareport or interreport navigation, for navigation to external resources like web pages and documents, and also to send e-mail. All of these features are enabled by using navigation properties that can be specified in the Textbox Properties or Image Properties dialog. First, open the Textbox Properties dialog by right-clicking the text box and selecting Properties from the pop-out menu. In the Textbox Properties dialog, click the Advanced button to show the Advanced Textbox Properties dialog, and then switch to the Navigation tab. In the Image Properties dialog, select the Navigation tab.

Bookmarks and Links

A bookmark is a text box or image in a report that can be used as a navigational link. If you want to allow the user to click an item and navigate to another item, assign a bookmark value to each of the target items. To enable navigation to a bookmark, set the Jump to bookmark property to the target bookmark.

Using bookmarks to navigate within a report is very easy to do. Each report item has a `BookMark` property that may be assigned a unique value. After adding bookmarks to any target items, use the Jump to Bookmark Selection list to select the target bookmark in the Properties for the Source item. This allows the user to navigate to items within the same report.

The Jump to URL option can be used to navigate to practically any report or document content on your report server, and files, folders, and applications in your intranet environment or on the World Wide Web. With some creativity, this may be used as a powerful, interactive navigation feature. It can also be set to an expression that uses links stored in a database, custom code, or any other values. It's more accurate to say that any URI (Uniform Resource Identifier) can be used since a web request is not limited only to a web page or document. With some creative programming, queries, and expressions, your reports could be designed to navigate to a web page, document, e-mail address, Web service request, or a custom web application, directed by data or custom expressions.

Just a word of caution: Reporting Services does not make any attempt to validate a URL passed in an expression. If a malformed URL is used, the Report Server will return an error, and there is no easy way to trap or prevent this from occurring. The most effective way to handle this issue is to validate the URL string before passing it to the Jump to URL property.

Drill-Through Reports

This powerful feature enables a text box or image to be used as a link to another report by passing parameter values to the target report. The target report can consist of a specific record or multiple records, depending on the parameters passed to the target report. The following example uses a Products by Category report, similar to the one used in the last example, to demonstrate the use of grouped tables. The Product Name text box is used to link to a report that will display the details of a single product record. The Product Details report is very simple. It contains only text boxes and an image bound to fields of a data set based on the Products table. This report accepts a `ProductID` parameter to filter the records and narrow down to the record requested.

In the Navigation tab of the Textbox Properties dialog box, select the Jump to report radio button, and select the target report from the drop-down list (see Figure 6-39).

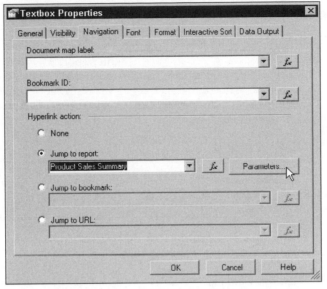

Figure 6-39

Any parameters you need to pass to the target report can be configured using the Parameters button. In the Parameters dialog, parameters for the target report are selected in the Parameter Name column. Values supplied from the current report are provided in the Parameter Value column, as you can see in Figure 6-40.

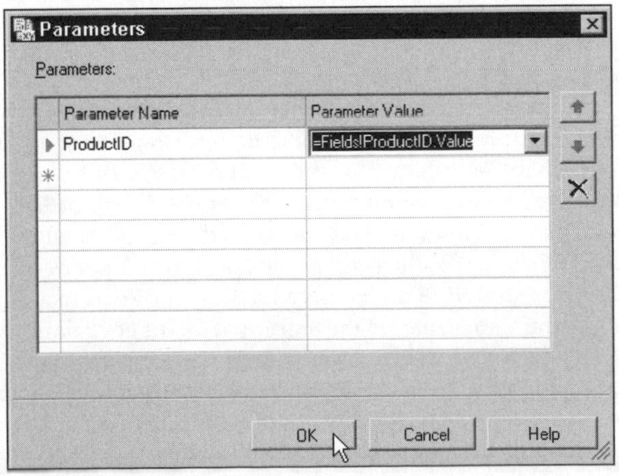

Figure 6-40

If you need to give a cue to the user that the item is a link, you may want to display text with an underline. The resulting reports provide drill-through functionality. When a product name is clicked on the main report, the viewer redirects to the detailed report for the specific product by passing the `ProductID` parameter value. This is shown in Figure 6-41.

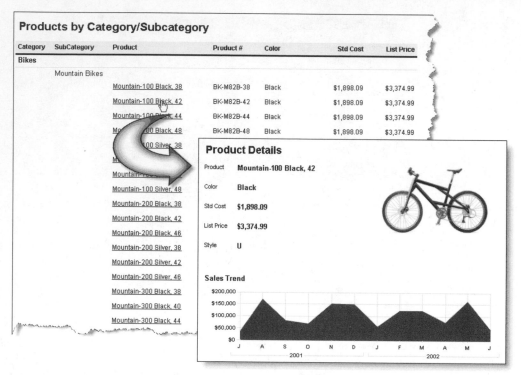

Figure 6-41

Recursive Relationships

Representing recursive hierarchies has always been a pain for reporting and often a challenge to effectively model in relational database systems. Examples of this type of relationship (usually facilitated through a self-join) may be found in the Employee table of the AdventureWorks sample database. Most reporting tools were designed to work with data organized in traditional multi-table relationships. Fortunately, our friends at Microsoft built recursive support into the reporting engine to deal with this common challenge. A classic example of a recursive relationship (where child records are related to a parent record contained in the same table) is the employee-manager relationship. The Employee table contains a primary key, `EmployeeID`, that uniquely identifies each employee record. The `ManagerID` is a foreign key that depends on the `EmployeeID` attribute of the same table, and it contains the `EmployeeID` value for the employee's *manager*. The only record that won't have a `ManagerID` would be the president of the company or any such employee who doesn't have a boss.

Representing the hierarchy through a query would be quite difficult. However, defining the data set for such a report is very simple. You simply expose the primary key, foreign key, employee name, and any other values that you want to include on the report.

To see how this works, create a new report and define a data set using the AdventureWorks shared data source. The name of the new data set will be `EmployeesAndManagers`. Enter this SQL expression into the third pane of the Query Builder:

```
SELECT
    Person.Contact.FirstName
  , Person.Contact.LastName
  , HumanResources.Employee.EmployeeID
  , HumanResources.Employee.ManagerID
FROM
    HumanResources.Employee
    INNER JOIN Person.Contact
    ON HumanResources.Employee.ContactID = Person.Contact.ContactID
ORDER BY
    Person.Contact.LastName
  , Person.Contact.FirstName
```

Add a table to the report in the Layout tab, and drag the `FirstName` field from the Dataset window to the first cell in the detail row. This will set the `DataSetName` property for you. A single group will provide all of the recursive functionality for the table. Click on the table to show the selection handles, and then click the selector to the left of the detail row. You're not adding a new group but simply using the detail group that already exists for this row. Right-click the detail row selector, and choose Edit Group from the menu. In the Details Grouping dialog, enter the Name as `table1_Details_Group_Employees`. In the first row of the Group on list box, select the expression `=Fields!EmployeeID.Value`. Drop down the Parent group list, and select the expression `=Fields!ManagerID.Value` and verify that your selections match Figure 6-42. The reporting engine recognizes this as a recursive grouping because both of these fields are in the same table. Click OK to close the dialog.

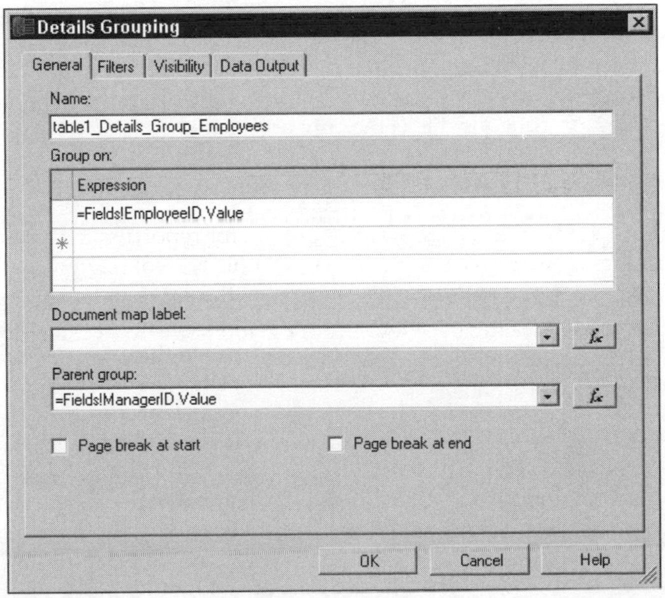

Figure 6-42

Now the fun begins; Reporting Services recognizes that recursive groupings have special characteristics. I use the Level() function to return the group level number within the recursive hierarchy. Each row is assigned an integer value that represents its relative position to parent and child rows in the hierarchy. You will also use a Count() function, indicating that you want the count of the recursive group's children.

Figure 6-43 shows the final solution. Note that for the first of the two function calls, detailed in the call-outs, you'll build this in two stages. I'll give you instructions to add and test only the Level() function and then you'll go back and add the Choose() function in a second pass.

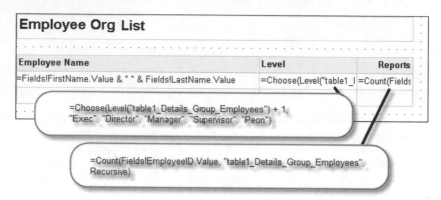

Figure 6-43

You want to see the employee's full name, so modify the expression as it appears in Figure 6-43 to show the FirstName, a space, and the LastName. Modify this column header and enter column headers for the second and third columns as Level and Reports, respectively. The Level column will show the employee's level within the organization and the Reports column will show the number reports they have (the number of employees who report to this employee.) All aggregate functions accept an optional group name for the scope argument which causes it to calculate the aggregation only within the scope of that group. For the Level() function this is the only argument.

In the second detail cell (labeled Level), set the Value property to:

```
=Level("table1_Details_Group_Employees") + 1
```

This returns an integer that I would like translated to a more meaningful value. Now, I'll embellish this expression so that it returns the employee level from the top of the food chain down (the number 1 represents an executive, 2 is a director, 3 is a manager, and so on). Passing the level number to the Choose() function, I can provide this translation:

```
=Choose(Level("table1_Details_Group_Employees") + 1, "Exec", "Director", "Manager",
"Supervisor", "Peon")
```

1 is added to this value because the Level() function returns 0 for the first level, 1 for the second, and so on. The expression for the third column will use the group name for the Count() function's scope argument and the Recursive keyword in the third argument. This indicates that the aggregate function should be applied to child rows of this group. Set the value to the expression:

```
=Count(Fields!EmployeeID.Value, "table1_Details_Group_Employees", Recursive)
```

Finally, you want each row's padding to be progressively greater based on the group level. Using the Level() function you can apply some simple math to the padding property value to get the desired result. Since padding values are expressed as a string value, you will concatenate the value pt to the end of a calculated numeric value.

Click on the first cell in the detail row to select the EmployeeName text box and in the properties window set the Padding_Left property to:

```
=Level("table1_Details_Group_Employees ") ^ 20 & "pt"
```

This will set the padding for the first level (level 0) to 0 points, the second to 20 points, and the third to 40 points, and so on. I've dressed up the header row using bold text, a border, and text alignment and added a title text box. Save the report and then select the Preview tab to view the results. The generated report should appear as shown in Figure 6-44.

Employee Org List		
Employee Name	**Level**	**Reports**
Ken Sánchez	Exec	289
David Bradley	Director	8
Wanida Benshoof	Manager	0
Kevin Brown	Manager	0
Mary Dempsey	Manager	0
Terry Eminhizer	Manager	0
Mary Gibson	Manager	0
Sariya Harnpadoungsataya	Manager	0
Jill Williams	Manager	0
John Wood	Manager	0
Terri Duffy	Director	13
Roberto Tamburello	Manager	12
Ovidiu Cracium	Supervisor	2
Thierry D'Hers	Peon	0
Janice Galvin	Peon	0
Gail Erickson	Supervisor	0
Jossef Goldberg	Supervisor	0
Dylan Miller	Supervisor	3
Diane Margheim	Peon	0
Gigi Matthew	Peon	0
Michael Raheem	Peon	0
Sharon Salavaria	Supervisor	0

Figure 6-44

Subreports

This feature is largely borrowed from Microsoft Access. Essentially, a subreport is a stand-alone report that is embedded into another report. Using parameters, you can link the contents of a subreport to the main report.

There are some limitations to the content and formatting that can be rendered within a subreport. For example, a multicolumn report may not be possible within a subreport (depending upon the rendering format used). If you plan to use multiple columns in a subreport, test your report with the rendering formats you plan to use.

There are generally two uses for subreports, which include embedding one instance of a separate report into the body of another report with an unassociated data source. The other scenario involves using the subreport as a custom data region to display repeated master and detail records in the body of the main report. From a design standpoint, this makes perfect sense. Using a subreport allows you to separate two related data sets and perhaps even data sources, linked in the same way that you would join tables in a SQL query. It allows you to reuse an existing report so that you don't have to redesign functionality you've already created. However, there may be a significant downside. If the master report will consume more than just a few records, this means that the subreport must execute its query and render the content many times. For large volumes of data, this can prove to be a very inefficient solution. Carefully reconsider the use of subreports with large result sets. It may be more efficient to construct one larger report with a more complex query and multiple levels of grouping rather than assume the cost of executing a query many times. I rarely use subreports in standard reporting scenarios. If I do, the main report is limited to one or a few records.

A subreport can be linked to the main report using a correlated parameter and field reference, so that it can be used like a data region, but this is not essential. A subreport could be used to show aggregated values unrelated to groupings or content in the rest of the report.

Creating a subreport is like creating any other report. You simply create a report and then add it to another report as a subreport. If you intend to use the main report and subreport as a *Master/Detail* view of related data, the subreport should expose a parameter that can be *linked* to a field in the main report. In the following walk-through, you'll build a simple report that lists products and exposes a subcategory parameter. The main report will list categories and subcategories and the product list report will then be used as a data region, like a table or list as in previous examples.

The first report, which will be used as a subreport, will include a list of products. The second report will consist of the product categories and subcategories and will contain the subreport, which renders a list of products for each subcategory.

1. Add a new report to your project called Product List Subreport.

2. On the Data tab, create a new data set called Product_List using the AdventureWorks database. Add the Product table to the data set and select the Name, StandardPrice, and ProductSubCategoryID columns to be output by the query. Sort the records by the Name column in ascending order.

3. Create a parameter for the ProductSubCategoryID column called @SubCategoryID. The easiest way to do this is to move the cursor to the grid column labeled Criteria on the row for the ProductSubCategoryID table column and type **= @SubCategoryID**. The SQL for the data set should look like this:

```
SELECT      Name
          , ListPrice
          , ProductSubcategoryID
FROM        Production.Product
WHERE       ProductSubcategoryID = @SubCategoryID
ORDER BY    Name
```

4. On the Layout tab, add a List item to the report.

5. From the Datasets window, drag the Name and ListPrice fields into the List item and arrange them horizontally to form a row with sufficient room for these values. Resize the list so that it is the height of one text box and about 4 inches wide. Place two text boxes to be column headings above the list and set their values to read Product and Price, as shown in Figure 6-45. Arrange the text boxes and the items in the list to line up, right justify the Price heading text box, and then resize the report body background to fit closely around the list.

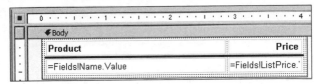

Figure 6-45

6. To dress up the report a bit, set the top border style for the list to be solid (in the Properties window, select BorderStyle|Top|Solid). Also set the Format property for the ListPrice text box to C2.

7. Add a new report called Product List Categories and create a new data set Product_List_Categories using the ProductCategory and ProductSubCategory tables. Leave the join in place, alias the name columns from both the tables, and sort by first the category name and then the subcategory name. The resulting SQL expression should look like the following:

```
SELECT      Production.ProductCategory.Name AS ProductCategory
          , Production.ProductSubcategory.Name AS SubCategory
          , Production.ProductSubcategory.ProductSubcategoryID
FROM        Production.ProductCategory
            INNER JOIN Production.ProductSubcategory
            ON Production.ProductCategory.ProductCategoryID
               = Production.ProductSubcategory.ProductCategoryID
ORDER BY    Production.ProductCategory.Name
          , Production.ProductSubcategory.Name
```

8. On the Layout tab, add a text box to be used for the report heading and a List item. Drag and drop the ProductCategory and SubCategory fields from the Dataset window into the list data region, with the Product_List_Categories data set selected. Size the list item to be about 6.5 inches wide by 1.5 inches tall (about 13 cm by 4 cm). Arrange the two new text boxes in two rows and staggered in the top area of the list. I'm going for roughly the same look as the previous report examples using two group headings.

9. Select the ProductCategory text box, and then find the HideDuplicates property in the Properties window. Change this property value to be True.

10. From the Solution Explorer, drag and drop the Product List Subreport report into the list data region below the text boxes. Resize the new subreport to be about the same size as the subreport in the designer. Mine is about 4.5 inches wide and 0.75 inches tall (7 cm by 2 cm) and place it under the second text box. Resize the list around the contained items. The report should be similar to Figure 6-46.

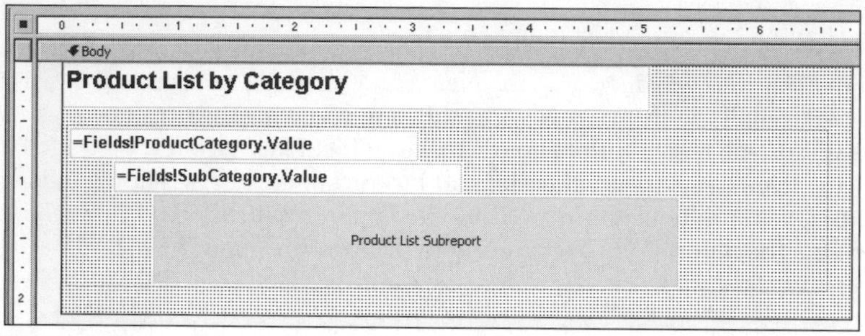

Figure 6-46

You need to use the subcategory parameter to associate the product list subreport with the outer list data region. Right-click the subreport and select Properties. In the Subreport Properties dialog, switch to the Parameters tab and select the `SubCategoryID` parameter in the first row of the parameters box. In the Parameter Value column, select `=Fields!ProductSubCategoryID.Value` in the drop-down list. See Figure 6-47.

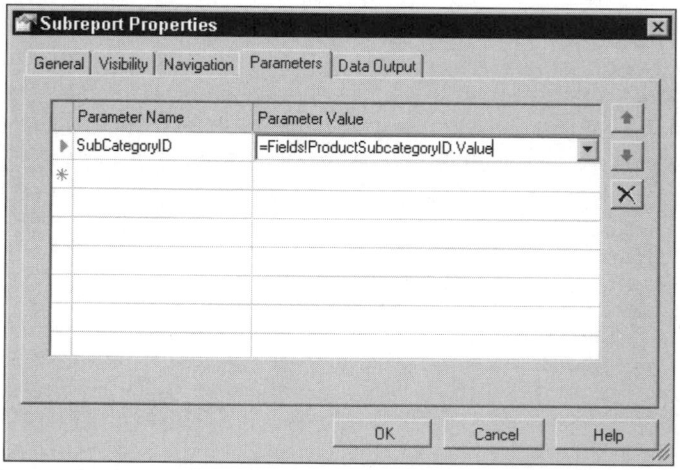

Figure 6-47

This completes the report design. The size and placement of the items in your subreport and the main report will likely be a little different from mine. Using lists and subreports typically makes the design process more ad hoc and artful than when using more rigid tables. Go back and check the size and placement of items so that they fit neatly within the subreport space. This often takes a few iterations of preview and layout to make the appropriate adjustments.

At this point, you should be able to preview the report and see the Category and Subcategory names followed by a list of related products, as shown in Figure 6-48.

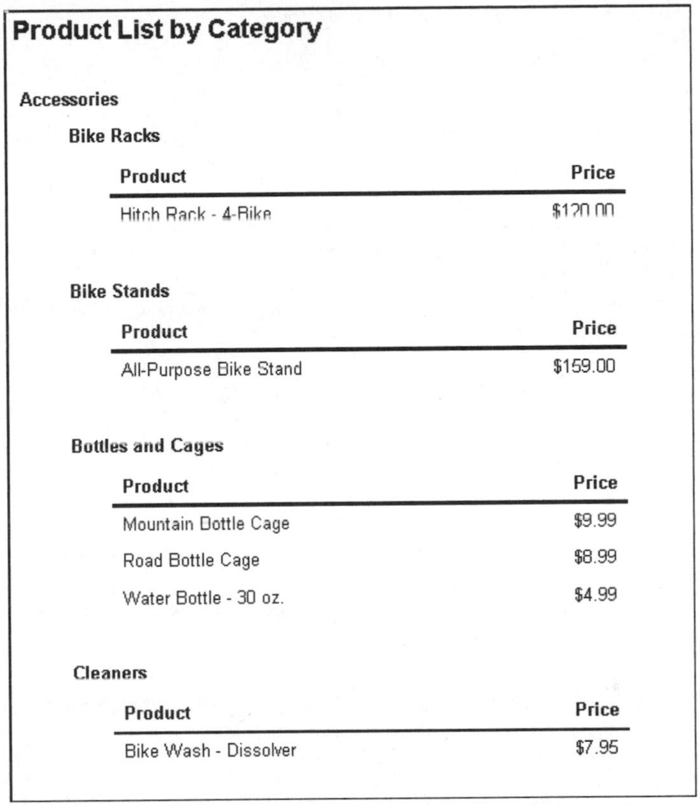

Product List by Category

Accessories

    Bike Racks

Product	Price
Hitch Rack - 4-Bike	$120.00

    Bike Stands

Product	Price
All-Purpose Bike Stand	$159.00

    Bottles and Cages

Product	Price
Mountain Bottle Cage	$9.99
Road Bottle Cage	$8.99
Water Bottle - 30 oz.	$4.99

    Cleaners

Product	Price
Bike Wash - Dissolver	$7.95

Figure 6-48

Designing Matrix Reports

As you saw in Chapter 4, a matrix is a cross-tab or pivot table. Just as the rows of a table are generated for the rows of the underlying result set, a matrix does the same thing for columns. Matrix data should have at least two groups with intersecting aggregate values. One group drives rows, while the other group creates columns. In the following example, my query returns sales order summaries for customers in different geographies, across different periods of time, and for customers who have different occupations. The geographical and time information (in multiple, related groups) will be displayed as rows, and the occupations will be columns. To make things even more interesting, I'll include two data points at each intersection: the order quantity and the average sales amount.

Pivot table queries can be quite complex and should use data sources optimized to handle large volumes of source data. SQL Server Analysis Services is ideal for these types of reporting solutions. My intention is to demonstrate the mechanics of the matrix report design rather than the complexity of the query. To follow along with this demonstration, the following T-SQL expression may be used:

```
SELECT      DimSalesTerritory.SalesTerritoryCountry AS Country
          , DimTime.CalendarYear AS Calendar_Year
          , DimTime.CalendarQuarter AS Calendar_Quarter
          , DimTime.EnglishMonthName AS Month
          , DimCustomer.EnglishOccupation AS Occupation
          , SUM(FactInternetSales.OrderQuantity) AS Order_Quantity
          , AVG(FactInternetSales.SalesAmount) AS Avg_Sales_Amount
          , SUM((FactInternetSales.SalesAmount - FactInternetSales.TotalProductCost)
                * FactInternetSales.OrderQuantity) AS Gross_Profit_Margin
FROM        DimSalesTerritory INNER JOIN FactInternetSales
              ON DimSalesTerritory.SalesTerritoryKey =
              FactInternetSales.SalesTerritoryKey
            INNER JOIN DimTime ON FactInternetSales.ShipDateKey = DimTime.TimeKey
            INNER JOIN DimCustomer
              ON FactInternetSales.CustomerKey = DimCustomer.CustomerKey
GROUP BY DimSalesTerritory.SalesTerritoryCountry
          , DimTime.CalendarYear, DimTime.CalendarQuarter
          , DimTime.EnglishMonthName, DimCustomer.EnglishOccupation
          , DimTime.MonthNumberOfYear
ORDER BY Country, Calendar_Year, Calendar_Quarter
          , DimTime.MonthNumberOfYear, Occupation
```

For simplicity, I've left the filter parameters out of the query. You'll see references to the data range parameter to show you what a finished report might look like. This query returns sorted values on three separate axes: Country, Time (Year, Quarter, and Month), and Occupation. These are used to define row and column groups. Figure 6-49 shows the basic report in the designer with the available fields in the Dataset window. When the matrix is placed in the report body, it has three drop zones.

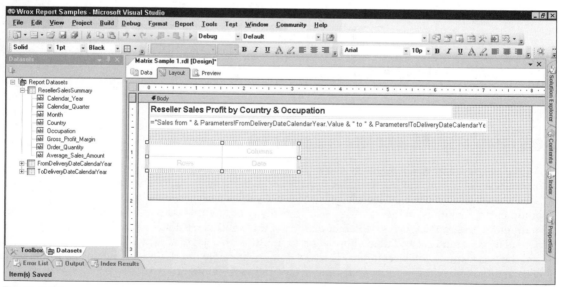

Figure 6-49

From the Dataset window, I drop my column axis field into the Columns drop zone. You can see in Figure 6-50 that the field reference doesn't use an aggregate function like First() or Sum(). This is because a group was automatically generated to support this column. You'll see the groups after all of the fields are placed into cells. Figures 6-50 through 6-54 show each of the fields added to a cell.

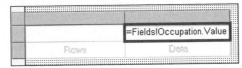

Figure 6-50

Now for the first row field: the Country.

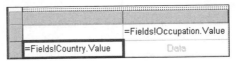

Figure 6-51

For each country, a group will display repeated date-related information. I drop the Calendar_Year field to the right of the Country. Note that a light-colored bar on the right edge of the existing text box indicates that a new group will be added.

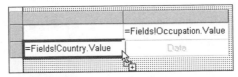

Figure 6-52

This pattern is repeated for the remaining fields. The row hierarchy now contains the Country, Calendar_Year, Calendar_Quarter, and Month fields. The Order_Quantity field is dropped into the center (or pivot) cell. Note that this field will be aggregated using the Sum() function by default. The expression can be changed to use any appropriate aggregation (such as Avg() or Count()),

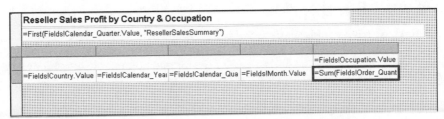

Figure 6-53

If another field is dropped into the pivot cell, it may be placed to either side of the existing text box. This adds an additional set of column headers to manage the two levels of column groups.

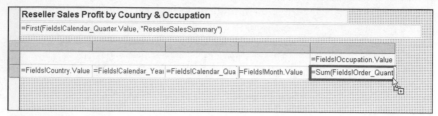

Figure 6-54

Figure 6-55 shows an unattractive report, but it contains data at the right intersect points. This is easily remedied by setting properties to adjust the text alignment (right-justify column headers over numeric and date values) and set borders and background colors. Different shades of gray borders and backgrounds will accent the data and provide just enough visual separation without being distracting.

Reseller Sales Profit by Country & Occupation

Q3 CY 2001

				Clerical		Management		Manual		Professional		Skille
				Qty	Avg Amt	Qty	Avg Amt	Qty	Avg Amt	Qty	Avg Amt	
Australia	CY 2001	Q3 CY 2001	July 2001	594	8129.732232 6087	594	9349.192067 5	594	8696.922853 48837	594	7479.353654	
			August 2001	1566	13879.85497 95455	1566	13723.90155 2809	1566	15461.10428 10127	1566	13571.41375 77778	
			September 2001	1236	15004.00317 65625	1236	12003.20254 125	1236	15741.90497 21311	1236	11855.01485 55556	
		Q4 CY 2001	October 2001	875	11957.13225 09804	875	11505.91971 32075	875	11727.1874	875	10514.03008 27586	
			November 2001	2352	20024.01358 96907	2352	18323.86149 24528	2352	18857.56619 61165	2352	17342.22605 53571	
			December 2001	1808	21239.43620 29412	1808	16991.54896 23529	1808	20059.46752 5	1808	16991.54896 23529	
	CY 2002	Q1 CY 2002	January 2002	613	10986.73722 2	613	9987.942929 09091	613	11688.01832 12766	613	8583.388454 6875	
			February 2002	1696	19335.21157 5	1696	18456.33832 15909	1696	19806.80210 12105	1696	15038.49789 16667	

Figure 6-55

Subtotals and Summaries

Each row group may have a subtotal or summary added when the group value changes. To evoke a subtotal on any group (rows or columns), right-click the group header cell and select Subtotal from the pop-up menu (see Figure 6-56). This adds a header cell for the subtotal row or column. These cells are indicated with a small green triangle in the upper-right corner.

A subtotal will render header and data cells, but the data cells are not displayed in the designer. By default, the style of the corresponding data cells is the same as the main intercept cell(s) but may be modified using the Properties window. Selecting the cell (using a standard left-click in the cell) selects the text box in the header cell, and properties may be modified as in any other text box. To select the subtotal properties, click the green triangle in the corner. Figure 6-57 shows the right-click menu for the subtotal selection, which has fewer menu choices than the text box.

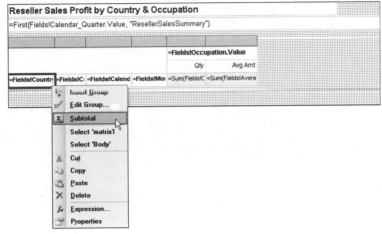

Figure 6-56

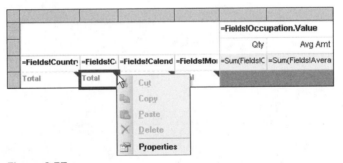

Figure 6-57

Verify that the subtotal has been selected by checking the object name drop-down list on the Properties window. Figure 6-58 shows the subtotal properties for the selected group. These properties affect only the data cells for this subtotal row.

Drill-Down in a Matrix

Setting up drill-down functionality for a matrix is similar to a table. Each group may be hidden and then expanded or collapsed (shown or hidden) based on a designated toggle item. Start at the deepest group level in the hierarchy. In Figure 6-59, I right-click the Month group header text box and select Edit Group to modify the group properties.

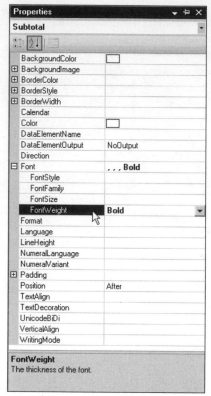

Figure 6-58

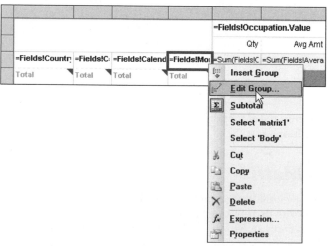

Figure 6-59

In the Grouping and Sorting Properties dialog (shown in Figure 6-60), I use the Visibility tab to set the group's `Hidden` property and the toggle item for the parent group. In my experience, this drop-down list may not show all available items as it should, assuming that the groups are set up correctly. Select or type the name of the preceding group header text box.

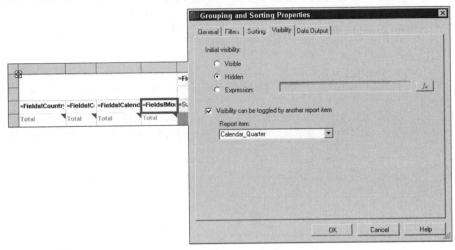

Figure 6-60

Figure 6-61 shows the finished matrix report with customer occupations across the top and the country and time period hierarchy along the left side. The drill-down features enable users to view aggregated totals for each country and then the year, quarter, and month. Under each occupation, a column displays the total number of orders and the average amount for all orders.

Reseller Sales Profit by Country & Occupation
Q3 CY 2001

			Clerical		Management		Manual		Professional		Skilled Manual	
			Qty	Avg Amt	Qty	Avg Amt	Qty	Avg Amt	Qty	Avg Amt	Qty	Avg Amt
Australia	Total		145,024	$494,346	145,024	$434,515	145,024	$512,973	145,024	$382,919	145,024	$450,817
Canada	CY 2001	Total	8,431	$101,669	8,431	$98,877	8,431	$101,883	8,431	$97,600	8,431	$97,733
	CY 2002	Total	42,633	$210,367	42,627	$211,126	42,626	$214,643	42,642	$197,603	42,655	$192,570
	CY 2003	Q1 CY 2003 Total	9,058	$39,714	9,058	$39,015	9,058	$39,951	9,058	$38,412	9,058	$37,542
		Q2 CY 2003 Total	14,136	$49,041	14,136	$48,936	14,136	$49,422	14,136	$46,815	14,136	$46,964
		Q3 CY 2003 July 2003	6,230	$18,709	6,230	$17,587	6,230	$18,709	6,230	$18,131	6,230	$16,910
		August 2003	10,038	$14,840	10,038	$13,125	10,038	$15,877	10,038	$12,054	10,038	$11,908
		September 2003	8,466	$12,349	8,466	$11,544	8,466	$14,023	8,466	$9,696	8,466	$9,968
		Total	24,734	$45,898	24,734	$42,256	24,734	$48,609	24,734	$39,880	24,734	$38,786
		Q4 CY 2003 Total	17,772	$32,762	17,772	$31,406	17,772	$39,234	17,772	$25,156	17,772	$24,777
		Total	65,700	$167,415	65,700	$161,614	65,700	$177,216	65,700	$150,263	65,700	$148,069
	CY 2004	Total	28,267	$60,945	28,267	$53,841	28,267	$71,810	28,267	$43,359	28,267	$44,430
	Total		145,031	$540,396	145,025	$525,458	145,024	$565,552	145,040	$488,826	145,053	$482,802
France	Total		146,737	$502,219	145,322	$555,651	146,074	$498,918	145,914	$535,512	145,464	$549,701
Germany	Total		146,815	$499,045	145,432	$552,315	146,740	$505,658	145,992	$531,477	145,532	$548,180
United Kingdom	Total		145,033	$486,394	145,024	$541,479	145,024	$497,623	145,024	$525,229	145,026	$527,418
United States	Total		146,503	$507,502	149,650	$461,555	146,128	$564,874	152,531	$398,527	151,832	$405,631

Figure 6-61

Chart Reports

The charting capabilities in Reporting Services are quite impressive and as easy to use as those in Excel or Access, and, in many ways, they are more powerful. The charting components are based on Dundas Charts, developed by Dundas Software. Dundas provides a suite of ASP.NET charting components that have been available for .NET developers for several years. A chart item is based on a data set just like any data range and can use groups, query parameters, and filters in much the same way as a table, list, or matrix.

So, why use a chart to present data? After all, isn't a chart simply a graphical representation of a group of numbers? Wouldn't rows and columns of values be just as effective? To fully understand the impact and perhaps the importance of presenting information graphically, it's important to understand the needs and objective of the report reader and how the information will be used. In Chapter 7, I discuss lessons learned about data presentation. For now, just consider some basic observations about report usage and the people who read these reports.

Analyzing information is usually a process rather than a single event. Regardless of the type of business or industry, users typically approach business information in stages. First it's important to consider the different roles of users in order to understand their respective stages of information discovery. Some may have a specific task they perform and the information they use will be focused on that task. Other users may be leaders and decision makers in various capacities, whose objectives are more broad and complex.

Consider the CEO whose first objective is often to find out whether there are any disasters to address. This executive isn't concerned with specific details or even short-term trends but in getting a meter reading on the business. After the CEO learns that there are no fires to put out, the next objective is to get a broad view of sales and productivity trends for different areas of the business. Typically, one of the most important questions addressed by effective business reporting solutions is How are we doing? Depending on the size and type of business, a high-level leader may also be interested in understanding some of the lower-level details regarding operations, production, sales, and other business specifics. Executives typically benefit from dashboard-type reports that provide high-level status information they use to take periodic business meter readings. Executives also need access to more detailed information to be used for occasional follow-up but will usually get their information from others.

Contrast the perspective of the CEO with the operational business leaders: the sales manager, marketing director, or production manager. These people need to have their finger on the pulse of specific business areas. They will be concerned with short- and long-term trends in their respective areas of responsibility. Questions to be answered for operational leaders might be What products or campaigns are successful and which are not? and Who are my top (and bottom) producers? Unlike the CEO, these individuals must be connected with every aspect of their microorganization and must be armed with detailed, accurate information so that they can make proactive decisions.

Consider that some users may need to have information spoon-fed to them in a specific format, while others may want to explore data, pivoting, sorting, and grouping it themselves.

Chart Types

Some of the more common chart types (like Column, Bar, Line, and Area) can be used for different views of the same data. Pie and doughnut charts present a more simplified view and work well with fewer dimensions. Other charts are more specialized and may be appropriate for multi-value data points, range values, and variances.

When a report is viewed, the chart output is rendered to a bitmap and streamed to a PNG-type image. This image is then linked or embedded in the report. There are nine general chart types available, and these are described in the following table.

Chart Type	Description
Column	This is a classic vertical bar chart with columns representing values along the Y-axis. Like-valued items along the X-axis are grouped together, and bars representing the same X-axis values in each group have the same colors or patterns. Series values may also be grouped and subgrouped. Columns can have point labels and the colored bars may be labeled using a legend. Columns may be arranged side by side (along the X-axis) or in front of one another (along the Z-axis.) Columns may appear to be extruded from their base using a rectangular or circular (cylindrical) shape.
Bar	This functionality is the same as a column chart turned 90 degrees. It has the advantage of more accurately depicting value comparisons for layouts where you have more available horizontal space.
Area	Like a column chart with a trend line drawn from one point to the next in the series. This type of chart is appropriate for a series of values that tend to progress over a relatively even plane that describes a "level," "up," or "down" trend. It is not at all appropriate for series values that tend to jump around. The solid shading of the charted area depicts a volume of data values.
Line	Like the area chart, but the area of the charted area isn't filled. This type of chart is useful for comparing multiple series (along the Z-axis) without obscuring trend lines behind a series.
Pie	The classic pie chart is an excellent tool for comparing relative values. Unlike bar, column, line, and area charts, the aggregate value isn't quantified. Users understand pie charts because they put comparative values into a proportional context and can drive quick decision support at a glance. Pie chart views can be exploded to visually separate each slide.
Doughnut	A doughnut is a pie with a hole in the middle. A three-dimensional doughnut rendering may expose smaller slices more clearly than a pie chart since each slice has four sides rather than three.
Scatter	Plots several points in a range (both X and Y) to show trends and variations in value. The result is more like a cloudy band of points rather than a specific aggregated point or line.
Bubble	This chart is a technique for charting points on three dimensions. Values are plotted using different-sized points, or bubbles, on a two-dimensional grid. The size of the bubble indicates the related value along the Z-axis.
Stock	This chart plots values vertically like a column chart. For each item along the Y-axis series, a vertical line indicates a start and end value for the range. A tick mark in the line can indicate a significant value in that range or an aggregation of the range. This type of chart is useful for showing trading stocks with opening, closing, and purchase values; wholesale, retail, and discount prices; and the like.

Column Charts

The following chart in Figure 6-62 is an example of a simple column chart. The X-axis series values are product categories, and the Y-axis values represent annual sales revenue. In this view, the legend at the bottom indicates the X-axis series values. Several visual elements can be modified to alter the color, shading, borders, text, formatting, labeling, and value placement. This figure shows generally default property settings.

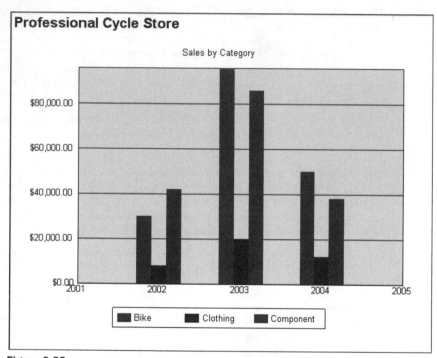

Figure 6-62

Figure 6-63 shows the same chart with 3-D modeling.

3-D modeling may be used to show data in a more interesting presentation, but this can also be distracting and less effective for analysis. Figure 6-64 shows a more extreme 3-D view of the same data with perspective. I've made a point to set this chart up with a fairly extreme 3-D and perspective view, just to show you what can be done. This type of view tends to distort the values, and the clustering (stacking the columns along the Z-axis) can hide some columns from view.

You have control over several 3-D properties to generate more realistic representation of the chart data. Be careful to maintain the appropriate balance between artistry and accuracy. Notice that it's difficult to quantify and distinguish the difference in height between the front-right column and the rightmost column in the back. The degree to which it makes sense to use these features will depend largely on the purpose of the chart. Is it sufficient to demonstrate that one data point is less than or greater than another, or do these points need to be strictly measurable? This type of view can be effective for making an impact, but a flatter view is usually more appropriate to maintain accuracy.

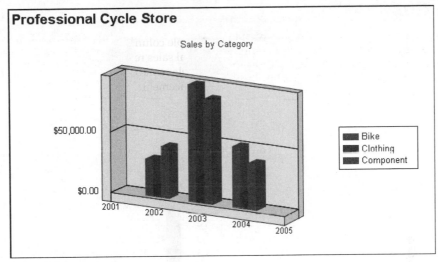

Figure 6-63

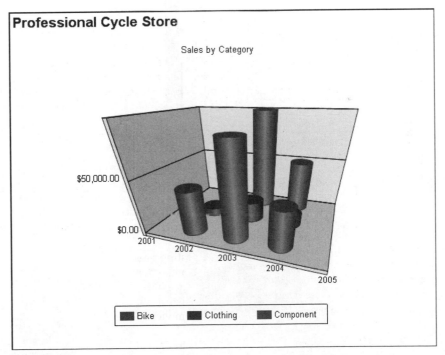

Figure 6-64

Figure 6-65 is a 3-D view with cylindrical columns arranged in a clustered formation. When used correctly and in appropriate moderation, this 3-D chart adds a sense of realism while remaining readable.

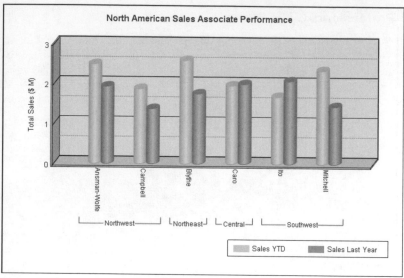

Figure 6-65

Stacked Charts

Column and bar charts may have their bars stacked. This appends the different-colored bars (for a like series value) into one bar with multiple colored bands. This may be an appropriate method for showing the accumulation of all values within the series point. The individual values are displayed in a different color as a percentage of the bar. In essence, each bar becomes like a linear pie chart (see Figure 6-66).

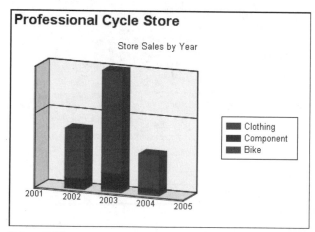

Figure 6-66

To emphasize the proportion of like values rather than the comparative accumulation, the 100% stacked view (not pictured) will make all of the bars in the chart the same length rather than depicting the sum of all the values in the bar.

Area and Line Charts

An area chart plots the values of each point and then draws a line from point to point to show the progression of values along the series. This is an effective method for analyzing trends and works well when values tend to climb, decline, or remain level in the series. This type of chart is accurate when data exists for all category values on the X-axis. It typically doesn't work well to express a series of values that are not in a relatively uniform plane. Figure 6-67 is an example of an area chart.

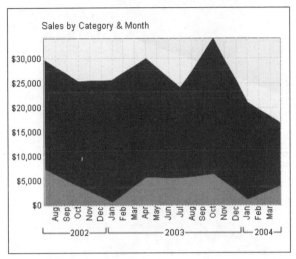

Figure 6-67

The line chart is a variation of an area chart using a line or ribbon rather than a solid area. The line chart works better than the area chart for comparing multiple categories for a series of values because one layer may obscure another in the area view. In the preceding example, the area chart works because values are sorted in a way that larger values are in the background and other points in the foreground are smaller; the trend decreases back to front.

Pie Charts

A pie chart is an excellent tool for comparing proportional values. Display options for a pie chart include exploded and 3-D views. The 3-D pie chart in Figure 6-68 clearly shows that Touring Bike sales are a small percentage, around 10% of total Bike Sales, and that Road Bike sales account for about half of the total sales. I call this piece "PacMan Gets a Root Canal."

A doughnut chart is a pie chart with a hole in it. This is a rather profound concept, isn't it? Actually, in cases where there may be several smaller slices, the donut chart can be a little easier to read and provides a little variation on an age-old chart theme. The chart shown in Figure 6-69 is the same as the previous chart without the exploded view and a legend showing the series labels.

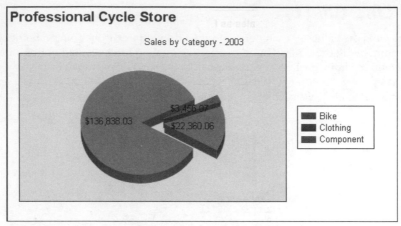

Figure 6-68

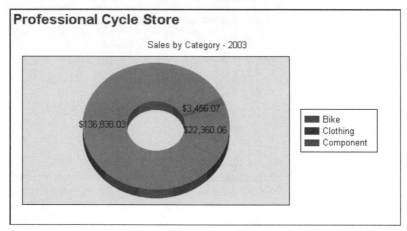

Figure 6-69

Pie charts are traditionally used to show multiple slices representing their data point percentage of the whole. In the usual form, data values grouped on another axis will result in slices automatically generated with the same style settings and contrasting colors from a standard color pallet. There are eight color pallets provided in the designer. Sometimes data may need to be presented as a percentage value or you may simply have two values and need to express one as a percentage of the other. This is possible by adding multiple Value groups to the chart with each representing a specific slice. In Figure 6-70 , only two values are presented. In this example, values in the data set exist for Bike Sales and Total Sales. Using an expression or a calculation in the query, subtracting Bike Sales from the total provides a value for Other Sales.

As you can see in Figure 6-71, I created a specific group for these two values. Another advantage of using this approach is that I can set the color and styles for each slice independently. You'll take a closer look at this and similar techniques in Chapter 7.

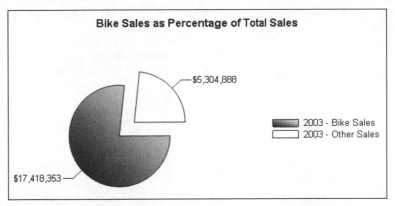

Figure 6-70

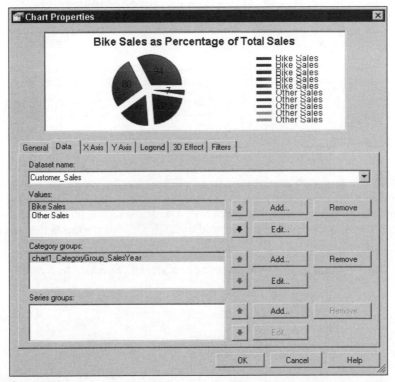

Figure 6-71

Bubble Charts

Bubble charts are essentially a point plotted in a grid representing three dimensions. The value of the Z-axis is expressed by the size of the bubble. Imagine that the bubble exists in a 3-D plane and will appear large if it is closer to you. Actually the "bubble" can be a circle, square, triangle, diamond, or cross shape.

This also means that a combination of shapes may be used to represent different data elements in the same chart space.

In Figure 6-72, employees' vacation and sick hours are plotted above their names. The number of vacation hours is represented by the bubble's vertical distance from the 0 baseline, and the number of sick hours is represented by the size of the bubble.

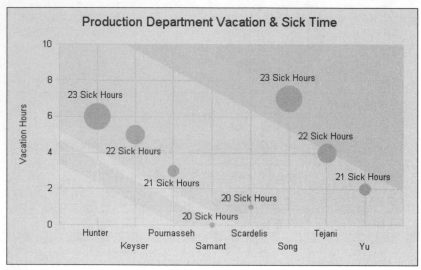

Figure 6-72

The chart shown in Figure 6-73 is a stock chart. As you see, for each product, a line is plotted to span a range of values and has a large tick mark to indicate the position of a value within the high–low range. In this example, the beginning (lowest point of the line) of the range is the standard cost of the product. The tick mark represents the last receipt cost, and the high range of the line is the list price.

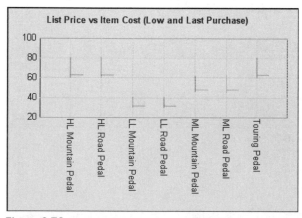

Figure 6-73

The Anatomy of a Chart

There is typically a lot of detail work involved in chart design and many properties to manage. Figure 6-74 shows the major property groups for charts. Although some charts have a few unique properties and some may not support all, generally these are shared across all chart types.

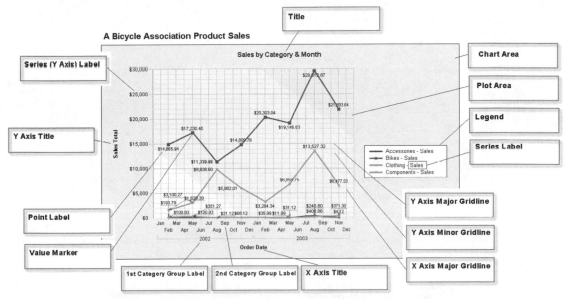

Figure 6-74

After the chart is placed in the report body, fields may be dragged from the Dataset window directly onto the chart design surface. At minimum, a chart should have one aggregated field for the value and one grouped field for the category. The category and series groups represent the X- and Y-axis in bar, column, line, area, and point charts.

Figure 6-75 shows four fields dropped onto this line chart in the designer. The ExtendedAmountSum field will provide the data point values. Distinct ProductCategory values will group data along the series. Two fields were dropped onto the chart category area. This creates two related groups on this axis.

Figure 6-76 shows the same chart configuration on the Data tab of the Chart Properties dialog. The chart groups created using the previous method may be modified here. Specific properties related to the category group(s) are accessible from the Grouping and Sorting dialog after you click the Edit button in this section.

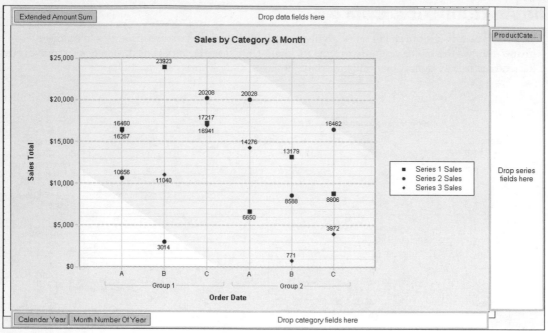

Figure 6-75

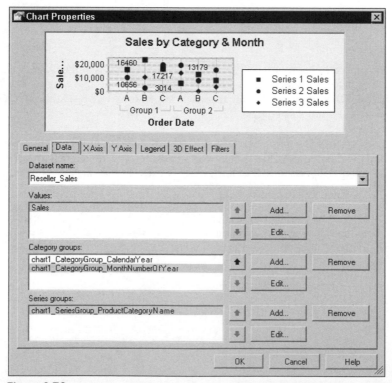

Figure 6-76

Chart Report Exercise

To get you started creating charts, we will create a column chart using sales information from AdventureWorks. This chart will include an added feature with a category group that shows sales associates grouped by their regions.

I will provide the data set SQL expression and the steps to set up the chart. You will need to take care of the standard report design details, which we covered in the earlier sections of this chapter.

To demonstrate a column or bar chart, we need a simple query with values to plot on two axes. We will also add a third value to categorize or group another set of values. To get started, add this SQL expression in a new data set using the AdventureWorks database:

```
SELECT      Person.Contact.LastName AS EmployeeName
          , Sales.SalesPerson.SalesYTD, Sales.SalesTerritory.Name AS TerritoryName
          , Sales.SalesPerson.SalesLastYear
FROM        HumanResources.Employee INNER JOIN Sales.SalesPerson
              ON Sales.SalesPerson.SalesPersonID = HumanResources.Employee.EmployeeID
            INNER JOIN Sales.SalesTerritory
              ON Sales.SalesPerson.TerritoryID = Sales.SalesTerritory.TerritoryID
            INNER JOIN Person.Contact
              ON HumanResources.Employee.ContactID = Person.Contact.ContactID
WHERE       (Sales.SalesPerson.SalesYTD > 0)
              AND (Sales.SalesPerson.SalesLastYear > 0)
              AND (Sales.SalesPerson.TerritoryID < 5)
ORDER BY Sales.SalesPerson.TerritoryID
```

Add a new Chart item to the report and resize it to fill an area about 7 inches (18 cm) wide by 5 inches (12 cm) tall.

Right-click the chart item in the report designer and select Column⇨Simple Column for the Chart Type.

When you drag fields onto the report item, drop zones are displayed in areas above, to the right, and below the report. These areas will change depending on the report type. Show the Fields window and drag these fields to these drop locations:

Field	Drop Zone Label
Sales YTD Sales Last Year	*Drop data fields here* (above the chart)
TerritoryName EmployeeName	*Drop category fields here* (below the chart)

Verify your results using this example. It's important that the fields are dropped in the order you see them in Figure 6-77. However, you can switch them later in the properties dialog.

Right-click the chart again, and select Properties to display the Chart Properties dialog.

On the General tab, give the chart the name SalesPerformanceChart and for the title, enter North American Sales Associate Performance (see Figure 6-78).

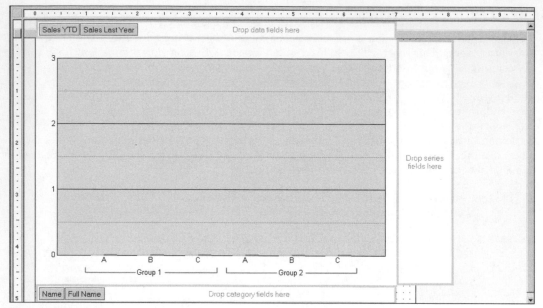

Figure 6-77

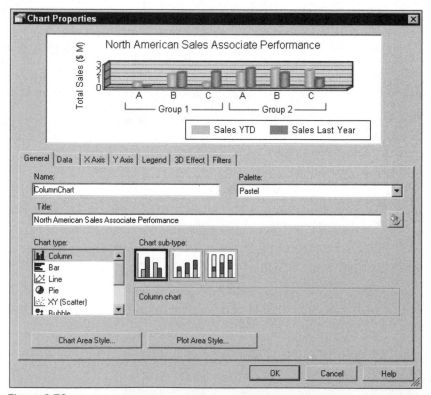

Figure 6-78

Note that the preview chart image on this dialog is the result of all completed property settings. I've made it a point to include it so that you get an idea about what we're trying to do. Yours should look similar to this when we've completed all of the settings.

On the Data tab, you should see your data set name and the fields you specified in the Values: list. The two items in the Category groups: list were auto-generated when you dropped the two fields into the category area.

Switch to the X Axis tab and check your settings against those in Figure 6-79.

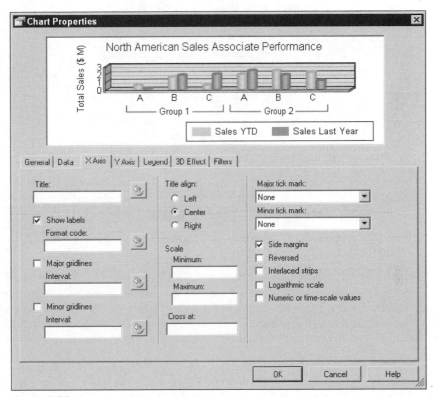

Figure 6-79

You're going to make several changes on the Y Axis tab. The title will be displayed along the left side of the chart as you see in the preview image. Set the title to Total Sales ($ M). For the Scale, set Minimum to 0 and Maximum to 3000000 and set the Format code·to ,,0 to indicate that this is to be a numerical value using comma thousand separators. By providing a range of values, the tallest column will be shorter that the top of the chart (unless it exceeds the maximum value.)

For the Gridlines, you want to show major and minor ticks using these specified values (see Figure 6-80).

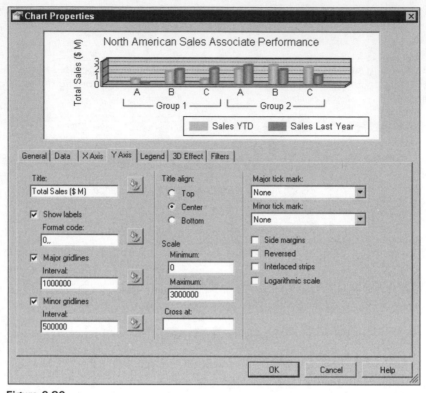

Figure 6-80

On the Legend tab, use properties to place the legend at the bottom, in the lower-right corner of the chart with labels arranged in a row (short and wide), as in Figure 6-81 Use Display Legend Inside Plot Area to maximize the size of the chart that works well on pie and doughnut charts that have free corner space. This, however, will often cause the legend to overlap the chart area for some types of charts.

Use the 3-D property settings at your discretion (see Figure 6-82). You often have to play with these settings to achieve the right balance between an effective 3-D rendering and an accurate display of data.

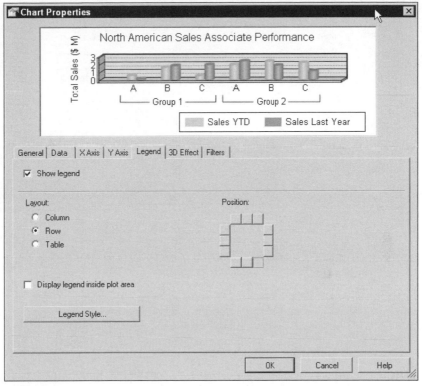

Figure 6-81

Realistic shading makes the 3-D chart appear to have a light source that casts shadows on the borders. The Orthographic property causes the 3-D effect to be slightly exaggerated. Clustered causes rows or columns at the same series point to be arranged in front of one another rather than side by side. Cylinder bars or columns are less traditional than block-style bars.

Click OK on the Properties dialog, save the report, and select the Preview tab to see the completed chart.

As you see in the example in Figure 6-83, having two related groups on the X-axis causes set lines to show the groupings, and two different values are plotted at each X-axis point using different-colored, cylindrical columns.

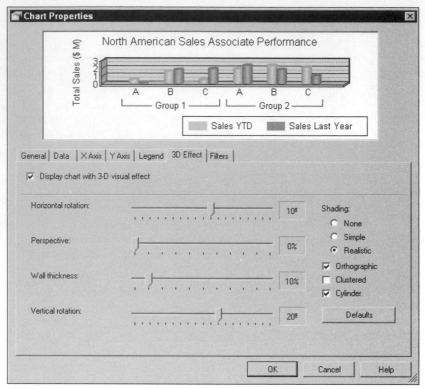

Figure 6-82

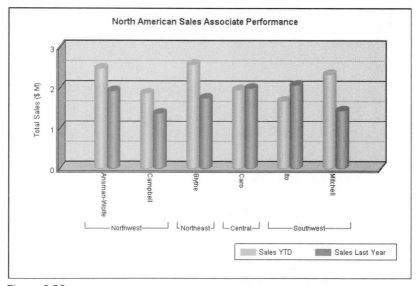

Figure 6-83

Custom Fields

Custom fields can be added to any report and can include expressions, calculations, and text manipulation. This might be similar in functionality to alias columns in a query or *view*, but the calculation or expression is performed on the report server after data has been retrieved from the database. Custom field expressions can also use Reporting Services global variables and functions that may not be available in a SQL expression.

Use the Dataset window in the Report Designer to select the data set you want to use. Right-click in the Dataset window, and select Add (see Figure 6-84).

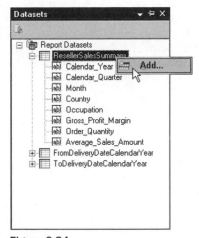

Figure 6-84

In the Add New Field dialog, enter the name you would like to use for the custom field. If you want to use an expression, select the `Calculated field` property, as shown in Figure 6-85, and then use the builder button to create the expression.

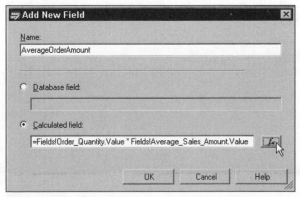

Figure 6-85

You may use the expression button to invoke the Expression Builder to use any functionality available within the design environment in addition to the database fields exposed by the data set query. These calculations will be performed on the report server rather than the database server.

Conditional Expressions

You've seen some simple examples of using expressions to set item values and properties in simple ways.

Let's take a look at one more example of a conditional expression, and then I'll discuss using program code to handle more complex situations. This will be a simple list of products with current inventory values. The Product table in the AdventureWorks database contains a ReorderPoint value that informs stock managers when they need to reorder products. If the inventory count falls below this value, you can set the inventory quantity to appear in red next to the name. Using a conditional expression in this manner is similar to using conditional formatting in Excel.

The following example will use a data set with the SQL expression:

```
SELECT     Product.Name, Product.ReorderPoint, ProductInventory.Quantity
FROM       ProductInventory INNER JOIN Product
           ON ProductInventory.ProductID = Product.ProductID
ORDER BY   Product.Name
```

A table bound to this data set has three columns: Name, ReorderPoint, and Quantity. On the Quantity text box in the detail row of the table, the `Color` property is set to an expression containing conditional logic instead of to a set value. You can use the Expression Builder or just type this expression into the properties window under the `Color` property:

```
=IIF( Fields!Quantity.Value < Fields!ReorderPoint.Value, "Red", "Black" )
```

I've also done the same thing with the `Font|FontWeight` property so that if the inventory quantity for a product is below the reorder point value, the quantity is displayed in both red and bold text.

Switch to the Preview tab to check the results; these should be as shown in Figure 6-86.

IIF() Is Your Friend

Even if you're not a programmer, learning a few, simple Visual Basic commands and functions will prove to be very valuable and will likely meet the vast majority of your needs. The most common and most useful function you're likely to use in simple expressions is the Immediate If function (`IIF`). As you saw in the previous example, the `IIF()` function takes three arguments. The first is an expression that returns either True or False. If the expression is True, the value passed into the second argument is returned. Otherwise (if the first expression is False), the third argument value is returned. Take another look at the expression used in the previous example:

```
=IIF( Fields!Quantity.Value < Fields!ReorderPoint.Value, "Red", "Black" )
```

Product Inventory / Reorder

Name	Reorder Point	Quantity
Adjustable Race	750	408
Adjustable Race	750	324
Adjustable Race	750	353
All-Purpose Bike Stand	3	144
AWC Logo Cap	3	288
BB Ball Bearing	600	585
BB Ball Bearing	600	443
BB Ball Bearing	600	324
Bearing Ball	750	427
Bearing Ball	750	318
Bearing Ball	750	364
Bike Wash - Dissolver	3	36
Blade	600	532
Blade	600	388
Blade	600	441
Cable Lock	3	252
Chain	375	236
Chain	375	192

Figure 6-86

If the expression `Fields!Quantity.Value < Fields!ReorderPoint.Value` yields a True result (where the `Quantity` is less than the `ReorderPoint`), the value `"Red"` is returned. Otherwise, the value returned is `"Black"`. You'll see more examples using this function in Chapter 7.

In cases where an expression may return more than two states, `IIF()` functions may be nested to form multiple branches of logic. In this example, three different conditions are tested:

```
=IIF( Fields!Quantity.Value < Fields!ReorderPoint.Value, "Red",
IIF(Fields!ListPrice.Value > 100, "Blue", "Black" ))
```

Let's analyze the logic: If `Quantity` is not less than the `ReorderPoint`, the third `IIF()` function argument is invoked. This contains a second `IIF()` function, which tests the ListPrice field value. If the value is greater than 100, the value `"Blue"` is returned. Otherwise, the return value is `"Black"`.

Beyond the simplest of nested functions, expressions can be difficult to write and to maintain. In addition to decisions structures, common functions may be used to format the output, parse strings, and convert data types. Count the opening and closing parentheses to make sure that they match. This is yet another example of where writing this code in a Visual Basic class library or forms project is helpful because of the built-in code-completion and integrated debugging tools. Consider using these other functions in place of nested `IIF()` functions.

The SWITCH() function accepts an unlimited number of expression and value pairs. The last argument accepts a value that is returned if none of the expressions resolve to True. I can use this in place of the previous nested IIF() example:

```
=SWITCH( Fields!Quantity.Value < Fields!ReorderPoint.Value, "Red",
Fields!ListPrice.Value > 100, "Blue", 1=1, "Black" )
```

Unlike the IIF() function, there is no "FalsePart" value. Each expression and return value is passed as a pair. The first expression in the list that evaluates to True causes the function to stop processing and return a value. This is why I included the expression "1=1". Since this expression will always evaluate to True, this becomes the catch-all expression that returns "Black" if no other expressions are True.

Visual Basic .NET supports many of the old-style VBScript and VB 6.0 functions as well as newer overload method calls. In short, this means that there may be more than one way to perform the same action. The following table contains a few other Visual Basic functions that may prove to be useful in basic report expressions.

Function	Description	Example
FORMAT()	Returns a string value formatted using a regular expression format code or pattern. Similar to the Format property but can be concatenated with other string values.	=FORMAT(Fields!TheDate.Value, "d") =FORMAT(Fields!TheDate.Value, "mm/d/yy")
MID(), LEFT() and RIGHT() .SUBSTRING()	Returns a specified number of characters from a specified position (if using MID()) and for a specific length. You can also use the .SUBSTRING() method.	=MID(Fields!TheString.Value, 3, 5) =LEFT(Fields!TheString.Value, 5) =Fields!TheString.Value.SUBSTRING(2, 5)
INSRT()	Returns an integer for the first character position of one string within another string. Often used with MID() or SUBSTRING() to parse strings.	=INSRT(Fields!TheString.Value, ",")
CSTR()	Converts any value to a string type. Consider using the newer TOSTRING() method.	=CSTR(Fields!TheNumber.Value) =Fields!TheNumber.Value.TOSTRING()
CDATE() CINT() CDEC() . . .	Type conversion function similar to CSTR(0) used to convert any compatible value to an explicit data type. Consider using the newer CTYPE() function to convert to an explicit type.	=CDATE(Fields!TheString.Value) =CTYPE(Fields!TheString.Value, Date)

Function	Description	Example
ISNOTHING()	Tests an expression for a null value. May be nested within an IIF() to convert nulls to another value.	=ISNOTHING(Fields!TheDate.Value) =IIF(ISNOTHING(Fields!TheDate.Value), "n/a", Fields!TheDate.Value)
CHOOSE()	Returns one of a list of values based on a provided integer index value (1,2,3, etc.)	=CHOOSE(Parameters!FontSize.Value, "8pt", "10pt", "12pt", "14pt")

There are hundreds of Visual Basic functions that could be used in some form, so this list is just a starting point. For additional assistance, view the online help index in Visual Studio, under Functions [Visual Basic]. This information is also available on the public MSDN library at http://www.msdn.Microsoft.com.

Using Custom Code

When you need to process more complex expressions, it may be difficult to build all of the logic into one expression. In such cases, you can write your own function to handle different conditions and call it from a property expression.

There are two different approaches for managing custom code. One is to write a block of code to define functions that are embedded into the report definition. This technique is simple, but the code will be available only to that report. The second technique is to write a custom class library compiled to an external .NET assembly and reference this from any report on your report server. This approach has the advantage of sharing a central repository of code, which makes updates to the code easier to manage. The downside of this approach is that the configuration and initial deployment is a bit tedious.

Why *Visual Basic*?

Before the .NET ("Dot Net") Framework was released in 2002, Microsoft offered two significant programming languages with very different capabilities. The C++ language was for very serious programming but required serious programming skills. The Visual Basic (VB) language has long been the flagship extension to practically all Microsoft desktop products. VB programming emphasizes simplicity and ease of use. Along with the framework, a new language, called C# ("C-sharp") was created to use all of the new .NET capabilities. The Visual Basic language underwent a major overhaul to bring it up to speed with the framework. One of the goals of the .NET platform was to separate the capabilities of the framework from the syntax of the languages. Since the inception of .NET, there has been a long-standing debate over the relative strengths and weaknesses of these two languages. Although there have been numerous articles and white papers comparing VB and C#, even industry experts have been reluctant to make broad statements about one language being superior to another. An unspoken belief among seasoned professionals is that C# is the "more serious" programming language.

At the prelaunch event for SQL Server 7.0 in 1998, Steve Ballmer offered career advice to the many database administrators in attendance. His advice was to learn Visual Basic programming. This seemed like a bold statement to make to the system admin (rather than the developer) community. Years later, this advice seems apropos given that Windows services—including the file and directory systems, web server, and database transformation services—may all be scripted and automated using Visual Basic code.

When Reporting Services was still in beta test phase, I was asked to make a presentation for the .NET Programmers' User Group at the Microsoft campus. When I announced that Reporting Services supports only Visual Basic embedded code, half the group was nearly transformed into a lynch mob—and I was looking for an exit. Why was VB chosen over C#? Was this an effort to "dumb down" or simplify report programming? Perhaps VB is the "lowest-common denominator" of the languages. At a lunch meeting with members of the Reporting Services product development team, I posed this question. Jason Carlson told me that they chose VB because it's a natural expression language. In most cases, conditional report logic must be processed in one line of code. The C# language, although powerful, tends to require multiple lines, whereas multiple functions can be nested in one line using a VB expression. I have used both languages, but as a longtime VB programmer, I was delighted to learn that VB was clearly a better choice for this job.

Using Custom Code in a Report

A report may contain embedded Visual Basic .NET code that defines a function you can call from property expressions. The code editor window is very simple and doesn't include any editing or formatting capabilities. For this reason, you may want to write the code in a separate Visual Studio project to test and debug before you place it into the report. When you are ready to add code, open the Report Properties dialog. You can do this from the Report menu. The other method is from the Report Designer right-click menu. Right-click the report designer outside of the report body and select Properties. On the Properties window, switch to the Code tab and write or paste your code in the Custom Code box.

The following example starts with a new report. Here is the code along with the expressions that you will need to create a simple example report on your own. The following Visual Basic function accepts a phone number or social security number in a variety of formats and outputs a standard U.S. phone number and properly formatted social security number (SSN). The Value argument accepts the value, and the Format argument accepts the value Phone or SSN. You're only going to use it with phone numbers, so you can leave the SSN branch out if you wish.

```
'*****************************************************************
'    Returns properly formatted Phone Number or SSN
'    based on Format arg & length of Value argument.
'    PT - 12/12/06
'*****************************************************************
Public Function CustomFormat(Value as String, Format as String) as String
      Select Case Format
      Case "Phone"
          Select Case Value.Length
          Case 7
              Return Value.SubString(0, 3) & "-" & Value.SubString(3, 4)
          Case 10
              Return "(" & Value.SubString(0, 3) & ") " _
                     & Value.SubString(3, 3) _
                     & "-" & Value.SubString(6, 4)
          Case 12
              Return "(" & Value.SubString(0, 3) & ") " _
                     & Value.SubString(4, 3) & "-" & Value.SubString(8, 4)
          Case Else
              Return Value
```

```
                End Select
        Case "SSN"
                If Value.Length = 9 Then
                        Return Value.SubString(0, 3) & "-" _
                                & Value.SubString(3, 2) & "-" & Value.SubString(5, 4)
                Else
                        Return Value
                End If
        Case Else
                Return Value
        End Select
End Function
```

The data set in this report gets its data from the Vendor and related tables in AdventureWorks and returns three columns: FirstName, LastName, and Phone. The SQL expression used to retrieve this information is as follows:

```
SELECT      Contact.FirstName, Contact.LastName, Contact.Phone
FROM        Vendor
            INNER JOIN VendorContact ON Vendor.VendorID = VendorContact.VendorID
            INNER JOIN Contact ON VendorContact.ContactID = Contact.ContactID
```

These three columns are used in a table bound to the data set. The Value property of the Phone column uses an expression that calls the custom function preceded by a reference to the Code object:

```
=Code.CustomFormat(Fields!Phone.Value, "Phone")
```

Figure 6-87 shows the report in design layout view. I didn't think you needed to see a preview of the report. It's a list of contacts with a properly formatted phone number. Trust me.

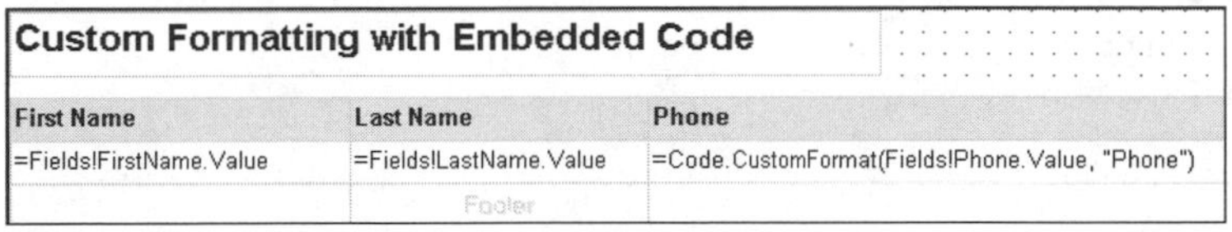

Custom Formatting with Embedded Code		
First Name	Last Name	Phone
=Fields!FirstName.Value	=Fields!LastName.Value	=Code.CustomFormat(Fields!Phone.Value, "Phone")
	Footer	

Figure 6-87

Using a Custom Assembly

Rather than embedding code directly into each report, using a custom assembly can be a central repository of reusable code to extend the functionality of multiple reports. In Reporting Services, custom assembly support is enabled by default. However, the code in the assembly will have restricted access to system resources. If you intend for the assembly to interact with the file system or perform data access, you will need to modify some configuration settings in order to grant the appropriate level of access to your code. We'll discuss these conditions after a simple walk-through to create an assembly that won't require any special settings.

To begin, create a class module project. You can write this code in any .NET language since it's going to be built into an assembly. The methods you create can be either static or instanced. It's a little easier to use static methods so that you don't have to manage the instancing and life of each object. This simply means is that you will declare public functions in your class using the `Static` keyword in C# or the `Shared` keyword in Visual Basic. Using the same code logic as in the previous example, the Visual Basic class code would look like this:

```vb
Public Class Report_Formats
    '********************************************************************
    '      Returns properly formatted Phone Number or SSN
    '      based on Format arg & length of Value argument.
    '      PT - 12/12/06
    '********************************************************************
    Public Shared Function CustomFormat(Value as String, Format as String) as String
        Select Case Format
        Case "Phone"
            Select Case Value.Length
            Case 7
                Return Value.SubString(0, 3) & "-" & Value.SubString(3, 4)
            Case 10
                Return "(" & Value.SubString(0, 3) & ") " _
                        & Value.SubString(3, 3) _
                        & "-" & Value.SubString(6, 4)
            Case 12
                Return "(" & Value.SubString(0, 3) & ") " _
                        & Value.SubString(4, 3) & "-" & Value.SubString(8, 4)
            Case Else
                Return Value
            End Select
        Case "SSN"
            If Value.Length = 9 Then
                Return Value.SubString(0, 3) & "-" _
                        & Value.SubString(3, 2) & "-" & Value.SubString(5, 4)
            Else
                Return Value
            End If
        Case Else
            Return Value
        End Select
    End Function
End Class
```

Save and build the class library project in Release configuration, and then copy the assembly (DLL) file to the `ReportServer\bin` folder. The default path to this folder is `C:\Program-Files\Microsoft SQLServer\MSSQL\Reporting Services\ReportServer\bin`.

In the Report Properties dialog (this is where you entered the code in the previous topic example), select the References tab and add the reference by browsing to the assembly file. The reference line shows metadata from the assembly, including the version number, as you can see in Figure 6-88.

To use a custom method in an expression, reference the namespace, class, and method using standard code syntax. The expression for the `CustomFormat` method should look like:

```
=Reporting_Component.Report_Formats.CustomFormat(Fields!Phone.Value, "Phone")
```

The report should look exactly as it did in the previous example.

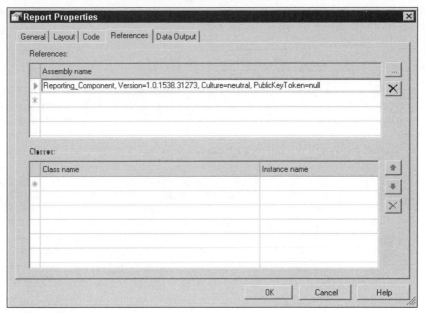

Figure 6-88

Custom Assembly Security

When using a custom assembly deployed to your report server, the assembly must run with the appropriate level of security access. This is a common challenge for all server-side .NET applications. A thorough discussion of this topic is beyond the scope of this book. If you are a seasoned developer, these should be familiar topics and if you are not, you should consult a .NET application developer to assist with the configuration of your custom assemblies.

In short, the steps to deploy and configure an assembly to run on your report server are not much different from any other remotely deployed component, and the permissions will depend on the resources used by the assembly. For example, a component that interacts with the local file system and consumes features of another component or database connections will require privileges to do so. The following are some of the more common steps to make custom assemblies more accessible:

❑   Build the assembly with a strong name. Use the SN.exe command-line utility to create a strongly named key pair, and then reference the generated key file within the AssemblyInfo class file in the class library project.

❑   Register the assembly in the Global Assembly Cache (GAC) on the report server. Not only does this elevate the trustworthiness for the assembly, it also provides downward version compatibility control.

❑   You may apply the AllowPartiallyTrustedCallers assembly attribute to allow the Reporting Services engine to call into this code.

❑   You can explicitly enable nondefault security permissions for the assembly using policy configuration files. Two files are used to manage these permissions. The rssrvpolicy.config file controls assembly permissions for the development and preview environment. The rspreviewpolicy .config file controls permissions on the Report Server.

For additional assistance with specific security considerations and configuration details, use SQL Server 2005 Books Online to look up the topic "Using Reporting Services Security Policy Files."

Errors, Warnings, and Debugging Code

When you preview or try to deploy a report, all of the expressions and embedded code in the report are cranked through the .NET Common Language Runtime debugger and native code compiler. If no errors are found, an assembly is built on the report server. This means that when reports execute, all of the expression and program code actually run from compiled binaries rather than from the Visual Basic source code.

Errors are listed in the task list if this process fails. The report designer has a quirk that can be a bit confusing until you get use to it. Along with errors that prevent the code compiling and report deployment, there is another set of information that shows up in this list. Some conditions may cause Reporting Services to be less than ecstatic with your code but not unhappy enough to prevent it from compiling. These are called warnings, and they appear on the task list below any errors. The confusing thing is that Visual Studio only displays this list when errors occur. This means that I can build a big, elaborate report that runs perfectly until I make one, small mistake in my code. When I try to preview this report, I may suddenly see 30 issues displayed on the task list. These may include "can't deploy shared datasource . . ." and "textbox42 has a BackgroundColor set to . . . which is invalid." If this happens to you, don't lose it . . . this is just the way the designer works. Those warnings were there all along. Visual Basic just didn't put the list in front of you until you committed a serious infraction. Start at the top of the list and work down until you see an error description that makes sense. Double-click this line. In most cases, this will go to the properties for the offending report item, allowing you to make the correction and move on.

When testing reports in the Visual Studio Report Designer, your custom assembly is loaded into memory when it is first invoked and may not be unloaded until you exit Visual Studio. This means that if you make code changes and redeploy the assembly, these changes may not be available to the report unless you cycle the Visual Studio application. There are two ways to work around this. The first is to make a point to deploy your report to your local report/web server and test it using the Report Manager. The other method is to use the stand-alone report preview utility and test it using the Report Manager.

I have found that under some conditions the report designer may display errors from other reports in the project or errors that may have been recently corrected. If you see behavior like this, close and reopen Visual Studio.

Designing for Mobility

The idea of making reports available in custom applications that run over the Internet or letting users access reports from desktop computers outside of the office opens many doors of opportunity that were not before possible. These capabilities are now very easy to achieve, but the promise of this technology doesn't stop there. This brings to mind the unforgettable words of Ron Popeil, ". . . but wait. There's more. . . ." Another very quotable figure, Bill Gates, announced in 2000 that the next generation of services from Microsoft would enable people to access information "any time, any place and on any device." This product fulfills that promise, making reports available to the next generation of mobile computing devices.

There are many different devices on the market that could be categorized as "mobile Internet devices" or "mobile network devices" capable of being used to view reports. These may include personal digital assistant (PDA) palm-sized or hand-held computers, enhanced pagers, or cell phones. The lines separating these devices are becoming quite blurred as the newest generation of cell phones can be used to surf the web and some PDAs now include integrated cell phones. There are even camcorders with built-in networking and web browsers! For this discussion we will limit the scope of these devices to the Windows-based units. However, some Palm OS devices may be used to view online content via a wireless corporate network or the World Wide Web and can be used to view offline documents in standard formats (such as PDF); we acknowledge that many of the capabilities we will discuss may also be supported on the Palm platform.

The challenges and opportunities for delivering mobile device–enabled reports are varied but fall into the following areas:

- ❑ Screen size
- ❑ Device, browser, and viewer capabilities
- ❑ Files portability
- ❑ File size restrictions

Current Windows-powered devices run a version of Windows CE called Pocket PC or Windows Mobile Smart Phone. The Pocket PC form factor has a screen resolution of 240 pixels wide by 320 pixels tall and features a number of scaled-down desktop applications (such as Pocket Word, Excel, Outlook, and Internet Explorer.) The Smart Phone screen is considerably smaller at 176 by 220 pixels and is designed to function primarily as a phone with some additional PDA features. An edition of the Pocket PC called the Pocket PC Phone Edition has integrated features to support units with a built-in cell phone. All Pocket PC devices have a touch screen interface and many of the Smart Phone units are controlled only by the phone's keypad. These devices, and many non-Windows cell phone devices, may be used to view online web content.

Screen Size

The most significant restriction for most mobile devices is the smaller screen size. The Pocket PC and Smart Phone will view web content with some client-side scripting support and will also cache recently viewed content for offline viewing. Most web pages designed for desktop computer users can be viewed on the tiny screen, but it requires the user to scroll extensively just to navigate a single page. Web-based reports created with Reporting Services are no exception. Most stock reports will likely work on a Pocket PC running Pocket Internet Explorer if they can be viewed in Internet Explorer on a desktop PC. The user experience, however, is often like watching a large-screen movie through a keyhole.

To design reports optimized for the mobile user, reports must be simplified and designed for smaller page size. Some dynamic reporting features (like drill-down and drill-through) may not be supported in all rendering formats. The comparable page size of the Pocket PC screen is about 3.25 inches (8.25 cm) wide. Simply scaling your mobile reports down to this width will resolve most screen resolution issues for mobile web users. Keep the font sizes small and avoid clutter, large graphics, and extra space.

Figure 6-89 is an example of a simple employee e-mail directory, created using a table data region on a narrow page:

Figure 6-89

The sample report shown above only has two columns, but it could easily have several. There is no need to restrict the functionality of your reports simply because users can't see all of the information at one time. Just keep in mind that when users navigate to the report, they will only see the information beginning in the top-left corner of the content. Design your reports with this in mind, placing the most important content near this entry point. Users can always scroll to find other information if the report is intuitive and easy to navigate. This is yet another reason to use interactive reporting features like drill-down.

Keep the report content size to a minimum as well. Regardless of the device or computer used to view reports, dial-up users will always suffer a significant performance penalty from large reports. Avoid unnecessary use of graphics and filter the data whenever possible. The Pocket PC phone device pictured here can connect to the Internet using either cell phone dial-up or a wireless network connection, but broadband wireless is typically only available in close proximity to a secure wireless access point. At best, cellular dial-up connection speeds are typically 14400 to 19200 bits per second. Figure 6-90 shows a product report with drill-down capabilities.

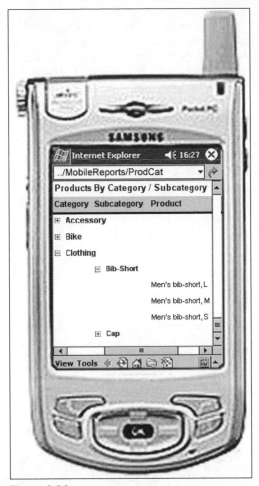

Figure 6-90

Offline Solutions

One of the challenges that mobile workers face on a number of levels is they typically don't have the opportunity to remain connected to a network or the Internet. Mobile devices are intended to give us the ability to cut ties with the corporate network and work without wires. At times, report users will need to render reports on their desktops or have them pushed out to files or e-mail via subscriptions — and then view the offline reports on the mobile device.

Typically, the best solution for offline reporting is to save the report to a document. Pocket Internet Explorer will store a cached copy of an HTML report if it has been viewed online. In the case of a drill-down report, the entire report content may not be stored in cache. When a cached drill-down report is viewed, exploring sections that have not been previously viewed may cause the device to try to connect and retrieve the newly requested content. Overall, caching HTML is not a comprehensive solution.

The PDF format is by far the most reliable method for transporting a report document and keeping content consistently formatted. After the report has been exported to a PDF document, it is a simple matter to drop the file into the synchronization folder on the partnering desktop and let ActiveSync copy it to the device. A pie chart, rendered to a PDF file, is illustrated in Figure 6-91. Unfortunately, Adobe Acrobat doesn't support the drill-down functionality in Reporting Services, so the report will need to be designed without dynamic drill-down and drill-through. The image format will also guarantee that the report will look and print consistently as the file is sent from place to place; however, files may be larger when rendered in PDF format.

Using the Excel rendering format is also an excellent medium for offline reports, but Pocket Excel also doesn't support drill-down. One advantage to using the Excel format is that users can make modifications to their local copy of the report content, sorting and formatting the data. A user can also add calculations and other content to extend the report for their own needs.

Figure 6-91

Best Practices and Tips

Report projects have the ability to stress the Visual Studio environment more than most any other types of application. Especially when using custom program code, errors can cause Visual Studio to—how do I say this?—become unhappy. Recovering from an error is usually the easy part. The tough part is when you have worked all day on a complex report and haven't saved your work for hours. You make one small change before clicking the Preview tab—and nothing happens. Visual Studio locks up and then you mutter some choice words before opening Windows Task Manager to kill the Visual Studio process and lose all of that work. Here's a simple solution: Click the Save All toolbar button (see Figure 6-92).

Figure 6-92

Click it often and especially click it after you make changes and before you preview your report.

As I mentioned earlier, if you have difficulty debugging complex expressions or custom Visual Basic code, take this code into a Visual Basic class library or forms application project in order to take advantage of the rich code completion and debugging tools offered in these Visual Studio projects.

- ❑ **Auto-Generated Aggregates:** Fix auto-generated aggregate expressions. If you are grouping data at the detail level and then you drag a field into the group header or footer, the report designer will apply aggregate functions unnecessarily. You can remove the function and parentheses in this case. Also, pay attention to the scope argument, passed in the second position to aggregate functions. If you build a report with one data set and then add another data set later on, you may need to add the scope information for report items not contained in a data range item.

- ❑ **Use Top Values in Charts:** Limiting the number of series values in charts will prevent crowding of the data points, bars, columns, or slices. Keep in mind that the test data you use when you design reports may not accurately reflect the data used in production. By restricting the number of rows or grouped values fed to chart reports, you can ensure that they will remain readable for your users when they are viewing real-world data.

- ❑ **Document Report Logic:** To document complex logic, properties, and expressions you can add text boxes to a report and hide them using the `Visibility|Hidden` property. This is also true with table columns used only for report design and testing. As a convention, I set the background color for comment items to yellow. This makes them easy to spot in the designer. I figure that any item with a bright yellow background ought to be hidden because no one in their right mind would put yellow text boxes on a report.

- ❑ **Search the RDL to Find or Fix Settings:** Large reports can often be difficult to debug because properties and expressions can get buried in the interface. Remember that all of these settings exist in one XML file. If you need to find an elusive property setting or replace all similar expressions with another, this can easily be done by using find-and-replace features in the RDL file. After making a backup copy of the report, right-click the report name in the Solution Explorer and select View Code from the pop-up menu. You can also use this technique to make modifications that would be difficult in the designer (like rearranging the order of groups). Just make sure you have a recovery plan if things don't work as expected.

Summary

We have covered a lot of ground in this chapter, building on the report design fundamentals you learned in the previous two chapters. You've learned to design several styles of reports using data sources and filtering techniques that exposed different design strategies.

❑ Data regions let you repeat and group data in a section of the report. The table organizes repeated data into specific rows and columns and provides inherent grouping capabilities with headers and footers. Using a list, you can achieve similar results with a little more formatting flexibility. With a subreport, you can essentially use a separately defined report as a data region and filter the data it contains with parameters and filters.

❑ Drill-down and drill-through reports use techniques that optimize screen space and allow the user to interact with the report. This is accomplished by expanding the groupings of a table or list or by using links to jump to an item, a bookmark, or another report. The document map provides a mini-drill-down report in a separate frame that may be used to easily find headings and category labels and navigate to them in the report. Recursive relationships are easy to manage and will produce multilevel groups using a single source or data.

❑ Charts are a powerful tool used to express aggregated values in a series and in multiple dimensions. Several chart types are available for different types of data and presentation formats.

❑ Reports utilize the power of the Visual Basic .NET programming language. Advanced formatting and calculations may be performed by adding programming code to your reports. This may be done by simply adding code in the report designer or by creating a compiled .NET assembly and adding a reference to the assembly in the report. Report properties may be set using expressions and program code to achieve conditional formatting.

❑ Developing reports for mobile users is a relatively simple task, keeping in mind the limits and capabilities of devices. Reports must be designed to fit smaller screen sizes and may be optimized for online or disconnected scenarios. Mobile reporting opens vast opportunities for traveling information workers using convenient wireless and synchronized devices.

7

Report Solution Patterns and Recipes

This chapter serves as a practical guide to designing reports and building reporting solutions in the real world. It contains several examples of advanced report designs as recipes to solve specific business problems. This is a high-level guide and not step-by-step instructions. You will use the techniques you've learned in the previous three chapters to implement specific functionality. I cover the following topics:

❑ Reporting project guidelines, key success factors, and the solution scope.

❑ Defining and managing report specifications and the development process phases.

❑ Migrating and converting reports from other reporting tools.

❑ Working with the strengths and limitations of the Reporting Services architecture.

❑ Recipes and models for several advanced reporting features and techniques.

In the previous chapters, you've learned what you can do and have been given a number of options to implement certain report functionality. After writing the first edition of this book over a year ago, I wanted to add a chapter that would be a practical guide to designing reports in the real world. I wanted this to be a sort of "street smart" guide about not what you *can* do but what you *should* do, based on the experience of those who have been doing this kind of work full-time, since this product became available. Over the past two years, I have spent the majority of my professional time building reporting solutions for consulting clients. Collectively, we've developed reporting solutions for a very large software producer, one of the world's largest media and entertainment companies, a global aerospace manufacturer, an international investment bank, utility companies, retail services, food services, telecommunications providers, and government agencies. I've made it a point to build the content for this chapter over time while working on different projects. These and other projects have afforded us challenging opportunities to discover effective patterns for designing a variety of report styles.

We have also had the opportunity to work closely with members of the Reporting Services product team at Microsoft to better understand the long-term goals for Reporting Services' features and capabilities. This has provided insight into the mechanics of the product's components and why they behave as they do. Without fully understanding the design goals in architecting this product, it's easy for a report designer to ask questions like Why does it work that way? . . . Why did that do that? Reporting Services has some limitations that may not make sense to the casual user. I've found that most advanced capabilities I would like to include in reports can be implemented but not necessarily using my chosen technique. As I've run up against limitations and have discussed these with the product architects and product managers, the answers are often in the vein of "that feature wasn't designed to work that way. You can accomplish the same thing by using this other feature or technique." My goal is to share these techniques and capabilities with you.

Unlike the previous chapters on report design, I'm not going to do much hand-holding in this chapter. By now, you should know how to use the features of the report designer and how to change properties, create queries, and use all of the report items. For each of the report design techniques that follow, I'll give you enough information to explain the concept and demonstrate the technique, but I won't walk you through the entire process from start to finish. This will save time and avoid redundancy with material covered in the previous chapters.

Reporting Project Requirement Guidelines

Reporting projects are a special breed of software solutions. In the software world, successful projects don't just happen without deliberate efforts to manage evolving requirements and to steer the creative effort. Whether you are a corporate application developer, an independent consultant, or the person who wears all the hats in the department, your project should have a sponsor who defines the requirements and takes delivery of the finished product. We could spend volumes discussing lessons learned about failed and successful projects. In short, the secrets of success nearly all come down to effective communication and the involvement of a customer stakeholder. We've discussed some of these principles and ideas in previous chapters. This section is a concise set of guidelines that you may consider using to help you and your project sponsor to cover the essentials.

Key Success Factors

Reporting projects have a much better chance of being successful when the business requirements are well defined and clearly communicated. In particular:

❑ Report specifications should be documented using a standard format for all reports.

❑ Report designers must understand the source data. In cases where the designer isn't familiar with the database design and business data, specific queries or stored procedures should be defined and prepared before report design.

❑ The database schema should be frozen before work begins.

❑ Accurate sample or real data should be available to support the design and testing of all reports.

These may seem like lofty goals. The fact is that oftentimes you may not be able to control all of these factors. Experience will help you to know where to draw the line between the situations where you should work with less-than-ideal conditions and situations in which you should put your foot down and insist that these conditions be met before you begin work. In any case, be sure to clearly communicate your concerns and the associated risks.

Solution Scope

Reports often have many dependencies on other parts of a solution and if these pieces aren't in place before reports are designed, this can hold up the report work and waste considerable time and money. Reporting solutions require that the right type of database is in place, that it has been populated with all of the data necessary to build the reports, and that the user and business report requirements are well defined and documented.

The scope of the solution should be understood before report work begins. Without a clear understanding of all the related components of the solution, the project can easily spin out of control, with more work being started than finished.

Common examples of solution scope challenges include:

❑ Report performance problems prompt database schema changes or the constructing denormalized fact tables containing duplicate data.

❑ Realizing that changing transactional data doesn't support reporting scenarios, the database is redesigned while in production.

❑ Database and report features are added as you go and not according to a predefined plan, causing each report to take on different behavior and features.

The process of periodic data extraction to populate the reporting database system is known as ETL (Extract, Transform, and Load). A separate data mart or data warehouse is created to store preaggregated decision-support data. A complex ETL process is created to periodically copy new data into the decision-support database.

Needless to say, if these kinds of issues aren't mitigated and managed, even simple projects may be doomed before they start. Ideally, a report designer should be on the receiving side of business requirements and should participate in helping to clarify the details rather than making up new requirements as the project moves along.

Reporting on Existing Data Sources

If you are walking into an environment where the databases already exist, you should carefully review and discuss the long-term viability of the solution with your project sponsor. If this is a small, simple database that isn't likely to grow significantly over its useful life, then you may be in good shape. However, small-database reporting solutions that perform well in test and design scenarios may not fare so well when loaded up with truckloads of data and accessed by many concurrent users.

The system should have a defined capacity and a plan to scale up when you need to support large volumes of data and high workloads.

Reporting on Transactional Sources

In even moderately sized systems, reporting on live data can often be challenging. If user applications are locking data rows and inserting new records while reports run, this creates resource contention and performance issues. Reporting on changing data can also be risky because the report can only capture a single moment in time, while this data continues to change.

Decision-support database systems are typically designed to be exclusively read-only and use data structures much simpler than those used by equivalent transactional databases. This optimizes report performance and keeps the data consistent for a set period of time. Users understand that they aren't looking at the most current data, but they know it should be accurate as of the end of business on the previous day.

One of the challenges when reporting on data in an existing database is that the database may not have been designed with your reporting requirements in mind. Even the simplest reporting requirements can often be difficult to meet without writing very complex queries. This can slow performance and only support a certain amount of data. For small and simple database systems, reporting on the same tables in a transactional database as the rest of the applications may be the easiest choice.

Building an End-to-End Reporting Solution

Using Reporting Services you can create an entire user experience by prompting for input parameters, customizing query operations, filtering, sorting, and using report item actions and navigation features. However, this all assumes that the data sources contain the necessary data in a form that is both accessible and scalable to meet future demands. If this isn't the case, what might have looked like a simple reporting project can take on a whole new dimension. Decision-support systems often involve a separate database that is populated at regular intervals from one or more transactional sources. Typically, scripts run during off hours to copy new data from the main database into a set of simplified tables designed especially for reporting. A *data mart* is a decision-support database used within a department or business unit to serve up report data to meet a set of specific business requirements. It could be as simple as a small set of denormalized tables in a relational database, or it could be a set of OLAP cubes in a hierarchal database system like Microsoft Analysis Services. Queries for OLAP reporting will be written in a hierarchal expression language, like MDX, rather than T-SQL.

Data warehouses and data marts are similar in principle but different in scale. A *data warehouse* is typically a large-scale, enterprise-wide system that meets the reporting needs of many business groups, and will nearly always be deployed as a specialized OLAP system.

An effective ETL process involves not only copying new data from one system to another but also transforming many rows from many source tables into preaggregated rows that describe specific facts. In the end, the decision-support data, populated by the ETL process, helps meet reporting business requirements as effectively as possible. Tools such as SQL Server Data Integration Services (formerly Data Transformation Services, or DTS) are often used to implement ETL.

Sample and Test Data

During report design, it is very important to work with data similar to that of report users. Sample or "mocked-up" data is often meaningless in a business context and doesn't exhibit the same characteristics as the real thing. This data should represent variety and should adhere to the same business rules as real data so that data grouping, sorting, and filtering features can be designed with predictable results. Where possible, production data (or at the very least, production-like data) should be used for report design and testing. Sensitive information can be scrubbed by using search-and-replace iterations and calculations to modify numeric and currency values. Report designers shouldn't be expected to enter their own data because they're too focused on the process to create effective test data. This is like expecting application developers to test their own code.

In addition to using real data, it's important to work with a manageable set of data so reports run quickly. Large data volumes can slow report design significantly. To design a bug-free report typically takes several iterations of testing after adding each feature. If it takes several minutes to render a report, this can slow the process by hours and days. When it takes a long time to test a report, I often find myself trying to use this downtime more effectively by working on other tasks. In the end, I find myself starting (more than finishing) multiple things on a slow-running machine. It's tough to keep track of all the loose ends, especially when queries are timing out and reports are crashing with errors.

Report Specifications

Work with your users and project sponsor to design a report specification template that addresses your unique business needs. Some reports may query data from multiple tables and users may not be familiar enough with the data structures to specify column names and keys for joins. In this case, you may need to involve a database expert to help with these requirements. Other reports may get their data from existing views or stored procedures, making this part of the process a whole lot easier.

I find that in some cases, where the project sponsor and users aren't familiar with the data structures, I am left to make assumptions about how the tables should be joined and queried. In these cases, the report specification becomes more of a checklist and a forum to validate assumptions and to answer questions. Ultimately, the burden must be left to the project sponsor to provide and approve the specific requirements for each report. This, of course, should be performed with the assistance and cooperation of the report designer as you discuss each feature. Remember that the key to success is effective communication. On larger projects or when reporting on more complex databases, you may need to separate the business requirements of the report from the technical specification, perhaps by using two separate documents to gather these requirements. In any case, the key is to involve users and business stakeholders in obtaining buy-off and validating the results.

The following sample report specification should work for most report projects and can be embellished for special needs. Replace the italicized text with appropriate responses and complete one complete copy for each report.

Report Specification for Description	*(Full Report Name)*		
Report Category or Group	*(Reports are often grouped by business function, features, or user audience.)*		
Priority	*(1 = High, 2 = Medium, 3 = Low)*		
Business Problems/Questions Answered			
Data Source	*[Database, table(s), stored proc., cube, etc.]*		
Fields *(Table columns and cube dimension members and measures are collectively called fields in Reporting Services. List all fields by name with the related report column title and data format.)*	Schema Field Name *(Actual table column or member name)*	Column Title *(Report column heading title)*	Format *(Currency, percent, date — short/long, decimal places, etc.)*

Table continued on following page

Row Heading(s)	*(If report format and data are not self-described, some sections of table row headings may require labels.)*		
Filtering	*(How is data filtered — that is, static filters, parameter-based filters, at database server, at report server?) List filtered fields and criteria.*		
Grouping	*(How is data grouped? Static; dynamic, based on parameter field selection; subgroups; are groups indented, formatted differently, and so on? If there are pivot/matrix reports, then there may be groups on rows and columns.) List the groups and the field(s) for each group.*		
Sorting	*(How is data sorted — static, parameter-based, subsorting within groups, clickable column headers, and so on?) List the sort field(s).*		
Parameters *(Parameters used for user input or selection may be presented in text boxes, check boxes, radio buttons, or drop-down lists. May be used to filter, group, sort, show and hide fields, items, rows, or columns)*	Parameter *(Parameter name)*	Source *(Source of value — that is, single value, static list, data set query)*	Default *(Default value)*
Calculations *(What calculations are performed in the report. Indicate operational order of precedence and conditions — i.e., if one or more values are 0 or null, what to do if divided by 0, negative results, etc.)*	*(Calculations may be performed in the data set query, on custom report fields, or in report items.)*		
Notes			

Development Phases

As with any software development project, each component or report should progress through a series of design and development phases. These may include prototyping or proof-of-concept, design, testing, and deployment. To keep reports organized, I find it helpful to create separate projects and folders and then graduate reports from one project to another as they are verified and pass testing criteria.

For each of these Visual Studio projects, within a master solution, create duplicate shared data sources. You can drag and drop reports from one project to another and then remove the previous report using the Solution Explorer. When you right-click the old report and choose the Remove option, the second Remove option will leave the file in the project folder and simply remove the entry from the project file. Since a new copy is created in the destination project, I advise choosing the Delete option so that you maintain only one copy of the report definition file.

For each report project, set the `TargetFolder` property to a deployment folder to a name that corresponds to the project name (that is, *Prototype Phase*, *Design Phase*, *Test Phase*, and *Completed Reports*). As you complete each report and move the RDL files between project folders, update a simple report progress summary list similar to the following sample.

Report Name	Requirements Complete	Prototype Complete	Queries Complete	Parameters Complete	Filtering/ Sorting Complete	Grouping Complete	Calculations Complete	Formatting Complete	Tested	Deployed
Product Downloads by Fiscal Month	✓	✓	✓	✓	✓	✓	✓	✓	✓	✓
Sales Channel Pipeline	✓	✓	✓	✓	✓	✓	✓			
Sales Analysis by Vendor	✓	✓	✓			✓				
Investment Summary	✓	✓	✓	✓	✓	✓	✓			

Finally, there is one last thing to remember about what *will* happen on practically every report project. In the beginning, your sponsor will tell you what reports and features they want and you'll work with them to capture all of the requirements in detail. Things will generally go pretty smoothly until they commence testing and you come up on a deadline. In the 11th hour, users will start asking for things and your sponsor will request changes. You'll learn of some minor misunderstandings you may have had about the early requirements and this will prompt even more changes. Some last-minute changes are inevitable in any project but when a change is requested, *it must be in writing*. Whether in hand-written form, in a document, or an e-mail message, keep and save these requests. You should be able to trace every new request back to an earlier requirement or obtain a clear understanding that it is a new requirement. If users request changes, you should have the project sponsor approve them. In the end, managing these changes will go a long way toward ensuring the success of your report project.

Migrating and Converting Reports

One of the most common scenarios in large businesses moving to Reporting Services is the desire to migrate or convert reports created using another reporting tool. Many large businesses that have existing applications will have reporting solutions in Crystal Reports, Business Objects, or Access reports. There has been a significant interest in "converting" Crystal Reports to Reporting Services reports. There are several challenges making this difficult to easily achieve.

Recognizing this need, some third-party report migration tools have been developed by companies that offer report migration services. In many cases, these do an effective job of moving Crystal Reports into SSRS Report Definition Language files. There is no single method for fully automating report conversion from Crystal Reports without some manual intervention. One of Reporting Services' greatest strengths is the ability to consolidate similar reports into one, to achieve a more flexible, single report. In many cases, several Crystal Reports or Access reports may be distilled into a handful of SSRS reports to address the same business challenges. There are several features that other reporting applications don't offer and by simply copying a report design from another tool, you will not take advantage of what Reporting Services has to offer. The best practice for report migration is to start, not just with existing reports, but with the user and business requirements, and meet them by effectively using the unique features in Reporting Services. With a large number of existing reports, report conversion can move this process along in large strides.

If you can use existing reports to model design elements, layout and formatting, calculation expressions, query strings, and connection information, this will likely save time and money when compared with starting over from scratch. However, you are almost guaranteed to find better ways to meet your requirements by considering a different approach, consolidating similar reports, and using updated features. The structure of these reports will often be different. Crystal Reports uses a banding approach for grouped data where the report itself defines grouped sections. By contrast, a Reporting Services report is simply a blank surface upon which report items are used to define data ranges for one or more data sets or query result sets. Since grouped data ranges may be implemented using a list, table, or matrix report item, depending on the need, there isn't a one-to-one correspondence between these report architectures. Crystal Reports also relies heavily on formulas and functions for mathematical calculations and conditional formatting, whereas Reporting Services allows designers and developers to use one of three techniques including Visual Basic in-line expressions, code-behind VB functions, or external .NET assemblies. This provides a great deal of flexibility to implement custom functionality. Converting all but the simplest expressions from Crystal Reports formulas to Visual Basic expressions would be nearly impossible. One of the most significant challenges for developers who might want to create and distribute a conversion application is a legal constraint imposed by Crystal/Business Objects. In order to programmatically query the structure of a Crystal Reports report this requires components licensed by Crystal Reports, and it prohibits their use for report conversion and distribution with third-party software.

Working with the Strengths and Limitations of the Architecture

Never assume that anything works the way you want it to. The late British comedic actor Benny Hill made the best presentation of this common joke and eternal truth by breaking the word *assume* into syllables to complete the phrase: *When you assume, you make an ___ out of _ and __*. Keep in mind that some of the chief goals of this product are to render reports in a variety of presentation formats utilizing server-side components. In doing so, a report rendered to a specific format may not take advantage of all the capabilities offered by that format, a client tool, or markup language. For example, reports rendered to HTML don't offer all of the advanced behavior you might implement in a custom-built web page with cascading style sheets and JavaScript. If you were to design a report in Microsoft Excel, you might design the workbook with formulas used to recalculate the spreadsheet rather than using literal values for summaries and totals. The general approach is that Reporting Services renders using methods to address the commonality of all these formats. There's always room for more features and advanced functionality. Some of these may be added to the product in later versions because this makes sense for mass consumption. Because of the modular architecture of Reporting Services, features can be added through custom programming extensions.

I think it's important to define boundaries, not to be critical but to better understand the possibilities and limitations. In software, we're always trying to do something new — something that has never been done before (at least not within a particular environment). To this end, there are some fundamental questions that can help you understand just how you might approach a problem, and whether a goal can be achieved within the constraints of your capabilities and resources. When I go into a new consulting opportunity, the first thing that I try to do is to take inventory of the skills necessary to get the job done and then let my client know where we stand: "I can do this . . . I've done that . . . I know someone who can help me with this . . . but I don't know much about that thing, and I don't know if I'm the right person to tackle it. I'll give it a shot, but we may need to consider bringing in another resource." After all, if I'm not honest with my clients, this could just turn out to be a bad experience for everyone, damaging my credibility and the business relationship with the client.

This is the approach I'd like to take in this section. Reporting Services can do some wonderful things, but it's important to understand the boundaries and limitations of certain features. Perhaps the same capability may be possible using another feature or perhaps you may be barking up the wrong tree entirely. You are not likely to build every conceivable type of report, and over time you will probably create a handful of reports using techniques that you will duplicate repeatedly as you build more reports of the same style. Therefore, not all of these reports may apply to you, but they may give you some ideas about new ways to solve old problems.

It's not easy to find the limits of most products. For some reason, that information isn't listed in the product specifications and documentation — at least not in bold type. I've had very little success going to a large software vendor asking: "Hey, tell me what your product *can't* do." Wouldn't it be nice when shopping for a car or a house, if the salespeople would just list the comparative shortcomings of their product? I think it would make the process so much easier. For this discussion, that is where I'd like to start. Some of the more recognizable limitations of the Reporting Service architecture are detailed below. This is by no means intended to be a complete list, nor is it a list of bugs or issues. It's simply a guideline of design constraints to be aware of when taking reports to the next level. I've also provided some common alternatives to implement desired functionality.

Area	Limitation	Alternatives
Data Presentation	In the report body or a group section, all fields must be aggregated, even if the data set only returns one row.	Use an aggregate function even if your query returns one row or all rows for the field return the same value. Typically, you should use the FIRST() function for character and date data and the SUM() function for numeric data.
	Page header and footer cannot reference field values.	Place hidden text boxes in the report body and then reference these in the ReportItems collection. Instead of a page header or footer, use a table header and footer or group header and footer. Set the footer to force a page break, and these rows effectively become page headers and footers.
	Subreports, used to relate Master/Detail records, cause performance and rendering problems.	Subreports work well for unrelated data or for a small set of master rows. The subreport's data set must be processed for every instance of a master row, resulting in performance and resource challenges. It is typically more efficient to build a single query, using joins and repeated values, and to use groups and nested report items rather than a subreport. If you do need to use a subreport, consider using report instance caching to improve performance if the underlying data doesn't change very often.
	Printing from the web browser isn't very reliable. It provides no control of the page orientation and margins cut off some information.	A client-side print control was introduced in Reporting Services 2000 SP2. This feature appears as a small printer icon in the upper right of the Report Manager toolbar. Clicking this icon will cause a client-side control to download and install to the user's computer. Once installed, this offers much greater control than printing directly from the browser. Rendering to other formats allows users to control print features from client applications (such as the Adobe Reader for PDF reports or Microsoft Excel).
Formatting	Conditional formatting expressions can be complicated and difficult to maintain, especially when repeated for multiple report items and fields.	Write a Visual Basic function in the Report Properties⇨Code window and call the function as an expression for each report item [for example, =Code.MyFunction(Fields!MyField.Value)].

Area	Limitation	Alternatives
	Aggregate functions don't return zero for summaries on nonexisting values. Our users want to see zeros.	Use a Visual Basic function to return a zero in place of an empty value [for example, =IIF(IsNothing(SUM(Fields!MyField.Value)), 0, SUM(Fields!MyField.Value))] Pass values to a Visual Basic function to convert null, empty string, or no value to a zero or another value. [for example, =Code.NullToZero(Fields!MyField.Value)]
	Standard formatting strings don't return values formatted the way I want to see them.	Format properties use the language of regular expressions, which are very capable but can be complicated. Conditional regular expressions can be obtained from a number of online resources or specialized technical books. Rather than modifying the format, create a Visual Basic function or expression called in the Value property. This can limit your ability to refer to the value of this report item in another expression (this is easy to work around). In related report items, refer to the Fields expression rather than this report item, or convert this report item value back to its native data type.
Rendering	Can't embed charts and subreports into the detail row of a table.	Create a group on a detail-level field. This effectively makes the group header or footer a detail row—which will support more embedded items. Remove unneeded rows from the table.
	PDF rendering doesn't support some bound items in page footers.	Use a table with a group footer set to repeat on each page. Place bound items in the group footer rather than the page footer.
	HTML rendering doesn't support some table design formatting. For example, narrow columns used for spacing and borders are padded with extra space.	This is a characteristic of HTML rendering and is not considered a bug. If reports require more exact tolerances, users should be instructed to use printer-friendly rendering formats like PDF and TIFF.
	Using images in place of borders causes extra vertical and horizontal padding and column misalignment.	Most rendering formats were not designed to use images in place of borders. Images placed in table cells will typically be padded. Report design is a little different from web design, and some of the techniques may not work. Reports should be tested in all common rendering formats when using images borders.

Table continued on following page

Area	Limitation	Alternatives
Actions	Reports don't support events like Access does. I want to count pages, rows, groups, and report item values, and call custom code when these "events" are fired.	Reporting Services doesn't support an event model at the design level. However, calling a function in a property of a report item can have a similar effect. Code is called in the order that items are rendered: left to right and top to bottom. You can use class module–level variables to manage values within the confines of one report rendering.
	Code variables aren't tracked across multiple "postings" of an interactive report. I need to keep track of values that are modified by code as my user interacts with a report.	Parameters may be used like QueryString values in a web page. When a user clicks on an item, the Action target can use an expression, which calls a custom Visual Basic function. This function can receive one or more parameter values or variables to process. The resulting value may be passed as a parameter to the same report, effectively posting back to itself with meaningful parameter values. The parameters may be used in expressions, modifying report and item properties to change properties or sort, group, hide, or show items.

Report Recipes

As we have endeavored to solve various business problems, we've learned to do some interesting things with Reporting Services. On consulting engagements, I often find myself in front of a client who is asking questions like "can you do this or that?" Almost inevitably, the answer is "yes," but the question becomes what the best method would be to meet the requirement. With a little outside-the-box thinking, a lot of interesting things are possible. This may involve some custom programming, embedding report items, or using customer application components in concert with Reporting Services.

In the following section, I've compiled a description of reporting challenges and solutions we've encountered, developing reports for our clients. For each "solution recipe," I provide a brief list of skills, techniques, and resources needed to apply the report feature. This should give you a good idea of how prepared you may be to use the techniques based on your skill set and the level of complexity. Some of these are easy to duplicate, whereas others require more advanced skills, which may include Transact-SQL and Visual Basic programming. These are not intended to be exercises or step-by-step instructions. I have made a point to provide enough information to demonstrate the concepts and techniques. However, to implement these solutions you will need to apply the skills you learned in the previous chapters.

Greenbar Reports

Once upon a time, most reports were printed on special continuous-feed paper. This paper is fan folded, with a perforation between each page, making it stackable in the input and output printer bins. The long scroll of pages has pin-feed holes on each side to feed it through and align each row with the mechanical print head. One of the common characteristics of this paper is that it has preprinted green bars for every other row of data. In more modern reports, this format remains popular to help readers visually separate each row of printed information. This typically involves using a light pastel background color for alternating table rows.

The Challenge:

❑   Reporting Services does not have a built-in alternating row color feature.

What you'll need:

❑   A Visual Basic function.

❑   Expressions used to call the function on the BackgroundColor property of row items.

I've seen a few different techniques used to implement this feature and they all require complex expressions or some use of Visual Basic programming. Fortunately, this isn't hard to do, even if you're new to VB programming. This technique involves using a VB function to return a different color for odd and even rows. Report items are rendered from top to bottom and then from left to right — as the carriage of a typewriter does (for the younger generation, a typewriter is sort of like a computer with moving parts). This means that custom code procedures and expressions associated with report item properties will always be executed in this order. In our solution, the start of a new row is indicated by passing a toggle flag when the function is called in the leftmost column's text box. The following Visual Basic code begins with a class module–level variable used to hold the odd-or-even row indicator between calls. As you can see, the bOddRow variable value is toggled between True and False on each call.

```
Private bOddRow As Boolean

'*********************************************************************
' -- Display green-bar type color banding in detail rows
' -- Call from BackGroundColor property of all detail row textboxes
' -- Set Toggle True for first item, False for others.
'*********************************************************************
Function AlternateColor(ByVal OddColor As String, _
        ByVal EvenColor As String, ByVal Toggle As Boolean) As String
    If Toggle Then bOddRow = Not bOddRow
    If bOddRow Then
        Return OddColor
    Else
        Return EvenColor
    End If
End Function
```

The program code is entered on the Code tab of the Report Properties dialog. To access this window, choose Report Properties from the Report menu while using the report designer's Layout tab. This is shown in Figure 7-1. After entering or making modifications to code, click the OK button to update the report definition.

For the BackgroundColor property of the first text box (in the leftmost column of the row), enter the following expression to call the custom code function:

```
=Code.AlternateColor("AliceBlue", "White", True)
```

The first parameter is the name of the background color for odd-numbered rows. The second is the background color for even-numbered rows. These two values may be the name of any standard web color (available from the color drop-down list in the designer). These may also be any one of about 16 million Pantone colors expressed in web-style hexadecimal format (for example, #FF8000 for orange and #9932CD for dark orchid).

273

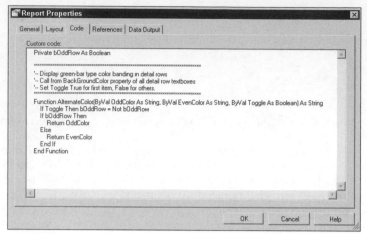

Figure 7-1

Creating a Greenbar Table

The first example I'll demonstrate uses a table with a single detail row. Every text box in the row contains an expression on the BackgroundColor property. This expression calls the AlternateColor custom function that returns the name of the color for this property. As you see in Figure 7-2 , the expression for the leftmost column passes the value True to toggle the odd/even row. For all other columns, the third argument value is False.

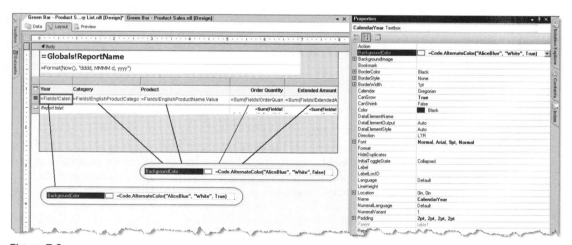

Figure 7-2

Figure 7-3 shows the report in preview. The AliceBlue color I chose for odd rows is subtle. Any combination of standard color names or hexadecimal values can be used. For example, the hex value #FF0000 is equivalent to the color Red.

Green Bar - Product Sales by Year by Category List

Sunday, August 21, 2005

Year	Category	Product	Order Quantity	Extended Amount
2001	Accessories	Sport-100 Helmet, Black	331	$6,681.73
2001	Accessories	Sport-100 Helmet, Blue	353	$7,118.43
2001	Accessories	Sport-100 Helmet, Red	319	$6,439.49
2001	Bikes	Mountain-100 Black, 38	312	$630,178.13
2001	Bikes	Mountain-100 Black, 42	297	$600,613.22
2001	Bikes	Mountain-100 Black, 44	315	$636,320.61
2001	Bikes	Mountain-100 Black, 48	273	$552,823.36
2001	Bikes	Mountain-100 Silver, 38	289	$589,558.27
2001	Bikes	Mountain-100 Silver, 42	263	$535,566.42
2001	Bikes	Mountain-100 Silver, 44	268	$545,086.40
2001	Bikes	Mountain-100 Silver, 48	225	$458,998.65
2001	Bikes	Road-150 Red, 44	52	$111,642.02
2001	Bikes	Road-150 Red, 48	52	$111,642.02
2001	Bikes	Road-150 Red, 52	52	$111,642.02
2001	Bikes	Road-150 Red, 56	178	$382,159.24
2001	Bikes	Road-150 Red, 62	109	$234,018.86
2001	Bikes	Road-450 Red, 44	157	$137,342.66
2001	Bikes	Road-450 Red, 48	52	$45,489.29
2001	Bikes	Road-450 Red, 52	352	$307,927.49
2001	Bikes	Road-450 Red, 58	281	$245,438.04
2001	Bikes	Road-450 Red, 60	161	$140,841.83
2001	Bikes	Road-650 Black, 44	136	$57,046.41
2001	Bikes	Road-650 Black, 48	63	$26,425.91
2001	Bikes	Road-650 Black, 52	346	$144,783.23
2001	Bikes	Road-650 Black, 58	263	$110,317.69
2001	Bikes	Road-650 Black, 60	138	$57,885.33
2001	Bikes	Road-650 Black, 62	64	$26,845.37

Figure 7-3

Creating a Greenbar Matrix

The pattern used for a matrix is very similar to a table. Since the matrix generates column cells dynamically, there is no way to specify a different expression for each column. If I wanted the row header to have an alternating background color, I could use the same technique as the table: toggling the odd/even flag explicitly on the row header text box. But, if the pivot cell is to be the leftmost item with an alternate background color on each row, this becomes more challenging. To work around this limitation, I define an extra row group on the same field expression as the previous group in the row hierarchy. Figure 7-4 shows the group definitions. The two row groups both use the same expression. This will cause the second group header text box to be repeated with each row. I'm going to hide this cell when I'm done.

Next, I set the BackgroundColor property using the same expression that I used in the table example. The second row header text box sets the AlternateColor function to toggle the odd and even rows. Since the pivot cell (the text box at the intersection of the row groups and column group) is repeated with the same background color for every column in a row, the second function argument is set to False (see Figure 7-5).

275

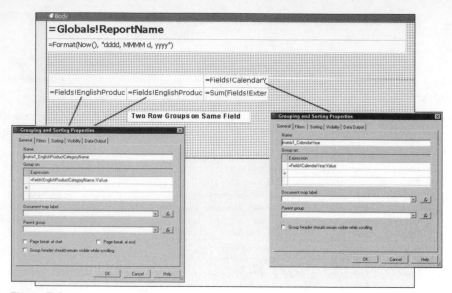

Figure 7-4

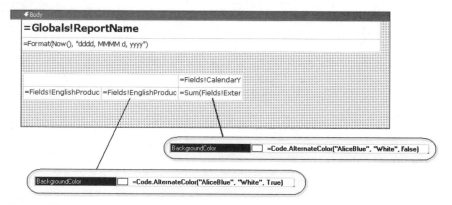

Figure 7-5

In Figure 7-6, I've reduced the width of this cell and I've also hidden it by setting the Visibility/ Hidden property to True. You actually can't completely eliminate all evidence of a cell but you can make it very narrow. I've set the GridSpacing property to .03125 (1/32 of an inch), so I could make this column as narrow as possible.

Figure 7-6

Figure 7-7 shows the end result. The utility cell causes a small gap between the row header and the remaining columns; alternate row colors are applied to the aggregate data cells.

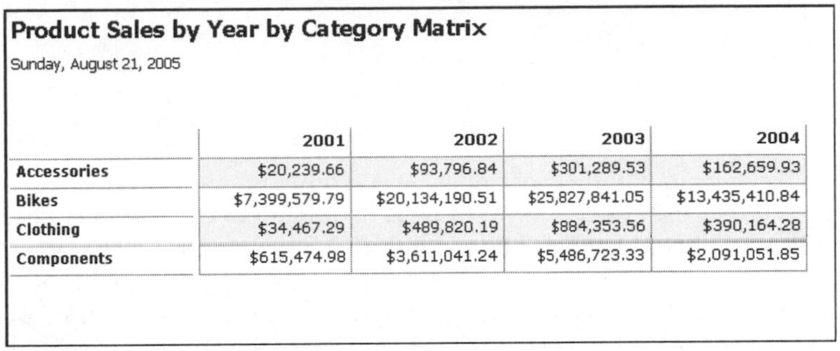

Product Sales by Year by Category Matrix

Sunday, August 21, 2005

	2001	2002	2003	2004
Accessories	$20,239.66	$93,796.84	$301,289.53	$162,659.93
Bikes	$7,399,579.79	$20,134,190.51	$25,827,841.05	$13,435,410.84
Clothing	$34,467.29	$489,820.19	$884,353.56	$390,164.28
Components	$615,474.98	$3,611,041.24	$5,486,723.33	$2,091,051.85

Figure 7-7

Multiple Criterion Report Filtering

Report design requirements may call for complex combinations of parameter values used to filter report data. Using Transact-SQL, you should be able to handle practically any advanced filtering criteria and filter the data before it reaches the report server. However, if you need to use report filtering to provide the same kinds of filtering support against data already cached by the data set query, the report designer has some significant limitations in this area. For example, let's say that my report has two parameters for filtering product records: ProductCategory and PriceRange. In this simplified example, the parameter values for both of my parameter lists are the same as the parameter label values.

The ProductCategory parameter list values are shown in the following table.

Parameter Value	Product Category Field Match
Bikes	Bikes
Components	Components
Clothing	Clothing
Accessories	Accessories
All Bike Related	Bikes and Components
All	All Categories

The PriceRange parameter list values are shown in the next table.

Parameter Value	Price Range Field Match
Less than 50	< 50
50 to 99	>= 50 AND < 100

Table continued on following page

Parameter Value	Price Range Field Match
100 to 499	>= 100 AND < 500
500 and Higher	>= 500
All	All Prices

Contending with the various combinations of these and other parameter values in the confines of the report designer's filtering user interface would be very difficult to do. The most flexible method is to write a separate Visual Basic function to handle the matching logic for each parameter and field combination. This code is called for each row. The function returns a value to be matched with a field in the row. If the values match, the row is returned. The following custom code is added to the report on the Code tab of the Report Properties dialog:

```
Function MatchProductCategory(ParamValue As String, FieldValue As String) As
String
    Select Case ParamValue
        Case "Bikes", "Components", "Clothing", "Accessories"
            Return ParamValue
        Case "All Bike Related"
            If FieldValue = "Bikes" Or FieldValue = "Components" Then
                Return FieldValue
            End If
        Case "All"
            Return FieldValue
    End Select
End Function

Function MatchPriceRange(ParamValue As String, FieldValue As String) As
Decimal
    Select Case ParamValue
        Case "Less than 50"
            If FieldValue < 50 Then Return FieldValue
        Case "50 to 100"
            If FieldValue >= 50 And FieldValue < 100 Then Return FieldValue
        Case "100 to 500"
            If FieldValue >= 100 And FieldValue < 500 Then Return FieldValue
        Case "500 and Higher"
            If FieldValue >= 500 Then Return FieldValue
        Case "All"
            Return FieldValue
    End Select
End Function
```

Using the Filters tab on the Dataset properties dialog, execute each of the functions, matching its return value to the corresponding field. Figure 7-8 shows this dialog.

This technique takes all of the complexity out of this simple dialog and puts it where it belongs: in program code. That environment gives you the control needed to contend with practically any set of business rules.

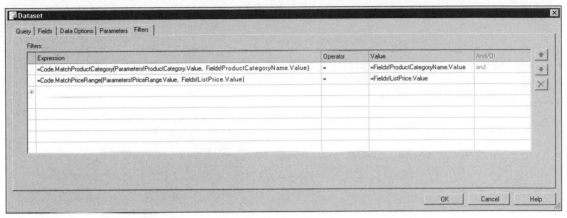

Figure 7-8

Multi-field Data Point Charts

The most common charting scenarios involve the use of one field value grouped across another field value, with data from multiple rows. The chart contains one data point for each group value and automatically generates colors or shades for each point. Most of the examples you'll find demonstrate various forms of single-field data point charting. However, there may be times when you need to chart multiple values from the same row. These may be different fields or calculated values based on one or more fields. One of the advantages to explicitly providing data for each point is the additional formatting control you have. You can specify the color, font characteristics, and labeling for each point individually.

What you'll need:

❑   A data set containing multiple, related fields with numeric values.

❑   A chart item with multiple data point expressions.

In this example, the report is filtered using a parameter to return only one row. Slices of the pie chart will represent the product cost and calculated profit from a single product record. Figure 7-9 shows the standard design-time preview of a pie chart. Don't pay any attention to the standard chart design view since ours isn't going to have five data point slices.

If no series or category groups are created, a field added to the value groups will result in only one data point. Depending upon the chart type, a data point is plotted as a slice, point, column, or bar. I'll create two value groups named Cost and Profit. These are visible on the Data tab of the Chart Properties dialog in Figure 7-10.

Since the entire pie circumference will represent the price of a product, the size of the cost and profit slices must be expressed as proportional values. The point labels (the value displayed on or near the plotted point) may be managed separately. For example, the point label could display the profit as a percentage rather than the actual currency value. Figure 7-11 shows the Value expression for the Cost group.

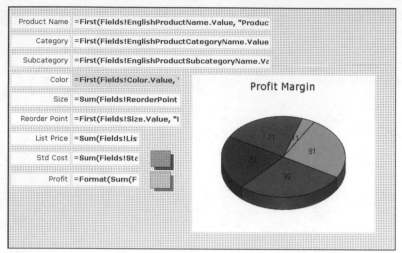

Figure 7-9

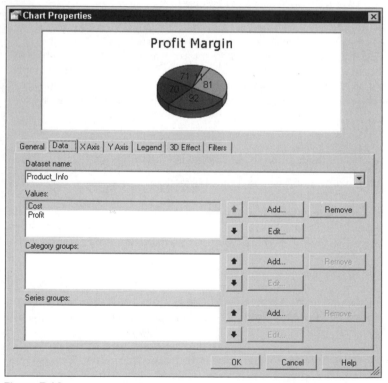

Figure 7-10

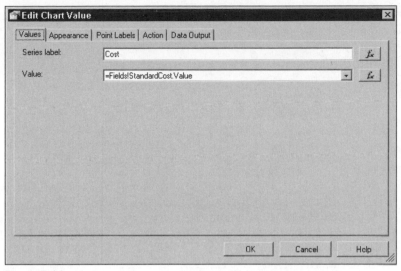

Figure 7-11

Rather than using a standard color palette, I can use a specific color for each data point. Figure 7-12 shows the Style Properties dialog, accessible form the Edit Chart Value window. Here, I set the color of this slice to SteelBlue.

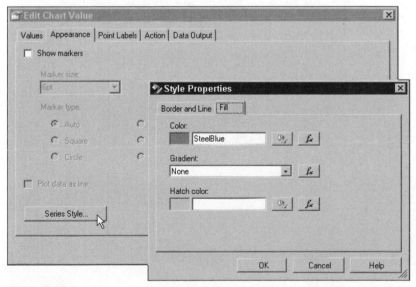

Figure 7-12

On the Point Labels tab, shown in Figure 7-13, I can set the display value and format. The regular expression C2 means that a localized currency value will be displayed with two decimal positions. The nine position buttons may be used to place the data point text labels on or near the pie slice using call-outs and connector lines.

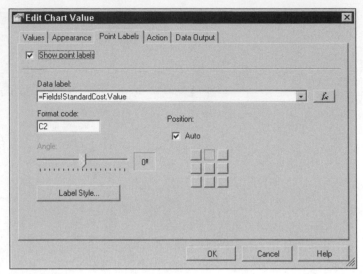

Figure 7-13

Figure 7-14 shows that the Profit data point value is calculated by subtracting the product cost from the price.

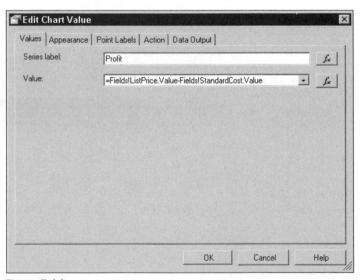

Figure 7-14

Figure 7-15 shows that the borders for both data points are set to black.

The Profit data point will be yellow. In Figure 7-16, this is set using the Style Properties dialog when editing this data point.

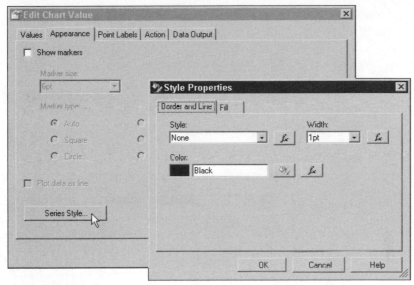

Figure 7-15

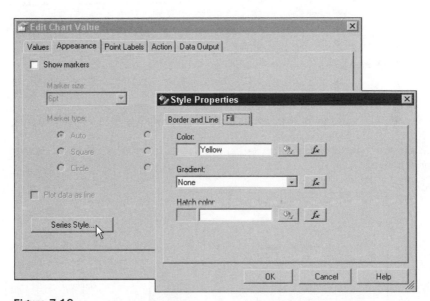

Figure 7-16

For the Profit data point label, I'd like to display both the profit value and the formatted percentage in parentheses. This will require a fairly complex expression. In Figure 7-17, you see the elements of this string concatenated together. When piecing multiple values together like this, numeric values need to be formatted separately. In this example, the Visual Basic Format() function is used to display the profit formatted as currency with two decimals and the percentage with no decimals.

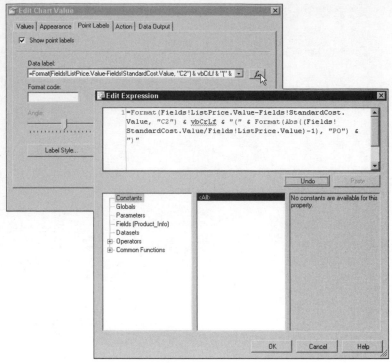

Figure 7-17

Incidentally, I like to see the line numbers in my code, so I've configured Visual Studio to show these. This option is available on the toolbar, under Tools➪Options➪Text Editor➪All Languages.

Figure 7-18 shows the report in preview. Rather than using the chart legend, I've created a custom key using colored rectangles.

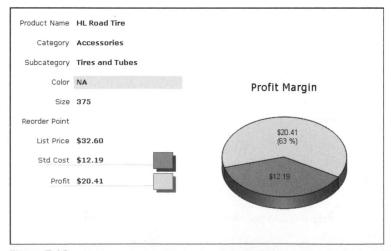

Figure 7-18

TOP X and "Other" Chart

Many standard chart formats have a limited capacity to effectively display more than a few series values. This can be remedied by capping the number of grouped values to a specific number of top values. However, a top 10 report may not accurately represent the entire data population. In addition to the top 10 slices, an additional slice represents everything else. This can be effective when the top 10 represent a significant portion of all values. Since each of the standard color palettes includes 16 colors, it at most makes sense to present the top 15 + 1 "other" slice aggregating the remaining rows.

Here's what you'll need:

- ❑ A custom query expression that combines two related result sets:
    - ❑ A specified number of top-rated values.
    - ❑ An aggregate row consisting of all remaining rows.
- ❑ A chart item used to present the combined result set.

Figure 7-19 shows the finished report, so you can see the concept before taking a look at the design technique. Note that there are 11 slices, 10 for the top 10–selling products and one for the sum of all remaining products.

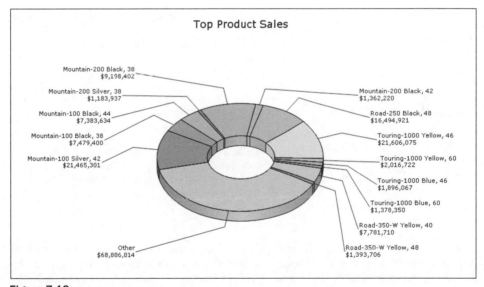

Figure 7-19

This technique doesn't require any special settings in the chart itself. The magic is all in the data set. This requires a little advanced SQL work. The following Transact-SQL query defines two different result sets, one for the top 10 rows and the other for everything else. To return the non–top 10 values, the top 10 query uses a subquery to exclude this selection for the entire result. The two results are combined using the SQL UNION statement:

```
-- Top 10 and Others:
SELECT Top10.ProductKey, Top10.ProductName
     , Top10.AmountSum
FROM (
     -- Top 10:
     SELECT TOP 10
              DimProduct.ProductKey
            , DimProduct.EnglishProductName AS ProductName
            , SUM(FactResellerSales.ExtendedAmount) AS AmountSum
     FROM    DimProduct INNER JOIN FactResellerSales
             ON DimProduct.ProductKey = FactResellerSales.ProductKey
             INNER JOIN DimTime
             ON FactResellerSales.OrderDateKey = DimTime.TimeKey
     GROUP BY DimProduct.ProductKey, DimProduct.EnglishProductName
     ORDER BY SUM(FactResellerSales.ExtendedAmount) DESC
     ) AS Top10
UNION
SELECT Other.ProductKey, Other.ProductName, Other.AmountSum
FROM (
     -- Others excluding the top 10:
     SELECT TOP 100 PERCENT
              -1 AS ProductKey, 'Other' AS ProductName
            , SUM(FactResellerSales.ExtendedAmount) AS AmountSum
     FROM    DimProduct INNER JOIN FactResellerSales
             ON DimProduct.ProductKey = FactResellerSales.ProductKey
             INNER JOIN DimTime
             ON FactResellerSales.OrderDateKey = DimTime.TimeKey
     WHERE   DimProduct.ProductKey NOT IN
             (
               SELECT TOP 10 DimProduct.ProductKey
               FROM    DimProduct INNER JOIN FactResellerSales
                       ON DimProduct.ProductKey =
                          FactResellerSales.ProductKey
                       INNER JOIN DimTime ON
                       FactResellerSales.OrderDateKey = DimTime.TimeKey
               GROUP BY DimProduct.ProductKey
               ORDER BY SUM(FactResellerSales.ExtendedAmount) DESC
             )
     ORDER BY SUM(FactResellerSales.ExtendedAmount) DESC
     ) AS Other
```

You should be mindful that this query must reselect data in the same tables multiple times and may not perform well with large tables. This solution can also be achieved using an upgraded version of the chart item available from Dundas Software. Dundas Chart for Reporting Services includes a similar feature that doesn't require complex query expressions.

Dynamic Images: Scales and Gauges

Images can be made to display different content under different conditions. Using expressions, the image report item may be used with a series of images to show progress gauges or indicators.

What you'll need:

- ❑ A series of gauge or scale images representing progressive values.
- ❑ An image item used to display one of the images.
- ❑ An expression used to translate integer values to the name of a corresponding image.

The Chart item outputs a static image that is embedded in the rendered report. In cases where you would like to use graphical output that a chart doesn't provide, you may use predefined graphics. The technique I'll demonstrate uses 11 image files, which represent a gauge with different values. Based on a data value, the image is replaced with a corresponding graphic. Images may be obtained from a database, from external files, or may be embedded within the report definition. Embedded images are convenient because they don't require special security or addressing deployment considerations. However, embedded images should be used with small image files to keep the report definition file size manageable.

The sales quota data in the AdventureWorksDW database didn't match up very well to the reseller sales totals, so I had to modify the quota values to get this demonstration to work. If you want to duplicate this query, I suggest that you back up the database and then modify some of the SalesAmountQuota values in the FactSalesQuota table so the results are more realistic.

Figure 7-20 shows 11 gauge graphic files I've created using Dundas Gauges. Each is saved in a folder as a PNG file. The file names also contain their value. This makes it easier to use an expression to derive the correct file name.

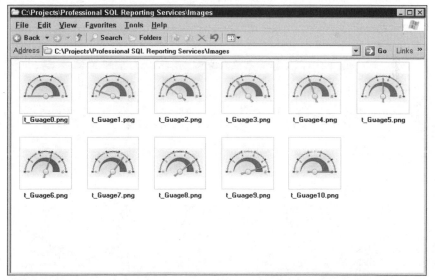

Figure 7-20

My data set query, shown in Figure 7-21, returns comparative quota and actual sales values grouped by year, quarter, and employee.

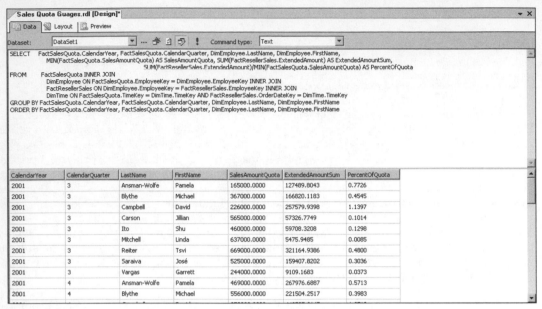

Figure 7-21

For simplicity, and because the image files are small, I'm adding them to the report definition. By default, each image is assigned the same name as the source file. These can by modified if necessary. Figure 7-22 shows the Embedded Images dialog, opened from the Report menu.

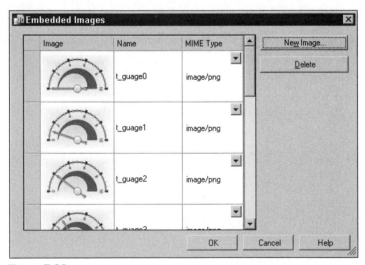

Figure 7-22

The report contains a table item with an image in one of the detail cells (see Figure 7-23). When the image item is dropped onto the report design surface, the Image Wizard is launched. The wizard selections aren't important and will be replaced with properties I'll set manually.

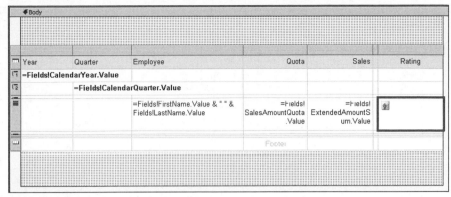

Figure 7-23

The Image items properties are set to use embedded images. I've set the image to `FitProportional` but this may be changed depending on the image size and characteristics. I typically use the Padding properties to provide margin space around the image cell. The image item's `Value` property will tie each row's sales quota value to a corresponding gauge.

A calculated column called PercentOfQuota returns a float value as a percentage (0.0 to 1.0). By multiplying this value and converting it to an integer, using the Visual Basic `CInt()` function, these values now correspond to my image file names (0 to 10). This expression concatenates this integer with the rest of the file name. To prevent an overflow condition, if the percentage value is greater than 1 (100%), the expression always returns the highest value, 10.

```
="t_guage" & IIF(Fields!PercentOfQuota.Value>1, "10",
CStr(CInt(Fields!PercentOfQuota.Value * 10 )))
```

Here's the final result, shown in Figure 7-24.

I'll use the same basic principle in the next example to produce a business scorecard.

Creating a Business Scorecard

This type of reporting scenario has quickly become a mainstay in enterprise business applications. Also known as executive dashboards, business scorecards provide summary level progress and success status information for business leaders.

What you'll need:

❑ A query expression with data-based or calculated target, budget, variance, and actual values.

❑ A multi-group table with drill-down features.

❑ Small images for use as progress indicators.

❑ An expression used to translate KPI and target values to indicator images.

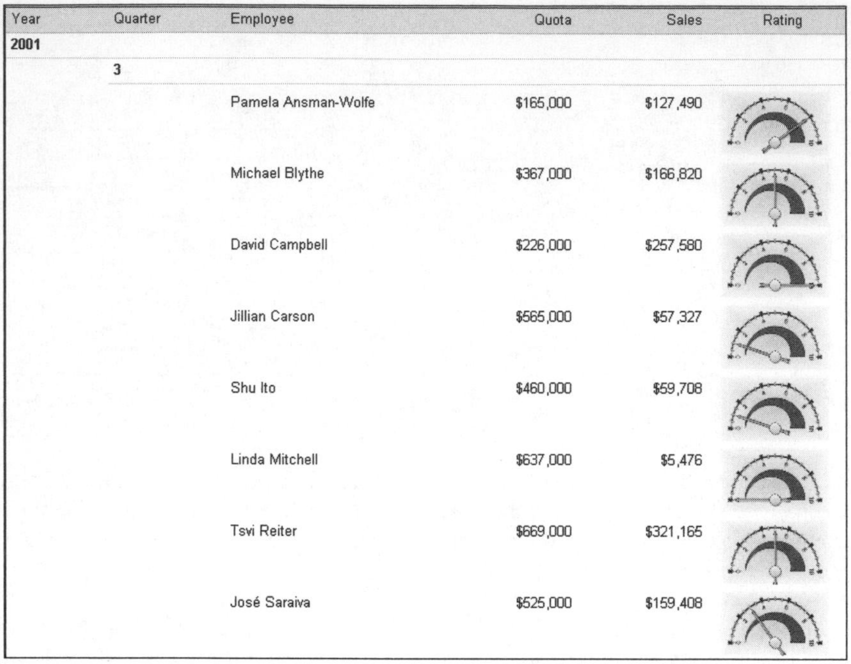

Year	Quarter	Employee	Quota	Sales	Rating
2001					
	3				
		Pamela Ansman-Wolfe	$165,000	$127,490	
		Michael Blythe	$367,000	$166,820	
		David Campbell	$226,000	$257,580	
		Jillian Carson	$565,000	$57,327	
		Shu Ito	$460,000	$59,708	
		Linda Mitchell	$637,000	$5,476	
		Tsvi Reiter	$669,000	$321,165	
		José Saraiva	$525,000	$159,408	

Figure 7-24

Executive Dashboards

To understand and appreciate the value of this type of reporting interface, you need to walk in the shoes of corporate business leaders. A typical corporate officer deals with a lot of people and a variety of information in a day and often needs to make immediate decisions based on this information. When moving from meeting to meeting, transaction-level details are too granular for most decisions. Business leaders need to know how the business is performing overall and whether there are areas of concern or notable success. I've sat in a lot of meetings with a general manager or director sitting on one side of the table and subject experts on another. The officer begins by saying "So, how are we doing?" The subject expert gives a lengthy presentation, stepping through PowerPoint slides, charts, graphs, and diagrams that depict trends and variances based on mountains of data. After the presentation, the officer concludes with the question: "So, how are we doing?" Scorecards and dashboards answer this all-important question using succinct summary values and simple graphical, symbolic progress indicators.

Although simplification is a key concept, scorecards go beyond just keeping reports simple. Trends and success indicators should be clear and easy to understand but should provide an avenue to discover more detail and to view related trends and summaries. These objectives are easily achieved using drill-down and drill-through report features.

Targets and KPIs

These are the fundamental concepts behind business scorecards. For any given measurement, a target is simply an objective value. Targets are often data-driven values such as a Budget, Quota, Baseline, or Goal. A KPI, or Key Performance Indicator, is a set of thresholds used to measure actual values with the target. KPIs may define banding indicators to signify a range of variances like poor, acceptable, and exceptional performance. KPI thresholds may be a single point, corresponding to the target, percentage, or fixed increment offsets with any number of indicator bands.

When considering longer-term trends, you may want to recognize the difference between a positive trend using a KPI and whether or not a value represents a successful outcome, as a KSI (Key Success Indicator). For example, sales for a particular product may have been unprofitable since it went on the market. If sales are rising, a KPI would show positive sales growth, whereas a KSI would indicate that the company is still in the red. We might simply define two targets, one to measure short-term progress and the other to measure overall profitability.

Indicators

Indicators are graphical icons, representing the state of an actual value with respect to a KPI band. On the scorecard, corresponding indicator icons might be red, yellow, and green symbols. Indicators are typically common symbolic metaphors such as traffic lights, colored shapes, progress bars, gauges, and directional arrows. Figure 7-25 shows some common indicator graphics embedded in a sample report.

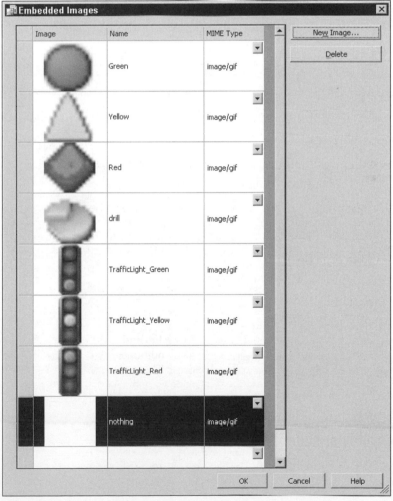

Figure 7-25

Calculating Variance

Variance is the difference between an actual and target value. If time variances will be used extensively, the queries used to make these calculations can be very intensive. Aggregating and calculating sales totals, for example, for a given month over last month, quarter, or year can require some heavy-duty query processing (even with a modest number of detail rows). Ideally, this type of data should be stored in a data mart or data warehouse with precalculated variance values stored in the database. The AdventureWorksDW database contains some preaggregated summary values, but as you can see, even for this simple report with only year-over-year variances, the query is fairly complex.

```sql
SELECT
    ThisYearSales.SalesTerritoryRegion
  , ThisYearSales.SalesTerritoryKey
  , ThisYearSales.CalendarYear
  , ThisYearSales.LastName
  , ThisYearSales.FirstName
  , ThisYearSales.EmployeeName
  , SUM(ThisYearSales.ExtendedAmount) AS ExtendedAmountSum
  , SUM(ThisYearSales.SalesAmountQuota) AS SalesAmountQuotaSum
  , SUM(LastYearSales.ExtendedAmountSum) AS ExtendedAmountSumLastYear
FROM (
    SELECT
        DimSalesTerritory.SalesTerritoryRegion
      , DimSalesTerritory.SalesTerritoryKey
      , DimTime.CalendarYear
      , DimEmployee.LastName
      , DimEmployee.FirstName
      , DimEmployee.EmployeeKey
      , DimEmployee.FirstName + ' ' + DimEmployee.LastName AS EmployeeName
      , FactResellerSales.ExtendedAmount
      , FactSalesQuota.SalesAmountQuota
    FROM DimEmployee INNER JOIN FactSalesQuota
        ON DimEmployee.EmployeeKey = FactSalesQuota.EmployeeKey
        INNER JOIN DimTime ON FactSalesQuota.TimeKey = DimTime.TimeKey
        INNER JOIN FactResellerSales
        ON DimEmployee.EmployeeKey = FactResellerSales.EmployeeKey
           AND DimTime.TimeKey = FactResellerSales.OrderDateKey
        INNER JOIN DimSalesTerritory
        ON DimSalesTerritory.SalesTerritoryKey =
           FactResellerSales.SalesTerritoryKey) AS ThisYearSales
        INNER JOIN
          ( SELECT
                FactResellerSales.EmployeeKey
              , DimTime.CalendarYear
              , DimSalesTerritory.SalesTerritoryKey
              , DimSalesTerritory.SalesTerritoryRegion
              , FactResellerSales.ExtendedAmount AS ExtendedAmountSum
            FROM FactResellerSales
                INNER JOIN DimTime
                ON FactResellerSales.OrderDateKey = DimTime.TimeKey
                INNER JOIN DimSalesTerritory
                ON DimSalesTerritory.SalesTerritoryKey =
                   FactResellerSales.SalesTerritoryKey
          ) AS LastYearSales
    ON LastYearSales.CalendarYear = ThisYearSales.CalendarYear - 1
```

```
           AND ThisYearSales.EmployeeKey = LastYearSales.EmployeeKey
           AND ThisYearSales.SalesTerritoryKey = LastYearSales.SalesTerritoryKey
    GROUP BY ThisYearSales.SalesTerritoryRegion, ThisYearSales.SalesTerritoryKey
       , ThisYearSales.CalendarYear, ThisYearSales.LastName, ThisYearSales.FirstName
       , ThisYearSales.EmployeeName
    ORDER BY ThisYearSales.SalesTerritoryRegion, ThisYearSales.CalendarYear
       , ThisYearSales.LastName, ThisYearSales.FirstName
```

When running complex queries like this one, you may need to increase the default connection timeout setting on the data source. The default setting is 15 seconds, which may not be sufficient for this query on all hardware. In a production application with data volumes greater than the sample database, I would recommend testing query performance and possibly using an Analysis Services database with cubes and precalculated aggregates. To populate the data warehouse, you will use queries similar to this one and store the results for later retrieval.

Figure 7-26 shows a simple table with two groups, on the SalesTerritory and CalendarYear fields. This table is much like several previous examples. The detail row is hidden by default, allowing for drill-down using the SalesTerritoryRegion text box. Two more images will serve as indicators. These are based on expressions used to change the indicator image.

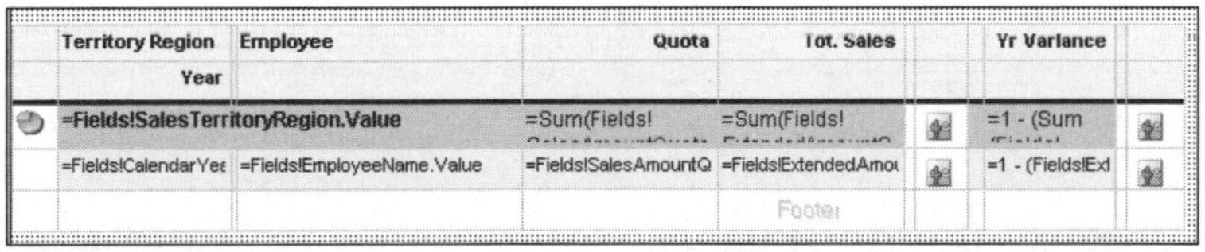

Territory Region	Employee	Quota	Tot. Sales		Yr Variance	
Year						
=Fields!SalesTerritoryRegion.Value	=Sum(Fields!	=Sum(Fields!		=1 - (Sum	
=Fields!CalendarYea	=Fields!EmployeeName.Value	=Fields!SalesAmountQ	=Fields!ExtendedAmou		=1 - (Fields!Ext	
			Footer			

Figure 7-26

You will notice that the images have a white background even though I've used background colors to separate the rows. I've only done this to simplify this example. I have simply added the images to the cells in the table header. If you want to use transparent images over a colored or shaded background, you will need to add rectangles to the header cells and then place images in the rectangles. This way, you can set the BackgroundColor property for each rectangle and take advantage of the image transparency. The final example, shown in Figure 7-30, uses this technique to fill the background color behind the scorecard indicator images.

Looking at the columns with text headers, the first column contains the SalesTerritoryRegion field in the first group header and the CalendarYear field in the detail row.

The second column contains the EmployeeName in the detail row.

The third text column is for the SalesAmountQuota field. The header uses the SUM() function to aggregate the details for the sales territory.

The forth text column contains total sales values, using the ExtendedAmount field.

The last column of text boxes, labeled Yr. Variance, calculates the total sales amount annual variance. In the header row, the expression uses the SUM() function. In the detail row, the SUM() function is omitted.

```
=1-(Sum(Fields!ExtendedAmountSumLastYear.Value)/
Sum(Fields!ExtendedAmountSum.Value))
```

The expression for the sales first set of indicators (the images column after total sales column) calls a Visual Basic function to apply the KPI threshold banding. Figure 7-27 shows this custom code.

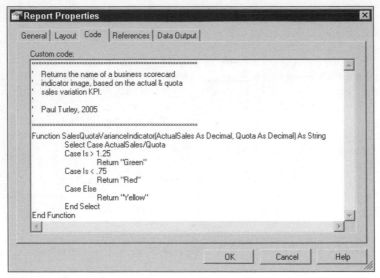

Figure 7-27

Since the image names for the green, yellow, and red indicators are Green, Yellow, and Red, these values are simply returned in the Value property of the image item using the following expression:

```
=Code.SalesQuotaVarianceIndicator(Sum(Fields!ExtendedAmountSum.Value),
Sum(Fields!SalesAmountQuotaSum.Value))
```

For variety, I've resolved the second indicator column images using only an in-line expression rather than using a custom function. This is the expression for the header row. The detail row expression is the same but without the SUM() function. As a rule, once I've decided to use custom code, I'll typically continue to use custom functions for all but the simplest expressions so that I can keep business logic in one place.

```
=IIF(Sum(Fields!ExtendedAmountSum.Value) /
Sum(Fields!ExtendedAmountSumLastYear.Value) < .8, "exclamation_small", "nothing")
```

This expression returns the name of an exclamation mark icon image when this year's sales amount is less than 80% of last year's. I created an image file called "nothing," which is a blank icon with a white background. Using this image effectively displays nothing in the image cell.

Synchronizing Charts and Related Report Items

One of the great advantages to the scorecard approach is that all the information is presented in a concise page. In order to make the best use of screen space, I can use a separate report item to show content related to the item selected in the scorecard.

Figure 7-28 shows the table and chart items. When I select a sales territory, by clicking on the small pie chart icon in the first column, I want to see sales trend information in a column chart. I've placed a chart to the right of the scorecard and have configured it as a column chart. I've also simplified the chart by removing the legend.

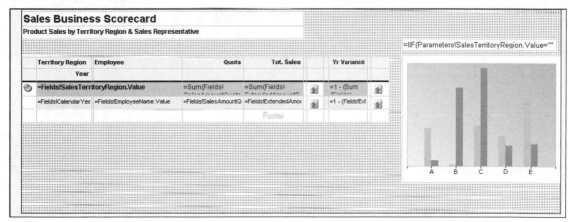

Figure 7-28

The chart content is synchronized using a report parameter. The `SalesTerritoryKey` parameter is used to filter the data set providing data to the chart. The `SalesTerritoryRegion` parameter is used to provide a title value for the text box above the chart. Figure 7-29 shows the Navigation properties for the pie icon used to synchronize the chart. Note that the Jump to report property is set to navigate back to this report, rerendering the same report with the new parameter values.

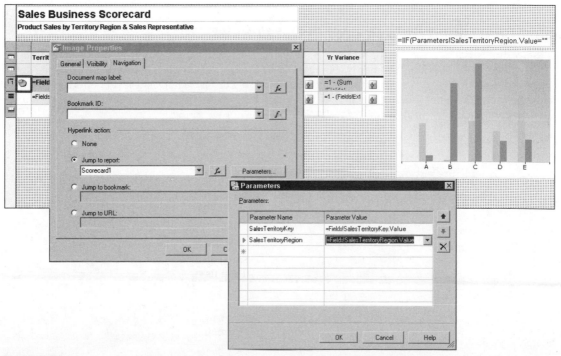

Figure 7-29

Figure 7-30 shows the rendered report with some region sections drilled open. I've clicked the pie icon next to the Southwest region to synchronize the chart and view sales trend details for the Southwest region. Again, note the background color fill behind the scorecard indicator images using the technique I mentioned earlier.

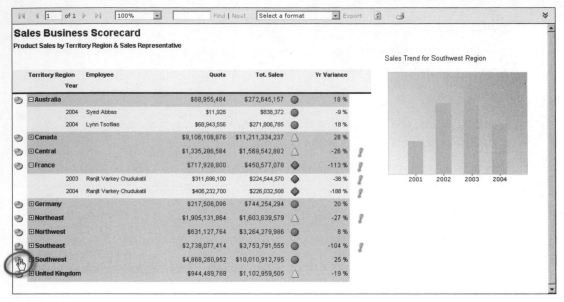

Figure 7-30

Using Charts and Data Ranges in Detail Rows

Reporting Services doesn't support the placement of charts and some other embedded report items in table detail rows. Working around this limitation is very easy and simply requires that a group be defined at the detail row level. You can either delete the detail row or resize it. Detail-level items are placed in the header row rather than the detail row. The following two sparkline chart examples will demonstrate this technique.

What you'll need:

❑ A table presenting a columnar set of values.

❑ A chart item embedded into a table group header cell.

Creating Sparklines

Edward Tufte, one of the most recognized experts on the subject of data visualization, presents the idea of sparklines. These are simple, word-sized graphics that are an alternative to large, busy charts used to communicate a simple trend or series of measurements. In order to be meaningful, sometimes charts need to have annotated gridlines, point labels, and legends. However, some charts can effectively serve their purpose without the use of supporting text labels. To illustrate observations like "sales are improving," "a product is profitable," or that a trend is cyclical, a simple trend chart needs little or no labeling. Sparklines are best used when embedded in text or other report formats.

What you'll need:

❏ A query expression used to return trend data.

❏ A small, simplified chart item.

❏ A table item to display master rows.

Column and line charts are best suited for this type of presentation. In the first of two examples, I'll use a column chart to show sports games scores for a team throughout the season. The first example uses data I had on hand from a project. The second example will use sample data from the AdventureWorks database.

Team Standings

The purpose of the chart, shown in Figure 7-31, is to quantify the team's relative position and win/loss trend rather than to show specific scores. For this I use a no-frills column chart. The data set returns a team name, game number, and score for each team. The column value will represent the number of points that won or lost the game. For example, a team that wins with a score of 5 to 3 would have a winning score of 2. If the team loses 3 to 4, their score would be -1.

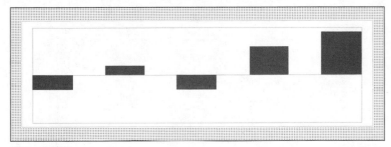

Figure 7-31

Figure 7-32 shows the category group. This plots columns along the X-axis, one for each game.

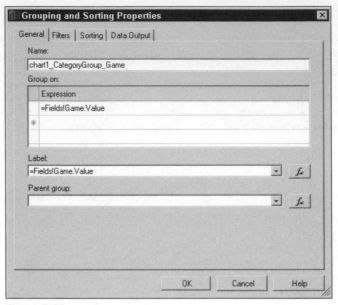

Figure 7-32

The value group uses the calculated score to plot the column above or below the line to indicate a win or loss. Figure 7-33 shows this calculation in the Edit Chart Value dialog.

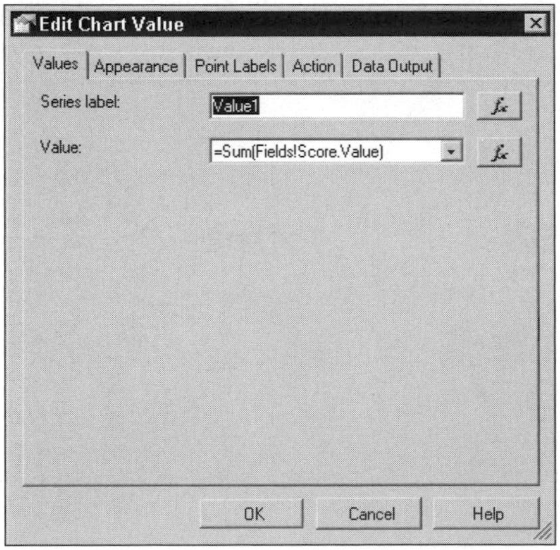

Figure 7-33

Figures 7-34 and 7-35 show the X-axis and Y-axis configuration. The X-axis grid lines, tick marks, and labels are removed to keep the chart simple.

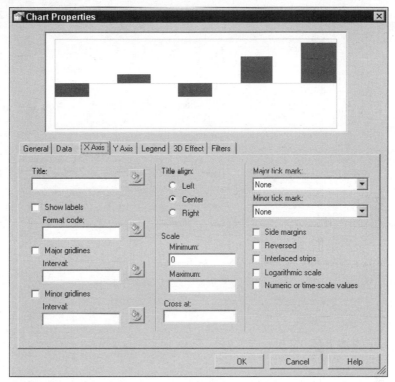

Figure 7-34

On the Y-axis, lines are displayed at the zero crosspoint, dividing wins and losses at 10 and -10 to render all chart instances at the same scale.

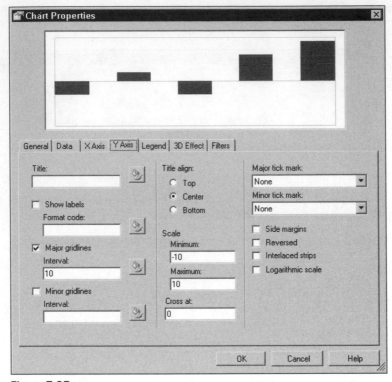

Figure 7-35

Since the chart will be quite small, border lines should be thin and subtle. Click the corresponding Style button to show the Style Properties dialog, shown in Figure 7-36. I'm using the Silver color (50% gray) and .5 point lines. These lines may not be displayed in the designer but should render correctly when the report is previewed or deployed.

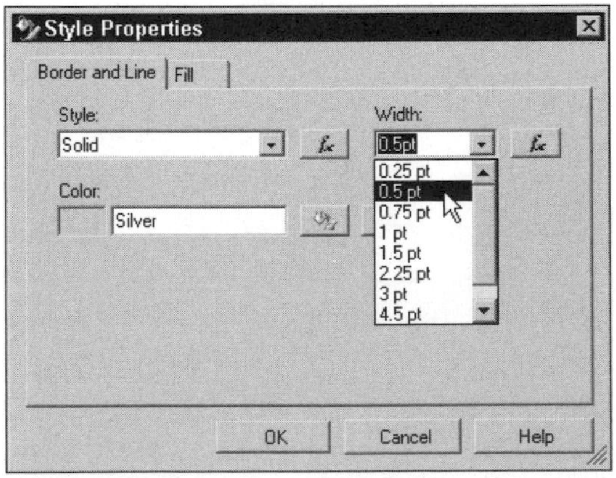

Figure 7-36

The chart is placed in a group header row within a table grouped on the team field. This will serve as the detail row, since a chart can't reside in a detail row. Figure 7-37 shows the finished report in design view.

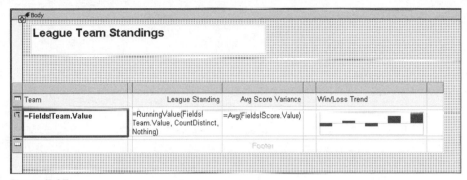

Figure 7-37

The finished report is shown in Figure 7-38. Each team's calculated league standing, average score variance, and win/loss trend sparkline chart are displayed in table rows.

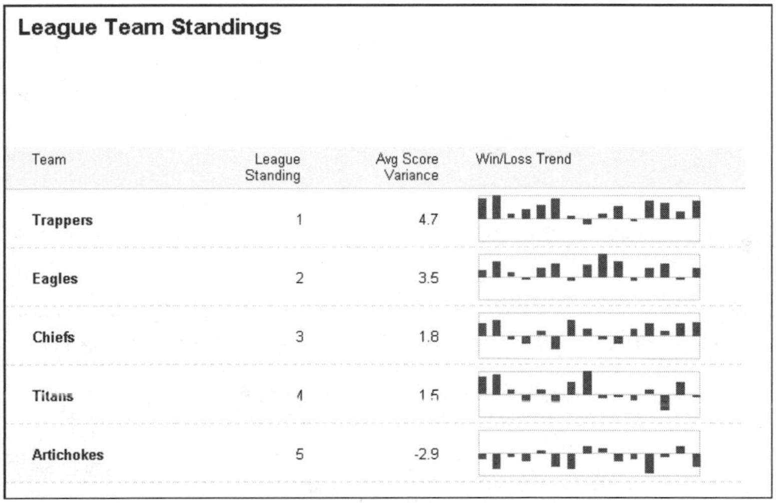

League Team Standings

Team	League Standing	Avg Score Variance	Win/Loss Trend
Trappers	1	4.7	
Eagles	2	3.5	
Chiefs	3	1.8	
Titans	4	1.5	
Artichokes	5	-2.9	

Figure 7-38

Sales Trends

This example shows product category sales on each row and sales by year in an associated line chart, plotting sales totals by month. This report's data set is based on a simple query that returns aggregated sales by year and month, and then by product category.

In Figure 7-39, I've added and set up the table and chart in separate areas of the report body. They're both bound to the same data set. After the table is configured, I'll add it to the table. As in the previous example, a group header row is used in place of the detail row.

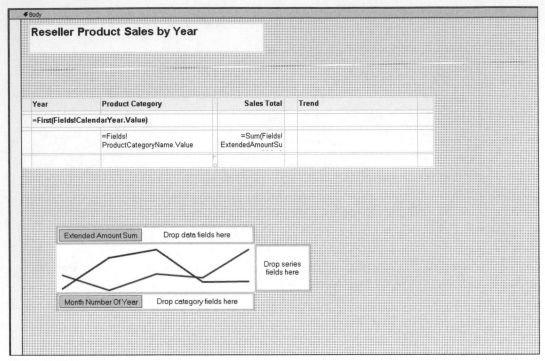

Figure 7-39

I've configured the chart with no gridlines or labels at all. Its purpose is to show relative sales trends, not specific values. In a production reporting solution, I might create a separate chart report, similar to the sparkline chart but with more detail. Figure 7-40 shows this report in design view.

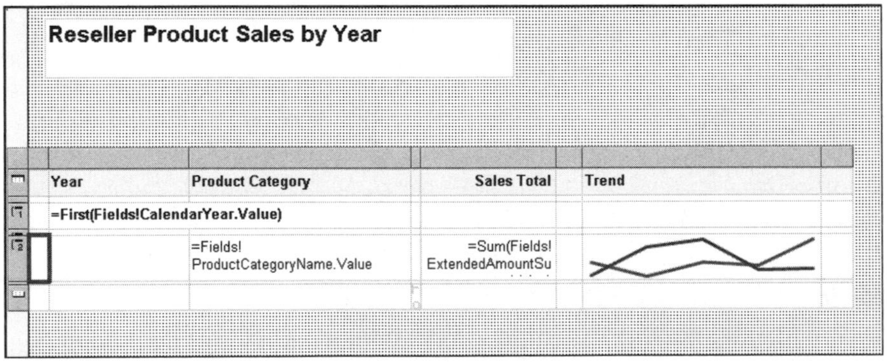

Figure 7-40

Finally, Figure 7-41 shows the finished report. The trend line shows sales total over the course of the year. Whether data points represented days, weeks, or months, the effect would be the same.

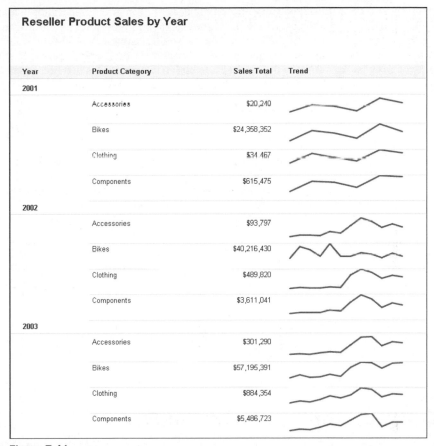

Figure 7-41

Using Field Values in Page Headers and Footers

Another limitation of the Reporting Services architecture is its inability to add data-bound items to page headers and footers. The reason for this is that the pagination of a report occurs after the data has been rendered. During the page formatting pass, items in the page header and footer areas have access to already rendered report items but not to data fields.

What you'll need:

❑   One or more hidden text boxes in the body of the report body.

❑   Text boxes in the page header or footer used to present field values.

❑   Expressions used to repeat values from the hidden item(s).

Displaying a single data-bound field value in a page header or footer is a fairly simple matter. Since report items in the page header can't refer to fields but can access report items, a hidden text box in the report body may be used as a surrogate field reference. You'll recall that a field-bound text box placed in the report body must use an aggregate function such as FIRST() or SUM(). Figure 7-42 shows a bound text box (with a gray background) in the report body above the table. This text box has been hidden as its purpose is only to be used by the corresponding text box in the page header.

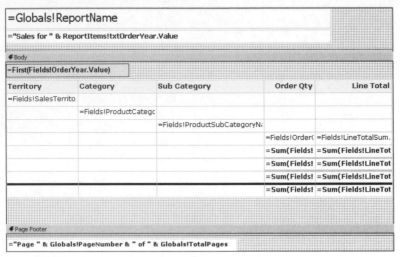

Figure 7-42

Group Continued in Page Header or Footer

Report items in a data range, such as a table or list, may also be referenced from items in the page header or footer. There are at least a couple of different techniques for repeating group values in a report header.

What you'll need:

❑ A table or other grouped data range item containing text box group headings.

❑ A text box in the page header or footer used to display the last group value.

❑ An expression used to refer to the previous group header text box.

In the following examples, I'll demonstrate two techniques. Figure 7-43 shows a report with a table item with groups, headers, and footers containing subtotals.

After the table header (shown with a light-gray background color), the first group has two header rows. The first row (with italicized text) is a hidden row used only to allow the text box in the report header to reference its value. The hidden row contains a text box named txtSalesTerritoryName, which is referenced from the page header text box within the First() aggregate function. This is necessary because the table header row may be repeated. I want the page header to show the value from the first instance on the page.

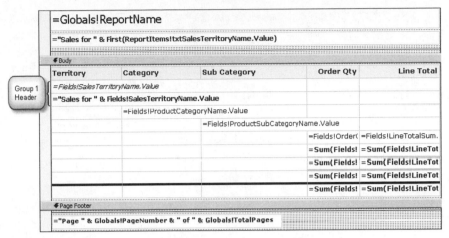

Figure 7-43

Dynamic Grouping

I get called in to consulting client sites often to rebuild a set of existing Crystal or Access reports in Reporting Services. They will typically have several reports for each data entity or table that are grouped, sorted, and filtered a little differently. This solution allows you to consolidate data groups for the same table into one report. The following example consolidates the reports Product Sales by Territory, Product Sales by Category, and Product Sales by Subcategory into one report with user-selectable field grouping.

What you'll need:

❑ A table presenting a columnar set of grouped values.

❑ A report parameter with a list of fields in the data set for sorting.

❑ A group expression using the report parameter to resolve the grouping field name.

❑ Heading and summary expressions referring to the dynamic group expression.

This works best with simple columnar reports that have one group. The dynamic grouping is based on a single parameter selection that returns the name of a field from the report's main data set. Figure 7-44 shows the settings for the GroupBy parameter. Note that the Value column for the parameter list contains the actual field names for selected fields in the data set.

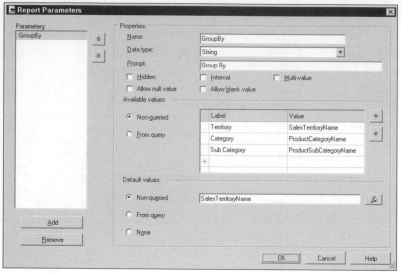

Figure 7-44

A group is defined in the table based on an expression that uses this parameter to resolve the field value. In the report header, I want to show the field name, and in the group header, I want to show the actual field value. To return the friendly field name that was displayed in the parameter drop-down list, I refer to the `Label` property of the parameter. You can see in Figure 7-45 that the field value is displayed using the compound expression: `=Fields(Parameters!GroupBy.Value).Value`. The inner reference `(Parameters!GroupBy.Value)` is resolved first to return the field name, which is passed to the outer expression `(Fields( <field name> ).Value )` to resolve the field value from the field name. I have found this technique useful in many different reports.

=Globals!ReportName			
="Grouped by " & Parameters!GroupBy.Label			
⁂Body			
=Parameters!GroupBy.Label	Product	Order Qty	Line Total
=Fields(Parameters!GroupBy.Value).Value			
	=Fields!ProductName.\	=Fields!Order(	=Fields!LineTotalSum.
		=Sum(Fields!	=Sum(Fields!LineTot
		=Sum(Fields!	=Sum(Fields!LineTot
⁂Page Footer			
="Page " & Globals!PageNumber & " of " & Globals!TotalPages			

Figure 7-45

Figure 7-46 shows the properties for the table group. The same expression you saw in the previous figure is used to define the group. On the Sorting tab of the Grouping and Sorting Properties dialog, shown in Figure 7-47, the sorting expression is set to match the group expression.

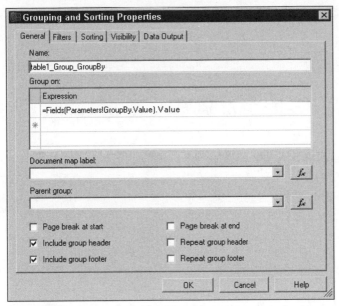

Figure 7-46

Since grouping should always be performed on values in the same sort order, the same expression is used on the Sorting tab.

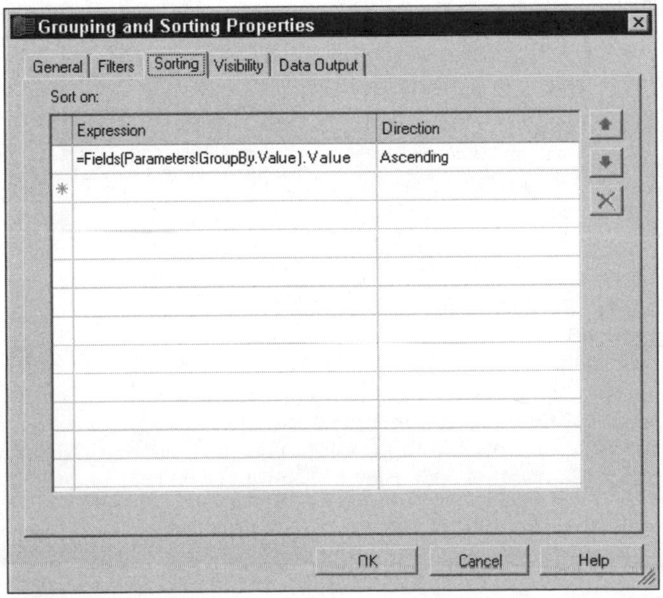

Figure 7-47

Sorting on Column Headers

Reporting Services for SQL Server 2000 doesn't include a specific feature for dynamic column sorting. Using parameters and report items navigation actions, text boxes and images can be made to act like hyperlinks that change parameter values, which may be used to change the sort order for a report or report item. A built-in feature was added to Reporting Services for SQL Server 2005 that effectively uses the same technique but manages everything internally. This feature does have its limits, though. I will demonstrate both techniques so you can decide whether you can do it the easy way or venture outside the box and be more creative.

Using the Interactive Sort Feature

This new feature in Reporting Services 2005 makes column sorting a snap. As you can see in Figure 7-48, the text boxes in a table header may be used to create an interactive sort for the table. The settings are fairly self-explanatory. Sorting may be set to the current group-level scope or a specific level can be specified. Using the Interactive Sort tab on the Textbox Properties dialog for each column header text box, check the box to enable sorting and specify a field expression.

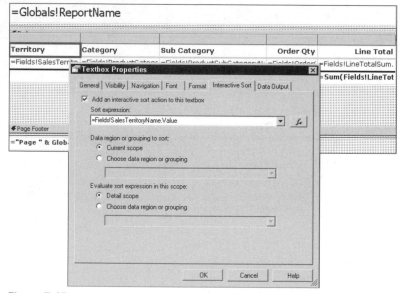

Figure 7-48

This is a very powerful feature with little design effort required. Figure 7-49 shows the report in preview with interactive sort enabled for the first three column headers. Small up/down icons are displayed next to each text box caption. This feature is simple but is limited to this view.

Column Sorting (Feature)				
Territory ⇅	Category ⇅	Sub Category ⇅	Order Qty	Line Total
Germany	Clothing	Bib-Shorts	2	$233.97
Germany	Clothing	Bib-Shorts	4	$233.97
Australia	Accessories	Bike Racks	8	$1,728.00
Australia	Accessories	Bike Racks	3	$648.00
Australia	Accessories	Bike Racks	6	$864.00
Australia	Accessories	Bike Racks	4	$288.00
Australia	Accessories	Bike Racks	7	$504.00
Australia	Accessories	Bike Racks	1	$4,344.00
Australia	Accessories	Bike Racks	5	$720.00
Canada	Accessories	Bike Racks	4	$1,440.00
Canada	Accessories	Bike Racks	7	$1,512.00
Canada	Accessories	Bike Racks	1	$4,104.00
Canada	Accessories	Bike Racks	10	$2,160.00
Canada	Accessories	Bike Racks	2	$1,296.00
Canada	Accessories	Bike Racks	5	$2,160.00
Canada	Accessories	Bike Racks	12	$3,273.98
Canada	Accessories	Bike Racks	6	$1,296.00
Canada	Accessories	Bike Racks	3	$432.00
Canada	Accessories	Bike Racks	8	$1,728.00
Canada	Accessories	Bike Racks	9	$648.00
Central	Accessories	Bike Racks	7	$504.00
Central	Accessories	Bike Racks	2	$432.00

Figure 7-49

Creating a Custom Column Sort Report

Building your own interactive sort feature has the advantage of using custom images and other sorting hotspots. The report user could click the text in the column header, an icon, or any other image of your choice and/or use parameter selections to change the report or item sort order. In the following example, I will use the column header text to sort by the chosen column and then show a custom image to indicate ascending or descending sort order.

What you'll need:

- ❑ A table item presenting a columnar set of values.

- ❑ Table heading or group heading items used as column sort toggle items.

- ❑ Thumbnail images used to indicate a column's sort direction.

- ❑ A set of report parameters used to manage the sort column name and direction.

- ❑ Action expressions used to modify report parameter values.

- ❑ Expressions used in the table or group Sort property, using report properties.

Figure 7-50 shows a simple table with text headings, a detail row, and totals in the report footer. You can see that I've placed images in separate columns and then merged the field text boxes. I do this so the up/down arrow images appear near the column header text. These columns are merged on the detail row so the fields have enough room. Each of the three sortable columns has text with underscores to indicate that these are links. This is just a visual effect until the navigation actions are set for these text boxes.

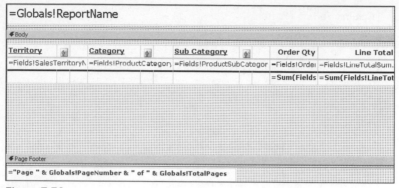

Figure 7-50

There are three small images embedded into the report. Figure 7-51 shows these embedded images. The no_arrow image (simply white space in the same dimensions as the arrow images) is used in place of an empty space. This is easier than changing the visibility property of the image item.

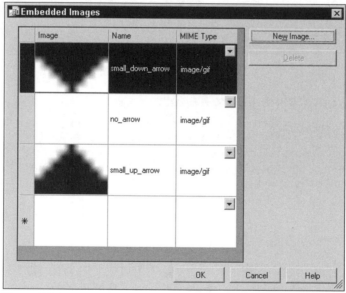

Figure 7-51

Just a quick aside: As in the Business Scorecard example, I have simply added the images to the cells in the table header. If you want to use transparent images over a colored or shaded background, you will need to add rectangles to the header cells and then place images in the rectangles.

Figure 7-52 shows the Report Parameters dialog with two parameters defined: SortField and SortDirection. For the report to render when it is first viewed, all parameters must have a default value. Since the parameters will be set when the user clicks the column header text, no other values need to be provided here.

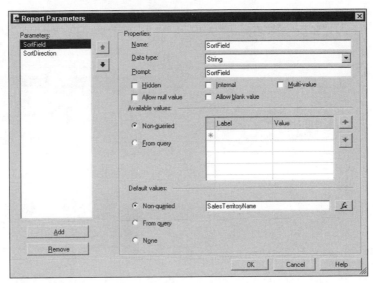

Figure 7-52

Next, I set the navigation properties for each column header text box separately. When the text box is clicked, the report navigates back to itself. I click the Parameters button on the Textbox Properties dialog Navigation tab to open the Parameters dialog shown in Figure 7-53. For each column header, the SortField parameter will be set to the name of the appropriate field and the SortDirection is set using an expression that toggles its value between "Ascending" and "Descending."

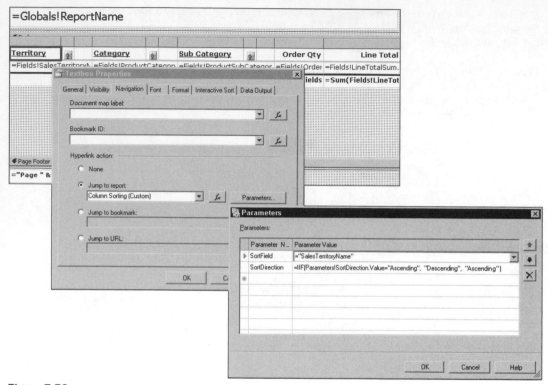

Figure 7-53

Next to each text box, I have placed an image item. Its value will correspond to the `SortDirection` parameter if the `SortField` value matches that table column. Figure 7-54 shows the Image item `Value` property expression. According to this logic, if the `SortField` parameter value matches this table column (SalesTerritoryName), then the appropriate arrow icon will be displayed based on the `SortDirection` parameter value. If the `SortField` parameter is for another column, the `"no_arrow"` white-space image is used.

In the Sorting properties for the table, shown in Figure 7-55, two expressions are used to test the `SortDirection` parameter. If the parameter value is "Ascending," then the first expression (on the Ascending line) returns the field value for the field name contained in the `SortField` parameter. Returning an empty string (`" "`) causes that sort expression to be ignored and enables the other (Ascending or Descending) expression.

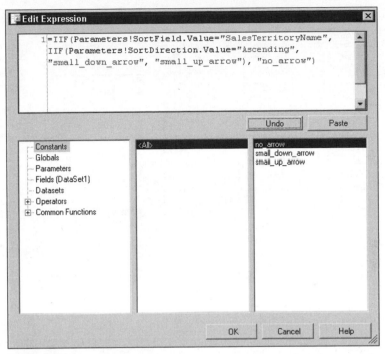

Figure 7-54

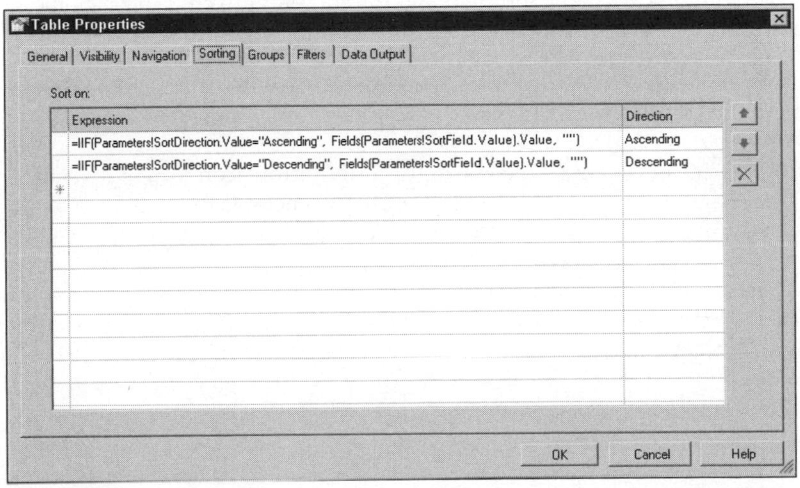

Figure 7-55

Figure 7-56 shows the report in preview mode after clicking the first column. Note the down arrow next to the Territory column header, which indicates that this column is sorted in Ascending order.

Column Sorting (Custom)

Territory ▼	Category	Sub Category	Order Qty	Line Total
Australia	Accessories	Bike Racks	8	$1,728.00
Australia	Accessories	Bike Racks	3	$648.00
Australia	Accessories	Bike Racks	6	$864.00
Australia	Accessories	Bike Racks	4	$288.00
Australia	Accessories	Bike Racks	7	$504.00
Australia	Accessories	Bike Racks	1	$4,344.00
Australia	Accessories	Bike Racks	5	$720.00
Australia	Accessories	Bike Stands	1	$5,088.00
Australia	Accessories	Bottles and Cages	4	$23.95
Australia	Accessories	Bottles and Cages	6	$35.93
Australia	Accessories	Bottles and Cages	3	$26.95
Australia	Accessories	Bottles and Cages	1	$6,615.73
Australia	Accessories	Bottles and Cages	2	$11.98
Australia	Accessories	Bottles and Cages	8	$23.95
Australia	Accessories	Cleaners	2	$9.54
Australia	Accessories	Cleaners	5	$47.70
Australia	Accessories	Cleaners	1	$969.90
Australia	Accessories	Cleaners	7	$66.78
Australia	Accessories	Cleaners	3	$42.93
Australia	Accessories	Cleaners	6	$28.62
Australia	Accessories	Cleaners	4	$19.08
Australia	Accessories	Fenders	1	$4,066.30

Figure 7-56

Clicking another column causes the sort field and the sort order to change. Click the same column again to toggle the sort order for that column (see Figure 7-57).

Column Sorting (Custom)

Territory	Category	Sub Category ▲	Order Qty	Line Total
Australia	Clothing	Vests	9	$342.90
Australia	Clothing	Vests	6	$457.20
Australia	Clothing	Vests	3	$228.60
Australia	Clothing	Vests	2	$228.60
Australia	Clothing	Vests	11	$1,191.08
Australia	Clothing	Vests	8	$304.80
Australia	Clothing	Vests	5	$952.50
Australia	Clothing	Vests	7	$800.10
Australia	Clothing	Vests	4	$457.20
Australia	Clothing	Vests	21	$696.75
Australia	Clothing	Vests	1	$4,800.60
Australia	Clothing	Vests	18	$597.22
Canada	Clothing	Vests	15	$995.36
Canada	Clothing	Vests	18	$597.22
Canada	Clothing	Vests	4	$1,371.60
Canada	Clothing	Vests	7	$1,333.50
Canada	Clothing	Vests	2	$533.40
Canada	Clothing	Vests	10	$1,143.00
Canada	Clothing	Vests	13	$469.21
Canada	Clothing	Vests	19	$630.40
Canada	Clothing	Vests	1	$4,216.40
Canada	Clothing	Vests	14	$4,042.46

Figure 7-57

Dynamic Fields and Columns

Under some conditions, you may need to display different field values in table columns. There are several ways this can be accomplished. One of the simplest methods to change column sources and values is to parameterize the query expression. This will work if you are using ad hoc SQL expressions but not if you are using preexisting stored procedures. Both of the techniques used in this example are more efficient, resolving fields and columns in the report without passing parameters back to the database server.

What you'll need:

❑   Data set query, including any source fields you need to consolidate into a dynamic column.

❑   A parameter with list values used for field selection.

❑   An expression defined on a custom field, referencing the parameter list values.

The first step is to include all of the source fields in the data set query. I want to define a custom field called Price that will dynamically be mapped to either of two existing data fields. The Product table contains two price fields, StandardCost and ListPrice, that represent the wholesale and retail product prices.

A report parameter named `PriceSource` is configured with the list values, Wholesale and Retail. These values are used to switch the custom field mapping between these two data fields. Figure 7-58 shows the custom field expression in the Add New Field dialog for the custom Price field.

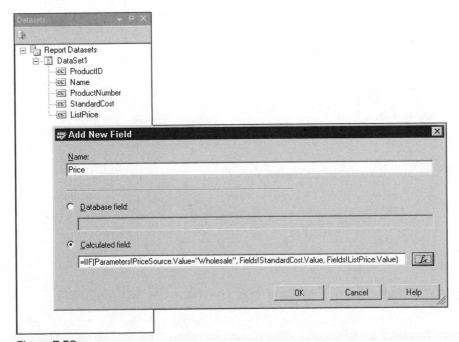

Figure 7-58

This custom field is simply used in the report, bound to a column in the table, as you can see in Figure 7-59.

=Globals!ReportName		
="Price Source: " & Parameters!PriceSource.Value		
Product Name	**Product Number**	**Price**
=Fields!Name.Value	=Fields!ProductNumber.Value	=Fields!Price.Value
	Footer	

Figure 7-59

Hiding and Showing a Row or Column

This technique is very simple. Using a parameter, a row or column may be dynamically shown or hidden using the `Visibility > Hidden` property. Instead of the custom field used in the previous example, both of the data fields could have been included in the report. The table columns then could be shown and hidden based on the parameter selection.

My example will hide or show a column based on a parameter selection. I've added a report parameter named `ShowProductNumber`. Figure 7-60 shows the expression used to manipulate the `Hidden` property for the selected column.

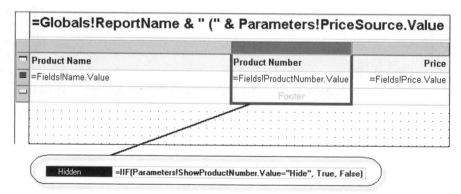

Figure 7-60

Modifying Data from a Report

In a meeting of the four authors of this book, we had a lengthy discussion about the appropriateness of this topic. I'll admit that the idea of modifying data from a report is a bit unusual. Dave said, "If you're going to show our readers how to manipulate data from a report, you ought to change the title of that section to 'How to Shoot Yourself in the Foot.'" He makes a good point, but under the right (and carefully restricted) circumstances, this can prove to be a very powerful and useful capability. Let me just say that if your report requirements have expanded to the point where you want to modify data from an interactive report, you should probably be meeting with the architects and developers of your entire database solution and carefully consider the best method to implement these features. It might be best to use an application front end better suited for that type of functionality. Yet, since the topic at hand is to demonstrate cool stuff you can do in reports, I'm going to show you what you *can* do. I'll leave it to you to decide what you *should* do.

"Data write-back" is a highly touted feature of data mining and data warehouse systems. There are a variety of situations where it may be beneficial to write back data to source tables. These may include inventory control, prices changes, or testing "what if" scenarios. Where possible, it's usually a good idea to write data to a staging or temporary table to preserve the state of important source data. You may then use join statements to correlate the original records with the modifications before (or instead of) committing changes to the source.

What you'll need:

❑ Permissions granted for the Report Server service user to modify data.

❑ A SQL stored procedure using a conditional query expression used to perform an update and return records.

❑ Report parameters used to pass data values into a data set using a stored procedure.

❑ Report item(s) with an action expression used to pass parameter values back to the report.

There are a few different methods to execute SQL script used to modify data. In the first of two examples, I'll use a stored procedure to perform both the data updates and to return results. After that, I'll separate these two query operations and use two separate reports to do the same thing.

Stored procedures are an excellent place to manage multiple operations and conditional business logic. The following script defines a stored procedure that accepts two input parameters used to modify price values for products matching a specified subcategory. If the @PriceIncrease parameter is zero or the @ProductSubCategoryID parameter value doesn't match values in the Product table, no modifications will be performed.

The second section of the procedure script returns a result set for all products and related categories and subcategories.

```
CREATE PROCEDURE spProductUpdatePrice
 @PriceIncrease           Float,
 @ProductSubCategoryID    Int
AS
 -- Update price:
 IF @PriceIncrease <> 0
 BEGIN
     UPDATE Production.Product SET ListPrice =
                              ListPrice + (ListPrice * @PriceIncrease/100)
     WHERE ProductSubCategoryID = @ProductSubCategoryID
 END

 -- Return products
 SELECT  Production.ProductSubcategory.Name AS ProductSubCategoryName,
```

```
            Production.Product.Name, Production.Product.ProductNumber,
            Production.Product.StandardCost, Production.Product.ListPrice,
            Production.Product.ProductSubcategoryID
FROM        Production.Product INNER JOIN
            Production.ProductSubcategory ON
            Production.Product.ProductSubcategoryID =
            Production.ProductSubcategory.ProductSubcategoryID
            AND
            Production.Product.ProductSubcategoryID =
            Production.ProductSubcategory.ProductSubcategoryID
WHERE       (Production.Product.ProductSubcategoryID = @ProductSubCategoryID)
ORDER BY Production.ProductSubcategory.Name, Production.Product.Name
```

In this example, a text box is used to set these parameters and perform the update. The sample report is shown in design view in Figure 7-61.

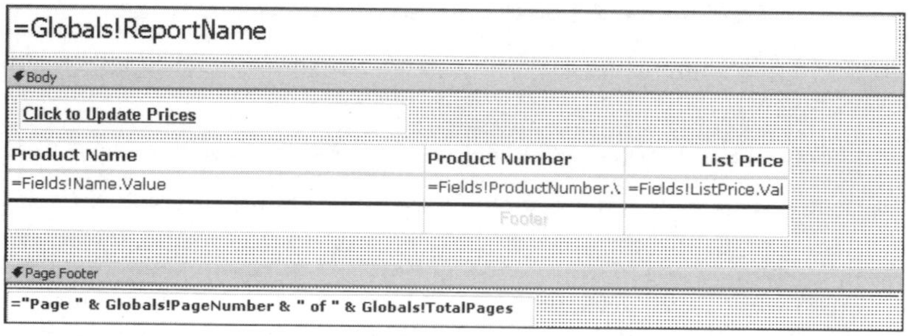

Figure 7-61

Figure 7-62 shows the Report Parameters dialog with two parameters matching those in the stored procedure. The SubCategoryID parameter is based on a list supplied by the ProductSubCategory table. In the example, I've predefined a list of price increase percentage values, shown in Figure 7-63. Note that the default value is zero, which allows the procedure to execute without modifying any product records.

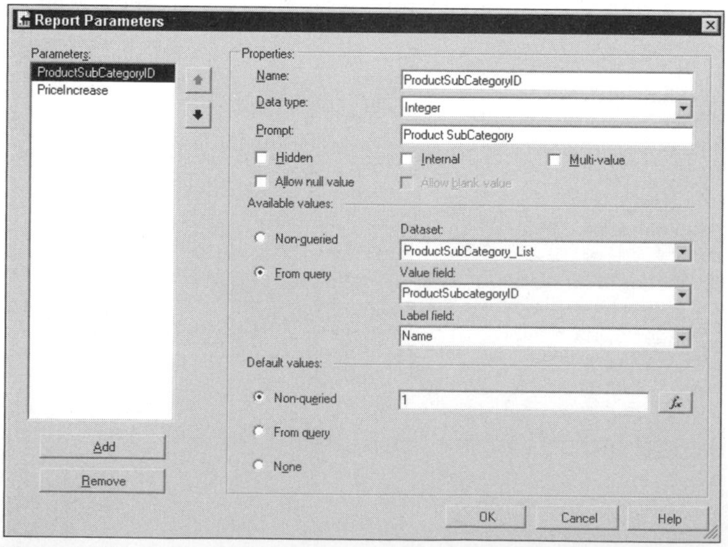

Figure 7-62

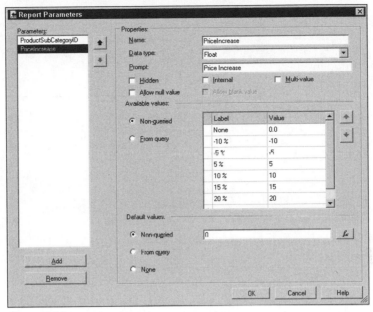

Figure 7-63

The final result is shown in Figure 7-64. In the Navigation properties for the text box, set the Jump to report action to the same report and then set the two parameters that were previously defined. This method is simple but offers limited control and user feedback.

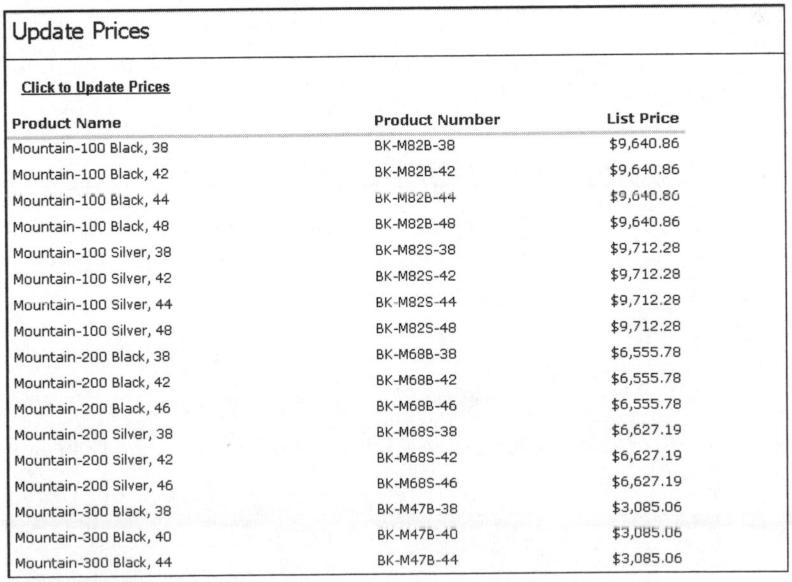

Product Name	Product Number	List Price
Mountain-100 Black, 38	BK-M82B-38	$9,640.86
Mountain-100 Black, 42	BK-M82B-42	$9,640.86
Mountain-100 Black, 44	BK-M82B-44	$9,640.86
Mountain-100 Black, 48	BK-M82B-48	$9,640.86
Mountain-100 Silver, 38	BK-M82S-38	$9,712.28
Mountain-100 Silver, 42	BK-M82S-42	$9,712.28
Mountain-100 Silver, 44	BK-M82S-44	$9,712.28
Mountain-100 Silver, 48	BK-M82S-48	$9,712.28
Mountain-200 Black, 38	BK-M68B-38	$6,555.78
Mountain-200 Black, 42	BK-M68B-42	$6,555.78
Mountain-200 Black, 46	BK-M68B-46	$6,555.78
Mountain-200 Silver, 38	BK-M68S-38	$6,627.19
Mountain-200 Silver, 42	BK-M68S-42	$6,627.19
Mountain-200 Silver, 46	BK-M68S-46	$6,627.19
Mountain-300 Black, 38	BK-M47B-38	$3,085.06
Mountain-300 Black, 40	BK-M47B-40	$3,085.06
Mountain-300 Black, 44	BK-M47B-44	$3,085.06

Update Prices

Click to Update Prices

Figure 7-64

The second method is a simple variation on the first. Add another report to the project and change the Jump to report action for the text box in the first report to the second report. The target report also contains the same parameters that were defined for the first report. The only difference is that there is no need to define parameter lists for either parameter. Figure 7-65 shows a simple report used to display the results of a simple update query.

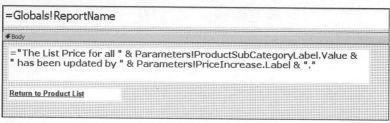

Figure 7-65

The data set for this report is simply the update script from the first section of the stored procedure:

```
IF @PriceIncrease <> 0
BEGIN
    UPDATE Production.Product SET ListPrice =
                                ListPrice + (ListPrice * @PriceIncrease/100)
    WHERE ProductSubCategoryID = @ProductSubCategoryID
END
```

The data set for the first report is only the SELECT statement (everything under the --Return Products label). The target report now performs the update when it renders and displays a simple message using the parameter values passed from the first report.

Consider using the next example with this method as a means to select a list of products and then update the prices only for the selected products.

Selected and Deselected Item List

A check box list is a universal metaphor for managing a list of selected and unselected items. Images may be used to create checked and unchecked boxes that are used to toggle the state of each item on the list.

What you'll need:

- ❏ A report parameter used to pass data values into a query expression.
- ❏ A query expression used to match selected key values with existing keys in the report data set.
- ❏ Report item(s) with an action expression used to pass parameter values back to the report.
- ❏ Expressions used to modify images or text to indicate selected and deselected rows.

Figure 7-66 shows the finished report; a list of products in a single row table, with a check box displayed in the first column.

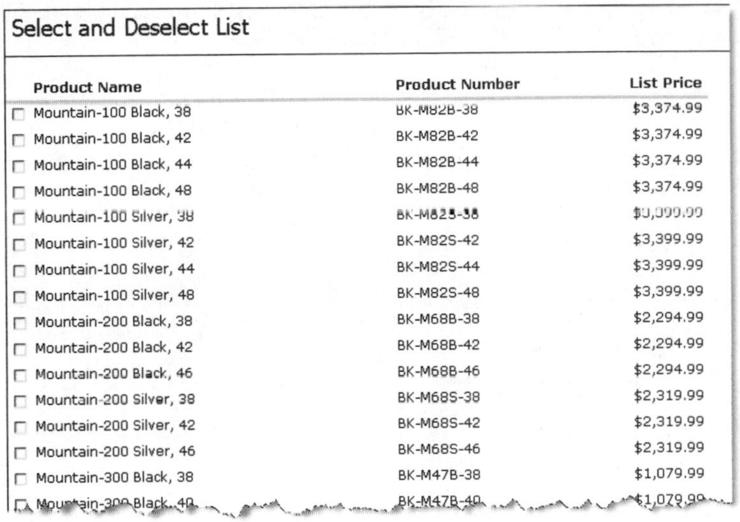

Select and Deselect List

Product Name	Product Number	List Price
Mountain-100 Black, 38	BK-M82B-38	$3,374.99
Mountain-100 Black, 42	BK-M82B-42	$3,374.99
Mountain-100 Black, 44	BK-M82B-44	$3,374.99
Mountain-100 Black, 48	BK-M82B-48	$3,374.99
Mountain-100 Silver, 38	BK-M82S-38	$3,399.99
Mountain-100 Silver, 42	BK-M82S-42	$3,399.99
Mountain-100 Silver, 44	BK-M82S-44	$3,399.99
Mountain-100 Silver, 48	BK-M82S-48	$3,399.99
Mountain-200 Black, 38	BK-M68B-38	$2,294.99
Mountain-200 Black, 42	BK-M68B-42	$2,294.99
Mountain-200 Black, 46	BK-M68B-46	$2,294.99
Mountain-200 Silver, 38	BK-M68S-38	$2,319.99
Mountain-200 Silver, 42	BK-M68S-42	$2,319.99
Mountain-200 Silver, 46	BK-M68S-46	$2,319.99
Mountain-300 Black, 38	BK-M47B-38	$1,079.99
Mountain-300 Black, 40	BK-M47B-40	$1,079.99

Figure 7-66

When the user clicks an unchecked box, a check appears and when a checked item is clicked, it is unchecked. This is a simple concept, but there is no check box item in the Report Designer Toolbox. As you can see in Figure 7-67, each check box (actually an image) is a navigation item. Clicking a checked or unchecked image cause the report to post back to itself, passing the selected ProductID to be added to or removed from a list of selected IDs stored in a report parameter.

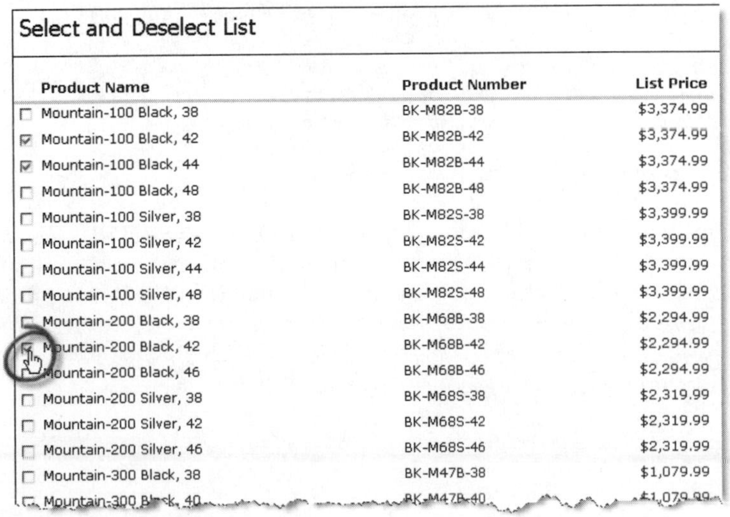

Select and Deselect List

Product Name	Product Number	List Price
Mountain-100 Black, 38	BK-M82B-38	$3,374.99
Mountain-100 Black, 42	BK-M82B-42	$3,374.99
Mountain-100 Black, 44	BK-M82B-44	$3,374.99
Mountain-100 Black, 48	BK-M82B-48	$3,374.99
Mountain-100 Silver, 38	BK-M82S-38	$3,399.99
Mountain-100 Silver, 42	BK-M82S-42	$3,399.99
Mountain-100 Silver, 44	BK-M82S-44	$3,399.99
Mountain-100 Silver, 48	BK-M82S-48	$3,399.99
Mountain-200 Black, 38	BK-M68B-38	$2,294.99
Mountain-200 Black, 42	BK-M68B-42	$2,294.99
Mountain-200 Black, 46	BK-M68B-46	$2,294.99
Mountain-200 Silver, 38	BK-M68S-38	$2,319.99
Mountain-200 Silver, 42	BK-M68S-42	$2,319.99
Mountain-200 Silver, 46	BK-M68S-46	$2,319.99
Mountain-300 Black, 38	BK-M47B-38	$1,079.99
Mountain-300 Black, 40	BK-M47B-40	$1,079.99

Figure 7-67

Two separate queries are necessary to keep track of selected and unselected values. These two queries are combined into one result set using the Transact-SQL UNION operator. The first of the two results returns the value 1 for the selected column for all of the selected products. The second result returns the value 0 for all remaining, unselected products. When these results are combined, the selected column is used as an indicator flag to produce the checked boxes.

The data set query is processed as a Visual Basic string expression so the list of selected ProductIDs may be concatenated into the expression. In the following script, note the reference to the ProductIDs report parameter. This parameter is defined in the Report Parameters dialog as a simple string-type parameter. The default value is set to = "". This allows the report to render without an explicit parameter value.

```
="SELECT ProductID, 1 AS Selected," &
" Production.ProductSubcategory.Name AS ProductSubCategoryName," &
" Production.Product.Name AS ProductName, Production.Product.ProductNumber," &
" Production.Product.StandardCost, Production.Product.ListPrice," &
" Production.Product.ProductSubcategoryID" &
" FROM   Production.Product INNER JOIN Production.ProductSubcategory" &
"     ON Production.Product.ProductSubcategoryID =" &
" Production.ProductSubcategory.ProductSubcategoryID AND" &
" Production.Product.ProductSubcategoryID =" &
" Production.ProductSubcategory.ProductSubcategoryID AND" &
" Product.ProductID IN (" & Parameters!ProductIDs.Value & ")" &
" WHERE   Production.Product.ProductSubcategoryID =" &
"         Parameters!ProductSubCategoryID.Value.ToString() & " " &
"UNION " &
" SELECT ProductID, 0 AS Selected," &
" Production.ProductSubcategory.Name AS ProductSubCategoryName," &
" Production.Product.Name AS ProductName, Production.Product.ProductNumber," &
" Production.Product.StandardCost, Production.Product.ListPrice," &
" Production.Product.ProductSubcategoryID " &
" FROM   Production.Product INNER JOIN Production.ProductSubcategory" &
"     ON Production.Product.ProductSubcategoryID =" &
" Production.ProductSubcategory.ProductSubcategoryID AND" &
" Production.Product.ProductSubcategoryID =" &
" Production.ProductSubcategory.ProductSubcategoryID AND" &
" Product.ProductID NOT IN (" & Parameters!ProductIDs.Value & ")" &
" WHERE   Production.Product.ProductSubcategoryID =" &
Parameters!ProductSubCategoryID.Value.ToString() &
" ORDER BY ProductName"
```

The report contains two embedded images, named checked and unchecked. These are simply screen captures of the two check box states that could be taken from any Windows application. Figure 7-68 shows the table with an image in the first column of the detail row. The Value property expression for the image item simply toggles between these two images based on the selected column Value on each row.

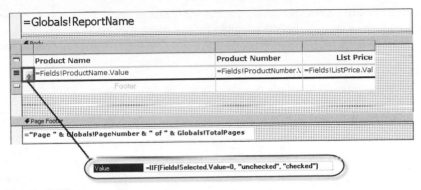

Figure 7-68

On the Navigation properties for the image, the report is posted back to itself using the Jump to report action. Figure 7-69 shows the Parameters dialog. The ProductIDs parameter is populated from a custom VB function that adds and removes the ID values to a comma-delimited list.

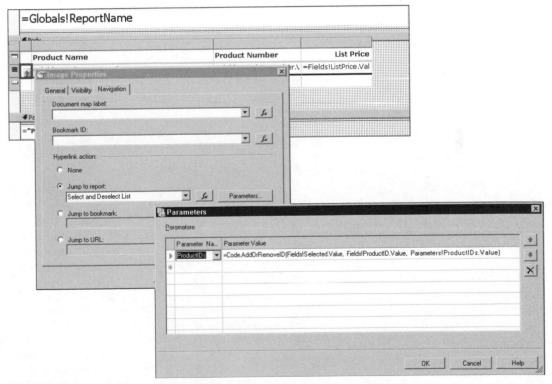

Figure 7-69

The custom code for this report is shown in Figure 7-70 . The `AddOrRemoveID()` function called on the navigation action of the image takes the current row's Selected value (1 or 0), the ProductID, and the current list of selected values. Depending on whether the current row's ID is selected, the item is either added or removed from the list.

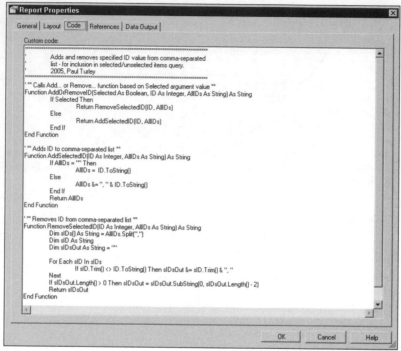

Figure 7-70

Using Advanced and Third-Party Report Items

In SQL Server Reporting Services 2005 the new Report Designer and product specification includes the ability for third-party vendors to integrate their own custom report items. Advanced charting components and other custom report items will allow you to take reports further using advanced and sophisticated features.

What you'll need:

❏   Dundas Chart for SQL Server Reporting Services.

The evaluation edition of Dundas Chart for Reporting Services may be downloaded from Dundas Software's web site at `www.dundasreporting.com`. This working edition enables all of the product features and displays a watermark message over each chart.

As I mentioned earlier, Dundas Chart, developed by Dundas Software Ltd., was used to create the integrated charting components in the out-of-the-box reporting capabilities of Reporting Services. This product was developed for the Microsoft .NET Framework and has been one of the leading charting components for Windows and Web application development. When the Microsoft Reporting Services product team decided to incorporate Dundas Chart into the Reporting Services product package, they simplified many reporting features. To keep things simple, some advanced features and capabilities were omitted for the standard charting features offered for reporting. Dundas Chart for Reporting Services contains the advanced features of the Dundas Chart stand-alone product. In this brief demonstration, I'll highlight just a few of many capabilities.

Figure 7-71 shows the Visual Studio Toolbox after the installation has been completed. The setup process adds a new Toolbox icon in addition to the Chart and other standard report items.

Figure 7-71

A chart is added to a report in the same manner as the standard chart item. The Dundas Chart designer has pretty much the same behavior. Fields may be dropped into target zones to create category, series, and data groups. The property dialog interface is also familiar and generally has the same tabs and features as the built-in chart item. In addition to basic features, you will find many enhancements on the property pages as well. Figure 7-72 shows the Advanced tab with object list dropped open. This enables you to view all of the chart objects with their properties and settings in one dialog.

One of the most useful features is the ability to combine multiple charts and chart types in the same space. Figure 7-73 shows a chart with two data point series: one for Internet sales and the other for reseller sales. Each of these series uses a different chart type: The reseller sales values are represented by columns and the Internet sales by lines.

Chart areas act as separate charts in the chart item space that may be coordinated and bound to the same or different data sets. In Figure 7-74, one donut chart displays the top values with one slice for "other" values. A second donut chart displays the details for the "other" slice. You can also see that more control is provided for the display characteristics of data point labels.

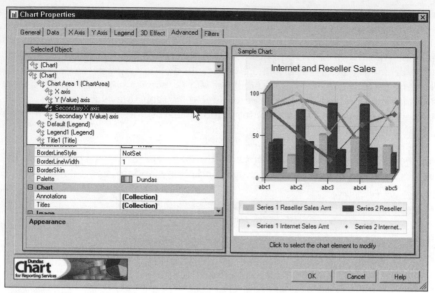

Figure 7-72

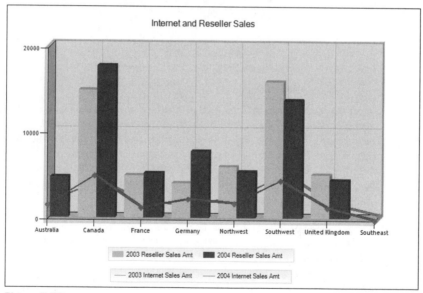

Figure 7-73

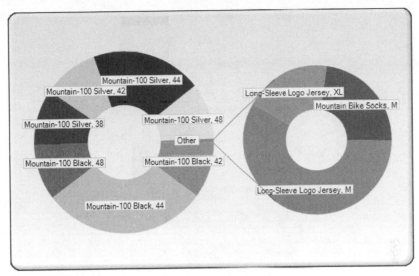

Figure 7-74

There are several unique and special-purpose charts. These may be combined and used in a variety of different ways to present data in graphical form. Thumbnail samples, in Figure 7-75, demonstrate a few of the advanced chart types and design concepts.

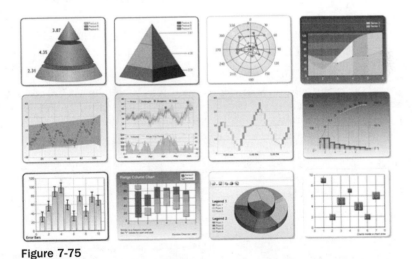

Figure 7-75

Figure 7-76 shows a sales pipeline funnel chart. This is a common metaphor, used in sales and Customer Relation Management systems, to track contacts and customers at all stages of the sales cycle.

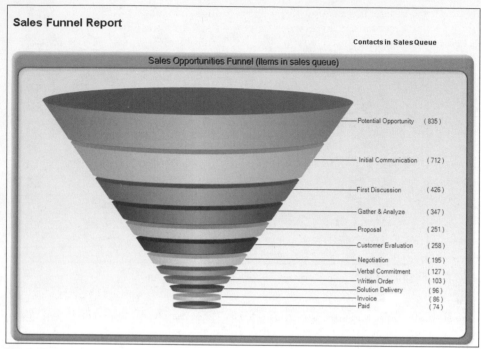

Figure 7-76

Dynamic Image Content

In Chapter 12, you learn how to integrate reporting into custom applications using a variety of rendering techniques. The following technique uses programmatic rendering to insert image content from another source. Many applications and components can render output in the form of an image. This content may be incorporated into reports using a variety of creative techniques. As with the previous examples, the purpose of this illustration is just to demonstrate the concept using one simple technique.

What you'll need:

❑   .NET programming skills.

❑   Visual Studio .NET

❑   A Visual Studio web application.

❑   Visual Basic .NET or C# code used to render reports and manage images and other binary report content.

The following example uses the Dundas Gauge ASP.NET web form control to render its content to an image file. Dundas Gauge can render a variety of attractive measurement dials, progress indicators, meters, scopes, clocks, and, of course, gauges, with tremendous control over the look and feel of specific visual and functional elements. This product would allow you to display data using familiar gauge and meter metaphors.

In this simple example, I use a simple thermometer gauge to display sales totals relative to a goal. Figure 7-77 shows a report containing an image item with the size and position of the gauge. It can contain any image content since it's only used as a placeholder. In this example, the image is separate from any other report content.

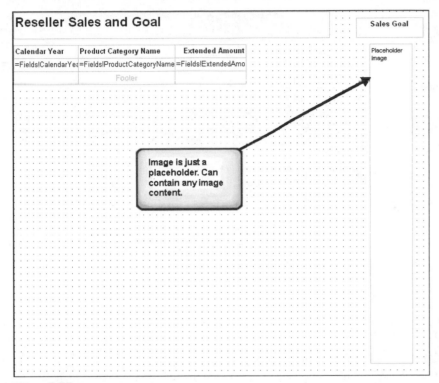

Figure 7-77

The actual ASP.NET web forms application includes two web forms, or pages. The first is used to render the gauge image to a file and the second is used to render the report. This page has no controls or content at design time. Program code running as it loads will fill the empty page with the report content and the gauge image as it is processed on the web server, before this content is sent to the web browser.

The first page contains the Dundas Gauge web form control. Figure 7-78 shows this control, configured as a thermometer, with the Gauge Wizard property page.

A standard button control is used to render the gauge to a file and then redirect the web application to the second page. The following Visual Basic .NET code runs on the Click event for this button. The first two lines, following the two comments, assign the gauge pointer (in this case, the thermometer bar) a value and then render the gauge to a PNG graphic file. In production, the value would most likely be obtained from a database query. Note that the file location maps to a web folder (report_images) under the default root web folder on the local web server.

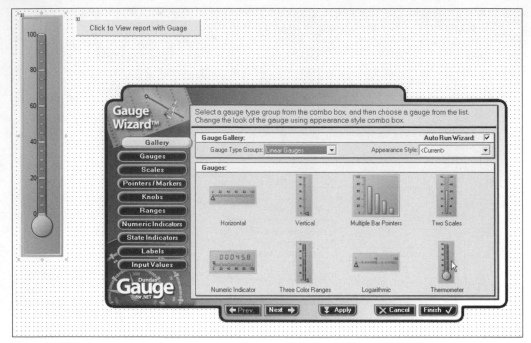

Figure 7-78

The last line of code redirects the web application to the second web form called GaugeReport_Viewer.aspx:

```
Private Sub Button1_Click(ByVal sender As System.Object, ByVal e As _
                                    System.EventArgs) _Handles Button1.Click
    '-- The gauge value is hard-coded in the example
    '-- In production, this would come from data or user-input
    Me.GaugeContainer1.LinearGauges(0).Pointers(0).Value = 65
    Me.GaugeContainer1.SaveAsImage("C:\inetpub\wwwroot\report_images\Gauge1.png", _
                                Dundas.Gauges.WebControl.GaugeImageFormat.Png)
    Response.Redirect("GaugeReport_Viewer.aspx")
End Sub
```

There is no need to show you the second page because it's completely blank. The only program code runs on the page Load event, which runs as the page object is loaded into memory on the web server and before the page content is sent to the client's web browser. First, take a look at the entire block of code. After this, I'll step you through each section of code separately and explain what's going on:

```
Private Sub Page_Load(ByVal sender As System.Object, ByVal e As System.EventArgs) _
        Handles MyBase.Load
    '*******************************************************************
    '   Replace report image with any custom image content.
    '   Paul Turley, 2005
    '*******************************************************************
    '-- Instantiate ReportingService object from web service reference:
```

```
       Dim rs As New localhost_RS.ReportingService
       rs.Credentials = System.Net.CredentialCache.DefaultCredentials

       '-- Resolve stream file location:
       Dim sDevInfo As String = _
             "<DeviceInfo><StreamRoot>/report_images/</StreamRoot></DeviceInfo>"

       '-- Declare variables to handle Stream ID value(s), report and image content:
       Dim sStreamIDs() As String
       Dim sStreamID As String
       Dim ReportBytes As Byte()
       Dim ImageBytes As Byte()

       '-- Render the report:
       ReportBytes = rs.Render("/RS_Play_Project/Report_With_Gauge", "HTML4.0", _
                        Nothing, sDevInfo, Nothing, Nothing, Nothing, _
                        Nothing, Nothing, Nothing, Nothing, sStreamIDs)

       '-- Get the image stream ID & rename the gauge image file using the stream ID:
       '-- This replaces the report image with the existing graphic file.
       sStreamID = sStreamIDs(0)
       Rename("C:\inetpub\wwwroot\report_images\Gauge1.png", _
                        "C:\inetpub\wwwroot\report_images\" & sStreamID)

       '-- Replace this web page's content with the rendered report content:
       With HttpContext.Current.Response
          .Clear()
          .BinaryWrite(ReportBytes)
          .End()
       End With
    End Sub
```

The first two lines of executable code invoke the Reporting Services web service and set up a security context. This is a standard practice for any web service request.

```
       '-- Instantiate ReportingService object from web service reference:
       Dim rs As New localhost_RS.ReportingService
       rs.Credentials = System.Net.CredentialCache.DefaultCredentials
```

The next line sets up the StreamRoot location. This tells the report where to obtain binary image content. Since I've already saved the gauge to a file location, this directs the report rendering engine to the same location as a relative URL path. When a report is rendered to HTML, each image is encoded with a unique identifier and a stream root or target. An HTML tag is created, which enables the web browser to request the image content from the server.

```
       '-- Resolve stream file location:
       Dim sDevInfo As String = _
             "<DeviceInfo><StreamRoot>/report_images/</StreamRoot></DeviceInfo>"
```

After declaring variables used to receive and manage the report and image content, the Render method actually processes the report. When a web page is sent to the web browser, it does so using the concept of streams. This may sound like a convoluted idea, but it's actually quite simple. A stream is simply a bunch of characters or bytes that flow from one location to another. To handle streams in program code, we send their contents to a byte or character array. This is really just a big bucket to stuff all of the content into so we can pull it back out and do something useful with it. Since the `Byte` data type can handle both character and binary content, I'm using two variables of this type to handle the report HTML content as well as the image binary content.

```
'-- Declare variables to handle Stream ID value(s), report and image content:
Dim sStreamIDs() As String
Dim sStreamID As String
Dim ReportBytes As Byte()
Dim ImageBytes As Byte()


'-- Render the report:
ReportBytes = rs.Render("/RS_Play_Project/Report_With_Gauge", "HTML4.0", _
                        Nothing, sDevInfo, Nothing, Nothing, Nothing, _
                        Nothing, Nothing, Nothing, Nothing, sStreamIDs)
```

The report content (all of the characters that compose the HTML report itself) reside in the byte array variable called `ReportBytes`. The `Render` method requires several arguments, most of which are unused, so I pass the value Nothing as a placeholder for each of these optional arguments. The last argument accepts a string array variable used to return the IDs for all of the images in the report.

Since I know that this report contains only one image, I'm simply using the first element in this array, `sStreamIDs(0)`, to obtain the ID assigned to the image content stream. Reporting Services assigns each stream a unique identifier. My code renames the gauge image file to this stream ID so that the report HTML's image tag points to the name and location of my image file.

```
'-- Get the image stream ID & rename the gauge image file using the stream ID:
'-- This replaces the report image with the existing graphic file.
sStreamID = sStreamIDs(0)
Rename("C:\inetpub\wwwroot\report_images\Gauge1.png", _
                   "C:\inetpub\wwwroot\report_images\" & sStreamID)
```

The last step is to send the report content to the web browser. This is achieved by calling the `BinaryWrite` method of the `Current.Response` object. This is ASP.NET speak for "this web page." In short, I'm simply stuffing the report content (all of the HTML) into the current web page and sending it down to the web browser.

```
'-- Replace this web page's content with the rendered report content:
With HttpContext.Current.Response
    .Clear()
    .BinaryWrite(ReportBytes)
    .End()
End With
```

The first round of content to hit the browser doesn't actually contain the image content. The StreamID and the stream URL are embedded into the HTML so that the browser can make a second request. This is why images always load after the text when you view a new web page.

Figure 7-79 shows the rendered report containing the gauge image.

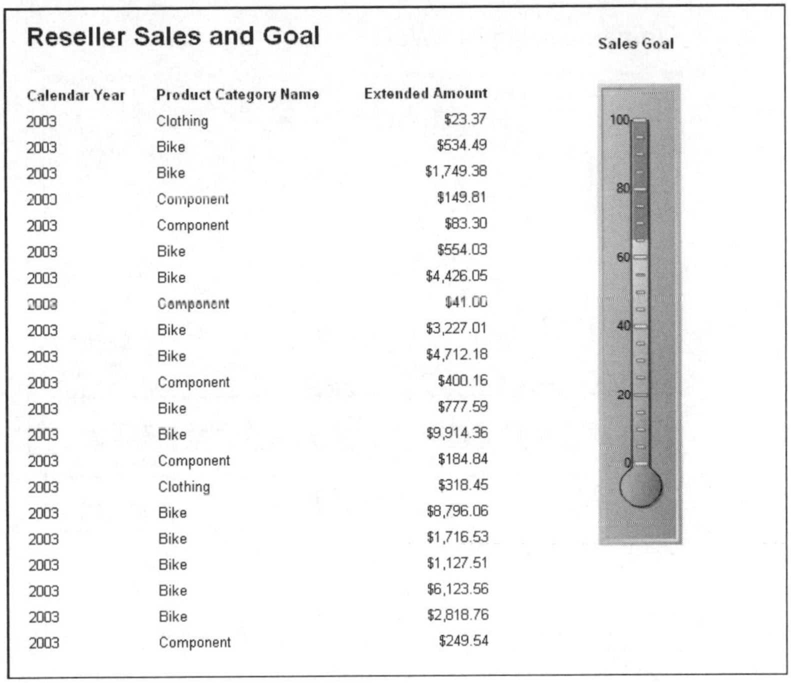

Reseller Sales and Goal

Sales Goal

Calendar Year	Product Category Name	Extended Amount
2003	Clothing	$23.37
2003	Bike	$534.49
2003	Bike	$1,749.38
2003	Component	$149.81
2003	Component	$83.30
2003	Bike	$554.03
2003	Bike	$4,426.05
2003	Component	$41.00
2003	Bike	$3,227.01
2003	Bike	$4,712.18
2003	Component	$400.16
2003	Bike	$777.59
2003	Bike	$9,914.36
2003	Component	$184.84
2003	Clothing	$318.45
2003	Bike	$8,796.06
2003	Bike	$1,716.53
2003	Bike	$1,127.51
2003	Bike	$6,123.56
2003	Bike	$2,818.76
2003	Component	$249.54

Figure 7-79

Figure 7-80 shows what my gauge image file looks like after this code runs and renames the file from its original name. This StreamID is what I call a BUN, or a Big Ugly Number.

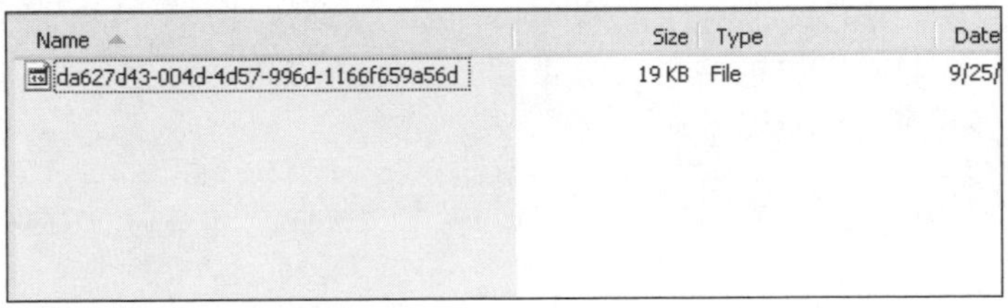

Name ▲	Size	Type	Date
da627d43-004d-4d57-996d-1166f659a56d	19 KB	File	9/25/

Figure 7-80

So what can you accomplish using this technique? Well, think about all of the useful things you can do with image content. Applications like Visio and MapPoint can easily output complex data to image files or file streams for use in reports.

Here are a couple of brief examples from a solution using the Microsoft MapPoint Server subscription service. Using Web Service calls, address and location information for some of the Hitachi Consulting offices are sent to the MapPoint Server Web Service. This returns a single image byte stream in much the same way as the Dundas Gauge control did in the previous example. The resulting map image, shown in Figure 7-81, is rendered to a report in a similar manner.

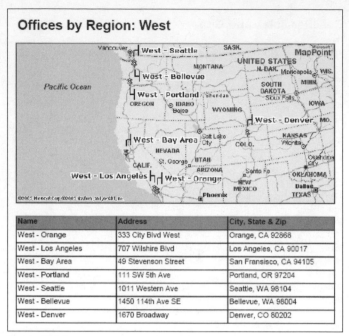

Offices by Region: West

Name	Address	City, State & Zip
West - Orange	333 City Blvd West	Orange, CA 92868
West - Los Angeles	707 Wilshire Blvd	Los Angeles, CA 90017
West - Bay Area	49 Stevenson Street	San Fransisco, CA 94105
West - Portland	111 SW 5th Ave	Portland, OR 97204
West - Seattle	1011 Western Ave	Seattle, WA 98104
West - Bellevue	1450 114th Ave SE	Bellevue, WA 98004
West - Denver	1670 Broadway	Denver, CO 80202

Figure 7-81

The next example uses a similar pattern but involves multiple image streams. These locations come from Employee records in the Northwind sample database. Using a query matched to the report data set, address information is sent to the MapPoint service in separate requests, resulting in separate map images. By iterating through each StreamID in the rendered report, placeholder images are replaced with these map images that appear in a table, alongside corresponding employee names. Figure 7-82 shows the rendered report with a map image displayed on each row.

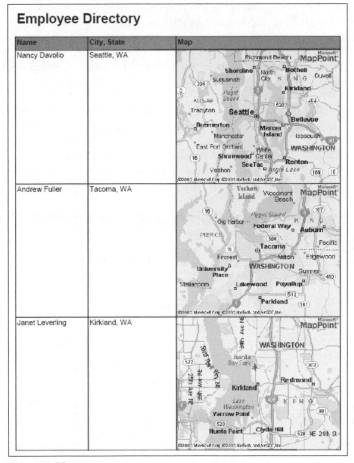

Figure 7-82

Using Advanced and Third-Party Controls for Parameter Selection

From a custom Windows or web application, you can replace the parameter selection interface with your own controls and interface.

What you'll need:

❑   Visual Studio 2005.

❑   A Windows form or Web form application project.

❑   Visual Basic .NET or C# programming skills.

❑   Any parameterized report.

Depending on the application type and the programming tools available, there are a few different ways to incorporate reporting into applications. Reporting Services now includes a `ReportViewer` control for .NET Windows forms and ASP.NET web forms projects. You can also use a `Frame` or an `IFrame` HTML tag to encapsulate a report in an ASP.NET project or in practically any other type of web application. Chapter 12 will explore a number of different scenarios and show you examples of custom program code used to implement them.

Using the `ReportViewer` control, the de facto parameter bar can be hidden and then standard or third-party controls may be used to prompt the user for parameter values. There are many advanced controls available for Windows and Web application development. Figure 7-83 shows a Windows form application that uses controls from the Infragistics NetAdvantage suite. Two `MonthView` controls are used for the date range selection. A pair of `UltraTree` controls allows countries to be selected by dragging and dropping flag icons from one list to another.

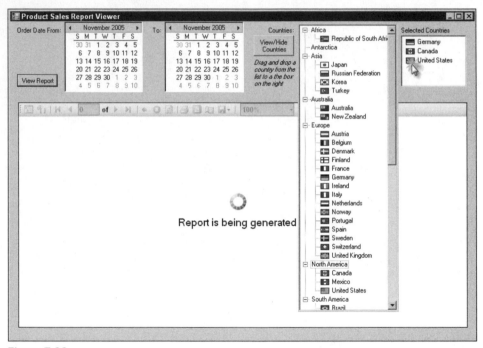

Figure 7-83

The nice thing about using ready-made, custom controls is that you can get a lot of bang for the buck and save yourself programming time. There are several good third-party control offerings from different companies. I've been using the Infragistics suite (available at `www.infragistics.com`) for several years. It's one of the most evolved and comprehensive, containing several dozen very capable and attractive controls that require little programming effort to implement impressive functionality.

The `ReportViewer` control rounds out the Reporting Services features by allowing reports to be tightly integrated into business applications with ease and tremendous flexibility. I encourage you to be creative and use your imagination to develop interesting report wrappers and parameter selection interfaces. Use advanced controls like these to enhance the user's experience and take reporting beyond out-of-the-box features.

Summary

With Reporting Services, you can create just about any type of report design that is required. Advanced solutions often take a bit of creative thought, and you may need to step outside the standard feature set to get there. Given the flexible architecture of this product, many compelling results can be achieved. In summary, this chapter covered the following topics:

❑   We began with a set of simple guidelines for gathering report requirements and managing your user and sponsor's expectations by creating a detailed specification for each report.

❑   The key success factors for reporting projects include a clear understanding of the entire solution scope and where reports fits into the picture. Requirements should be specified before you begin, and requirement changes must be documented and approved.

❑   When you understand the limitations and capabilities of the Reporting Services platform, you will find interesting ways to achieve your reporting goals. You saw several examples of how requirements can be addressed by applying some of the techniques discussed in earlier chapters. You also saw several advanced techniques involving the creative use of the flexible architecture of this very capable product. Most advanced capabilities require the use of some Visual Basic programming and extending most features requires only simple expressions.

❑   The reporting interface can be enhanced using Custom Report Items, such as Dundas Chart for Reporting Services. Using ASP.NET web form controls, user input and parameter selection can be enhanced to provide a richer user experience. Through programmatic rendering and image manipulation, reports may be enhanced to include dynamic graphical content, extending capabilities beyond standard reporting features.

By now, you should have a few tricks up your sleeve to answer reporting requirements with some nifty features. With your imagination and a little experimentation, you're likely to find the right techniques for your solutions by building on what you've learned here.

Part III

Enabling End
User Reporting
with Report Builder

Reporting Services
Report Models

This chapter looks at building a Reporting Services Report Model. A Report Model is the key component behind performing ad hoc end user queries. Using a Report Model, users can easily navigate through either a SQL Server database or an Analysis Services database. To better understand how Report Models are built and what features they include, you will do a simple walk-through using the AdventureWorksDW database.

This chapter covers:

- ❑ Creating Reporting Services Report Models.
- ❑ Working with Report Model data sources.
- ❑ Creating Report Model Data Source Views.
- ❑ Setting Report Model properties.
- ❑ Deploying Report Models.
- ❑ Creating Report Models for Analysis Services.

Getting Started

To begin, open up the SQL Server Business Intelligence Development Studio (Development Studio for short). In the Development Studio, you can create a number of business intelligence projects. Go to File⇨New⇨Project, and select the Report Model project template as shown in Figure 8-1.

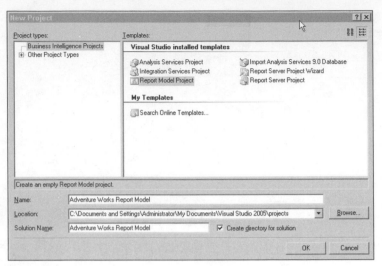

Figure 8-1

Once you have opened a new Report Model project, there are three folders within the Solution Explorer:

❑ Data Sources contains connection information to one or more SQL Server databases.

❑ Data Source Views contains logical representations of SQL Server databases.

❑ Report Models contains models that translate SQL Server structure into user-friendly entities and attributes.

The next sections walk you through each of these three major components: data sources, Data Source Views, and Report Models.

Creating the Report Model Data Source

Data sources contain information for connecting to a SQL Server database. Reporting Services reports created with Visual Studio can use any of the .NET managed data providers. However, Report Models can only be created against SQL Server and Analysis Services. This is understandable considering each different connection type (SQL, Oracle, and so on) requires its own semantic query processor to translate Report Models into the underlying query syntax. In the 2005 release, Microsoft has no plans to support other data sources.

To create a new data source, navigate to the Solution Explorer, right-click on the Data Sources folder, and select Add New Data Source, as illustrated in Figure 8-2.

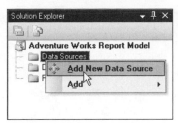

Figure 8-2

When adding a new data source, the Data Source Wizard is initiated. This wizard will step you through the creation of a SQL Server connection. After moving past the welcome screen, select the New... button to open the Connection Manager window. Figures 8-3 and 8-4 walk you through creating a new connection to the AdventureWorksDW database.

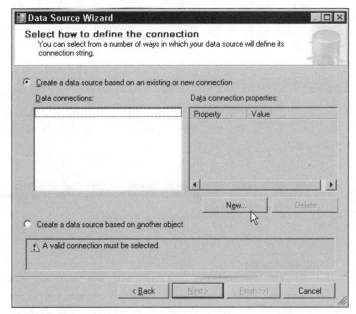

Figure 8-3

Once you have set up the new connection, continue through the Data Source Wizard by clicking Next. The final screen of the wizard will let you assign a name to your data source. In this scenario, you can leave the default name "Adventure Works DW" and click Finish, as shown in Figure 8-5.

The Connection Manager and Data Source Wizard are now common components used throughout projects in the Business Intelligence Studio. Once you have created a Connection Manager, it will be available for use in Analysis Services and Integration Services projects.

Now that the data source has been created, you can move on to creating the Data Source View.

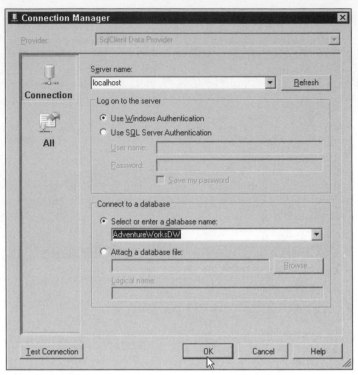

Figure 8-4

Figure 8-5

Building a Data Source View

Data Source Views represent a logical layer above the database schema. Within a Data Source View, you can create primary keys and foreign key relationships as well as calculated values. Building a well-defined Data Source View is one of the key steps to creating a Report Model. All Report Models must be based on information retrieved from the Data Source View. In this section, you look at building the Data Source View, working with productivity features and the code behind a Data Source Views.

To create a data source view, navigate to the Solution Explorer, right-click on the Data Source Views folder, and select Add New Data Source View. Figure 8-6 illustrates adding a new Data Source View.

Figure 8-6

The first step to creating a Data Source View is specifying the data source. Only one data source can be defined per Data Source View. Figure 8-7 illustrates selecting the AdventureWorksDW connection created earlier in the chapter.

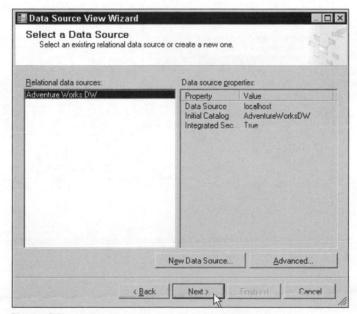

Figure 8-7

After selecting the data source, the Data Source View Wizard allows you to select tables and views defined in the data source. In this example, you select a limited number of tables from the AdventureWorksDW database, but there is no limitation that prevents you from selecting all available tables and views. Select the following tables as illustrated in Figure 8-8.

- ❑ DimProduct
- ❑ DimProductCategory
- ❑ DimProductSubcategory
- ❑ DimGeography
- ❑ DimTime
- ❑ FactResellerSales
- ❑ DimReseller
- ❑ DimSalesTerritory

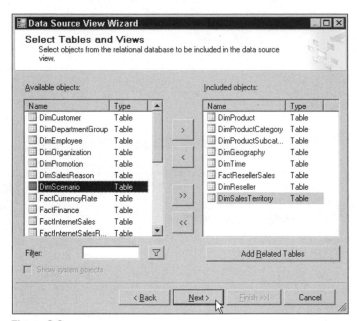

Figure 8-8

Later in this section, you look at creating new diagrams within the Data Source View to help group logical subject areas within a large set of tables.

The final step in the Data Source View Wizard allows you to name the view. In this example, give the view the name "Adventure Works DW DSV," as illustrated in Figure 8-9, and click Finish to complete the wizard.

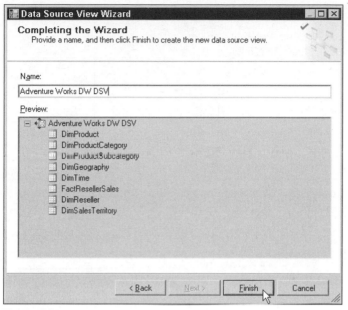

Figure 8-9

In the next sections, you look at working with Data Source Views after completing the Data Source View Wizard.

Manipulate the Data Source View

The Data Source View Wizard is a nice starting point for getting your main tables established, but in most situations, the Data Source View will need to be massaged a little. This section describes how to create additional diagrams to organize your views, adding new relationships, and working with named queries.

Data Source View Diagrams

The example Data Source View in this chapter uses only a small number of tables. In a relatively small database application, the number of tables can often be substantial. When dealing with a large number of tables, it often becomes difficult to organize them in a single relational diagram. To help alleviate some of this confusion, Microsoft has included the ability to create multiple relational diagrams within a single Data Source View. Start by opening the AdventureWorksDW DSV.dsv Data Source View created earlier in the chapter by double-clicking on it in the Solution Explorer. In the upper-left corner of the Data Source View designer, you should notice a pane called Diagram Organizer. You will use the Diagram Organizer to create new diagrams. Figure 8-10 illustrates adding a new diagram to the Data Source View created earlier in this chapter.

After clicking New Diagram, you can rename the diagram to "Products." Now that you have added a new diagram to the project, you can simply drag tables from the Tables window to include them in the diagram. All the tables listed in the Tables window represent the objects contained within the Data Source View. Diagrams are simply a logical representation to ease editing of the objects. If you make a change to a table in one diagram, it will be reflected on all other diagrams the table is associated with.

Figure 8-10

Figure 8-11 illustrates the Products diagram using the DimProduct, DimProductSubCategory, and DimProductCategory tables. This diagram will now simplify the management of the related product tables.

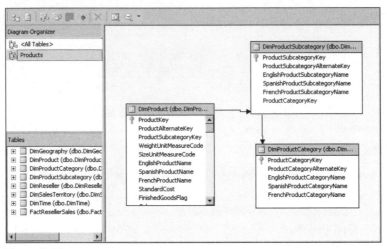

Figure 8-11

Building Data Source View Relationships

In a Data Source View, you can also work with primary key–foreign key relationships within a data source. Creating new primary key–foreign key relationships is often necessary if the underlying database does not already contain the relationships. Relationships created in the Data Source View are only logical relationships, so this will not impact the underlying database.

The FactResellerSales table in the AdventureWorksDW database contains three time-related columns: OrderDateKey, ShipDateKey, and DueDateKey. These columns relate to the DimTime table based on the TimeKey column. Open the "<All Tables>" diagram by clicking on it in the Diagram Organizer pane, as illustrated in Figure 8-12.

In this diagram, you should notice the three relationships from FactResellerSales to DimTime. To examine how the relationship is defined, double-click on the arrows connecting the two tables. In this example, you can click on the leftmost arrow connecting to DimTime to view the FactResellerSales.ShipDateKey to DimTime.TimeKey relationship, as illustrated in Figure 8-13.

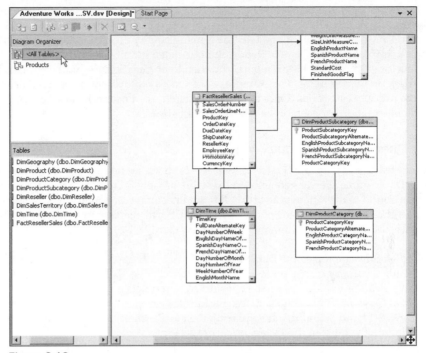

Figure 8-12

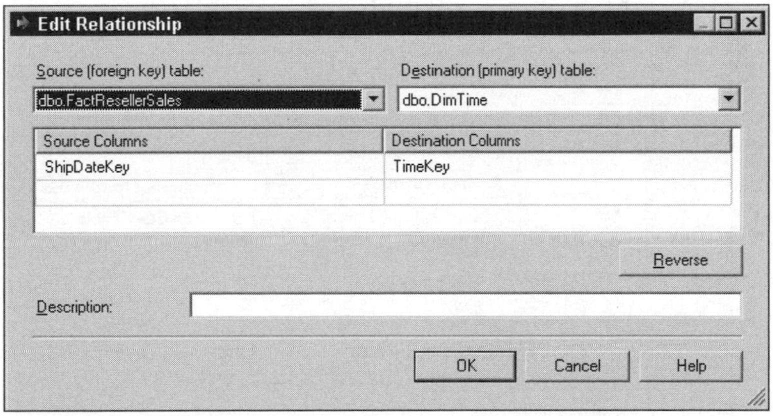

Figure 8-13

Within the Edit Relationship window, you can specify table and columns used as both the primary and foreign key. You can also reverse relationships if they were created incorrectly and add a meaningful description.

Relationships in the Data Source View are extremely important in a Report Model. These relationships will later be used to create *roles* within the Report Model. A role allows a user to navigate from one section of the Report Model to another and tells the semantic query processor how to retrieve data. Roles are also used to implement a feature of Report Builder called Infinite Drill Through. This feature allows the report developer to create a single report, and then Reporting Services will create reports at runtime when users click on related items. For example, a user could build a report that contains Sales Amount for each of the product categories. Once the report is deployed, a user can click on a product category and see sales information for each of the related subcategories.

Using Named Queries in Data Source Views

Another major feature of the Data Source View is its ability to use named queries. When a table or view is added to a Data Source View, a reference to that table or view is created. If the table or view schema changes, items bound to the schema can break. It is not uncommon in applications to have column names or table names change during the life of the application. So, to alleviate this issue, queries instead of direct references can be created within the Data Source View.

Queries offer flexibility on top of the Data Source View. If a column name changes in the underlying database schema, the query can be updated to reflect this change. Column names can be aliased and breaking changes can be avoided. It can be considered best practice to change your Data Source View tables to Named Queries. There is no negative performance impact, so the flexibility you gain is well worth it. Figures 8-14 and 8-15 illustrate replacing the FactResellerSales table with a new named query by right-clicking on the table in the Data Source View.

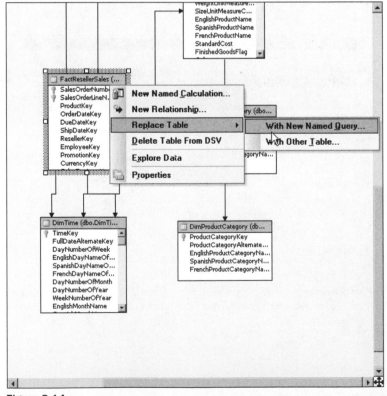

Figure 8-14

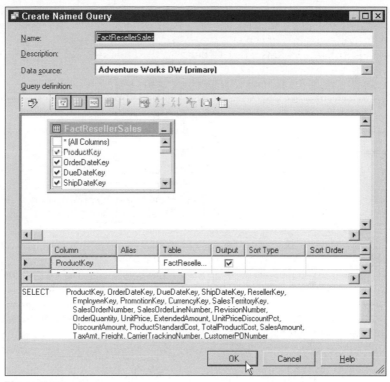

Figure 8-15

Now that you have seen some of the core features around creating a Data Source View, you will look at the XML code generated by the designer.

Data Source View Code Behind

All of the source files created in a Report Model project are stored as XML files. This is important for a couple of reasons. First, the use of XML allows developers to easily manipulate files through programmatic interfaces such as the .NET System.Xml assembly. Second, Report Model developers can now use standard source control systems such as Visual Source Safe to store their projects. This offers the advantage of versioning to Business Intelligence projects. If a mistake is made while updating a file, users of a source control system can simply revert their changes and avoid costly and sometimes error-prone rework.

In this section, you will take a look at the XML behind a Data Source View. If you have worked with Typed data sets in ADO.NET, the XML schema should look very familiar. To view the XML behind a Data Source View, right-click on the AdventureWorksDW DSV.dsv file in the Solution Explorer and click View Code. Figure 8-16 illustrates viewing the XML behind the AdventureWorksDW DSV created earlier in this chapter.

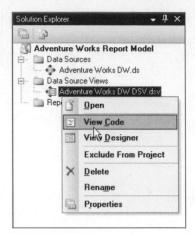

Figure 8-16

The Data Source View XML starts with both an ID tag and a Name tag. The ID tag is the object name given to the Data Source View. When new objects, such as a Report Model, are associated with the Data Source View, they will reference the value in the ID tag. If the ID values is changed after objects are associated with the Data Source View, those items will be unable to read from it. The Name tag is the friendly name displayed in the Business Intelligence Development Studio interface. This value can be updated as needed without breaking other items. By default, the ID and Name tag will have the same value.

The next major section of the Data Source View is contained within the Annotation tag. Each Annotation tag contains information about how the Data Source View should be displayed within the designer. Annotation tags also contain information related to how initial relationships were established within the Data Source View. Once the Data Source View is created, the Annotations section does not include any information crucial to the function of the view; it is solely for display purposes. So, if you delete the entire section, the Report Model will continue to function. However, you will not have a very pretty designer to work in.

Following the Annotations tag is the DataSourceID tag. This tag represents a reference to the ID tag in one of the project's data sources. Modifying this tag can break the relationship between the two objects.

The next tag in the document is the Schema tag. This tag contains the core definition of the Data Source View. It breaks down into two major areas: elements and relationships.

The document starts with one main element tag. This tag represents the entire Data Source View as a single complex type. Within the main element tag are element tags for each of the individual tables. The table element tags contain the name of the object as well as a query or reference to the underlying table. Within each element tag for a table are element tags for the table's different columns. The column element tags contain the columns name, data type, and other defining properties.

After moving through all of the table element tags, you will find a variable list of tags for each unique constraint within the Data Source View. These tags contain information about primary keys defined within the view. Each constraint will have an indication of its type as well as an xpath reference to its related table and column.

The final section of the Data Source View XML contains information about the references defined between the tables in the view. This section is enclosed in an `xs:annotation` tag. Unlike the `Annotation` tags discussed earlier, this tag cannot be removed without affecting the view's behavior. Each primary key–foreign key relationship is identified with a `Relationship` tag. The `Relationship` tag contains a name for the relationship as well as references to columns within the Data Source View.

Now that you have seen how to create a relational data source connection and Data Source View, let's take a look at generating the Report Model.

Building the Report Model

In this section you look at the Report Model Wizard and build a simple model based off of the AdventureWorksDW database. Once the model is created, you will look at different ways to improve your Report Model. Finally, you will look at deploying the model for end users to work with.

Report Model Wizard

All Report Models start by using the Report Model Wizard. This wizard will step through selecting the relational data source as well as the Data Source View. However, the final step of the wizard runs the Model Generation Rules. These rules are key to creating a layer that is easily understood by the end user.

Let's first take a look at adding a new Report Model to our project. To add a new Report Model, right-click on the Report Models folder in the Solution Explorer and select Add New Report Model. Figure 8-17 illustrates adding a new model.

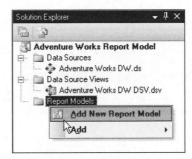

Figure 8-17

Adding a new Report Model invokes the Report Model Wizard. The first step in the wizard has you select your Data Source View. Figure 8-18 illustrates selecting the AdventureWorksDW `DSV.dsv` Data Source View created earlier in this chapter.

The Data Source View dialog will display a list of all Data Source Views associated with a SQL Server connection. It is possible to add other Data Source Views to your Report Model project. However, only SQL Server can be used to generate a model. Later in this chapter, creating Report Models using Analysis Services is discussed.

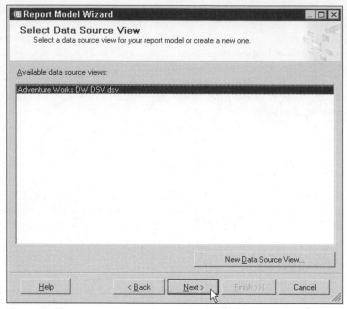

Figure 8-18

After selecting a Data Source View, you will see the Report Model Rules Generation dialog. This dialog is key to creating the Report Model. It allows you to select all of the rules that will be applied to the underlying Data Source View. Figure 8-19 shows the Report Model Rules Generation dialog.

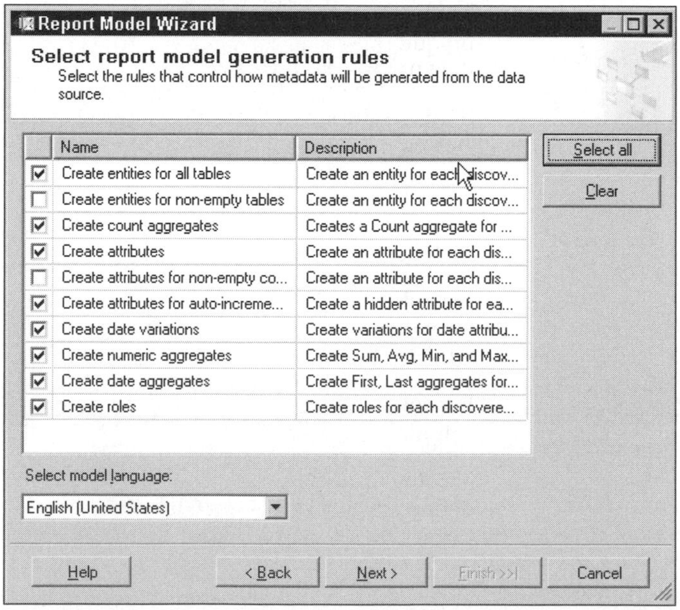

Figure 8-19

The Report Model is generated by going through two passes of rules defined on the Report Server. The implementation of the rules can be found at the following location:

```
<install drive>\Program Files\Microsoft SQL Server\MSSQL.<instance>\Reporting
Services\Report Server\ModelGenerationRules.smgl
```

The following table shows each of the rules and describes how they are implemented against the Data Source View.

Pass 1

Name	Description
Create entities for all tables.	Builds Report Model entities for any tables contained in the Data Source View. System tables and the dtproperties table are excluded from the Model Generation Wizard.
Create entities for nonempty tables.	Build report model entities only for tables that have a row count greater than 0.
Create count aggregates.	For each entity in the Report Model, a count aggregate is added. If the Data Source View contains a table named Product, an entity called Product will be created along with an attribute #Product that represents the count of rows within the Product table.
Create attributes.	Creates attributes for each column in a table that is not a foreign key and not an auto-increment column.
Create attributes for nonempty columns.	Creates only attributes for columns that contain data. A query against the data source is required to identify the number of unique values stored in a given column. If that number is greater than 0, the column is included.
Create attributes for auto-increment columns.	If this option is selected, auto-increment columns are also included as attributes of an entity.
Create date variations.	For columns that have a data type of DateTime, additional attributes are added for the day, month, quarter, and year of each date.
Create numeric aggregates.	For columns of type Integer, Float, and Decimal, attributes for Sum, Average, Min, and Max aggregates of the column are added.
Create date aggregates.	For columns of type DateTime, Min, and Max, aggregates of the column are added.
Create roles.	Creates a role for each primary key–foreign key relationship defined in the Data Source View.

Table continued on following page

Pass 2

Name	Description
Lookup entities.	Once the attributes are created through Pass 1, Pass 2 looks at each attribute to identify if it is eligible to become a lookup. By default, lookups are added to columns that are not aggregated (`DateTime`, `Integer`, `Float`, `Decimal`) and are not auto-increment columns.
Small lists.	Drop-down lists are created for entities with less than 100 rows.
Large lists.	Filter lists are created for entities with greater than 500 rows.
Very large lists.	Requires that large entities (greater than 5,000 rows) have mandatory filters.
Set identifying attributes.	Identifying attributes are columns that can uniquely identify items in the entity. Identifying attributes are determined based on a combination of non-null requirements, data types, and use as a foreign key.
Set default detail attributes.	Default detail attributes are identified as those attributes most likely to further define an entity. Default detail attributes are also defined based on a combination of non-null requirements, data types, and use as a foreign key.
Role name only.	Looks at identifying attributes and determines the role name to be used in role definitions.
Numeric/date formatting.	Sets the default sort direction to Descending for numeric and date attributes.
Integer/decimal formatting.	Sets the default formatting for `Integer` and `Decimal` type attributes to general number format.
Float formatting.	Sets the default formatting for `Float` type attributes to 2 decimal places.
Date formatting.	Sets the default formatting for `DateTime` type attributes to the general date format.
Discourage grouping.	Discourages grouping of items that have a unique occurrence of greater than 80%.
Dropdown value selection.	Creates drop-down selections for attributes that have greater than 0 and less than 200 unique values.

After selecting the generation rules, the wizard moves to the Update Statistics dialog. This dialog presents two options: Update statistics before generating and Use current statistics in the data source view. The statistics this dialog is referring to are not statistics from the underlying database. They are statistics from the Data Source View. These statistics include properties such as the max length of a column. The Report Model designer uses this information to help create the new Report Model.

Statistics on a Report Model only need to be updated when the database changes. So, for the first run of the wizard, it is suggested that you select the Update statistics before generating option. Any further passes through the wizard can simply use the information then stored in the Data Source View.

Completing the Report Model Wizard requires two steps. The first step is to name the model. In this example, give your Report Model the name "Adventure Works DW Model." The second step is to run the Rules Generation Wizard. Figure 8-20 illustrates the first step in the completion screen.

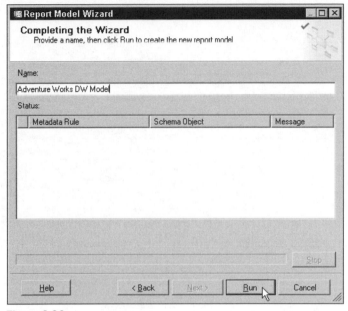

Figure 8-20

To start the Model Wizard, click on the Run button. Running the wizard can take a few moments. As it is generated you will see an output of all the rules that are applied. You should see all of the tables identified in the Data Source View as well as their corresponding columns. Figure 8-21 show the wizard after running against our Data Source View created earlier.

In Figure 8-21 you should notice the wizard running through PASS 1 of the modeling rules. The table DimProduct is listed first and has been created as an entity. From there a count aggregate for the table is created, as well as attributes for each of the columns.

After clicking Finish in the Report Model Wizard, you will see a new file in the Solution Explorer with the extension smdl. smdl stands for Semantic Model Definition Language. "smdl" is the XML schema used to represent a Reporting Services Report Model. The next section will explore the makeup and editing of the Report Model.

Working with Reporting Services Report Models

To understand the Report Model, you will explore the model created in the previous section. In this section, you will add the DimEmployee table to your Report Model. The first step to adding the DimEmployee table is to edit the AdventureWorksDW DSV.dsv Data Source View. Open the Data Source View by double-clicking on it in the Solution Explorer. Right-click on the design surface and select Add/Remove Tables, as illustrated in Figure 8-22.

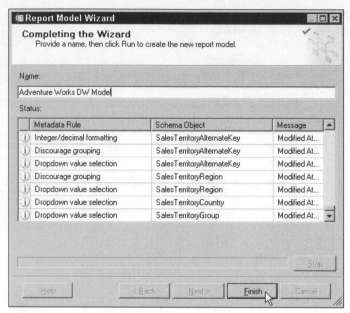

Figure 8-21

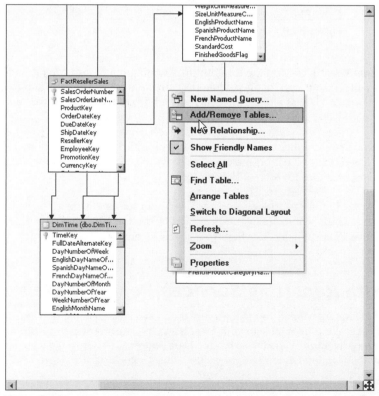

Figure 8-22

In the Add/Remove Tables dialog, select the table DimEmployee and move it to the Included objects, as illustrated in Figure 8-23.

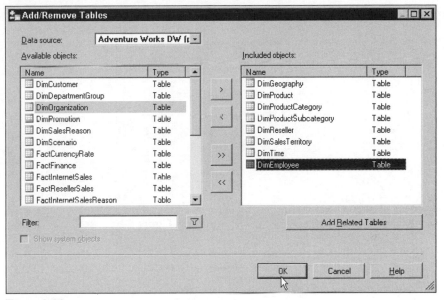

Figure 8-23

Click OK to close the Add/Remove Tables dialog, save and close the Data Source View, and return to the Adventure Works DW Model.smdl designer.

To add `DimEmployee` attributes to your Report Model, right-click on the Model node and select New/Entity, as illustrated in Figure 8-24.

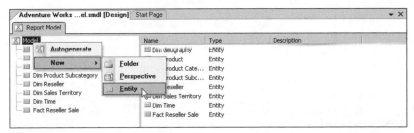

Figure 8-24

Right-click on the new entity, select Rename and rename it "Dim Employee." Before you can generate the new Dim Employee entity, you must set its Binding property. The Binding property tells the Report Model which table or view in the Data Source View contains the attributes for the entity. Using the Properties window, modify the Dim Employee entity's Binding property to use the DimEmployee table as illustrated in Figure 8-25.

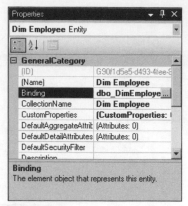

Figure 8-25

Now that you have bound the new entity, you are ready to generate its model. Right-click on the Dim Employee entity and select Autogenerate, as illustrated in Figure 8-26.

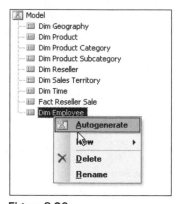

Figure 8-26

You will be prompted with a warning that says "Regenerating an existing model item cannot be reversed." In this case, that is perfectly acceptable because you have not done any modifications to the Dim Employee entity. If this were an existing entity that you had made modifications to, you would not want to auto-generate the model. For this example, select "Yes" from the warning dialog. Click through the Report Model Wizard dialog using the defaults and notice that it is the same dialog as illustrated above when you first created the Report Model. When you are finished running the wizard, you should have a completed entity like Figure 8-27.

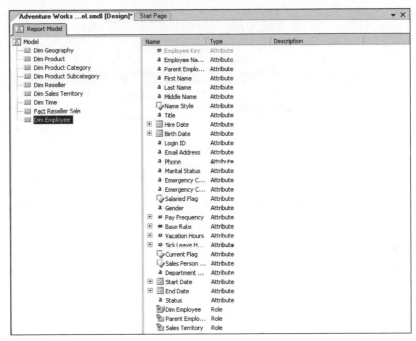

Figure 8-27

The final step in adding the Dim Employee entity is to define its Identifying Attributes. In this case, `EmployeeKey` will uniquely identify the entity. To set the Identifying Attributes, navigate to the Properties window and click on the builder button for the `IdentifyingAttributes` property. This will launch the AttributeReference Collection Editor, as shown in Figure 8-28.

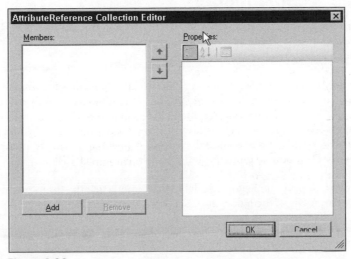

Figure 8-28

To add the EmployeeKey, click the Add button and select "# Employee Key" from the list Fields. Click OK to close the dialog and the resulting AttributeReference Collection Editor should appear as shown in Figure 8-29.

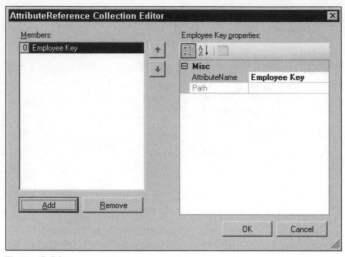

Figure 8-29

Click OK to apply the property setting and save the Report Model.

Now that you have seen how to create and manipulate a Report Model, you will look at deploying the model to the Report Server.

Deploying the Report Model

Report Models are deployed to a central Report Server in much the same way as Reports. The smdl file, along with the data source, is published via the Reporting Services Web service. Once the Report Model is published, it can be used by end users.

One slight difference between the deployment of models and reports is the number of folders that are created. In reports, you deploy to a single target folder. With report models, you can deploy to both a target Data Source folder and target Model folder. By default, these are simply set to Data Sources and Models, respectively. To change the target folders, right-click on the Report Model project in the Solution Explorer and select Properties. From there, you will see properties for the different folder locations as well as the Overwrite Data Source property and Deployment Server URL.

Once you are ready to deploy the Report Model to the server, click the Build menu and select Deploy *<project name>*. Deployment of the model consists of two steps: building the model and sending the deploy command.

Building the model consists of checking expression syntax, validating the availability of files, verifying IDs of related objects, and performing other types of validation activities. If the project is verified, the process will continue with the deployment of the package.

To deploy the package, SQL Server Business Intelligence Development Studio invokes the Reporting Services Web service. The Reporting Services Web service contains methods for publishing to the server. When you are deploying a project, you are really deploying the smdl file. This file will be stored in the ReportServer database in the Catalog table. Whenever users make a request for the model, Reporting Services will simply read it back from the database. No file is actually stored on the server's file system.

To check that the project has deployed successfully, open SQL Management Studio and connect to your Report Server. Under the home folder, you should see a Data Source and Models folder now created. If you expand the Models folder, you will see your project listed.

Now that the Report Model has been created and deployed, you can move on to creating reports using the Report Builder. Chapter 9 will walk you through using the Report Builder to allow end user development of reports.

Building Report Models from Analysis Services Databases

The bulk of this chapter discussed building Reporting Services Report Models using SQL Server. It is also possible, and in my opinion much simpler, to create Report Models using Analysis Services. Creating a Report Model from Analysis Services requires the initial creation of an Analysis Services database. Creating Analysis Services databases is outside the scope of this text, so you will use the Adventure Works DW Analysis Services sample provided with SQL Server 2005.

To create a Report Model from an Analysis Services database, you do not need to use the Business Intelligence Development Studio. Most of the work that was done to create a Report Model from SQL Server is the same type of work that is done to create an Analysis Services database. So, all you need to do is create a connection to the Analysis Services database in Report Manager and then generate the model from it. The first step is to open the Report Manager in the web browser. The default location is http://localhost/reports.

From Report Manager, click on the New Data Source button to launch the New Data Source entry page. In the New Data Source page, simply give the data source a name as connection string to the Analysis Services database as illustrated in Figure 8-30. Make sure that you set the appropriate connection string for your database and specify "Windows integrated security" for the Connect using setting. Once you have entered the correct settings, click OK to create the data source.

Once your data source is created, edit it by clicking on it in the Report Manager page. If you used the settings from Figure 8-30, the data source should be labeled "Adventure Works DW AS." In the Data Source edit page, you should be able to scroll to the bottom and see a Generate Model button, as illustrated in Figure 8-31.

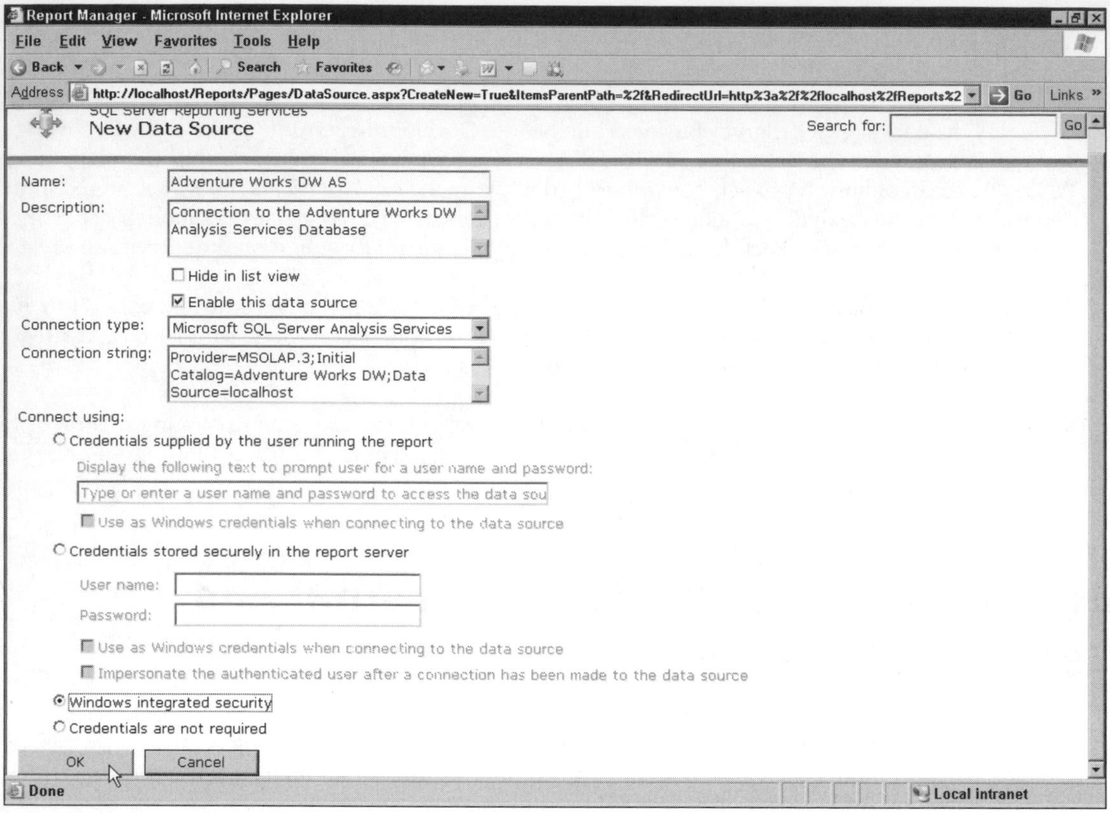

Figure 8-30

Clicking on the Generate Model button will take you to a new page that allows you to name the Report Model and specify its location. For this example, name the model "Adventure Works DW AS Report Model" and click OK, as illustrated in Figure 8-32.

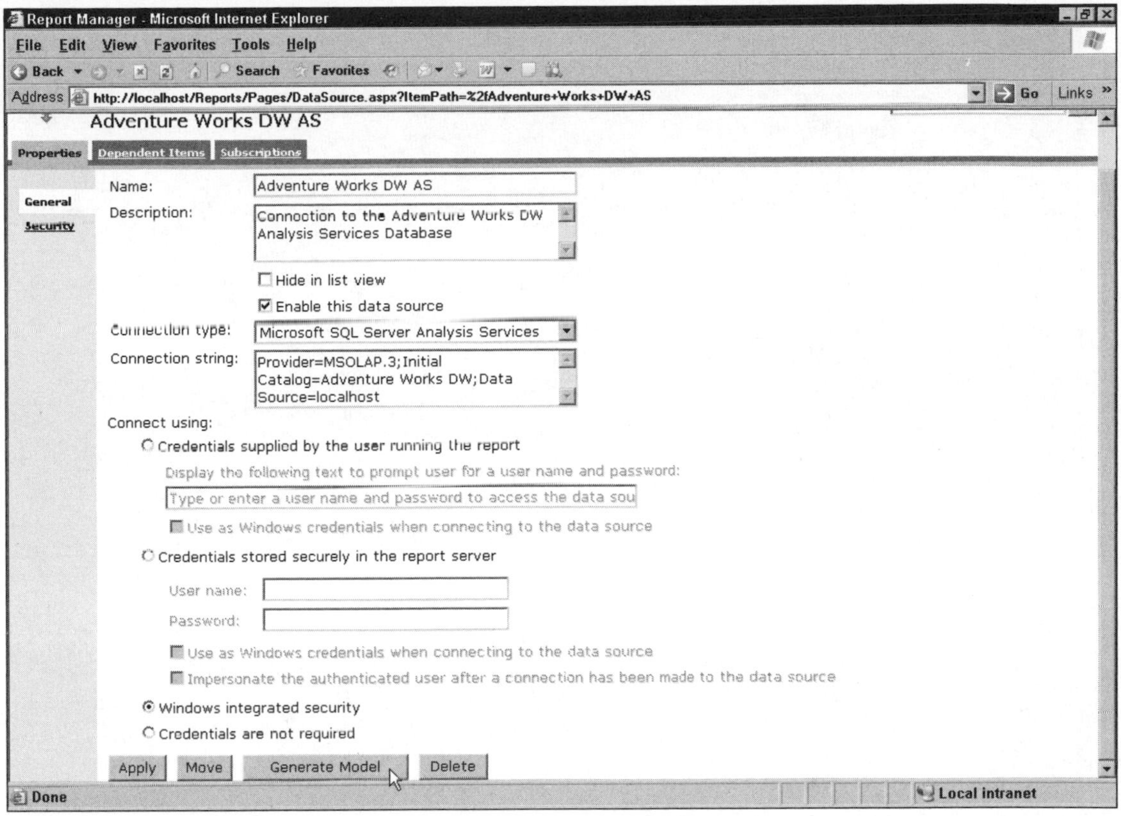

Figure 8-31

Reporting Services uses the Analysis Services definition to generate the Report Model. Analysis Services Database already contains relationship information as well as formatting and aggregates. For this reason, you do not have to go through all of the steps necessary to create a Report Model from SQL Server. Once the model is created you can use it just like a SQL Server base Report Model. Chapter 9 discusses using the Report Builder to create reports from Report Models.

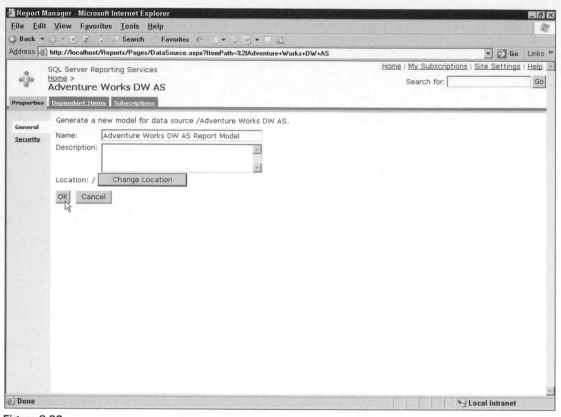

Figure 8-32

Summary

In this chapter, you took a look at creating Reporting Services Report Models. You started by creating a data source within your Report Model project. A data source in a Report Model project can connect to a SQL database. Other databases are not currently supported.

After you created a data source, you looked at adding a Data Source View. The Data Source View is a logical representation of the underlying database. It allows you to add a level of abstraction from our source. You then created named queries to help shield your model from database changes as well as create diagrams to more easily view certain objects.

Once the Data Source View was in place, you could run the Report Model Wizard. The Report Model Wizard runs through a number of steps, but the key process is the Model Rules Generation. You saw what rules are implemented and how they use the underlying Data Source View to create objects.

After running the Report Model Wizard, you looked at editing the Report Model. The Report Model is an XML-based file known as the Semantic Model Definition Language (SMDL). This file is made up of three major components: entities, attributes, and roles. Entities generally represent tables in the Data Source View. Attributes generally represent columns, and roles represent relationships between entities.

When the model is completed, you can deploy it to the Report Server. Deployment consists of two steps: build and deployment. Building the project checks to make sure the model is syntactically valid. Deploying the project invokes the Reporting Services Web service and publishes the `smdl` file to the server.

Once the Report Model is deployed, users can start building reports. After reading this chapter, you should now have an understanding of:

❑ The types of data sources that can be used for Report Models. Analysis Services, and SQL Server.

❑ How Data Source Views are created and some best practices around using named queries.

❑ How Report Models are generated and where you can find information about generation rules.

❑ How Report Models are deployed to the report server.

❑ How Report Model are created for Analysis Services databases.

In the next chapter, you look at the Report Builder client and see how it can be used against an existing model.

Report Builder

This chapter looks at performing ad hoc reporting. In March 2004, Microsoft purchased a company by the name of ActiveViews. ActiveViews had a technology that allowed users to build a user-friendly model on top of their data. This model has become the backbone of ad hoc reporting in Reporting Services.

As you move through this chapter, you will be introduced to the Report Builder application. The Report Builder application has a familiar Microsoft Office interface for building reports. You will also see how to use different report layouts to fulfill various reporting needs. Once you understand the report layouts, you will move on to formatting and filtering data. The chapter ends with a few administrative items you need to be aware of when deploying this tool to your users.

In this chapter, you learn:

- ❑ What Report Builder is and how it can be used.
- ❑ How to create reports with Report Builder.
- ❑ How to format Report Builder reports.
- ❑ How to add filtering and sorting to your reports.
- ❑ How to create calculations in a report.
- ❑ Administration tasks with Report Builder.

Building Report Models

Report Models are the key to creating ad hoc reports. They represent the semantic layer on top of your SQL Server of Analysis Services data. Report models help users easily identify data elements as well as navigate their relationships.

In the previous chapter, you built a Report Model using the AdventureWorksDW database. In this chapter, you will leverage that model to create your own ad hoc reports.

If you have not built a Report Model up to this point, I suggest reviewing the material in the previous chapter and familiarizing yourself with the process. Above and beyond creating reports, building the model is the single most important aspect of doing ad hoc analysis. Without a solid model, users will most likely find creating reports confusing and time-consuming.

Working with the Report Builder

In this section you look at accessing the Report Builder tool. Once you are familiar with the application, you will move on to building your own reports.

Accessing the Report Builder

Ad hoc reporting in Reporting Services uses a Windows smart client application. Smart client applications combine the rich user interface of a Windows application with the ease of deployment found in web applications. To run a smart client application, users navigate to a web server. From the web server, the executable and any dependencies are loaded onto the client machine. The smart client then runs on the user's local machine and can access all of the local resources. When an update to the application is available, the smart client application downloads the new bits and is ready to go.

Microsoft decided that to effectively develop ad hoc reports, users would need more functionality than a traditional web application can provide. For this reason, Report Builder was introduced using smart client technology.

There are two methods available for accessing the Report Builder. First, you can access the Report Builder through the following URL:

```
http://servername/reportserver/ReportBuilder/ReportBuilder.application
```

You will need to replace *servername* with the name of your report server and *reportserver* with the name of the Report Server virtual directory. Using this URL, you could create your own buttons to launch the Report Builder application.

The second method for accessing the Report Builder is through the Report Manager web interface. When you navigate to Report Manager (`http://servername/reports`), you will see a Report Builder button as illustrated in Figure 9-1. Click on the Report Builder button to launch the smart client application.

When you click the Report Builder button, the smart client application verifies that you have the required prerequisites to run the application. To run the Report Builder, your users will need version 2.0 of the Microsoft .NET Framework.

After the Report Builder application is downloaded, you should see a new application in your Start menu. You can now use the resulting shortcut to launch Report Builder. Opening and saving reports will require a connection to the Report Server.

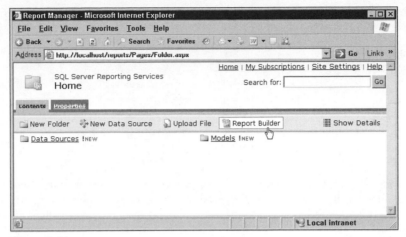

Figure 9-1

In the next section, you look at building Reporting Services reports using the Report Builder.

Building a Report

Once you launch the Report Builder, you will be presented with a dialog to select a Report Model. As was discussed in the previous chapter, Report Models are the key component for creating ad hoc reports. They represent an easy-to-use representation of your data.

The list of Report Models presented represents all Report Models that you have access to on the given Report Server. You might also notice a + next to some of the Report Models. You can expand the Report Model node to view any perspectives associated with the model. Perspectives are views of the Report Model that present a subset of information to the user.

To start designing reports, select the Adventure Works DW Report Model. In the previous chapter, you created a small Report Model from the AdventureWorksDW database. You will use this model through-out the rest of this chapter. If you have not deployed the Report Model, please walk through the Report Model chapter.

After selecting a Report Model, the Report Builder will present four main windows:

❑ Explorer

❑ Fields

❑ Report Layout

❑ Designer

The Explorer window displays a list of Entity collections from the Report Model. As you select items in the Explorer window, you will notice that the Fields window updates to display all of the available Attributes for the selected Entity. You will use the Explorer and Fields windows to construct your first report.

Before you build your report, you need to decide what type of layout is appropriate. In the Report Layout window, you are presented with three options:

❑ Table

❑ Matrix

❑ Chart

Let's take a look at creating reports with three different layout types.

Table Layout

To understand the table report layout, you will create a simple report that shows Products in the hierarchy (Product Category, Product Subcategory, Product Name) with their associated Sales Amount and Order Quantity. This will build a base around working with related data as well as aggregated values.

To start, select the Adventure Works DW Model and Table layout from the Getting Started window (see Figure 9-2).

Figure 9-2

Once you have selected the Table layout, you will notice that the design window displays a base report with one column. You want to start building your report based on the Product Category, Product Subcategory, and Product Name hierarchy. Start at the lowest level of the hierarchy and work your way up. English Product Name is the lowest level of detail required, so you start with that field. Select the Dim Product node from the Explorer window. This will refresh the fields list with all the attributes of Product. Select English Product Name from the list and drag it onto the table in the design window. Figure 9-3 illustrates adding the Product Name field.

Now that English Product Name has been added to the report, you should notice a change in the Explorer window as shown in Figure 9-4. Selecting the Product Name field told the Report Builder that you were going to use the Product entity for this report. The change in the Explorer window shows all of the related entities to Product. In this model, Product Subcategory and Reseller Sales have a direct relationship to product.

The next step in building the report is the addition of Product Subcategory and Product Category. You are moving from the lowest level of detail to the highest, so your next field will be English Product Subcategory. To add the field, select the English Product Subcategory node from the Explorer window. This should change the field list to display Product Subcategory attributes. Select English Product Subcategory Name and drag it to the left of Product Name, as illustrated in Figure 9-5.

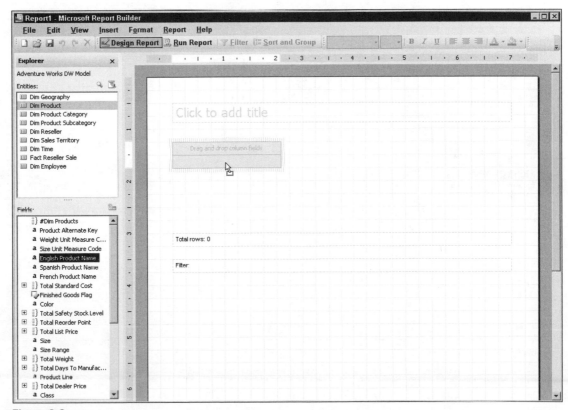

Figure 9-3

Figure 9-4

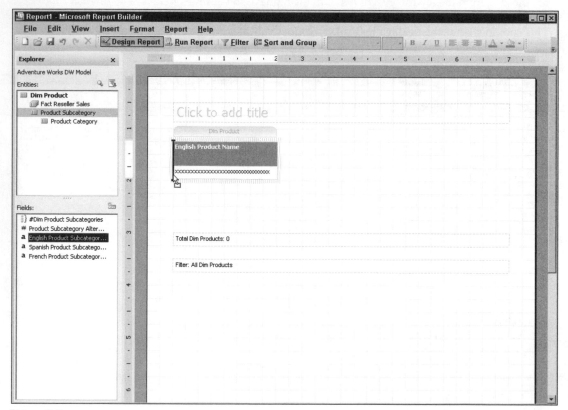

Figure 9-5

To finish the Product hierarchy, click on the Product Category node in the Explorer and add the English Product Category Name field to the left of Product Subcategory Name. You can also repeat these steps to add Total Sales Amount and Total Order Quantity from the Fact Reseller Sales as Product node. Figure 9-6 illustrates the finished layout.

Notice that Report Builder recognized the hierarchy between Product Name, Product Subcategory, and Product Category. Based on the hierarchy, it created subtotals for each of the levels. You might have noticed that the English Product Name total is unnecessary since it is the lowest level of detail. There are a number of formatting improvements that you can make. After discussing the different types of layouts, you will come back to formatting your reports. For now, save this report as "Table Layout Product Sales."

Click on the Save button in the application toolbar to save the report. Clicking the Save button will present a list of folders located on the Report Server. Reports from the Report Builder are always saved on the Report Server. Saving reports to the Report Server requires publish permissions. Required permissions are covered later in this chapter.

Now that you have created a basic Table report, you will look at the next layout option, Matrix.

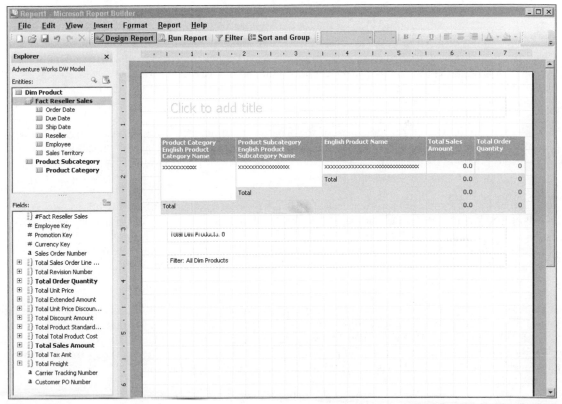

Figure 9-6

Matrix Layout

The Matrix layout is very similar to the Table layout. Both deal with a report as rows and columns. However, the Matrix report allows you to dynamically change the number of columns based on the data returned. This differs from the static column layout of a table.

The ability to expand a report across columns is sometimes referred to as a cross-tab or pivot table. I tend not to use the term pivot table as it can be confused with the flexibility available from pivot tables in Microsoft Excel. A matrix changes its columns based on the data returned. It does not give users the ability to change layout on the fly like Microsoft Excel.

That being said, it is a very powerful layout. It will allow you to build very dynamic reports. Some of the most common examples I see are reports based on time. These examples could include displaying products along the rows with the weeks for a month across the columns. Weeks in a month are a prime candidate for the matrix. Depending on how the calendar for a particular year works out, months can potentially have four or five weeks. Dynamically expanding your columns in a regular table to accommodate this type of variation can be extremely difficult. With a matrix report, you simply and automatically bring back the appropriate data and the report layouts.

The downside of a matrix report is printing. Anytime you want something to print well, you need to be able to control the page width. Length is less of an issue because data can simply continue on to the next page without losing continuity. However, if the columns fall off to the right of the page, it is often difficult to line items back up again. You can increase a report's width, but when you deal with a matrix report, you will never know with certainty how wide the report will be. For that reason, I always set the expectation of my users that if the columns can dynamically grow, there is no guarantee of a beautiful print layout.

Now that you've walked through some of the benefits and trade-offs of the matrix report, let's take a look at creating one. You will again use the Adventure Works DW Report Model. In this section, you create a report that displays Total Sales Amount with Product Categories along your rows and Year (based on Order Date) across your columns.

To start, on the Report Builder menu, select File and New. In the Getting Started window, select the Adventure Works DW Model and the Matrix (cross-tab) Report Layout, as illustrated in Figure 9-7.

After selecting the Matrix layout, the design window will load with the Matrix template. The Matrix template is similar to that of the table. However, it is broken down into three distinct areas: Rows, Columns, and Totals.

In this scenario, you want to display Product Categories along your rows. To access the Product Categories, you need to select Dim Product Category from the Explorer Window. Once Product Categories is selected, the Field List will include the English Product Category Name attribute. To add it to your report, click on English Product Category Name and drag it to the report layout section that says "Drag and drop row groups." Figure 9-8 illustrates adding the Product Category Name to the rows.

Figure 9-7

The second piece of information you want to display in this report is the Year (based on order date) across your columns. The Order Date field you need is located in the Reseller Sales entity. As the report is now, you cannot see the Reseller Sales entity. This is because Product Category has no direct relationship with Reseller Sales. Product Category is related to Reseller sales through the Product and Product Subcategory entity. So, to navigate to Order Date, you will need to select Dim Product Subcategories from the Explorer window, then Dim Products, next Fact Reseller Sales, and finally Order Date. Figure 9-9 illustrates the movement through this hierarchy.

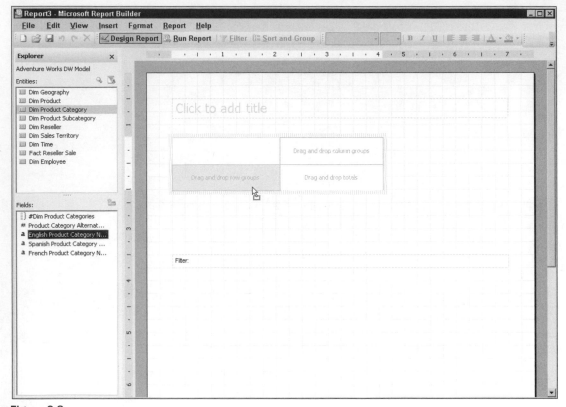

Figure 9-8

Figure 9-9

Now that you have accessed the Order Date field from the Report Model, you can add Year to the columns of your report. In the field list you will see a number of different attributes that define Order Date. One of those attributes is the Calendar Year. This breakdown was defined when the Report Model was created and allows the user to easily use different date variations in their reports. To add Calendar Year to the report, click on the Calendar Year field and drag it to the report designer area labeled "Drag and drop column groups," as illustrated in Figure 9-10.

The final item you need to add to the report is a data element to total. In this scenario, you are using Total Sales Amount from the Reseller Sales entity. After adding the Calendar Year field to the report, the Explorer displays all of the other attributes related to Fact Reseller Sale in the field list. Select Total Sales Amount and drag and drop it on the report area labeled "Drag and drop totals." Once you have added the final field, you should see a report layout similar to the one in Figure 9-11.

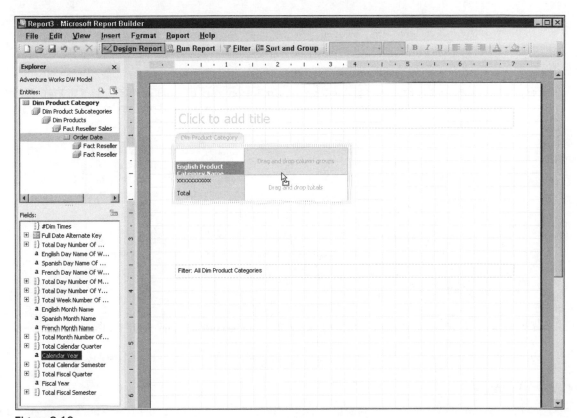

Figure 9-10

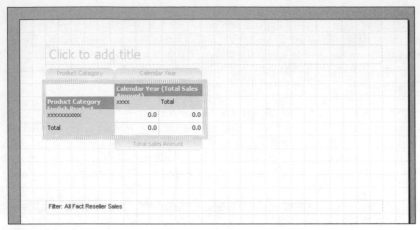

Figure 9-11

To view the results of the report, click the Run Report button from the toolbar. As shown in Figure 9-12, you can see that the calendar years are repeated across the columns based on the data returned.

Product Category: English	Calendar Year (Total Sales Amount)				
	2001	2002	2003	2004	Total
Accessories	20235.3646	92735.3534	296532.8766	161794.3332	571297.9278
Bikes	7395348.6266	19956014.6741	25551775.0727	13399243.1836	66302381.5570
Clothing	34376.3353	485587.1546	871864.1866	386013.1626	1777840.8391
Components	615474.9788	3610092.4719	5482497.2893	2091011.9184	11799076.6584
Total	8065435.3053	24144429.6540	32202669.4252	16038062.5978	80450596.9823

Figure 9-12

You can save the Matrix report as "Matrix Layout Product Sales" using the Save button.

Now that you have seen the Table and Matrix layout, you will move on to the Chart layout.

Chart Layout

The chart layout allows you to graphically display information in your report. There are a number of different chart types that you can choose from including bar charts, line charts, and pie charts. The charting component in Reporting Services is supplied by Dundas. Dundas specializes in data visualization and has a number of graphical components that can be embedded in applications.

To start the chart report, select File and New from the Report Builder menu. In the Getting Started window, select the Adventure Works DW Model and the Chart Report Layout. Figure 9-13 illustrates creating a new chart report.

Figure 9-13

For the chart report, you want to display a pie chart with Total Order Quantity broken down by Sales Territory Region. By default, the chart type is set to a bar chart. To change the chart type, right-click on the chart in the designer and select Chart Type, Pie, Simple Pie. Figure 9-14 illustrates changing the chart type.

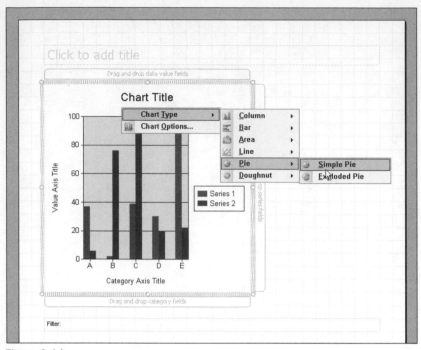

Figure 9-14

Once you have selected the chart type, the chart in the designer surface exposes the drop areas for data fields. Charts have three different drop areas: data value fields, series fields, and category fields. Data value fields represent the information that will determine how the chart area is drawn. For bar charts, it will represent the length of the bars. For your pie charts, it will represent the size of the pie pieces. Series fields are used to display multiple values side by side in the chart. Category fields will define the overall grouping of the chart.

In this scenario, you want to display Total Order Quantity by Sales Territory Regions. Start by selecting Fact Reseller Sale in the Explorer window. From the field list, select Total Order Quantity and drag it to the "Drag and drop data value fields" section in the chart. Figure 9-15 illustrates adding Order Quantity to the chart.

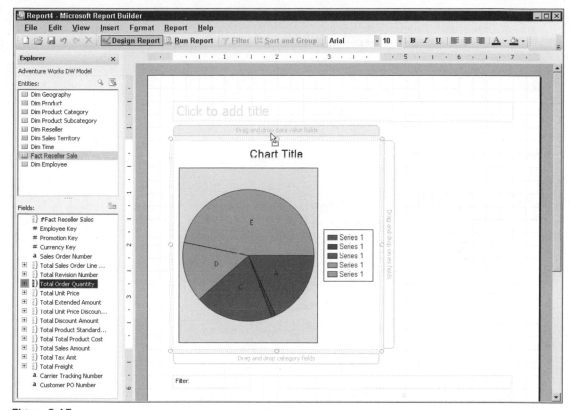

Figure 9-15

Now that you have added Total Order Quantity, you can add your Sales Territory Regions. From the Explorer, select Sales Territory. Drag the Sales Territory Region field from the field list, and drop it on the "Drag and drop category fields" area of the chart. Figure 9-16 illustrates adding the Sales Territory Region.

Once you have added both fields to the chart, select Run Report from the toolbar. You should now see Order Quantity broken down by Sales Territory Region. Figure 9-17 shows the rendered chart report.

I won't say that this is the ugliest report I have ever created, but it is darn close. You can save this report as "Chart Order Quantity by Sales Territory Region." The next section covers sprucing up the reports through different formatting options. This should allow you to create something you wouldn't be embarrassed to distribute to users.

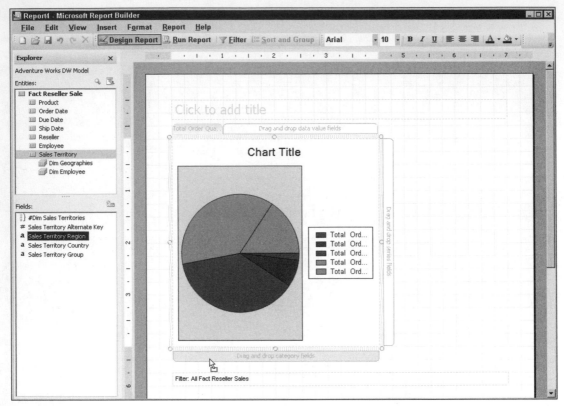

Figure 9-16

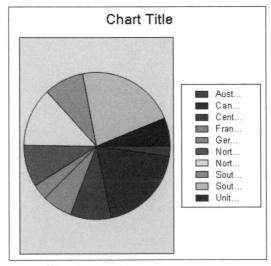

Figure 9-17

Formatting a Report

Now that you have seen the different types of report layouts, you will look at formatting your reports. You will start by looking at adding text elements to the reports, move on to editing field names and widths, and, finally, work with fonts, borders, and alignment.

Adjusting Text

Let's start by adding a title to the table report created in the previous section. To open the existing report, click the Open button in the Report Builder toolbar and open the Table Layout Product Sales report.

In the report designer, you should notice a text box at the top of the designer. This text box is available for adding titles to your report. To edit the title, simply click on the text box to get a cursor. Once you have the cursor, simply type the title for the report. In this example, you use the title "Product Sales." Figure 9-18 shows the table report with the new title.

Figure 9-18

Now that your report has a title, you want to go ahead and clean up the formatting for the rest of the table. Start by cleaning up the column headers. To modify the column headers, simply click on the header to display the cursor. Once you have the cursor, type in the new header text. Change your columns to the following:

❑ Category

❑ Subcategory

❑ Product Name

❑ Sales Amount

❑ Order Quantity

Figure 9-19 illustrates the new column headings.

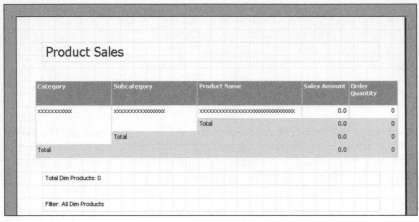

Figure 9-19

Column Width, Alignment, and Number Formatting

Now that your text is displayed correctly, you need to work on the layout of the fields. If you preview the report, you will notice that the Category and Subcategory column widths are larger than necessary to accommodate the text returned from the query. You'll want to reduce those columns to give a little better presentation. To decrease the column width, simply select the table by clicking on it and then hover your cursor between the columns. When you move your cursor between the columns, it will change to indicate that you can modify the width. Click between the columns and move the mouse right or left to increase or decrease the width of the columns.

Once you have adjusted the column widths, you might also notice that the alignment of the Sales Amount and Order Quantity column headers is incorrect. Number fields are right aligned, and it is good practice to do the same with their respective column headers. In our report, they are left aligned. To clean this up, highlight the Sales Amount and Order Quantity cell. To highlight both cells at once, click on Sales Amount, hold down the shift key, and click on Order Quantity. Once you have selected both cells, click the Right Justify button in the toolbar, as illustrated in Figure 9-20.

Now that you have your numbers formatted correctly and the alignment set, you'll take a look at working with the font and background color.

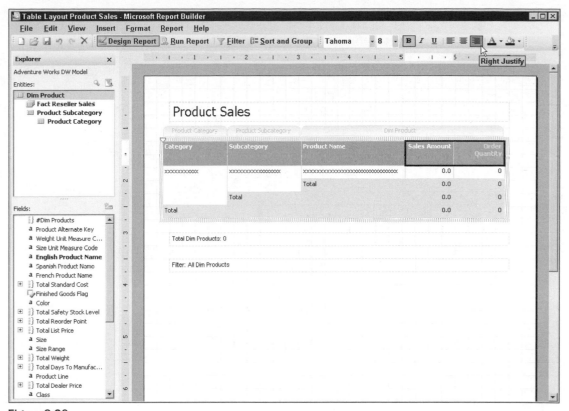

Figure 9-20

Font and Background Color

In your report, there are three levels to the Product hierarchy. To improve the report, you will modify the font for the top level elements as well as alter the background color for the individual products.

To set the font in our reports, you can simply use the Report Builder toolbar. In the sample report, click the Category field text box directly beneath the "Category" column header, and set the font to 12 pt, as shown in Figure 9-21.

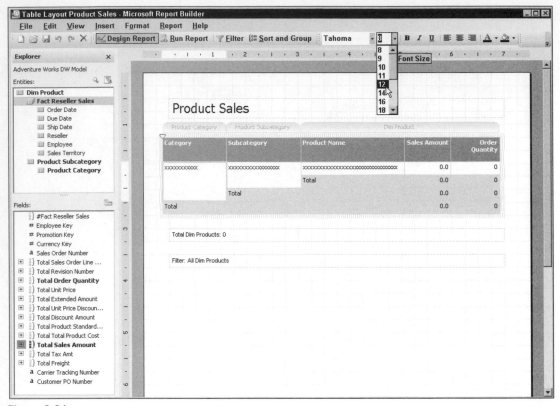

Figure 9-21

You can repeat the same process to set the Subcategory font to 10 pt. This should allow you to more easily distinguish the different levels.

The second formatting feature you'll explore is how to set the background color for a set of items. In this scenario, you want to format the Product Name items. You will set the background color to Light Turquoise. To set the background color, select the Product Name, Sales Amount, and Order Quantity detail lines by clicking on the text boxes directly under the column headers and holding down the Shift key. Once you have highlighted the desired cells, use the Fill Color button in the toolbar to select Light Turquoise. Figure 9-22 illustrates setting the background color.

There are a number of formatting features that you can add to your reports. Now that you have given your report a nice look, you need to clean up the data a little. One thing you might have noticed in your report is that a number of rows come back with no data. There is also no distinct sort order defined in the report. In the next section, you look at how to filter out those empty rows and how to update the sort order.

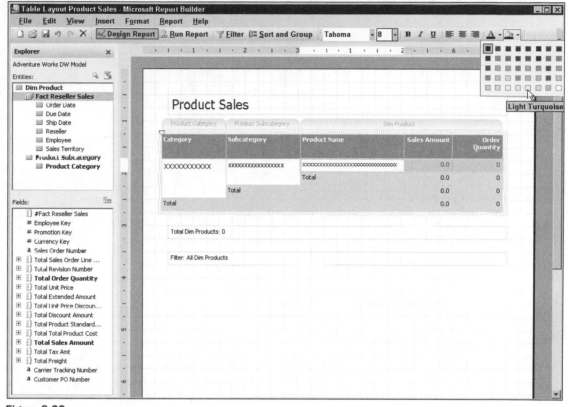

Figure 9-22

Filtering and Sorting Reports

Another key set of features for any reporting tool is the ability to filter and sort the data. In this section, you look at removing empty rows from your report, giving users the option to filter the report based on a given time period and sorting the report alphabetically based on Product Name.

Filtering

First thing to do is simply remove all of the empty data rows. In the Report Builder toolbar, you will see a button labeled "Filter." Clicking on this button will bring up the Filter Data dialog. Figure 9-23 shows this window.

There are three main windows within the Filter data window: Entities, Fields, and the filter list. The Entities and Fields windows should be familiar from previous sections in this chapter. They contain the data Elements and related Attributes in our Report Model. You should notice that your Entities window is already limited to items related to Dim Product, since this is the information contained within your report.

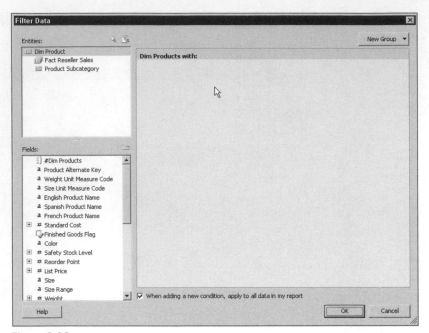

Figure 9-23

The majority of the filtering functionality will be handled in the filter list on the right side of the Filter Data dialog. The first item that should be pointed out is the title over the filter list. In this scenario, it displays the text "Dim Products with." If you click on the text, you will be presented with a drop-down list like that shown in Figure 9-24.

The drop-down in Figure 9-24 presents four options: All of, Any of, None of, and Not all of. "All of" represents a logical AND condition. All of the expressions in the filter list must be true to return a result set. "Any of" represents a logical OR condition. If any one of the conditions in the filter list is true, the data row is returned. "None of" represents a logical Exclusive AND condition. If all of the conditions are false, the data row is returned. The final item, "Not all of," represents a logical Exclusive OR condition. If any one of the conditions is true, but not all of them, then the data is returned. Let's put these into some real terms.

For this scenario, you will use the "All of" option. You will create conditions to test if Sales Amount is not empty and Order Quantity is not empty. If both of those statements are true, you want to return the data row. You will add this filter after examining the other filter types.

An "Any of" report might be something like "Show me all of the sales for people in the United States and Canada." You could add filters to specify Country equal to Canada or Country equal to United States. "Any of" these two values would be acceptable.

"None of" could be used in a reverse scenario from the previous example. You might want to see sales for people not in the United States or Canada. In that example, you would set filters for Country equals Canada or Country equals United States. If either of those conditions is true, you would want to remove them from the report.

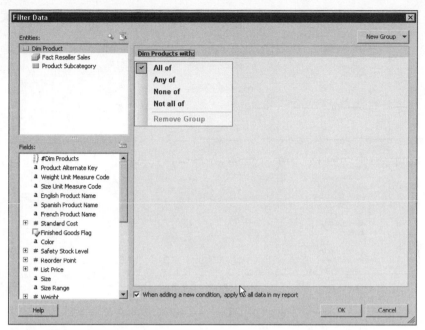

Figure 9-24

The last condition, "Not all of," is a little more difficult. Let's say that you want to find customers who purchase only one of a list of products that normally are purchased together. For example, you want to see people who purchase Bikes but not Helmets, or purchase Helmets but not Bikes. In this scenario, you would set filters for Product equals Bikes or Product equals Helmets and set the overall condition to "Not all of." Your result set would contain only those people who have purchased one of the products but not both.

Now that you have seen the different conditional statements, you will add the filter for removing empty data rows. There are two elements that you need to test: Sales Amount and Order Quantity. If they are both empty, then you will remove them from the report.

Start by selecting "Fact Reseller Sales" in the Entities window. The field list now contains the Reseller Sales attributes. Click and drag "Sales Amount" over to the filter list (large gray area on the right side of the dialog). You can click on the word "equals" and select "Not." In the text box to the right of "not equal to," set the value to 0. You can do the same with Order Quantity by dragging it from the Field list to the filter list.

You should notice that Order Quantity does not have a text box to enter criteria in. When the report model was generated, it found a small number of unique values for Order Quantity. Because there were a limited number of items, it decided to make it a lookup field. This is probably more appropriate for items like Product, but it does illustrate the point.

To filter out empty Order Quantities, select "equals" and change it to "Is Empty." Finally, click again on "Is Empty" and select "Not." The resulting filter should look like Figure 9-25.

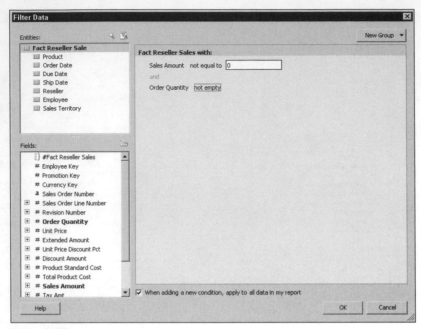

Figure 9-25

If you run the report, you should notice that the empty data rows have been removed.

Along with adding individual filters, you can also add groupings. Grouping helps nest logical conditions together. If you click on the New Group button in the Filter Data window, you will notice the same four filters outlined earlier in this section. Within the group, you can then add multiple conditions that are evaluated together.

The second filter you want to add is the ability for the user to select a date range. You will use Order Date in this example. Go back to the report design view and click the "Filter" button. To add the order date, select Order Date in the Entities window. You should see a list of attributes related to Order Date. Drag "Full Date Alternate Key" onto the filter list and change the condition from "equals" to "On or After." Since you want a range of dates, you will take "Full Date Alternate Key" again and drag it into the filter list, this time changing "equals" to "On or Before." The final step is to allow the user to select a value. Click on either one of the Date filters, and select "Prompt" from the drop-down. Repeat the same step on the other date. When you have it all set, your filter list should look like Figure 9-26. Note that you will need to fill in default dates in order for the query to run properly.

For this example, I simply entered in a large date range. If you click on the date drop-down list, you will see an item at the bottom of the calendar labeled "Relative Date." Hovering over "Relative Date" exposes a large list of possible time periods. Using the relative dates, you can modify the report to display Product Sales for the last 60 days. You can click the OK button and run the report to see the updated results.

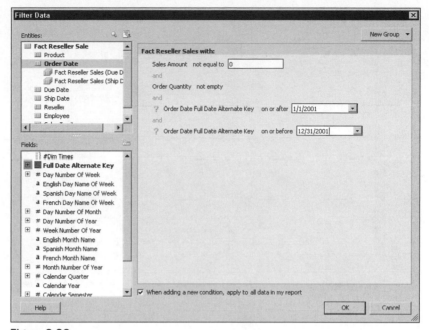

Figure 9-26

Sorting

The final item to look at in your report is the sort order. It is important in many cases that the user is presented with information that is easily navigable. Right now your report simply shows a list of products in alphabetical order. It might be more useful to show those products with the largest sales amount first.

To add a sort to your report, you first need to click the "Sort and Group" button in the Report Builder toolbar. When you open the Sort dialog, you should see a listing of all the groups available in a report. In this scenario, you have Product Category, Product Subcategory, and Product.

Within your report the item that you will be sorting is Product. To sort Products, select Product in the "Select Group" list. For the "Sort by" criteria, you will specify Sales Amount in descending order. Figure 9-27 shows the finished sorting.

You can add multiple sorts for a single item by adding additional values in the sort dialog. When you run the report, you should notice that within each Product Subcategory the Products are sorted by Sales Amount in descending order.

You have now seen all of the core features required to create a report. You've covered the different types of report layouts, adding fields to your reports, formatting numbers, fonts, and backgrounds, and, finally, setting filters and sorting the reports. In the next section, you will look at working with expressions inside reports.

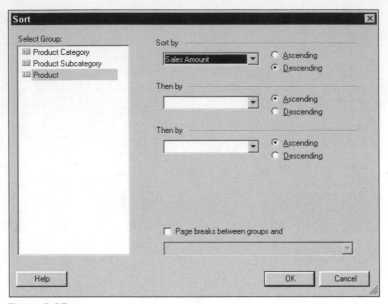

Figure 9-27

Adding Calculations with Expressions

A major advanced feature of Report Builder is the ability to add expressions to your reports. Expressions allow you to add custom fields, modify filters, and modify report results. In this section, you look at adding a new custom field to your report. In the process, you will learn about the main areas of the expression editor and how they are used.

For this section, you will continue to use the Table Layout Product Sales report. Make sure that the report is open in design view with the Explorer window and Fields list on the left-hand side. Above the field list is an icon to add new fields. You want to add a field to your report that calculates the Average Price based on Sales Amount divided by Order Quantity. Click on the new field button, shown in Figure 9-28, to bring up the formula editor, shown in Figure 9-29. Be sure that Reseller Sales is selected in the Explorer window.

Figure 9-28

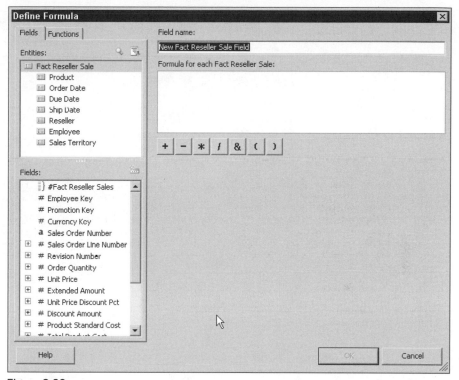

Figure 9-29

The Formula window has three main sections: Fields, Functions, and the expression editor. Fields is the same dialog you have seen throughout Report Builder. It is broken down into Entities and Fields. The Functions tab presents a list of all available functions within Report Builder. The functions are grouped by types. So, you will find AND, OR, and NOT under the logical folder. As well, you will find AVG, SUM, and COUNT under the aggregates folder. The expression editor contains a Field name text box to define the name of your calculation and the Formula text box for setting the calculation logic.

To define your expression for Average Price, take the Total Sales Amount (expand the Sales Amount field to see this) divided by the Total Order Quantity (under Order Quantity). It is important that you use the Total and not simply Sales Amount or Order Quantity. The Total allows you to define your average calculation at different levels without having to rework the formula. Figure 9-30 shows the completed Average Price calculation.

Once you have added the formula, you can add it to your report like any other field. Simply click on the field in the Field list, and drag it onto the report table. The final layout, including Average Price, should look similar to Figure 9-31.

Now that you have seen how to create reports with Report Builder as well as working with formatting, filters and expressions, you will take a look at a few administrative requirements.

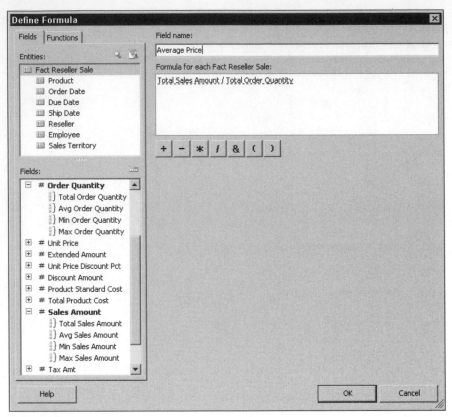

Figure 9-30

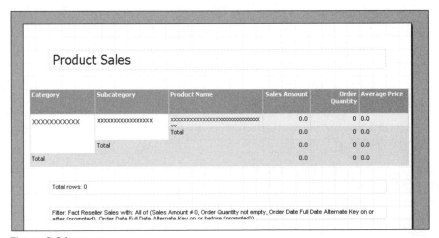

Figure 9-31

Administration

This section covers a few topics on administration and Report Builder. First, it looks at the client machine requirements, then it discusses permissions required to save reports, and finally it outlines strategies for organizing user reports.

The first thing pointed out in this chapter is that the Report Builder is not just a simple web application. Report Builder is a Windows client delivered over the Internet. To support this functionality, users will have to have the Microsoft .NET 2.0 Framework. Microsoft has no plans to ship Report Builder to support earlier versions of the .NET Framework.

When using the Report Builder, users save reports to the Report Server. In order to save rdl files (the structured file created by the Report Builder), a user must have publish permissions. Using Report Manager, you can grant permissions on different folders and set the user role to Publisher. Publisher is a default item-level role created when Reporting Services is installed. This role will have sufficient item-level permissions to add and remove reports. However, it also has permissions to create folders, remove models, and handle a few other tasks that you might not want your users to perform.

If you are concerned about giving users too high a level of permissions, there are two approaches you can use either independently or together. The first approach is to create your own item-level role. Within the role, you can limit the users' actions to simply managing reports. This will eliminate their ability to move or delete folders, data sources, and other items. If you still want more granular control, you can take advantage of the My Reports feature. This feature can be enabled from either Management Studio or Report Manager. By enabling My Reports, you give the users their own personal folder. They can publish content, add folders, and generally have control over their own small area in the Report Server. This feature has been available since Reporting Services 2000; however, there was never a real need for it. With the Report Builder, I believe it will become a much more popular option.

For more information on setting permissions, take a look at the administration chapters later in this book.

Summary

In this chapter, you looked at creating ad hoc reports. Ad hoc reports require two major components. First, you need a semantic model that puts your data into a user-friendly form. You saw that Reporting Services 2005 has a Report Model project that will help you create a user-friendly model. Second, users will need an easy-to-use tool with familiar interfaces. You saw that the Report Builder provides both a rich user experience and a familiar Microsoft Office–like look and feel.

After reading this chapter, you should have an understanding of :

❑   How to create new reports with Report Builder.

❑   How the different layouts can be used to create interesting reports.

❑   How to format report items.

Chapter 9

❑   How to add filtering and sorting capabilities to your reports.

❑   How to add calculations to your reports.

Ad hoc reports have been a feature sadly lacking from Reporting Services. It is our most common reason for implementing competing products. With the introduction of the Report Builder, Microsoft shows that it is committed to building an enterprise-level reporting tool.

Part IV

Administering Reporting Services

Chapter 10: Report Management

Chapter 11: Report Server Administration

10

Report Management

Once a report has been created, it must be published to the Report Server so that it can be viewed by report users. Publishing reports to the server doesn't have to be done from Visual Studio, although that will typically be the developer's choice. Report Server managers have other tools available to perform that task. Once a collection of reports and other content is out on the server, it will need to be managed. Basic tasks like creating content folders and publishing reports and other resources to those folders will need to be performed by users. Administrators and content managers need ways to control user access, automate report generation, and create historical archives. In this chapter, you read about:

- ❑   The four types of Report Server content and how to work with them.
- ❑   The stages of report execution and how to optimize them.
- ❑   How to automate report delivery and server management.

As you'll see, you can also create your own custom interfaces for your users. In this chapter, you'll also read about how to secure your reports and other content. First, though, you look at where everything goes and how to get to it.

Report Server Content

Content is stored in the Report Server using a hierarchal metaphor. The content itself is managed in a SQL Server database.

Folders represent the structure and relationship of content in the Report Server database. Folders are containers for items and other folders. Items are stored as content in the Report Server database. Reports and data sources are examples of different items that are stored there. Report content can reference data source content, for example, to perform work as part of a process. Images, documents, and other resources are also accessed this way. The folder structure you build is typically based on how your user groups are defined.

The root of the folder hierarchy is the Home folder. Each item in the database automatically inherits the user permissions of the parent folder it's contained in.

There are four types of content items stored in the database:

❑ Report

❑ Folder

❑ Data Source

❑ Resource

You'll read details about all these items throughout the rest of this chapter.

Managing Content Items

Generally, content in the Report Server database isn't worked directly. In other words, you typically don't work with content by manipulating records in the Report Server database tables using Transact-SQL or SQL Server Enterprise Manager. The functionality to work with the database content is abstracted and provided through other interfaces. Graphical user, command-line, and programmatic interfaces are all available. Depending on the requirements, several approaches can be taken to performing management tasks.

Two primary tools are provided for performing content management tasks. The Report Manager web application is both a management tool and report viewer. Integration with SQL Server Management Studio also provides a Windows forms environment for managing the Report Server, and custom applications can expose their own interfaces to those same functions. These tools enable you to configure common management properties such as report execution, subscriptions, and security. Let's explore each.

Report Manager

Report Manager is a web-based management application included with Reporting Services. It's built using ASP.NET and interfaces with the Report Server using the Web Service API.

The Report Manager application resides on a web server and is accessed using a web browser. It provides a management interface for the contents in the Report Server database. The Report Manager web application works against another ASP.NET web application, which is the Report Server Web Service interface. Figure 10-1 shows the stack between the Report Server and the client browser when using the Report Manager application.

You could even build your own version of the Report Manager by creating an application that works against the same Reporting Services Web Service API. You can use the Report Manager to:

❑ Create folders and folder structures to act as containers for report collections.

❑ Create and modify data sources, and add additional resources to the Report Server database.

❑ Implement an identity-based security model, controlling access to Reporting Services resources.

❑ Configure automated report generation and delivery.

Client Browser

Report Manager ASP.NET
Web Application

Reporting Services Web
Service API

Report Server
Database

Figure 10-1

Access to all reports and resources can be flexibly managed. For example, a user can be provided access to reports that run on demand based on values supplied by that user, or they may be restricted to viewing static reports delivered by subscription. The task of managing content can also be broken up among multiple roles, each responsible for managing the functions of different reports or other resources. Using the Report Manager, you can perform create, read, update, and delete operations on the most frequently accessed content in the Report Server database.

There's a link to the Report Manager on your Start⇨Programs menu, or you can point your browser to the Report Server URL. The default address for that is

```
http://<ServerName>/reports
```

Be sure to replace <ServerName> with the server hosting the Report Manager application. If that's your local machine, then localhost works. In a production installation, the name of the virtual directory containing the Report Manager may be different from the default /reports. If that's the case in your environment, you'll also need to specify that virtual directory rather than /reports. Figure 10-2 shows a screen shot of the URL and the Report Manager's home page.

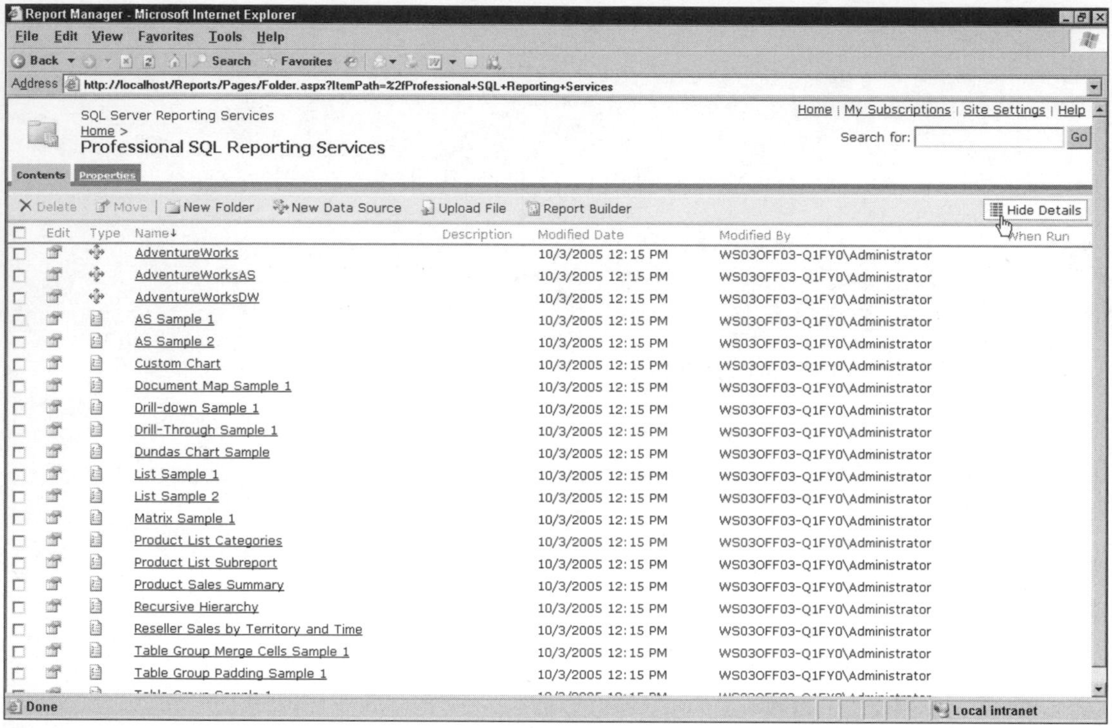

Figure 10-2

This particular screen shot shows the Report Manager in Details view, similar to the Details view in Windows Explorer. This view provides quick access to the properties of items contained in a folder. You can switch to Details view by clicking the Details button on the right side of the Report Manager toolbar. Also, you may have noticed that the URL in the screen shot uses FormalCasing. URLs are not case sensitive, so don't feel like you have to capitalize the address when typing. For example, appending the server name with /reports provides the same results as using /Reports. When Reporting Services performs the browser redirect, it replaces your typed URL with its own. The Report Manager application is covered in more detail throughout this chapter.

SQL Server Management Studio

SQL Server Management Studio is a new management interface that's included with SQL Server 2005. Its interface contains modules for different types of SQL Server components, providing a single point of management for them. Reporting Services is one that's been integrated into the Management Studio. It provides access to a superset of Report Manager functions. You can perform the most common management tasks using this application just as you would in Report Manager. The Management Studio (shown in Figure 10-3) will be a familiar interface for database managers, who are as likely to be involved in managing Report Server content as anyone else.

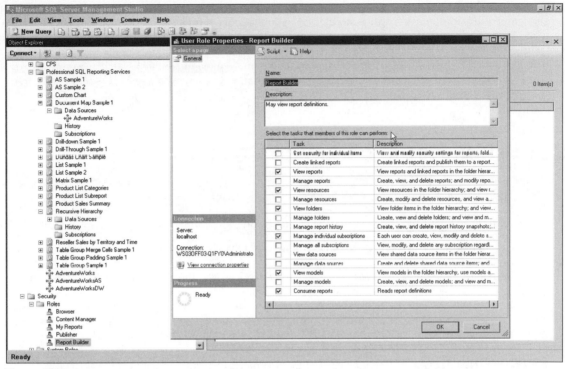

Figure 10-3

This particular image shows the dialog box for editing the properties of the Report Builder role. You can see the specific tasks that are enabled for this particular role. Right-click context menus are available throughout the Management Studio interface and make accessing common tasks quick and straightforward.

Other Utilities

A number of other useful utilities are also provided with Reporting Services. Most of these are accessed at the command prompt or programmatically. These include:

- ❑ Script Host utility
- ❑ Server Configuration utilities
- ❑ Encryption Key Management

Working with the key utilities is covered later in this chapter.

Programmatic Interfaces

Web services are encapsulations of programming logic that can be called using standard Internet protocols. Because Reporting Services is a Web service, its functionality can be invoked by any client that can send it a properly formatted request and work with the returned response. Developers can easily build applications that incorporate Reporting Services functionality. There are many custom interfaces being used in production today. Products developed by independent software vendors (ISVs) work against the same Web Service interface.

You can also use that same capability to automate common management tasks such as migrating reports from testing to production environments. The "Automating Content Management" section later in this chapter provides an example.

Securing Report Server Content

A core function of Report Server management is ensuring that only authorized users have access to sensitive information. In Reporting Services, security is based on two essential elements:

❑ Identifying who or what is attempting to perform an action, then

❑ Determining whether that user has permission to perform that action on the resource

For example, to view the Report Manager you must first log in to the system where Report Manager is running, and then you must have the correct permissions to view the Report Manager application. By default, anyone belonging to the Everyone group can view Report Manager, so the application is available to a wide group of users. Regardless of this, you still have to log in and be authenticated as belonging to that group.

Reporting Services uses a role-based security model, which can be implemented and managed through the Report Manager interface, SQL Server Management Studio, and the provided programmatic interfaces.

In Report Manager, security is addressed at two levels:

❑ **System-level:** This type of security addresses the tasks required to administrate the Report Server globally.

❑ **Item-level:** This type of security addresses the tasks that can be performed on an individual item in the Report Server database.

If you've worked with configuring users and groups in SQL Server, you're already familiar with adding users and groups to role definitions. Let's take a closer look at how to use it in Report Manager.

Role-Based Security

Reporting Services does not authenticate users. It relies on the outside network for that function. Although it natively integrates with Windows authentication, you can extend the application to incorporate your own custom or other third-party security appliances. The Report Server takes the authenticated users and categorizes them into groups and then grants permissions to the users based on those groups, or roles.

Reporting Services installs with a default set of permissions in place. These permissions provide the initial settings, so you can go in and start defining the implementation of your own security policy. Called Default security, it's configured so that users who belong to the local Administrator group are given System Administrator role permissions, and Windows users belonging to the Everyone group are added to the Browser role. You'll need to edit the default security settings to support other Windows users and groups, depending on the permissions needed for users to accomplish their tasks.

Tasks

Tasks are the specific actions that can be performed by a user. The permission to perform a task is either granted or revoked. Roles are defined by the combination of tasks granted to users who belong to it. In Reporting Services, tasks fall into two general categories: system tasks and item tasks.

System-level tasks are actions on the Reporting Services system as a whole, whereas item-level tasks are actions on items such as folders and reports that are contained in the Report Server database. The two groups essentially form separate security zones, each containing different task items. For example, Manage Report Server Security is a system task, while View Reports is an item task. These two groups of tasks define the item roles and system roles.

In Reporting Services, tasks are predefined. They cannot be changed, nor can you add custom tasks. Different combinations of tasks are called roles.

Roles

Users are granted permission based on their role. A number of roles are predefined in Reporting Services. You can add a user or Windows group to a role in Report Manager. For example, you can add a user to the Content Manager role, which grants them sufficient permission to manage the content in the Report Server database. A role definition is the unique set of task permissions it holds.

Like tasks, there are system-level and item-level roles. Different forms are used to configure each type, which are each accessed from the Site Settings page. There are two system-level roles:

❑ **System Administrator:** This role has task permissions to enable them to manage Report Manager site security and Report Server jobs.

❑ **Site User:** This role can view basic information on the site, including report properties and shared schedules.

Local Administrators on a machine belong to the System Administrator role and so always have access to the system. If you want to secure reports and other content from specific users with high-level permission sets like this, then you'll have to set security at the item level.

There are four predefined item-level roles:

❑ **Browser:** This role can navigate to reports and run them. Specific permissions include:

    ❑ View Folders

    ❑ View Reports

    ❑ Manage individual subscriptions

❑ **My Reports:** This role allows users to create, view, and manage reports in their My Reports folder. Examples of tasks this user can perform include:

    ❑ Create linked reports

    ❑ Manage folders

    ❑ Manage report history

❑ **Publisher:** Users can publish content to the Report Server database. This role includes these tasks:

    ❑ Manage folders

    ❑ Manage reports

    ❑ Manage data sources

❑ **Content Manager:** This role has permission to all item-level tasks, including:

    ❑ Set security for individual items

    ❑ Manage individual subscriptions

    ❑ Manage all subscriptions

If the predefined roles provide the particular combination of tasks you need for a user, you can create your own roles. Report Manager is used to create a new role definition. A good way to do that is by copying an existing role definition. Go to a current role definition and click the Copy button, and then modify your new role.

New roles can be added in Report Manager or SQL Server Management Studio. Figure 10-4 shows the creation of a new role in the Management Studio.

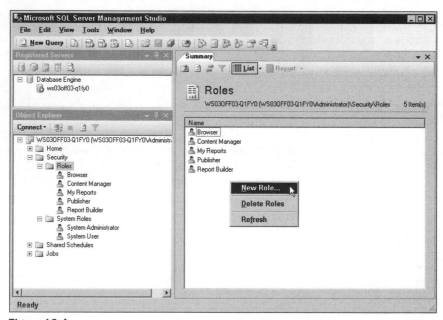

Figure 10-4

Generally, you shouldn't need to create many new roles. Having too many roles can quickly become a management headache, especially if you start modifying role definitions that are already in use. When you've got a lot of content stored on the server, it can become difficult to tell what effects your changes will have.

To create a new role definition, you'll need to have permission to manage system security policy. An example of the steps required to create a new role definition follows:

1. In Report Manager, click the Site Settings link. It's a global link in the upper-right corner of the page.

2. Click the Configure item-level role definitions link. Note that you also have the ability to configure system-level roles.

3. Click the New Role button on the options toolbar. You'll be brought to the New Role form.

4. Give your new role the name Demo User. It's a good practice to use a name that matches the job function or title for the group you're creating. The name can include spaces and special characters, though it can't be more than 256 characters long.

5. Type Role to demonstrate item-level security for the description. The description should make it easy for administrators who create role assignments to understand what purpose the role is intended for. Ideally, the description should describe the role responsibilities. Providing a complete description keeps an administrator from having to open a role definition just to figure out what task permissions it has.

6. Check the View folders, View reports, and View resources check boxes. Figure 10-5 shows the completed New Role form.

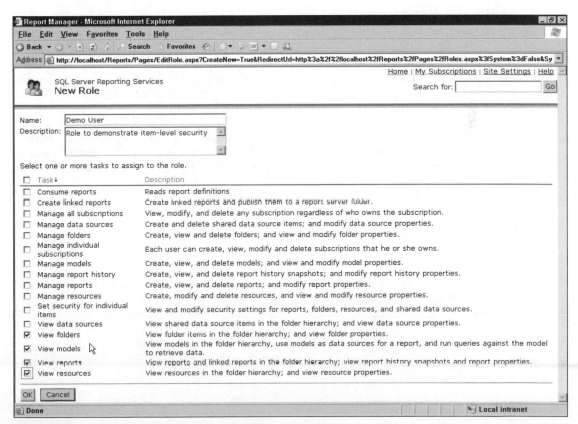

Figure 10-5

7. Click OK to save the new role into the Report Server database. You'll see the new role and its description listed on the Item-Level Roles page.

The Demo User role is now ready for user or group accounts to be added. You can go back in and modify the task permissions, if needed, but have your changes ironed out before adding users. Remember that many management headaches have started with modifying a role after users have already begun using it. If desired, you can also delete the role by clicking the Delete button on the Edit Role form. The Copy button will open a new Edit Role form with the same task permissions already selected. This way, you can easily extend an existing role to create a new one.

Creating a new role definition is straightforward, but it's important to be careful and not go overboard. Note how changing task permissions affects users. When you remove tasks or delete a role entirely, the change applies to every item in every folder in the Report Server database. A role can be associated with a single item as well as an upper-level folder and all its children. There isn't any way to easily view how the web of user roles and permissions affect their access to different reports and folders, so use care when modifying existing role definitions. Whenever possible, start with an existing definition, and extend permissions only as required.

You then add users to the role to create what's called a *role assignment*, described in the next section.

Role Assignments

Ultimately, access to the Report Server content is controlled by role assignments. Role assignments are created when you add a Windows domain account to a role definition. Remember that Report Server doesn't perform its own authentication; it relies on Windows to perform that function. Report Manager is used to map Windows users and groups to Reporting Services role definitions. As you've seen, each role is a unique collection of permissions. When a user attempts to perform an action, Report Server checks the roles that the user belongs to, to determine whether or not to allow the action.

Reporting Services creates its own role assignments when it implements the default security policy upon installation. Default security allows members of the local Administrators group to perform administrative actions on the Report Server database, while restricting users in the Everyone group to viewing items only.

You add users and groups to roles at the item level. The user or group that you want to grant permissions to must be a Windows User or belong to a Windows Group. Remember that Reporting Services doesn't perform its own authentication of users — it relies on the Windows operating system for that function.

Creating role assignments is how you bring life to your role definitions. Role assignments are created in place, meaning that you must be looking at the properties for a specific item before you can make a role assignment for it. The following steps show how to create a new role assignment:

1. Open Report Manager and navigate to a folder containing sample reports.
2. Be sure you're viewing the Contents tab of the folder. On the Options toolbar, click the Show Details button.

3. Click the Properties icon for your report. The icon is in the Edit column on the left side of the page. Click it to go to the Properties pages of the report.

4. In the left navigation area, click the Security link to view the security properties page for the report.

5. On the Options toolbar, click the Edit Item Security button. You'll see a message box displaying a security message, as seen in Figure 10-6.

6. Click OK on the message box. The page view will change, adding new buttons on the options toolbar, as shown in Figure 10-7.

7. Click the New Role Assignment button to view the New Role Assignment form.

8. In the Group or user name field, type the user name you log in with.

9. Locate the Demo User role, and click the check box next to it. This will add you as a user to the Demo User role, and you now have the permissions of that role on that report item. This role permission set is in addition to the one you are currently using as you perform this exercise. Note that you can click a role to view its task permissions. Figure 10-8 shows a completed form.

10. Click OK to apply the new assignment.

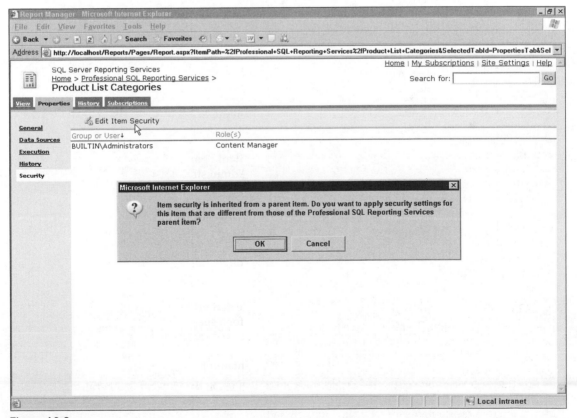

Figure 10-6

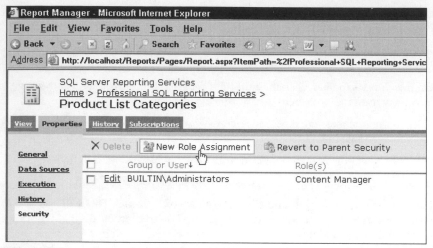

Figure 10-7

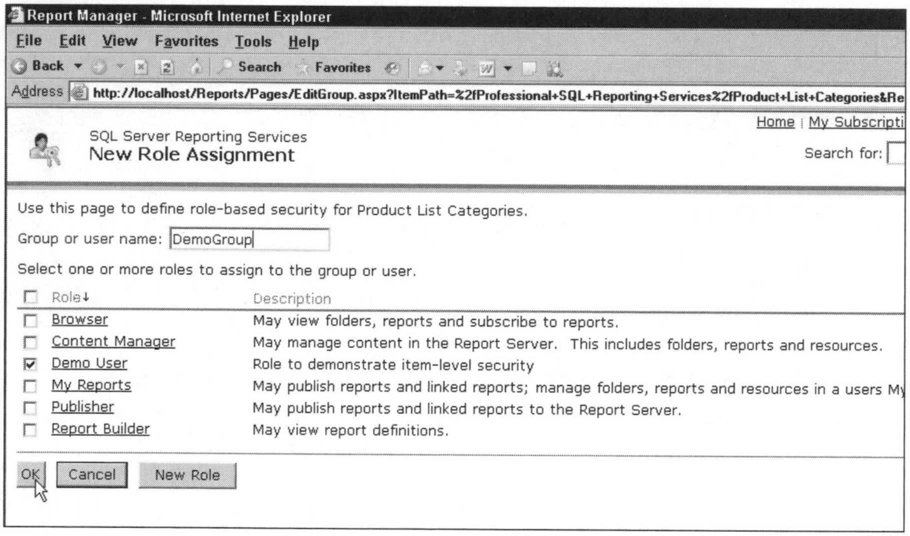

Figure 10-8

Note that you can easily revert back to the security settings of the parent folder by clicking the Revert to Parent Security button. That will cause the security settings for the report to be set back to *mirror* those of the parent folder. Subfolders inherit the security characteristics of their parent, so the security settings of the Home folder effectively establish the default settings for the rest of the tree unless overridden by a child in the structure. For example, the My Reports folder has different permission settings than the Home folder. It's a good practice to grant limited permissions on the Home folder because of the inheritance of security settings down the folder hierarchy. It's also a good idea to bear in mind that when modifying the role assignments for a folder, your new settings can affect items much further down in the folder hierarchy.

You can add multiple users and groups to a role assignment, though you can add a specific named group or user to a role only once. A user can belong to multiple groups or roles. The permissions then combine for that user. For example, let's say that Mary belongs to the domain Department Managers and that both Mary's and Department Managers' rights have been assigned to a folder, then she'll have the combined permissions of both Mary and Department Managers for that folder (and its contents).

Role definitions are applied across the system. Modifying them can have unforeseen consequences unless careful consideration is given to the effects of that change. If a user needs certain permissions on an item in the Report Server database, it may be better to address the issue at the item level rather than the role level. Modifying the role definition affects all assignments to that role and in every location that the role has access.

Creating roles and role assignments aren't an everyday task, but it's important to know what happens when you do make or modify one. Let's look at a couple of other important security topics.

Security Inheritance

When security is set on a folder, those settings also apply to all the items in that folder—including sub-folders. By default, Report Manager opens to the Home folder—which represents the root of the folder hierarchy. The security settings on that folder set the baseline for every other folder, report, data source, and other resource in the Report Server database.

Item-Level Security

Role assignments apply to what are called securable objects. These are items that can have role assignments applied to them, specifically reports, data sources, and other resources.

- ❑ **Reports:** Permission to view the report and perform other actions, such as changing report properties. Stored versions of a report, including history and snapshots, have the same permission sets as their parent reports and cannot be changed.

- ❑ **Data Sources:** Permission to modify property settings.

- ❑ **Other Resources:** Only individual resources like shared images can be secured. Items embedded within a report have the same permission sets as their parent reports and cannot be changed.

Folders are container items that can also have permission applied. The permissions apply to the folder and all the items within it, unless overridden by an individual item.

System-Level Security

In Report Manager, a distinction is made between two groups of actions that can be performed: actions performed on the system and actions performed on items. They are referred to as system-level and item-level actions, or tasks. System-level tasks are actions that apply to the Reporting Services system as a whole, whereas item-level tasks are actions that can be performed on items such as folders and reports that are contained in the Report Server database. The two groups essentially form separate security zones, each containing different permission sets. Typically, system tasks are performed by administrators, and item tasks are performed by users.

The next section covers sitewide security settings in more detail.

Site Settings

The Site Settings form is accessed by clicking the Site Settings link in the top-right corner of the Report Manager interface. Site Settings is where you can configure default settings for the site and enable different features of the Report Manager. Usually, you won't have access to this form unless you're a member of the System Administrator role.

Here, you can change the name that's displayed in the top-left corner of every page in the Report Manager. My Reports can be enabled here, as you'll read about shortly. First, let's briefly cover the other site property settings on this form.

Properties

Sitewide settings are accessed using the site settings link at the top right of the Report Manager window. Figure 10-9 shows the Site Settings page:

Report History

This property defines the number of previously run reports to keep archived. Although this sets the default report history value for all reports, this value can be overridden by individual reports. You'll read more about configuring report histories in the "Snapshots and History" section later in this chapter.

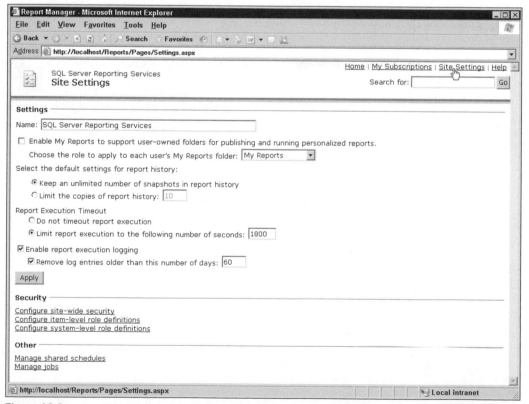

Figure 10-9

Execution Timeout

Execution timeout is the length of time the Report Server will continue attempting to execute a report. When the timeout value elapses, execution will stop and rendering or delivery of the report will not occur. This value can be overridden in individual reports.

Report Logging

By default, Report Server logs information about report execution. The Report Log contains values such as delivery format, the parameters used, and server processing time. The Report Log is not viewable in the Report Manager; a SQL Server DTS package is used to obtain values from the log. For more information on viewing report logs, see Chapter 11.

My Reports

My Reports is a folder that allows users to manage their own content. It provides a central location for the management of user-specific content and subscriptions rather than having to navigate through the public folders for regularly generated and referenced reports. My Reports is disabled by default.

Enabling My Reports lets users create and delete their own folders and reports and create personal reports. A personal report is one that's meant for an individual user and not intended for widespread use. The report may not conform to corporate guidelines for published reports, for example. My Reports provides flexibility by allowing users to create and use reports without worrying about the potential impact on other users. Figure 10-10 shows the broad scope of permissions a user has (by default) on content in their My Reports folder.

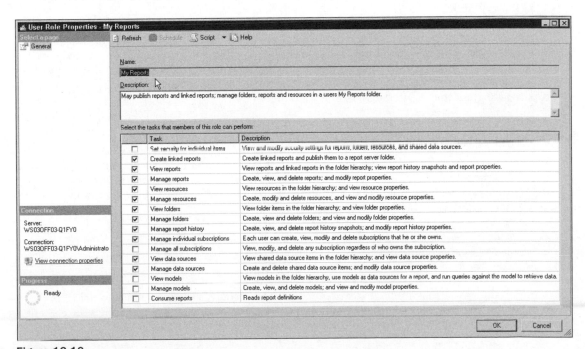

Figure 10-10

This view is from SQL Server Management Studio. To view it yourself in the Management Studio, first ensure that SQL Server Management Studio is connected to your Report Server instance. Once you're viewing the Reporting Services component, right-click the My Reports role in the Object Explorer window and select Properties. This option may not be available if My Reports has not been enabled on your server, or if your permission set does not allow access to that folder.

One My Reports folder is created for each user. Users don't have access to the My Reports folders of other users; only Report Server administrators can do that. Using My Reports, you can upload reports and other resources as well as publish reports you've created using the report designer or other tool. Anonymous users do not have access to a My Reports folder.

To access My Reports, the user simply clicks the My Reports folder or link in Report Manager. Alternately, they can navigate their browser to `http(s)://<server_name>/My Reports`. The users identity is checked, and the browser is then redirected to `/users/<username>/My Reports`.

`/My Reports` is redirected to `http://localhost/Reports/Pages/Folder.aspx?ItemPath=%2fMy+Reports&ViewMode=List`.

It's important to keep in mind that there's a My Reports folder and a My Reports role. The My Reports role defines permissions the user has in their My Reports folder. System administrators can change the permission set for all roles including My Reports. Because of that, your capabilities may be different from those just described. It's a good practice to reserve a specific role for accessing My Reports to help ensure a consistent user experience when using it. It's easy to create a shortcut to your My Reports folder, creating a portal to the reports you frequently need to work with. Functionally, the My Reports folder provides a secure area for users who need to manage and view reports as part of their regular work responsibilities.

If you're not careful, creating folders and modifying their security settings can degrade into an ad hoc combination of configuration settings for different folders and users. That type of unplanned structure can be difficult to manage and maintain. Making the My Reports folder available to users allows them to manage settings in the context of their own My Reports folder rather than modifying individual folder properties to grant the required permissions for different users.

Securing My Reports

Let's say that access rights have been granted to a user for My Reports. The user creates folders to organize their content and places their commonly accessed reports within them. If rights to the My Reports folder is then revoked, you might think that the user no longer has access to the folders and their content. In fact, that may or may not be the case.

Consider the possible ways to prevent users from accessing their My Reports folder. First, you can clear the Enable My Reports check box under Site Settings. That removes the My Reports folder from the Home folder contents.

It's important to note that although clearing the check box removes the My Reports folder from the display, it doesn't actually prevent access to the My Reports folder content. If a user knows the content structure and the path to a folder, he or she can still navigate to the location directly.

Another way to prevent access to the contents of My Reports is to modify the role definition used for accessing My Reports. Clearing all the task permissions will effectively lock it down and prevent a user from accessing its contents. Unfortunately, it also denies access to anyone else in that role (who doesn't already have permissions granted through other role memberships).

Finally, My Reports can be secured by removing the user's Windows account from My Reports role membership. This is the most effective way of locking out individual users, without creating potentially far-reaching side effects.

Managing Reports

Once you've laid the foundation for the Report Server content by configuring the system settings, you're ready to begin working with items that are stored on the server. Folders represent the hierarchical structure of the database content, and items are contained within them. In this section, you'll read about setting the properties for items in the database and how to publish content. First, though, let's take a closer look at working with the folders themselves.

Working in Folders

When you deploy reports from Visual Studio using the report designer, you can publish content to any folder in the hierarchy. You can also specify that a new folder be created for your content, which will be created when your content is deployed. You control the report destination by setting the target folder property in the project properties dialog box. Project properties can be accessed by right-clicking on the project in the Solution Explorer window and selecting Properties.

Once the report is deployed, you can use Report Manager to create additional folders and move the content from folder to folder. Create new folders in Report Manager by navigating to the location where you would like the new folder. Once there, click the New Folder button on the toolbar. The Report Manager then displays a page where you can name the folder and add a description.

Security Inheritance

When you create a new folder, it automatically has the same security settings as its parent folder. By changing folder permissions, you can override the parent folder settings and define your own values. The changed values will, in turn, be applied to the contents of that folder. This application of parent settings continues to the deepest level of the folder structure. The use of configuration settings that are inherited by child nodes is used extensively in .NET.

Moving Content between Folders

There are times when it's necessary to move content after it's been deployed. This is particularly true early in the life of a Report Server deployment. You can minimize this by planning an effective directory structure for your organization *before* deploying reports.

To move a report, go to the property pages for the report. Clicking the Move button on the toolbar will take you to a page where you can specify the target location for the report item.

Report Properties

Each report has basic properties for values such as which data source to use during processing. These properties can be set by developers at design time or by users when the content is in production. Report Manager provides an easy-to-use interface for working with report property settings. This section provides an overview of the report property pages.

The easiest way to access the properties of a report in Report Manager is to view the contents of a folder in Details view. Begin by accessing the folder where your report is located. There's a Show Details button on the right end of the Report Manager toolbar. This button reads Show Details or Hide Details, depending on the current view state (see Figure 10-2 earlier in the chapter). In Details view, you can access report properties without causing the report to begin processing. Click the properties icon for your report, and you'll be taken directly to the property pages for that item.

Execution

Depending on the scenario, you can control how often reports are executed. For example, you might base execution on how often the source data changes or how long a report takes to run. If a report takes longer than users are willing to wait, you can save the report and the data for delivery to the users later. You'll be able to take a "snapshot" of the data at a point in time, and improve the performance of your server as a result. Figure 10-11 shows a sample Execution property page for a report.

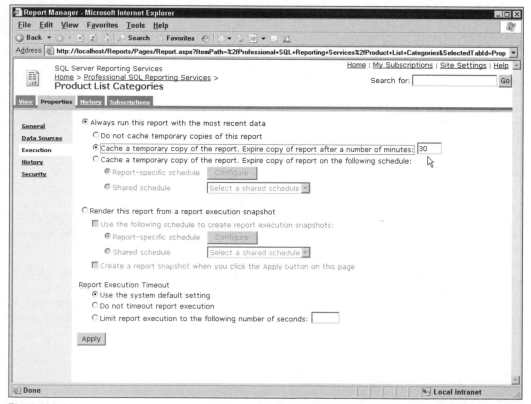

Figure 10-11

For Figure 10-11, I selected the option to have copies of the report added to the cache in ReportServerTempDB. This means that a copy of the report will be kept in cache for the number of minutes specified. Thirty minutes is the default. Once the report has run, the cached copy will be rendered for users instead of going through the entire report generation process. This can save resources on the server and processing time for your users. This is covered in more detail in the "Managing Report Execution" section later in this chapter.

Parameters

If your report takes input parameters, this property page will also be available to users who have "Update Parameters" permission on the report. In Report Manager, this page is used to indicate if a user should be prompted for a value, whether the parameter has a default value, and what text is used to prompt the user. Figure 10-12 shows a sample Parameters page.

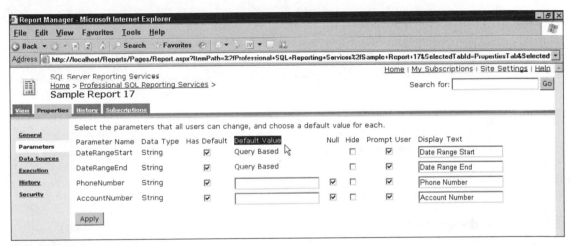

Figure 10-12

The following table provides descriptions of the parameter properties.

Property	Description
Has Default	When the check box is selected, the parameter has a default value — even if the user doesn't enter one.
Default Value	What's displayed here will vary depending on the parameter. For example, in Figure 10-12 the four parameters are string data types. Two provide text boxes for default values; if the Has Default check box is cleared, these controls will be disabled. Two of the parameters display "Query Based." This means the default value used for the report comes from a T-SQL query, which is also used to populate the control with possible options for the user when the report runs.
Null	Used to indicate whether a null value is allowed for this parameter. This will be disabled if Has Default is cleared.

Table continued on following page

419

Property	Description
Prompt User	You can hide parameters from users by selecting this check box. This is a great way to provide data-specific reports for different users.
Display Text	Allows you to change the prompt for improved readability and user comprehension when running the report.

Subscriptions

Using the subscription properties of a report, you can configure how users view a report. Subscriptions can be set up for an individual user or broadcast to many users. For example, Report Server administrators can create subscriptions that automate report execution and deliver rendered reports to user e-mail inboxes or posted to file shares on the company network. The types of subscriptions and working with them are covered later in this chapter.

Data Sources

Data sources are used to specify the sources of data to be used in the report. For example, you can indicate that the queries in a report connect to a SQL Server or Oracle database. Data sources are wrappers for connection strings. A *connection string* tells the server what server the source database is on, and what database on that server to reference.

Credentials are an important data source property. Depending on your execution requirements, you can specify whether or not the login credentials should be stored in the Report Server database. Finally, reports can use a shared data source or a data source that is specific to an individual report. Figure 10-13 shows the Data Sources property page for a report.

Data sources are covered in more detail in "Working with Data Sources" later in this chapter.

Security

As you learned earlier in this chapter, you enable end user access to specific reports or folders using the security properties for a folder or content item. When working with reports, you can also control which data an end user can view within that report. For more information on working with security settings in Report Manager, refer to "Securing Report Server Content" earlier in this chapter.

Linked Reports

Linked reports are extensions of standard, published reports. They're a reliable, flexible way to customize report output for different users. For example, you can use linked reports to create regional sales reports based on the national report. Simply create a linked report for each region, and then specify unique parameter values for each linked report.

A linked report is a configuration profile for a report that can store a separate set of configuration settings. Because they're based on already published reports, you can leverage that report design to create different views of the same source data. They use the parent report data source and rdl file, but you can modify the execution, parameter, subscription, and security properties without affecting the parent report. Creating a linked report is done from the General property page of the report you want to use as the base report. Provide a new name for your report, and modify the report parameters as needed for the target users.

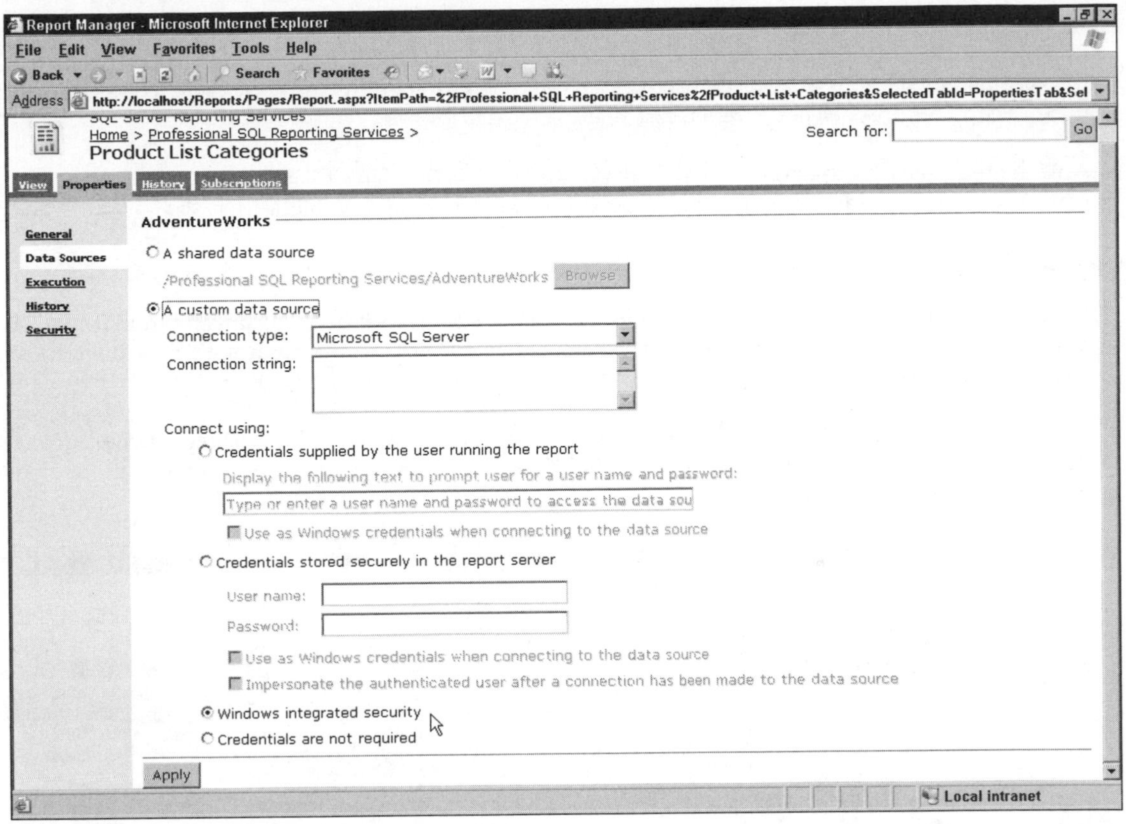

Figure 10-13

Publishing Reports

Report publishing is done by different users, and different tools are available to suit the needs of each. For example, graphical user interfaces (GUIs) are provided for administrators, and programmatic API's are provided for developers. This section covers the most common tools and techniques for report publishing.

Publishing with Report Manager

Publishing with Report Manager, because it's an ASPX web application, allows users the flexibility of publishing content using their browser. You can also manage existing content using this interface.

To upload a completed report to Report Manager, simply navigate to the location where you want the report deployed. Once there, click the Upload File button on the toolbar.

Publishing from Visual Studio

You can publish content to the Report Server database from the development environment. Use the standard Visual Studio deployment options, easily accessed by right-clicking an item in the Solution Explorer window. First, I'll cover deployment from Windows Explorer.

Manual Deployment

In this scenario, you simply copy the rdl and other resource files from one location to another using the file system and Windows Explorer. Select the solution items to deploy, and copy them to the target location. To copy reports, select the report rdl file.

Add the resource files to a third-party source control application. This is also typically done using some sort of tool that provides a combination of security and versioning capabilities.

Solution Explorer Deployment

Visual Source Safe integration with Visual Studio allows source control access directly from the development environment. To work on a file, first check the item out from source control. Edit the item, and then check it back in for inclusion in the next build.

A couple of project properties are important when using the Solution Explorer to deploy your project items. You can access these properties by right-clicking the project name in the Solution Explorer window. Figure 10-14 shows an example.

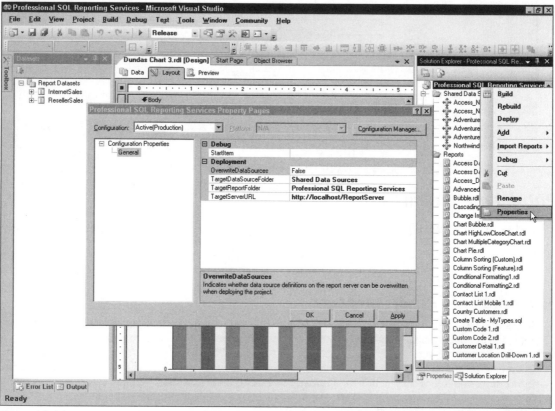

Figure 10-14

The Deployment properties available here include:

❑ **Target Report and Data Sources Folders:** Here, you can indicate the destination folders for your reports and data sources. Leaving the `TargetDataSourceFolder` property blank will cause the data Sources to be deployed to the same folder as the reports.

❑ **Overwrite Data Sources:** Indicates whether to replace any existing data sources with the data sources in your project that have the same name. In Figure 10-14, the `OverwriteDataSources` property still has the default value of False. You can tell that because the value is not in bold font — when a value is changed from the default, the font is changed to bold. Be careful about changing this from the default value, particularly when deploying to a production server.

The level in the project you select to begin a deployment from has an effect on what items are deployed. For example, you can publish every project in a solution by deploying at the solution level. Selecting the project and deploying from there will deploy all the data sources, reports, and any other content in that project. You can deploy an individual item by right-clicking the item in the Solution Explorer window and selecting Deploy from the context menu.

Programmatic Deployment

This involves making calls against the Reporting Services Web service using program code. As long as the messages exchanged with the Report Server are understood by both endpoints, it doesn't matter what language or platform the client uses.

You can write scripts, for example, that automate the repetitive task of deploying reports. Many of the common management tasks can be scripted. Once scripted, a process can then be automated to run on a schedule. You can easily deploy multiple reports, data sources, or other resources using this technique. To do that, you use the RS.exe utility.

You can also create a custom application to act as the user interface for deploying content. By using the Reporting Services Web Services API, your application can perform the same functions. You'll read more about creating scripts and working against the Web Services API at the end of this chapter.

Updating Reports

To update a report, the rdl file is changed and then republished. Doing that replaces the report definition previously stored in the ReportServer database. Replacing an existing rdl file does not overwrite any parameter changes that were made in Report Manager though, even if they were changed in the newly deployed report. It also does not change any security, subscription, or other report execution settings. In Report Manager, updating a report is done exactly the same as uploading a new one — using the Upload File button on the Report Manager toolbar. Uploading files using Report Manager must be done in the destination folder for that item.

Working with Data Sources

Data sources are wrappers for connection strings. Connection strings contain information about what server the source database is on, what database to look for, what credentials to use when authenticating to the database server, and so on. Data sources are generally created by the report author and added to the database content along with the report definition. At times, it may be necessary to adjust data source properties for existing reports. When a database gets moved to a new machine, for example, you may need to update data sources referencing that database to point them at the new machine.

Data sources are used by reports and by data-driven subscriptions. They are managed using Report Manager, SQL Server Management Studio, and program code. If you are not versed in the practice of creating a connection string or Transact-SQL expressions, it is recommended that you use the report designer to create these expressions. The connection string and query expressions may be copied from the respective designer tool and pasted into these text boxes. File paths must also be typed into these pages, as no browsing feature is offered.

There are two types of data sources: private and shared, which are covered in the following sections.

Private Data Sources

This type of data source is for use by a single report and is embedded within the report definition. Since private data sources are part of the report definition file (.rdl), modifications to the Data Source properties must be made using the report designer, or some other tool that can generate the correct XML. When making changes in the report designer, the author can choose to overwrite the existing Data Source properties in the Report Server database.

Shared Data Sources

These items are separate from report definitions. Shared data sources are intended for use by reports and subscriptions that retrieve similar data sets, giving you the ability to configure and manage a single data source for use by multiple reports. For example, if the connection string for a data source changes, that property only needs to be changed in one place. In that case, there's no need to worry about whether each dependent report is updated and retested. Updating and management is all performed at a single location, rather than within multiple reports.

When working with shared data sources in Report Manager, you can view the items using that data source. Those are called Dependent Items and are listed under the Dependent Items tab for the data source, as shown in Figure 10-15.

Subscriptions dependent upon that shared data source are also listed, under the Subscriptions tab for the data source.

Creating Data Sources

Both types of data sources can be created in Report Manager. Data sources are created in place, meaning you must navigate to the location in Report Manager where you want the data source to be located. To create a private data source, go to the Data Source property page of the report. To create a shared data source, go to the folder where you want it to live and click the New Data Source button on the toolbar. That will bring you to the New Data Source page, as shown in Figure 10-16.

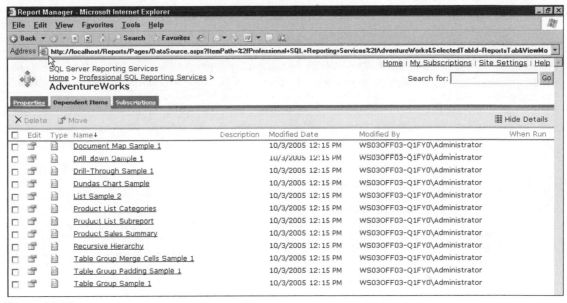

Figure 10-15

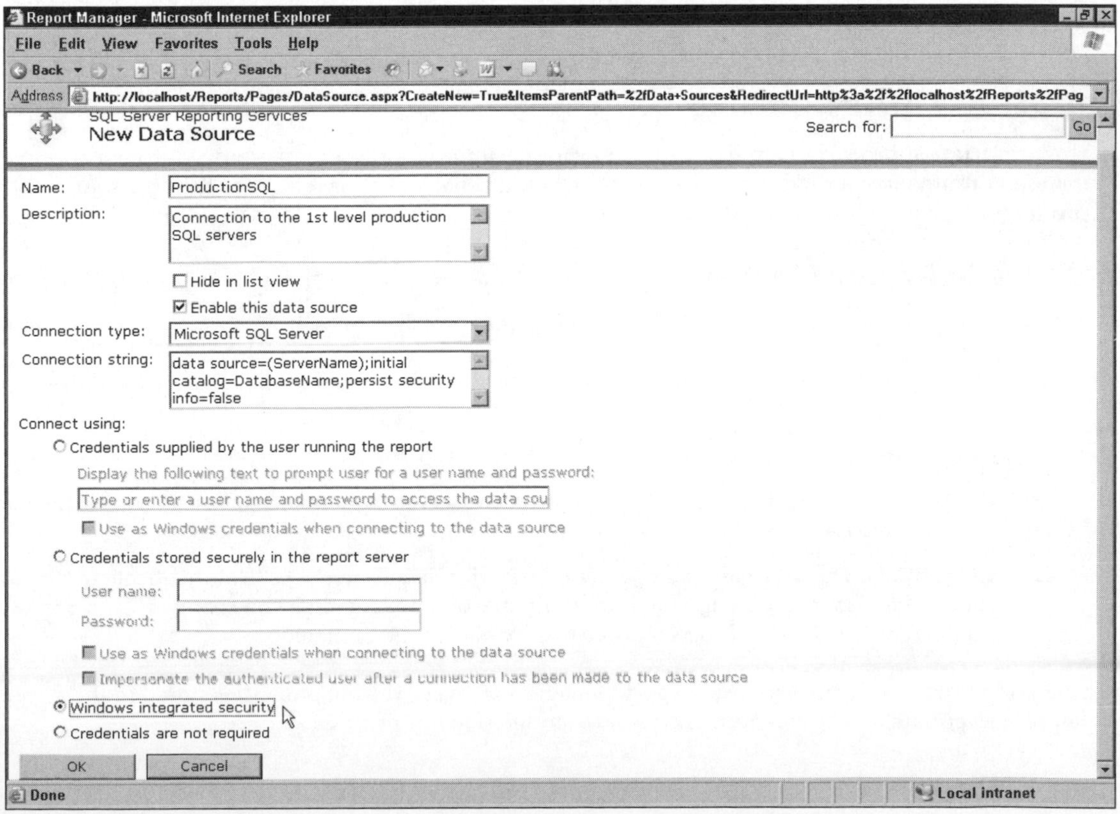

Figure 10-16

Data Source Credentials

When the Report Server connects to a source database to retrieve data, authorization is performed on the credentials it provides. Those credentials can be obtained from the user when the report is run, or they can be values previously stored in the Report Server database. On-demand reports can run using credentials supplied by the user at runtime or just use their current Windows account to authenticate. Scheduled reports, however, must use credentials stored in the database. When a report run is not triggered by a user — such as reports run on a schedule — credentials can't be supplied by a user. When reports are run on the server, Reporting Services must still authenticate itself to a database to retrieve source data. Setting up a Windows user account specifically for this can help to resolve issues by providing trails in places like server logs.

Credentials Supplied by the User

Here, the user will be prompted for a user name and password each time he or she runs a report. The credentials can be used to identify the user as a Windows account holder or passed directly to SQL Server so that it can perform its own authentication and authorization. Users can provide Windows or SQL credentials, depending on whether your SQL Server is configured for Integrated Windows or SQL Server security.

Credentials Stored Securely

Data sources used by cached reports (either cached instances or report snapshots) must use stored credentials. This information is stored in encrypted form with the shared data source or the report definition in the Report Server database.

Updating Data Sources

Updating data sources is a common task. For example, if the report solution is moved from a development environment to a production environment, you'll usually also need to point the data source at the production database server and database.

Updating in Report Manager

You can change these Data Source properties from Report Manager or SQL Server Management Studio:

- ❑ **Data Source Name:** Use a unique name that makes it easy to tell what database the data source points to.

- ❑ **Connection Type:** SQL Server, Oracle, OLEDB, and so on.

- ❑ **Connection String:** This includes the name of the server the source database is on and the name of that database.

- ❑ **Credentials:** The user name and password that this data source uses to authenticate to the source database server. This is an important one, because any time you change a Data Source property you're required to reenter the user password. Be prepared.

Changing Data Source properties in Report Manager will overwrite the properties stored in the ReportServer database. The report `rdl` file isn't modified in this process.

Note that the changes you make to a shared data source using Report Manager overwrite the data source properties previously held in the ReportServer database. If the report is redeployed, the Report Manager settings remain. This can cause confusion if testing reveals a bug in a report, which is sent back to the developer for rework. If the developer changes the report data source and redeploys the report, the previous settings in Report Manager take precedence. To get around this, first delete the report from the ReportServer database, and then redeploy the report.

Managing Report Execution

When a user requests a report, the Report Server begins a process. The process, like other processes, is made up of a series of discreet operations or tasks. Understanding how reports are executed will help you make effective decisions to optimize your server capabilities and user experience. This section covers techniques you can use to improve the performance of your report server.

Report Execution Process

For this topic, I'll divide the execution process into three major pieces (shown in Figure 10-17): data retrieval, intermediate report generation, and rendered report.

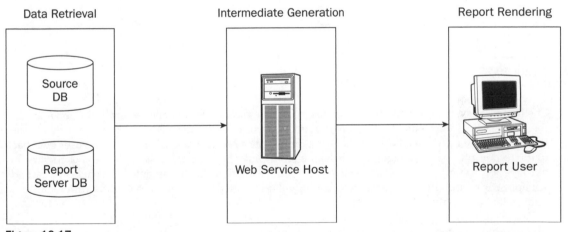

Figure 10-17

To process a report request, the Report Server pulls up the report definition from the ReportServer database and the data set from the source database. When those two are brought together, the report and the data exist in a format that can be persisted. From that intermediate state, reports can be rendered for viewing by the user.

You can allow the process to execute each time or arrange to have portions of the process executed ahead of time. For example, you can cache an intermediate version of a sales report in anticipation of a higher user load every Monday morning. Before I cover that, though, let's take a closer look at the process when a user initiates the process.

On-demand Report Generation

After a report is deployed to the Report Server, its definition is stored in the ReportServer Database. Before the final rendered report is created, an image of the report and its data is produced on the server in an *intermediate report format*. The intermediate report describes the placement of the report elements before it is rendered to a specific output format. Figure 10-18 provides an example of the result of when a user has initiated the report generation process.

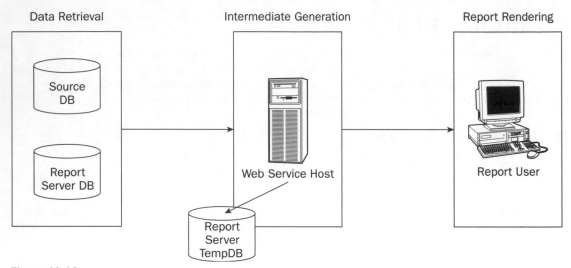

Figure 10-18

The Report Server connects to the databases to retrieve the source data and report definition and then creates the intermediate version of the report. A copy of the intermediate report is written to the ReportServerTempDB database for that user, defined as a browser session. If that same user goes back to the folder in Report Manager and clicks the report link again, he or she will get the cached version of the report, saving database connections and processing time. Each user gets his or her own cached version. For reports that take parameters, a different intermediate report is cached for different parameter combinations.

The intermediate rendering format is the foundation of report caching. When a report is cached, the intermediate format image is written to disk in the ReportServerTempDB database (one of the two databases that compose the Report Server). This enables the report data and definition to be retrieved with one connection and then output in different formats (or multiple times in the same format). A single cached instance can produce different outputs based on report parameters that filter data on the cached data. The final rendering is performed against the intermediate format using a designated rendering extension.

Working with Cached Instances

Data sources used by cached reports (either cached instances or report snapshots) must use stored credentials. This information is stored in encrypted form with the shared data source or the report definition in the ReportServer database.

If the report is rendered from a cached instance, this means that data presented in the report could potentially be out of date without the user's realizing it. For this reason it may be a good idea to update cached instances frequently, especially for a transactional database, where data may change often. In the case of a data warehouse, it might make sense to synchronize cached report updates with batch data updates to the warehouse database.

Cached reports are configured to expire after a specific period or on a schedule, after which the report cache is flushed and the report is cached again on the next request. The cache will also be flushed automatically when a report definition is modified and redeployed, caching options are changed, or the report is deleted. Configure cache with Report Manager or Management Studio.

Using Parameters

If a report is configured to cache report instances when a user first requests the report with a unique combination of parameter values (assuming that the report takes parameters), the intermediate form of the report and its data are stored in the ReportServer database. Each unique combination of parameters may produce a separate cached instance. A significant difference between a cached instance and a snapshot is that a cached instance is created the first time a user requests the report with unique parameters. A different cached instance is created for different report input parameters.

Be careful when using this technique. You can easily wind up with many versions of a report being held in the report server cache, quickly consuming resources. A better approach you might consider is keeping a single cached instance on hand and creating views of the data using the technique described in the following section.

Using Filters

Reports can apply a number of query and filtering techniques to the data. Typically, these include using parameterized queries in the database (by using either ad hoc SQL statements or stored procedures) and filtering data in the report, or a combination of the two.

Report filters are applied when the report is rendered for the user. Different users can have different views of the same data, by filtering the data based on user identity. Applying different filters does not cause a new cached instance to be created. Because of that, the report server can handle a greater number of report requests and respond to them more quickly.

Data Source Credentials

In order to set up any implementation of caching, security credentials must be provided for the data source of a report. This is called storing credential securely on the report server. If you are using shared data sources, this only needs to be set up once on the shared data source.

Snapshots and History

A *snapshot* is a static, cached copy of a rendered report. Snapshots are created before users want to view a report and are usually created and refreshed on a defined schedule. Because snapshots are created beforehand, users cannot interactively supply parameter values. Reports that require parameters must be configured with these values ahead of time. This can be done in the Visual Studio report designer, though you'll typically use Report Manager or SQL Server Management Studio.

Report snapshots may be placed into history. This means that when another snapshot is created for a report, it doesn't overwrite the previous snapshot. Any of these individual snapshots for the same report may be retrieved from history until the history is cleared or reaches its maximum size. Reports may manually or automatically be placed into history based on a schedule when a snapshot is created.

The following table compares the features of various types of cached reports.

	Cached Instance	Snapshot	History
Creation	Created with the first user request using a unique combination of parameters.	Created on a schedule before the first user requests the report.	Like a standard snapshot; history entries can be created on a schedule or snapshots may be added to history manually by users.
Lifespan	Cache automatically expires after a designated time has elapsed or based on a designated schedule.	A report snapshot is overwritten when the next scheduled snapshot is created.	History entries don't typically expire but may be overwritten when a designated number of history entries have been reached.
Typical Scenarios	To optimize performance and conserve resources when the report runs using different parameter values.	For static reports that do not require user interaction, a snapshot can be created with preselected parameter values. It's not optimal if reports have several parameter options.	Preserves snapshots for archival and future reference. Appropriate for keeping a static view of data that changes.

Often, a particular report needs to be generated at a predetermined interval. For example, let's say a sales report must be generated monthly. If the report were created at the end of January, users would want to see the January report throughout February. They do not expect the February data to be seen in the January report. These types of reports are best created upfront, without waiting for the first user to request it, because the report is expected to be available at the end of January. Therefore, you can now instruct Reporting Services to create the report proactively and keep it ready for users.

Snapshots for a report are set up on the Execution property page for a report. Figure 10-19 shows an example of a snapshot configuration.

In this example, the report is being configured to create snapshots on a report-specific schedule. Users will view reports that have been rendered from the most recent snapshot.

Using Parameters and Filters

Report parameters that are derived from query parameters cause data to be filtered at the data source. Additional report parameters may be added to filter data on the report server using filter expressions. Unlike query parameters that will cause multiple report instances to be cached (each instance for a different combination of parameters), filter parameters in a cached instance simply filter the data stored with the cached report. Filter expressions are applied to the cached data and will not cause additional instances to be cached.

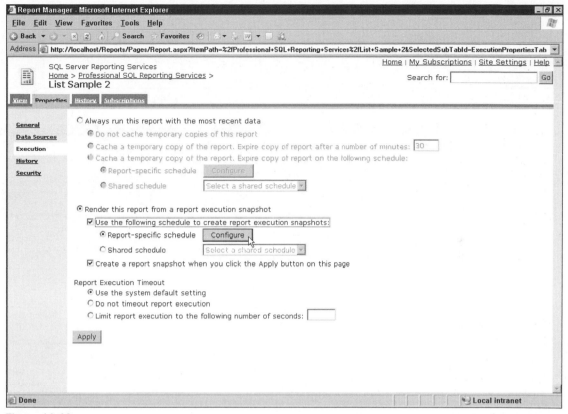

Figure 10-19

Since report snapshots (and subscriptions) are executed without the user's interaction, all parameter values must be supplied beforehand. This is set up in the report configuration, so they're readily available to the processing engine at runtime. Reports configured to execute as a cached instance, on the other hand, can be interactive and so do not require parameter values to be stored.

Like cached instances, filters can be applied to snapshots. The snapshot has already been created, and a filter then reduces the result set that the report viewer actually sees rendered in the report. When used with query parameters, filters provide a great deal of flexibility during report rendering. A snapshot can freeze data at a particular point and then filter on the fly for different users.

Report History

Report snapshots may be placed into history. This means that when another snapshot is created for a report, it doesn't overwrite the previous snapshot. Any of these individual snapshots for the same report may be retrieved from history until the history is cleared or reaches its maximum size. Reports may manually or automatically be placed into history based on a schedule when a snapshot is created.

To help manage disk space, you can specify the number of reports kept in the archive. This can be done either globally across all reports or for individual reports. When the number of reports in an archive has reached its limit, it will no longer add new snapshots. If you desire, you can also choose to keep an unlimited number of snapshots in the report history.

To configure report histories globally, use the Site Settings page in Report Manager, as shown in Figure 10-20.

Configuring the history for an individual report is done using the History property page of the report.

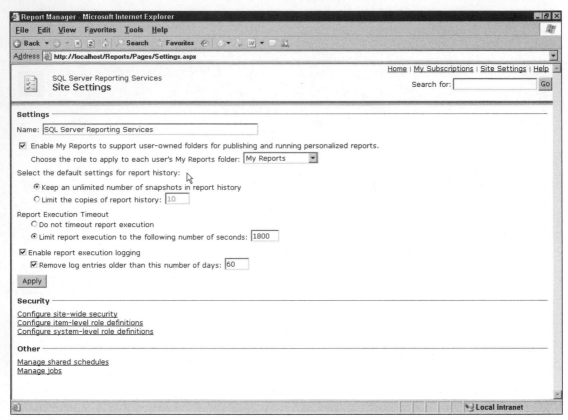

Figure 10-20

Scheduling Reports

Scheduling is used in a number of areas in Reporting Services. For example, scheduling is used to execute a report and create a snapshot. Like a regular report, the snapshot can then be placed in the report History or delivered to users by e-mail or other method.

There are two kinds of schedules to work with: shared schedules and private schedules.

Shared schedules can be used across multiple reports. *Private schedules* are scoped to an individual report and are not shared. Shared schedules are managed centrally by a user with sufficient permissions.

Private schedules, on the other hand, are not handled centrally and require the user to manage each schedule individually. Schedules can also be managed programmatically. In that case, shared and private schedules are handled the same.

The scheduling mechanism is based on the *SQL Server Agent*, which fires and executes events at specific times. When the subscription is triggered, SQL Server Agent adds an entry to the database queue, where it's polled by the Reporting Services Windows service. There are advantages to using both types of scheduling options. Let's take a closer look at working with shared schedules.

Creating a shared schedule makes it easier to schedule multiple events to run at the same time, and individual schedules don't have to be set up for each event. This may be an appropriate solution when you need to run several reports during off-peak hours when the server isn't busy with live user requests. Although this may be more convenient, a significant penalty is realized when the server tries to run demanding jobs at the same time. For reports that are long, perform complex calculations, or consume a lot of data, you may want to stagger the schedules to prevent this condition.

Delivering Reports

Reports can be delivered to users in multiple ways and rendered in multiple formats. Rendering in multiple formats occurs quickly, because the intermediate report format shortcuts most of the original report processing as discussed earlier. Out of the box, reports can be rendered in these formats:

❑   **HTML:** For static snapshots.

❑   **DHTML (the default):** Allows dynamic behavior such as expanding report sections.

❑   **PDF:** Adobe Acrobat is needed on the client to view the file.

❑   **DOC:** Microsoft Word.

❑   **XLS:** Microsoft Excel; test well, especially if your report has dynamic behavior.

❑   **CSV:** Standard comma-delimited format.

The rendering format is specified by the user at runtime or when a subscription is configured. Reports can be rendered in Web or Windows applications, or delivered to an end point for easy user access.

Two delivery options are provided: e-mail delivery and file share delivery.

E-Mail Delivery

Delivering reports by e-mail requires that a configured SMTP server is available. When Reporting Services is first installed, the Setup Wizard prompts for the mail server name and address information. If you launch the setup wizard again, it will not prompt for this information.

To modify or set the e-mail server information, you can edit the `RSReportServer.config` file or use SQL Server Management Studio. When working directly with the configuration file, e-mail options are set under the `RSEMailDPConfiguration` element in the Delivery section of this file. For more information on modifying configuration settings, see Chapter 11.

File Share Delivery

Specifying a file share subscription is very simple. On the Subscriptions link for a report, click Add Subscription. On the Report Delivery Options page, under Delivered By, select Report Server File Share from the drop-down list (see Figure 10-21).

Enter a valid Universal Naming Convention (UNC) file path into the Path text box. A local file system path is not acceptable input. If you are entering a local path, follow these steps:

1. Using Windows Explorer, create a file share for the local path. This is easily done by right clicking on the folder and selecting Sharing. Create the share using the Sharing tab.

2. Using the Permissions options on the Sharing tab, grant a user read and write access to this shared folder.

3. Click OK on the Sharing Permissions dialog to accept the file share settings.

4. In Windows Explorer, navigate to My Network Places (or Network Neighborhood in Windows NT). Continue to drill down to the network share on the server. Typically, this will be under `Entire Network\ Microsoft Windows Network\ (your domain or workgroup name)\ (server name)\ (file share name)`.

5. Copy the path from the address box in Windows Explorer and paste it into the Path text box.

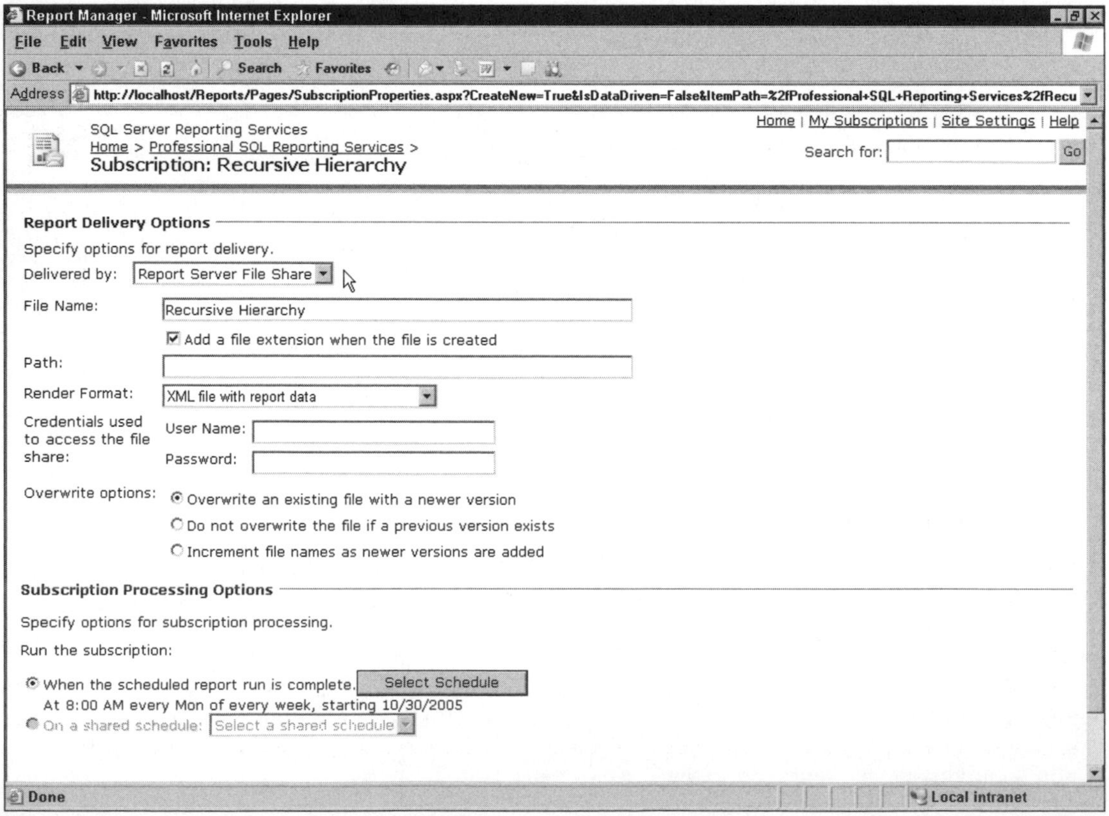

Figure 10-21

The UNC path should be in the form \\server name\share name. Although it is not usually recommended, you can use an administrative user's credentials to write the subscription output file. In this case, you could use an administrative share (such as c$) rather than create a new share. In any case, the system administrator should be involved in this decision.

Pocket PC Report File Updates

If you would like to have a subscription that updates file-based reports for a Pocket PC device, you can output report files across the network to the synchronization folder for a device. When a mobile device partnership is created using Microsoft ActiveSync on a user's personal computer, a folder is designated for automatic file synchronization. Any files that are modified or written to this folder will be automatically synchronized with the Pocket PC device. This folder is found under the user's My Documents folder and is typically named (mobile device name) My Documents. For example, if your device name were Freds Pocket PC, the synchronization folder would be named Freds Pocket PC My Documents. Any subfolders are also synchronized, so you could create a subfolder called Reports and write report files to this location.

When creating file shares for machines across the network, the My Documents folder location can be remapped by the user and is profile-specific. The default location for My Documents is C:\Documents and Settings\(user profile name)\My Documents. Make sure that the user writing to the remote computer from the Report Server has been granted write access to the output folder.

Report Subscriptions

As a manager, you may need to do a biweekly status report for your people. When you travel, you might like to have a current, up-to-date employee directory on your PDA at all times. As new items are added to your product line or pricing changes, you'd like the updated product catalog in front of your people, so they're never working with outdated information. Using subscriptions makes all of this possible, simply and easily.

Using a combination of the Reporting Services Windows service and SQL Server Agent, the subscription engine renders a report anytime you want it. It renders it in the format you need and delivers it using the method you choose — either by e-mail or to a file in any folder. When delivering reports via e-mail, you can specify that a link to the report be embedded in the e-mail or the entire rendered report.

A common subscription management task is to verify that subscriptions are running as scheduled. The outcome of subscription events is recorded in the server's Application Log, and more specific details are written to individual log files with the date/time stamp in each file name. Over time, hundreds of these files may be produced and should be moved off to a backup machine and/or deleted.

Events in the Application Log are recorded with the Source property value of Report Server and SQL Server Reporting Service. There is no method to directly read or consolidate the individual log files. However, Reporting Services ships with SQL script files, which will enable you to import this data into tables for analysis using SQL Server Integration Services. These files are contained on the product CD in the Extras folder.

Simplified subscription log information is easy to obtain in the Report Manager. To get information for a specific report, select the Subscription tab for that report. The status for the last execution is displayed for each subscription and snapshot. A summary view of all reports accessible to the current user is also available on the My Subscriptions tab. These execution summaries can be used to diagnose subscription errors including service- and permission-related problems.

Snapshot-Triggered Subscriptions

Subscriptions can be triggered when a snapshot gets updated rather than being directly tied to a schedule. If the snapshot is refreshed on a schedule, this effectively will cause the subscription to deliver a report on the schedule for the snapshot. Since snapshots can also be updated manually, using this technique can guarantee that users receive updated reports regardless of the method used to refresh the snapshot. For example, at the end of each month, after you bulk-load new data into your decision-support database, you update the related snapshots. Triggering subscriptions on the snapshot updates brings the process into balance without concern for the coordination of scheduled events.

The option to create a snapshot-triggered subscription is available only when the report execution is based on a subscription. After setting up a snapshot for your report, add a subscription. Under the Subscription Processing Options, select the radio button to run the subscription when the report content is refreshed.

Schedule-Triggered Subscriptions

The most common type of subscriptions are based on a shared or individual schedule. Schedule options vary, depending on how frequently you want the schedule to trigger a report run. Figure 10-22 shows an example of a daily schedule.

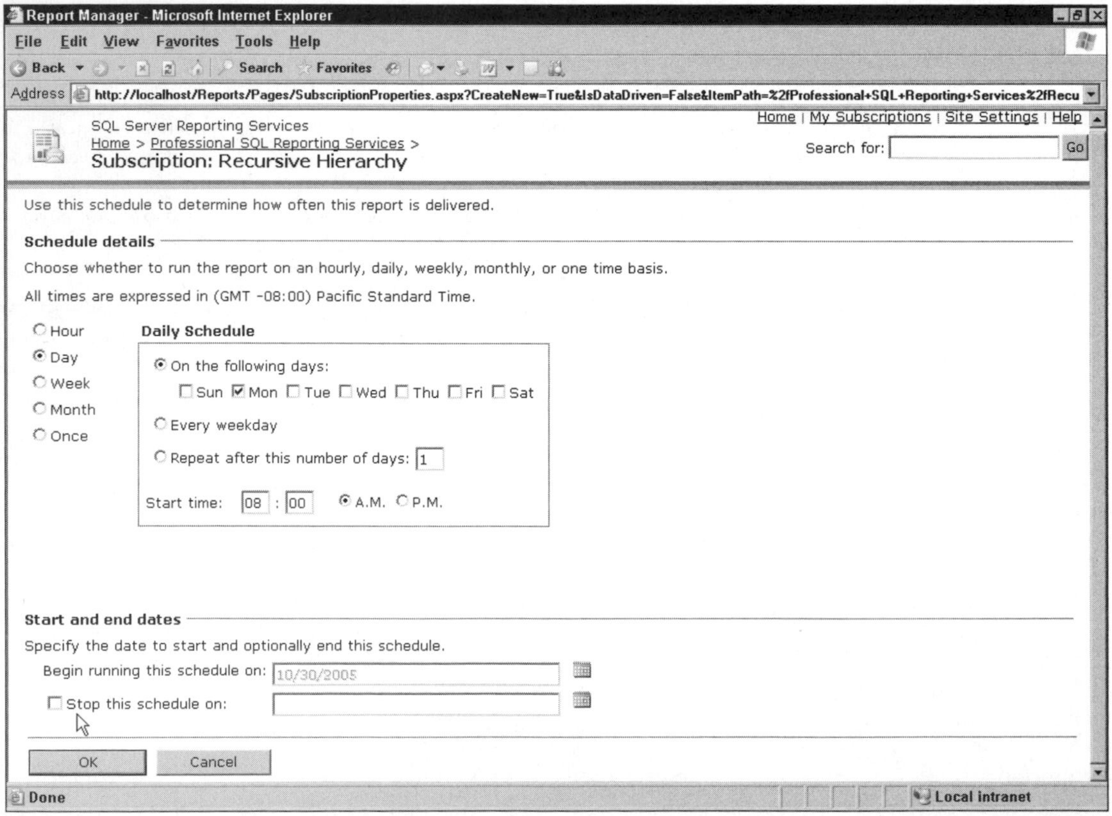

Figure 10-22

In this case, the report is scheduled to run at 8:00 am every Monday, based on the date/time settings of the server.

Data-Driven Subscriptions

A data-driven subscription is a subscription where the report recipient information is provided by a query. In addition to the list of recipients, several subscription-specific properties can be based on values returned by a query as well. For example, you can deliver reports to multiple users in multiple rendered formats. The list of users can be dynamic, and each can receive customized content. This makes some very interesting and creative solutions possible.

Reporting Services doesn't provide a database by default, so you do have to do a little work to prepare a data-driven subscription, but it's actually quite simple. The data can be stored in practically any form as long as the necessary values are available in columns returned by the query. At the very least, the only requirement is a list of names or e-mail addresses.

Delivery settings and parameters may use either static values (assigned when the subscription is created) or values returned from a query. The query could also return information that can be used to customize a report; this implies that for every subscription recipient, a report may be rendered in a different format, sent to a different file share, or sent using a different subject line, priority flag, and so on.

These subscriptions can be set to run on a predefined schedule, or they can be triggered by the execution of a snapshot. You can also "deliver" data-driven subscriptions to cache by simply specifying the Null Delivery Provider in the subscription properties.

Automating Content Management

Because Reporting Services is a Web service, the functionality it exposes can be accessed and consumed using code. Code can be set to run on a schedule, enabling tasks to be performed unattended. Examples of common tasks that can be done using code include:

- ❑ Duplicating settings between servers.
- ❑ Migrating content from test to production environments.
- ❑ Changing shared data sources.
- ❑ Canceling running jobs.

The next sections in this chapter look at automating two tasks that you've already read about in this chapter: subscription management and report deployment.

Automating Subscription Management

The Reporting Service Web service object exposes methods for managing subscriptions. Remember that *web methods* (programmatic methods for a `webservice` class) don't support overloaded calls or optional arguments. For arguments that don't require a value, you can pass a `Null` (C#) or `Nothing` (VB).

Let's look at a few examples of some subscription management routines. To obtain a list of subscriptions with associated properties for a report, you can use the `ListSubscriptions` method and use it by passing in a report name. This returns a collection of `Subscription` objects.

You'll build a sample application to view and create subscriptions. I'm not going to take you through this example step by step, but I will give you enough information to reproduce the subscription-related code. As you can see in Figure 10-23, I've added two `ComboBoxes`, two `Buttons`, and a `ListView` control to a form in a Windows application project.

The `Panel` and the other controls at the bottom will be used later to create new subscriptions. The Panel is invisible, and the New Subscription button is disabled. The click event of the Get Subscription button enables the other button because you create the `ReportService` object in this event.

The `ListSubscriptions` event takes two optional arguments. Now, if you were paying attention, you would have caught that web methods don't support optional arguments! In this sense, arguments that don't have required values can accept the value `Nothing` (VB) or `null` (C#), making these methods somewhat polymorphic (behaving differently under different conditions); this method behaves like this. If you pass the path and report name for the `Report` argument, all subscriptions are returned. If you pass the user name for the *Owner*, subscriptions owned by this user are returned, and if you pass nothing, all subscriptions on the server are returned. I've written some conditional statements that check the two combo boxes and pass the appropriate values.

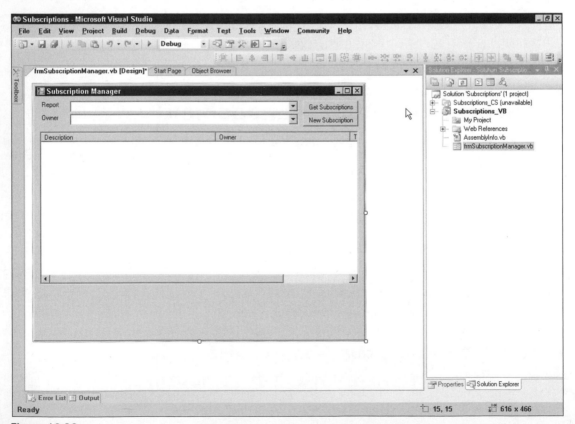

Figure 10-23

In the declaration section of the form class module, you declare an object variable for the Web service proxy class. The code to implement this in VB is as follows:

```
Private rs As New localhost_RS.ReportingService
```

The code in C# is as follows:

```
private localhost_RS.ReportingService rs = new localhost_RS.ReportingService();
```

The Get Subscription button uses two object variables to hold the report path name and/or owner name supplied by the user. You use object type variables so you can pass the value Nothing (VB) or null (C#) in case no values are provided.

After attaching the current user's security credentials to the Web service proxy object, you use the ListSubscriptions method to iterate through each subscription object and write associated properties to list and view subitems. The ListView control will show each of these values in separate columns if displayed in Detail mode. The last step is to enable the New Subscription button. This button will be used in the next example. The code to implement this in VB and C# follows:

VB

```
Private Sub btnGetSubscriptions_Click( _
                ByVal sender As System.Object, ByVal e As System.EventArgs) _
                Handles btnGetSubscriptions.Click
    Dim subscr As localhost_RS.Subscription
    Dim strReport As String = IIf(Me.cboReport.Text <> "", Me.cboReport.Text, _
                                Nothing)
    Dim strOwner As String = IIf(Me.cboOwner.Text <> "", Me.cboOwner.Text, Nothing)

    rs.Credentials = System.Net.CredentialCache.DefaultCredentials
    '-- Loop through subscriptions collection, add to listview
    For Each subscr In rs.ListSubscriptions(strReport, strOwner)
       Dim ListItem As New ListViewItem
       With ListItem
          .Text = subscr.Description
          .SubItems.Add(subscr.Owner)
          .SubItems.Add(subscr.EventType)
          .SubItems.Add(subscr.LastExecuted)
          .SubItems.Add(subscr.Status)
       End With
       Me.lstvwSubscriptions.Items.Add(ListItem)
    Next
    '-- Enable new subscription button
    Me.btnNewSubscription.Enabled = True
End Sub
```

C#

```
private void btnGetSubscriptions_Click(object sender, System.EventArgs e)
{
    string strReport = null;
    string strOwner = null;
    if(this.cboReport.Text!= "")
    {
```

```
        strReport = this.cboReport.Text;
    }
    if(this.cboOwner.Text!= "")
    {
        strOwner = this.cboOwner.Text;
    }
    rs.Credentials = System.Net.CredentialCache.DefaultCredentials;

    foreach (localhost_RS.Subscription subscr in rs.ListSubscriptions(strReport,
            strOwner))
    {
        ListViewItem  ListItem = new ListViewItem();
        ListItem.Text = subscr.Description;
        ListItem.SubItems.Add(subscr.Owner.ToString());
        ListItem.SubItems.Add(subscr.EventType.ToString());
        ListItem.SubItems.Add(subscr.LastExecuted.ToShortDateString());
        ListItem.SubItems.Add(subscr.Status.ToString());
        this.lstvwSubscriptions.Items.Add(ListItem);
    }
    this.btnNewSubscription.Enabled = true;
}
```

You can add a new subscription using the `CreateSubscription` method. Arguments passed to this method are as follows:

- `ExtensionSettings`: This argument is required and can be a little tricky. The `ExtensionSettings` object contains two properties. The `Extension` property is a string indicating the type of delivery extension. The `ParameterValues` property is an object of type `ParameterValueOrFieldReference` that contains an array of `ParameterValue` objects. Each element is a name/value pair. Depending on the subscription type, a different list of parameter name/value pairs is passed using this array. These parameters correspond to the items presented on the Report Delivery Options section of the Snapshot page in Report Manager.

- `EventType`: This argument takes a string to set either `TimedSubscription` or `SnapshotUpdate`.

- `MatchData`: This argument accepts multiple types and values depending on the `EventType` argument; these include the `ScheduleID` for a shared schedule or a string containing the XML element content for the schedule. Shared schedule information may be obtained using the `ListSchedules` method to enumerate the server's schedules.

- `Parameters`: This argument is an array of `ParameterValue` objects. It is used to supply report parameters as name/value pairs.

Now, let's put it all together in a sample application. Using the same form as the previous example, I've placed two text boxes, two combo boxes, and a button on the `Panel` control at the bottom of the form, as shown in Figure 10-24.

At the top of this form, the New Subscription button was enabled at the end of the Get Subscriptions button-click event code. In the click event of this button, you set the Visible property of the panel to True and get a list of shared subscriptions that have been created on the Report Server, adding the Description for each schedule to the Schedule combo box. For the following code, you'll look at VB and C# language examples side by side:

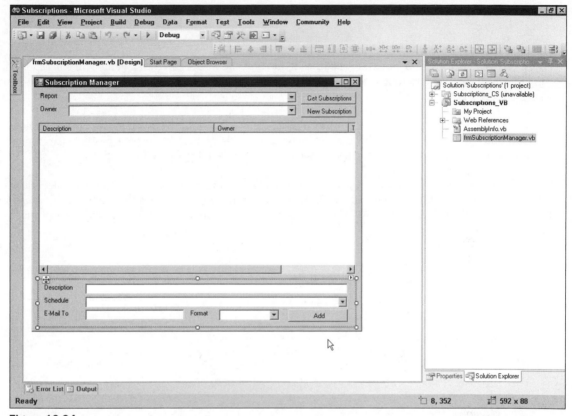

Figure 10-24

VB

```vb
Private Sub btnNewSubscription_Click( ByVal sender As System.Object, _
                                      ByVal e As System.EventArgs) _
                              Handles btnNewSubscription.Click

    Me.Panel1.Visible = True

    Dim sched As localhost_RS.Schedule
    For Each sched In rs.ListSchedules
        Me.cboSchedules.Items.Add(sched.Description)
    Next
End Sub
```

C#

```csharp
private void btnNewSubscription_Click(object sender, System.EventArgs e)
{
    this.Panel1.Visible = true;
    foreach (localhost_RS.Schedule sched in rs.ListSchedules())
    {
```

```
            this.cboSchedules.Items.Add(sched.Description);
        }
    }
```

After a schedule is selected from the schedule combo box, the `SelectedIndex` value will correspond to the index of the corresponding schedule. Let's use this to obtain the `ScheduleID` value and pass it to the `CreateSubscription` method.

After entering a description, recipient e-mail address, and selecting a rendering format, the user clicks the Add Subscription button. In this click event, you set up the values and objects passed as arguments to the `CreateSubscription` method. Let's see how to do this in the following sections.

The selected item in the Schedule combo box corresponds to a member of the `Schedules` collection returned by the `ListSchedules` method. There is only one method to obtain these items, so you use a loop to resolve the selection and exit when the counter variable matches the `SelectedIndex` property of the combo box.

VB

```
'-- Get selected schedule
Dim sched As localhost_RS.Schedule
Dim iSchedCounter As Int16
For Each sched In rs.ListSchedules
    iSchedCounter += 1
    If iSchedCounter = Me.cboSchedules.SelectedIndex() Then Exit For
Next
```

C#

```
//-- Get selected schedule
localhost_RS.Schedule scheduleItem = null;
Int16 iSchedCounter = 0;
foreach (localhost_RS.Schedule sched in rs.ListSchedules())
{
    iSchedCounter += 1;
    if (iSchedCounter == this.cboSchedules.SelectedIndex)
    {
        scheduleItem = sched;
        break;
    }
}
```

You can now obtain the `ScheduleID` property of the `Schedule` object using the `sched` variable.

Next, you create an `ExtensionSettings` object and set its `Extension` property to indicate that this subscription will use the e-mail delivery extension as follows.

VB

```
        Dim extset As New localhost_RS.ExtensionSettings
        extset.Extension = "Report Server Email"
```

C#

```
localhost_RS.ExtensionSettings extset = new localhost_RS.ExtensionSettings();
extset.Extension = "Report Server Email";
```

Now we move on to the extension-specific properties of the ExtensionSettings object. The ParameterValues property is set to an object of type ParameterValueOrFieldReference and is a five-element array. You also create five corresponding ParameterValue objects. For each of these objects, you set the Name and Value properties and then add them to the array.

VB

```
'-- Create Parameter Values array
Dim ParamVals(5) As localhost_RS.ParameterValueOrFieldReference
extset.ParameterValues = ParamVals

'-- Populate the Extension Parameters
Dim pvTo As New localhost_RS.ParameterValue
pvTo.Name = "TO"
pvTo.Value = Me.txtEMailTo.Text
extset.ParameterValues(0) = pvTo
Dim pvIncludeRpt As New localhost_RS.ParameterValue
pvIncludeRpt.Name = "IncludeReport"
pvIncludeRpt.Value = "True"
extset.ParameterValues(1) = pvIncludeRpt

Dim pvRenderFormat As New localhost_RS.ParameterValue
pvRenderFormat.Name = "RenderFormat"
pvRenderFormat.Value = Me.cboRenderFormat.Text
extset.ParameterValues(2) = pvRenderFormat
Dim pvPriority As New localhost_RS.ParameterValue
pvPriority.Name = "Priority"
pvPriority.Value = "NORMAL"
extset.ParameterValues(3) = pvPriority

Dim pvSubject As New localhost_RS.ParameterValue
pvSubject.Name = "Subject"
pvSubject.Value = "@ReportName was executed at @ExtensionTime"
extset.ParameterValues(4) = pvSubject
```

C#

```
//-- Create Parameter Values array
localhost_RS.ParameterValueOrFieldReference[] ParamVals = new
        Subscriptions_CS.localhost_RS.ParameterValueOrFieldReference[5];
extset.ParameterValues = ParamVals;

//-- Populate the Extension Parameters
localhost_RS.ParameterValue  pvTo = new localhost_RS.ParameterValue();
pvTo.Name = "TO";
pvTo.Value = this.txtEMailTo.Text;
extset.ParameterValues[0] = pvTo;

localhost_RS.ParameterValue  pvIncludeRpt = new localhost_RS.ParameterValue();
pvIncludeRpt.Name = "IncludeReport";
```

```
        pvIncludeRpt.Value = "true";
        extset.ParameterValues[1] = pvIncludeRpt;

        localhost_RS.ParameterValue  pvRenderFormat = new
                                               localhost_RS.ParameterValue();
        pvRenderFormat.Name = "RenderFormat";
        pvRenderFormat.Value = this.cboRenderFormat.Text;
        extset.ParameterValues[2] = pvRenderFormat;

        localhost_RS.ParameterValue  pvPriority = new localhost_RS.ParameterValue();
        pvPriority.Name = "Priority";
        pvPriority.Value = "NORMAL";
        extset.ParameterValues[3] = pvPriority;

        localhost_RS.ParameterValue  pvSubject = new localhost_RS.ParameterValue();
        pvSubject.Name = "Subject";
        pvSubject.Value = "@ReportName was executed at @ExtensionTime";
        extset.ParameterValues[4] = pvSubject;
```

The report you are using doesn't require any parameters, so you have everything necessary to actually create the subscription. Call this method by passing Nothing in place of a Parameters array.

VB

```
    '-- Create the Subscription (no report parameters in last arg)
    rs.CreateSubscription(Me.cboReport.Text, _
                          extset, _
                          Me.txtDescription.Text, _
                          "TimedSubscription", _
                          sched.ScheduleID, _
                          Nothing)
```

C#

```
    //-- Create the Subscription (no report parameters in last arg)
    rs.CreateSubscription(this.cboReport.Text,
                          extset,
                          this.txtDescription.Text,
                          "TimedSubscription",
                          scheduleItem.ScheduleID,
                          null);
```

Now let's look at the entire routine put together. Here's all of the Add Subscription button-click event code in both VB and C#:

VB

```
Private Sub btnAddSubscription_Click(ByVal sender As System.Object, _
                             ByVal e As System.EventArgs)
                             Handles btnAddSubscription.Click

    '-- Get selected schedule
    Dim sched As localhost_RS.Schedule
    Dim iSchedCounter As Int16
    For Each sched In rs.ListSchedules
```

```
            iSchedCounter += 1
            If iSchedCounter = Me.cboSchedules.SelectedIndex() _
                            Then Exit For
        Next

        Dim extset As New localhost_RS.ExtensionSettings
        extset.Extension = "Report Server Email"

        '-- Create Parameter Values array
        Dim ParamVals(5) As localhost_RS.ParameterValueOrFieldReference
        extset.ParameterValues = ParamVals

        '-- Populate the Extension Parameters
        Dim pvTo As New localhost_RS.ParameterValue
        pvTo.Name = "TO"
        pvTo.Value = Me.txtEMailTo.Text
        extset.ParameterValues(0) = pvTo
        Dim pvIncludeRpt As New localhost_RS.ParameterValue
        pvIncludeRpt.Name = "IncludeReport"
        pvIncludeRpt.Value = "True"
        extset.ParameterValues(1) = pvIncludeRpt

        Dim pvRenderFormat As New localhost_RS.ParameterValue
        pvRenderFormat.Name = "RenderFormat"
        pvRenderFormat.Value = Me.cboRenderFormat.Text
        extset.ParameterValues(2) = pvRenderFormat
        Dim pvPriority As New localhost_RS.ParameterValue
        pvPriority.Name = "Priority"
        pvPriority.Value = "NORMAL"
        extset.ParameterValues(3) = pvPriority
        Dim pvSubject As New localhost_RS.ParameterValue
        pvSubject.Name = "Subject"
        pvSubject.Value = "@ReportName was executed at @ExtensionTime"
        extset.ParameterValues(4) = pvSubject

        '-- Create the Subscription (no report parameters in last arg)
        rs.CreateSubscription(Me.cboReport.Text, _
                            extset, _
                            Me.txtDescription.Text, _
                            "TimedSubscription", _
                            sched.ScheduleID, _
                            Nothing)
    End Sub
```

C#

```
private void btnAddSubscription_Click(object sender, System.EventArgs e)
{
    //-- Get selected schedule
    localhost_RS.Schedule scheduleItem = null;
    Int16 iSchedCounter = 0;
    foreach (localhost_RS.Schedule sched in rs.ListSchedules())
    {
        iSchedCounter += 1;
        if (iSchedCounter == this.cboSchedules.SelectedIndex)
```

```
                {
                scheduleItem = sched;
                break;
                }
        }
        localhost_RS.ExtensionSettings  extset = new localhost_RS.ExtensionSettings();
        extset.Extension = "Report Server Email";

        //-- Create Parameter Values array
        localhost_RS.ParameterValueOrFieldReference[] ParamVals = new
        Subscriptions_CS.localhost_RS.ParameterValueOrFieldReference[5];
        extset.ParameterValues = ParamVals;

        //-- Populate the Extension Parameters
        localhost_RS.ParameterValue  pvTo = new localhost_RS.ParameterValue();
        pvTo.Name = "TO";
        pvTo.Value = this.txtEMailTo.Text;
        extset.ParameterValues[0] = pvTo;

        localhost_RS.ParameterValue  pvIncludeRpt = new localhost_RS.ParameterValue();
        pvIncludeRpt.Name = "IncludeReport";
        pvIncludeRpt.Value = "true";
        extset.ParameterValues[1] = pvIncludeRpt;
        localhost_RS.ParameterValue  pvRenderFormat = new
                                                localhost_RS.ParameterValue();
        pvRenderFormat.Name = "RenderFormat";
        pvRenderFormat.Value = this.cboRenderFormat.Text;
        extset.ParameterValues[2] = pvRenderFormat;

        localhost_RS.ParameterValue  pvPriority = new localhost_RS.ParameterValue();
        pvPriority.Name = "Priority";
        pvPriority.Value = "NORMAL";
        extset.ParameterValues[3] = pvPriority;

        localhost_RS.ParameterValue  pvSubject = new localhost_RS.ParameterValue();
        pvSubject.Name = "Subject";
        pvSubject.Value = "@ReportName was executed at @ExtensionTime";
        extset.ParameterValues[4] = pvSubject;

        //-- Create the Subscription (no report parameters in last arg)
        rs.CreateSubscription(this.cboReport.Text,
                extset,
                this.txtDescription.Text,
                "TimedSubscription",
                scheduleItem.ScheduleID,
                null);
}
```

Using Script

Using script, you can perform almost any task in a .NET application, but scripts are run at the command line in text mode. A Reporting Services script file is written using VB code and has nearly all the capabilities of a console application.

You will use the GetSubscriptions button code from the Subscription Manager application above. However, there are some modifications for this to work in console mode rather than as a Windows form. The VBScript code is saved in a file called List_Subscriptions.rss.

```
Sub Main()
   Dim subscr as Subscription
   Console.WriteLine()
   Console.Write("Report: ")
   Dim strReport as String = Console.ReadLine()
   Console.Write("Owner: ")
   Dim strOwner as String = Console.ReadLine()
   rs.Credentials = System.Net.CredentialCache.DefaultCredentials
   If sReport = "" Then strReport = Nothing
   If sOwner = "" Then strOwner = Nothing

   Console.WriteLine()
   Console.WriteLine("**********************************************************")
   Console.WriteLine("Subscriptions for:")
   Console.WriteLine("Report: " & sReport)
   Console.WriteLine("Owner:  " & sOwner)
   Console.WriteLine("----------------------------------------------------------")
   For Each subscr In rs.ListSubscriptions(strReport, strOwner)
        Console.WriteLine(subscr.Description)
   Next
   Console.WriteLine("----------------------------------------------------------")
End Sub
```

In a Reporting Services script, the Reporting Service Web service is invoked automatically, and all related classes are accessible without additional references. As you can see in this code, you declare a Subscription object using the variable subscr.

Using the Console object, you use the ReadLine method to obtain a value from the user and the Write and WriteLine methods to send text to the console (command line).

You can use two string variables, sReport and sOwner, to capture input from the user and then convert these values to object types using the variables oReport and oOwner. This is necessary so you can pass the Nothing value to the ListSubscriptions method in case the user doesn't provide a value. Next, you iterate through the Subscriptions collection and write out the list to the console.

Scripting can ease the content and server management process. The "Creating Scripts" section of this chapter covers scripting in more detail.

Automating Report Deployment

A great time to automate a process is when deploying reports or migrating content from one environment to another. For example, moving reports from development to test, and then again from test to production environments. Once in production, you may need to deploy content across multiple servers in a farm. Scripting is a "write it once, cash it as many times as you like" kind of tool that's good to have in your toolbox. We take a detailed look at a script that deploys reports in the next section.

Creating Scripts

Many repetitive tasks on Report Server administration and management can be automated using script files. An example that was covered in the last topic is managing subscriptions. You can also copy reports from one server to another and then schedule the script to run when network traffic is low. By using scripts, the security configuration can be updated on a remote machine, or the settings of a single report can be copied to multiple reports on a server — or across a server farm.

Reporting Services provides a WMI interface to the configuration files for the Report Server instance and the Report Manager application. Much like the command-line utilities, these classes provide a way to programmatically perform application management. For example, you can change the credential values and authentication mechanisms that the Report Server uses to connect to the database. The same classes can be used to perform actions on remote machines.

As you may know, the configuration files are XML files. The next time the application runs, the .NET Common Language Runtime (CLR) will apply the new values in the configuration file. The Report Server configuration file is programmatically accessed through the `MSReportServer_ConfigurationSetting` class, and the Report Manager Interface web application configuration file is available through the `MSReportServerReportManager_ConfigurationSetting` class. Both classes are accessed through the WMI interface.

Script files can be created using a text editor, Visual Studio, or SQL Server Management Studio. The file that contains the automation code is a Unicode or UTF-8 text file with a `.rss` file extension. The code itself is written in VB. We'll cover automatically generated scripts at the end of this chapter; in the meantime, let's look at how to build your own.

Using the RS WMI Provider

Invoking the RS utility is as simple as typing `rs` or `rs.exe` at the command prompt and supplying the required values. The two required values are the script to run (`/i` argument) and the server to run the script against (`/s` argument).

The syntax for using the RS utility is:

```
rs /i <inputFile> /s <serverURL> [/u <username>] [/p <password>] [/l <timeout>]
[/b] [/v <var=value>] [/t]
```

The arguments (parameters) can be indicated by using the / or – symbols. For example, the input file value can be provided using –i or /i and the filename. It's a matter of personal preference and, in some cases, the company style guide. The arguments themselves are case insensitive except for the password value. You can have as many spaces as you want between the argument indicator and the value you're providing.

The script file must be a fully qualified path to the `rss` file. For example, let's say that your scripts are located in the `C:\ReportServer\Scripts` directory. If you navigate to that location in the command window, the path value that you'll provide to the RS utility will be as simple as the filename itself.

The `serverURL` value is made up of the protocol, server, and virtual directory to execute the script. By default, the RS utility will attempt to connect to the resource using `https`. If you specify `http`, the RS utility will only use `http`. If you specify `https` and it's not supported on the server, the RS utility will return an error.

By default, the RS utility will authenticate against the target Report Server instance using the credentials provided by the user running the script. Both the user name and password arguments are optional arguments and can be used to provide different credentials. The script itself can provide credential values through the `rs` object, but hardcoded credentials are a security threat. It's better to have the script authenticate credentials passed by the user at runtime; the user name must include the domain name and user account.

The `timeout` value is an optional argument and is used to specify the number of seconds before the connection to the server times out. The default value is eight seconds. Providing a value of zero means the connection never times out.

If you want your script to run as a batch, you can indicate that by using the optional /b argument. Batches are particularly useful when you need to be sure that the same action is performed on multiple machines; for example, when running a script against multiple machines in a server farm. A batch runs as a type of minitransaction where failure of commands within the script causes the batch to roll back. This argument doesn't take any values. The RS utility default behavior is to run scripts without creating a batch.

Your VB script can also contain variables with user-provided values. These variables are not declared in the script and are available globally to any member within the script. The values are supplied using /v arguments for each variable, which are provided as `name=value` pairs. The following code shows an example:

```
rs /i DeployReports.rss /s http://localhost/reportserver/reportservice.asmx /v
targetURL= http://localhost/reportserver/reportservice.asmx
```

The quotation marks around the value are optional unless the value contains spaces. The /v argument is optional unless your script uses a variable value that's not declared in the script. If the script takes an argument that the user doesn't supply, the script will not compile.

The /t argument is also optional; it turns on tracing to view request processing and capture information about returned errors.

When your script runs, the RS utility creates an instance of the scripting engine to run it. The VB scripting engine uses the same code base as VB, so you have access to standard VB functionality from within your script. You'll take a closer look at the hosting environment capabilities and limitations throughout the rest of this chapter.

Creating a Script Using Code

Although Visual Studio is not required for script execution or development, it's ideal for development because the developer has the support of syntax highlighting, code completion, and *IntelliSense*. The development environment provides sophisticated debugging capabilities, and the file can be managed as part of a Visual Studio 2005 project.

Visual Studio is a robust development tool that's familiar to most .NET developers. Its IntelliSense, code completion, and debugging capabilities help ease the development of `rss` scripts as well. If you plan on creating multiple scripts for the RS utility, it can be helpful to group the individual script projects under a single solution. To do that, simply start with a blank solution and add script projects as needed.

In Visual Studio, select File⇨New⇨Blank Solution from the menu bar. This will open the New Project dialog box.

Name the blank solution rsUtilities, and click OK to create the solution. You now have a container for all your RS utility script projects. To add the first project, right-click the solution in the Solution Explorer and select Add⇨New Project to open another New Project dialog box. This time select Visual Basic Projects in the Project Types pane. You'll see the various prebuilt project templates in the right pane. Choose the Console Application template and give the project an appropriate name, in this case, DeployReports.

Click OK to close the dialog box and add the project to the solution. The `Module1.vb` file will open in the code window. Notice that the file already includes the `Main` method contained in a module called `Module1`. Rename the `Module1.vb` file to `DeployReports.vb` in the Solution Explorer.

Now that the rough framework is in place, let's further define the environment you'll be working in.

Adding Imports Statements

Remember, you only have access to certain namespaces from within the `rss` script. The RS hosting utility provides the namespace access. The script file itself does not contain any `Imports` statements. The console application template includes several `Imports` statements already, and you'll need to modify those to suit the project.

To do this, right-click the DeployReports project in the Solution Explorer and select Properties. That will bring up the DeployReports Property Pages box. In the Common Properties folder in the left pane, click the Imports group. Notice that in the Project imports box, five namespaces are already listed:

❑ Microsoft.VisualBasic

❑ System

❑ System.Collections

❑ System.Data

❑ System.Diagnostics

Select and remove all but the System and System.Diagnostics namespaces. The System.Diagnostics namespace is included for debugging purposes. Then, add System.IO, System.Web.Services, and System.Xml. Your new imports list will include:

❑ System

❑ System.Diagnostics

❑ System.IO

❑ System.Web.Services

❑ System.Xml

Adding the Web Reference

Now you'll need to modify the assembly references for the project. First, remove the references that are not needed. In the Solution Explorer, open the References folder to view the current assembly references. Remove the System.Data reference by right clicking it and selecting Remove from the context menu. Then right-click the References folder, and select Add Reference.

In the Add Reference dialog box, ensure that you're viewing the .NET tab. Select the System.Web .Services.dll assembly by clicking the component name, and then click the Select button. That will add the component to the list of Selected Components in the bottom list box. Click OK to add the reference to your project.

For development, you'll also need to reference the Reporting Services Web service. To do that, right-click the References folder in the Solution Explorer and select Add Web Reference to bring up the Add Web Reference dialog box. This form contains a browser pane, an address bar, and a couple of other items. In the address bar, type the URL of the Report Server you want to code against. The default URL is http<s>://<servername>/reportserver/reportservice.asmx.

If you've pointed at a valid Web service, the Add Reference button will be enabled. Before you click it, however, give the web reference a name; in this case, the reference is called ReportServer.

Clicking the Add Reference button invokes the wsdl.exe utility. The wsdl.exe checks the WSDL document for the Web service and creates a proxy class that acts as your local interface to the remote Web service. You're creating a Web service proxy in the same way that the RS utility creates it for your hosted script. Now you can code against that Web service as if it were a local object because in proxy form, it is a local object.

A Sample Deployment Script

Here's an example of a script used to migrate content from one environment to another. It works against the RS utility described earlier, and is structured to work in that environment. You'll need to wrap this code in a console application for it to run in Visual Studio 2005.

The Main method is the entry point into the application, and is where the bulk of the work is done. Three helper subs are called from Main(). The credentials for the current user are passed to the utility to provide a security context. Variables are also set up to hold destination values for the source data and target. The target folder is then created.

```
Sub Main()
    rs.Credentials = System.Net.CredentialCache.DefaultCredentials

    Dim dataSourceName As String = "reportsdb"
    Dim folderName As String = "Company Reports"
    Dim folderPath As String = "/" & folderName

    'create the folder "Company Reports"
    Try
        rs.CreateFolder(folderName, "/", Nothing)
        Console.WriteLine("Company Reports folder created.")
```

Both the reports and the data source are being deployed in this script. Here, the data source is created in the new folder.

```
'add the datasource "reportsdb" to the "Company Reports" folder
        Dim csrdb As New DataSourceDefinition
        csrdb.ConnectString = "Initial Catalog=reportsdb;Data Source=localhost"
        csrdb.Extension = "SQL"
        csrdb.CredentialRetrieval = CredentialRetrievalEnum.Integrated

        rs.CreateDataSource(dataSourceName, folderPath, True, csrdb, Nothing)

        Console.WriteLine("reportsdb data source created.")
    Catch ex As System.Exception
    End Try
```

Now the code goes to the source folder and loops through each `rdl` file and deploys it.

```
        'upload the rdl files
        Dim files() As String
        files = Directory.GetFiles _
(Directory.GetCurrentDirectory() & "\Catalog Items")
        Dim len As Integer = files.Length - 1
        Dim i As Integer

        'loop through each file.
        For i = 0 To len
            'load the file into a byte array
            Dim fs As FileStream = File.Open(files(i), FileMode.Open)

            Dim data(fs.Length - 1) As Byte
            fs.Read(data, 0, fs.Length)

            'retrieve the report name
            Dim itemName As String = GetShortFileName(files(i))
            Dim extension As String = GetExtension(files(i))

            If extension = "rdl" Then
                'create the report
                rs.CreateReport(itemName, folderPath, True, data, Nothing)
            Else
                Dim mimeType = GetMimetype(files(i))
                rs.CreateResource _
(itemName, folderPath, True, data, mimeType, Nothing)
            End If
            Console.WriteLine(itemName & " was created in: " & folderPath)

        fs.Close()
        Next
```

Changing the `Data Source` property for multiple deployed reports can be a hassle. Here that task has been added to the script, automating that part of the process as well.

```
        'set the datasources to "reportsdb"
        Dim reference As New DataSourceReference
        reference.Reference = folderPath & "/" & dataSourceName

        Dim items As CatalogItem() = rs.ListChildren(folderPath, False)
        For Each item As CatalogItem In items
            If item.Type = ItemTypeEnum.Report Then
                Dim dataSources As DataSource() = _
rs.GetReportDataSources(item.Path)
                For Each dataSource As DataSource In dataSources
                    dataSource.Item = reference
                Next
                rs.SetReportDataSources(item.Path, dataSources)
                Console.WriteLine(item.Name & " datasource was updated")
            End If
        Next
    End Sub
```

These are the helper functions that provide string parsing and mime type checking:

```
    Private Function GetShortFileName(ByVal fullFileName As String) As String
        'get the report name
        Dim slashPos As Integer = fullFileName.LastIndexOf("\")
        Dim dotPos As Integer = fullFileName.LastIndexOf(".")
        Dim retVal As String = fullFileName.Substring _
(slashPos + 1, dotPos - slashPos - 1)
        Return retVal
    End Function

    Private Function GetExtension(ByVal fullFileName As String) As String
        Dim retVal As String = fullFileName.Substring _
(fullFileName.LastIndexOf(".") + 1)
        Return retVal
    End Function

    Private Function GetMimetype(ByVal fullFileName As String) As String
        Dim extension As String = GetExtension(fullFileName)
        Dim retVal As String

        Select Case extension
            Case "htm"
                retVal = "text/html"
            Case "html"
                retVal = "text/html"
            Case "xml"
                retVal = "text/xml"
            Case "csv"
                retVal = "text/plain"
            Case "tif"
                retVal = "image/tif"
            Case "tiff"
                retVal = "image/tif"
```

```
        Case "gif"
            retVal = "image/gif"
        Case "bmp"
            retVal = "image/bmp"
        Case "jpg"
            retVal = "image/jpeg"
        Case "jpeg"
            retVal = "image/jpeg"
        End Select

        Return retVal
    End Function
```

Generating Scripts

SQL Server Management Studio is a handy source for procedures and snippets of code to use in your own scripts. Many actions can be saved as script. The scripts are complete enough to run on their own, and run against the same RS utility. To capture a script, simply perform an action in SQL Server Management Studio and then find the Script button. Figure 10-25 shows an example of changing a schedule.

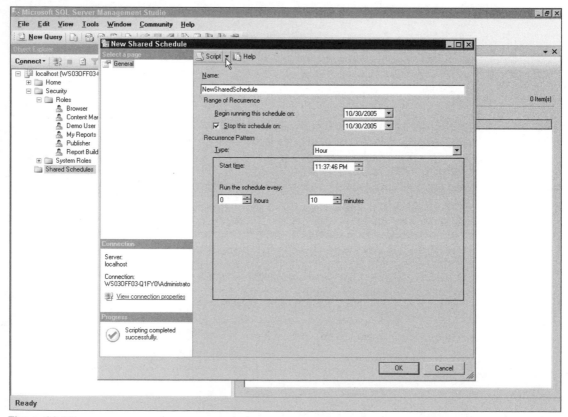

Figure 10-25

The output for the script, chosen from the Script drop-down menu in that screen shot, was sent to the Clipboard. This is the script that was created:

```
Public Overridable Sub Main()
    CreateSchedule
End Sub

Private Sub CreateSchedule()

    Dim Name As String = "NewSharedSchedule"
    Dim ScheduleDefinition As _
Microsoft.SqlServer.ReportingServices2005.ScheduleDefinition = New _
Microsoft.SqlServer.ReportingServices2005.ScheduleDefinition
    ScheduleDefinition.StartDateTime = New Date
    ScheduleDefinition.EndDate = New Date
    ScheduleDefinition.EndDateSpecified = true
    Dim Item As Microsoft.SqlServer.ReportingServices2005.MinuteRecurrence = New _
Microsoft.SqlServer.ReportingServices2005.MinuteRecurrence
    Item.MinutesInterval = 10
    ScheduleDefinition.Item = Item

    RS.CreateSchedule(Name, ScheduleDefinition)
End Sub
```

It seems like nearly anything can be picked up as a script. If you're inclined, play around in the Management Studio to see what handy snippets you can come across. It's definitely worth stopping there to jump-start your own script for that next repetitive task.

Summary

Content managers can have a significant effect on the report end user experience. Whether it's performing tasks such as configuring users and implementing security policies or configuring global settings, managing reports and other Report Server content can involve many more skills than simply uploading new reports to the server.

In this chapter, you read about the four types of Report Server content: reports, folders, data sources, and other resources. Those items are secured using item-level security. Global system settings are considered system-level security.

The two types of data sources are private and shared. Private data sources are embedded within a report RDL file, whereas shared data sources are external to a report. Schedules can also be private or shared and are run by the SQL Server Agent. Shared schedules and data sources provide single points of management for all reports that use them. Use private schedules and data sources on an as-needed basis.

It's important to understand the report execution process to get the most from your servers and provide the best user experience. Caching, snapshots, linked reports, and subscriptions are tools you can use to manage the report execution process.

Some key points to take away include:

❑ Consider your security policy when deciding on the structure of your Report Server content. Keep in mind that nested folders inherit their parent security settings.

❑ Exercise care when creating new user roles. Keep things simple, and provide users with the least permissions they need to perform their tasks.

❑ Work with caching to reduce server loads and improve the user experience. Whenever possible, render reports from cached instances. Linked reports can provide narrowed views of the data contained in a base report.

❑ Use scripting to automate repetitive tasks such as migrating content and configuring server farms.

You should now have a good understanding of how to work with the content in the Report Server. But what about the bigger picture, like deployment scenarios? The next chapter takes a closer look at the tools and techniques used to administer a Reporting Services installation.

11

Report Server
Administration

This chapter is for people who need to install Reporting Services and manage the instances that are in production. This frequently includes staff from different IT departments such as the web, database, and operations sides of the house. One reason for that is the nature of reporting services applications themselves — part web application, part database application, and part Windows application.

For example, let's say you're the IT manager for your company. Your responsibilities include administrating the reporting system. A group of reports has been developed for the management meetings that take place at the beginning of each month. As historical data and the number of users increases, the early-in-the-month load has begun to slow the server down noticeably. Some managers have asked if there's anything that can be done to speed up report processing during that period. In this case, you might take advantage of the report server's ability to create and store snapshots of reports to decrease server load and the time it takes to render reports.

Another typical requirement in this scenario is for the new reports to be accessible only by the department managers. In this case, you might take advantage of the role-based security model used by Reporting Services. First, create a Windows group called Department Managers and add the department managers to it. Then, back in Report Manager, grant that group read access to the report folder while preventing access by all others.

A common Reporting Services scenario is the use of SharePoint as a reporting portal. Less common is exposing Reporting Services reports to external users through a custom web application. You'll take a look at considerations for outward-facing reporting requirements later in this chapter. In addition, this chapter covers:

❑   Deployment scenarios for Reporting Services.

❑   The configuration tools and utilities provided.

Chapter 11

❑   Backup and restore procedures.

❑   Monitoring a Reporting Services instance for best performance.

Your exploration of report server administration begins with a look at the server components and requirements. Then I'll address different deployment environments and configuration. Once the environment is in place, you'll read about backup and restore procedures. The chapter rounds out with approaches to server monitoring and strategies to increase server performance.

Deploying Reporting Services

There are a number of different types of Reporting Services deployments. The two most common scenarios are single box installation and multiple box deployments.

❑   Installing pretty much everything on a single machine. For smaller organizations and some development environments, this configuration works great. The machine has IIS and a SQL Server instance both running locally. For production use, Reporting Services Standard Edition provides support for most users in this category. One exception to note, however, is that data-driven subscriptions are not supported in the Standard Edition. Data-driven subscriptions allow you to broadcast reports to users listed in a database table. For developers, Reporting Services Developer Edition provides all the capabilities of the Enterprise Edition but isn't suitable for production machines.

❑   Installing the Report Server on one machine and the Report Server database on another. This type of installation is common. For example, let's say you already have an existing reporting infrastructure and want to begin using Reporting Services. In that case, you would run the Reporting Services setup as usual—but point the installation to your existing SQL Server data store. Later on, you may need to point the Report Server instance to another database. This type of installation can also have significant impact on Report Server performance. You'll read much more about that later in this chapter.

Other common types of installations include adding another Reporting Services instance to a web farm cluster and performing installations using the command line or script. You'll read more about all of these in this chapter as well.

When installing Reporting Services, setup allows you to:

❑   Create a new server instance. During a new install, you provide input values that are written into the Report Server configuration files for retrieval later. Registry keys are added, virtual directories are created in IIS, new databases are created, and data is encrypted and stored.

❑   Change an existing installation. This will allow you to remove individual components from or add them to an existing report server instance. If any or all of the components you specify are already installed, they'll be uninstalled and then reinstalled.

❑   Remove the server components. This will remove all the report server components and machine changes from the computer, except for files that contain user data. It's important to remember that the Report Server database and log files remain after running uninstall.

Before I talk about what those deployment configurations look like, let's look at what kinds of bits are getting deployed.

Reporting Services Components

Reporting Services is a Web service application that exposes functionality through a number of programmatic interfaces. Because it's a Web service, it runs as an ASP.NET web application hosted by IIS. Reporting Services also includes Windows services components to help with report scheduling and delivery.

Installed components include tools you can use to manage a Report Server instance right out of the box. However, because of the programming interfaces provided, you can replace the stock tools with custom applications that work better for you. You can create applications to view, design, and manage reports by working against the provided APIs. Create new data-bound controls to add impact and functionality to reports. Build a new processing extension to render reports in Rich text. There are many ways to take advantage of the open architecture Microsoft has provided in the product, and several are demonstrated in this book.

At a high level, Reporting Services can be viewed as three main components: the Report Server, the Report Server database, and the client tools. Figure 11-1 shows the relationship between these major components.

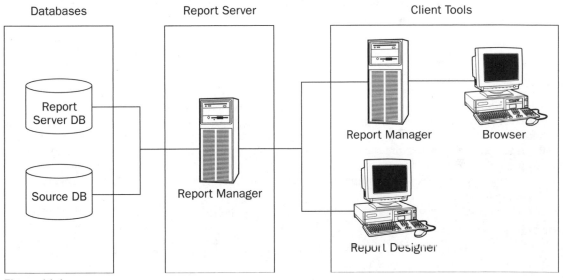

Figure 11-1

To get a better handle on the tools that are provided, let's look at the main server components that they work against.

Server Components

In addition to these, Books Online for Reporting Services is installed. Those are your local help files. Remember that help is also available on the Microsoft Developer Network (MSDN) site; you'll just need to dig a bit more for the information you're looking for. A helpful site for keeping track of Knowledge Base articles and other Microsoft support info on a particular technology is KBAlertz.com. The automated e-mail notifications of new content posted on Microsoft's web site can be helpful even if you have an MSDN subscription.

The three main components of Reporting Services are distributed across a server layer, client layer, and data layer. The Report Server core elements make up the server, the database catalog is contained in the database layer, and various developer and management applications compose the client layer.

Report Server

This is the primary component of Reporting Services and makes up the server layer. The Report Server is a process Web service that oversees the objects and subprocesses it takes to respond to the incoming calls to its exposed web method interfaces.

Those incoming calls are typically in the form of Simple Object Access Protocol (SOAP) or URL (`http://`) requests. Processing a report can include security checks, query execution, expression evaluation, and final report generation. The interface exposed by the Web service includes methods used to implement security policies, as well as manage database and cache content.

The Report Server itself is made up of discreet components. The processing of a report can make use of data processing, security, rendering, and other extensions to the core processing engine.

The Report Server is composed of two services, which are used to handle different aspects of report processing. These are the Web service and the Windows service.

The ASP.NET Web service is responsible for report processing. It handles incoming requests to its Web Service API and manages those sessions. The processing of a request can include executing, processing, and rendering a report.

The Windows service handles the scheduling and delivery of reports. It triggers scheduled report runs, including subscriptions and snapshots. The delivery of reports using e-mail or file share is also handled here. You can extend the delivery options by creating your own components that work with the exposed interfaces and plug them into the existing architecture.

Extending Reporting Services components is covered in Chapter 13. For now, take a look at the Report Server Catalog.

Reporting Services Catalog

The catalog serves as the data layer in Reporting Services. Two SQL Server databases form the catalog: ReportServer and ReportServerTempDB.

❑   **ReportServer:** The ReportServer database is where information about the reports is stored. That includes report definitions, report metadata, data source definitions, snapshots, and history. This is also where security settings like users, policies, and roles are kept. Account information, scheduling, and delivery settings are also kept here. Some of these values are encrypted before being written to the database. This database is vital to the operation of your report server and should be included in your regular database backup procedures. Always back up this database.

The data here is not directly accessible. You get access to the database content through the various Reporting Services programmatic interfaces, to enforce rules on the data. A number of utilities are included with Reporting Services to help with the management of the ReportServer content, and we'll cover those throughout the rest of this chapter.

❑ **ReportServerTempDB:** As its name implies, the ReportServerTempDB database is where more temporary information is stored. Short-life-span data includes information to manage user sessions and cached report data.

This database differs from the ReportServer database. If the ReportServerTempDB database is lost, the Report Server will automatically rebuild it. The data in the previous instance is lost, but it was only temporary anyway. Depending on how heavily you rely on caching, for example, you may see slower response times from the server until the cache is rebuilt.

Client Applications

Client applications access the server via the SOAP and URL requests. The Report Manager application that comes standard with Reporting Services is one example. Many third-party software vendors also offer their own client applications for creating and working with reports. These apps work against the same Report Server API as the intrinsic tools do. Let's take a look at the client tools included with Reporting Services.

Client Components

A variety of client applications are included with Reporting Services. Third-party applications are also available to suit specific uses. These client apps include the Report Designer, Report Builder, SQL Server Management Studio, and the Reporting Services Configuration Manager.

❑ **Report designer:** Report designer is the authoring tool that's integrated with Visual Studio 2005. Visual Studio must already be installed on the machine for the report designer to install. The report project file extension (.rptproj) is also registered with the operating system to open the report designer in Visual Studio by default. From Visual Studio, reporting projects can be managed in Visual Source Safe to provide version and access control.

❑ **Web browser:** On the client, a web browser is commonly used to view and manage reports. When running reports, DHTML is the default rendering format, so viewing them in a web browser like Internet Explorer 6 or better is a natural. Since Report Manager is an ASP.NET web application, managing report server content and viewing rendered reports can both be done using the same web browser. Report Manager, if you'll recall, is the tool included with Reporting Services to help manage content in the report server database. It's discussed in detail in Chapter 10.

❑ **Report Builder:** This tool allows a developer to create report models, from which users can create their own reports. The Report Builder is covered in Part III.

❑ **SQL Server Management Studio:** SQL Server Management Studio is a new "one-stop" shop for a variety of SQL Server management tasks. Opening the application brings up the Connect to Server dialog box, where you can select the Reporting Services server to work with.

Once the Management Studio is open, you have access to all the normal tasks needed to manage the Report Server content, just as in the Report Manager web application. From this interface, you can create and modify schedules and perform other typical Report Server management tasks. Figure 11-2 shows an example of modifying the Data Source properties of a report in SQL Server Management Studio.

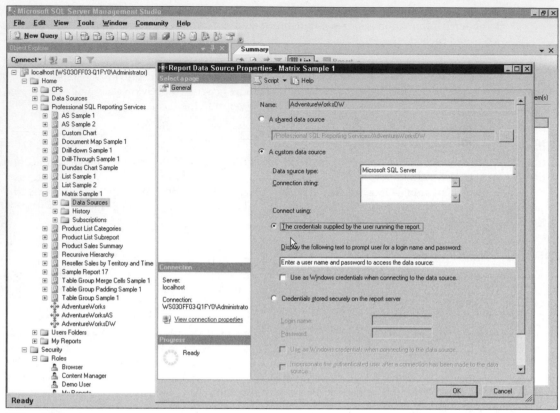

Figure 11-2

You can also modify security settings and role permissions, as shown in Figure 11-3.

The client tools included with Reporting Services provide all the functionality you need to manage a basic Reporting Services installation. However, they aren't your only options. These tools work against open application programming interfaces that you can use yourself. If needed, you can create a client component that's a better fit for your particular requirements. Extending the capabilities of Reporting Services isn't limited to the server components.

The Report Server Configuration Manager is a client tool specifically for working with the many configuration settings available. The Configuration Manager is covered in the "Configuration Tools" section of this chapter.

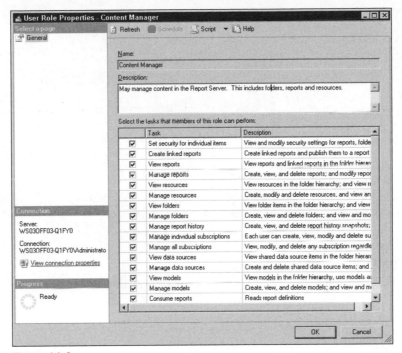

Figure 11-3

The Report Server

The purpose of this chapter isn't to recite the requirements info readily available from Microsoft but to give you an understanding of what's going on before you get there. In general, most managers of business and enterprise environments are already pretty well set for hardware or are aware of holes in their existing infrastructure. If in doubt about your particular needs, contact a Microsoft rep or regional office to help sort things out. To install, the Reporting Services installation process needs to be pointed to a licensed instance of SQL Server.

❑ **Computer processor:** PC with an Intel or compatible Pentium II 500 MHz or higher processor. At the time of this writing, our development boxes run 1.8-GHz Pentiums. For production boxes, dual processors will give you a big bang for the performance buck. Reporting Services supports quad processor boxes for intensive applications. If you're running quad-proc boxes, be sure to ask Microsoft about Reporting Services tweaks you may want to make in order to get the most from your server. Running Reporting Services on a multiple-processor machine will mean that SQL Server is also running on that box. Depending on your licensing agreement, additional processors may also require additional SQL Server licenses.

❑ **RAM:** Forget what it says on the box; you'll want 512 MB minimum. Personally, I've got 1.5 gig running on my development machines and 2 gigs on single-processor production boxes. It's hard to go wrong by adding more RAM.

❑ **Hard disk space (by component):**

❑ Report Server and Report Manager applications: 50 MB

❑ Microsoft .NET Framework: 100 MB

❑ Samples, AdventureWorks database, and Books Online: 145 MB

Requirements numbers can vary quite a bit from installation to installation, depending on how you intend to use the service. If you're doing a web farm installation for a heavily used portal, for example, expect your hardware requirements to go up quickly. If you're unfamiliar with enterprise reporting installations, it may be helpful to enlist some help from Microsoft or other knowledgeable resource to be sure you're getting the most out of your investment.

Another useful tool is Microsoft's Baseline Security Analyzer. It can check the security level of your network servers and client machines and is especially handy if you wear multiple hats such as both developer and server administrator.

Installation Directory

The default installation directory for Reporting Services components is one level below the default location of SQL Server:

```
C:\Program Files\Microsoft SQL Server\MSSQL\Reporting Services
```

By default, the Report Server is installed one level below that, in the \ReportServer directory. That folder contains a subdirectory, \bin, where the executables and assemblies are located. You can change the installation path of the Report Server during setup. Best practice is to use a Secure Socket Layer (SSL) certificate to create a secure SSL connection across the gap between the reporting service server and client application.

Service Credentials

At one point during setup, you'll need to provide the credentials used by the Report Server. The user name and password are used as credentials for the service as it performs tasks and connects to the Report Server database. You can choose to have the Report Server use a systems account as well. If values are not provided, then Reporting Services defaults to these settings in the following table.

Operating System	Service Account
Windows XP and 2000	Local System
Windows Server 2003	Network Service

IIS Virtual Directory

A virtual directory is created in Internet Information Services (IIS 5 or greater) to receive incoming HTTP requests. IIS routes the incoming request to the Report Server, which then processes the data contained in the body of the request. Once the request has been processed, a response can be sent back to the client application. The outgoing response is also handled by IIS. The default virtual directory for the Report Server Web service is:

```
http://<server_name>/reportserver
```

Navigating to the `asmx` file in that directory brings you to the Web service itself: `http://<server_name>/reportserver/reportservice.asmx`.

Chapter 12 covers working with the Web service in depth.

Remember that Report Manager, the report management and viewing tool, is a separate application from the Report Server. It also has its own virtual directory in IIS, located at:

```
http://<server_name>/reports
```

Navigating to that address will bring up the Home page in Report Manager. Anytime you want easy access to information about virtual directories and IIS in general, trip over to IIS help by pointing your browser to:

```
http://<server_name>/iishelp
```

There's a lot more you can do with URLs and URL addressing. We'll discuss those in depth in the next chapter. In the meantime, let's cover a critical area for Reporting Services and IIS: securing client communication with the report server.

During installation of Reporting Services, setup provides an option to Use SSL connections when retrieving data on these virtual directories. For most installations, this option should be selected. While most every component of the Reporting Services process has layers of security protecting it, the communication between the client application and the Report Server Web service remains open and vulnerable to attack. An effective strategy to use against this type of threat is to use SSL.

SSL secures the data during transmission by encrypting it. Although there's a small performance hit, the benefit is peace of mind. Even if the transmission is snagged and read, the contents remain secure. To enable SSL on your IIS instance, you install an SSL Certificate.

There are two types of SSL Certificates: Those that are obtained from another authority, and those that you declare for yourself. Subordinate Certificates are signed by a "trusted' certificate authority. You purchase the certificate and install it on your web server. Client browsers will recognize the named certificate authority and display the lock symbol in the status bar.

Declaring yourself as a Root Certificate Authority gives you the ability to create SSL connections without conferring with a higher authority. It's a simple process to install a certificate this way. The drawback is that client browsers won't trust your certificate and will display a warning to the user each time they visit the site—unless extra security settings are made in each client browser. For more on setting up SSL Certificates, see `msdn.microsoft.com`.

IIS virtual directories can be created and managed in the Reporting Services Configuration Manager, which is discussed later in this chapter. In the meantime, let's briefly look at log files and delivery settings.

Log files

During the setup process, the Report Server creates a folder for log files. It's located one level below the Reporting Services install directory, in the following:

```
C:\Program Files\Microsoft SQL Server\MSSQL.3\Reporting Services\LogFiles
```

Like a typical log file, each contains information about Report Server events, warnings, and errors. There's a separate trace log file that's created for each day. The log file contains all the entries for that day, beginning at midnight. The local time of the computer is used to determine when midnight is and is also used to name the file. It's good to know that Reporting Services doesn't remove any previously generated log files, but that can also be a problem as disk space gets used up. Figure 11-4 shows a typical Report Server log file.

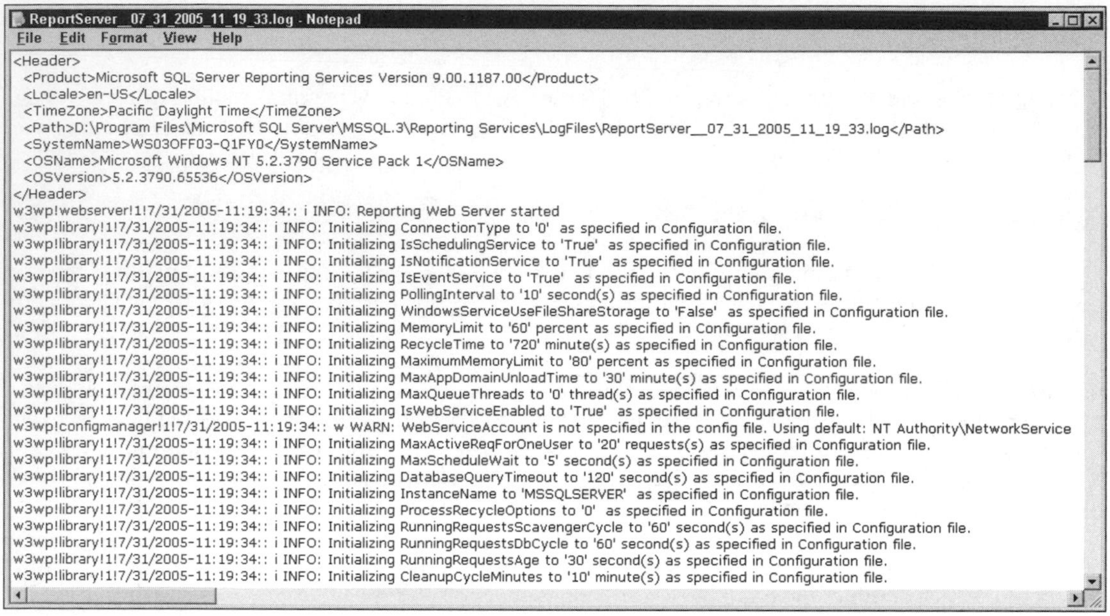

ReportServer__07_31_2005_11_19_33.log - Notepad

File Edit Format View Help

```
<Header>
  <Product>Microsoft SQL Server Reporting Services Version 9.00.1187.00</Product>
  <Locale>en-US</Locale>
  <TimeZone>Pacific Daylight Time</TimeZone>
  <Path>D:\Program Files\Microsoft SQL Server\MSSQL.3\Reporting Services\LogFiles\ReportServer__07_31_2005_11_19_33.log</Path>
  <SystemName>WS03OFF03-Q1FY0</SystemName>
  <OSName>Microsoft Windows NT 5.2.3790 Service Pack 1</OSName>
  <OSVersion>5.2.3790.65536</OSVersion>
</Header>
w3wp!webserver!1!7/31/2005-11:19:34:: i INFO: Reporting Web Server started
w3wp!library!1!7/31/2005-11:19:34:: i INFO: Initializing ConnectionType to '0'  as specified in Configuration file.
w3wp!library!1!7/31/2005-11:19:34:: i INFO: Initializing IsSchedulingService to 'True'  as specified in Configuration file.
w3wp!library!1!7/31/2005-11:19:34:: i INFO: Initializing IsNotificationService to 'True'  as specified in Configuration file.
w3wp!library!1!7/31/2005-11:19:34:: i INFO: Initializing IsEventService to 'True'  as specified in Configuration file.
w3wp!library!1!7/31/2005-11:19:34:: i INFO: Initializing PollingInterval to '10' second(s) as specified in Configuration file.
w3wp!library!1!7/31/2005-11:19:34:: i INFO: Initializing WindowsServiceUseFileShareStorage to 'False'  as specified in Configuration file.
w3wp!library!1!7/31/2005-11:19:34:: i INFO: Initializing MemoryLimit to '60' percent as specified in Configuration file.
w3wp!library!1!7/31/2005-11:19:34:: i INFO: Initializing RecycleTime to '720' minute(s) as specified in Configuration file.
w3wp!library!1!7/31/2005-11:19:34:: i INFO: Initializing MaximumMemoryLimit to '80' percent as specified in Configuration file.
w3wp!library!1!7/31/2005-11:19:34:: i INFO: Initializing MaxAppDomainUnloadTime to '30' minute(s) as specified in Configuration file.
w3wp!library!1!7/31/2005-11:19:34:: i INFO: Initializing MaxQueueThreads to '0' thread(s) as specified in Configuration file.
w3wp!library!1!7/31/2005-11:19:34:: i INFO: Initializing IsWebServiceEnabled to 'True'  as specified in Configuration file.
w3wp!configmanager!1!7/31/2005-11:19:34:: w WARN: WebServiceAccount is not specified in the config file. Using default: NT Authority\NetworkService
w3wp!library!1!7/31/2005-11:19:34:: i INFO: Initializing MaxActiveReqForOneUser to '20' requests(s) as specified in Configuration file.
w3wp!library!1!7/31/2005-11:19:34:: i INFO: Initializing MaxScheduleWait to '5' second(s) as specified in Configuration file.
w3wp!library!1!7/31/2005-11:19:34:: i INFO: Initializing DatabaseQueryTimeout to '120' second(s) as specified in Configuration file.
w3wp!library!1!7/31/2005-11:19:34:: i INFO: Initializing InstanceName to 'MSSQLSERVER'  as specified in Configuration file.
w3wp!library!1!7/31/2005-11:19:34:: i INFO: Initializing ProcessRecycleOptions to '0'  as specified in Configuration file.
w3wp!library!1!7/31/2005-11:19:34:: i INFO: Initializing RunningRequestsScavengerCycle to '60' second(s) as specified in Configuration file.
w3wp!library!1!7/31/2005-11:19:34:: i INFO: Initializing RunningRequestsDbCycle to '60' second(s) as specified in Configuration file.
w3wp!library!1!7/31/2005-11:19:34:: i INFO: Initializing RunningRequestsAge to '30' second(s) as specified in Configuration file.
w3wp!library!1!7/31/2005-11:19:34:: i INFO: Initializing CleanupCycleMinutes to '10' minute(s) as specified in Configuration file.
```

Figure 11-4

From the developer perspective, you can get a lot of troubleshooting information from a combination of the log files and the stack trace. If you're a local administrator and are running Internet Explorer on the server, stack trace info is available by right-clicking the error page in the browser window and selecting View Source.

You can also tweak how log entries are made and kept. Changing those settings can have an effect on how your server behaves. You'll read about what settings to change and how to set them later in this chapter, in the section "Exploring the Execution Log."

Delivery Settings

Reporting Services includes a delivery extension so reports can be distributed by e-mail. The delivery settings include a Simple Mail Transfer Protocol (SMTP) server address and an e-mail address for the From: field. This typically occurs when a subscription has been created and the user requests e-mail delivery. The e-mail itself can contain the actual report in static HTML or can contain a link to the report in Report Manager.

The delivery setting must be the valid hostname of an SMTP server. If you're using Microsoft Exchange, use the name of the SMTP gateway; don't use the name of the Exchange server here or you'll get errors during subscription processing. Use an IP address like 192.168.0.1 or other DNS-resolvable name. Remember to include the domain name if necessary.

Server Configurations

There are two basic types of Reporting Services server configurations: Local Catalog and Remote Catalog. The difference between them is where the Report Server database is located. A variation of the remote catalog is distributed deployment. Since these are by far the most common types of Reporting Services environments, let's take a closer look at them.

Local Catalog

This is the simplest configuration for a Reporting Services deployment. In this environment, the Reporting Services databases are installed on the same server as Reporting Services. That is to say, SQL Server and IIS are both running on the same box. Figure 11-5 shows a diagram of this type of deployment.

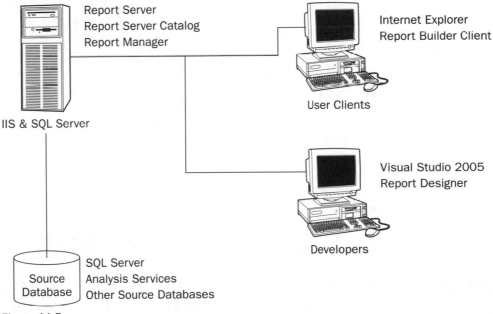

Report Server
Report Server Catalog
Report Manager

IIS & SQL Server

Internet Explorer
Report Builder Client

User Clients

Visual Studio 2005
Report Designer

Developers

Source Database

SQL Server
Analysis Services
Other Source Databases

Figure 11-5

In this example, the source data — that is, the data displayed in the report — is on a separate machine from the report server. The source data can be on SQL Server 2005 or any other data source that you can connect with and get a result set returned to then work with in Reporting Services. The Report Server instance and the Report Server Catalog live on the same server, which has both IIS and SQL Server running on it. The client machines connect to the single report server to upload, view, and manage reports. This type of deployment works best for light server loads.

Remote Catalog

In this configuration, the Report Server Catalog has been broken out onto its own machine. The Catalog, you may recall, is comprised of both the ReportServer and ReportServerTempDB databases. Moving the Report Server Catalog off of the machine hosting the report server instance greatly improves report server performance. It can handle more client requests more quickly this way. Figure 11-6 shows an example environment.

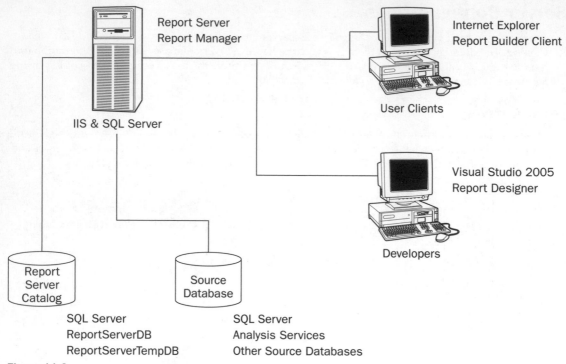

IIS & SQL Server

Report Server
Report Manager

Internet Explorer
Report Builder Client

User Clients

Visual Studio 2005
Report Designer

Developers

Report
Server
Catalog

SQL Server
ReportServerDB
ReportServerTempDB

Source
Database

SQL Server
Analysis Services
Other Source Databases

Figure 11-6

Just moving the Report Server Catalog off the machine that has Reporting Services installed will net you a noticeable increase in performance. The Report Server Catalog and the source database can be on the same database server, separate from the machine that IIS is running on.

Web Farm Deployment

Reporting Services is an ASP.NET web-based application. For a long time, customers have been scaling such web-based applications using scale-out. A few reasons scale-out has proven to be popular is that it:

❑ Enables customers to incrementally add (or remove) capacity as needed.

❑ Offers a very affordable, manageable, and flexible way to add/remove that capacity.

❑ Allows heavy workloads to be balanced across multiple commodity servers.

❑ Inherently offers a certain degree of fault tolerance.

Customer input drives the features and capabilities that Microsoft designs into products and Reporting Services is no exception. Reporting Services was built with the knowledge that most people would decide to deploy it across a multiple servers. As a result, Reporting Services scales very well in a web farm configuration. Deploying Reporting Services to an environment that includes clustered IIS and SQL Servers allows your report servers to handle all but the most extreme request load. Figure 11-7 shows an example configuration.

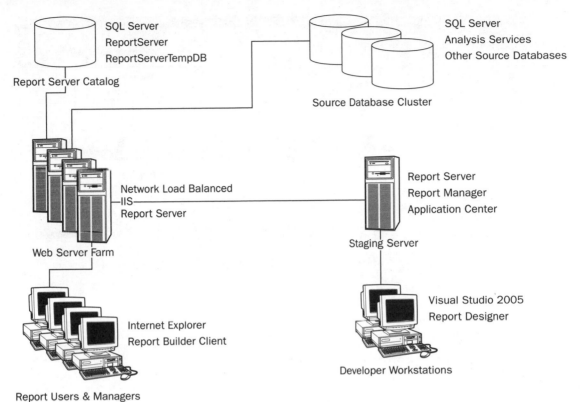

Figure 11-7

Once each of the report server instances has been created, they'll each have to be initialized in order to participate in the web farm. Initialization is done using the RSConfigTool. Figure 11-8 shows the Initialization page and that one server is currently initialized.

In a Reporting Services web farm, coordination between each of the Report Server instances is done by having them access a single Reporting Services catalog. A great way to scale out your Reporting Services implementation is to use a dedicated SQL Server instance to host the report server databases. Taking it a step further, implementing a web farm with Network Load Balancing in an IIS server cluster can handle very high-response loads. ASP.NET applications in that kind of environment can be tweaked to handle high capacity reliably and securely. If the reports are mission critical, deploy the report server database in a server cluster configured for failover, to reduce the risk of server downtime on the data side.

If you're anticipating a high load on your report server, as is covered in the "Monitoring and Performance" section later in this chapter, the report server delivers good performance returns on two- and four-processor machines. Because of that, consider using fast dual- or quad-processor machines to host the report server components. If you still need more capacity, increase the amount of RAM on the report server. High server loads will also increase the use of the Report Server databases, so keep an eye on your database server hard drive capacities as well.

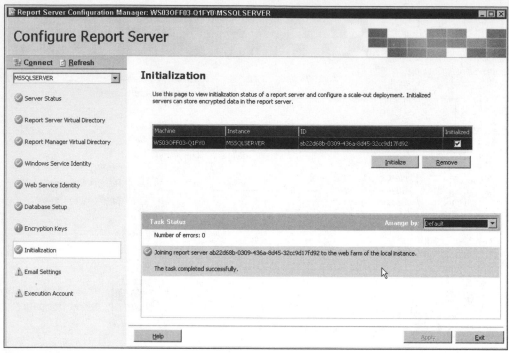

Figure 11-8

Command-Line Installation

Installing Reporting Services can also be done from the command line. This technique is especially useful when performing multiple installs, as in a web farm deployment. Using scripts, the deployment process can be automated. This allows the installations to run unattended and with identical settings used for each report server instance.

To run setup.exe from the command line, first navigate to the location of the executable file on the file system. Then, use the switches to indicate which components to install. To get a summary of the switches available, invoke help by adding the /? switch at the command prompt. Use switches to supply the required installation parameters as well. Be sure to provide values for all required properties or the install will fail. If the components you specify are already installed, they'll be uninstalled and then reinstalled. Note that in order to perform an unattended installation, /qn must be specified, or else the regular installation GUI will be displayed.

Configuration Tools

To configure settings in Reporting Services means working in a variety of environments, such as XML and database files. Like many of the applications that run on the .NET Framework, Reporting Services makes extensive use of XML. Other settings are kept encrypted in the ReportServer database. To help make configuring the server an easier task, Microsoft has provided utilities that abstract the details of making configuration changes. Let's take a closer look at working with those configuration files and utilities.

Configuration Utilities

There are basically two ways to tweak configuration file settings using the tools provided by Microsoft. You can use the utilities from the command line or use the Report Server Configuration Manager GUI.

The utilities are console applications that use switches to specify arguments and parameters that you need to pass in. To run them directly, open a command prompt and navigate to where the executable is located. Most of these utilities are located in:

```
C:\Program Files\Microsoft SQL Server\90\Tools\Binn
```

The utilities are:

- ❏   `Rsconfigtool.exe`

- ❏   `Rsconfig.exe`

- ❏   `Rskeymgmt.exe`

- ❏   `Rs.exe`

Each has a specific purpose, which is covered in the next sections.

Reporting Services Configuration Tool

The Reporting Services Configuration Tool is the one to use when configuring Reporting Services installations. It touches most of the components of a Reporting Services instance, including SQL Server and the file system. Many of the operations are performed using the underlying WMI interfaces. You can use the graphical user interface (GUI) version or invoke it using code. Code can be run using the command-line interface or a code file. This tool is the army knife that can handle most of the tasks needed to configure and maintain your report server.

You can launch the tool from the Start menu by running `rsconfigtool.exe` from the command line or from the SQL Server Management Studio. When you first open the tool, a dialog box opens so you can select which report server instance to connect with, as shown in Figure 11-9.

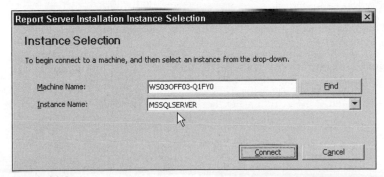

Figure 11-9

The Management Studio is an excellent single point of management for a report server. It provides an easy-to-use interface, as shown in Figure 11-10.

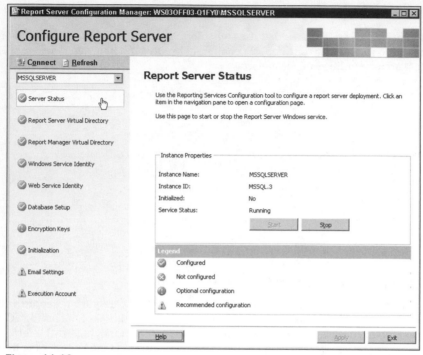

Figure 11-10

It even helps guide you to a level of configuration through the use of icons for each configuration section. The legend for them is:

❑ **Configured:** The settings on this page have values. Does not necessarily mean that the report server works as intended.

❑ **Not Configured:** Values must be provided for settings contained here or you'll have reduced functionality.

❑ **Optional Configuration:** Optional configuration settings, except in the case of backing up the encryption key. That one should be a recommended configuration.

❑ **Recommended Configuration:** Set these up to get the most from your server.

Rsconfig.exe

Credential information that Report Server uses when logging into the catalog database is kept encrypted in the Report Server `RSReportServer.config` file. Because the values are encrypted, you need to use a utility to work with them. For example, let's say you need to go in and reset the credentials used by the report server to connect to the report server database. You can perform that task using the GUI tools or from the command line, using the console application `reconfig.exe`.

The syntax for using the utility is:

```
Rsconfig.exe (-e | -c) [-m machinename][-i instancename][-s servername][-d
databasename][-a authmethod][-u username][-p password][-t]
```

Either the parameter e or c must be supplied; the others are optional. The following table describes each property.

Switch	Parameter	Description
-c	connection	Sets the connection information to the report server database.
-e	executionaccount	Sets the unattended execution account used by the report server when executing reports.
-m	machinename	The UNC path to the machine being configured; localhost is the default.
-i	Instancename	Name of the Reporting Services instance; MSSQLSERVER is the default.
-s	Servername	The name of the SQL Server that the Report Server catalog is on.
-d	databasename	The name of the SQL Server catalog database.
-a	authmethod	Use SQL or Windows authentication.
-u	username	The credential user name; usually either a SQL or Windows user.
-p	password	The credential password; usually either a SQL or Windows password.
-t		The trace switch to include trace information in error messages; for development use only.

Rskeymgmt.exe

Similar to the rsconfig.exe utility, this one also handles encryption duties for data in the report server catalog. Rskeymgmt.exe is used to encrypt and decrypt the encryption key. That key is used, in turn, to encrypt and decrypt the other data in the catalog. By encrypting the encryption key, you're essentially locking the key to the safe in a vault instead of leaving it lying around for someone to potentially pick up and use. The utility help file provides a list of the parameters that can be supplied, along with the syntax to use when performing action such as creating a backup copy of the Report Server encryption key. You can access the help file by typing this at a command prompt:

```
Rskeymgmt.exe /?
```

Rs.exe

This is the host application used to run scripts for managing your report server. Scripts can be used to automate many tasks. The utility is covered in depth in Chapter 10.

Configuration Files

The .NET platform makes extensive use of XML. One of those uses is to hold application configuration settings. These are well-formed XML files, made up of elements and attributes to contain the properties and property values each application uses. If the file is not well formed, the file is considered invalid and the server component won't run. The root element for these files is Configuration. The following table shows the main configuration files for the primary server components.

Server Component	Configuration File	Default Location
Report Server	RSReportServer.config	Files\Microsoft SQL Server\MSSQL\Reporting Services\ReportServer
Report Manager	RSWebApplication.config	Program Files\Microsoft SQL Server\MSSQL\Reporting Services\ReportManager
Report Designer	RSReportDesigner.config	Program Files\Microsoft SQL Server\90\Tools\Report Designer

Although the XML files are just text files and can be modified, it's safer to use the Reporting Services Configuration Tool. That way, you're sure of keeping the file well formed and don't inadvertently risk losing important settings.

Backup and Restore Procedures

The importance of backing up can't be over emphasized. Even for relatively small installations, think of how many hours have been spent configuring the server and building reports. Losing that wouldn't be good, so be safe — back up your data. Disaster recovery is something you want to be ready for, because when the disaster happens (however large or small) it's too late to prepare.

For Reporting Services, you'll need to plan on backing up two items in particular: the catalog and the encryption key. First, you'll read about backing up the Report Server databases. Then, you'll take a look at the role of encryption keys and the process to use when backing them up.

Backing Up the Report Server Catalog

Earlier in this chapter the structure of the Report Server catalog data was covered. It consists of two SQL Server databases, ReportServer and ReportServerTempDB. Typically, you'll use the backup utilities in SQL Server to actually perform the backup. However, only one of the catalog databases needs to be backed up.

You may remember that the ReportServer database is the key data store. Permanent data is persisted there. Report definitions are kept there, along with report snapshots and security information. The ReportServer database is the one database that you don't want to lose.

The ReportServerTempDB database, however, holds short-term data. Browser-specific session data and cached instances are examples of the data it contains. In fact, the Report Server anticipates that it may go down at some point. Once operations are up, the Report Server automatically restores the temporary database.

The thing to know about losing ReportServerTempDB this is that you'll also lose snapshots that were cached. They won't be added to cache again until a user requests the report or the schedule runs again. Users may end up triggering report runs that would normally be rendered from cached snapshots. If that happens, you may see higher server loads until the cache is restored.

If you're not the database administrator for the catalog data, be sure to communicate with whoever that person is. Depending on the backup procedures used by your organization, it may not be wise to assume that the ReportServer database is being backed up each night along with everything else. The DBA may have to manually add the database to the backup routine.

Restoring the ReportServer database is done using the utilities provided with SQL Server. The process is straightforward, using SQL Server Management Studio to restore the database with the backup file.

Backing Up the Encryption Key

There are two types of encryption: symmetric and asymmetric. Reporting Services uses symmetric encryption to protect sensitive data, including credentials. The symmetric encryption process uses a single key value to encrypt and decrypt the data. Several processes in Reporting Services use the key to access and store critical information.

Though the data is secure, it's only as secure as the key. If the key is compromised, the data may also be compromised. To secure the encryption key, it's encrypted using its own utility and kept in the ReportServer database. That utility is rskeymgmt.exe.

It's important to understand why backing up the encryption key is crucial. Connection information, credentials, and server accounts are all stored as encrypted values. Because the key that's used to unlock all that data is itself encrypted, you can't just pull it from the database and use it. If you lose the key, everything that was encrypted using it is also lost. Back up the key and keep it in a safe place.

Back up your encryption key right after installing Reporting Services, and if you haven't done it yet, now's a good time. The rskeymgmt.exe utility is executed from the command line and uses switches to specify input parameters:

❑   -e: The "extract" command, to get the encryption key.

❑   -f: The path and file to write the encryption key to.

❑   -p: The password associated with the key file.

The easiest way to do the backup is with the Reporting Services Configuration Tool, described earlier in this chapter. Remember to back up the key on *all* report servers.

Many common server management tasks are made easier using the graphical Report Server Configuration Manager interface. Clicking the Encryption Keys button in the application provides quick access to the standard encryption key tasks, as shown in Figure 11-11.

Figure 11-11

Clicking the Backup button allows you to enter the password and file location for the backup, as shown in Figure 11-12.

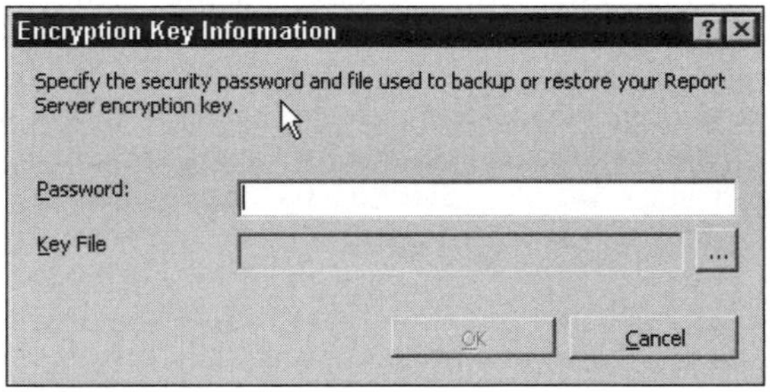

Figure 11-12

Restoring the key is just as easy—just click the Restore button, enter your password, and point it to the backup file. Keep the key file in a safe place. Keep the password safe as well because you need it to restore the key.

Monitoring and Performance

As reports are deployed to the report server and users begin accessing reports more frequently, the load on the report server can cause report processing to slow. This can happen from multiple users requesting reports at a peak load time, such as Monday mornings, or from the resources consumed by large, complex reports. Because Reporting Services is essentially an ASP.NET web application, there are a number of ways to increase server performance. For example, choosing the best deployment scenario can go a long way in helping your server handle higher loads. Additionally, there are a number of techniques particular to Reporting Services that you can employ to get the most from your server. This section looks at ways to leverage those techniques, beginning with a brief review of the report execution process. Then you'll read about the unique capabilities of caching in Reporting Services and look at ways to quantify the performance of your server.

Report Execution

We include a brief overview of the report generation process here to set the stage for the rest of the chapter. Much of what can be done by way of server monitoring and performance management is based on leveraging points in the execution process. For example, there are attributes specific to SQL databases and ASP.NET applications that you can address. To begin this discussion, we'll revisit the topic of report execution. Generally speaking, there are two types of report execution.

User-triggered

The first type of report execution is user-triggered. It's also called on-demand execution and is the report execution process running in response to some user action. Typical user actions include viewing a page in Report Manager or on a SharePoint site or clicking a link in an e-mail. Frequently, the entire report generation process is initiated — from connecting to the database for the rdl file to connecting to the source database for query data and generation of the intermediate report format to finally rendering the report to the user. With this type of on-demand report, report execution is typically performed using the credentials of the person who triggered the report. There's a way to improve performance of user-triggered reports, which you'll explore after looking at timer-triggered reports.

Timer-triggered

The other type of report execution is timer-triggered. With this type of report processing, SQL Server Agent triggers the call to the report server. Report execution is performed using credentials that were previously entered when the schedule was set up. Report subscriptions can be delivered to users in a variety of rendering formats. Database-driven subscriptions take that one step further by delivering the report to multiple users using potentially different rendering formats for each.

What timer-triggered and user-triggered processes have in common is the ability to take advantage of caching.

Caching

Caching is a mechanism that's used to improve the effective performance of a machine. The results of processing can be temporarily stored in cache (pronounced "cash") for later retrieval and possibly further processing. Later, typically on a schedule or when the underlying data changes, the cache is refreshed.

Typically, data is read from a slower, persistent data source and cached in a faster, temporary storage space. When the same data is needed later, it's retrieved from the faster-to-access cache. Bypassing the trip to the data stores allows the server to respond to more requests more quickly, increasing both performance and scalability.

Remember that two database accesses occur with each report process: once to the Report Server catalog for the rdl file content and then to the specified data source to retrieve a result set for use in the report. Once those two are brought together, generation of the report can begin.

Both user-triggered and timer-triggered report execution share a common stage in their processing. This stage occurs after the Report Server has gone to the report catalog to retrieve the rdl file and then gone to the source database to retrieve a result set for the report query. When the data and the report file are combined, ready to generate a rendered report, that's the moment when the report exists in prerender limbo. The Report Server has the ability to cache this prerendered report snapshot. The snapshot itself is static, in that any reports rendered from it will all be based on the same data result set. Rendering the report to the user no longer requires round trips to the databases. That has potentially large implications for increasing server scalability and performance.

Many performance counters are included with Reporting Services, including ones to monitor cache use. For example, the "cache read miss" counter shows the number of times the server went to access data in cache, but it wasn't there. One example of that is when the cached version has expired. Missing cache data would cause the server to run the report process again, from initial catalog query to report rendering. You'll read more about using performance counters later in this chapter.

Reporting Services also performs session caching. User sessions are maintained between the client and the server when exchanging HTTP messages. These are user-specific, and data is not shared across sessions. When a report is viewed, the report is added to the session cache for that user. The ReportServerTempDB database is used to hold this type of short-lived data. The user must refresh the report in order to see changes in the data that might have occurred since the report was first requested by that user. Refreshing the report is done using the Refresh button on the report toolbar in Report Manager. Refreshing the browser does not force a report refresh — it only causes a reload of the cached report.

It's important to know that cached instances are temporary and *must expire*. They expire:

❑ According to a predefined interval, like every 10 minutes.

❑ According to a report-specific or shared schedule.

❑ By forced expiration, such as when the ReportServerTempDB is restarted.

Reporting Services doesn't force a limit to the number of cached instances you can have, but your hardware will certainly have its limits. SQL Server Agent handles scheduling duties for the report server and also takes care of timing out items in cache. When planning your security policy, remember that cached instances must use credentials that are stored on the server.

Exploring the Execution Log

One of the first ways to troubleshoot and monitor report execution is by going through the Report Server Execution Log. When a report is executed, log information is written to the ReportServer database. This info is helpful, for example, when you want to see how often a report is run or who is requesting the report.

A number of attributes are recorded for each report execution. These include:

❑   Data retrieval time, which is the time (in milliseconds) spent executing the query.

❑   Processing time, which is the time (again in milliseconds) spent processing the report — including calculating subtotals, applying grouping and sorting, and so on.

❑   Rendering time, regardless of the rendered format.

❑   Source, which is the source of the rendered report. This may include processing reports using live data, cached, snapshot, or history report sources.

Reporting Services stores this data in the ExecutionLog table in the ReportServer database. Because the data in the table isn't easy to understand in raw form, an Integration Services package is provided to export the log data to another location for viewing. You can also use SQL Server Agent to schedule the Integration package to run according to a predefined schedule.

Three other main log files are maintained by Reporting Services. The default folder location for these files is:

```
C:\Program Files\Microsoft SQL Server\MSSQL\Reporting Services\ LogFiles
```

The log files contain information about errors, warnings, and events for different Reporting Services components. The name and description of these files are listed in the following table:

Log File	Description
ReportServerService_<timestamp>.log	Contains logged information about the Reporting Services Web service.
ReportServerWebApp_<timestamp>.log	Contains logged information about the Report Manager web application.
ReportServer_<timestamp>.log	Contains logged information about the Report Server processing engine.

Adjusting Execution Log Settings

The ReportingServicesService.exe.config file contains settings that configure how tracing is performed. By default, the file is located in:

```
C:\Program Files\Microsoft SQL Server\MSSQL.3\Reporting Services\ReportServer\bin
```

Here's a sample of the XML content you'll find in this file:

```
<configuration>
 <configSections>
       <section name="RStrace"
type="Microsoft.ReportingServices.Diagnostics.RSTraceSectionHandler,Microsoft.Repor
tingServices.Diagnostics" />
 </configSections>
 <system.diagnostics>
        <switches>
```

479

```
                    <add name="DefaultTraceSwitch" value="3" />
            </switches>
    </system.diagnostics>
    <RStrace>
            <add name="FileName" value="ReportServerService_" />
            <add name="FileSizeLimitMb" value="32" />
            <add name="KeepFilesForDays" value="14" />
            <add name="Prefix" value="tid, time" />
            <add name="TraceListeners" value="debugwindow, file" />
            <add name="TraceFileMode" value="unique" />
            <add name="Components" value="all" />
    </RStrace>
      <runtime>
         <legacyImpersonationPolicy enabled="true"/>
      </runtime>
    </configuration>
```

Notice the child element of the switches tag. Right now, the DefaultTraceSwitch has a value of 3. This means quite a bit of detail is going to be written to the log. Possible values for this setting are in the next table:

Element	Description	Values
DefaultTraceSwitch	This sets how much detail is written to the trace log files. Unless you have a good reason to turn it off, it's best to leave tracing enabled.	0 = Disables tracing 1 = Logs exceptions and restarts 2 = Logs exceptions, restarts, warnings 3 = Logs exceptions, restarts, warnings, status messages (default) 4 = Verbose mode
FileSizeLimitMb	This is the max size for trace logs, in megabytes.	0 to max integer (a way big number); the default is 32.
KeepFilesForDays	The life span in days for the trace log files. After that, it's deleted.	0 to max integer again; the default for this one is 14.

Status messages are generated through normal processing. The log files can get quite large, if not kept under control. Changing the DefaultTraceSwitch value to 2 will slow the rate at which the files grow, while still giving you a good degree of information when things start behaving badly.

> While you can modify the config file to rename the log file or increase or decrease trace levels, don't modify any of the other settings.

Performance Counters

Reporting Services includes performance counters for the two core Report Server functions: the Report Server Web service and the Windows service. Remember that the Report Server handles report processing, and the Windows service is responsible for report scheduling and delivery.

The best way to access these counters is through Administrative Tools, as shown in Figure 11-13.

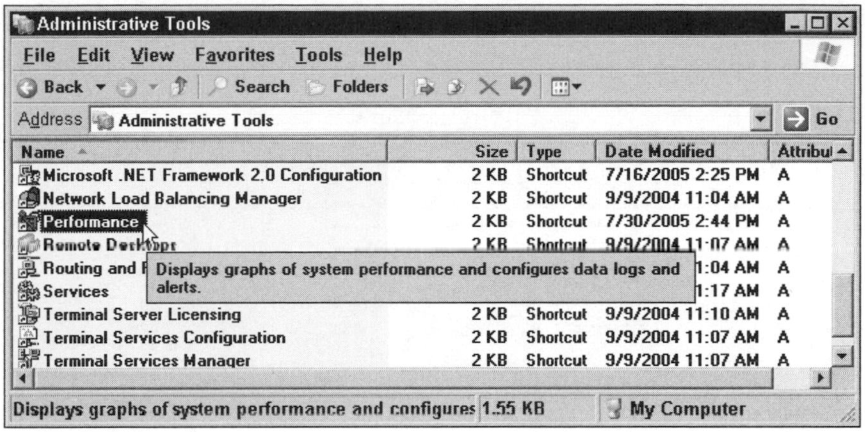

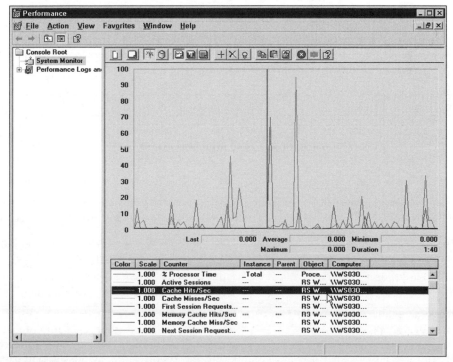

Figure 11-13

You can get to Administrative Tools through the Start menu or the Control Panel. Select Administrative Tools⇨Performance to open the performance monitor, or perfmon for short. When System Monitor is selected in the tree view pane on the left, you can view the performance trace for selected counters in the display on the right. Figure 11-14 shows perfmon in action.

Figure 11-14

There are 18 different performance monitors provided for the Report Server Web service and 27 counters for the RS Windows service. To access the counters, right-click the display window in perfmon and select "Add Counters..." from the context menu. That brings up the Add Counters dialog box, where you can choose which counters to view. When Reporting Services is installed on a machine, two of the Performance Objects available are RS Windows service and RS Web Service, as shown in Figure 11-15.

Figure 11-15

Once one of the two Performance Objects is selected, you'll have access to the individual counters exposed by each of them. The following table lists commonly used counters for the Web and Windows services, but is just a selection of the counters available.

Performance Counter	Counter Description
RS Web Service	
Active Sessions	Number of active sessions being managed.
Report Requests Report Server.	Number of active requests being handled by the
Reports Executed/Sec	Number of reports being executed per second.
Cache Hits/Sec	Number of times per second data is being pulled from Report Server catalog.
Cache Misses/Sec	Number of times per second that requests couldn't be returned from the Report Server catalog.
Memory Cache Hits (and Misses) / Sec	How many times per second that reports are being retrieved from in-memory cache (or not being retrieved). When data is pulled from in-memory cache, the Report Server avoids a round trip to the database.

Performance Counter	Counter Description
Total Cache Misses	The total number of times that requests could not be returned from the Report Server catalog. Like other "Total" counts, this one is reset when the service restarts. This one can help determine if you've got enough memory and hard drive capacity.
RS Windows Service	
Delivers/Sec	Number of report deliveries per second, regardless of the delivery method.
Cache Hits/Sec (Semantic Model)	Number of times per second for cached models.
Total App Domain Recycles	Total number of times the application domain has been recycled.
Total Deliveries	Total number of deliveries that have been made.
Total Reports Executed	The total number of reports that have been processed.
Total Requests	Total number of incoming requests that have been processed; there are typically more requests than processed reports.

Another component of Reporting Services, the Report Manager, does not have its own performance counters. The Report Manager is an ASP.NET web application that works with the report server by sending requests to the Report Server Web Service. Microsoft provides two key performance objects: ASP.NET and ASP.NET Applications. These two objects expose performance counters like Request Wait Time and Requests Queued, which can help narrow down where a bottleneck might be.

Note that the Reporting Services Web service is also an ASP.NET application, so those monitors can help keep an eye on it as well. Other system monitors that can provide valuable insight into how your server environment is handling its workload include:

❑ .NET CLR Data

❑ .NET CLR Memory

❑ Memory

❑ System

The .NET CLR counters read the Common Language Runtime (CLR) of the .NET Framework. The CLR is essentially the runtime engine that manages the applications running on the .NET Framework. This includes providing services such as garbage collection, security checking, and application isolation.

For insight into how SQL Server is handling its side of things, use a combination of perfmon and SQL Server Profiler to monitor the Reporting Services catalog and the data source databases. You'll want to include both the Report Server catalog and the data source databases, which could easily be on different machines.

Summary

Microsoft has improved the management tools in this edition of Reporting Services, making server administration mostly straightforward. How you configure your Reporting Services environment will affect the number of incoming requests your servers can handle.

To increase the capacity of your report server, one of the first things to look at is deploying the ReportServer and ReportServerTempDB databases to a remote instance of SQL Server.

Some other things to keep in mind when considering a Reporting Services deployment include:

❑ As much as possible, render reports from cached data rather than live data.

❑ Be reasonable when defining report requirements. Large, complex reports consume server resources and may not be the best way to meet user needs.

❑ Use scheduling to process reports during off-peak times to reduce anticipated server loads.

❑ Use tools such as Query Analyzer and SQL Profiler to improve query performance.

❑ Consider linked reports to reduce database round trips. Linked reports can provide users with a subset of data by leveraging the filtering, grouping, and aggregate function capabilities of the report server.

Lastly, consider scaling out in addition to scaling up. If you'll remember, scaling up is the addition of more capacity within a server. For example, by adding processors to create dual- or quad-processor machines. Scaling out is adding more machines to spread the load and has been popular for Reporting Services installations. Scaling out can be a flexible, cost-effective way of incrementally adding and removing additional capacity. When anticipating a seasonal spike in reporting loads, for example, adding relatively inexpensive commodity servers will not only help balance the load but will also provide an additional degree of fault tolerance.

The next chapter takes a closer look at working programmatically with the report server, to enable viewing reports in custom client applications.

Part V

Reporting Services Integration and the Reporting Services Web Services

12

Integrating Reporting Services into Custom Applications

The main focus of Reporting Services is to be a flexible reporting tool that can be easily incorporated in different applications. There are a number of scenarios where the report viewer provided by Reporting Services will not meet report delivery needs. For example, many organizations maintain corporate reporting portals. In these situations, developers might need a way to display numerous reports in a web environment. Reporting Services can also be embedded into any line of business applications. Developers might want to use Reporting Services to create invoices or purchase orders directly from their applications. For other organizations, the default Report Manager might not provide a secure enough method of accessing reports.

All of these issues can be solved with the features available in Reporting Services. In this chapter, you will take a look at four methods of rendering reports from Reporting Services. They are:

❑ Using URLs to access reports.

❑ Using the Reporting Services Web service to programmatically render reports.

❑ Using the `ReportViewer` controls to embed reports.

❑ Using SharePoint to display reports.

URL access allows you to quickly incorporate Reporting Services reports in applications such as web portals. Programmatic rendering allows for creating custom interfaces. Developers can do anything from implementing their own security architecture around Reporting Services to creating their own parameter interface.

In this chapter you learn about:

❑ The syntax and structure for accessing Reporting Services through the URL.

❑ The reporting items that can be accessed through the URL.

❑ The parameter options that can be passed to the URL to control report output.

❑ Creating a Windows application that renders reports to the file system.

❑ Creating a web application that returns rendered reports to the browser.

❑ Easily embedding reports in a Windows application using controls.

❑ Adding report browsing and rendering to your SharePoint sites.

URL Access

Reporting Service's main means for accessing reports is through HTTP requests. These requests can be made through URLs in a web browser or a custom application. By passing parameters in the URL, you can specify the report item, set the output format, and perform a number of other tasks. In the next few sections, you will look at the features available through URL requests, URL syntax, passing parameters, and setting the output format.

URL Syntax

The basic URL syntax is as follows:

```
http://server/virtualroot?[/pathinfo]&[prefix:]param=value[&[prefix:]param=value]
...n]
```

The parameters in the syntax are as follows:

❑ server: Specifies the instance of Report Server you would like to access. To access your local machine, you can either type the machine name or use the localhost alias.

❑ virtualroot: Specifies the IIS virtual directory you specified during the setup. When installing Reporting Services, you must enter two virtual directories: one for the Report Manager and one for the Reporting Services Web service. By default, the virtual directory you would access is reportserver.

❑ pathinfo: After specifying the server and virtual directory to the Reporting Services Web service, you can pass a number of parameters to access report objects. The first parameter you pass is pathinfo, which specifies the path to the resource you want to access. To access the root of the Report Server, you can simply place a single forward slash (/).

Once you have listed the path, you can pass various parameters. These parameters will depend on the type of object you are referencing. Reports will have a number of parameters to specify properties such as the rendering format. Each parameter is separated by an ampersand (&) and contains a name=value pair for the parameter.

Here is a quick look at retrieving the list of items under the Professional SQL Reporting Services folder.

```
http://localhost/reportserver?%2fProfessional+SQL+Reporting+Services&rs:Command=
ListChildren
```

Now that you've taken a look at the basic URL syntax, let's see how it is implemented in each of the Reporting Services objects.

Accessing Reporting Services Objects

URL requests are not limited to just reports. You can access a number of Reporting Services items. These include:

- ❑ Folders
- ❑ Data Sources
- ❑ Resources
- ❑ Reports

In this section, you will look at accessing each of the items listed above. You will go through sample URLs and look at items provided in the Professional SQL Reporting Services project.

Folders

Accessing folders will be your starting point for looking at URL requests. Let's take a look at the simplest URL request you can make:

```
http://localhost/reportserver
```

That URL is redirected to the default Home page in Report Manager. With this request, you can see a listing of all reports, data sources, resources, and folders in the root directory of the Reporting Server, as shown in Figure 12-1. To access another server, simply replace localhost with the name of the server.

To see how other folder URL requests work, simply click on any of the <dir> links. Clicking the Professional SQL Reporting Services link will give you the following URL:

```
http://localhost/reportserver?%2fProfessional+SQL+Reporting+Services&rs:Command=
ListChildren
```

This URL contains the following items:

- ❑ **Path to the report:** %2fProfessional+SQL+Reporting+Services
- ❑ **Command to list the contents of the directory:** rs:Command=ListChildren

You'll take a closer look at the URL parameters in the "Reporting Services URL Parameters" section later in the chapter.

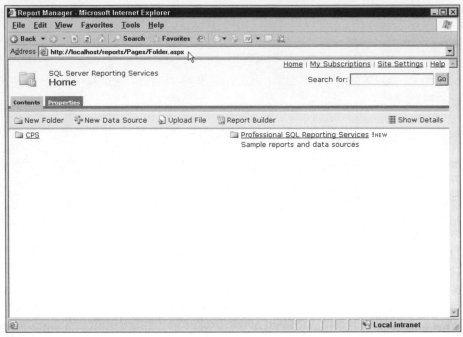

Figure 12-1

Data Sources

Through URL requests, you can also view the contents of data sources. Let's again take a look at the Professional SQL Reporting Services folder. Enter the following URL to view the contents of this folder:

```
http://localhost/reportserver?%2fProfessional+SQL+Reporting+Services&rs:Command=
ListChildren
```

You'll see the listing of items, as shown in Figure 12-2.

You will notice that one of the items listed is AdventureWorks. You can tell that this item is a data source by the <ds> tag next to the item name. If you follow the AdventureWorks link, you will be able to view the contents of that data source. Figure 12-3 shows the AdventureWorks data source contents.

Let's take a look at the URL used to view the AdventureWorks data source: `http://localhost/ reportserver?%2fProfessional+SQL+Reporting+Services%2fAdventureWorks2000&rs:Command= GetDataSourceContents`

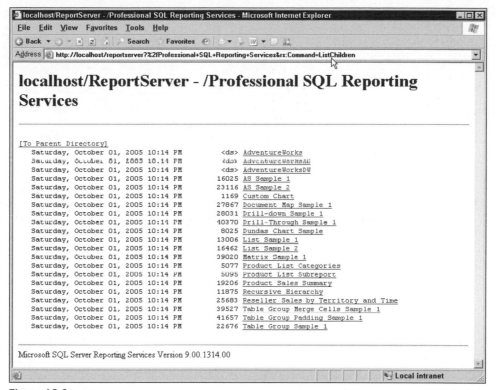

Figure 12-2

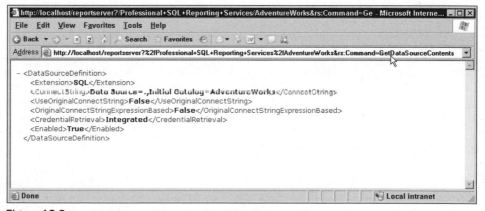

Figure 12-3

This URL contains the following items:

❑ **Path to the data source:**
   `%2fProfessional+SQL+Reporting+Services%2fAdventureWorks2000&`

❑ **Command to view the data source content:** `rs:Command=GetDataSourceContents`

Viewing the data source enables you to quickly see how your data source is configured. Notice that this information is returned in XML format. This allows you to easily work with the data source information. If you have your own reporting application that shares a single connection, you could use this URL to dynamically load this data source information. This information could then be used to make other database connections in your application.

Resources

Resources are items that you use in your reports, such as images or additional resources that have been added to your Report Server folder, such as Word and Excel documents. You can use URLs to access resources stored in the Report Server. Depending on the type of resources you reference, either you will be prompted to open or save a file, such as a Word or Excel document, or the resource will be rendered directly in the browser. In the Professional SQL Reporting Services folder, a resource for the Adventure Works logo is added. This image can be directly rendered in your browser. Let's take a look at the following URL:

```
http://localhost/reportserver?%2fProfessional+SQL+Reporting+Services%2fAdventure+
Works+Logo&rs:Command=GetResourceContents
```

The URL contains the following contents:

❑ **Path to the resource:**
   `%2fProfessional+SQL+Reporting+Services%2fAdventure+Works+Logo`

❑ **Command to retrieve the resource content:** `rs:Command=GetResourceContents`

You can use this information in other applications. If you want to reference the Adventure Works logo from a web page, you could simply set the `src` attribute of an image tag (`<img>`) to reference the earlier URL.

Resources can also be incredibly handy for storing documents. In your reporting solution, you might want to store *readme* files to accompany your reports. You can store these documents as resources on the Report Server and then apply different properties to them, such as security. Your application could then point to the resource URL to allow downloading of the document.

Reports

The most important objects you can access through the URL are your reports. This section provides a quick look at the syntax for accessing reports. Later we'll discuss the various parameters you can pass to change things such as report parameters, output formats, and other items.

The basic syntax for accessing a report is very similar to accessing all of your other resources. You should first specify a path to the report and then provide the commands for its output. Let's look at the basic URL for accessing your Customer Product List by Category report:

```
http://localhost/ReportServer/Pages/ReportViewer.aspx?%2fProfessional+
SQL+Reporting+Services%2fProduct+List+Categories&rs:Command=Render
```

View the Customer Product List by Category report, as shown in Figure 12-4.

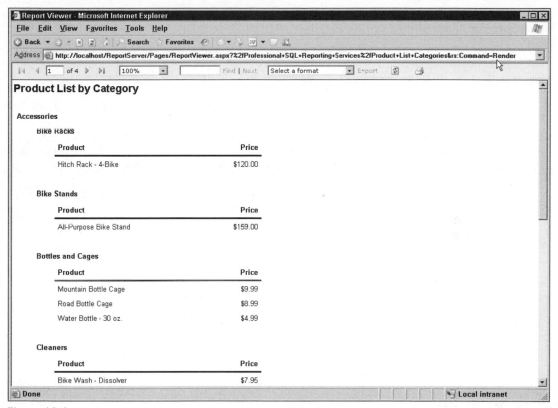

Figure 12-4

The URL contains the following contents:

❑ **Path to the resource:**
   %2fProfessional+SQL+Reporting+Services%2fProduct+List+Categories

❑ **Command to retrieve the resource content:** rs:Command=Render

Using URLs is the easiest and most convenient way to embed Reporting Services reports in your applications. You can simply create your own links that point to the various report URLs. You are probably saying to yourself, "That's nice! I can access a report, but how do I pass parameters and change the output format?" In the next section, you'll take a look at all the possible parameters you can pass through the URL, including setting report parameters and output format.

Reporting Services URL Parameters

Now that you have seen the basics of obtaining items from your Report Server using URLs, let's take a look at passing some parameters. The next few sections will move through how parameters are passed to Reporting Services and what values for these parameters are available. The majority of the parameter functionality will be focused on report rendering, but some items will also apply to your data source, resources, and folder.

Parameter Prefixes

The first thing you need to take a look at is the different parameter prefixes in Reporting Services. There are four main parameter prefixes in Reporting Services: `rs`, `rc`, `dsp`, and `dsu`. The following sections will take a look at these prefixes in detail.

rs Prefix

In the earlier examples, you saw the parameter `rs:Command`. This parameter contains the prefix `rs`. The `rs` prefix is used to send commands to the Report Server. The following URL shows an example of the `rs` prefix being used to call the Command parameter and pass the `ListChildren` argument to it:

```
http://localhost/reportserver?%2fProfessional+SQL+Reporting+Services&rs:Command=
ListChildren
```

rc Prefix

The second main parameter prefix in Reporting Services is the `rc` prefix. This prefix is used to interact with the given report output format. For example, if you are outputting your report as HTML, you can control the HTML viewer. You can use this prefix to pass parameters that do things such as hide toolbars or control the initial state of toggle items. The following URL calls the Product Sales Pivot report and turns off the parameter inputs:

```
http://localhost/reportserver?%2fProfessional+SQL+Reporting+Services%2fProduct+
List+Categories&rs:Command=Render&rc:Parameters=False
```

dsu and dsp Prefixes

Parameter prefixes can also be used to send database credentials. Use the `dsu` prefix to pass the data source user name and `dsp` to pass the data source password. In any Reporting Services report, you could incorporate multiple data sources. So, you need a way to specify which data source the credentials should be passed to. That's where the prefixes come in. The full syntax to use these prefixes is as follows:

```
[dsu | dsp]:datasourcename=value
```

If you want to pass the user name guest with a password guestPass to your AdventureWorks data source, you will use the following URL parameters:

```
&dsu:AdventureWorks=guest&dsp:AdventureWorks=guestPass
```

Be aware that these credentials will be passed unencrypted over the Internet and will be visible to the end user. You can encrypt the URL using the Secure Sockets Layer (SSL) on your web server. This will prevent the information from being sent unencrypted but will not prevent the end user from viewing the credentials that you pass. Make sure that you consider these factors in your reporting solution architecture.

Now that you have seen the different parameter prefixes in Reporting Services, we'll move on to the available parameters that can be used with the `rs` and `rc` prefixes.

Parameters

First, let's take a look at the parameters that can be used with the `rs` prefix. The following table lists the three available values and their uses:

Parameter	Use
Command	The Command parameter is used to send instructions to the Report Server about the item being retrieved. Available values return the report item and set session timeout values.
Format	The Format parameter is used when rendering reports. Any rendering formats available on the report server can be passed using this parameter.
Snapshot	The Snapshot parameter is used to retrieve historical report snapshots. Once a report has been stored in snapshot history, it is assigned a time/date stamp to uniquely identify that report. Passing this time/date stamp will return the appropriate report.

Now that you have seen the different `rs` parameters, let's take a look at some of their available values.

Command Parameter

The Command parameter is your main parameter for setting the output of a given report item. It can also be used for resetting a user's session information, which guarantees that a report is not rendered from the session cache. Here is a listing of the possible values that can be passed to the `Command` parameter:

Value	Use
GetDataSourceCredentials	The GetDataSourceCredentials command can be used to return data source information in an XML format. You can use this parameter on shared data sources.
GetResourceCredentials	This command returns the binary of your Reporting Services resources, such as images, via the URL.
ListChildren	Used in combination with a Reporting Services folder. This lets you view all the items in a given folder.
Render	Allows you to render the report using the URL. Probably the most frequently used command.
ResetSessionTimeout	Can be used to refresh a user's session cache. Because Reporting Services works typically via HTTP, it is crucial for the server to maintain state information about the user. However, if you want to ensure that a report is executed each time the user views a report, this state information needs to be refreshed. Use this parameter to reset the user's session and remove any session cache information.

Format Parameter

The Format parameter is the main parameter for controlling the report output. The available values for this parameter are determined by the different rendering extensions available on your report server. The following table shows the output formats available with the default installation of Reporting Services:

Value	Output
Web Formats	
HTML3.2	HTML version 3.2 output. Used for older browsers.
HTML4.0	HTML version 4.0. This format is supported by newer browsers, such as Internet Explorer 4.0 and above.
MHTML	MHTML standard output. This output format is used for sending HTML documents in e-mail. Using this format will embed all resources, such as images, into the MHTML document instead of referencing external URLs.
Print Formats	
IMAGE	The IMAGE format allows you to render your reports to a number of different graphical device interfaces (GDI) such as BMP, PNG, GIF, or TIFF.
PDF	The Portable Document Format (PDF) can be used for viewing and printing documents.
Data Formats	
EXCEL	Excel output. Users can use this format to further manipulate report data.
CSV	Comma Separated Value (CSV) format. CSV is a standard data format and can be read by a wide variety of applications.
XML	Extensible Markup Language (XML) format. XML has become a standard data format, used by many different applications.
Control Format	
NULL	The NULL provider allows you to execute reports without rendering. This can be very useful when working with reports that have cached instances. You can use the NULL format to execute the report for the first time and then store the cached instance.

When you set the rendering formats via the URL, the report will either be rendered directly in the browser, or you will be prompted to save the output file. Let's take a look at rendering the Customer Product List by Category report in PDF format. Enter the following URL using the rs:Format=PDF parameter:

```
http://localhost/ReportServer/Pages/ReportViewer.aspx?%2fProfessional+SQL+
Reporting+Services%2fProduct+List+Categories&rs:Command=Render&rs:Format=PDF
```

Figure 12-5 shows the output.

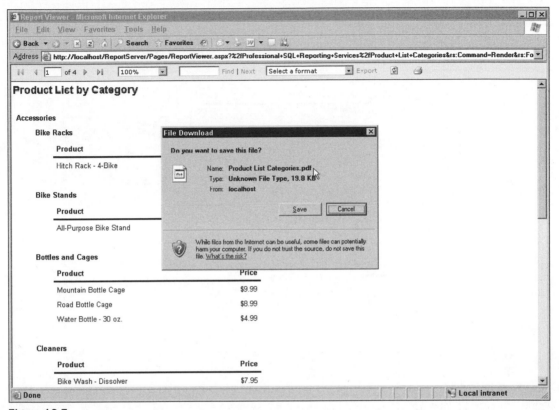

Figure 12-5

Notice that the browser will now prompt you to save the rendered report. This can be easily incorporated into your own custom applications or portals. You can simply give your users a link containing the rs:Format parameter and automatically output the correct format.

Setting Device Information

Now that you have seen the various output formats available in Reporting Services, you need to take a look at the different device information settings for the various formats. The Format parameter allows you to specify the type of format you want, but each format has specific settings that can be useful to you. For example, if you specify the IMAGE format, you get an output in TIFF. What if you wanted a bitmap or JPEG image? Well, to output in a different image format, all you need to do is to just specify device information when passing the URL. Take a look at outputting your Customer Product Sales Pivot report in JPEG format using the following URL (Figure 12-6 shows the output).

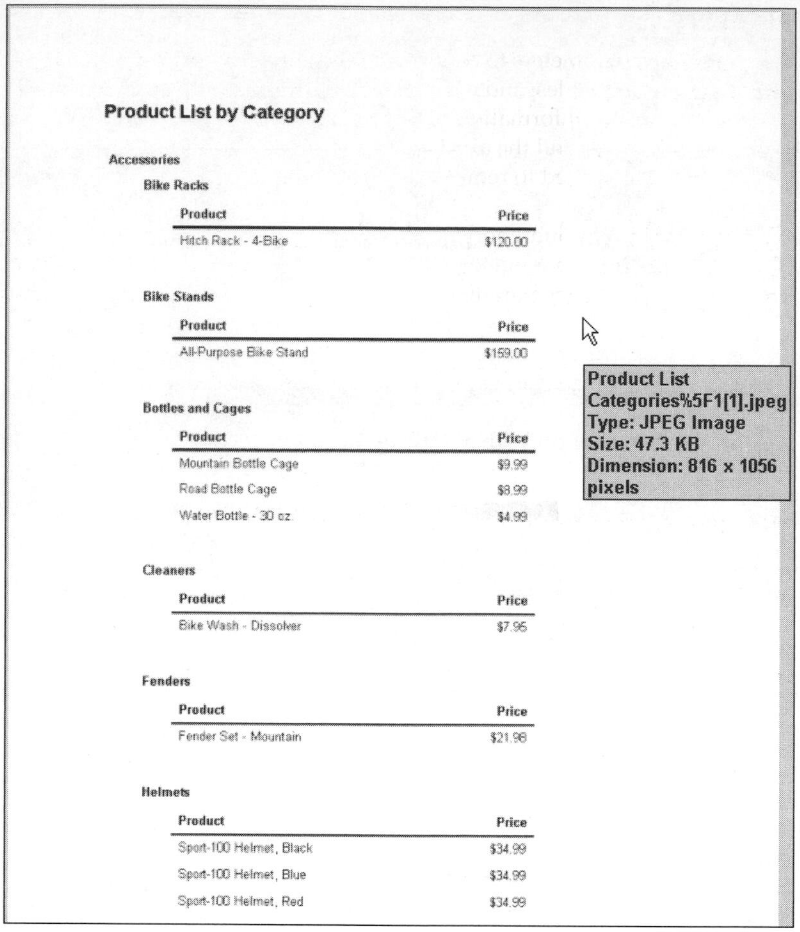

Figure 12-6

Notice that the file type sent back to you is a JPEG image. There are numerous device information settings you can use for each of the rendering extensions. Each device information setting is prefixed using the `rc` prefix. The following syntax can be used for passing device information:

```
http://server/virtualroot?/pathinfo&rs:Format=format&rc:param=value[&rc:param=
value...n]
```

Now that you have seen the different output formats and commands you can pass to Reporting Services, let's take a look at passing information to your individual reports.

Passing Report Information through the URL

The previous sections illustrated how a URL can be used to control report rendering. In the next section, you look at how a URL can be used to control report execution. This section starts with an explanation of passing report parameters. These are the parameters that you define while authoring your report. Finally, you'll see how historical snapshots can be rendered using the URL.

Report Parameters

Many of your reports have parameters to control all kinds of behavior. You can use parameters to alter your query, filter datasets and tables, and even change the appearance of your reports. Reporting Services allows you to pass this information directly via a URL request. In the earlier section, you saw a lot about the parameter prefixes and the available values that can be sent to the Reporting Services. With report parameters, you simply need to remove the prefix and directly call the parameter name.

In this example, the Product List Subreport accepts one parameter: `SubCategoryID`. You might want to allow your users to update these parameters through a custom interface you define. When you call the report, you will need to provide the parameter value in the URL as shown here:

```
http://localhost/ReportServer/Pages/ReportViewer.aspx?%2fProfessional+SQL+Reporting+
Services%2fProduct+List+Subreport&rs%3aCommand=Render&SubCategoryID=1
```

Let's take a look at calling the report with a `SubCategoryID` of 1 (see Figure 12-7).

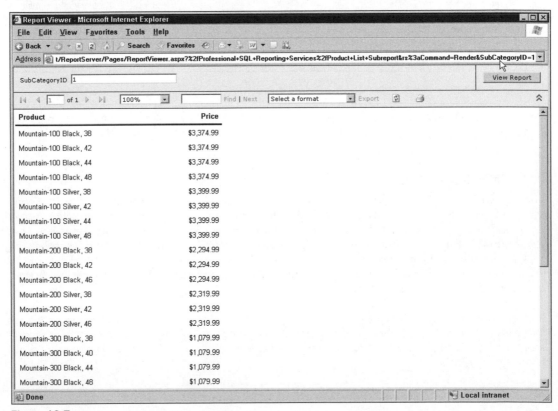

Figure 12-7

Notice that by passing the parameters in your URL, the HTML viewer updates to reflect the values. The parameter name that you use in the URL is defined in the report definition. Since your Report Parameter is called SubCategoryID, that name is used in your URL.

Now that you have seen how to pass report parameters to the URL, let's look at passing snapshot IDs to render historical execution snapshots.

Rendering Snapshot History

One of the major features of Reporting Services is the ability to create execution snapshots of reports. Say you have a report where the data updates on a monthly basis. Once the data is updated, it does not change for another month. A perfect example of this would be monthly financial statements. If your data changes only once a month, there is no reason to query your database every time you need a report. So, you can use execution snapshots to store this information after the query has been executed. Going along the same lines as a monthly report, what should happen when your data updates from, say, January to February? You don't want to lose the January snapshot once the February information is available. That is where historical snapshots come into play. When you create the February snapshot, you go and add January to the snapshot history and so on for each subsequent month.

Now that you have execution snapshots stored in history, you need some way to access them. Reporting Services gives you a very easy way to do this. As you have already seen, each report has a report path that can be used to render the report. To render a historical snapshot, you simply need to add a parameter for the historical snapshot ID.

The syntax to pass your snapshot ID is as follows:

```
http://server/virtualroot?[/pathinfo]&rs:Snapshot=snapshotid
```

The snapshot ID for your historical snapshot will be the time and date stamp of when the report was added to the history. The time is adjusted to GMT based on the time zone where the historical snapshot was added.

URL Rendering Summary

Through URL rendering, you have seen the various commands that can be passed to Reporting Services that can be used to control the report item display, the format to use, and snapshot information using the rs prefix. Once you have created your commands for the Report Server, you can pass parameters specific to the output format. Using the rc prefix and the device information parameters, you can specify things such as encoding and what items to display in the HTML viewer. After you have specified the report item, you need to know how to output it. You can pass parameters to your report by simply passing the parameter name and value combination.

In the next section, let's take a look at the second part of rendering Reporting Service reports. You can use URLs for simple web applications and web portals, but sometimes you need finer control over report access and rendering. To achieve this, we'll use the Reporting Service Web service to programmatically render your reports.

Programmatic Rendering

There are several ways that reports may be integrated into custom Windows forms and web applications. These include:

- ❏ Link to a report in web browser window using a URL rendering request.

- ❏ Replace web page content with a report by using SOAP rendering to write binary content to the web Response object.

- ❏ Use SOAP rendering to write report content to a file.

- ❏ Embed a report in an area of a web page by setting the source of a frame or IFrame tag.

- ❏ Use the ReportViewer control in a Windows form or Web form application.

Rendering using a URL is very handy and easy to implement in many situations, but it does have its limitations. When rendering from the URL, you have to make sure that you use the security infrastructure provided with Reporting Services. For some applications, such as public web sites, you might want to implement your own security. In that case, rendering from the URL will not provide the functionality you need. In this section, you will take a look at rendering reports using the Reporting Services Web service.

You'll connect to the Reporting Services Web service, return a list of available reports, retrieve their parameters, and finally render the report. Let's take a look at three implementations of programmatic rendering. The first implementation is using a Windows form to render reports to a file. This will help you to understand the basic principles without a lot of interface work. The second implementation will take you through rendering through an ASP.NET page. You'll see some of the items that need to be considered when working through a web application. Last, you'll read about the ReportViewer controls embed reports in a Windows application using one.

Common Scenarios

Before you look at the actual programming code for rendering reports, it is important to understand a couple of scenarios where it is reasonable to do so. There are two scenarios that are commonly experienced while working with clients. They do not represent the *only* scenarios where you would write your own rendering code but do illustrate how and when custom code can be used. Let's look at each of these scenarios.

Custom Security

Probably the biggest question I get when working with clients is How do I use Reporting Services if I don't want to implement their security infrastructure? Reporting Services requires you to connect to reports using a Windows identity. In many organizations, this is just not possible. They have mixed environments or nontrusted domains that do not allow for identification to the Report Server. Some clients also have large-scale authentication and authorization infrastructures already implemented.

You can still use Reporting Services in these situations. Using your own security infrastructure involves creating both authentication and authorization code in your environment. After you have determined that a user can access a report, a Windows identity that you define can be used to connect to reports. To hide this security implementation, the Reporting Services Web service can be employed. You can render reports directly to a browser or file without passing the original user identity to the Report Server.

Server-Side Parameters

Although URL rendering is by far the easiest way to incorporate Reporting Services in your applications, it does have some limitations. When you send information via a URL, it is very easy for a user to change that URL or see what it is that you pass.

By using the Reporting Services Web service, you can easily hide the details of how you retrieve report information. Parameters are passed through your code instead of the URL. This gives you complete control over how that information is retrieved without exposing it to the users. Let's take a look at your first rendering application.

Rendering through Windows

In this section, we'll take a look at the mechanics of rendering using the Reporting Service Web service. We are going to build a simple Windows application that returns a list of reports from the report server. Once we have the list of reports, we'll use the Web service to return a list of report parameters. After entering any report parameters, we'll render the report to a file. These steps will illustrate the main components of rendering through program code.

Building the Application Interface

To start, you need to build your application interface. Let's start by building a simple Windows form; for this example, I've added labels, text boxes, and buttons for basic functionality. Figure 12-8 shows the design view of your form.

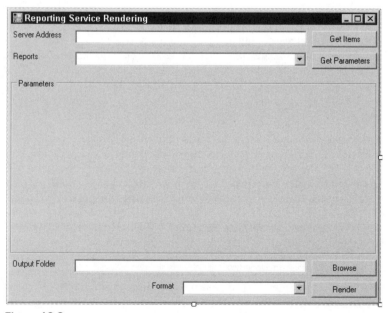

Figure 12-8

This form will allow you to query a given Report Server to return a list of reports. Once it has returned the reports, you can use it to access a list of parameters for the reports. Finally, you'll need to render the report to a given folder location.

Setting Up the Reporting Service Web Service

Before you can get into rendering reports, you need to set up a reference to the Reporting Service Web service. Once you have created your web reference, you can start to develop the application. The next few figures show you how to create a reference to the Web service. Start by adding a web reference to your project.

Open the Solution Explorer and right-click on the References folder. Click the Add Web Reference menu item, as in Figure 12-9. That will open the Add Web Reference dialog.

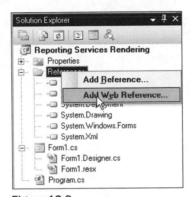

Figure 12-9

In the Add Web Reference dialog, enter the location of Web service in the URL dialog. This URL will depend on the Report Server name and the installed location of the Report Server virtual directory. By default, the Report Server virtual directory is located under the root as /reportserver. For the default virtual directory on a local machine, enter the following URL:

`http://localhost/reportserver/reportservice.asmx?wsdl`.

Once you have entered the URL, hit Enter to view a description of the Web service. Enter a name for the new web reference and click Add Reference. I've named mine RSService. The dialog should look like Figure 12-10 when filled in.

Now that you have referenced the Web service, you are ready to start writing your code. The first thing you can do is add a `using` (C#) or `Imports VB.` (VB) statements to your code. The first part of the `using` statement will be the application name followed by the web reference name. I have called my C# project `Rendering` and my VB project `RenderingVB`.

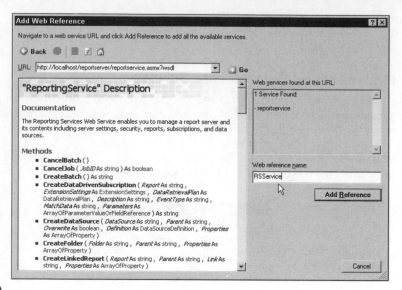

Figure 12-10

C#

```
using System;
using System.Drawing;
using System.Collections;
using System.ComponentModel;
using System.Windows.Forms;
using Rendering.RSService;
```

VB

```
Imports System
Imports System.Drawing
Imports System.Collections
Imports System.ComponentModel
Imports System.Windows.Forms
Imports RenderingVB.RSService
```

After you have added the `using` or `Imports` statement, you need to create an instance of the `ReportingService` object. This is the main object that will be used to retrieve a list of reports and their associated parameters and then render the report. At the top of the Windows form class code, create the declarations shown in the following sections. The class declaration is included for clarity.

C#

```
public class frmMain : System.Windows.Forms.Form
{
        private ReportingService _rs = new ReportingService();
```

VB

```
Public Class frmMain
    Inherits System.Windows.Forms.Form
    Private _rs As New ReportingService
```

Next, you need to set the security credentials that will be used by Reporting Services. In your code, pass the credentials of the currently logged-on user. If you already have your own custom authentication and authorization method in place, you could pass a system identification you define instead of the current user.

Open the Form Load event in the windows form; this is a suitable place for setting the credentials. Inside this event, set the ReportingService object's Credentials property to System.Net.CredentialCache.DefaultCredentials. This will give the Web service the credentials of the currently logged-on user.

C#

```
_rs.Credentials = System.Net.CredentialCache.DefaultCredentials;
```

VB

```
_rs.Credentials = System.Net.CredentialCache.DefaultCredentials
```

The final piece you need to add to the Form Load event is the code to populate your drop-down list. This code will add all the format names to the list along with appropriate extensions for each. Let's begin by creating a small class that helps you populate the drop-down:

C#

```
/*  Helper class for format extensions. */
private class Format
{
    private string _name;
    private string _extension;

    public Format(string name, string extension)
    {
        _name = name;
        _extension = extension;
    }

    public string Name
    {
        get{return _name;}
    }

    public string Extension
    {
        get{return _extension;}
    }
}
```

VB

```vb
'  Helper class for format extensions.
Private Class Format
    Private _name As String
    Private _extension As String

    Public Sub New(ByVal name As String, ByVal extension As String)
        _name = name
        extension = extension
    End Sub

    Public ReadOnly Property Name() As String
        Get
            Return _name
        End Get
    End Property

    Public ReadOnly Property Extension() As String
        Get
            Return _extension
        End Get
    End Property
End Class
```

With these classes you can finish off your FormLoad event code. Add the few last lines of code to populate your format combo box:

C#

```csharp
private void frmMain_Load(object sender, System.EventArgs e)
{
    rs.Credentials = System.Net.CredentialCache.DefaultCredentials;
    //load the format values
    Format[] formats = new Format[7];
    formats[0] = new Format("Excel", ".xls");
    formats[1] = new Format("HTML3.2", ".html");
    formats[2] = new Format("HTML4.0", ".html");
    formats[3] = new Format("XML", ".xml");
    formats[4] = new Format("CSV", ".csv");
    formats[5] = new Format("PDF", ".pdf");
    formats[6] = new Format("IMAGE", ".tif");

    cboFormat.DataSource = formats;
    cboFormat.DisplayMember = "Name";
    cboFormat.ValueMember = "Name";
}
```

VB

```vb
Private Sub frmMain_Load(ByVal sender As Object, _
    ByVal e As System.EventArgs) Handles MyBase.Load

    _rs.Credentials = System.Net.CredentialCache.DefaultCredentials
```

```
     'load the format values
     Dim formats(6) As Format
     formats(0) = New Format("Excel", ".xls")
     formats(1) = New Format("HTML3.2", ".html")
     formats(2) = New Format("HTML4.0", ".html")
     formats(3) = New Format("XML", ".xml")
     formats(4) = New Format("CSV", ".csv")
     formats(5) = New Format("PDF", ".pdf")
     formats(6) = New Format("IMAGE", ".tif")

     cboFormat.DataSource = formats
     cboFormat.DisplayMember = "Name"
     cboFormat.ValueMember = "Name"
 End Sub
```

You have now created an instance of the `ReportingService` object, passed the logged-on user's credentials to it, and populated the format drop-down list. In the next section, we'll take a look at connecting to the Report Server and retrieving a list of available reports.

Retrieving Report Information

Now that you have set up the Reporting Service Web service, you need to retrieve your list of reports. To do this, specify the Report Server you want to query and then call the `ListChildren` method of the `ReportingService` object. `ListChildren` returns a list of all items, including data sources, resources, and reports. Once you have retrieved the list, you will need to pull out only report items. Finally, you will add the report items to the drop-down.

Let's start by setting the URL to your Report Server. Open the click event of the Get Items button to start your code. Remember that `_rs` is your reference to the Web service.

C#

```
_rs.Url = txtServer.Text + "/ReportService.asmx";
```

VB

```
_rs.Url = txtServer.Text & "/ReportService.asmx"
```

The preceding code uses the server location specified in the Server Address text box concatenated with the reference to the Reporting Service Web service.

Once the URL for the Web service is set, you can get the list of reports. Create an array of `CatalogItem` objects and then call the `ListChildren` method. This method takes two parameters: the folder path on the Report Server and a Boolean value indicating whether or not to recur the directory.

C#

```
CatalogItem[] items;
items = _rs.ListChildren("/", true);
```

VB

```
Dim items() As CatalogItem
items = _rs.ListChildren("/", True)
```

The last step is to loop through the returned list of items and add them to a drop-down list. Similar to how the formats were loaded, create a class to help data-bind the report items. Let's take a look at the code for this class.

C#

```csharp
private class ReportItem
{
    private string _name;
    private string _path;

    public ReportItem(string name, string path)
    {
        _name = name;
        _path = path;
    }

    public string Name
    {
        get{return _name;}
    }

    public string Path
    {
        get{return _path;}
    }
}
```

VB

```vb
Private Class ReportItem
    Private _name As String
    Private _path As String

    Public Sub New(ByVal name As String, ByVal path As String)
        _name = name
        _path = path
    End Sub

    Public ReadOnly Property Name() As String
        Get
            Return _name
        End Get
    End Property

    Public ReadOnly Property Path() As String
        Get
            Return _path
        End Get
    End Property
End Class
```

Using the `ReportItem` class just created, you can now add the report catalog items to the combo box. The following code is for the `GetItems` button click event, including populating the report drop-down.

C#

```csharp
private void btnGetItems_Click(object sender, System.EventArgs e)
{
    //set the path to the report server
    _rs.Url = txtServer.Text + "/ReportService.asmx";

    //return a list of items from the report server
    CatalogItem[] items;
    items = _rs.ListChildren("/", true);

    //populate your report combo box
    cboReports.Items.Clear();
    foreach(CatalogItem item in items)
    {
        if(item.Type == ItemTypeEnum.Report)
        {
            cboReports.Items.Add(new ReportItem(item.Name, item.Path));
        }
    }

    cboReports.DisplayMember = "Name";
    cboReports.ValueMember = "Path";
}
```

VB

```vb
Private Sub btnGetItems_Click(ByVal sender As Object, _
    ByVal e As System.EventArgs) Handles btnGetItems.Click

    'set the path to the report server
    _rs.Url = txtServer.Text & "/ReportService.asmx"
    'return a list of items from the report server
    Dim items() As CatalogItem
    items = rs.ListChildren("/", True)
    'populate your report combo box
    cboReports.Items.Clear()
    Dim item As CatalogItem
    For Each item In items
        If item.Type = ItemTypeEnum.Report Then
            cboReports.Items.Add(New ReportItem(item.Name, item.Path))
        End If
    Next item
    cboReports.DisplayMember = "Name"
    cboReports.ValueMember = "Path"
End Sub
```

You will now be able to open your form and return a list of report items. In the next section, you will look at retrieving the parameters for a report.

Retrieving Report Parameters

The next area of programmatic rendering consists of retrieving a list of parameters for your report. This bit of code can be used in a number of scenarios. The parameter interface that is provided by Reporting Services works well for simple parameters. However, it does not handle many things, like multiselect parameters or more advanced interfaces such as calendar controls. Being able to return a list of parameters allows you to create your own dynamic interface.

In the following example, we will create a simple list of parameters. For each parameter, we will dynamically add a label control and text box to your form. This example will also include the `GetParameters` click event to run your code. First thing you need to do is identify the report that is selected in your report drop-down list.

C#

```
ReportItem reportItem = (ReportItem)cboReports.SelectedItem;
```

VB

```
Dim reportItem As ReportItem = CType(cboReports.SelectedItem, ReportItem)
```

This creates a new `ReportItem` variable using the selected item of your combo box. The `ReportItem` class created in the previous section contains a `Name` and `Path` property. You can use this `Path` property to retrieve your list of parameters.

To return your list of parameters, call the `GetReportParameters` method or the `ReportingService` object. This method has two functions. It returns a list of parameters and can validate parameters against the available values defined when creating the report. Let's take a look at the arguments of the `GetReportParameters` method:

❑ `Report`: This is the path to the report you want to retrieve.

❑ `HistoryID`: The ID used to identify any historical snapshots of your report.

❑ `ForRendering`: This Boolean argument can be used to retrieve the parameters that were set when the report was executed. For example, you might create a snapshot of your report or receive it in an e-mail subscription. In both cases, the report is executed before the user views it. By setting the `ForRendering` property to `true`, you can retrieve these values and use them in your own custom interface.

❑ `ParameterValues`: The `ParameterValues` argument can be used to validate the values assigned to a parameter. This can be useful in guaranteeing that the parameter values you pass to your report match the parameter values accepted by the report.

❑ `Credentials`: The database credentials to use when validating your query-based parameters.

Since you are not working with historical reports or validating values, a number of the properties will not be set. The following code can be used for calling the `GetReportParameters` method.

C#

```
ReportParameter[] parameters;
parameters = _rs.GetReportParameters(reportItem.Path, null, false, null, null);
```

VB

```
Dim parameters() As ReportParameter
        parameters = _rs.GetReportParameters(reportItem.Path, Nothing, False, _
                        Nothing, Nothing)
```

The last piece of work to do is to create a user interface for your parameters. The `ReportParameter` objects returned by Reporting Services contain information useful for creating a custom interface. Some of the key properties include the parameter data type, prompt, and valid values. All of these can be used to define your own interface. Finish your code by simply adding a label and text box to your form for each `ReportParameter`. Following is the completed `GetParameter` click event code.

C#

```csharp
private void btnParameters_Click(object sender, System.EventArgs e)
{
    //return the list of parameters for the report item
    ReportItem reportItem = (ReportItem)cboReports.SelectedItem;
    ReportParameter[] parameters;
    parameters = _rs.GetReportParameters(reportItem.Path, null, false, null,
                                    null);
    //add the parameters to the parameter list UI
    int left = 10;
    int top = 20;
    foreach(ReportParameter parameter in parameters)
    {
        Label label = new Label();
        TextBox textBox = new TextBox();

        label.Text = parameter.Prompt;
        label.Left = left;
        label.Top = top;

        textBox.Name = parameter.Name;
        textBox.Text = parameter.DefaultValues[0];
        textBox.Left = left + 150;
        textBox.Top = top;
        top +=25;

        grpParamInfo.Controls.Add(label);
        grpParamInfo.Controls.Add(textBox);
    }
}
```

VB

```vb
Private Sub btnParameters_Click(ByVal sender As Object, ByVal e As _
    System.EventArgs) Handles btnParameters.Click

    'return the list of parameters for the report item
    Dim reportItem As ReportItem = CType(cboReports.SelectedItem, ReportItem)

    Dim parameters() As ReportParameter
    parameters = _rs.GetReportParameters(reportItem.Path, Nothing, _
```

```
                                                              False, _Nothing, Nothing)
        'add the parameters to the parameter list UI
        Dim left As Integer = 10
        Dim top As Integer = 20
        Dim parameter As ReportParameter
        For Each parameter In parameters
            Dim label As New Label
            Dim textBox As New TextBox
            label.Text = parameter.Prompt
            label.Left = left
            label.Top = top

            textBox.Name = parameter.Name
            textBox.Text = parameter.DefaultValues(0)
            textBox.Left = left + 150
            textBox.Top = top
            top += 25

            grpParamInfo.Controls.Add(label)
            grpParamInfo.Controls.Add(textBox)
        Next parameter
    End Sub
```

Now that you have retrieved your list of reports and built a parameter list, let's take a look at outputting the report to a file.

Rendering a Report to a File System

In this section, you'll take a look at rendering your report to a file. Using the `ReportingService` object's `Render` method, you can retrieve a byte array that contains the final report. This byte array can be used in a number of different ways. In this example, you will write the byte array to a file by using the file system object. Later you will take a look at another example that writes the byte array to the HTTP `Response` object.

Before you get into the rendering code, look at the different parameters of the `Render` method shown in the following table.

Parameter	Data Type	Description
Report	String	Path to the report in Reporting Services.
Format	String	Output format of the report.
HistoryID (optional)	String	History ID used to render the report from a historical snapshot.
DeviceInfo	String	Information used by a specified rendering format. For example, specifying the image type (gif, .jpeg) with the IMAGE format.
Parameters	ParameterValue Array	Input parameter value array used to process the report.

Parameter	Data Type	Description
Credentials	DataSource Credentials Array	Array of data source credentials used to connect to the data sources for a report. These credentials contain the username, login password, and the data source name.
ShowHideToggle	String	Changes initial toggle state of the report.
Encoding (out)	String	Output returned from Reporting Services containing the encoding of the report. The encoding parameter is used to correctly decode the returned byte array.
MimeType (out)	String	Output returned from Reporting Services containing the MIME type of the underlying report. Useful when rendering a report to the web. The MIME type can be passed to the Response object to ensure that the browser correctly handles the document returned.
ParametersUsed (out)	ParameterValue Array	Output of parameter values used to execute the report. Can include query parameters used for the creation of an execution snapshot. Important when developing the application user interface.
Warnings (out)	Warning Array	Output of any warning returned from Reporting Services during report processing.
StreamIDs (out)	String Array	Output of the stream IDs that can be used with the RenderStream method.

The parameters of the Render method are similar to the values that can be passed using URL rendering. In your Windows application, you will be mostly interested in the Report, Format, and Encoding parameters. These parameters allow you to correctly return your report and stream it to the file system.

Now that you have seen the basics around the Render method, let's take a look at the code you need to write for your Render button click event. The first thing you need to do in your code is retrieve the selected report and output format. Use the Format and ReportItem classes created earlier to retrieve the selected items in your drop-downs.

C#

```
Format format = (Format)cboFormat.SelectedItem;
ReportItem reportItem = (ReportItem)cboReports.SelectedItem;
```

VB

```
Dim format As Format = CType(cboFormat.SelectedItem, Format)
Dim reportItem As ReportItem = CType(cboReports.SelectedItem, ReportItem)
```

You need to retrieve the input parameters specified by the user. Then, you need to create a new function that loops through the text boxes you've created earlier to retrieve their values and return an array of ParameterValue objects.

C#

```csharp
private ParameterValue[] GetParameters()
{
    ArrayList controls = new ArrayList();

    //get the values from the parameter controls
    int len = grpParamInfo.Controls.Count;
    for(int i=0;i<len;i++)
    {
        if(grpParamInfo.Controls[i] is TextBox)
        {
            controls.Add(grpParamInfo.Controls[i]);
        }
    }

    //add the control information to parameter info objects
    len = controls.Count;
    ParameterValue[] returnValues = new ParameterValue[len];
    for(int i=0;i<len;i++)
    {
        returnValues[i] = new ParameterValue();
        returnValues[i].Name = ((TextBox)controls[i]).Name;
        returnValues[i].Value = ((TextBox)controls[i]).Text;
    }

    return returnValues;
}
```

VB

```vb
Private Function GetParameters() As ParameterValue()
    Dim controls As New ArrayList

    'get the values from the parameter controls
    Dim len As Integer = grpParamInfo.Controls.Count
    Dim i As Integer
    For i = 0 To len - 1
        If TypeOf grpParamInfo.Controls(i) Is TextBox Then
            controls.Add(grpParamInfo.Controls(i))
        End If
    Next i

    'add the control information to parameter info objects
    len = controls.Count - 1
    Dim returnValues(len) As ParameterValue
        For i = 0 To len
            returnValues(i) = New ParameterValue
            returnValues(i).Name = CType(controls(i), TextBox).Name
            returnValues(i).Value = CType(controls(i), TextBox).Text
        Next i

    Return returnValues
End Function
```

You can now use the `GetParameter` function to build an array of input parameters. You can add the following code to your `Render` click event to retrieve the input parameters.

C#

```
ParameterValue[] parameters = GetParameters();
```

VB

```
Dim parameters As ParameterValue() = GetParameters()
```

Now that you have your list of input parameters, you are almost ready to call the `Render` method. For this, you need to declare variables that will be used for the MIME type, encoding, output parameters, warnings, and stream IDs. These are all output parameters of the `Render` method. This step is necessary when working in C# but can be avoided in VB by passing `Nothing` into the unused parameters. The final variable you will need for the `Render` method is an array of bytes. This byte array can then be written to the file system.

C#

```
string encoding;
string mimeType;
ParameterValue[] parametersUsed;
Warning[] warnings;
string[] streamIds;

//render the report
byte[] data;
data = _rs.Render(reportItem.Path, format.Name,
        null, null, parameters, null, null, out encoding, out mimeType,
        out parametersUsed, out warnings, out streamIds);
```

VB

```
Dim encoding As String
Dim mimeType As String
Dim parametersUsed() As ParameterValue
Dim warnings() As Warning
Dim streamIds() As String

'render the report
Dim data() As Byte
data = _rs.Render(reportItem.Path, format.Name, Nothing, Nothing, _
        parameters, Nothing, Nothing, encoding, mimeType, _
        parametersUsed, warnings, streamIds)
```

Finally, you need to take the byte array returned from the `Render` method and write it to the file system. Use the output path specified in the output text box along with the report name and format file extension to open a file stream. Following is the entire `Render` button click event along with the final piece of code for writing the file to the file system.

C#

```csharp
private void btnRender_Click(object sender, System.EventArgs e)
{
    //get the format and report item from the comboboxes
    Format format = (Format)cboFormat.SelectedItem;
    ReportItem reportItem = (ReportItem)cboReports.SelectedItem;

    //set up variables needed to call render method
    ParameterValue[] parameters = GetParameters();

    string encoding;
    string mimeType;
    ParameterValue[] parametersUsed;
    Warning[] warnings;
    string[] streamIds;

    //render the report
    byte[] data;
    data = _rs.Render(reportItem.Path, format.Name,
            null, null, parameters, null, null, out encoding, out mimeType,
            out parametersUsed, out warnings, out streamIds);
    //create a file stream to write the output
    string fileName = txtOutputLocation.Text + "\\" +
    reportItem.Name + format.Extension;

    System.IO.FileStream fs = new System.IO.FileStream(fileName, System.IO.FileMode
                            .OpenOrCreate);

    System.IO.BinaryWriter writer = new System.IO.BinaryWriter(fs);
    writer.Write(data, 0, data.Length);
    writer.Close();
    fs.Close();
    MessageBox.Show("File written to: " + fileName);
}
```

VB

```vb
Private Sub btnRender_Click(ByVal sender As Object, ByVal e As System.EventArgs) _
                    Handles btnRender.Click

    'get the format and report item from the comboboxes
    Dim format As Format = CType(cboFormat.SelectedItem, Format)
    Dim reportItem As ReportItem = CType(cboReports.SelectedItem, ReportItem)
    'set up variables needed to call render method
    Dim parameters As ParameterValue() = GetParameters()
    Dim encoding As String
    Dim mimeType As String
    Dim parametersUsed() As ParameterValue
    Dim warnings() As Warning
    Dim streamIds() As String

    'render the report
    Dim data() As Byte
    data = _rs.Render(reportItem.Path, format.Name, Nothing, Nothing, _
```

```
                    parameters, Nothing, Nothing, encoding, mimeType, _
            parametersUsed, warnings, streamIds)
    'create a file stream to write the output
    Dim fileName As String = txtOutputLocation.Text & "\" & reportItem.Name & _
                        format.Extension

    Dim fs As New System.IO.FileStream(fileName, System.IO.FileMode.OpenOrCreate)

    Dim writer As New System.IO.BinaryWriter(fs)
    writer.Write(data, 0, data.Length)
    writer.Close()
    fs.Close()
    MessageBox.Show(("File written to: " + fileName))
End Sub
```

Now that you have completed the code for rendering the application, let's try it out. You need to build and run the project. When the form opens, enter your server information in the Server Address text box and click the Get Items button that you can see in Figure 12-11.

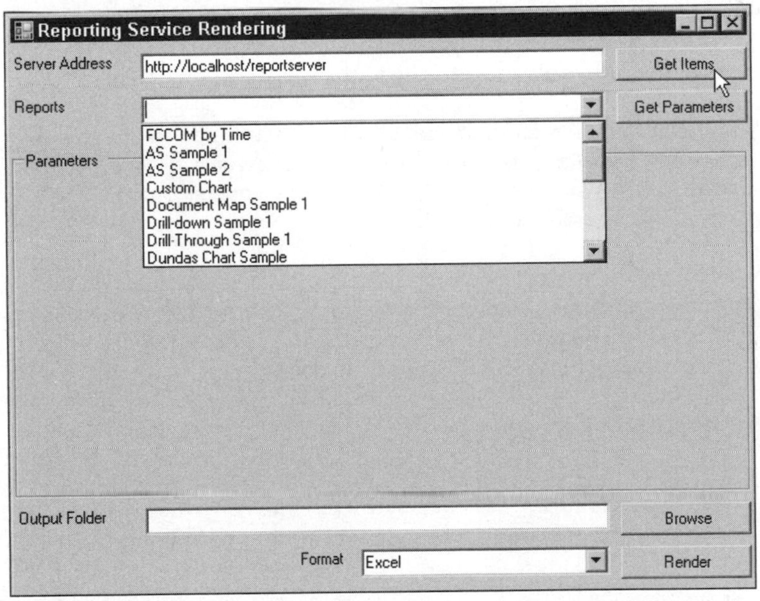

Figure 12-11

Select a report that takes parameters, and click the Get Parameters button. Finally, enter the Output Folder (C:) and the rendering Format as PDF. Once these items have been specified, you can click the Render button to render your report. When the rendering is complete, you will receive a message box letting you know that the file has been written to the specified location, as shown in Figure 12-5, earlier in this chapter.

You can now search for and open your saved file in Adobe Acrobat.

Rendering a Report to the File System Summary

In this section, you learned the basic steps of rendering a report to the file system:

❑ Using the `ReportingService` object's `ListChildren` method to return a list of reports.

❑ Using the `ReportingService` object's `GetReportParameters` method to return a list of report parameters.

❑ Using the `Render` method of the `ReportingService` object to output your report in a given format.

These basic steps can be used in numerous applications to render a report. Using these methods, users can create their own custom list of reports, customer report parameter pages, and output the report using the returned byte array. In the next section, you will use some of these same steps to render a report to the web via the `Response` object.

Rendering to the Web

In the preceding section, you saw the mechanics of rendering to a file system. However, most of today's applications are written for the web. Along with URL requests, you can also use the Reporting Services Web Service to render reports programmatically to the web.

While doing this, most of your steps will be identical to rendering to the file system; you simply change the interface. Using the `ListChildren` method, developers can easily bind reports to an ASP.NET data grid or create a tree view of available reports. Likewise, developers could also use the `GetParameters` method to create their own parameter interface.

Since you have seen both the `ListChilden` and `GetParameters` methods, in this section, you will work more with the specifics around developing ASP.NET applications. You'll look at changes that can be made to the `web.config` file to pass credential information to Reporting Services. Then you will look at the mechanics of rendering to the ASP.NET `Response` object.

Using Integrated Authentication

There are two main components to every security model: authentication and authorization. In Reporting Services, you can use Windows Integrated Security within an ASP.NET application to authenticate users. Before you start your example, you need to ensure that your application is configured to use Integrated Security.

After creating a new ASP.NET web application, you need to open IIS and change some settings of the virtual directory. Make sure that the Anonymous Access has been turned off and Integrated Windows authentication has been turned on in IIS.

In the sample created for this chapter, the virtual directory created in IIS is called `WebRenderingCS` and `WebRenderingVB` for the C# and Visual Basic projects, respectively. To set the virtual directories to use integrated authentication, you need to check their settings in IIS. Using Integrated Authentication in an ASP.NET web application is the easiest way to take advantage of the security features in Reporting Services. Using this method allows developers to concentrate on other areas of an application without having to build their own authentication mechanism. It also allows for taking full advantage of the Reporting Services role-based security model.

After updating the IIS settings to use Integrated Authentication, you will have to make some modifications to your ASP.NET web application.

Modifying the web.config File

In the web application created for this demonstration, you want to pass the user's security credentials to the Reporting Services Web service. To accomplish this, you have to allow your ASP.NET application to *impersonate* the currently logged-on user. Setting up impersonation requires adding the following line of code to the web.config file; place this line after the authorization tag in the file:

```
<identity impersonate="true" />
```

Setting Up the Reporting Service Web Service

Just as in any Windows application, you need to set a reference to the Reporting Services Web service. The details for creating the reference are identical to those found in the "Rendering through Windows" section, so we will not go into the details here.

For this example, I've added a web reference to http://localhost/reportserver/ reportservice.asmx?wsdl and named it RSService.

Rendering to the Response Object

Now that you have set up Integrated Authentication and modified the web.config file, you're ready to write some code. In this application, you will have one page that takes in a report path and format from the URL. You'll use this information to call the Render method of the Reporting Services object and write that information back to the response stream.

This sample will use one ASP.NET page called Render.aspx. Place your code sample in the Page_Load event of the page. This would be a logical approach when developing an application around Reporting Services. It allows you to have one point of entry to the Report Server. The page could then be referenced from other areas of an application.

Let's add some code to the page's Page_Load event to retrieve the report path and format from the HTTP Request:

C#

```
string path = Request.Params["Path"];
string format = Request.Params["Format"];
```

VB

```
Dim path As String = Request.Params("Path")
Dim format As String = Request.Params("Format")
```

Now that you have the report path and format, you can start setting up the ReportingService object. This is an instance of the Web service reference, similar to what you did in the Windows application. Like you did with the Windows application, you will create an instance of the ReportingService object and then set the credentials to the credentials of the currently logged-on user.

C#

```
//create the ReportingService object
ReportingService rs = new ReportingService();

//set the credentials to be passed to Reporting Services
rs.Credentials = System.Net.CredentialCache.DefaultCredentials;
```

VB

```
'create the ReportingService object
Dim rs As New ReportingService

'set the credentials to be passed to Reporting Services
rs.Credentials = System.Net.CredentialCache.DefaultCredentials
```

Once the ReportingService object has been created and your credentials set, you can go ahead and render the report. You will create variables to pass any report parameters (none in this example) and capture the reports encoding, MIME type, parameters used, warnings, and stream IDs. The key output parameter, which you'll render your report through, is the MIME type. This parameter will tell the HTTP Response what type of document is being passed back. The following code renders your report to the web application. You should notice that it is identical to the code used in the Windows application.

C#

```
ParameterValue[] parameters = new ParameterValue[0];
string encoding;
string mimeType;
ParameterValue[] parametersUsed;
Warning[] warnings;
string[] streamIds;

//render the report
byte[] data;
data = rs.Render(path, format, null, null, parameters, null, null,
        out encoding, out mimeType, out parametersUsed,
        out warnings, out streamIds);
```

VB

```
Dim parameters As ParameterValue()
Dim encoding As String
Dim mimeType As String
Dim parametersUsed As ParameterValue()
Dim warnings As Warning()
Dim streamIds As String()

'render the report
Dim data As Byte()
data = rs.Render(path, format, Nothing, Nothing, parameters, _
                 Nothing, Nothing, encoding, mimeType, parametersUsed, _
                 warnings, streamIds)
```

The Render method of the ReportingService object passes back a byte array that can be used in a number of ways. For the web, you will write this information directly back to the HTTP Response object. Before you write back the data though, you need to set some information about the report, namely, the report MIME type and a filename. You will start by assembling a filename for the report. To do this, you use the name of the report followed by an extension that you determine using the value returned in the MIME type parameter. Following is a sample function for determining a file extension based on the MIME type. There are a number of MIME types that can be passed back from Reporting Services that are not shown here, so you might want to add more code to this function for your application needs.

C#

```csharp
string GetExtension(string mimeType)
{
    string retVal="";

    switch(mimeType)
    {
        case "text/html": //HTML3.2, HTML4.0
            retVal = "html";
            break;
        case "multipart/related": //MHTML
            retVal = "html";
            break;
        case "text/xml":  //XML
            retVal = "xml";
            break;
        case "text/plain":  //CSV
            retVal = "csv";
            break;
        case "image/tiff":  //IMAGE
            retVal = "tif";
            break;
        case "application/pdf":  //PDF
            retVal = "pdf";
            break;
        case "application/vnd.ms-excel": //EXCEL
            retVal = "xls";
            break;
    }
}
```

VB

```vb
Public Function GetExtension(ByVal mimeType As String) As String
    Dim retVal As String

    Select Case mimeType
        Case "text/html"  'HTML3.2, HTML4.0
            retVal = "html"
        Case "multipart/related"  'MHTML
            retVal = "html"
        Case "text/xml"  'XML
            retVal = "xml"
```

```
            Case "text/plain"    'CSV
                retVal = "csv"
            Case "image/tiff"    'IMAGE
                retVal = "tif"
            Case "application/pdf"    'PDF
                retVal = "pdf"
            Case "application/vnd.ms-excel"    'EXCEL
                retVal = "xls"
        End Select


        Return retVal
    End Function
```

Now that you have a function to return the appropriate file extension, you can construct a complete file-name. Following is the code to use the report path information along with the MIME type to create the filename.

C#

```
string extension = GetExtension(mimeType);
string reportName = path.Substring(path.LastIndexOf("/") + 1);
string fileName = reportName + "." + extension;
```

VB

```
Dim extension As String = GetExtension(mimeType)
Dim reportName As String = path.Substring(path.LastIndexOf("/") + 1)
Dim fileName As String = reportName & "." & extension
```

Finally, you need to put it all together by writing the data and file information back to the Response object. For this, you:

1. Start by clearing out any information that is already in the response buffer.

2. Set the content type of the response equal to the MIME type of your rendered report.

3. If your report is in a format other than HTML, be sure to attach your filename information to the response.

4. Finally, use the BinaryWrite method to write the rendered report byte array directly to the Response object.

Following is the completed code for the Page_Load event:

C#

```
private void Page_Load(object sender, System.EventArgs e)
{
    //get the path and output format from the query string
    string path = Request.Params["Path"];
    string format = Request.Params["Format"];

    //create the ReportingService object
```

```
ReportingService rs = new ReportingService();

//set the credentials to be passed to Reporting Services
rs.Credentials = System.Net.CredentialCache.DefaultCredentials;

ParameterValue[] parameters = new ParameterValue[0];
string encoding;
string mimeType;
ParameterValue[] parametersUsed;
Warning[] warnings;
string[] streamIds;

//render the report
byte[] data;
data = rs.Render(path, format, null, null, parameters, null, null,
        out encoding, out mimeType, out parametersUsed,
        out warnings, out streamIds);
//determine if format is rendered to the web or a file.
string extension = GetExtension(mimeType);
string reportName = path.Substring(path.LastIndexOf("/") + 1);
string fileName = reportName + "." + extension;
//write the report back to the Response object
Response.Clear();
Response.ContentType = mimeType;
//add the file name to the response if it is not a web browser format.
if(mimeType!="text/html")
    Response.AddHeader("Content-Disposition", "attachment; filename=" +
                    fileName);

Response.BinaryWrite(data);
}
```

VB

```
Private Sub Page_Load(ByVal sender As System.Object, ByVal e As System.EventArgs)_
                Handles MyBase.Load

    'get the path and output format from the query string
    Dim path As String = Request.Params("Path")
    Dim format As String = Request.Params("Format")

    'create the ReportingService object
    Dim rs As New ReportingService

    'set the credentials to be passed to Reporting Services
    rs.Credentials = System.Net.CredentialCache.DefaultCredentials

    Dim parameters As ParameterValue()
    Dim encoding As String
    Dim mimeType As String
    Dim parametersUsed As ParameterValue()
    Dim warnings As Warning()
    Dim streamIds As String()


    'render the report
```

```
      Dim data As Byte()
      data = rs.Render(path, format, Nothing, Nothing, parameters, _
            Nothing, Nothing, encoding, mimeType, parametersUsed, _
            warnings, streamIds)

      'determine if format is rendered to the web or a file.
      Dim extension As String = GetExtension(mimeType)
      Dim reportName As String = path.Substring(path.LastIndexOf("/") + 1)
      Dim fileName As String = reportName & "." & extension

      'write the report back to the Response object
      Response.Clear()
      Response.ContentType = mimeType
      'add the file name to the response if it is not a web browser format.
      If mimeType <> "text/html" Then
          Response.AddHeader("Content-Disposition", "attachment; filename=" &
                              fileName)
      End If
      Response.BinaryWrite(data)
  End Sub
```

This example quickly demonstrates some of the key pieces of code that can be used to render reports to the web. You first need to set the security context for the application by configuring Windows Integrated authentication and allowing impersonation from your application. Next, you retrieve a report from Reporting Services by specifying the report path and format. Finally, you use the rendered report data along with its associated MIME type to render the report using the HTTP `Response` object.

Now that the code for your web application is complete, let's take a look at using your `Render.aspx` page. You can use a simple query string to render your report. A sample query string that renders the Employee List report from the Professional Reporting Services sample reports in HTML 4.0 format is as follows:

```
http://localhost/WebRenderingCS/Render.aspx?Path=%2fProfessional+SQL+Reporting+Serv
ices%2fEmployee_List&Format=HTML4.0
```

This URL does the following:

❑   It calls the `Render.aspx` page from your C# project.

❑   It passes in the required parameters: the path (`Professional SQL Reporting Services/Employee List`) and the Format (HTML 4.0).

If you place this URL into Internet Explorer, you'll get the HTML output shown in Figure 12-12.

Notice that when you enter HTML 4.0 as the output format, the report data is rendered directly in the browser. In your code, set the MIME type of your HTTP Response to `text/html` in this scenario. When the browser receives the response, it recognizes the MIME type and renders it directly to the browser.

Let's take a quick look at rendering in a format that does not go directly to the browser. Use the following URL to render the same Employee List report but in the EXCEL format:

```
http://localhost/WebRenderingCS/Render.aspx?Path=%2fProfessional+SQL+Reportin
g+Services%2fEmployee_List&Format=EXCEL
```

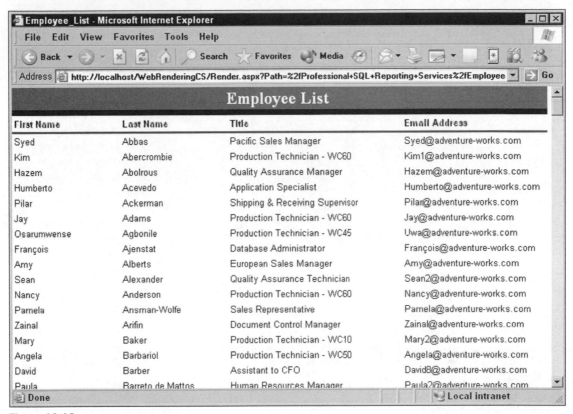

Figure 12-12

Figure 12-13 shows the result.

Notice this time that when you set the format to EXCEL, you are prompted to save to the file system. In this case, the MIME type needs to be set to `application/vnd.ms-excel`. You also need to add header information to the `Response` object that contains the filename `Employee_List.xls`. The MIME type notifies Internet Explorer that you are sending a file, and the added header gives it the appropriate filename.

In this section, you saw some of the base mechanics around rendering a report using an ASP.NET application. To start with, you need to pass the currently logged-on user's credentials. This is accomplished by setting the application virtual directory to use Integrated Windows authentication and then modifying the `web.config` file for the application to use impersonation. In the code, you need to call the Reporting Services Web service to retrieve the report along with content information such as MIME type. Once you have the binary report data, you can write that information directly back to the `Response` object.

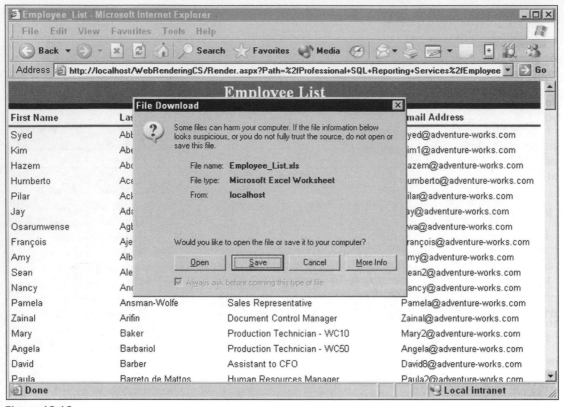

Figure 12-13

Using the ReportViewer Control

The ReportViewer control is by far the most flexible and, in most cases, the easiest technique for adding a report to your .NET application user interface. Two separate but very similar controls are available for .NET Windows forms and ASP.NET Web forms applications. All of the user interface attributes you have seen in the Report Manager and Designer Preview tab may be managed using properties of the control and may be set at design time in the properties window, or at runtime using program code.

The ReportViewer controls are client-side control that does not need a SQL Server instance to be used. The only dependency of the control is the .NET Framework 2.0. To install the Report Server does require a SQL Server license, however. The controls are redistributable, packaged as an msi.

The source data used by the control can come from any data source, not just SQL Server. The ReportViewer controls themselves have no knowledge of where the data comes from. Your application brings in the data from whatever source you choose and makes it available to the ReportViewer controls in the form of ADO.NET DataTables or custom business objects. The ReportViewer controls don't even know how to connect to databases or execute queries. By requiring the host application to supply the data, the

`ReportViewer` controls can be used with any data source. That includes relational, nonrelational, and non-database data sources.

Two different report execution scenarios are supported in both types of the `ReportViewer` control. The first is where standard, Report Server reports are deployed and executed on the report server and then viewed in the control as you would expect. The other is using the `ReportViewer` control as a mini-report-hosting engine that allows reports to execute in your application without needing a connection to the report server. This requires a version of the report definition file that's been retrofitted for client-side execution. The file is an RDLC file, with C standing for client-side processing.

Both RDL and RDLC formats have the same XML schema, but RDLC files allow some elements to contain empty values. RDLC files also contain information that the `ReportViewer` control uses to generate data-binding code. Once you've constructed an RDLC file in the Visual Studio Report Designer, you can then use the SQL Server Report Designer to add values for the empty elements. Simply change the file extension from `rdlc` to `rdl`, and add the missing values. Typically, the query text will need to be supplied.

Embedding a Server-Side Report in a Windows Application

In the following exercise, I'll take you through the steps to view a server-side report in a Windows forms application using the `ReportViewer` control. The properties and methods of the Web form version of the control are nearly identical, making your code transportable between Windows and Web application projects. In the first pass through the example project, I'll be demonstrating Visual Basic .NET code. At the end of the section, I'll show you code in C# that works the same way but sets the property values programmatically.

As you know, the report rendering interface can generate a number of toolbar options and parameter prompts. You may either use these default UI elements or replace them with your own. In the latter case, it would make sense to hide the default prompts. In the example, I will hide the parameter bar and feed parameters to the `ReportViewer` using controls on my form.

I've created a report called Product Sales Detail drill-down that contains two `Date` type parameters used to define a range of sales order dates for filtering. These parameters are named `OrderDateFrom` and `OrderDateTo`. The details of the report definition are unimportant for this demonstration.

First, I'll add a form to my Visual Studio 2005 Windows Application project. Although the Report Server is a component of SQL Server 2005, the `ReportViewer` control is not. The `ReportViewer` control is only included in Visual Studio 2005. Because of that, the `ReportViewer` must be added to the Control Toolbox in Visual Studio 2005. With the form in design view, right-click the Toolbox and select Choose Items... from the context menu. The Choose Toolbox Items dialog is shown in Figure 12-14. Check the `ReportViewer` control with the namespace Microsoft.Reporting.WinForms. Note that the ReportViewer web forms control is also displayed in this dialog.

Depending on your needs, it may be necessary to instantiate classes in your code from the ReportViewer namespace. To add a reference for this namespace to your project, right-click the project name in the Solution Explorer and select Add Reference.... The Add Reference dialog is shown in Figure 12-15. The items listed are similar to those shown previously in Figure 12-14. Highlight the component named Microsoft.ReportViewer.WinForms, and then click the OK button.

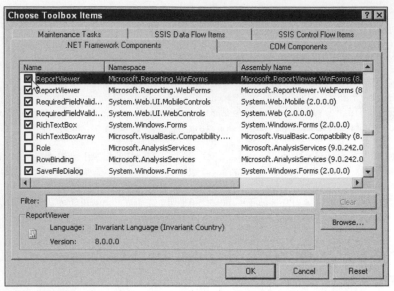

Figure 12-14

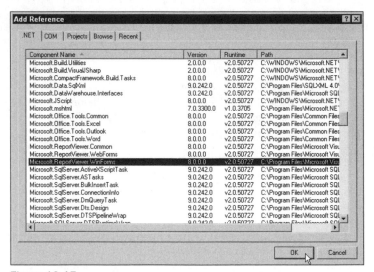

Figure 12-15

Figure 12-16 shows part of the form Designer Toolbox. The ReportViewer control icon now appears along with the rest of the form controls.

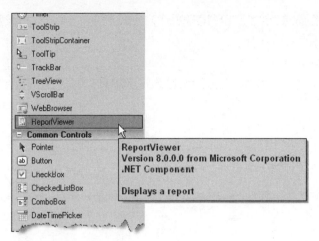

Figure 12-16

Drag and drop the `ReportViewer` onto the form. Resize and anchor it to meet your needs. In the form shown in Figure 12-17, I have added two labels and `DateTimePicker` controls for my two parameters. I've also added a button to run the code that will set these parameters and display the report.

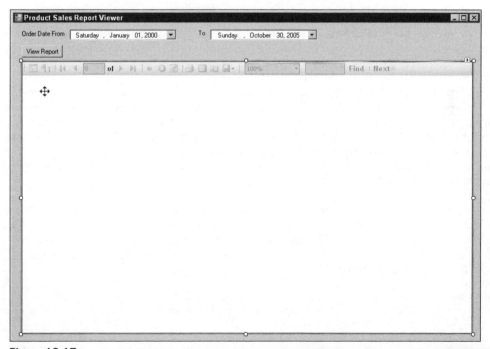

Figure 12-17

First, I'll set all of the `ReportViewer` properties at design time using the properties window. After that, I'll demonstrate the code that will set the same properties at runtime.

The report you want to display is the value entered for the `ReportPath` property, as shown in Figure 12-18.

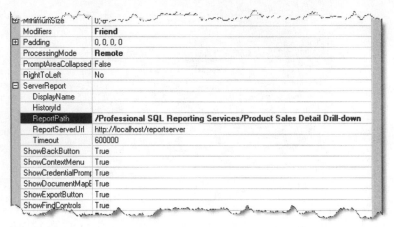

Figure 12-18

The `ReportPath` property is the report location in the Report Server hierarchy. In this case, I've selected a report on my local machine to display in the `ReportViewer` control. The location of the Report Server is set using the `ReportServerUrl` property. The default Report Server URL is also displayed in Figure 12-18.

Since you're going to use the Report Server for processing, set the `ProcessingMode` property to Remote. That will use the Report Server to retrieve source data that will be used in the report. In Remote mode, the `ReportViewer` controls display reports that are hosted on a SQL Server 2005 Report Server. The source data for those reports can come from any appropriate data source, not just SQL Server. This behavior is normal report processing behavior. Setting the processing mode is shown in Figure 12-19.

With everything except the parameters set using the properties window, the only necessary code sets the parameters and executes the report.

Parameters are managed as an array of `ReportParameter` objects. Note that the reference to the Microsoft.Reporting.WinForms namespace is used to instantiate this object. Since the report has two required parameters, the array is declared with a maximum element index of 1 to provide two elements. Each of the elements is populated by passing the parameter name and value to each of the two the `ReportParameter` constructors.

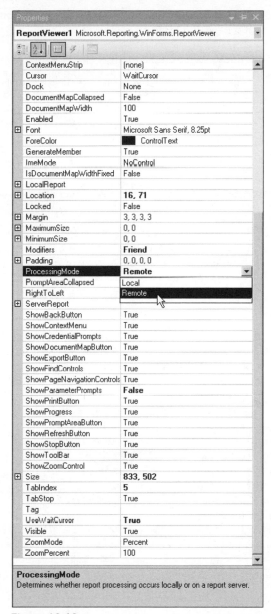

Figure 12-19

The report parameters are populated by passing the array to the `SetParameters` method of the `ServerReport` object.

Finally, the ReportViewer's `RefreshReport` method causes report execution to begin.

```vb
Private Sub btnViewReport_Click(ByVal sender As System.Object, _
                    ByVal e As System.EventArgs) Handles btnViewReport.Click

    Dim Param(1) As Microsoft.Reporting.WinForms.ReportParameter
    Param(0) = New Microsoft.Reporting.WinForms.ReportParameter("OrderDateFrom", _
                    Me.dtOrderDateFrom.Value)
    Param(1) = New Microsoft.Reporting.WinForms.ReportParameter("OrderDateTo", _
                    Me.dtOrderDateTo.Value)

    Me.ReportViewer1.ServerReport.SetParameters(Param)
    Me.ReportViewer1.RefreshReport()

End Sub
```

In Figure 12-20 you can see the result. The report is displayed in the `ReportViewer` control embedded on the form. The standard report parameter bar and prompts are not displayed in the top of the viewer since they were suppressed using the related `ReportViewer` properties.

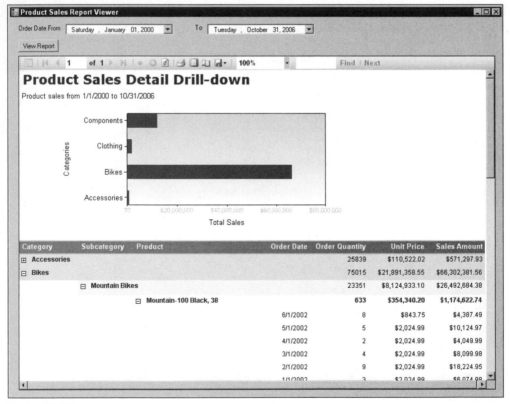

Figure 12-20

Setting Properties at Runtime

All of the `ReportViewer` parameters may be set at runtime using programming code rather than the properties window. The following is the only code required for this demonstration. The report server URL and path for the report are set using string type variables. In this sample code, I've encapsulated the code in a method that can be called from a button click event.

```
Private Sub ViewReport()

    Dim sReportServerURL As String = "http://LocalHost/ReportServer"
    Dim sReportPath As String = _
            "/Professional SQL Reporting Services/Product Sales Detail Drill-down"

    Dim Param(1) As Microsoft.Reporting.WinForms.ReportParameter
    Param(0) = New Microsoft.Reporting.WinForms.ReportParameter("OrderDateFrom", _
                    Me.dtOrderDateFrom.Value)
    Param(1) = New Microsoft.Reporting.WinForms.ReportParameter("OrderDateTo", _
                    Me.dtOrderDateTo.Value)

    With Me.ReportViewer1
        .ProcessingMode = Microsoft.Reporting.WinForms.ProcessingMode.Remote
        With .ServerReport
            .ReportServerUrl = New Uri(sReportServerURL)
            .ReportPath = sReportPath
            .SetParameters(Param)
        End With

        .ShowParameterPrompts = False
        .ShowPromptAreaButton = False
        .RefreshReport()
    End With

End Sub
```

Here's the same functionality in C#:

```
private void ViewReport()
{
    string sReportServerURL = "http://LocalHost/ReportServer";
    string sReportPath =
            "/Professional SQL Reporting Services/Product Sales Detail Drill-down";

    Microsoft.Reporting.WinForms.ReportParameter[] Param;
    Param[0] = new Microsoft.Reporting.WinForms.ReportParameter("OrderDateFrom",
                        this.dtOrderDateFrom.Value.ToString());
    Param[1] = new Microsoft.Reporting.WinForms.ReportParameter("OrderDateTo",
                    this.dtOrderDateTo.Value.ToString());

    reportViewer1.ProcessingMode = Microsoft.Reporting.WinForms.ProcessingMode.Remote;
    reportViewer1.ServerReport.ReportServerUrl = new Uri(sReportServerURL);
```

```
reportViewer1.ServerReport.ReportPath = sReportPath;
reportViewer1.ServerReport.SetParameters(Param);
reportViewer1.ShowParameterPrompts = false;
reportViewer1.ShowPromptAreaButton = false;
reportViewer1.RefreshReport();
}
```

The ReportViewer controls provide an easy-to-implement way of embedding reports in your custom Web and Windows applications. Unfortunately, you still have to code the rest of the application in order to provide users with an all-around solution. There's an in-between option, where reports can be made available to users without going through the Report Manager application. That in-between option is SharePoint.

SharePoint Web Parts

SharePoint sites are Web-based applications that provide a single point of entry for information across an enterprise. Better yet, sites can be created without any programming. Windows SharePoint sites can be created by anyone with sufficient permissions. The functionality is made available through Windows SharePoint Services. Multiple SharePoint sites can be aggregated into portals through the use of SharePoint Portal Server. A fundamental SharePoint concept is the Web Part. Web Parts can be thought of as modular elements containing functionality that is added to the user interface. Web Parts typically display specific information and can be moved around the Web page. For example, SharePoint comes with Web Parts that can display images and list files. They have a consistent format, with a customizable title bar and a Web Part menu available on the right side of it. SharePoint is a natural for corporate reporting portals.

Reporting Services Web Parts includes two Web Parts: the Explorer for navigating through the report server content and the Viewer for viewing rendered reports. They work by way of an IFrame that's been embedded into the Web Parts. The Report Manager application uses an IFrame to display reports as well. The Reporting Services Web Parts expose a slightly smaller set of functionality than the full Report Manager interface. Like regular Web Parts, the Reporting Services Web Parts provide a standard context menu from the title bar.

Report Explorer Control

The Report Explorer Web Part provides a way to navigate around the content in the Report Server database. Clicking a report link in the Report Explorer displays the report. There are two ways the report can be displayed: in linked or stand-alone mode. When linked to a ReportViewer control, the report renders in that control. When in stand-alone mode, the report is rendered in a new browser window. Which mode you choose typically depends on how much screen real estate you have available. If the Report Explorer is not linked to a Report Viewer Web Part, it opens a new browser window to display reports. Connected mode simply means that data is passed between the two Web Parts.

Like Report Manager, the Report Explorer Web Part has a Details view. When in this view, you can create or edit a subscription to a report. It also provides bread-crumb-trail navigation and sortable columns. In the Report Explorer, however, only folders, reports, and resources are displayed. You don't have access to Data Sources from the Report Explorer.

ReportViewer Control

The `ReportViewer` control is used to display rendered reports. You can interact with reports as you would in Report Manager, using links within the report and DHTML functionality for collapsing report sections. For drill-down reports, the target report displays in the same Report Viewer Web Part. Drill-through reports, however, are rendered in a new browser window. Depending on the layout of the report and the size of the Web Part on the page, only a portion of the report may be visible. You'll need to use the scroll bars to view the rest of the report. As with standard Web Parts, you can change the size of the Report Viewer on the page in the Tool Pane. The Tool Pane is a configuration window that lets you set property values for Web Parts displayed on the SharePoint page.

Like the Report Explorer Web Part, the Viewer can be used in connected or stand-alone mode. In connected mode, clicking a link in the Report Explorer renders the report in the Viewer. With the Report Viewer in stand-alone mode, it doesn't have the Explorer pointing it to a report for rendering. You'll have to provide the path to the report manually. The report path is set using the Tool Pane. Though this might not seem very user-friendly, it has a purpose. Once the report path has been set, the Viewer can then display the report without user-initiated input or action.

Report parameters are displayed at the top of the Viewer content area. This parameters section expands to display the report parameters, with the standard Report Manager toolbar below it. Using the toolbar, reports can be exported in either Excel or PDF format.

Summary

In this chapter, we saw three ways to render reports from Reporting Services. The first part of the chapter focused on rendering reports via URL requests. The second part looked at rendering reports programmatically through the Reporting Services Web service. In the last part, you used the `ReportViewer` control to easily embed reports in a Windows application.

URL rendering gives you a quick way to add Reporting Services reports to your own applications. You can add Reporting Services reports to custom portals or create your own custom report links in other applications.

Rendering reports directly through an ASP.NET application can be very helpful. It allows developers to create their own interface for items such as parameters. A key point to remember is that Report Manager uses the same Reporting Services Web Service that we used in the examples in this chapter. So, anything that you can do from the Report Manager can also be done through your own code. This adds an incredible amount of flexibility for developers of custom applications.

This chapter has shown you how to:

❑ Use simple URL query strings to access reports.

❑ Programmatically work with the Reporting Services Web Service API.

❑ Embed reports into custom Windows and Web applications.

❑ Work with the `ReportViewer` control in Visual Studio 2005.

Since the Reporting Services API is implemented as a Web service, you can call it from a number of different types of applications, including .NET Windows applications, ASP.NET web applications, and .NET console applications. You can even use this Web service from Visual Basic 6.0, VBA applications using Microsoft's SOAP library, or essentially any application that can send a properly formatted request to the report server. This flexibility allows for the creation of a number of applications, including those that use custom security or pass parameter information stored in other application databases.

With Reporting Services Web service and the varied ways to access its functionality, developers can quickly and easily incorporate Reporting Services into their own custom-built applications.

13

Extending Reporting Services

As you learned in Chapter 3, Reporting Services is a robust and scalable product for enterprise report processing. In addition, Microsoft has created Reporting Services using a modular extensible architecture that gives users the ability to customize, extend, and expand the product to support their enterprise business intelligence (BI) reporting needs. This chapter introduces you to most of the areas within Reporting Services that allow customization and some of the reasons that you may wish to extend the product. The basic requirements for implementing each type of extension are discussed followed by a detailed example of creating and deploying a data processing extension.

In this chapter, you will learn about the extensibility of Reporting Services and the areas that currently support customization. These include:

❑   Extensibility options.

❑   Reasons for extending SQL Server Reporting Services.

❑   How to create custom extensions.

❑   How to install custom extensions.

Reporting Services currently supports extending its behavior in the following areas:

❑   **Data processing extensions:** Custom processing extensions allow you to access any type of data using a consistent programming model. This option is for you if you cannot access your data using one of the currently supported providers (ODBC, OLE DB, Oracle, and SQL).

❑   **Delivery Extensions:** Earlier in the managing reports chapter, we discussed "subscribing to a report." During this process, one of the required options is the method of delivery. Do you want the report sent to your cell phone in image format, or perhaps delivered to a file share for your perusal at a later date? The ability to extend SSRS with delivery extensions allows you to choose.

Delivery extensions allow you to deliver reports to users or groups of users according to a schedule. E-mail and network file shares are the delivery mechanisms currently built into the product.

Creating a delivery extension is really a two-part process. You must create the extension itself, as well as a UI tool to manage the extension if you want it to be usable from the SSRS Report Manager. The difficulty in creating a delivery extension is primarily a function of the delivery mechanism.

❑ **Rendering Extensions:** Rendering extensions control the type of document/media that gets created when a report is processed. Theoretically, you could have Report Services create any type of media given the ability to extend the product in this area. Microsoft provides the following rendering extensions out of the box:

 ❑ **HTML:** The HTML extension will generate HTML 3.2 for use with older browsers and HTML 4.0 for browsers that support the dynamic HTML standard.

 ❑ **MHTML:** MHTML is another HTML standard that was created to allow disconnected viewing of HTML documents. All the images in the page are encoded into the document, which increases its size but allows it to be viewed both online and offline.

 ❑ **Excel:** The Excel extension creates Excel-specific MHTML.

 ❑ **CSV:** The Comma Separated Values emit the data fields separated by a comma. The first row of the CSV results contains the field names for the data.

 ❑ **Image:** The image extension allows you to export reports as images in the EMF, GIF, JPEG, PNG, TIFF, and WMF formats.

 ❑ **PDF:** This extension allows the generation of reports in the PDF format.

❑ **Security Extensions:** In its first release, Reporting Services only supported Integrated Windows Security for report access. This was a pretty big problem for some enterprise players. Most companies have heterogeneous networks with multiple operating systems and products. In a perfect world, all of our networks, applications, and resources would support some form of "*single sign-on,*" or at least would allow us to build this ourselves. If Microsoft wanted SQL Server to be a key part of an Enterprise Business Intelligence platform, it had to play nice with others.

Microsoft fixed this problem in service release one. The release contained full documented security extension interfaces and an example using forms-based security. You may now implement your security model using SSRS.

Extension through Interfaces

Reporting Services uses common interfaces or "extension points" to allow expanding the product in a standard way. Enforcing the requirement that RS extension objects must implement certain interfaces allows Reporting Services to interact with different object types without knowledge of their specific implementation. This is a common object-oriented programming technique used to abstract the design from the implementation.

For an in-depth study of this topic, look at the "Creational Patterns" section of Design Patterns (Addison Wesley).

What Is an Interface?

Most C/C++ developers are intimately familiar with interfaces. The entire COM programming model is based upon them. Visual Basic developers have used them as well, but the VB6 programming environment hides this. Seasoned .NET developers are also familiar with the use of Interfaces, as we use them to interact with the FCL (Framework Class Libraries). In fact, Reporting Services itself is exposed to developers through a web service interface. In order to provide complete coverage of extending Reporting Services, a definition and explanation of interfaces is required.

So what is an *interface?* An interface is a predefined code construct that forms a contract between software components and defines how they communicate.

That sounds great, but what does it mean? It simply means that in order to adhere to the contract defined by an interface, all extension components must contain certain methods, properties, and so on.

In Reporting Services specifically, it means that every single extension component must contain certain methods defined by the IExtension interface. Other interface implementations may be required as well, depending on the type of extension you are trying to create.

Interface Language Differences

There are differences in the way that VB.NET and C# require interface methods to be declared. C# supports "implicit" interface definitions. If the method names and signatures match those of an interface implemented by the class, then the class methods are automatically mapped to their associated interface definitions. I chose IDisposable for this example because many of the classes you will create are required to implement it.

C#

```
public class TestClass : IDisposable
{
  public void Dispose() //this method is automatically mapped to IDisposable.Dispose
  {
      //write some code to dispose of non-memory resources
  }
}
```

VB.NET requires explicit interface implementation. In order to be mapped correctly, VB.NET requires that you specify that the method is implementing a certain interface. This is done with the Implements keyword as follows:

VB.NET

```
Public Class TestClass
    implements IDisposable

    Public Sub Dispose() Implements IDisposable.Dispose
            'write some code to dispose of non-memory resources
    End Sub
End Class
```

There are new features in Visual Studio 2005 that make this distinction almost unnecessary. Microsoft has a new feature I call Interface AutoComplete. When you indicate that a class should implement a certain interface, Visual Studio can jump in and create wrapper methods for all of the properties, methods, and so on that are required for that interface (see Figure 13-1). This saves a huge amount of typing and is a great productivity enhancement when creating objects designed to "plug in" to an existing framework.

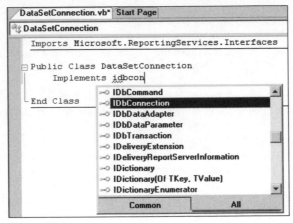

Figure 13-1

Microsoft is also attempting to build "best practices" into Visual Studio. While the two examples shown above are technically correct in that they implement IDisposable, they do not implement the IDisposable design pattern shown in the .NET Framework SDK. When I allow Visual Studio 2005 to do the heavy lifting, it creates a more feature-complete implementation that includes consideration for cascading object chains and explicit release of memory and nonmemory resources. Visual Studio would create code similar to the following for IDisposable. I did take liberties with the comments to make it easier to read.

VB.NET

```
Public Class TestDispose
    Implements System.IDisposable

    Private disposed As Boolean = False

    'IDisposable
    Private Overloads Sub Dispose(ByVal disposing As Boolean)
        If Not Me.disposed Then
            If disposing Then
                ' TODO: put code to dispose managed resources
            End If
            ' TODO: put code to free unmanaged resources here
        End If
        Me.disposed = True
    End Sub


    'IDisposable Support
    'Don't change
    Public Overloads Sub Dispose() Implements IDisposable.Dispose
```

```
      ' Don't change. Put cleanup code
      'in Dispose(ByVal disposing As Boolean) above.
        Dispose(True)
        GC.SuppressFinalize(Me)
    End Sub

    'Don't change
    Protected Overrides Sub Finalize()
        Dispose(False)
        MyBase.Finalize()
    End Sub

End Class
```

You will be using this Interface AutoComplete feature for the remainder of this chapter. If you are using Visual Studio 2003, you will have to create these methods manually, or download the source and revert to the old "cut and paste." The generated code for IDisposable is suitable for demonstration purposes, so I won't repeat this code for each object but simply indicate that it is required.

Data Processing Extensions — a Detailed Look

Reporting Services allows you to access data from traditional data sources such as relational databases using the existing .NET data providers. The following providers are supplied as part of the .NET Framework supplied by Microsoft:

❑   ODBC

❑   OLE DB

❑   Oracle

❑   SQLClient

Data processing extensions are components that allow you to access data for use within Reporting Services. If that implies a ".NET data provider" to you, then congratulations are in order. These two types of data access objects are very similar and are based on a common set of interface definitions. If you have already built a custom .NET data provider, you may use that provider with Reporting Services with no modification. However, you also can extend your existing provider to provide additional functionality.

To begin, we need to discuss the similarities and differences between a standard .NET data provider and a Reporting Services data processing extension. Let's start with some architectural information about data providers in general, and then dive into the details of creating a custom data processing extension. The .NET Framework has a data access object model that is very similar to that used in traditional COM-based ADO. The ADO.NET object model is displayed below in Figure 13-2.

Prior to Service Pack 1 of SSRS on SQL2000, Reporting Service data providers were essentially the same as the ADO data providers, except for the fact that Microsoft had implemented wrapper classes around the .NET providers in order for them to meet the Reporting Service extension interface requirements. The Reporting Services requirements were a subset of the data provider requirements. The programming paradigm was the same as well.

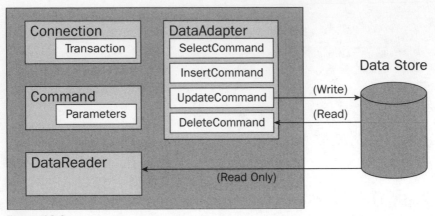

Figure 13-2

With Service Pack 1 came the ability to customize and extend the security model of Reporting Services. This required adding a few things to the object model.

The basic steps for working with a data source are:

❏ Make a connection to a data source.

❏ Issue a command to manipulate data.

❏ Retrieve the results of your query.

These actions map directly to the objects above, although a `DataAdapter` implementation is not needed because Reporting Services only *reads* the data.

The following table summarizes the objects that are normally created in a data processing extension and provides a description of the object responsibilities.

Object	Description
Connection	Establishes a connection to a specific data source.
Command	Executes a command against a data source. Exposes a `Parameters` collection and can execute within the scope of a transaction.
DataReader	Provides access to data using a forward-only, read-only stream.
DataAdapter (not required)	Responsible for retrieving data and for resolving updates with the data source. This object is not required for a Reporting Services data processing extension because Reporting Services only needs to *read* the data to create reports.

Each of these objects contains implementation-specific code needed to create a connection, issue commands, or read and update data. Microsoft has enforced a consistent data access mechanism by basing these objects on a set of standard interfaces. Figure 13-3 shows the interfaces that may be implemented when creating a data processing extension, although not all of them are required.

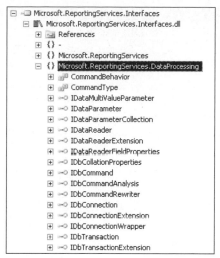

Figure 13-3

You may build a minimalist `DataExtension` by implementing the required interfaces shown in the following table and add additional behavior by implementing the optional interfaces.

Required Interfaces	Description
IDbConnection	Unique session with a data source.
IDbCommand	Represents query command methods to be executed against a data source.
IDataParameter	Methods to support passing parameters to a Command object.
IDataParameterCollection	Collection of parameters.
IDataReader	Methods used to read a forward-only read-only data stream.
IExtension	Reporting Services specific Interface that supports localization and is implemented by all SSRS extensions.

Optional Interfaces	Description
IDataReaderExtension	Used to provide `Resultset`-specific aggregation information.
IDbCommandAnalysis	Analysis Services–specific extension.
IDbConnectionExtension	Unique session with a data source.
IDbTransaction	Local transaction (nondistributed).
IDbTransactionExtension	Reporting Services–specific interface that supports localization and is implemented by all SRS extensions.

Creating a Custom Data Processing Extension

Creating a full-blown data provider is no trivial task. The goal of this walk-through is to familiarize you with the .NET data access mechanism, as well as help you create and install a custom Reporting Services data processing extension. Our implementation is simplified in that it does not support transactions or the use of parameters, and many of the methods are empty unless code is explicitly required. All of the images shown were created using the Visual Basic IDE. The code snippets will be given in both languages unless there is a reason to do otherwise.

The Scenario

After the release of Reporting Services for SQL 2000 and the first edition of this book, it seemed that everywhere that I went, I was asked the same question: Why doesn't Reporting Services allow me to consume existing `DataSet` objects? Alas, I had no answer.

It seems that a lot of companies have internal data silos. (Really?) Well, the complaint was that after going to the trouble of getting different internal organizations to expose needed data via Web services, you were unable to *easily* use it in a report.

After the release of Service Pack 1, the Books Online documentation contained an example extension that used some of the dataset's intrinsic properties to allow you to query a `DataSet` object and limit the resulting rows based upon certain criteria. The only problem was that you were unable to do complex filtering or limit the columns returned by a query. This example demonstrates one way that you might give yourself the filtering and sorting that you need.

Creating and Setting Up the Project

Let's start by creating our project. Create the Project by choosing File⇨New⇨Project. Change the name of the Project to `DataSetDataExtension`. Use the Class Library template. After your project is created, you need to set up your environment to help you work. The Visual Basic IDE tends to hide some things from you, so you are going to make some changes to help our C# brethren following along. The first thing you want to do is show all of your references. The default behavior of VB.NET is to hide them. Choose Project⇨Show All Files from the menu. The Explorer tab should now show you all of your project references.

Next, you need to add the references to the required SSRS dlls. The `Microsoft.ReportingServices` `.DataProcessing` namespace is needed to implement the data processing extension interfaces, and the `Microsoft.ReportingServices.Interfaces` namespace is needed to implement the `IExtension` interface. Both of these namespaces are defined in the same dll, `Microsoft.ReportingServices` `.Interfaces.dll`. The location of extensions and their dependencies is a subdirectory below the installation directory of SQL Server itself. I will refer to the SQL Server installation path as *InstallPath*. The directory for the SSRS extensions dll that you need is *InstallPath*`\MSSQL.3\Reporting Services\` `ReportServer\bin`. On my machine this directory is `C:\Program Files\Microsoft SQL Server\` `MSSQL.3\Reporting Services\ReportServer\bin`. Choose Project⇨Properties from the menu. Browse to the appropriate directory and add the reference. Your Solution Explorer window should now look something like that shown in Figure 13-4.

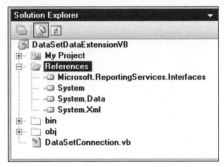

Figure 13-4

The name of the assembly needs to be changed to reflect your custom namespace. Choose Project⇨ Properties from the menu. At this point, you may either choose to put the fill in the root namespace for you components or put it in your code. The example code contains the namespaces directly. This was another way for me to avoid IDE problems as shown in Figure 13-5.

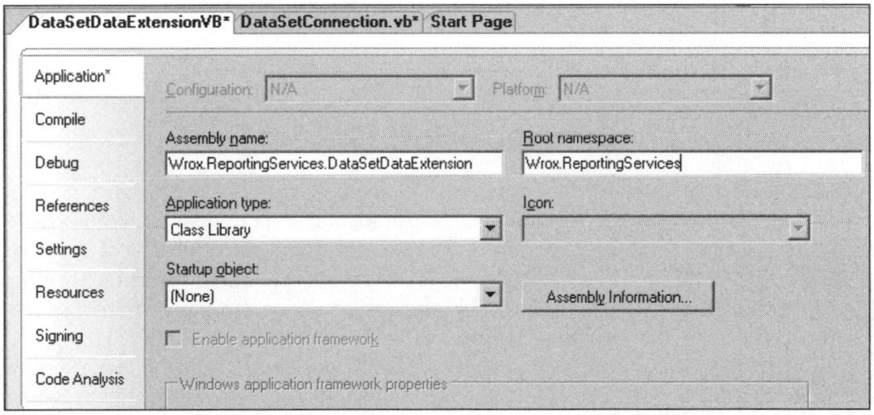

Figure 13-5

Most of the classes created for this project have common requirements. Most of them have empty default constructors, and all of them require the use of some common namespaces. The code below is a skeleton of how each class should look after you create it. Replace the italicized "*ClassName*" with the name of the class you are working on. This will allow you to concentrate only on the differences between the objects that will be created in your data extension project.

Notice the use of an alias for the System.Data namespace. You will be working with DataSet objects in this example that are defined in System.Data. To support the SSRS interface requirements you must have a reference to Microsoft.ReportingServices.DataProcessing where IExtension is defined. Because the common data interfaces are defined in both namespaces, you need an alias to avoid name collisions. This namespace is not needed in the DataSetParameter or DataSetParameterCollection classes.

C#

```
Using System;
using Microsoft.ReportingServices.DataProcessing;
using FCLData = System.Data;

namespace Wrox.ReportingServices.DataSetDataExtension
{
    public class DataSetClassName
    {
    }
}
```

VB.NET

```
Imports System
Imports Microsoft.ReportingServices.DataProcessing
Imports FCLData = System.Data

Namespace Wrox.ReportingServices.DataSetDataExtension
    Public Class DataSetClassName

    End Class
End Namespace
```

Creating the DataSetConnection Object

The connection object is responsible for connecting to the data source and providing a mechanism for accessing both the data processing extension-specific transaction and command objects. These responsibilities are enforced through the IDbConnection interface. Because the connection object is the extension entry point and will be the first object in the extension that will deal with SQL Reporting Services, it also is required to support Iextension, as discussed previously. Because the connection object is usually responsible for connecting to a unmanaged resource, it is required to implement IDisposable. The aggregate interface for all these others is IDbConnectionExtension, which is what you will implement. A diagram created with the new Visual Studio class designer is in Figure 13-6 shown below. Having the class designer within Visual Studio makes it easier both to implement and understand the relationships between objects in a complex system.

To add the DataSetConnection class to the project, choose Project➪Add Class from the menu. Change the name of the class to DataSetConnection. Open the file, and indicate that the class should implement the IDbConnection Extension interface, as discussed earlier. Visual Studio will jump in and create all of the wrapper methods for you. Because you will be doing file IO and using regular expressions to parse your ConnectionString property, you need to add those namespaces to this class.

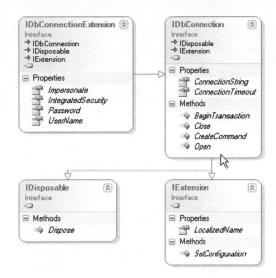

Figure 13-6

C#

```
using System;
using System.IO;
using System.Text.RegularExpressions;
using Microsoft.ReportingServices.DataProcessing;
```

VB.NET

```
Imports System
Imports System.IO
Imports System.Text.RegularExpressions
Imports Microsoft.ReportingServices.DataProcessing
```

Variable Declarations

In order to maintain state for your connection object, you need to declare some member variables. The `connString` variable will hold the connection string that will be used to connect to the data source. The `localName` variable should hold a localized name of the current extension used to list the extension as a data source option in the user interface of tools such as Visual Studio or SQL Management Studio. The filename variable will hold the path to the `DataSet` object persisted as XML.

C#

```
private string m_userName;
private string m_password;
private bool m_integrated;
private string m_impersonate;
private string m_connectionString = String.Empty;
private string m_localizedName = "DataSet Data Source";
private string m_fileName;

internal FCLData.DataSet dataSet;
```

VB.NET

```
Private m_impersonate As String
Private m_integrated As Boolean
Private m_password As String
Private m_userName As String
Private m_connectionString As String = String.Empty
Private m_localizedlName As String = "DataSet Data Source"
Private m_fileName As String

Friend dataSet As FCLData.DataSet = Nothing
```

Constructors

The `DataSetConnection` object has an empty default constructor, as well as an overloaded constructor that allows the developer to create the object and initialize the connection string in one line of code.

C#

```
public DataSetConnection(string connectionString)
{
    this. m_connectionString = connectionString;
}
```

VB.NET

```
Public Sub New(ByVal connectionString As String)
Me m_connectionString = connectionString
End Sub
```

Implementing IDbConnectionExtension

`IDbConnectionExtension` adds support for extending the SSRS security model. The interface definition is shown below. Notice the unusual use of `WriteOnly` properties.

C#

```
public interface IDbConnectionExtension : IDbConnection, IDisposable, IExtension
{
    // Properties
    string Impersonate { set; }
    bool IntegratedSecurity {get; set; }
```

```
        string Password { set; }
        string UserName { set; }
}
```

VB.NET

```
Public Interface IDbConnectionExtension
      Implements IDbConnection, IDisposable, IExtension

      ' Properties
      WriteOnly Property Impersonate As String
      Property IntegratedSecurity As Boolean
      WriteOnly Property Password As String
      WriteOnly Property UserName As String
End Interface
```

Impersonate Property

Windows supports the idea of *impersonation*. This is the idea that a process of execution can "assume" the identity of a set of assigned security credentials. The Impersonate property allows the assignment of a string representing the user account whose security context the process should run under.

C#

```
public string Impersonate
{
      set { m_impersonate = value; }
}
```

VB.NET

```
Public WriteOnly Property Impersonate() As String
   Implements IDbConnectionExtension.Impersonate
      Set(ByVal value As String)
            m_impersonate = value
      End Set
End Property
```

IntegratedSecurity Property

The IntegratedSecurity property indicates whether or not you want the extension to run using Windows security for both authentication (identifying the user), and authorization (denying/granting a user permission to perform certain actions).

C#

```
public bool IntegratedSecurity
  {
      get{ return m_integrated;}
      set {m_integrated = value;}
  }
```

VB.NET

```
Public Property IntegratedSecurity() As Boolean
     Implements IDbConnectionExtension.IntegratedSecurity
       Get
            Return m_integrated
       End Get
       Set(ByVal value As Boolean)
            m_integrated = value
       End Set
End Property
```

UserName/Password Properties

The UserName and Password properties are used during the Reporting Services authentication process. The UserName/Password pair are authenticated against either the Windows credential store or some custom store you provide. Next, an object that implements IPrincipal is created and assigned to the current thread of execution. That object contains the user's identity and role membership information and is used to authorize user access to system resources (the data source). Good security practice dictates that this information be available for the shortest time possible—thus the use of read-only properties.

C#

```
public string Password
 {
        set { m_password = value; }
 }

public string UserName
 {
        set { m_userName = value; }
 }
```

VB.NET

```
Public WriteOnly Property Password() As String
  Implements IDbConnectionExtension.Password
        Set(ByVal value As String)
             m_password = value
        End Set
End Property

Public WriteOnly Property UserName() As String
  Implements IDbConnectionExtension.UserName
        Set(ByVal value As String)
             m_userName = value
        End Set
End Property
```

Implementing IDbConnection

The IDbConnection interface is the standard mechanism that data providers use to control the use of the connection object. These properties and methods help you make changes to the connection settings, open and close the connection, and associate the connection with a valid transaction. Your connection object does not support transactions due to its read-only nature and because you are working against a file system, which is not a resource manager.

C#

```
public interface IDbConnection : IDisposable, IExtension
    {
        IDbTransaction BeginTransaction();
        IDbCommand CreateCommand();
        void Open();
        void Close();
        string ConnectionString { get; set; }
        int ConnectionTimeout { get; }
    }
```

VB.NET

```
Public Interface IDbConnection
    Inherits IDisposable, IExtension
      Function BeginTransaction() As IDbTransaction
      Function CreateCommand() As IDbCommand
      Sub Open()
      Sub Close()
      Property ConnectionString() As String
      Property ConnectionTimeout() As Integer
End Interface
```

BeginTransaction Function

The BeginTransaction function is primarily responsible for initiating a new transaction and returning a reference to a valid, implementation-specific transaction object. The file system, which is our data store, does not support transactions, but this method is required by the interface. You need to ensure that the developer who will use your object in code is aware of that fact. This is done by throwing a NotSupportedException.

C#

```
public IDbTransaction BeginTransaction()
    { //example doesn't support transactions
      throw new NotSupportedException("Transactions not supported");
    }
```

VB.NET

```
Public Function BeginTransaction() As IDbTransaction _
    Implements IDbConnection.BeginTransaction
        'example doesn't support transactions
      Throw New NotSupportedException("Transactions not supported")
End Function
```

CreateCommand Function

The CreateCommand function is responsible for creating and returning a reference to a valid implementation-specific Command object. The method uses an overloaded constructor of your custom Command object in order to pass that object a reference to the current connection.

C#

```csharp
public IDbCommand CreateCommand()
    { // Return a new instance of the implementation-specific command object
      return new DataSetCommand(this);
    }
```

VB.NET

```vbnet
Public Function CreateCommand() As IDbCommand _
     Implements IDbConnection.CreateCommand
         'Return a new instance of the implementation specific command object
            Return New DataSetCommand(Me)
End Function
```

Open Method

In a full data provider implementation, the Open method is used to make a data source–specific connection. Your implementation will use the Open method to create an instance of a generic data set object from the Framework Class Libraries and fill it from the filename provided in our ConnectionString property.

C#

```csharp
public void Open ()
{
        this.dataSet = new FCLData.DataSet ();
        this.dataSet.ReadXml (this.m_fileName);
}
```

VB.NET

```vbnet
Public Sub Open() Implements IDbConnection.Open
      Me.dataSet = New FCLData.DataSet
      Me.dataSet.ReadXml(Me.m_fileName)
End Sub
```

Close Method

The Close method is used to close your data source–specific connection. You are going to use the Close method to release the DataSet object that you have in memory.

C#

```csharp
public void Close ()
{
        this.dataSet=null;
}
```

VB.NET

```vbnet
Public Sub Close() Implements IDbConnection.Close
      set the connection state to close and return
        Me.dataSet = Nothing
End Sub
```

ConnectionString Property

The ConnectionString property allows you to set the connection string through code. The property uses a private variable to store the current connection string, which is used to provide the information needed to connect to the data source. Most developers are familiar with this property because of its frequent use in both traditional ADO and ADO.NET. The ConnectionString property is used to indicate the file that you are going to parse. The user of your data processing extension should input the path to the file they wish to parse into the connection string. You are storing the connection string in the private member variable m_connString.

C#

```csharp
public string ConnectionString
    {
        Get {return m_connectionString;}
        Set {m_connectionString = value;}
    }
```

VB.NET

```vbnet
Public Property ConnectionString() As String _
        Implements IDbConnection.ConnectionString
        Get
                Return m_connString
        End Get
        Set(ByVal Value As String)
                m_connString = Value
        End Set
End Property
```

You want to enforce that the value passed into the ConnectionString property meets your criteria for supplying the information needed to connect to the data source. You want to enforce that the string is in the format:

```
FileName=c:\FileName.xml
```

You will accomplish this through the use of regular expressions. You need to modify the Set accessor to reflect this change. First, you are going to execute that static/shared Match method of the Regex class. You are passing in an expression that basically says "Parse the connection string and make matches on character arrays that are preceded by FileName= and are not composed of beginning of line characters or semicolons." All that is left is test to see if the filename is valid, and, if so, assign it to your private file-name variable. Your code should resemble that below.

C#

```csharp
set
{
    this.m_connectionString = value;
    Match m = Regex.Match (value, "FileName=([^;]+)", RegexOptions.IgnoreCase);
    if (!m.Success)
    {
        throw (new ArgumentException ("'FileName=<filename>' must be present in the
        connection string and point to a valid DataSet xml file", "ConnectionString"));
    }
```

```csharp
    if(!File.Exists(m.Groups[1].Captures [0].ToString ()))
    {
      throw (new ArgumentException("Incorrect Filename","ConnectionString"));
    }
    this.m_fileName = m.Groups[1].Captures [0].ToString ();
}
```

VB.NET

```vbnet
Set(ByVal Value As String)
    Me.m_connectionString = Value
    Dim m As Match = Regex.Match(Value, "FileName=([^;]+)",
                RegexOptions.IgnoreCase)
    If Not m.Success Then
        Throw (New ArgumentException("'FileName=<filename>' must be present string
and point to a valid DataSet xml file", "ConnectionString"))
    End If
    If Not File.Exists(m.Groups(1).Captures(0).ToString) Then
        Throw (New ArgumentException("Incorrect FileName", "ConnectionString"))
    End If
    Me.m_fileName = m.Groups(1).Captures(0).ToString
End Set
```

ConnectionTimeout Property

The ConnectionTimeout property allows you to set the timeout property of the connection. This is used to control how long the interval for connecting to the source should be before an error is thrown. Your class does not actually use this value, but it is implemented for consistency and due to interface requirements. Returning a value of 0 indicates that there is an infinite timeout period.

C#

```csharp
public int ConnectionTimeout
    {
        get
        {   // Returns the connection time-out value.
            // Zero indicates an indefinite time-out period.
            return 0;
        }
    }
```

VB.NET

```vbnet
Public ReadOnly Property ConnectionTimeout() As Integer _
        Implements IDbConnection.ConnectionTimeout
        Get       ' Returns the connection time-out value.
                  ' Zero indicates an indefinite time-out period.
                  Return 0
        End Get
End Property
```

Creating the DataSetParameter Class

The DataSetParameter class is not needed until the command class is created, but because of that dependency you do need to create it. The parameter object is used to send parameters to the command object that can be used in executing commands against the data source. Despite the fact that this class is not used to perform any work, the interface requirements of the command class force you to create it. This class also has interface requirements; it is required to support the IDataParameter interface defined in the Reporting Services data processing extension assembly.

To add the DataSetParameter class to the project, choose Project⇨Add Class from the menu and change the name to DataSetParameter.

Declarations

The following declarations are used internally to hold both the value and the name of the parameter. The name is stored in a string variable called m_parameterName. Because the value variable might contain any type of value, the m_value is declared as an Object type.

C#

```
String   m_parameterName;
Object   m_value;
```

VB.NET

```
Dim m_parameterName As String
Dim m_value As Object
```

Implementing IDataParameter

The IDataParameter interface enforces that your custom parameter class allow a programmer to get and set the name and value of the current parameter.

C#

```
public interface IDataParameter
    {
        string ParameterName { get; set; }
        object Value { get; set; }
    }
```

VB.NET

```
Public Interface IDataParameter
    Property ParameterName() As String
    Property Value() As Object
End Interface
```

Modify the class code to force the DataSetParameter class to implement IDataParameter using the AutoComplete technique. Your code should resemble the following. The wrappers for all of your interface methods should have been created automatically.

C#

```
namespace Wrox.ReportingServices.DataSetExtension
{
    public class DataSetDataParameter : IDataParameter
    {
```

VB.NET

```
Namespace Wrox.ReportingServices.DataSetExtension
    Public Class DataSetParameter
        Implements IDataParameter
```

ParameterName Property

The ParameterName property is used to store the name of the parameter in a string variable called m_parameterName. This field is typically used to map to parameters in stored procedures but is unused in this implementation.

C#

```
public String ParameterName
    {
        get { return m_parameterName; }
        set { m_parameterName = value; }
    }
```

VB.NET

```
Public Property ParameterName() As String _
        Implements IDataParameter.ParameterName
            Get
                Return m_parameterName
            End Get
            Set(ByVal Value As String)
                m_parameterName = value
            End Set
End Property
```

Value Property

The Value property is similar to the name created earlier in that it is not actually used. The value is stored in an object variable called m_value.

C#

```
public object Value
    {
        get { return m_value; }
        set { m_value = value; }
    }
```

VB.NET

```
Public Property Value() As Object _
        Implements IDataParameter.Value
            Get
                Return m_value
            End Get
            Set(ByVal Value As Object)
                m_value = Value
            End Set
End Property
```

Creating the DataSetParameterCollection Class

The DataSetParameterCollection class is simply a collection of parameter objects. Although you could have created a custom collection class that implements all of the required methods, an easier route exists. The IDataParameterCollection interface is basically a subset of the IList interface used to define other objects in the .NET Framework. By using an object already available, you reduce the required coding effort considerably.

To add the DataSetParameterCollection class to the project, choose Project⇨Add Class from the menu. Change the name of the class to DataSetParameterCollection.

There is no need to create custom constructors or member variables for use in your collection class. This is because you can use the internal variables and constructors that exist inside the ArrayList base class that this class inherits from. The properties that you create will be mapped directly to properties and methods that exist in the ArrayList class.

Namespaces

The DataSetParameterCollection class uses the standard namespaces discussed earlier. There is an additional namespace that is needed because of the use of ArrayList. You must add the System.Collections namespace and a private variable for our internal collection.

C#

```
using System;
using Microsoft.ReportingServices.DataProcessing;
using System.Collections;
```

VB.NET

```
Imports System
Imports Microsoft.ReportingServices.DataProcessing
Imports System.Collections
```

Implementing IDataParameterCollection

It would have been really elegant to create the DataParameterCollection with the Generics feature in .NET 2.0. I chose not to use this because creating an object wrapper around an ArrayList should work with all versions of the .NET Framework. The IDataParameterCollection interface defines a custom Add method as well as provides methods to access the members of this collection through the IEnumerable interface. The ArrayList base class implements this interface. Your class will use the internal ArrayList class properties and methods to service its needs.

C#

```csharp
public interface IDataParameterCollection : IEnumerable
    {
        int Add(IDataParameter parameter);
    }
```

VB.NET

```vbnet
Public Interface IDataParameterCollection
    Inherits IEnumerable
    Function Add(ByVal parameter As IDataParameter) As Integer
End Interface
```

C#

The modified code in C# is:

```csharp
namespace Wrox.ReportingServices.DataSetDataExtension
{
    public class DataSetDataParameterCollection : IDataParameterCollection
    {
        ArrayList paramList;
```

VB.NET

The modified code in VB.NET is:

```vbnet
Namespace Wrox.ReportingServices.DataSetDataExtension

    Public Class DataSetDataParameterCollection
        Implements IDataParameterCollection

        Private paramList As ArrayList
```

Since most of the functionality of the DataSetDataParameterCollection class exists through the paramList reference, all that needs to be done is to create the wrapper Add method required by the IDataParameter interface. This method is used by the internal collection to add parameters to an instance of the collection object.

C#

```csharp
public int Add(IDataParameter value)
    {
        return (paramList.Add (value));
    }
```

VB.NET

```
Public Overloads Function Add(ByVal value As IDataParameter) As Integer _
     Implements IDataParameterCollection.Add

     Return (paramList.Add(value))

End Function
```

Creating the DataSetCommand Class

The command object is responsible for sending commands to the data source. This is enforced by making the object implement the IDbCommand interface, which supplies a standard mechanism for passing in commands to be executed against the data source as well as parameters that might be needed in the process of executing these commands. It also defines a property that allows the developer to associate the command with a transaction object. Your implementation is simplified in that it does not support transactions or parameters.

In your implementation, this class is where the majority of the work is done. You need to process the command text to know what data the user wants. You must validate that this text conforms to your requirements, and then you need to create the internal data reference that will supply the data for the data reader object to process. You are going to be using some of the built-in behaviors of the System.Data.DataSet class to satisfy your needs.

To add the DataSetCommand class to the project, choose Project⇨Add Class from the menu. Change the name of the class to DataSetCommand. Use the Interface Autocomplete feature to have Visual Studio create the wrappers for the methods that you will implement. Most of the functionality that exists in this extension will live in this class.

Variable Declarations

Since, most of our work is done in this class, it make sense that most of our code is also. First, you need to create variables to hold your property data. This class is actually going to be a wrapper around some of the built-in DataSet functionality, so you will need reference variables for the data set objects as well as other variables used for text parsing and the like. In order to not be repetitive, I will discuss the variables in more depth where they are used.

C#

```
// property variables
int m_commandTimeOut=0;
string m_commandText = String.Empty;
DataSetConnection m_connection;
DataSetParameterCollection m_parameters;

 //dataset variables
string tableName= String.Empty;
FCLData.DataSet dataSet = null;
internal FCLData.DataView dataView = null;

// regex variables
MatchCollection kwc = null;
```

```
Match fieldMatch= null;
//regex used for getting keywords
Regex keywordSplit = new Regex(@"(Select|From|Where| Order[ \s] +By)",
                RegexOptions.IgnoreCase| RegexOptions.Multiline
                | RegexOptions.IgnorePatternWhitespace | RegexOptions.Compiled);
// regex used for splitting out fields
Regex fieldSplit = new Regex(@"([^ ,\s]+)",
                RegexOptions.IgnoreCase | RegexOptions.Multiline
                | RegexOptions.Compiled|RegexOptions.IgnorePatternWhitespace);

//constants
const int selectPosition = 0;
const int fromPosition = 1;
const int wherePosition = 2;
const int orderPosition = 3;
const string tempTableName = "TempTable";

//internal variables
int keyWordCount=0;
bool filtering = false;
bool sorting = false;
bool useDefaultTable = false;
```

VB.NET

```
'property variables
Private m_cmdTimeOut As Integer = 0
Private m_commandText As String = String.Empty
Private m_connection As DataSetConnection
Private m_parameters As DataSetParameterCollection = Nothing

'dataset variables
Private tableName As String = String.Empty
Private dataSet As FCLData.DataSet
Friend dataView As FCLData.DataView

'regex variables
Private kwc As MatchCollection
Private fieldMatch As Match
Private tableMatch As Match
Private keywordSplit As Regex = New Regex("(Select|From|Where| Order[ \s] +By)",
        RegexOptions.IgnoreCase Or RegexOptions.Multiline Or
        RegexOptions.IgnorePatternWhitespace Or RegexOptions.Compiled)
Private fieldSplit As Regex = New Regex("([^ ,\s]+)", RegexOptions.IgnoreCase Or
        RegexOptions.Multiline Or RegexOptions.Compiled Or
        RegexOptions.IgnorePatternWhitespace)

'Constants
Private tempTableName As String = "TempTable"
Private selectPosition As Integer = 0
Private fromPosition As Integer = 1
Private wherePosition As Integer = 2
Private orderPosition As Integer = 3

'internal variables
```

```
Private keyWordCount As Integer = 0
Private filtering As Boolean = False
Private sorting As Boolean = False
Private useDefaultTable As Boolean = False
```

Constructors

You want the users of your processing extension to be forced to create the Command object either through the CreateCommand method of the IDbConnection interface or by passing in a valid DataSetConnection object as a parameter. The purpose of this is to ensure that you have access to the underlying DataSet object created and parsed in the connection process. This can be done by deleting or not providing an empty default constructor. This prevents the developer from creating the DataSetCommand object without the correct initialization. In the constructor, you want to get a reference to the DataSet that you opened from the file system in your connection object.

C#

```csharp
internal DataSetCommand(DataSetConnection conn)
{
        this.m_connection = conn;
        this.dataSet = this.m_connection.dataSet;
        this.m_parameters = new DataSetParameterCollection();
}
```

VB.NET

```vbnet
Friend Sub New(ByVal conn As DataSetConnection)

        Me.m_connection = conn
        Me.dataSet = Me.m_connection.dataSet
        Me.m_parameters = New DataSetParameterCollection
End Sub
```

Implementing IDbCommand

The required interface for all Command objects is called IDbCommand. It consists of methods that allow the developer to pass commands and parameters to the Command object. The most interesting method in our implementation is the CommandText method where you will parse the command string provided by the user and return the appropriate data.

C#

```csharp
public interface IDbCommand : IDisposable
    {
        void Cancel();
        IDataReader ExecuteReader(CommandBehavior behavior);
        string CommandText { get; set; }
        int CommandTimeout { get; set; }
        CommandType CommandType { get; set; }
        IDataParameter CreateParameter();
        IDataParameterCollection Parameters { get; }
        IDbTransaction Transaction { get; set; }
    }
```

VB.NET

```
Public Interface IDbCommand
    Inherits IDisposable
    Sub Cancel()
    Function ExecuteReader(ByVal behavior As CommandBehavior) As IDataReader
    Property CommandText() As String
    Property CommandTimeout() As Integer
    Property CommandType() As CommandType
    Function CreateParameter() As IDataParameter
    Property Parameters() As IDataParameterCollection
    Property Transaction() As IDbTransaction
End Interface
```

Now that you have created the method wrappers and created all of the variables that you need to work, you may begin implementing your IDbCommand methods.

Cancel Method

The Cancel method is typically used to cancel a method that has been *queued*. Most implementations of data providers are multithreaded and support the issue of multiple commands against the data store. You have only created this method to support the IDbCommand interface requirements and should inform the developer of your lack of support by throwing a NotSupportedException.

C#

```
public void Cancel()
    {        // not supported
      throw new NotSupportedException();
    }
```

VB.NET

```
Public Sub Cancel() _
      Implements IDbCommand.Cancel
      'not supported
       Throw New NotSupportedException
End Sub
```

ExecuteReader Function

The ExecuteReader method returns an extension-specific reader object to the caller so that it can loop through and read the data. The DataSetCommand object creates an instance of your custom reader object by executing this method. A reference to your custom data reader is then returned. Your implementation actually builds a temporary table with a schema built based on the query issued by the user. You don't want to fill this temporary table unless the user actually requests the data, so you are checking to see if it is a schema-only command. You are also checking to see if the user indicated that they want all of the fields available from the data source. If that is the case, you use the default DataTable, which already contains all of the data.

C#

```
public IDataReader ExecuteReader (CommandBehavior behavior)
  {
    if(!(behavior == CommandBehavior.SchemaOnly) && !useDefaultTable)
```

```
    {
       FillView();
    }
    return (IDataReader) new DataSetDataReader(this);
 }
```

VB.NET

```
    Public Function ExecuteReader(ByVal behavior As CommandBehavior) As IdataReader
        Implements IDbCommand.ExecuteReader
        If Not (behavior = CommandBehavior.SchemaOnly) AndAlso Not useDefaultTable Then
                    FillView()
        End If
        Return CType(New DataSetDataReader(Me), IDataReader)
    End Function
```

CommandText Property

Reporting Services does not manually create a separate command object. It uses the CreateCommand method of the IDBConnection interface to return an implementation-specific command object. You will be using the CommandText property to help us build the data schema that we will return, as well as filling your data source for use of Reporting Services. This method has been broken down into methods reflecting the actual work being done and to facilitate this discussion. Notice the ValidateCommandText method. This method is the entry point for your text-parsing and table-building process.

C#

```
public String CommandText
  {
     get
     {
         return (this.m_commandText);
     }
     set
     {
         ValidateCommandText(value);
         this.m_commandText = value;
     }
  }
```

VB.NET

```
    Public Property CommandText() As String Implements IDbCommand.CommandText
        Get
             Return (Me.m_commandText)
        End Get
        Set(ByVal value As String)
             ValidateCommandText(value)
             Me.m_commandText = value
        End Set
    End Property
```

The `ValidateCommandText` method is used to parse the command text to ensure that it meets the requirements for the extension. The first step is to apply the `keywordSplit` regular expression that was defined in the member variable section. The regular expression is "`(Select|From|Where| Order[ \s] +By)`", which could be translated into English as: Match the keywords "Select," "From," "Where," and "Order," where each is followed by the word "By," but allow spaces and nonvisible characters between them. After you have parsed the statement, you can make some basic assumptions based upon the number of matches. At a minimum, you require that the user tell you the field names and the table name that he or she wants to pull the information from. This means that you must have a `Select` keyword followed by a field list and a `From` keyword followed by a table name, and thus the minimum keyword count is two. If you have a keyword count greater than two, you know that the user has either given you a filtering criteria such as `Where userID = 3` or a sort criteria such as `Order by lastname ASC`. You can find out which by checking the value in the third position. If that value is a `Where` clause, then you can assume that the user wants filtering. If it is not, assume that sorting is the order of the day. If the count if four, you know that both filtering and sorting are needed.

C#

```csharp
private void ValidateCommandText(string cmdText)
{
        kwc = keywordSplit.Matches (cmdText);
        keyWordCount = kwc.Count;
        switch(keyWordCount)
        {
        case 4:
            sorting = true;
            filtering = true;
            break;
        case 3:
            if(kwc[keyWordCount -1].ToString().ToUpper() =="WHERE")
                filtering=true;
            else
                sorting=true;
                break;
        case 2:
                break;
        default:
                throw (new ArgumentException ("Command Text should start with
'select <fields> from <tablename>'"));
                }

        ValidateTableName(cmdText);
        ValidateFieldNames(cmdText);
        if(filtering)
        {
                ValidateFiltering(cmdText);
        }
        if(sorting)
        {
                ValidateSorting(cmdText);
        }
}
```

VB.NET

```vbnet
Private Sub ValidateCommandText(ByVal cmdText As String)
        kwc = keywordSplit.Matches(cmdText)
        keyWordCount = kwc.Count
        Select Case keyWordCount
            Case 4
                sorting = True
                filtering = True
                ' break
            Case 3
                If kwc(keyWordCount - 1).ToString.ToUpper = "WHERE" Then
                    filtering = True
                Else
                    sorting = True
                End If
            Case Else
                Throw (New ArgumentException("Command Text should start with
'select <fields> from <tablename>'"))
        End Select
        ValidateTableName(cmdText)
        ValidateFieldNames(cmdText)
        If filtering Then
            ValidateFiltering(cmdText)
        End If
        If sorting Then
            ValidateSorting(cmdText)
        End If
    End Sub
```

The next step in the process is validating that the table name and the field names provided by the user are valid. You have created methods specifically for this purpose. Shown below is the ValidateTableName method. In the member declaration section constant values were created indicating the assumed positions of the keywords within the command text. The table name must immediately be followed by the From keyword. You then use the position of that keyword to locate the table name. Next, you check to see if your internal DataSet contains this table. If so, the table name is valid; otherwise, it is invalid.

C#

```csharp
private void ValidateTableName(string cmdText)
{
 //Get tablename
 //get 1st match starting at end of from
  fieldMatch = fieldSplit.Match(cmdText,
                    (kwc[fromPosition].Index) + kwc[fromPosition].Length+1);
  if(fieldMatch.Success)
  {
        if(this.dataSet.Tables.Contains(fieldMatch.Value))
        {
        this.tableName = fieldMatch.Value;
        }
        else
```

```
        {
                throw new ArgumentException("Invalid Table Name");
        }
    }
}
```

VB.NET

```
Private Sub ValidateTableName(ByVal cmdText As String)
        fieldMatch = fieldSplit.Match(cmdText, (kwc(fromPosition).Index) +
kwc(fromPosition).Length + 1)
        If fieldMatch.Success Then
            If Me.dataSet.Tables.Contains(fieldMatch.Value) Then
                Me.tableName = fieldMatch.Value
            Else
                Throw New ArgumentException("Invalid Table Name")
            End If
        End If
    End Sub
```

The next step is to validate the field names. You also want users to be able to use the * character to indicate that they want all of the fields without having to list them individually. This is standard SQL syntax. You need to parse all of the text between the Select statement and the From statement. This is done using the constant values created earlier to signify character position and a regular expression to pull out exactly what you are interested in. The fieldSplit regular expression look like "([^ ,\s]+)", which reads in English: Match all character groups that do not contain spaces, commas, and nonvisible white space and have spaces at the end. If the first field is an asterisk, you know that the user wants all fields. This means that you do not have to build a temporary table to reflect the schema and that you can use the table they requested in the From portion of the text. If the first field is not an asterisk, you must build a temp table reflecting the schema of the data that you will return. To avoid problems with a user changing the fields, and the temp table previously existing, you will simply test for its existence each time and remove it if you must. Next, you check to see whether the field names exist in your main table by testing to see whether the column names exist. If they do, the column is valid and you add a column with this name to your new temp table. You continue to do this as long as the field names are valid. If an invalid field is submitted, you throw an exception to make the user aware of their mistake.

C#

```
public void ValidateFieldNames(string cmdText)
{
//get fieldnames
//get first match starting at the last character of the Select
// with a length from that position to the from
fieldMatch = fieldSplit.Match(cmdText,
        (kwc[selectPosition].Index + kwc[selectPosition].Length+1),
        (kwc[fromPosition].Index -
        (kwc[selectPosition].Index+kwc[selectPosition].Length+1)));

if(fieldMatch.Value=="*")  // all fields, use default view
{
    this.dataView = this.dataSet.Tables[this.tableName].DefaultView;
    this.useDefaultTable = true;
}
```

```
    else   //custom fields :  must build table/view
    {
        this.useDefaultTable = false; //don't use default table
        //remove table if exists - add new
        if(this.dataSet.Tables.Contains(tempTableName))
        {
            this .dataSet.Tables.Remove(tempTableName);
        }
         FCLData.DataTable table = new FCLData.DataTable(tempTableName);
        //loop through column matches
        while(fieldMatch.Success)
        {
        if(dataSet.Tables[tableName].Columns.Contains(fieldMatch.Value))
            {
FCLData.DataColumn col = this.dataSet.Tables[tableName].Columns[fieldMatch.Value] ;
table.Columns.Add(new FCLData.DataColumn(col.ColumnName,col.DataType));
fieldMatch = fieldMatch.NextMatch();
            }
            else
            {
            throw new ArgumentException("Invalid column name");
            }
      }
  //add temptable to internal dataset and set view to tempView;
  this.dataSet.Tables.Add(table);
  this.dataView =  new FCLData.DataView(table);
  }
}
```

VB.NET

```
Private Sub ValidateFieldNames(ByVal cmdText As String)
    fieldMatch = fieldSplit.Match(cmdText, (kwc(selectPosition).Index +
kwc(selectPosition).Length + 1), (kwc(fromPosition).Index -
kwc(selectPosition).Index + kwc(selectPosition).Length + 1)))

    If fieldMatch.Value = "*" Then
       Me.dataView = Me.dataSet.Tables(Me.tableName).DefaultView
       Me.useDefaultTable = True
    Else
       Me.useDefaultTable = False
       If Me.dataSet.Tables.Contains(Me.tempTableName) Then
            Me.dataSet.Tables.Remove(Me.tempTableName)
       End If
       Dim table As FCLData.DataTable = New FCLData.DataTable(Me.tempTableName)
    While fieldMatch.Success
       If Me.dataSet.Tables(Me.tableName).Columns.Contains(fieldMatch.Value) Then
            Dim col As FCLData.DataColumn =
dataSet.Tables(tableName).Columns(fieldMatch.Value)
                    table.Columns.Add(New FCLData.DataColumn(col.ColumnName,
col.DataType))
                    fieldMatch = fieldMatch.NextMatch
                Else
                    Throw New ArgumentException("Invalid column name")
                End If
```

```
                    End While
                    Me.dataSet.Tables.Add(table)
                    Me.dataView = New FCLData.DataView(table)
                End If
            End Sub
```

Assuming that the table name is valid and all of the requested fields are valid, you will use the temp table you have built to satisfy data access requirements. The only thing left to do is add the new table to the existing data set.

You have now validated all the parts of your query except the filtering and sorting criteria. In the CommandText method you test whether filtering and sorting are enabled based upon your keyword count. If they are enabled, you execute a method that uses the internal behavior of the DataSet class to do the work. In the ValidateFiltering method, you need to parse out the text based upon the keyword count. You either need to grab all of the text after the Where clause, or if an order clause exists, you need to stop there.

C#

```csharp
public void ValidateFiltering(string cmdText)
 {
 if(filtering)
    {
        StringBuilder sbFilterText = new StringBuilder();
        int startPos =0;
        int length =0;

        startPos = (kwc[wherePosition].Index + kwc[wherePosition].Length+1);
        if(keyWordCount ==3)  //no "order by" - Search from Where till  end
        {
            length = cmdText.Length-startPos;
        }
        else // "order by" exists -  search from where  position to "order by"
        {
            length =  kwc[orderPosition].Index - startPos;
        }

        sbFilterText.Append(cmdText.Substring(startPos,length));
        this.dataView.RowFilter = sbFilterText.ToString();
    }
 }
```

VB.NET

```vbnet
Private Sub ValidateFiltering(ByVal cmdText As String)
    If filtering Then
        Dim sbFilterText As StringBuilder = New StringBuilder
        Dim startPos As Integer = 0
        Dim length As Integer = 0
        startPos = (kwc(wherePosition).Index + kwc(wherePosition).Length + 1)
        If keyWordCount = 3 Then
            length = cmdText.Length - startPos
```

```
        Else
              length = kwc(orderPosition).Index - startPos
        End If
      sbFilterText.Append(cmdText.Substring(startPos, length))
      Me.dataView.RowFilter = sbFilterText.ToString
    End If
End Sub
```

After you parse the text, you will use the `DataView.RowFilter` property to filter out results. Simply apply the string that you have extracted to the `RowFilter`, and the `DataView` class takes care of the rest. The same technique is applied to get ordering.

C#

```csharp
public void ValidateSorting(string cmdText)
    {
        if(sorting)
        {
            StringBuilder sbFilterText = new StringBuilder();
            int startPos =0;
            int length =0;
            //start from end of 'Order by' clause
            startPos = (kwc[orderPosition].Index +
kwc[orderPosition].Length+1);

            length =  cmdText.Length - startPos;

            sbFilterText.Append(cmdText.Substring(startPos,length));
            this.dataView.Sort = sbFilterText.ToString();
        }
    }
```

VB.NET

```vbnet
Private Sub ValidateSorting(ByVal cmdText As String)
    If sorting Then
        Dim sbFilterText As StringBuilder = New StringBuilder
        Dim startPos As Integer = 0
        Dim length As Integer = 0
        startPos = (kwc(orderPosition).Index + kwc(orderPosition).Length + 1)
        length = cmdText.Length - startPos
        sbFilterText.Append(cmdText.Substring(startPos, length))
        Me.dataView.Sort = sbFilterText.ToString
    End If
End Sub
```

CommandTimeout Property

The `CommandTimeout` property is used to specify how long the command object should wait for the results of an executed command before throwing an exception. You are not actually using this value, but it must be implemented due to interface requirements. Just return a zero value to indicate timeouts are not supported.

C#

```
public int CommandTimeout
    {   // Implemented the Property for consistency but it is not used.
        get  { return 0; }


    }
```

VB.NET

```
Public Property CommandTimeout() As Integer _
        Implements IDbCommand.CommandTimeout
            Get
                Return 0
            End Get
            Set(ByVal Value As Integer)

            End Set
End Property
```

CommandType Property

Most data processing extensions allow the developer to pass in a command as text, or they can pass in a fully initialized command object for the Execute reader method to examine and use. The DataSetCommand class only accepts text, and any other type will cause your component to throw a NotSupported exception.

C#

```
public CommandType CommandType
    {    // supports only a text commandType
        get { return CommandType.Text; }
        set { if (value != CommandType.Text) throw new NotSupportedException(); }
    }
```

VB.NET

```
Public Property CommandType() As CommandType _
        Implements IDbCommand.CommandType
            Get
                Return CommandType.Text
            End Get
            Set(ByVal Value As CommandType)
                If Value <> CommandType.Text Then
                    Throw New NotSupportedException
                End If
            End Set
        End Property
```

CreateParameter Function

The CreateParameter returns an extension-specific parameter to the command object. The method must be supported due to the interface requirements, although it is not actually used. The DataSetParameter object is a simple class that implements another interface called IDataParameter, which allows it to be returned as an object of the interface type.

C#

```
public IDataParameter CreateParameter()
    { //return DataSetDataParameter
            return new DataSetDataParameter();
    }
```

VB.NET

```
Public Function CreateParameter() As IDataParameter _
        Implements IDbCommand.CreateParameter
            Return New DataSetDataParameter
End Function
```

Parameters Property

The Parameters property returns a collection that implements the IDataParameterCollection interface. Your custom collection class is the DataSetParameterCollection and satisfies these requirements. The Parameters property allows the developer to index into the Parameters collection to set or get the parameter values.

C#

```
public IDataParameterCollection Parameters
    {
            get
            {
                    Debug.WriteLine ("IDBCommand: Retrieving parameters list");
                    return this.m_parameters;
            }
    }
```

VB.NET

```
Public ReadOnly Property Parameters() As IDataParameterCollection Implements
IDbCommand.Parameters
        Get
            Debug.WriteLine("IDBCommand: Retrieving parameters list")
            Return Me.m_parameters
        End Get
    End Property
```

Creating the DataReader Object

The data reader in our implementation does nothing more than read properties of our internal DataView. The behavior of the data reader is enforced by the IDbDataReader interface, which supplies methods to indicate the number, names, and types of the fields that will be read. It also allows the object to actually access the data.

To add the DataSetDataReader class to the project, choose Project➪Add Class from the menu. Change the name of the class to DataSetDataReader. After adding the class, add the custom namespace and edit the class definition.

Declarations

The variables of the DataSetDataReader hold all the information that you will use to build the properties supported by the DataSetDataReader class. The m_currentRow variable is used to store the value of the current row as the data is being read from your CSV data file. The string array m_names contains the names of the fields that will be read, while the m_types array provides access to the type of data that will be read. As the data is read, it will be loaded into an array of the object type called m_cols. Data from the file will be read by an internal StreamReader class called sr.

C#

```
FCLData.DataView dataView;
DataSetCommand dataSetCommand = null;
int currentRow= -1;
```

VB.NET

```
Private dataView As FCLData.DataView = Nothing
Private dataSetCommand As dataSetCommand = Nothing
Private currentRow As Integer = -1
```

Implementing IDbDataReader

The IDbDataReader interface enforces consistency in working with data. It provides properties and methods that allow you to examine the data and its types as well as the Read method that will actually do the dirty work.

C#

```
public interface IDataReader : IDisposable
    {
        Type GetFieldType(int fieldIndex);
        string GetName(int fieldIndex);
        int GetOrdinal(string fieldName);
        object GetValue(int fieldIndex);
        bool Read();
        int FieldCount { get; }
    }
```

VB.NET

```
Public Interface IDataReader
    Inherits IDisposable
    Function GetFieldType(ByVal fieldIndex As Integer) As Type
    Function GetName(ByVal fieldIndex As Integer) As String
    Function GetOrdinal(ByVal fieldName As String) As Integer
    Function GetValue(ByVal fieldIndex As Integer) As Object
    Function Read() As Boolean
    Property FieldCount() As Integer
End Interface
```

You need to modify your class definition to force the custom DataSetDataReader class to support the interface requirements.

C#

```
namespace Wrox.ReportingServices.DataSetDataExtension
{
    public class DataSetDataReader : IDataReader
    {
        internal int          currentRow;
```

VB.NET

```
Namespace Wrox.ReportingServices.DataSetDataExtension
    Public Class DataSetDataReader
        Implements IDataReader
```

GetFieldType Function

This property returns the type of data at a particular position within the stream that is being read. This data is used to allow the developer to store the data being read in the correct data type upon retrieval from the data reader.

C#

```
public Type GetFieldType (int fieldIndex)
{
        return( this.dataView.Table.Columns[fieldIndex].DataType);
}
```

VB.NET

```
Public Function GetFieldType(ByVal fieldIndex As Integer) As Type Implements
IDataReader.GetFieldType
        Return (Me.dataView.Table.Columns(fieldIndex).DataType)
End Function
```

GetName Function

The GetName method allows the developer to retrieve a data field from the DataReader object by passing in the name of the field to be read.

C#

```
public String GetName (int fieldIndex)
{
        return this.dataView.Table.Columns[fieldIndex].ColumnName;
}
```

VB.NET

```
Public Function GetName(ByVal fieldIndex As Integer) As String Implements
IDataReader.GetName
        Return( Me.dataView.Table.Columns(fieldIndex).ColumnName)
End Function
```

GetOrdinal Function

The GetName method allows the developer to index the data based on its position within the DataReader stream.

C#

```
public int GetOrdinal (String fieldName)
{
        return( this.dataView.Table.Columns[fieldName].Ordinal);
}
```

VB.NET

```
    Public Function GetOrdinal(ByVal fieldName As String) As Integer Implements
IDataReader.GetOrdinal
            Return (Me.dataView.Table.Columns(fieldName).Ordinal)
End Function
```

GetValue Function

The GetValue function retrieves the actual value from the data stream. All of these methods are typically used together. The developer pulls the type information from the stream, creates variables of the correct type to hold this data, and gets the values of the data using the GetValue function.

C#

```
public object GetValue (int fieldIndex)
 {
        return( this.dataView [this.currentRow] [fieldIndex]);
 }
```

VB.NET

```
Public Function GetValue(ByVal fieldIndex As Integer) As Object Implements
IDataReader.GetValue

            Return (Me.dataView(Me.currentRow)(fieldIndex))
End Function
```

Read Method

The Read method is the workhorse of the DataSetDataReader class. The function loops through the current DataView. If a line is successfully read, this is indicated to the user of your extension by incrementing the row count variable m_currentRow and by returning a Boolean value. As long as true is returned, data is successfully read. False is returned when the internal view hits the end of the result set.

C#

```
public Boolean Read ()
        {
        this.currentRow ++;
        if (this.currentRow >= this.dataView.Count)
        {
                return (false);
```

```
        }
              return (true);
        }
```

VB.NET

```
Public Function Read() As Boolean Implements IDataReader.Read
          System.Threading.Interlocked.Increment(Me.currentRow)
          If Me.currentRow >= Me.dataView.Count Then
              Return (False)
          End If
          Return (True)
     End Function
```

FieldCount Property

The FieldCount property returns the number of fields or columns available in each row of data that the Read method returns.

C#

```
public int FieldCount
{ // Return the count of the number of columns,
          get { return m_fieldCount; }
    }
```

VB.NET

```
Public ReadOnly Property FieldCount() As Integer Implements IDataReader.FieldCount
    Get

          Return (Me.dataView.Table.Columns.Count)
        End Get
End Property
```

Installing the DataSetDataProcessing Extension

After creating your custom data processing extension, you must install it to enable access. The installation process is two steps.

❑   Installing and configuring the extension.

❑   Configuring extension security.

This particular extension is used both by the Reporting Server and the report designer itself, which requires us to install it in two locations. It must be installed on the report server and the workstation used to design the reports.

Server Installation

Reporting Services has a standard location where extensions should be installed. This location is a subdirectory below the installation directory of SQL Server itself. I will refer to the SQL Server installation path as InstallPath. On my machine, this directory is C:\Program Files\Microsoft SQL Server\.

The directory that you will install the extension into is the `bin` directory of the report server: `InstallPath\MSSQL.3\Reporting Services\ReportServer\bin`. Copy your custom data processing extension assembly into this directory. The extension is now in the correct location, but you need to inform Reporting Services of its presence. This is done by editing the configuration file that Reporting Services uses for its settings. This file is called `RSReportServer.config` and is located in the parent directory. Open this file and look for the `<Data>` section. Within this section, you should see entries similar to the following:

```
<Data>
    <Permissions>
        <PermissionSet class="System.Security.NamedPermissionSet" version="1"
                    Unrestricted="true" Name="FullTrust"
                    Description="Allows full access to all resources"/>
    </Permissions>
    <Extension Name="SQL"
        Type="Microsoft.ReportingServices.DataExtensions.SqlConnectionWrapper,
            Microsoft.ReportingServices.DataExtensions"/>
    <Extension Name="OLEDB"
        Type="Microsoft.ReportingServices.DataExtensions.OleDbConnectionWrapper,
            Microsoft.ReportingServices.DataExtensions"/>
    <Extension Name="ORACLE"
        Type="Microsoft.ReportingServices.DataExtensions.OracleClient
          ConnectionWrapper,Microsoft.ReportingServices.DataExtensions"/>
    <Extension Name="ODBC"
        Type="Microsoft.ReportingServices.DataExtensions.OdbcConnection
            Wrapper,Microsoft.ReportingServices.DataExtensions"/>
    <Extension Name="DATASET"
Type="Wrox.ReportingServices.DataSetDataExtension.DataSetConnection,Wrox.ReportingS
ervices.DataSetDataExtension"/>
    </Data>
```

Add the `DataSet` entry that you see in the highlighted code snippet. The `Name` tag is the unique name you want users to see when they select your extension. The `Type` element contains the entry point for your extension (the first object created and the one that is required to implement the `IExtension` interface), followed by the fully qualified name of your extension. Save the file. Reporting Services will now recognize your extension, but you must change the security policy to give the extension the permissions that it needs to do its job.

Server Security configuration

The security policy file is located in the same directory as the server configuration file. Simply locate the file called `rssrvpolicy.config`. This file contains the security policy information for SSRS, and an entry should be made that looks similar to the following:

```
    </CodeGroup>
    <CodeGroup  class="UnionCodeGroup"  version="1" PermissionSetName="FullTrust"
    Name="WroxSRS" Description="Code group for my DataSet data processing
    extension">
    <IMembershipCondition class="UrlMembershipCondition"
    version="1"Url="C:\Program Files\Microsoft SQL Server\MSSQL.3\Reporting
    Services\ReportServer\bin\Wrox.ReportingServices.DataSetDataExtension.dll" />
    </CodeGroup>
```

WorkStation Installation

The next task is installing the extension on your development machine so that you can use it in the report designer. The process for installing the extension into the report designer is much the same as the server, with the exception of the file names and locations. This is also done by copying the file to a specific directory of your development machine and making an entry in the configuration file so that the designer is aware of the extension.

Copy your extension to the `C:\Program Files\Microsoft Visual Studio 8\Common7\IDE\PrivateAssemblies` directory. All of the files needed for workstation configuration are located here. The configuration file of the designer is called `RSReportDesigner.config`. Insert the same information that you inserted at the server-side extension at the end of the `<Data>` section in this file.

```
<Data
 <Extension Name="ODBC"
Type="Microsoft.ReportingServices.DataExtensions.OdbcConnection
Wrapper,Microsoft.ReportingServices.DataExtensions"/>
<Extension Name="DATASET"
Type="Wrox.ReportingServices.DataSetDataExtension.DataSetConnection,Wrox.ReportingS
ervices.DataSetDataExtension"/>
</Data>
```

There is one additional requirement in this file. You must also tell Visual Studio what designer to use with your extension. I chose not to implement a custom designer class but to use the Generic Query Designer provided by Microsoft instead. Your query is based on SQL, so this works well. Make an entry in the `<Designer>` section that immediately follows the `<Data>` section.

```
<Extension Name="DataSet"
Type="Microsoft.ReportingServices.QueryDesigners.GenericQueryDesigner,Microsoft.Rep
ortingServices.QueryDesigners"/>
```

WorkStation Security Configuration

The next step is to set up the security policy so the extension will run in the designer correctly. The required file is called `rspreviewpolicy.config`. Add an entry resembling the following into this file.

```
<CodeGroup   class="UnionCodeGroup"   version="1" PermissionSetName="FullTrust"
Name="WroxSRS" Description="Code group for my DataSet data processing
extension">
<IMembershipCondition class="UrlMembershipCondition" version="1" Url=" C:\Program
Files\Microsoft Visual Studio 8\Common7\IDE\PrivateAssemblies
\Wrox.ReportingServices.DataSetDataExtension.dll" />
</CodeGroup>
```

Testing the DataSetDataExtension

In order to test the extension, a report that uses the custom extension must be created. You must also create a `DataSet` file to contain your data or use the one provided in the sample code. The code is generic enough that you may use it against any serialized data set. The file included in the example is just a `Select * from DimCustomer` run against the `AdventureWorksDW` database and persisted from a data set object.

Add a new project to your existing solution. Create the project by choosing File⇨Add Project⇨New Project. If the development environment is set up correctly, you will see the Business Intelligence template folder. Choose the Report Server Project Wizard template. Change the name of the project to `TestReport` and click OK. This will launch the Report Wizard. Click Next. The Select Data Source page will appear. Leave the default data source name, and click on the Type drop-down box. Your new `DataSetDataExtension` should now be available. Using a `FileName` attribute, enter the physical path to your serialized dataset into the Connection String text box. When you are done, the result should resemble Figure 13-7.

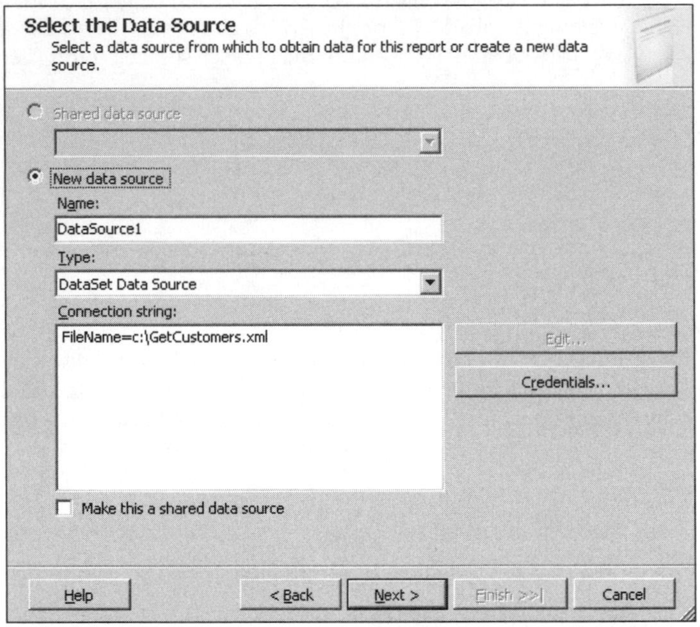

Figure 13-7

Next, you need to indicate the credentials that you wish to use. Click on the Credentials button, which will cause the Credentials windows to be displayed. Instruct the data source to use Windows integrated security by selecting the radio button (see Figure 13-8).

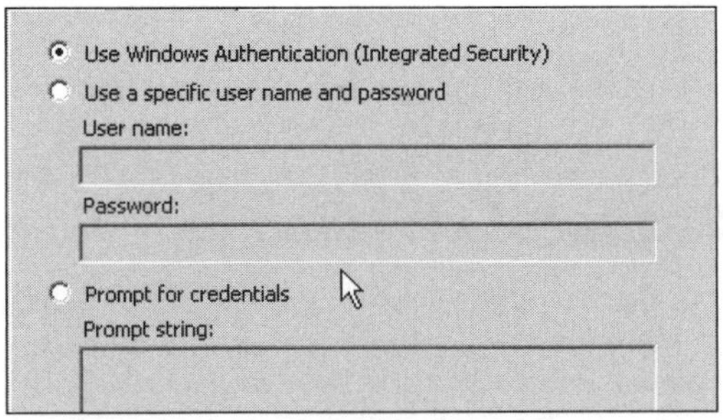

Figure 13-8

After you have set both the type and connection string, you are ready to set up the basic data query. The dataset that I used included a table called DimCustomer that I want to query. Enter **Select * from DimCustomer** into the query window if you are using the sample provided or some statement that works on your specific data. The query should resemble the text shown in Figure 13-9.

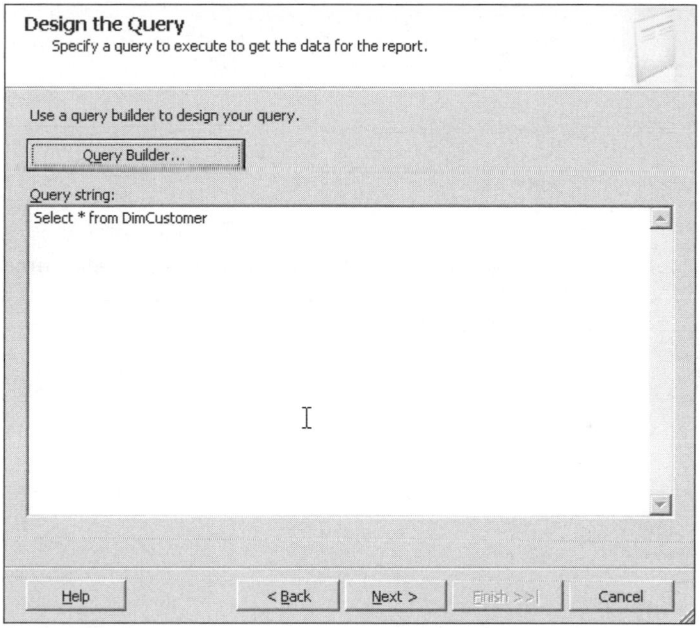

Design the Query
Specify a query to execute to get the data for the report.

Use a query builder to design your query.

Query Builder...

Query string:

Select * from DimCustomer

| Help | | < Back | Next > | Finish >> | Cancel |

Figure 13-9

Simply finish the wizard by choosing your report style and the fields that you are interested in. I chose the tabular report type. I then selected three fields and put them into the detail list. I chose the default report style, and the resulting report is shown in Figure 13-10.

Figure 13-10

Next, you need to see if our extension actually returns data. Click on the Preview tab. The resulting data should resemble Figure 13-11.

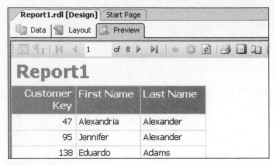

Figure 13-11

Now you know that our extension works. You can experiment with the field-limiting and -sorting functionality by clicking on the Data tab. This brings up the data designer where you can enter more advanced queries and test the results (see Figure 13-12).

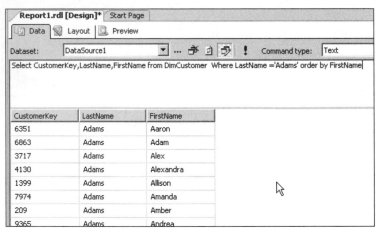

Figure 13-12

Summary

In this chapter, you learned about the extensibility of Reporting Services and the areas that currently support customization. Specifically, you learned:

❑ What extensibility options are available.

❑ Reasons for extending SQL Server Reporting Services.

❑ How to create custom extensions.

❑ How to install custom extensions.

Along with the extensibility options available in SQL Reporting Services, you also learned about some of the business opportunities created. Microsoft has created a flexible, powerful reporting solution that allows you to modify its behavior by implementing the interfaces required by the particular extension type. This functionality is sure to create a third-party market for tools, as well as allow the enterprise developer to create custom solutions for the unique needs of their business.

Also discussed was the data access methods used by the .NET Framework and specifically how to create a custom data processing extension to work with nonrelational data. The example is very simple and does not stand alone as an application—although it could be easily extended to provide additional functionality such as support for parameters. The primary purpose of the example is to familiarize you with the requirements for creating and installing an extension. This type of extension was chosen because it is used on the server for report processing and on the developer machine for report creation.

Migrating Access Reports

The following Access report controls, property settings, and other report elements will be converted to report items in SQL Server Reporting Services if supported.

Controls

Control	Converted to Item
Label	Textbox
Textbox	Textbox
Option Group	(unsupported)
Toggle Button	(unsupported)
Option Button	(unsupported)
Check Box	(unsupported)
Combo Box	(unsupported)
List Box	(unsupported)
Command Button	(unsupported)
Image	Image
Unbound Object Frame	(unsupported)
Bound Object Frame	(unsupported)
Page Break	(unsupported)
Tab Control	(unsupported)

Table continued on following page

Control	Converted to Item
Sub form	Subreport
Sub report	Subreport
Line	Line
Rectangle	Rectangle
ActiveX Controls	(unsupported)

Property Settings

Property	Supported
BackColor	Yes
BackStyle	Yes
BorderColor	Yes
BorderStyle	Yes
BorderWidth	Yes
BottomMargin	Yes
CanGrow (section)	No
CanGrow (textbox)	Yes
CanShrink (section)	No
CanShrink (textbox)	Yes
Caption	Yes
DecimalPlaces	No
FastLaserPrinting	No
Filter	No
FilterOn	No
FontBold	Yes
FontItalic	Yes
FontName	Yes
FontSize	Yes
FontUnderline	Yes
FontWeight	Yes
ForceNewPage	Yes
ForeColor	Yes

Property	Supported
Format	No
FormatConditions	No
GrpKeepTogether	No
Height	Yes
HideDuplicates	Yes
Hyperlink	Yes
IsHyperlink	Yes
IsVisible	Yes
KeepTogether (group)	Yes
KeepTogether (section)	No
Left	Yes
LeftMargin	Yes
LineSlant	Yes
LineSpacing	Yes
LinkChildFields	Yes
LinkMasterFields	Yes
NewRowOrCol	Yes
NumeralShapes	No
Orientation	No
PageFooter	Yes
PageHeader	Yes
Pages	Yes
PaintPalette	No
PaletteSource	No
Picture	Yes
PictureAlignment	No
PicturePages	No
PictureSizeMode	No
PictureTiling (image)	No
PictureTiling (report)	Yes
ReadingOrder	Yes

Table continued on following page

Property	Supported
RepeatSection	Yes
RightMargin	Yes
RunningSum	Yes
ScrollBars	No
SizeMode	Yes
SpecialEffect	No
TextAlign	Yes
Top	Yes
TopMargin	Yes
Vertical	No
Width	Yes

Functions

Nearly all common expression functions (VBA and Access SQL) are supported by Reporting Services or have Visual Basic .NET equivalents. The following domain aggregate functions are not supported and do not have equivalent functionality. Equivalent aggregate functions exist in Transact SQL, but these need to be applied within a query rather than on item properties.

Function	Supported
DAvg	No
DCount	No
DFirst	No
DLast	No
DLookup	No
DMax	No
DMin	No
DStDev	No
DStDevP	No
DSum	No
DVar	No
DVarP	No

Report Elements

Element	Supported	Comment
VBA Code Modules	Yes	
Events	No	
Parameterized queries	Yes	
Express functions	Yes	Reporting Services supports most VBA or Access SQL functions that are allowed in Access property expressions. All supported functions are converted to the Visual Basic .NET equivalents. The most significant functions commonly used in Access expressions and not supported by Reporting Services are the domain aggregate functions.
Access data source — Access tables	Yes	Connection string refers to the original Access database.
Access data source — linked tables	No	Connection string refers to the original Access database not the source of the linked tables.
Remote data source in Access Data Project (ADP)	Partial	ODBC and OLEDB sources are supported, but certain characters are not allowed in names (';', '<', or '>')
Group Section	Yes	Appropriate sorting and grouping properties are applied to detail sections. Nested groupings are created for additional group sections.
Field names and variables	Yes	Names are converted according to Reporting Services rules. Field names that are the same as control/item names are modified, and names containing spaces are modified. Any variable names that don't correspond to fields are converted to report parameters.
Image formats	Yes	All image formats are converted to BMP and stored as embedded images

During report conversion, the Access database or project is opened during the report conversion process. Although the conversion engine handles most unsupported conversion issues gracefully, errors can cause the process to stall under some conditions. In this case, the Access database may be left with open locks on it, and you won't be able to open the database. In such a case, delete the corresponding ldb file after closing Visual Studio. In extreme cases, you may need to reboot the computer first.

Reporting Services Object Model

Reporting Services exposes its application program interface (API) through the Reporting Services Web service that interacts with the actual Reporting Server. This appendix is meant to be a quick reference to the programmatic functionality that Reporting Services exposes through this Web service.

Relevant code for both C# and VB.NET has been provided in this chapter. Book formatting constraints may cause the code lines to wrap. However, note that the VB.NET code lines should reside on one line in the code editor, even though no underscore has been inserted in such cases.

CancelBatch

This method cancels a batch of commands that are created by using CreateBatch and associated with a particular BatchID. The BatchID can be changed to a value equal to the BatchID that was generated when the batch was created through the BatchHeaderValue property of the Web service. When CancelBatch is called, any calls associated with that BatchID value cannot be executed.

C#

```
public void CancelBatch();
```

VB.NET

```
Public Sub CancelBatch()
```

CancelJob

A job is a task that a report server is actively processing. CancelJob cancels execution of a job by passing in the JobID associated with that job.

C#

```
public bool CancelJob(string JobID);
```

VB.NET

```
Public Function CancelJob(ByVal JobID As String) As Boolean
```

CreateBatch

The CreateBatch method creates a batch that allows the execution of multiple methods within the scope of a single transaction. Upon execution, this method returns a BatchID. This batch identifier is used to group commands and can be accessed through the BatchHeaderValue property of the Web service.

C#

```
public string CreateBatch();
```

VB.NET

```
Public Function CreateBatch() As String
```

CreateDataDrivenSubscription

This method creates a data-driven subscription for a specified report. It requires passing in the extension settings for the preferred delivery mechanism, as well as the DataRetrievalPlan and event type that will cause the report to be delivered. The return value is a unique identifier for the new subscription.

C#

```
public string CreateDataDrivenSubscription(string Report, ExtensionSettings
ExtensionSettings, DataRetrievalPlan DataRetrievalPlan, string Description, string
EventType, string MatchData, ParameterValueOrFieldReference[] Parameters);
```

VB.NET

```
Public Function CreateDataDrivenSubscription(ByVal Report As String, ByVal
ExtensionSettings As ExtensionSettings, ByVal DataRetrievalPlan As
DataRetrievalPlan, ByVal Description As String, ByVal EventType As String, ByVal
MatchData As String, ByVal Parameters As ParameterValueOrFieldReference()) As
String
```

CreateDataSource

This method creates a new data source in the Reporting Server database. It is sensitive because it contains user name and password information, and depending on the settings of the server, may require that it be executed only over SSL.

C#

```
public void CreateDataSource(string DataSource, string Parent, bool Overwrite,
DataSourceDefinition Definition, Property[] Properties);
```

VB.NET

```
Public Sub CreateDataSource(ByVal DataSource As String, ByVal Parent As String,
ByVal Overwrite As Boolean, ByVal Definition As DataSourceDefinition, ByVal
Properties As Property())
```

CreateFolder

The CreateFolder method creates a logical folder on the reporting server in which items such as reports or data sources may be placed. If you are creating a nested folder hierarchy, then you must pass in the full path of the parent folder. In addition, you must pass a collection of custom properties for the folder. These properties can be used to search by or provide detailed information about the folder.

C#

```
public void CreateFolder(string Folder, string Parent, Property[] Properties);
```

VB.NET

```
Public Sub CreateFolder(ByVal Folder As String, ByVal Parent As String, ByVal
Properties As Property())
```

CreateLinkedReport

A linked report is defined as a report that does not contain a full report definition in the reporting server and is primarily created for the purpose of being included in other reports. This method creates a report and requires that you pass in the name of the linked report, the path of the report, the path to the report definition upon which you are basing the report, and the report properties.

C#

```
public void CreateLinkedReport(string Report, string Parent, string Link,
Property[] Properties);
```

VB.NET

```
Public Sub CreateLinkedReport(ByVal Report As String, ByVal Parent As String, ByVal
Link As String, ByVal Properties As Property())
```

CreateModel

Creates a report model used to define the information in the database in business terms. The model is used by the Report Builder.

C#

```
public Warning[] CreateModel(string Model, string Parent, byte[] Definition,
Property[] Properties);
```

VB.NET

```
Public Function CreateModel(ByVal Model As String, ByVal Parent As String,
Definition As Byte(), ByVal Properties As Property()) as Warning()
```

CreateReport

The CreateReport method adds a new report to the Reporting Server database. It requires that you pass in the path where you want the report to be created, a Boolean value indicating whether you want an existing report with the same name to be overridden, the report itself, and any custom properties that you would like applied to the report.

C#

```
public Warning[] CreateReport(string Report, string Parent, bool Overwrite, byte[]
Definition, Property[] Properties);
```

VB.NET

```
Public Function CreateReport(ByVal Report As String, ByVal Parent As String, ByVal
Overwrite As Boolean, ByVal Definition As Byte(), ByVal Properties As Property())
As Warning()
```

CreateReportHistorySnapshot

A snapshot of a report is a view of that report frozen at a certain point in time. This method generates a report history snapshot of a specified report. All the subreport items and parameters are also stored as history. A string is returned which is a unique snapshot identifier.

C#

```
public string CreateReportHistorySnapshot(string Report,[out]  Warning[] Warnings);
```

VB.NET

```
Public Function CreateReportHistorySnapshot(ByVal Report As String, ByRef Warnings
As Warning()) As String
```

CreateResource

This method adds a new resource to the Reporting Server database. It requires that you pass in the resource, the parent directory, a Boolean value indicating whether to overwrite an existing resource with the same name, the MIME-type of the resource, and any properties that you want to specify.

C#

```
public void CreateResource(string Resource, string Parent, bool Overwrite, byte[]
Contents, string MimeType, Property[] Properties);
```

VB.NET

```
Public Sub CreateResource(ByVal Resource As String, ByVal Parent As String, ByVal
Overwrite As Boolean, ByVal Contents As Byte(), ByVal MimeType As String, ByVal
Properties As Property())
```

CreateRole

This method creates a new security role in the Reporting Server database. The required fields are a string role name, a description of the role, and a collection of tasks that you want the role to perform represented by task IDs.

C#

```
public void CreateRole(string Name, string Description, Task[] Tasks);
```

VB.NET

```
Public Sub CreateRole(ByVal Name As String, ByVal Description As String, ByVal
Tasks As Task())
```

CreateSchedule

The CreateSchedule method allows the developer to create a shared schedule that can be used by a subscription to deliver reports. The name of the schedule and a ScheduleDefinition object that describes the schedule are the required parameters. The return value is a unique schedule ID that identifies the newly created schedule.

C#

```
public string CreateSchedule(string Name, ScheduleDefinition ScheduleDefinition);
```

VB.NET

```
Public Function CreateSchedule(ByVal Name As String, ByVal ScheduleDefinition As
ScheduleDefinition) as String
```

CreateSubscription

Creates a subscription for a specified report in the Reporting Server database. The required parameters are the name of the report, the delivery extension to use, a user-friendly description, the event that will cause the subscription to be run, and match data that is needed by the EventType object. This method returns a unique subscription ID for the newly created subscription.

C#

```
public string CreateSubscription(string Report, ExtensionSettings
ExtensionSettings, string Description, string EventType, string MatchData,
ParameterValue[] Parameters);
```

VB.NET

```
Public Function CreateSubscription(ByVal Report As String, ByVal ExtensionSettings
As ExtensionSettings, ByVal Description As String, ByVal EventType As String, ByVal
MatchData As String, ByVal Parameters As ParameterValue()) As String
```

DeleteItem

The DeleteItem method deletes a specified item from the Reporting Server database as well as any objects that are related to that item, such as properties, subscriptions, or snapshots. It takes the full path to the item to be deleted as a string parameter.

C#

```
public void DeleteItem(string Item);
```

VB.NET

```
Public Sub DeleteItem(ByVal Item As String)
```

DeleteReportHistorySnapshot

This method deletes an individual report history snapshot for a specified report. It requires that you pass in the path to the report and an identifier for the specific history to be removed.

C#

```
public void DeleteReportHistorySnapshot(string Report, string HistoryID);
```

VB.NET

```
Public Sub DeleteReportHistorySnapshot(ByVal Report As String, ByVal HistoryID As String)
```

DeleteRole

It deletes a specified role from the Reporting Server database. In addition, all the policies associated with this role are also deleted. It requires you to pass in the name of the role to be deleted.

C#

```
public void DeleteRole(string Name);
```

VB.NET

```
Public Sub DeleteRole(ByVal Name As String)
```

DeleteSchedule

The DeleteSchedule method deletes a specific schedule from the Reporting Server database. Any reports that were scheduled to run based on this schedule will no longer be processed. It requires passing in a string value representing the ID of the schedule.

C#

```
public void DeleteSchedule(string ScheduleID);
```

VB.NET

```
Public Sub DeleteSchedule(ByVal ScheduleID As String)
```

DeleteSubscription

This method allows the user to delete a subscription to a specified report. Executing the method requires the subscription ID of the subscription to be deleted.

C#

```
public void DeleteSubscription(string SubscriptionID);
```

VB.NET

```
Public Sub DeleteSubscription(ByVal SubscriptionID As String)
```

DisableDataSource

This method allows the developer to disable a specific data source. Reports and subscriptions that use the specified data source will not run. It requires passing in the name of the data source that is to be disabled.

C#

```
public void DisableDataSource(string DataSource);
```

VB.NET

```
Public Sub DisableDataSource(ByVal DataSource As String)
```

EnableDataSource

This method enables a data source that was previously disabled.

C#

```
public void EnableDataSource(string DataSource);
```

VB.NET

```
Public Sub EnableDataSource(ByVal DataSource As String)
```

ExecuteBatch

A batch Identifier is returned when the CreateBatch Method is used. To execute a batch, the developer sets the BatchHeaderValue property of the Web service proxy class to the appropriate batch ID. All methods that are associated with this batch ID will execute within the scope of a single database transaction.

C#

```
public void ExecuteBatch();
```

VB.NET

```
Public Sub ExecuteBatch()
```

FindItems

FindItems returns items that match the specified search criteria. The required parameters are the folder to search, logical operators AND or OR, and a collection of search conditions. The return value is the CatalogItem collection.

C#

```
public CatalogItem[] FindItems(string Folder, BooleanOperatorEnum BooleanOperator,
SearchCondition[] Conditions);
```

VB.NET

```
Public Function FindItems(ByVal Folder As String, ByVal BooleanOperator As
BooleanOperatorEnum, ByVal Conditions As SearchCondition())As CatalogItem()
```

FireEvent

FireEvent causes an event to be fired. Required parameters are the event to be fired and the data required by the event.

C#

```
public void FireEvent(string EventType, string EventData);
```

VB.NET

```
Public Sub FireEvent(ByVal EventType As String, ByVal EventData As String)
```

FlushCache

FlushCache invalidates the cache for an individual report. The name of the report is the only parameter passed to this method.

C#

```
public void FlushCache(string Report);
```

VB.NET

```
Public Sub FlushCache(ByVal Report As String)
```

GenerateModel

Generates a default Model for a shared DataSource.

C#

```
public Warning[] GenerateModel(string DataSource, string Model, string Parent,
Property[] Properties);
```

VB.NET

```
Public Function GenerateModel(ByVal DataSource As String, ByVal Model As String,
ByVal Parent As String, ByVal Properties As Property()) As Warning()
```

GetCacheOptions

This method returns the cache configuration for a report and the ExpirationDefinition settings that describe when the cached copy of the report expires. The return value is a Boolean value indicating whether the report is in the cache or not.

C#

```
public bool GetCacheOptions(string Report, [out] ExpirationDefinition Expiration);
```

VB.NET

```
Public Function GetCacheOptions(ByVal Report As String, [out] ByRef Expiration As
ExpirationDefinition) As Boolean
```

GetDataDrivenSubscriptionProperties

This method returns the properties of a data-driven subscription. The required parameter is the ID of the subscription. The other parameters are declared but not initialized. They will be returned with valid values representing the settings of the subscription. They are the extension settings, the data retrieval plan, a description of the subscription, the current status of the subscription, the type of event that causes the subscription to fire, and the match data for the event.

C#

```
public string GetDataDrivenSubscriptionProperties(string DataDrivenSubscriptionID,
[out] ExtensionSettings ExtensionSettings, [out] DataRetrievalPlan
DataRetrievalPlan, [out] string Description, [out] ActiveState Active, [out]
string Status, [out] string EventType, [out] string MatchData, [out] ref
ParameterValueOrFieldReference[] Parameters);
```

VB.NET

```
Public Function GetDataDrivenSubscriptionProperties(ByVal DataDrivenSubscriptionID
As String,[out] ByRef ExtensionSettings As ExtensionSettings, [out] ByRef
DataRetrievalPlan As DataRetrievalPlan, [out] ByRef Description As String, [out]
ByRef Active As ActiveState, [out] ByRef Status As String, [out] ByRef EventType As
String, [out] ByRef MatchData As String, [out] ByRef Parameters As
ParameterValueOrFieldReference())
```

GetDataSourceContents

GetDataSourceContents returns a DataSourceDefinition object representing the contents of a data source. The required parameter is the name of the data source.

C#

```
public DataSourceDefinition GetDataSourceContents(string DataSource);
```

VB.NET

```
Public Function GetDataSourceContents(ByVal DataSource As String) As
DataSourceDefinition
```

GetExecutionOptions

This method returns the execution options and associated settings for an individual report. The required parameters are the name of the report and an uninitialized ScheduleDefinition object. This object will be returned with its properties set to the values for the report. The return value is an enum datatype that indicates whether the report is based on live data or a snapshot.

C#

```
public ExecutionSettingEnum GetExecutionOptions(string Report, [out]
ScheduleDefinitionOrReference Schedule);
```

VB.NET

```
Public Function GetExecutionOptions(ByVal Report As String,[out] ByRef Schedule As
ScheduleDefinitionOrReference) As ExecutionSettingEnum
```

GetExtensionSettings

This method requires that you pass in the name of an extension. The return value is an array of known parameters for the specific extension.

C#

```
public ExtensionParameter[] GetExtensionSettings(string Extension);
```

VB.NET

```
Public Function GetExtensionSettings(ByVal Extension As String)As
ExtensionParameter()
```

GetItemDataSourcePrompts

Gets the prompts associated with a particular item.

C#

```
public DataSourcePrompt[] GetItemDataSourcePrompts(string Item);
```

VB.NET

```
Public Function GetItemDataSourcePrompts(ByVal Item As String) as
DataSourcePrompt()
```

GetItemDataSources

Returns a DataSource collection associated with a particular item in the report catalog.

C#

```
public DataSource[] GetItemDataSources(string Item);
```

VB.NET

```
Public Function GetItemDataSources(ByVal Item As String) as DataSource()
```

GetItemType

It retrieves the type of an item, if it exists in the Reporting Server database. The required parameter is the name of the object. The return value is an enumeration representing the type of object.

C#

```
public ItemTypeEnum GetItemType(string Item);
```

VB.NET

```
Public Function GetItemType(ByVal Item As String) as ItemTypeEnum
```

GetModelDefinition

Returns the Model definition for a particular catalog item.

C#

```
public byte[] GetModelDefinition(string Item);
```

VB.NET

```
Public Function GetModelDefinition(ByVal Item As String) as Byte()
```

GetModelItemPermissions

Retrieves the permissions associated with a particular ModelItem.

C#

```
public string[] GetModelItemPermissions(string Model,string ModelItemID);
```

VB.NET

```
Public Function GetModelItemPermissions(ByVal Model As String, ModelItemID as
String) As String()
```

GetModelItemPolicies

Retrieves the policies associated with a particular ModelItem as well as a Boolean value indicating whether the object inherits from its parent.

C#

```
public Policy[] GetModelItemPolicies(string Model, string ModelItemID, out bool
InheritParent);
```

VB.NET

```
Public Function GetModelItemPolicies(ByVal Model As String, ByVal ModelItemID as
String, [out] InheritParent as Bool) as Policy()
```

GetPermissions

GetPermissions returns a string array containing a list of user permissions that are associated with a particular item in the Reporting Server database. The required input parameter is a string representing the name of the item.

C#

```
public string[] GetPermissions(string Item );
```

VB.NET

```
Public Function GetPermissions(ByVal Item As String) As String()
```

GetPolicies

GetPolicies returns an array of Policy objects that are associated with a particular item as well as a Boolean value indicating whether the item inherits those policies from its parent.

C#

```
public Policy[] GetPolicies(string Item, [out] ref bool InheritParent);
```

VB.NET

```
Public Function GetPolicies(ByVal Item As String, [out] ByRef InheritParent As
Boolean) As Policy()
```

GetProperties

GetProperties returns property values for a particular report object. You need to pass in an array of Property objects with names initialized, and the method returns those objects with their values set.

C#

```
public Property[] GetProperties(string Item, Property[] Properties);
```

VB.NET

```
Public Function GetProperties(ByVal Item As String, ByVal Properties As Property())
As Property()
```

GetRenderResource

GetRenderResource returns the resource for a specified rendering extension format. It requires that you pass in the format to use for processing device-specific information and the MIME-type of the resource. It returns the resource as a base-64 encoded byte array.

C#

```
public byte[] GetRenderResource(string Format, string DeviceInfo,[out]  string
MimeType);
```

VB.NET

```
Public Sub GetRenderResource(ByVal Format As String, ByVal DeviceInfo As String,
[out] ByRef MimeType As String) as Byte()
```

GetReportDefinition

This method retrieves the report definition for a report in base-64-encoded byte format. It can then be converted into Report Definition Language for use in tools such as Visual Studio.

C#

```
public byte[] GetReportDefinition(string Report);
```

VB.NET

```
Public Function GetReportDefinition(ByVal Report As String)As Byte()
```

GetReportHistoryLimit

This method returns an integer that indicates the number of snapshot history reports to maintain. The required parameters are the name of the report, a Boolean value that will be altered in the method to reflect whether the report has its own limit or uses the system limit, and an integer that will be returned with the value of the current system limit.

C#

```
public int GetReportHistoryLimit(string Report, [out] bool IsSystem, [out] int
SystemLimit);
```

VB.NET

```
Public Function GetReportHistoryLimit(ByVal Report As String, , ByRef IsSystem As
Boolean, ByRef SystemLimit As Integer) as Integer
```

GetReportHistoryOptions

This method returns the report history snapshot options and properties that are generated for a report by passing in the report name. The method returns a Boolean variable that indicates whether the report allows the creation of manual snapshots. The property information is retrieved by output parameters, which indicate whether snapshots have been kept and a schedule definition is associated with the report.

C#

```
public bool GetReportHistoryOptions(string Report,[out] bool
KeepExecutionSnapshots, [out] ScheduleDefinitionOrReference Schedule);
```

VB.NET

```
Public Function GetReportHistoryOptions(ByVal Report As String,[out] ByRef
KeepExecutionSnapshots As Boolean, [out] ByRef Schedule As
ScheduleDefinitionOrReference) as Boolean
```

GetReportLink

The GetReportLink method returns the full path of the report, the report definition of which is used for the specified linked report. The only parameter is the name of the report referred for the report definition.

C#

```
public string GetReportLink(string Report);
```

VB.NET

```
Public Function GetReportLink(ByVal Report As String) As String
```

GetReportParameters

This method returns report parameters for a specified report. The first parameter is the name of the report. The next two parameters are used together. If a HistoryId is provided and the ForRendering parameter is set to true, the returned properties belong to a snapshot of the provided report. The ParameterValues argument can be used to verify valid parameters against a report. The Credentials parameter returns the credentials to use to validate and check the parameters.

C#

```
public ReportParameter[] GetReportParameters(string Report, string HistoryID, bool
ForRendering, ParameterValue[] Values, DataSourceCredentials[] Credentials);
```

VB.NET

```
Public Function GetReportParameters(ByVal Report As String, ByVal HistoryID As
String, ByVal ForRendering As Boolean, ByVal Values As ParameterValue(), ByVal
Credentials As DataSourceCredentials()) As ReportParameter()
```

GetResourceContents

This method requires the developer to pass in the resource that needs retrieval. The method returns a MIME-type and the value of the resource as a base-64-encoded byte array.

C#

```
Public byte[] GetResourceContents(string Resource, [out]  string MimeType);
```

VB.NET

```
Public Function GetResourceContents(ByVal Resource As String, ByRef MimeType As
String) As Byte()
```

GetRoleProperties

This method returns a collection of tasks associated with a given role. The description string argument will return containing the description for the role.

C#

```
public Task[] GetRoleProperties(string Name,[out]  string Description);
```

VB.NET

```
Public Function GetRoleProperties(ByVal Name As String, ByRef Description As
String) as Task()
```

GetScheduleProperties

This method returns a Schedule object containing the schedule definition for a single shared schedule by passing in a specific schedule ID.

C#

```
public Schedule GetScheduleProperties(string ScheduleID);
```

VB.NET

```
Public Function GetScheduleProperties(ByVal ScheduleID As String) As Schedule
```

GetServerDateTime

This method is described in the documentation. It supposedly returns the current date and time of the computer that is running the report server scheduler. It exists in the internal Reporting Server classes but is not exposed through the WSDL-generated proxy class.

C#

```
public DateTime GetServerDateTime();
```

VB.NET

```
Public Function GetServerDateTime()
```

GetSubscriptionProperties

The GetSubscriptionProperties method returns a subscription and the associated information for a specified report in the Reporting Server database. The required parameters are the name of the report, a delivery extension object, a string to hold a user-friendly description, an Event object, and match data that is needed by the EventType object. It also returns a string representing the owner of the subscription. All of the parameters except the subscription have no initial value but return the settings for the subscription after the method executes.

C#

```
public string GetSubscriptionProperties(string SubscriptionID, [out] ref
ExtensionSettings ExtensionSettings, [out] ref string Description, [out] ref
ActiveState Active, [out] ref string Status, [out] ref string EventType, [out] ref
string MatchData, [out] ref ParameterValue[] Parameters);
```

VB.NET

```
Public Function GetSubscriptionProperties(ByVal SubscriptionID As String,[out]
ByRef ExtensionSettings As ExtensionSettings, [out] ByRef Description As String,
[out] ByRef Active As ActiveState, [out] ByRef Status As String, [out] ByRef
EventType As String, [out] ByRef MatchData As String, [out] ByRef Parameters As
ParameterValue()) as String
```

GetSystemPermissions

This retrieves a string array representing the system permissions of the current user. An example of a valid permission is the Create Roles permission.

C#

```
public string[] GetSystemPermissions();
```

VB.NET

```
Public Function GetSystemPermissions() As String()
```

GetSystemPolicies

This method returns an array of `Policy` objects representing groups and associated roles.

C#

```
public Policy[] GetSystemPolicies();
```

VB.NET

```
Public Function GetSystemPolicies() As Policy()
```

GetSystemProperties

This method requires passing in an array of `Property` objects with names initialized to the properties that you are interested in. The method returns this array of properties with their values from the system, indicating the system status.

C#

```
public Property[] GetSystemProperties(Property[] Properties) ;
```

VB.NET

```
Public Function GetSystemProperties(ByVal Properties As Property()) As Property()
```

InheritModelItemParentSecurity

Indicates that the Model should inherit its security attributes from its parent.

C#

```
public void InheritModelItemParentSecurity(string Model, string ModelItemID);
```

VB.NET

```
Public Sub InheritModelItemParentSecurity(ByVal Model As String, ByVal ModelItemID
As String)
```

InheritParentSecurity

This method deletes all the policies associated with an item, thereby causing it to inherit policies from its parent.

C#

```
public void InheritParentSecurity(string Item);
```

VB.NET

```
Public Sub InheritParentSecurity(ByVal Item As String)
```

ListChildren

This method returns a `CatalogItem` array, given a string value representing a specified folder. A Boolean value that indicates whether the search should be recursive and traverse the entire directory structure of the path below the specified folder is also required.

C#

```
public CatalogItem[] ListChildren(string Item, bool Recursive);
```

VB.NET

```
Public Function ListChildren(ByVal Item As String, ByVal Recursive As Boolean) As
CatalogItem()
```

ListDependantItems

This method returns a `CatalogItem` array, given a string value representing a specified folder. A Boolean value that indicates whether the search should be recursive and traverse the entire directory structure of the path below the specified folder is also required.

C#

```
public CatalogItem[] ListDependantItems(string Item);
```

VB.NET

```
Public Function ListDependantItems(ByVal Item As String) As CatalogItem()
```

ListEvents

This method returns an array of events that are defined on the report server.

C#

```
Public Event[] ListEvents();
```

VB.NET

```
Public Function ListEvents() As Event()
```

ListExtensions

It returns a list of `Extension` objects that are configured for a given extension type such as delivery, rendering, or data. The parameter is an enumeration representing all of the extension types.

C#

```
public Extension[] ListExtensions(ExtensionTypeEnum ExtensionType );
```

VB.NET

```
Public Function ListExtensions(ByVal ExtensionType As ExtensionTypeEnum)As
Extension()
```

ListJobs

Method returns an array of `Jobs` that represent information about currently running jobs on the report server.

C#

```
public Jobs[] ListJobs();
```

VB.NET

```
Public Function ListJobs()As Job()
```

ListModelDrillthroughReports

Lists drill through reports associated with a particular model item.

C#

```
public ModelDrillthroughReport[] ListModelDrillthroughReports(string Model, string
ModelItemID);
```

VB.NET

```
Public Function ListModelDrillthroughReports (ByVal Model As String, Byval
ModelItemID as String) As ModelDrillthroughReport()
```

ListModelItemChildren

Returns an array of ModelItems associated with a particular model.

C#

```
public ModelItem[] ListModelItemChildren(string Model, string ModelItemID,bool
Recursive);
```

VB.NET

```
Public Function ListModelItemChildren (ByVal Model As String, Byval ModelItemID as
String, Recursive as Boolean) As ModelItem()
```

ListModelPerspectives

Lists `ModelItems` available to a particular user.

C#

```
public ModelCatalogItem[] ListModelPerspectives(string Model);
```

VB.NET

```
Public Function ListModelPerspectives (ByVal Model As String) As ModelCatalogItem()
```

ListReportHistory

This method returns an array of report history snapshots and their properties for a specified report.

C#

```
public ReportHistorySnapshot[] ListReportHistory(string Report);
```

VB.NET

```
Public Function ListReportHistory(ByVal Report As String)As ReportHistorySnapshot()
```

ListRoles

It returns an array of Roles defined on the report server from which their names and descriptions can be extracted.

C#

```
public Roles[] ListRoles(SecurityScopeEnum SecurityScope);
```

VB.NET

```
Public Function ListRoles(ByVal SecurityScope as SecurityScopeEnum) As Role()
```

ListScheduledReports

This method returns an array of reports that are associated with a shared schedule.

C#

```
public CatalogItem[] ListScheduledReports(string ScheduleID);
```

VB.NET

```
Public Function ListScheduledReports(ByVal ScheduleID As String)As CatalogItem()
```

ListSchedules

This method returns an array containing all the shared schedules on the report server.

C#

```
public Schedule[] ListSchedules();
```

VB.NET

```
Public Function ListSchedules()As Schedule()
```

ListSecureMethods

It returns a string array of methods that require a secure connection when invoked.

C#

```
public string[] ListSecureMethods();
```

VB.NET

```
Public Function ListSecureMethods() As String()
```

ListSubscriptions

The `ListSubscriptions` method returns an array of `Subscription` objects that have been created for a given report for a specific user. This array includes both standard and data-driven subscriptions.

C#

```
public Subscription[] ListSubscriptions(string Report, string Owner);
```

VB.NET

```
Public Function ListSubscriptions(ByVal Report As String, ByVal Owner As String) As
Subscription()
```

ListSubscriptionsUsingDataSource

This method returns a list of subscriptions associated with a given data source.

C#

```
public Subscription[] ListSubscriptionsUsingDataSource(string DataSource);
```

VB.NET

```
Public Function ListSubscriptionsUsingDataSource(ByVal DataSource As String) As
Subscription()
```

ListTasks

This method returns an array of `Task` objects from which item task information may be extracted. An example of an item-level task is viewing a folder or a report.

C#

```
public Task[] ListTasks(SecurityScopeEnum SecurityScope);
```

VB.NET

```
Public Function ListTasks(ByVal SecurityScope as SecurityScopeEnum) As Task()
```

LogonUser

Creates an active session for the user with the specified credentials.

C#

```
public void LogonUser(string userName, string password, string authority);
```

VB.NET

```
Public Sub LogonUser(userName as String, password as String, authority as string)
```

Logoff

Logs off the current user making requests.

C#

```
public void Logoff();
```

VB.NET

```
Public Sub Logoff()
```

MoveItem

The `MoveItem` method moves or renames an item in the Reporting Server database; required parameters are the original location and the destination path.

C#

```
public void MoveItem(string Item, string Target);
```

VB.NET

```
Public Sub MoveItem(ByVal Item As String, ByVal Target As String)
```

PauseSchedule

This method pauses the execution of a given shared schedule. The required parameter is the associated schedule ID.

C#

```
public void PauseSchedule(string ScheduleID);
```

VB.NET

```
Public Sub PauseSchedule(ByVal ScheduleID As String)
```

PrepareQuery

This method returns a data set containing the fields retrieved by the delivery query for a data-driven subscription. The parameters are the data source to be used, the data definition object, and a Boolean value to indicate whether the data definition has changed.

C#

```
public DataSetDefinition PrepareQuery(DataSource datasource, DataSetDefinition
dataset, [out] bool changed);
```

VB.NET

```
Public Function PrepareQuery(ByVal DataSource As DataSource, ByVal DataSet As
DataSetDefinition, [out] ByRef Changed As Boolean) as DataSetDefinition
```

RegenerateModel

Causes a model to be regenerated based on changes to the underlying data definition.

C#

```
public Warning[] RegenerateModel(string Model);
```

VB.NET

```
Public RegenerateModel( ByVal Model as String) as Warning()
```

RemoveAllModelItemPolicies

Removes all policies associated with a particular model item.

C#

```
public void RemoveAllModelItemPolicies(string Model);
```

VB.NET

```
Public Sub RemoveAllModelItemPolicies(ByVal Model as String)As String
```

ResumeSchedule

This method is used to resume from a shared schedule that has been paused.

C#

```
public void ResumeSchedule(string ScheduleID);
```

VB.NET

```
Public Sub ResumeSchedule(ByVal ScheduleID As String)
```

SetCacheOptions

This method configures caching options for a specified report. Parameters of the report, whether to create a cache of the report, and an expiration definition or date that controls how long the report is in the cache are passed to this function.

C#

```
public void SetCacheOptions(string Report, bool CacheReport, ExpirationDefinition
Expiration);
```

VB.NET

```
Public Sub SetCacheOptions(ByVal Report As String, ByVal CacheReport As Boolean,
ByVal Expiration As ExpirationDefinition)
```

SetDataDrivenSubscriptionProperties

This method sets the properties of a data-driven subscription.

C#

```
public void SetDataDrivenSubscriptionProperties(string DataDrivenSubscriptionID,
ExtensionSettings ExtensionSettings, DataRetrievalPlan DataRetrievalPlan, string
Description, string EventType, string MatchData, ParameterValueOrFieldReference[]
Parameters);
```

VB.NET

```
Public Sub SetDataDrivenSubscriptionProperties(ByVal DataDrivenSubscriptionID As
String, ByVal ExtensionSettings As ExtensionSettings, ByVal DataRetrievalPlan As
DataRetrievalPlan, ByVal Description As String, ByVal EventType As String, ByVal
MatchData As String, ByVal Parameters As ParameterValueOrFieldReference())
```

SetDataSourceContents

This replaces the contents of an existing data source. The parameters are the name of the source and a data definition object defining all the source properties.

C#

```
public void SetDataSourceContents(string DataSource, DataSourceDefinition
Definition);
```

VB.NET

```
Public Sub SetDataSourceContents(ByVal DataSource As String, ByVal Definition As
DataSourceDefinition)
```

SetExecutionOptions

This method sets the execution options and the associated execution properties for an individual report. The first parameter is the name of the report, followed by an enumeration indicating whether the report should be executed in real time or scheduled. The third parameter, Schedule, is only used if the execution is scheduled.

C#

```
public void SetExecutionOptions(string Report, ExecutionSettingEnum
ExecutionSetting, ScheduleDefinitionOrReference Schedule);
```

VB.NET

```
Public Sub SetExecutionOptions(ByVal Report As String, ByVal ExecutionSetting As
ExecutionSettingEnum, ByVal Schedule As ScheduleDefinitionOrReference)
```

SetItemDataSources

Sets the DataSources associated with a particular catalog item.

C#

```
public void SetItemDataSources(string Item, DataSource[] DataSources);
```

VB.NET

```
Public Sub SetModelDefinition(Item as String, DataSources as DataSource())
```

SetModelDefinition

Sets the DataSources associated with a particular Model item.

C #

```
public Warning[] SetModelDefinition(string Model, byte[] Definition);
```

VB.NET

```
Public Function SetModelDefinition(Model as String, Definition as Byte()) as
Warning()
```

SetModelDrillthroughReports

Associates drill-through reports with a particular Model item.

C#

```
public void SetModelDrillthroughReports(string Model, string ModelItemID,
ModelDrillthroughReport[] Reports);
```

VB.NET

```
Public Sub SetModelDrillthroughReports(Model as String, ModelItemID as String,
Reports as ModelDrillthroughReport())
```

SetModelItemPolicies

Associates policies with a particular Model item.

C#

```
public void SetModelItemPolicies(string Model, string ModelItemID, Policy[]
Policies);
```

VB.NET

```
Public Sub SetModelItemPolicies(Model as String, ModelItemID as String, Policies as
Policy())
```

Reporting Services Object Model

SetPolicies

This method sets the policies that are associated with a specified item. The required parameters are the item and an array of `Policy` objects to place on the specified item.

C#

```
public void SetPolicies(string Item, Policy[] Policies);
```

VB.NET

```
Public Sub SetPolicies(ByVal Item As String, ByVal Policies As Policy())
```

SetProperties

This sets the properties that are associated with a specified item. The required parameters are the item for which you will set properties and an array of `Property` objects to place on the specified item.

C#

```
public void SetProperties(string Item, Property[] Properties);
```

VB.NET

```
Public Sub SetProperties(ByVal Item As String, ByVal Properties As Property())
```

SetReportDefinition

The `SetReportDefinition` method is used to change a report definition for a specified report. The required parameter is the name of the report, followed by an array of bytes that are the report definition. The return value is an array of warnings informing the developer of problems that occur.

C#

```
public Warning[] SetReportDefinition(string Report, byte[] Definition);
```

VB.NET

```
Public Function SetReportDefinition(ByVal Report As String, ByVal Definition As Byte()) As Warning()
```

SetReportHistoryLimit

This allows the developer to specify the number of snapshots of a report that the report server retains. The required parameters are the name of the report and a Boolean value indicating whether the default system limit should be used or a specific limit.

C#

```
public void SetReportHistoryLimit(string Report, bool UseSystem, int HistoryLimit);
```

VB.NET

```
Public Sub SetReportHistoryLimit(ByVal Report As String, ByVal UseSystem As
Boolean, ByVal HistoryLimit As Integer)
```

SetReportHistoryOptions

This method allows the developer to set report history options that control snapshot creation and lifetime. The required parameters are the name of the report, a Boolean value that controls whether manual snapshots can be created, and a Boolean value indicating whether snapshot histories should be maintained. You also need to pass in the schedule the snapshot should be created against.

C#

```
public void SetReportHistoryOptions(string Report, bool
EnableManualSnapshotCreation, bool KeepExecutionSnapshots,
ScheduleDefinitionOrReference Schedule);
```

VB.NET

```
Public Sub SetReportHistoryOptions(ByVal Report As String, ByVal
EnableManualSnapshotCreation As Boolean, ByVal KeepExecutionSnapshots As Boolean,
ByVal Schedule As ScheduleDefinitionOrReference)
```

SetReportLink

A linked report does not contain a full report definition. This method allows you to specify the report that contains the full definition for the report. A linked report may be linked to more than one report definition.

C#

```
public void SetReportLink(string Report, string Link);
```

VB.NET

```
Public Sub SetReportLink(ByVal Report As String, ByVal Link As String)
```

SetReportParameters

This method allows the developer to specify parameters for a report that it needs in order to be processed. The parameters are the name of the report and a collection of parameters, the names of which must match those defined in the report.

C#

```
public void SetReportParameters(string Report, ReportParameter[] Parameters);
```

VB.NET

```
Public Sub SetReportParameters(ByVal Report As String, ByVal Parameters As
ReportParameter())
```

SetResourceContents

Resources such as images are stored as byte arrays. The SetResourceContents method allows the developer to replace the contents of an existing resource by passing in a byte array representing the new value. The required parameters are the resource to be accessed, the byte array that contains the value, and the MIME-type of the resource.

C#

```
public void SetResourceContents(string Resource, byte[] Contents, string MimeType);
```

VB.NET

```
Public Sub SetResourceContents(ByVal Resource As String, ByVal Contents As Byte(),
ByVal MimeType As String)
```

SetRoleProperties

This method allows the developer to associate a group of tasks with a specified role. The required parameters are the role name and the array of tasks to associate with the role.

C#

```
public void SetRoleProperties(string Name, string Description, Task[] Tasks);
```

VB.NET

```
Public Sub SetRoleProperties(ByVal Name As String, ByVal Description As String,
ByVal Tasks As Task())
```

SetScheduleProperties

This method allows the developer to set the properties of a shared schedule. The required parameters are the name of the report, the schedule ID, and a schedule definition object that contains the schedule properties for the report.

C#

```
public void SetScheduleProperties(string Name, string ScheduleID,
ScheduleDefinition ScheduleDefinition);
```

VB.NET

```
Public Sub SetScheduleProperties(ByVal Name As String, ByVal ScheduleID As String,
ByVal ScheduleDefinition As ScheduleDefinition)
```

SetSubscriptionProperties

This method allows the developer to set the properties of a shared subscription. The required parameters are the name of the report, the subscription ID, delivery-specific setting information, a description of the subscription, the event that causes the subscription to run, match data used by the specific type of event used, and the parameters for the report.

C#

```
public void SetSubscriptionProperties(string SubscriptionID, ExtensionSettings
ExtensionSettings, string Description, string EventType, string MatchData,
ParameterValue[] Parameters);
```

VB.NET

```
Public Sub SetSubscriptionProperties(ByVal SubscriptionID As String, ByVal
ExtensionSettings As ExtensionSettings, ByVal Description As String, ByVal
EventType As String, ByVal MatchData As String, ByVal Parameters As
ParameterValue())
```

SetSystemPolicies

This allows the developer to set system policies by passing in an array of Policy objects.

C#

```
public void SetSystemPolicies(Policy[] Policies);
```

VB.NET

```
Public Sub SetSystemPolicies(ByVal Policies As Policy())
```

SetSystemProperties

This method allows the developer to set system properties by passing in an array of Property objects.

C#

```
public void SetSystemProperties(Property[] Properties);
```

VB.NET

```
Public Sub SetSystemProperties(ByVal Properties As Property())
```

UpdateReportExecutionSnapshot

This method creates a report history snapshot for a specified report.

C#

```
public void UpdateReportExecutionSnapshot(string Report);
```

VB.NET

```
Public Sub UpdateReportExecutionSnapshot(ByVal Report As String)
```

ValidateExtensionSettings

This method allows the developer to validate the Reporting Services extension settings. The required parameters are the name of the extension and an array of parameter values to verify. The method returns an array of extension parameter objects with initialized values if they are valid, and error messages if they are not.

C#

```
public ExtensionParameter[] ValidateExtensionSettings(string Extension,
ParameterValueOrFieldReference[] ParameterValues);
```

VB.NET

```
Public Function ValidateExtensionSettings (ByVal Extension As String, ByVal
ParameterValues As ParameterValueOrFieldReference()) Values As ExtensionParameter()
```

Public Properties

The Reporting Services Web service proxy class contains several properties that are used to control how Reporting Services handles various requests. These properties and a description of their impact on Reporting Services are discussed.

BatchHeaderValue

This value is used to group multimethod operations against the Reporting Services Web service.

C#

```
public BatchHeader BatchHeaderValue { get; set; }
```

VB.NET

```
Public Property BatchHeaderValue() As BatchHeader
```

ItemNamespaceHeaderValue

This value is used to retrieve properties for a specific item by setting either the ID or the name of the property in the ItemNamespaceHeader.

C#

```
public ItemNamespaceHeader ItenNamespaceHeaderValue { get; set; }
```

VB.NET

```
Public Property ItemNamespaceHeaderValue() As ItemNamespaceHeader
```

ServerInfoHeaderValue

This property contains server-related information such as the edition of Reporting Services and the version information.

C#

```
public ServerInfoHeader ServerInfoHeaderValue { get; set; }
```

VB.NET

```
Public Property ServerInfoHeaderValue() As ServerInfoHeader
```

C

Transact SQL Command Syntax Reference

A significant portion of this text is used with permission from Beginning Transact SQL, *available from Wrox Press.*

SQL Server recognizes up to four parts of object names. Depending upon the context of an expression, some parts may or may not be necessary when referencing an object. When script runs on a different server or when using a different database, related object names may be required. Note that SQL Server 2005 recognizes the schema name in the third position, while SQL Server 2000 recognizes the object owner name in the same position. If you are using SQL Server 2000, substitute the owner for the schema.

Object Reference	Use and Context
`object`	In the context of the local database, on the same server. Object is owned by the dbo user (SQL Server 2000) or part of the dbo schema (SQL Server 2005) and there are no duplicate object names.
`schema.object`	In the context of the local database, on the same server. Object may be owned by a user other than dbo (SQL Server 2000) or part of a specific schema. Duplicate object names that have different owners or schema names are permitted. Also uses a standard convention for clarity.
`database..object`	In the context of the same or different database on the same server. Without specifying the owner or schema, assumes the dbo owner or schema.
`database.schema.object`	A three-part name fully describes an object on the same server, in the same or different database.

Table continued on following page

Object Reference	Use and Context
`server.database.schema.object`	A four-part name is valid in the context of a remote server or the local server, in the local or a different database, and for any user or schema.
`server.database..object`	The database owner or schema in the third position can be omitted to use the default dbo owner or schema.
`server..schema.object`	The database name may be omitted to use the default database on that server. This is a not a typical practice.
`server...object`	Omitting the database and owner or schema name uses the default database and the default dbo user or schema. This is not a typical practice.

Transact-SQL Commands, Clauses, and Predicates

Following are the core components of the Transact-SQL language. New commands for SQL Server 2005 are explicitly called out in this section.

WITH

This is a new method in SQL Server 2005 for defining an alias for the result set returned by a SELECT expression.

```
WITH MyCTE
AS
( SELECT * FROM Product WHERE ListPrice < 1000 )
```

Optionally, column aliases can be defined in parentheses following the Common Table Expression (CTE) name:

```
WITH MyCTE ( ID, ProdNumber, ProdName, Price )
AS
( SELECT
    ProductID
  , ProductNumber
  , Name
  , ListPrice
  FROM Product WHERE ListPrice < 1000
)
```

SELECT

Return all columns from a table or view:

```
SELECT * FROM table_name
```

Return specific columns from a table or view:

```
SELECT Column1, Column2, Column3 FROM table_name
```

Column alias techniques:

```
SELECT Column1 AS Col1, Column2 AS Col2 FROM table_name
SELECT Column1 Col1, Column2 Col2 FROM table_name
SELECT Col1 = Column1, Col2 = Column2 FROM table_name
```

Literal values:

```
SELECT 'Some literal value'
SELECT 'Some value' AS Col1, 123 AS Col2
```

Returning an expression value:

```
SELECT (1 + 2) * 3
```

Returning the result of a function call:

```
SELECT CONVERT( VarChar(20), GETDATE(), 101 )
```

TOP

Return a fixed number of rows:

```
SELECT TOP 10 * FROM table_name ORDER BY Column1
SELECT TOP 10 Column1, Column2 FROM table_name ORDER BY Column2
```

Return a fixed number of rows with the ties for last position. If the value in the *nth* row is the same as the subsequent row(s), these rows are also returned.

```
SELECT TOP 10 WITH TIES Column1, Column2 FROM table_name ORDER BY Column2
```

Return a percentage of all available rows:

```
SELECT TOP 25 PERCENT * FROM table_name ORDER BY Column2
SELECT TOP 25 PERCENT Column1, Column2 FROM table_name ORDER BY Column2
```

For SQL Server 2005 only, substitute a variable or expression for a top values number:

```
DECLARE @TopNumber Int
SET @TopNumber = 15
SELECT TOP @ TopNumber * FROM table_name ORDER BY Column2
```

Top values–based on an expression:

```
SELECT TOP (SELECT a_column_value FROM some_table) * FROM another_table
```

SELECT INTO

Create and populate a table from a result set:

```
SELECT Column1, Column2 INTO new_table_name FROM existing_table_or_view_name
```

FROM

Single table query:

```
SELECT * FROM table_name
```

Multi-table join query:

```
SELECT *
FROM table1.key_column INNER JOIN table2 ON table1.key_column = table2.key_column
```

Derived table:

```
SELECT DerTbl.Column1, DerTbl.Column2
FROM
    ( SELECT Column1, Column2 FROM some_table ... ) AS DerTbl
```

WHERE

Exact match:

```
SELECT ... FROM ...
WHERE Column1 = 'A literal value'
```

Not NULL:

```
SELECT ... FROM ...
WHERE Column1 IS NOT NULL
```

Any trailing characters:

```
SELECT ... FROM ...
WHERE Column1 LIKE 'ABC%'
```

Any leading characters:

```
SELECT ... FROM ...
WHERE Column1 LIKE '%XYZ'
```

Any leading or trailing characters:

```
SELECT ... FROM ...
WHERE Column1 LIKE '%MNOP%'
```

Placeholder wildcard:

```
SELECT ... FROM ...
WHERE Column1 LIKE '_BC_EF'
```

Criteria using parentheses to designate order:

```
SELECT ... FROM ...
WHERE
    (Column1 LIKE 'ABC%' AND Column2 LIKE '%XYZ')
    OR
    Column3 = '123'
```

GROUP BY

All nonaggregated columns in the SELECT list must be included in the GROUP BY list:

```
SELECT COUNT(Column1), Column2, Column3
FROM ... WHERE ...
GROUP BY Column2, Column3
```

Designating order:

```
SELECT COUNT(Column1), Column2, Column3
FROM ... WHERE ...
GROUP BY Column2, Column3
ORDER BY Column2 DESC, Column3 ASC
```

HAVING

Filter results based on values available after the aggregations and groupings are performed:

```
SELECT COUNT(Column1), Column2, Column3
FROM ... WHERE ...
GROUP BY Column2, Column3
HAVING COUNT(Column1) > 5
```

UNION

Combine multiple results with the same column count:

```
SELECT Column1, Column2 FROM table1_name
UNION
SELECT Column1, Column2 FROM table2_name
```

Combine literal values and query results:

```
SELECT -1 AS Column1, 'A literal value' AS Column2
UNION
SELECT Column1, Column2 FROM table1_name
```

Include nondistinct selection (UNION performs SELECT DISTINCT by default):

```
SELECT Column1, Column2 FROM table1_name
UNION ALL
SELECT Column1, Column2 FROM table2_name
```

EXCEPT and INTERSECT

Select the differences (EXCEPT) or common values (INTERSECT) between two queries:

```
SELECT * FROM TableA EXCEPT SELECT * FROM TableB
```

```
SELECT * FROM TableA INTERSECT SELECT * FROM TableB
```

ORDER BY

Order a result set by one or more column values. The default order is ascending. If ordering by more than one column, each column can have a different order.

```
SELECT * FROM table_name ORDER BY Column1
```

```
SELECT * FROM table_name ORDER BY Column1 DESC, Column2 ASC
```

COMPUTE (BY)

The COMPUTE and COMPUTE BY clauses generate totals that are appended to the end of an aggregate query result set. These clauses are not very useful in applications because the aggregated results are not in relational form and cannot be utilized in a dataset.

```
SELECT ProductID, SalesOrderID, OrderQty
FROM SalesOrderDetail
ORDER BY ProductID, SalesOrderID
COMPUTE SUM(OrderQty)
```

FOR Clause

The FOR clause is used with either the XML or BROWSE option in a SELECT statement. However, the BROWSE and XML options are completely unrelated. FOR XML specifies that the result set is returned in XML format. FOR BROWSE is used when accessing data through the DB-Library so that rows can be browsed and updated one row at a time in an optimistic locking environment. There are several requirements when using the FOR BROWSE option. For more information consult the SQL Server Books Online under the topic "Browse Mode."

```
SELECT * FROM table_name FOR XML {XML Option}
```

```
SELECT * FROM table_name FOR BROWSE
```

OPTION Clause

The OPTION clause is used in a SELECT statement to provide a query hint that will override the query optimizer and specify an index or specific join mechanism to be used along with other hint options. As a rule, this is not a recommended practice but may be useful in rare cases to influence query processing and performance.

```
OPTION (HASH JOIN)

OPTION ( OPTIMIZE FOR (@ProductCategory = 'Widget') )
```

CASE

CASE evaluates one or more expressions and returns one or more specified values based on the evaluated expression.

```
SELECT expression = CASE Column
WHEN value THEN resultant_value
WHEN value2 THEN resultant_value2
. . .
ELSE alternate_value
END
FROM table

SELECT value =
        CASE
        WHEN column IS NULL THEN value
        WHEN column {expression true} THEN different_value
        WHEN column {expression true} and price {expression true} THEN other_value
        ELSE different_value
        END,
       column2
FROM table
```

INSERT

Adds a new row to a table:

```
INSERT table (column list)
VALUES
(column values)

INSERT table
SELECT columns FROM source expression

INSERT table
EXEC stored_procedure
```

UPDATE

Updates selected columns in a table:

```
UPDATE table SET column1 = expression1, column2 = expression2
WHERE filter_expression
```

Update a table based on the contents of another table:

```
UPDATE table SET column1 = expression
FROM table INNER JOIN table2
ON table.column = table2.column
WHERE table.column = table2.column
```

DELETE

Deletes selected rows from a table:

```
DELETE table
WHERE filter_expression
```

Deletes rows from a table based on the contents of a different table:

```
DELETE table
FROM table INNER JOIN table2
ON table.column = table2.column
WHERE column = filter_expression
```

DECLARE @local_variable

This creates a named object that temporarily holds a value with the data type defined in the declaration statement. Local variables have scope only within the calling batch or stored procedure. The value of a local variable can be set with either a SET or SELECT operation. SELECT is more efficient and has the advantage of populating multiple variables in a single operation, but the SELECT operation cannot be confined with any data retrieval operation.

```
DECLARE @local_variable AS int
SET @local_variable = integer_expression

DECLARE @local_variable1 AS int, @local_variable2 AS varchar(55)
SELECT @local_variable1 = integer_column_expression, @local_variable2 =
character_column_expression FROM table
```

SET

The SET operator has many functions, from setting the value of a variable to setting a database or connection property. The SET operator is divided into the categories listed in the following table:

Category	Alters the Current Session Settings For
Date and time	Handling date and time data
Locking	Handling Microsoft SQL Server locking
Miscellaneous	Miscellaneous SQL Server functionality
Query execution	Query execution and processing
SQL-92 settings	Using the SQL-92 default settings
Statistics	Displaying statistics information
Transactions	Handling SQL Server transactions

LIKE

LIKE is a pattern-matching operator for comparing strings or partial strings.

Compare a string value where the compared string is anywhere in the string:

```
SELECT * FROM table WHERE column1 LIKE '%string%'
```

Compare a string value where the compared string is at the beginning of the string:

```
SELECT * FROM table WHERE column1 LIKE 'string%'
```

Compare a string value where the compared string is at the end of the string:

```
SELECT * FROM table WHERE column1 LIKE '%string'
```

Compare a string value where a specific character or character range is in the string:

```
SELECT * FROM table WHERE column1 LIKE '[a-c]'
SELECT * FROM table WHERE column1 LIKE '[B-H]olden'
```

Compare a string value where a specific character or character range is not in the string:

```
SELECT * FROM table WHERE column1 LIKE '[M^c]%' -Begins with M but not Mc
```

ALTER TABLE

Alter the structure of a table by adding or removing table objects such as Constraints, Columns, and Partitions or enabling and disabling Triggers.

```
ALTER TABLE table_name ADD new_column int NULL
ALTER TABLE table_name ADD CONSTRAINT new_check CHECK (check expression)
ALTER TABLE table_name DISABLE TRIGGER trigger_name
ALTER TABLE table_name ENABLE TRIGGER trigger_name
```

CREATE DATABASE

Create a database and all associated files:

```
CREATE DATABASE new_database
ON (
   NAME - 'logical_name',
   FILENAME = 'physical_file_location',
   SIZE = initial_size_in_MB,
   MAXSIZE = max_size_in_MB, --If no MAXSIZE specified unlimited growth is assumed
   FILEGROWTH = percentage_OR_space_in_MB)
LOG ON
( NAME = 'logical_log_name',
   FILENAME = 'physical_file_location',
   SIZE = initial_size_in_MB,
   MAXSIZE = max_size_in_MB, --If no MAXSIZE specified unlimited growth is assumed
   FILEGROWTH = percentage_OR_space_in_MB)
COLLATE database_collation
```

CREATE DEFAULT

Create a database-wide default value that can then be bound to columns in any table to provide a default value.

```
CREATE DEFAULT default_name AS default_value
--bind the default to a table column
sp_bindefault default_name, 'table.column'
```

CREATE PROCEDURE

Create a new stored procedure:

```
CREATE PROC proc_name @variable variable_data_type ...n
AS
...procedure code
```

CREATE RULE

Create a database-wide rule, much like a check constraint, that can then be bound to individual columns in tables throughout the database.

```
CREATE RULE rule_name AS rule_expression
--bind the Rule to a table column
sp_bindrule rule_name, 'table.column'
```

CREATE TABLE

Create a new table:

```
CREATE TABLE table_name (
Column1 data_type nullability column_option,
Column2 data_type nullability column_option,
Column3 data_type nullability column_option,

--Column_option = Collation, IDENTITY, KEY...
```

Create a new partitioned table:

```
CREATE TABLE partitioned_table_name (col1 int, col2 char(10))
Column1 data_type nullability column_option,
Column2 data_type nullability column_option,
Column3 data_type nullability column_option

ON partition_scheme_name (column)
```

CREATE TRIGGER

Create a new trigger on a table that fires AFTER a DML (Data Manipulation Language) event or INSTEAD OF a DML event.

```
CREATE TRIGGER trigger_name
ON table_name FOR dml_action -INSERT, UPDATE or DELETE
AS
...trigger_code
CREATE TRIGGER trigger_name
ON view_or_table_name INSTEAD OF dml_action -INSERT, UPDATE or DELETE
AS
...trigger_code
```

CREATE VIEW

Creates a new view:

```
CREATE VIEW view_name
AS
...Select Statement
```

CREATE SCHEMA

Creates a new schema in SQL Server 2005 with the option of specifying a non-dbo owner with the AUTHORIZATION clause.

```
CREATE SCHEMA schema_name AUTHORIZATION user_name
```

CREATE PARTITION FUNCTION

Creates a partition function in SQL Server 2005 to use in physically partitioning tables and indexes.

```
CREATE PARTITION FUNCTION partition_function_name ( input_parameter_type )
AS RANGE LEFT --or RIGHT
FOR VALUES (value1, value2, value3, ...n)
```

CREATE PARTITION SCHEME

This creates a partition scheme in SQL Server 2005 to use in physically partitioning tables and indexes.

```
CREATE PARTITION SCHEME partition_scheme_name
AS PARTITION partition_function_name
TO (filegroup1, filefroup2, filefroup3, ...n)
```

Script Comment Conventions

In-line comment:

```
SELECT ProductID, Name AS ProductName    -- Comment text
```

Single-line comment:

```
/* Comment text */
-- Comment text
```

Comment block:

```
/****************************************************
    spProductUpdateByCategory
    Created by Paul Turley, 5-21-06
    nospam@sqlreportservices.com
    Updates product price info for a category

    Revisions:
    5-22-06 - Fixed bug that formatted C:
              drive if wrong type was passed in.
****************************************************/
```

Reserved Words

Reserved words should generally not be used as names of objects. Reserved words are typically easy to see when using either Query Analyzer or SQL Server Management Studio. Both of these tools change the color of reserved words to blue, but for whatever reason, not all reserved words are recognized by Query Analyzer and Management Studio and color-coded. To make matters worse, some words are color-coded blue even when they are not really reserved words. Also, if the object names are delimited with double quotation marks or square brackets, which they often are if using a graphical tool to create queries, then they won't show up color-coded at all. However, use of a nondelimited reserved word, whether it is blue or not, will always cause a syntax error to be raised. You will know when you have placed a nondelimited reserved word in your script when you receive the error "Incorrect syntax near the keyword 'keyword'." Keep in mind that if the decision is made to use a keyword in an object name, you will be forced to delimit that keyword every time it is used in the future.

The following key words have significant meaning within Transact-SQL and should be avoided in object names and expressions. If any of these words must be used in a SQL expression, they must be contained within square brackets [ ].

ADD	EXCEPT	PERCENT
ALL	EXEC	PLAN
ALTER	EXECUTE	PRECISION
AND	EXISTS	PRIMARY
ANY	EXIT	PRINT
AS	FETCH	PROC
ASC	FILE	PROCEDURE
AUTHORIZATION	FILLFACTOR	PUBLIC
BACKUP	FOR	RAISERROR
BEGIN	FOREIGN	READ
BETWEEN	FREETEXT	READTEXT
BREAK	FREETEXTTABLE	RECONFIGURE
BROWSE	FROM	REFERENCES
BULK	FULL	REPLICATION
BY	FUNCTION	RESTORE
CASCADE	GOTO	RESTRICT
CASE	GRANT	RETURN
CHECK	GROUP	REVOKE
CHECKPOINT	HAVING	RIGHT
CLOSE	HOLDLOCK	ROLLBACK
CLUSTERED	IDENTITY	ROWCOUNT

COALESCE	IDENTITY_INSERT	ROWGUIDCOL
COLLATE	IDENTITYCOL	RULE
COLUMN	IF	SAVE
COMMIT	IN	SCHEMA
COMPUTE	INDEX	SELECT
CONSTRAINT	INNER	SESSION_USER
CONTAINS	INSERT	SET
CONTAINSTABLE	INTERSECT	SETUSER
CONTINUE	INTO	SHUTDOWN
CONVERT	IS	SOME
CREATE	JOIN	STATISTICS
CROSS	KEY	SYSTEM_USER
CURRENT	KILL	TABLE
CURRENT_DATE	LEFT	TEXTSIZE
CURRENT_TIME	LIKE	THEN
CURRENT_TIMESTAMP	LINENO	TO
CURRENT_USER	LOAD	TOP
CURSOR	NATIONAL	TRAN
DATABASE	NOCHECK	TRANSACTION
DBCC	NONCLUSTERED	TRIGGER
DEALLOCATE	NOT	TRUNCATE
DECLARE	NULL	TSEQUAL
DEFAULT	NULLIF	UNION
DELETE	OF	UNIQUE
DENY	OFF	UPDATE
DESC	OFFSETS	UPDATETEXT
DISK	ON	USE
DISTINCT	OPEN	USER
DISTRIBUTED	OPENDATASOURCE	VALUES
DOUBLE	OPENQUERY	VARYING
DROP	OPENROWSET	VIEW
DUMMY	OPENXML	WAITFOR

Table continued on following page

DUMP	OPTION	WHEN
ELSE	OR	WHERE
END	ORDER	WHILE
ERRLVL	OUTER	WITH
ESCAPE	OVER	WRITETEXT

ODBC Reserved Words

Although ODBC Key Words are not strictly prohibited, as a best practice to prevent driver inconsistencies, they should be avoided. These are listed in the following table.

ABSOLUTE	EXEC	OVERLAPS
ACTION	EXECUTE	PAD
ADA	EXISTS	PARTIAL
ADD	EXTERNAL	PASCAL
ALL	EXTRACT	POSITION
ALLOCATE	FALSE	PRECISION
ALTER	FETCH	PREPARE
AND	FIRST	PRESERVE
ANY	FLOAT	PRIMARY
ARE	FOR	PRIOR
AS	FOREIGN	PRIVILEGES
ASC	FORTRAN	PROCEDURE
ASSERTION	FOUND	PUBLIC
AT	FROM	READ
AUTHORIZATION	FULL	REAL
AVG	GET	REFERENCES
BEGIN	GLOBAL	RELATIVE
BETWEEN	GO	RESTRICT
BIT	GOTO	REVOKE
BIT_LENGTH	GRANT	RIGHT
BOTH	GROUP	ROLLBACK
BY	HAVING	ROWS
CASCADE	HOUR	SCHEMA

CASCADED	IDENTITY	SCROLL
CASE	IMMEDIATE	SECOND
CAST	IN	SECTION
CATALOG	INCLUDE	SELECT
CHAR	INDEX	SESSION
CHAR_LENGTH	INDICATOR	SESSION_USER
CHARACTER	INITIALLY	SET
CHARACTER_LENGTH	INNER	SIZE
CHECK	INPUT	SMALLINT
CLOSE	INSENSITIVE	SOME
COALESCE	INSERT	SPACE
COLLATE	INT	SQL
COLLATION	INTEGER	SQLCA
COLUMN	INTERSECT	SQLCODE
COMMIT	INTERVAL	SQLERROR
CONNECT	INTO	SQLSTATE
CONNECTION	IS	SQLWARNING
CONSTRAINT	ISOLATION	SUBSTRING
CONSTRAINTS	JOIN	SUM
CONTINUE	KEY	SYSTEM_USER
CONVERT	LANGUAGE	TABLE
CORRESPONDING	LAST	TEMPORARY
COUNT	LEADING	THEN
CREATE	LEFT	TIME
CROSS	LEVEL	TIMESTAMP
CURRENT	LIKE	TIMEZONE_HOUR
CURRENT_DATE	LOCAL	TIMEZONE_MINUTE
CURRENT_TIME	LOWER	TO
CURRENT_TIMESTAMP	MATCH	TRAILING
CURRENT_USER	MAX	TRANSACTION
CURSOR	MIN	TRANSLATE
DATE	MINUTE	TRANSLATION

Table continued on following page

DAY	MODULE	TRIM
DEALLOCATE	MONTH	TRUE
DEC	NAMES	UNION
DECIMAL	NATIONAL	UNIQUE
DECLARE	NATURAL	UNKNOWN
DEFAULT	NCHAR	UPDATE
DEFERRABLE	NEXT	UPPER
DEFERRED	NO	USAGE
DELETE	NONE	USER
DESC	NOT	USING
DESCRIBE	NULL	VALUE
DESCRIPTOR	NULLIF	VALUES
DIAGNOSTICS	NUMERIC	VARCHAR
DISCONNECT	OCTET_LENGTH	VARYING
DISTINCT	OF	VIEW
DOMAIN	ON	WHEN
DOUBLE	ONLY	WHENEVER
DROP	OPEN	WHERE
ELSE	OPTION	WITH
END	OR	WORK
END-EXEC	ORDER	WRITE
ESCAPE	OUTER	YEAR
EXCEPT	OUTPUT	ZONE
EXCEPTION		

Future and Miscellaneous Reserved Words

The following table contains keywords that may be reserved currently or in future editions of SQL Server. As a convention, these words should be avoided in user-defined objects, table, and column names.

ABSOLUTE	FOUND	PRESERVE
ACTION	FREE	PRIOR
ADMIN	GENERAL	PRIVILEGES
AFTER	GET	READS

AGGREGATE	GLOBAL	REAL
ALIAS	GO	RECURSIVE
ALLOCATE	GROUPING	REF
ARE	HOST	REFERENCING
ARRAY	HOUR	RELATIVE
ASSERTION	IGNORE	RESULT
AT	IMMEDIATE	RETURNS
BEFORE	INDICATOR	ROLE
BINARY	INITIALIZE	ROLLUP
BIT	INITIALLY	ROUTINE
BLOB	INOUT	ROW
BOOLEAN	INPUT	ROWS
BOTH	INT	SAVEPOINT
BREADTH	INTEGER	SCROLL
CALL	INTERVAL	SCOPE
CASCADED	ISOLATION	SEARCH
CAST	ITERATE	SECOND
CATALOG	LANGUAGE	SECTION
CHAR	LARGE	SEQUENCE
CHARACTER	LAST	SESSION
CLASS	LATERAL	SETS
CLOB	LEADING	SIZE
COLLATION	LESS	SMALLINT
COMPLETION	LEVEL	SPACE
CONNECT	LIMIT	SPECIFIC
CONNECTION	LOCAL	SPECIFICTYPE
CONSTRAINTS	LOCALTIME	SQL
CONSTRUCTOR	LOCALTIMESTAMP	SQLEXCEPTION
CORRESPONDING	LOCATOR	SQLSTATE
CUBE	MAP	SQLWARNING
CURRENT_PATH	MATCH	START
CURRENT_ROLE	MINUTE	STATE

Table continued on following page

CYCLE	MODIFIES	STATEMENT
DATA	MODIFY	STATIC
DATE	MODULE	STRUCTURE
DAY	MONTH	TEMPORARY
DEC	NAMES	TERMINATE
DECIMAL	NATURAL	THAN
DEFERRABLE	NCHAR	TIME
DEFERRED	NCLOB	TIMESTAMP
DEPTH	NEW	TIMEZONE_HOUR
DEREF	NEXT	TIMEZONE_MINUTE
DESCRIBE	NO	TRAILING
DESCRIPTOR	NONE	TRANSLATION
DESTROY	NUMERIC	TREAT
DESTRUCTOR	OBJECT	TRUE
DETERMINISTIC	OLD	UNDER
DICTIONARY	ONLY	UNKNOWN
DIAGNOSTICS	OPERATION	UNNEST
DISCONNECT	ORDINALITY	USAGE
DOMAIN	OUT	USING
DYNAMIC	OUTPUT	VALUE
EACH	PAD	VARCHAR
END-EXEC	PARAMETER	VARIABLE
EQUALS	PARAMETERS	WHENEVER
EVERY	PARTIAL	WITHOUT
EXCEPTION	PATH	WORK
EXTERNAL	POSTFIX	WRITE
FALSE	PREFIX	YEAR
FIRST	PREORDER	ZONE
FLOAT	PREPARE	

Transact SQL System Variables and Functions

A significant portion of this text is used with permission from Beginning Transact SQL, *available from Wrox Press.*

Variables and functions are often used interchangeably. SQL Server Books Online documents some variables as if they were functions. However, it's important to note that variables return a value, whereas functions process specific business logic and many functions accept input arguments. Optional arguments are denoted using square brackets.

System Global variables

The system-supplied global variables are organized into these categories:

- ❑ Configuration
- ❑ Cursor
- ❑ System
- ❑ System Statistics

Configuration

Variable Name	Return Type	Description
@@DATEFIRST	TinyInt	Returns the system setting for the first day of the week. 1 = Monday, 2 = Tuesday, 3 = Wednesday, 4 = Thursday, 5 = Friday, 6 = Saturday, 7 = Sunday. U.S. default is 7.
@@DBTS	VarBinary	The last assigned unique TimeStamp value.
@@LANGID	SmallInt	The current language ID for the server. (US English = 0, German = 1, French = 2, and so on).
@@LANGUAGE	nVarChar	The current language string for the server. Returns the language name in the native language form (US_English, Deutsch, Français, Dansk, Español, Italiano, and so on).
@@LOCK_TIMEOUT	Int	Lock timeout setting for the current session in milliseconds.
@@MAX_CONNECTIONS	Int	The maximum concurrent connections setting for the server.
@@MAX_PRECISION	TinyInt	The maximum precision setting for decimal and numeric types. Default is 38 significant digits (total to the left and right of the decimal point).
@@MICROSOFTVERSION	Int	Returns an internal tracking number used by product development and support groups at Microsoft.
@@NESTLEVEL	Int	The current number of nested stored procedure or trigger calls. This may be used to limit cascading and/or recursive calls prior to reaching the system limit of 32 recursive calls.
@@OPTIONS	Int	The set of query-processing options for the current user session. Multiple options are combined mathematically using bitwise addition (that is, If SELECT @@OPTIONS & (512 + 8192) > 0 ...). Any combination of option values may be added to determine whether all these options are enabled.

Variable Name	Return Type	Description
		Option values: 1 = DISABLE_DEF_CNST_CHK 2 = IMPLICIT_TRANSACTIONS 4 = CURSOR_CLOSE_ON_COMMIT 8 = ANSI_WARNINGS 16 = ANSI_PADDING 32 = ANSI_NULLS 64 = ARITHABORT 128 = ARITHIGNORE 256 = QUOTED_IDENTIFIER 512 = NOCOUNT 1024 = ANSI_NULL_DFLT_ON 2048 = ANSI_NULL_DFLT_OFF 4096 = CONCAT_NULL_YIELDS_NULL 8192 = NUMERIC_ROUNDABORT 16384 = XACT_ABORT
@@REMSERVER	nVarChar	Name of the remote server if executing remote procedures.
@@SERVERNAME	nVarChar	Name of the current server.
@@SERVICENAME	nVarChar	Name of the Windows service for the current SQL Server instance.
@@ID	Int	The process/session ID assigned to the current user's connection.
@@TEXTSIZE	Int	The current value of the TEXTSIZE option for a query returning data from a Text, nText, or Image type.
@@VERSION	nVarChar	Returns a text string with detailed information about the current version of SQL Server. This includes the major version, build number, service pack, and copyright information.

Cursor

Variable Name	Return Type	Description
@@CURSOR_ROWS	Int	The row count for the currently open cursor. Used for explicit cursor processing following an OPEN command. If an asynchronous cursor is opened, the row count will not be known and this variable returns –1.
@@FETCH_STATUS	Int	Used as a flag to indicate whether the open cursor has navigated past the last row (EOF). Status values include: 0 = Normal fetch operation –1 = Fetch past last row or unsuccessful –2 = Fetched row has been removed

System

Variable Name	Return Type	Description
@@ERROR	Int	Value of the most recent error within the current user session. Error numbers (from the sysmessages table) are used to determine the status of an error condition.
@@IDENTITY	Numeric	Value of the most recently generated identity value. This is typically the result of an identity column insert.
@@ROWCOUNT	Int	Number of rows affected by, or returned by, the last operation.
@@TRANCOUNT	Int	Number of currently active transactions. Used to determine the number of nested transactions. The maximum number of nested transactions is 11.

System Statistical

Variable Name	Return Type	Description
@@CONNECTIONS	Int	The total connects that have been opened or attempted since the SQL Server service was last started.
@@CPU_BUSY	Int	The total time in milliseconds that the server has not been idle since the SQL Server service was last started.
@@IDLE	Int	The total time in milliseconds that the server has been idle since the SQL Server service was last started.
@@IO_BUSY	Int	The total time in milliseconds that the server has performed physical disk I/O operations since the SQL Server service was last started.
@@PACK_RECEIVED	Int	The total number of network packets received by the server since the SQL Server service was last started.
@@PACK_SENT	Int	The total number of network packets sent by the server since the SQL Server service was last started.
@@PACKET_ERRORS	Int	The total number of network packet errors that have occurred since the SQL Server service was last started.
@@TIMETICKS	Int	The number of milliseconds per CPU tick. Each tick takes 1/32 of a second.
@@TOTAL_ERRORS	Int	The total number of disk read/write errors that have occurred, while performing physical disk I/O, since the SQL Server service was last started.
@@TOTAL_READ	Int	The total number of physical disk reads that have occurred since the SQL Server service was last started.
@@TOTAL_WRITE	Int	The total number of physical disk writes that have occurred since the SQL Server service was last started.

System Functions

The system functions are organized into these categories:

- ❑ Aggregation
- ❑ Checksum
- ❑ Conversion
- ❑ Cursor
- ❑ Date
- ❑ Image/Text
- ❑ Mathematical
- ❑ Metadata
- ❑ Ranking
- ❑ Security
- ❑ System
- ❑ System Statistics

Aggregation

Function Name	Return Type	Description
AVG()	(numeric — depends on input)	Calculates the arithmetic average for a range of column values. Internally, this function counts rows and calculates the sum for all non-null values in the column and then divides the sum by the count. Returns the same numeric data type as the column.
COUNT()	Int	Counts all non-null values for a column. The row count is returned using COUNT(*) regardless of null values.
COUNT_BIG()	BigInt	Same as COUNT() but returns a BigInt type rather than an Int type.
GROUPING()	Int	Used in conjunction with ROLLUP and CUBE operations in a GROUP BY query, this function returns 0 to indicate that it is on a detail row and 1 to indicate a summary row.
MAX()	(numeric or date — depends on input)	Returns the largest value in a range of column values.
MIN()	(numeric or date — depends on input)	Returns the smallest value in a range of column values.

Table continued on following page

Function Name	Return Type	Description
STDEV()	Float	Calculates the standard deviation for a range of non-null column values.
STDEVP()	Float	Calculates the standard deviation over a population for a range of non-null column values.
SUM()	(numeric — depends on input)	Calculates the arithmetic sum for a range of non-null column values. If all values are NULL, returns NULL.
VAR()	Float	Calculates the statistical variance for a range of non-null column values. If all values are NULL, returns NULL.
VARP()	Float	Calculates the statistical variance over a population for a range of non-null column values. If all values are NULL, returns NULL.

Checksum

Function Name	Return Type	Description
CHECKSUM()	Int	Calculates a checksum value for a row or range of column values. This function accepts a single column name, a comma-delimited list of columns, or * to use the entire row. Accepts columns of all types except Text, nText, Image, Cursor, and Sql_Variant. The returned value itself is meaningless but will consistently yield the same result for a column or row unless a value changes. String comparisons are case insensitive.
BINARY_CHECKSUM()	Int	Calculates a checksum value for a row or range of column values. This function accepts a single column name, a comma-delimited list of columns or, * to use the entire row. Accepts columns of all types except Text, nText, Image, Cursor, and Sql_Variant. The returned value itself is meaningless but will consistently yield the same result for a column or row unless a value changes. String comparisons are case sensitive.
CHECKSUM_AGG()	Int	Calculates a single checksum value for a range of Int type column values. When applied to the result of the CHECKSUM() or BINARY_CHECKSUM() functions, returns a scalar (single value) checksum value for the entire range of values. May be used to detect value changes over a table or range of column values.

Conversion

Function Name	Return Type	Description
CAST()	(returns a specified type)	Converts a value to a specified data type. CAST(the_value_AS_the_type)
CONVERT()	(returns a specified type)	Converts (and optionally formats) a value to a specified data type. Formatting may be applied to numeric and date types. CONVERT(the_type, the_value) or CONVERT(the_type, the_value, format_number)

Cursor

Function Name	Return Type	Description
CURSOR_STATUS()	SmallInt	Returns the status of a previously opened cursor. 1 = Open and populated, 0 = Contains no records, −1 = Closed, −2 = No cursor or de-allocated, −3 = Doesn't exist

Date

Function Name	Return Type	Description
DATEADD()	DateTime or SmallDateTime (depending on input type)	Returns a date value (DateTime or SmallDateTime) from a date value added by X number of date interval units. Units may be Year, Quarter, Month, DayOfYear, Day, Hour, Minute, Second, or Millisecond.
DATEDIFF()	Int	Returns an integer representing the difference between two date values (DateTime or SmallDateTime) in specified date interval units. Units may be Year, Quarter, Month, DayOfYear, Day, Hour, Minute, Second, or Millisecond.
DATENAME()	nVarChar	Similar to DATEPART(). Returns a character string representing the specified date part for a date value. The Datepart parameter is the same as the DATEDIFF() interval and includes Year, Quarter, Month, DayOfYear, Day, Hour, Minute, Second, or Millisecond.
DATEPART()	Int	Similar to DATENAME(). Returns an integer representing the specified date part for a date value. The Datepart parameter is the same as the DATEDIFF() interval and includes Year, Quarter, Month, DayOfYear, Day, Hour, Minute, Second, or Millisecond.

Table continued on following page

Function Name	Return Type	Description
DAY()	Int	Returns the day part for a date as an integer.
GETDATE()	DateTime	Returns the current date and time value.
GETUTCDATE()	DateTime	Returns the current date and time value, for the Universal Time Zone, based on the server's time zone settings. UTC is the same as Greenwich Mean Time (GMT).
MONTH()	Int	Returns the month part for a date as an integer.
YEAR()	Int	Returns the year part for a date as an integer.

Image/Text

Function Name	Return Type	Description
PATINDEX()	Int	Returns the character index (first position) for a character string pattern occurring within another character string. Similar to CHARINDEX() but supports wildcards.
TEXTPTR()	VarBinary	Returns a VarBinary text pointer handle to be used with the READTEXT(), WRITETEXT(), and UPDATETEXT() functions. Used for performing special operations on Text, nText, and Image type column data.
TEXTVALID()	Int	Used to verify a VarBinary text pointer value, obtained from the TEXTPTR() function.

Mathematical

Function Name	Return Type	Description
ABS()	(numeric — same type as input)	Returns the absolute value for a numeric value.
ACOS()	Float	Computes the arccosine (an angle) in radians.
ASIN()	Float	Computes the arcsine (an angle) in radians.
ATAN()	Float	Computes the arctangent (an angle) in radians.
ATN2()	Float	Computes the arctangent of two values in radians.
CEILING()	(numeric — same type as input)	Returns the smallest integer value that is greater than or equal to a number.
COS()	Float	Computes the cosine of an angle in radians.
COT()	Float	Computes the cotangent of an angle in radians.
DEGREES()	(numeric — same type as input)	Converts an angle from radians to degrees.

Function Name	Return Type	Description
EXP()	Float	Returns the natural logarithm raised to a specified exponent. Result is in exponential form.
FLOOR()	(numeric — same type as input)	Returns the largest integer value that is less than or equal to a number.
LOG()	Float	Calculates the natural logarithm of a number using base-2 (binary) numbering.
LOG10()	Float	Calculates the natural logarithm of a number using base-10 numbering.
PI()	Float	Returns the value for pi.
POWER()	Float	Raises a value to a specified exponent as FLOAT(the_value, the_exponent).
RADIANS()	(numeric — same type as input)	Converts an angle from degrees to radians.
RAND()	Float	Returns a fractional number based on a randomizing algorithm. Accepts an optional seed value.
ROUND()	(numeric — same type as input)	Rounds a fractional value to a specified precision.
SIGN()	Float	Returns –1 or 1 depending on whether a single argument value is negative or positive.
SIN()	Float	Computes the sine of an angle in radians.
SQRT()	Float	Returns the square root of a value.
SQUARE()	Float	Returns the square (n^2) of a value.
TAN()	Float	Computes the tangent of an angle in radians.

Metadata

Function Name	Return Type	Description
COL_LENGTH()	Int	Returns the length of a column from the column name.
COL_NAME()	sysname (nVarChar)	Returns the name of a column from the object ID.
COLUMNPROPERTY()	Int	Returns a flag to indicate the state of a column property.

Table continued on following page

645

Function Name	Return Type	Description
DATABASEPROPERTY()	Int	This function is maintained for backward compatibility with older SQL Server versions. Returns a flag to indicate the state of a database property.
DATABASEPROPERTYEX()	SqlVariant	Returns a numeric flag or string to indicate the state of a database property.
DB_ID()	SmallInt	Returns the database ID from the database name.
DB_NAME()	nVarChar	Returns the database name from the database ID.
FILE_ID()	SmallInt	Returns the file ID from the file name.
FILE_NAME()	nVarChar	Returns the file name from the file ID.
fn_listextendedproperty()	Table	Returns a table object populated with extended property names and their settings.
FULLTEXTCATALOGPROPERTY()	Int	Returns a flag to indicate the state of a full-text catalog property.
FULLTEXTSERVICEPROPERTY()	Int	Returns a flag to indicate the state of a full-text service property.
INDEX_COL()	nVarChar	Returns the name of a column contained in a specified index, by table, index, and column ID.
INDEXKEY_PROPERTY()	Int	Returns a flag to indicate the state of an index key property.
INDEXPROPERTY()	Int	Returns a flag indicating the state of an index property.
OBJECT_ID()	Int	Returns an object ID from the object name.
OBJECT_NAME()	nChar	Returns an object name from the object ID.
OBJECTPROPERTY()	Int	This function allows you to get property information from several different types of objects. It is advisable to use a function designed to query specific object types, if possible. Returns a flag indicating the state of an object property.

Ranking (SQL Server 2005)

Function Name	Return Type	Description
DENSE_RANK()	Int	Returns a running incremental value based on an ORDER BY clause passed into the function. Doesn't preserve the ordinal position of the row in the list if there are ties.

Function Name	Return Type	Description
NTILE(n)	Int	Returns an evenly distributed ranking value, dividing the result into a finite number of ranked groups.
RANK()	Int	Returns a running incremental value based on an ORDER BY clause passed into the function. Preserves the ordinal position of the row in the list with duplicate values for ties followed by subsequent skips.
ROW_NUMBER()	Int	Returns a running incremental value based on an ORDER BY clause passed into the function.

Security

Function Name	Return Type	Description
fn_trace_geteventinfo()	Table	Returns a table type populated with event information for a specified trace ID.
fn_trace_getfilterinfo()	Table	Returns a table type populated with information about filters applied to a trace for a specified trace ID.
fn_trace_getinfo()	Table	Returns a table type populated with trace information for a specified trace ID.
fn_trace_gettable()	Table	Returns a table type populated with file information for a specified trace ID.
HAS_DBACCESS()	Int	Returns a flag indicating whether the current user has access to a specified database.
IS_MEMBER()	Int	Returns a flag indicating whether the current user is a member of a Windows group or SQL Server role.
IS_SRVROLEMEMBER()	Int	Returns a flag indicating whether the current user is a member of a database server role.
SUSER_SID()	VarBinary	Returns the security ID for a specified user name.
SUSER_SNAME()	nVarChar	Returns the user name for a specified security ID.
USER_ID()	SmallInt	Returns a user name for a specified user ID.
fn_trace_geteventinfo()	Table	Returns a table type populated with event information for a specified trace ID.

String Manipulation

Function Name	Return Type	Description
ASCII()	Int	Returns the numeric ASCII character value for a standard character.
CHAR()	Char	Returns the ASCII character for a numeric ASCII character value.
CHARINDEX()	Int	Similar to PATINDEX(), returns the index (character position) of the first occurrence of a character string within another character string.
DIFFERENCE()	Int	Returns the numeric difference between two character strings based on the consensus Soundex values.
LEFT()	VarChar	Returns the leftmost X characters from a character string.
LEN()	Int	Returns the length of a character string.
LOWER()	VarChar	Converts a character string to all lowercase characters.
LTRIM()	VarChar	Removes leading spaces from the left side of a character string.
NCHAR()	nChar	Like the CHAR() function, returns the Unicode character for a numeric character value.
PATINDEX()	Int	Returns the index (first character position) for the first occurrence of characters matching a specified pattern within another character string. Wildcard characters may be used.
QUOTENAME()	nVarChar	Returns a character string with square brackets around the input value. Used with SQL Server object names so that they can be passed into an expression.
REPLACE()	(character or binary types, depending on input)	Returns a character string with all occurrences of one character or substring replaced with another character or substring.
REPLICATE()	VarChar	Returns a character string consisting of a specified number of repeated characters.
REVERSE()	VarChar	Returns a character string with all characters in reverse order.

Function Name	Return Type	Description
RIGHT()	VarChar	Returns a specific number of characters from the rightmost side of a character string.
RTRIM()	VarChar	Removes trailing spaces from the right side of a character string.
SOUNDEX()	Char	Returns a four-character alphanumeric string representing the approximate phonetic value of a word, based on the U.S. Census Soundex algorithm.
SPACE()	Char	Returns a character string consisting of a specified number of spaces.
STR()	Char	Returns a character string value that represents a converted numeric data type. Three arguments include the value, the overall length, and the number of decimal positions.
STUFF()	(character or binary types, depending on input)	Returns a character string with one string placed into another string at a given position and for a specified length.
SUBSTRING()	(character or binary types, depending on input)	Returns a portion of a character string from a specified position and for a specified length.
UNICODE()	Int	Returns the numeric Unicode character value for a specified character.
UPPER()	VarChar	Converts a character string to all uppercase characters.

System

Function Name	Return Type	Description
APP_NAME()	nVarChar	Each session is associated with an application name, passed to the database server by explicit program code or by the driver or data provider.
COALESCE()	(same type as input)	Returns the first non-null value from a comma-delimited list of expressions.
COLLATIONPROPERTY()	Sql_Variant	Returns the value of a specific property for a specified collation. Properties include CodePage, LCID, and ComparisonStyle.

Table continued on following page

Function Name	Return Type	Description
CURRENT_TIMESTAMP()	DateTime	This function returns the current date and time and is synonymous with the GETDATE() function. It exists for ANSI-SQL compliance.
CURRENT_USER()	Sysname (VarChar)	This function returns the name of the current user and is synonymous with the USER_NAME() function.
DATALENGTH()	Int	Returns the number of bytes used to store or handle a value. For ANSI string types, this will return the same value as the LEN() function, but for other data types, the value may be different.
ENCRYPT()	VarChar	Returns a hexadecimal value as a character string from a character string value. The result is a one-way encrypted value. This value can be read by the database engine (in the case of an object script definition) but cannot be decrypted.
Fn_Get_SQL()	Table	Returns a table populated with the full text of a query based on a process handle. This value is stored in the sysprocesses table referencing a SPID. This function was introduced with SQL Server 2000 SP3.
Fn_HelpCollations()	Table	Returns a table type populated with a list of collations supported by the current version of SQL Server.
Fn_ServerSharedDrives()	Table	Returns a table type populated with a list of drives shared by the server.
Fn_VirtualFileStats()	Table	Returns a table type populated with I/O statistics for database files, including log files.
FORMATMESSAGE()	nVarChar	Returns an error message from the sysmessages table for a specified message number and comma-delimited list of parameters.
GETANSINULL()	Int	Returns the nullability setting for the database, according to the ANSI_NULL_DFLT_ON and ANSI_NULL_DFLT_OFF database settings.
HOST_ID()	Char	Returns the workstation ID for the current session.

Function Name	Return Type	Description
HOST_NAME()	nChar	Returns the workstation name for the current session.
IDENT_CURRENT()	Sql_Variant	Returns the last identity value generated for a specified table regardless of the session and scope.
IDENT_INCR()	Numeric	Returns the increment value specified in the creation of the last identity column.
IDENT_SEED()	Numeric	Returns the seed value specified in the creation of the last identity column.
IDENTITY()	(same as input)	Used in a SELECT . . . INTO statement to insert an explicitly generated identity value into a column.
ISDATE()	Int	Returns a flag to indicate whether a specified value is, or is capable of being converted to, a date value.
ISNULL()	(same as input)	Determines whether a specified value is null and then returns a provided replacement value.
ISNUMERIC()	Int	Returns a flag to indicate whether a specified value is, or is capable of being converted to, a numeric value.
NEWID()	UniqueIdentifier	Returns a newly generated UniqueIdentifyer type value. This is a 128-bit integer, globally unique value, usually expressed as an alphanumeric hexadecimal representation (such as 89DE6247-C2E2-42DB-8CE8-A787E505D7EA). This type is often used for primary key values in replicated and semi-connected systems.
NULLIF()	(same as input)	Returns a NULL value when two specified arguments have equivalent values.
PARSENAME()	nChar	Returns a specific part of a four-part object name.
PERMISSIONS()	Int	Returns an integer whose value is a bitwise map indicating the permission or combination of permissions for the current user on a specified database object.

Table continued on following page

Function Name	Return Type	Description
PWDCOMPARE()	Int	Compares an encrypted value with an unencrypted character string value. May be used to compare the encrypted and unencrypted forms of a password to determine whether they match. Returns 1 for a match and 0 for no match.
PWDENCRYPT()	VarChar	Returns the encrypted form of a character string in hexadecimal form. May be used to encrypt a password for storage. This value cannot be decrypted using SQL Server tools or Transact-SQL commands.
ROWCOUNT_BIG()	BigInt	Like the @@ROWCOUNT variable, returns the number of rows either returned by or modified by the last statement. Returns a BigInt type.
SCOPE_IDENTITY()	Sql_Variant	Like the @@IDENTITY variable, this function returns the last Identity value generated but is limited to the current session and scope (stored procedure, batch, or module).
SERVERPROPERTY()	Sql_Variant	Returns a flag indicating the state of a server property. Properties include Collation, Edition, Engine Edition, InstanceName, IsClustered, IsFullTextInstalled, IsIntegratedSecurityOnly, IsSingleUser, IsSyncWithBackup, LicenseType, MachineName, NumLicenses, ProcessID, ProductLevel, ProductVersion, and ServerName.
SESSION_USER	nChar	Returns the current user name. Function is called without parentheses.
SESSIONPROPERTY()	Sql_Variant	Returns a flag indicating the state of a session property. Properties include: ANSI_NULLS, ANSI_PADDING, ANSI_WARNINGS, ARITHABORT, CONCAT_NULL_YIELDS_NULL, NUMERIC_ROUNDABORT, and QUOTED_IDENTIFIER.
STATS_DATE()	DateTime	Returns the date that statistics for a specified index were last updated.
SYSTEM_USER	nVarChar	Returns the current user name. Function is called without parentheses.
USER_NAME()	nVarChar	Returns the user name for a specified User ID.

Index

X

Y

Z